A

HISTORY OF

SONG

Edited by

DENIS STEVENS

RADIUS BOOK/HUTCHINSON

HUTCHINSON & CO (Publishers) LTD
178–202 Great Portland Street, London W1

London Melbourne Sydney
Auckland Johannesburg Cape Town
and agencies throughout the world

First published 1960
Radius edition 1971

This book has been set in Bembo type, printed in Great Britain
on white M.F. paper by Taylor Garnett Evans & Co
and bound by Wm. Brendon, of Tiptree, Essex

ISBN 0 09 104680 7 (cased)
0 09 104681 5 (paper)

Contents

Foreword

THIS book is concerned with secular art-song as perceived from two main angles: historical depth and geographical breadth. History, however, is a bottomless pit, and even geography has its limitations. Thus the reader who seeks for information on Chinese songs or the songs of the ancient Greeks will certainly fail to find it in these pages, from which the music of ancient times and of non-western countries has had to be excluded for reasons of space. On the other hand, the reader or singer who wishes to follow the changing patterns and styles and fashions of art-song from mediaeval Europe to the Europe and Americas of our own day will be able to do so in reasonable detail.

No single writer or scholar could ever hope to cover such a vast repertory and deal sympathetically and knowledgeably with every part of it. For this reason the present book has been entrusted to a group of writers, each of whom has set forth, in his own way (though within the general framework of the initial plan) an account of some aspect of song related to his own specialized studies and experience. Some sections will reveal for the first time that buried musical treasure so frequently sought but seldom found, and because it has been buried the writers have felt bound to give accurate information about books, articles, and editions well outside the normal stock range of even the largest music shop. Other chapters deal with songs that may be

relatively familiar to musicians and generally easy of access, and here
the bibliographical aids will dwindle since their presence would to a
large extent be superfluous.

If this book suggests new departures and new additions to the
repertory of singers who feel hemmed in by a narrow range of musical
style, it will have fulfilled one of its principal aims and objects. If it
assists the musician and musical historian to grasp the essential continuity
of a genre that has flourished with particular vigour during the past
millennium, some part of the editor's hopes will have been realized.
He offers his sincere thanks to contributors for their patience and
co-operation, and to his publishers for their unfailing assistance,
understanding, and courtesy at all stages in the writing and production
of this book.

Professor Gustave Reese was kind enough to read *The Middle Ages*
in page proof, and Professor Donald Grout performed a similar
service in connection with *The Renaissance*; the remainder of the book
benefited not a little from the experienced eye of Mr. Deryck Cooke.
Such errors as may still be discovered are the exclusive property of the
Editor, who will quash relentlessly any and every attempt to copy them.

DENIS STEVENS

Acknowledgements

GRATEFUL acknowledgement is made to the following publishers for permission to quote extracts from the songs mentioned:

AMERICAN COMPOSERS' ALLIANCE: *Vigil* (Ben Weber), *The Hound of Heaven* (Gideon); BELA BARTÓK ARCHIVES: 'Five Songs' Op. 15; BOELKE-BOMART: 'Two Sonnets', 'Du' (Babbitt); BOOSEY & HAWKES: *Go, lovely rose* (Barab); 'Eight Hungarian Folk-Songs', 'Twenty Hungarian Folk-Songs', 'Five Songs' Op. 16, 'Four Songs', 'Hungarian Folk-Songs' with Kodály, (Bartok); *Serenade, Canticle I* (Britten); 'Eight Epitaphs' (Chanler); 'Twelve Poems of Emily Dickinson', 'Old American Songs' (Copland); 'Seven Songs' Op. 6, 'Five Songs' Op. 9, 'Three Songs' Op. 14 (Kodály); *Roza* (Medtner); *The Ugly Duckling* (Prokofiev); *On a Summer Morning* (Somervell); 'Four Hymns' (Vaughan Williams); BOTE & BOCK: *Frühlingsfeier* (R. Strauss); BREITKOPF & HAERTEL: *Das Heiligste* (Schoeck); CHAPPELL: *She is far from the land* (F. Lambert); CHESTER: *Calmes, aux quais déserts* (Jongen); DONEMUS: *Meiliedje* (Pijper); DURAND: *L'hiver a cessé* (Fauré), *Les deux guerriers* (Messiaen), 'Chansons Madécasses' (Ravel); ELKAN-VOGEL: *Billy in the Darbies* (Diamond); ELKIN: *A Song of Wine* (Scott); CARL FISCHER: *Velvet People* (Bacon); FREDERICK HARRIS: *A maiden yonder sings* (Sibelius); HEUGEL: 'Expressions lyriques' (Massenet); JOBERT: *Le Tombeau des Naiades* (Debussy); KALMUS-UNIVERSAL EDITION: 'Falun' (Bartók), *Machines Agricoles* (Milhaud), *Słowik* (Szymanowski), 'Drei Gesänge' (Webern); MEXICANAS DE MUSICA: *Madre mía, quando muera* (Galindo); MUSIC PUBLISHERS' HOLDING CORPORATION: *I got rhythm* (Gershwin); NOVELLO: *Ich bin der Welt abhanden gekommen* (Mahler), *Through the Ivory Gate* (Parry); OXFORD UNIVERSITY PRESS: *Sleep* (Warlock), *Quel espoir de guarir* (Guedron-Warlock); OXFORD UNIVERSITY PRESS AND THE DELIUS TRUSTEES: *Twilight Fancies* (Delius); POLSKIE WYDAWNICTWO MUZYCZNE: *Wiem ja coś* (Niewiadomski); THEODORE PRESSER: *On the Antipodes; Soliloquy* (Ives); RICORDI AMERICANA: *Gato* (Ginastera); RICORDI: *Follow Your Saint* (Thomson);

9

Giovane Bella (Casella); *Quel rosignol* (Pizzetti); ROUART LEROLLE: *Seguidille* (Falla), *Suray Surita* (Sas); G. SCHIRMER, *Knoxville: Summer of 1915* (Barber), *The First Snowfall* (Griffes): *Pirate Story* (Homer); SOUTHERN MUSIC PUBLISHING COMPANY: *Chatterton* (Diamond); SUVINI ZERBONI: *La primavera* (Dallapiccola); UNION MUSICAL ESPAÑOLA: *La Maja de Goya* (Granados); UNIVERSAL-VIENNA: *Haja, Haja*; 'Magyar Nepzene' (Kodály).

Owing to the fact that in some instances control of copyright has changed hands two or three times since original publication, it has been impossible to verify details of the actual owner, especially when letters requesting permission to quote have remained unanswered. Apologies are offered to any publisher who has been inadvertently omitted from the above list, which is believed at the time of going to press to be as complete as possible.

Trägt die Sprache schon Gesang in sich, oder lebt der Ton erst getragen von ihr? Eins ist im andern und will zum andern. Musik weckt Gefühle, die drängen zum Worte. In Wort lebt ein Sehnen nach Klang und Musik.

Clemens Krauss: libretto for Richard Strauss's Capriccio

Musick and Poetry have ever been acknowledg'd Sisters, which walking hand in hand, support each other; as Poetry is the harmony of Words, so Musick is that of Notes; and as Poetry is a Rise above Prose and Oratory, so is Musick the exaltation of Poetry. Both of them may excell apart, but sure are most excellent when they are join'd, because nothing is then wanting to either of their Perfections: for thus they appear like Wit and Beauty in the same Person.

Henry Purcell: preface to The History of Dioclesian

The Middle Ages

The Middle Ages

GILBERT REANEY

T HE history of song is obviously as old as the history of mankind, but unfortunately we have to depend on musical notation to decipher the oldest known songs. It is not quite so obvious a fact that musical notation only occurs where civilization and culture are highly developed. What this means is that, apart from a few fragments in Greek notation, European music is represented only by the notation which developed from about the seventh century A.D. Moreover, our earliest musical sources are not earlier than the ninth century. Another factor which particularly interests the subject in question is that clerics were the main propagators of musical notation; hence most of the earliest preserved western music is church music. A few very early songs have been preserved of secular origin, but for the most part the notation is too rudimentary for a transcription to be possible. This is particularly disappointing, since the dates attributable to these compositions show that they go back to the seventh century in some cases. These are naturally enough in Latin and consist of only one part. Indeed part-music of a secular character is not notated till the thirteenth century, though it is clear that early secular song in general had an improvised accompaniment. Of the existing very early Latin songs, there are six odes by Horace, some fragments of the Aeneid, some poems by Boethius and a number of laments for such personages as the Visigothic king Chindasvinthus (d. 652) and queen Reciberga (d.c. 657), duke Eric of Friuli (d. 799), Charlemagne (d. 814) and his son Hugo of St. Quentin (d. 844). In addition, there is a piece about the battle of Fontenoy (841), another concerning the destruction of the monastery of Glonnes near Saumur and other historical compositions.

By sheer coincidence Horace's ode to Phyllis happens to have the same melody as the famous hymn *Ut queant laxis*,[1] which Guido of Arezzo (d.c. 1050) used to instil the sol-fa syllables into his pupils. Another piece, a pilgrim's song *O Roma nobilis*, has been preserved in one source in alphabetical notation on staves.[2] The piece has a rugged dignity of its own, though it appears that the original text was a love-song entitled *O admirabile Veneris ydolum*. Most of these early pieces seem to sound best in duple rhythms, though there is little indication of the correct type of measure to use in the music. Another popular composition addressed to the nightingale bears out this hypothesis by its heavy accents on the first and third beat of a $\frac{4}{4}$ bar. This song *Aurea personet lyra* seems to suggest in its text that the organ was used in its performance. Another interpretation of the word 'organica' would be doubling the melody at the fourth or fifth below. Anyhow, the work is a vigorous one and deserved its celebrity.

Ex. 1

These pieces already lead us into the tenth and eleventh century. Between this period and the thirteenth century comes the era of the Goliards, the wandering scholars, students and clerics in minor orders who left behind a body of secular Latin songs of all kinds best represented by the *Carmina Burana*, an invaluable collection which originated in the library of the monastery of Benediktbeuren.[3] There are even a few German texts among these songs, which are unfortunately all notated without staves, so that a transcription into modern notation is only possible from other musical sources, if these exist. Although drinking songs exist among these works, others, with their moral content,

---

[1] Publ. by G. Reese, *Music in the Middle Ages* (1940), p. 150 after R. Haas, *Aufführungspraxis der Musik* (1930), p. 87.

[2] J. Westrup, *Medieval Song*, in *New Oxford History of Music* II (1954), p. 221.

[3] Complete edition of the texts by A. Hilka and O. Schumann, 3 vols. (1930–41).

come into the category of religious music. Satirical and love-songs are not easy to classify, but all these pieces, even when they border on the sacred, may be considered here because they are Latin songs of undoubted musical value. Duets and trios will not be included in this assessment, but the essential fluidity of medieval performance practice means that a piece which is monodic in one source may have a second part in another manuscript and a third one in still other sources. Nevertheless, there are many such works, usually called conductus, which are essentially monodies, and these might well have been accompanied solos, a simple accompaniment being improvised on the monastery organ or some other instrument. However this may be, it is certainly true that a long monodic conductus like *Veritas, equitas* has the melody of a Provençal lay, and it is clear that Troubadour songs usually had an improvised accompaniment on harp or viol.[4]

A piece like this already brings us up against another problem, that of rhythm. By the thirteenth century the use of the stave had become general, and so there is no question about what the actual notes of a composition may be. But a measured notation of Troubadour and Trouvère songs or monodic or polyphonic conductus is the exception rather than the rule. A few late sources prove that triple time was general, especially in the form of the six rhythmic modes. One of these usually governs the form of a composition rhythmically, so that a piece falls into a basic pattern which is repeated strictly throughout the work. Stops are generally made at the end of a line of verse, though with short lines two or three often form a rhythmic group. In modern terms the rhythmic patterns are:

These fit into ⅜ or ⅝ bars. The lay just mentioned may well be used as an example because, chameleon-like, its melody was used for the Provençal lay *Gent menais*, the French lay *Flour ne glais* by Gautier de Coincy and the Latin conductus *Veritas, equitas*, whose text is by Chancellor Philippe (d. 1236) of Paris. The fourth stanza exemplifies the second mode but *Gent menais* is long and changes mode.

Ex. 2

A Jhe - su lo   rei   prec qu'a leis m'au - trei, qu'el 'es   la __   plus va - len - ta.

[4] Cf. the references in Th. Gérold, *La Musique au moyen âge* (1932), p. 381ff.

More typical is a cheerful first mode melody like *Fas et nefas ambulant*,[5] which is taken from the *Carmina Burana*. The sequence was mainly a religious form of poetry and music characterized by metrically paired stanzas set to identical music, but there are secular examples. A fine one is *Axe Phebus aureo*,[6] also from the *Carmina Burana*. The melody has a lot of repeated notes which give it a fine swing, and the C major tonality could hardly be more pronounced. For beauty and breadth of phrasing, the conductus cannot be beaten as a form of medieval song, though obviously not every piece is on the same high level. We are hampered too by the lack of modern editions of these remarkable compositions, which are as varied in form as in melody and subject-matter. There are strophic conductus and through-composed conductus, others have sequence form, and again others have an initial or concluding coloratura passage. The subject-matter of many conductus is moralizing in character, like *O mens, cogita*, whose melody is of a jewel-like perfection in its balance of ascending and descending movement. Historical compositions come into the same category, carrying on the tradition of the early laments already mentioned. The death of king Philip Augustus of France in 1223 is lamented in *Alabaustrum frangitur* and *O mors que mordes*, while the coronation of his son at Reims in the same year is celebrated in *Beata nobis gaudia*.[7] *Turmas arment christicolas* bewails the assassination of Albert of Louvain, bishop of Liège, and *In rama sonat gemitus* the exile of Thomas à Becket (d. 1170).

The Troubadours

Whether the monodic conductus were performed with or without accompaniment, it is quite clear that vernacular songs of the twelfth and thirteenth centuries were accompanied by an instrument of some kind as a general rule, though there was no rule forbidding solo performance without accompaniment. The exact nature of these accompaniments is hard to determine, since only the solo voice-part is given in the manuscripts. The instruments are clearly depicted in contemporary illustrations in the hands of practising musicians, and descriptions of performances constantly mention viols, harps, bagpipes, shawms,

[5] W. Lipphardt, article *Carmina Burana*, in *Die Musik in Geschichte und Gegenwart* II (1952), col. 854.

[6] idem, *Unbekannte Weisen zu den Carmina Burana*, in *Archiv für Musikwissenschaft* XII (1955), p. 137f.

[7] L. Schrade, *Political Compositions in French Music of the 12th and 13th Centuries*, in *Annales Musicologiques* I (1953), p. 56.

trumpets, flutes and many other instruments. These were not standard-ized in shape or size, but certain of them were particularly popular and used in specific types of song. The viol was especially favoured, because it was very versatile, had quite a wide compass, and could be plucked or bowed. The professional instrumentalist was called a *jongleur* or minstrel, and he might be called upon to play lays, conductus, chansons, or independent dance pieces. He generally played and sang at the same time, and it is reasonable to suppose that, in the early days of counter-point, accompaniments were of a simple character. They might include drone basses, doubling at the unison, fifth or octave and a simultaneous but slightly ornamented performance of the voice-part.

On the highest level, such accompaniments might include simple counterpoint and imitative preludizing. The alternation of voice and instrument was a means of achieving variety, even though the same music might be repeated. The real pitfall in providing accompaniments for this type of song is obviously over-sophistication and complexity. In dance-music we might expect that such percussion instruments as drums, cymbals, tambourines and the like would employ as complex rhythms as, say, native African music. However this may be, even as late a writer as Thoinot Arbeau in the sixteenth century gives only the simplest drum patterns for dances.[8] The harp and rote (an instrument like the lyre) were other popular *jongleur* instruments, but unfortunately it is not so easy to obtain these for modern performances as it is a viol or even a viola. The same is true of the portative organ, an organ small enough to be carried about, played with one hand and blown with the other. This instrument however was not at the height of its popularity till the fourteenth century, and flutes, recorders, lutes, guitars, psalteries and many another instrument were employed when they were available. Under the circumstances, we can hardly go wrong if we perform accompaniments on the viol, the ubiquitous minstrel instrument, while bearing in mind the many other possibilities which exist.

Troubadours and Trouvères are not only distinguished by the diversity of their language, for the Troubadours preceded the Trouvères by about a century, but they have much in common, since the Trou-vères obviously continued Troubadour art. The language of the Troubadours was Provençal and their home the south, while the more northerly Trouvères wrote in the language whose home was the Ile de France. It is true that a number of the Troubadours were nobles, and this is the case with the first known Troubadour, Guillaume IX of

[8] Cf. E. Ferand, *Die Improvisation in der Musik* (1938), p. 395.

Aquitaine, but they were not always so fortunately placed. Thus the old idea that the Troubadours were all men of the upper class while the Trouvères were of lower birth is to be discounted. Similarly, it was thought that the princely Troubadours often wrote only the words of their songs, the music being set by *jongleurs*, but again one cannot generalize. As for the question of the origins of Troubadour song, that too is probably unanswerable. One can but put forward a few suggestions. The cult of woman, or courtly love as it has been called, was one of the main subjects of Troubadour verse. However women were treated in fact in the Middle Ages (and they were actually no more than chattels), in song they were placed on so high a pedestal that no mere man could hope to gain their love. This unusual idea could hardly originate anywhere outside the church, and the tremendous influence exercised by the worship of the Virgin Mary must be seen at work here. In the same way, church music must have made its mark on secular song, for most Troubadour works have little in common with what we know of earlier secular songs. Still, it is true enough that Guillaume IX had little conception of courtly love, and Marcabru, another early Troubadour, was actually a woman-hater. His stirring crusading song *Pax in nomine Domini* still has the rough vigour of the earliest Latin songs we know.

Ex. 3

Pax - in no-mi - ne Do - mi - ni! Dist Mar - ca - brus lou vers e͏̀l son. Au - jatz que di._

The recent publication of a complete edition of all Troubadour melodies[9] makes available to the scholar and performer 300 melodies, of which only a handful are anonymous. The lives of many of these composers have been made known by unreliable biographies of the Troubadours,[10] but in a good many cases the most satisfactory evidence is the poetry of their songs. Guiraut de Bornelh is a good example. He was born about 1140 near Périgueux and died soon after 1200. During the summer months he travelled from one castle to another, accompanied by two singers, who performed his songs. He was what might be called nowadays a self-made man, for his origins were lowly and his education due entirely to his own efforts in the long winter months. His songs themselves inform us who were his patrons, for he obviously was welcomed by the kings of Leon, Aragon and Navarre

[9] F. Gennrich, *Der musikalische Nachlass der Troubadours* (1958).
[10] J. Boutière and H. Schultz, *Biographies des Troubadours* (1950).

and by most of the nobility of Provence. The hothouse character of Troubadour poetry is nowhere more evident than in the so-called 'trobar clus', which Guiraut seems to have cultivated at first. This art for the initiated is reminiscent of our own times with its obscure style and difficult terminology.

Guiraut soon realized that the popularity of his songs depended on their being understood by wider circles, and he set out consciously to make them understood by everybody. In this he seems to have had great success, for he was known as the master of the Troubadours. His extant works are manifold and include 52 love-songs, 17 sirventes, 3 tensos, an alba, a pastourelle, a romance and a puzzle poem. The music shares the fate of that of many Troubadors, for only four pieces have been noted down. The most famous is the Alba *Reis glorios*,[11] which is justly famous. It represents a form in which lovers are generally waiting for the dawn. Here the lady is praying to God that he will look after her companion, whom she has not seen all night, and soon it will be dawn. The opening invocation is a masterpiece of simple dignity. Indeed, the mood throughout is one of quiet devotion, resignation and trust.

Of the other forms mentioned above, the sirventes is a song of service, moral or political in character, often about the crusades. The melody of these poems had often been used before. The tenso is the Provençal equivalent of the North French *jeu-parti*, a dialogue concerning problems of courtly love. This so-called dispute was a feature of the courts of love and the minstrel contests. The nobility entertained themselves at the former and the musicians practised to entertain the nobility at the latter. The idea was to discuss in the manner of a debate some point which might conceivably (or inconceivably!) arise between two lovers. It was a kind of sport, but the competitors had to be versed in poetry, music and logical reasoning. The pastourelle is not merely a pastoral song. It concerns a shepherd and his shepherdess and the trouble caused by a third party, an amorous knight. Contrary to what has often been thought, the idea of poetic and musical structure does not generally enter into the titles of Troubadour forms. It is rather the subject-matter that counts. In the cases mentioned this is obvious enough, but even general titles like *canso* or *vers* are distinguised by the matter more than by the form, since the only Provençal treatise dealing seriously with types of song, 'Las leys d'amors', considers the *canso* as

---

[11] Gennrich, p. 65; also available in Reese, p. 215 and W. Apel and A. T. Davison, *Historical Anthology of Music* I (2nd ed. 1949), p. 15f.

a love song and the *vers* a more serious piece.[12] Structurally, however, both forms have five or more stanzas and one or two semi-stanzas or envoys. In any case, the Provençal writers strove to give each new song a distinct form, though certain features indicate that the origin of the fourteenth century Ballade is to be found in some of the *cansos*.[13]

The Provençal ballada, on the other hand, is more like the virelai or the Italian ballata. Unfortunately, only one example exists with music, but this splendid work obviously attained some popularity since it was used as a basis for a three-part Latin conductus.[14] This already probably dates it as early as 1200. The rhythm stamps it as a dance-song and in any case the words 'let us dance' and the chorus-like interjections 'Eia' are clear enough indications of the piece's destination. The title *A l'entrada del tens clar* shows the piece is just one of the medieval spring songs which exist.[15]

Bernart de Ventadorn (c. 1125–1195) is one of the best of the Troubadours and combines a great talent for music with an equally superior gift for poetry. He was another Troubadour of lowly birth, for his father was a servant and his mother a maid in the castle of count Eble de Ventadorn. It appears that he was called to England in the mid-twelfth century by Eleanor of Aquitaine, the art-loving wife of Henry II. In the past she has been credited with the dissemination of Troubadour art in France, but obviously many factors have to be taken into account in this respect, not least the fact that long-distance travel was common in the Middle Ages. Furthermore, Troubadour poetry and music was also imitated in Germany and Italy as well as in Northern France. Bernart's poems are elevated in tone but straightforward to read. They are full of a simple joy in nature and a quiet regard for woman and love.

Ex. 4

Lan - can vei la fol - ha jos dels al - bres —— cha - zer, cui que pes· ne
No cre-zatz qu'eu vol - ha flor ni— fol - hà —— ve - zer, car vas me s'or-

dol - ha a me— deu bo— sa - ber.
-gol - ha so qu'eu plus volh a - ver.

[12] R. H. Perrin, *Some Notes on Troubadour Melodic Types*, in *Journal of the American Musicological Society* IX (1956), p. 14.

[13] G. Reaney, *Concerning the Origins of the Rondeau, Virelai and Ballade Forms*, in *Musica Disciplina VI* (1952), p. 164.

[14] *Veris ad imperia*, publ. by F. Gennrich, *Grundriss einer Formenlehre des mittelalterlichen Liedes* (1932), p. 85.

[15] Gennrich, *Troubadours*, p. 222; also available in *New Oxford History of Music* II, p. 241f.

The famous song of the lark *Can vei la lauzeta mover*[16] and the almost equally celebrated *Lancan vei la folha* (Ex. 4), are just two examples of the influence of birds, trees, and flowers in Bernart's poetry. The music accompanying them is spring-like too, but there is a slightly melancholy touch in it, corresponding with Bernart's own mood, presumably caused by the disdain of his beloved. Melancholy and even depression is indeed the prevailing mood of Troubadour poetry, for the lady of the poet's choice is always unyielding and even harsh towards her lover, on top of which there is the irritation caused by wagging tongues. Peire d'Auvergne, another Troubadour, actually makes fun of Bernart in his *Amics Bernartz*[17] in the same way that Dowland was later to be laughed at as the ever doleful Dowland. Peire can't believe that Bernart can be so sad when he can see how happy the nightingale is in his song. At least, the nightingale must be more successful in love than Bernart.

Folquet de Marseille (c. 1155–1231) was actually a member of a wealthy Genoese family, but he came to live in Marseilles when he was still a boy. He did not need to compose to earn money, but as an artist he was greatly admired by the highest society, which included king Alfonso II of Aragon and the viscount of Marseilles. His complete works are not extensive, but the majority are set to music. There are fourteen love songs, two crusading songs, a tenso, a *planh* or lament and a cobla. Quite apart from his amorous poetry glorifying noble ladies of his time in the language of courtly love, he wrote political works furthering the cause of the crusades. Richard the Lion Heart's decision to take part in the third crusade is greeted by him with approval and Richard's entry into Marseilles in 1190 forms the subject of another work. All the music that has been preserved is for the love-songs and these are mostly in the style whereby every phrase of the composition is a new one. For the Troubadours his compass is a wide one, nearly an octave and a half. As the texts are more refined than earlier poems, so the music tends to be more ornamented too. This is particularly the case with *Al quan gen vens*,[18] which at one point has a descending scale of a whole octave. More typical is *Tant m'abellis l'amoros pensamens*[19] with its opening on a repeated A and Dorian tonality. It is interesting to find that, when Folquet decided to end his life in a monastery, after which he became abbot in 1201 and bishop of Toulouse in 1205, he abandoned conventional love-poetry and turned to more religious and moralizing material.

Of course, there were many other Troubadours, including such

[16] Gennrich, *Troubadours*, p. 43; also available in *New Oxford History of Music* II, p. 236f.
[17] Gennrich, *Troubadours*, p. 45.   [18] ibid, p. 81.   [19] ibid, p. 90.

famous names as Jaufré Rudel, Bertran de Born, Peire Vidal, Arnaut Daniel, Gaucelm Faidit, Peirol, Raimbaut de Vaqueiras, Raimon de Miraval, Uc de Saint Circ and Aimeric de Peguillan. Raimbaut, who died in 1207, is particularly famous for his *Kalenda maya*,[20] a spring song which, according to the legend, he composed to the melody he had just heard played as a dance-tune on the viols. Quite apart from the importance of this anecdote in clarifying medieval methods of composition, the melody itself is a stirring one and well worth singing. Bertran de Born was a political adventurer, and it is not surprising that he left twenty-seven sirventes, a genre which has much to do with diplomacy. Unfortunately, only one melody[21] has been preserved, as with Raimbaut d'Orange, Beatritz de Dia, Jordan Bonel, Peire Raimon de Toulouse, Uc Brunec, Cadenet and several other Troubadours. Arnaut Daniel, who flourished c. 1200, exercised great influence on later Troubadours and on such famous Italian writers as Dante and Petrarch because of his excellence in the *trobar clus*, but even he has left us only two pieces with music.

Guiraut Riquier (c. 1230–1300), often called the last of the Troubadours, was more fortunate, since no less than forty-eight songs have come down with music.[22] He was not however so lucky in other ways, since he lived at a time when princely courts found it difficult to support minstrels and composers. Indeed, after the so-called Albigensian Crusade, the courtly love of the Troubadours was to some extent looked upon as sinful. Still, Guiraut found shelter at the court of Henry II, count of Rodez, where he could indulge in the old game of poetic disputes. None of his 21 tensos has any music, but 22 love-songs, 13 sirventes, 7 religious songs, 3 retroenchas, a crusading song, a prayer and a *planh* have all been notated. The songs with the name *Belh Deport* in the text were written for the wife of the viscount of Narbonne between c. 1250 and 1265. Many of his songs have the initial repeat which we associate with the later French Ballade. Perhaps the highly ornamented style is a sign of decline, but it also has a certain appeal, as in the prayer to Christ *Jhesus Cristz filh de Dieu*.[23] The lament for the viscount of Narbonne *Ples de tristor*[24] is not quite so florid, but is probably a more moving work. Another religious song *Quis tolgues*[25] has a remarkably ornamented closing couplet, which gradually descends a whole octave. Although there are few anonymous songs in

[20] ibid, p. 100; conveniently available in Apel and Davison, p. 16.
[21] Gennrich, *Troubadours*, p. 49.
[22] ibid, p. 185–219.   23 ibid, p. 201.   24 ibid, p. 208.   25 ibid, p. 212.

Provençal, some of them are astoundingly fine compositions, such as the folk-like *L'altrier m'iere levaz*[26] and the lively first mode *Ara lausetz, lauset, lauset.*[27] Pieces like *Amors m'art con fuoc*[28] and *Dona, pos vos ai chausida*[29] have the ABBAA form of the Italian ballata and may have been the models for this important fourteenth-century form.

There are three lays among the anonymous Troubadour compositions[30] but this form was more cultivated in the north. The Breton origins of this type of song are suggested by the frequent mention of Breton origin in the songs themselves, but it is possible that the relationship between French and Breton lays was a very distant one. The question is very difficult, but it would seem that the Breton lay was a narrative work after the manner of the *chanson de geste*, while the French works are lyric compositions. The *chanson de geste*, the long heroic poem so popular from the eleventh to the thirteenth century in France, simply repeated a phrase of music long enough to encompass one line of text rather in the style of a primitive incantation.[31] Whether the Breton lays were in fact of this kind will probably never be known, but the French works are lengthy lyric poems employing a variety of stanzas and very short lines of verse. The music of the lays tends to make use of repetition and melodic sequence so that the notes will last out. The material of which the melodies are made up seems to come from a common pool, and one can frequently trace phrases from other songs in them. Nevertheless, these pieces are especially interesting from a modern point of view because of their relative length and variety. Some thirty of these compositions exist with music, though the majority are anonymous.[32]

Among the composers of lays are Gautier de Dargiès, Guillaume le Vinier and Thibaut de Navarre. By no means all the lays are secular. One of the sacred lays, which may well be based on an earlier melody, is Ernoul le Vieux's *Lai de l'Ancien et du Nouveau Testament*,[33] with its repetitions of the most elementary motifs. A typical example of an early lay is the *Lai des pucelles*.[34] Once one has accepted the necessity for repetitions of short motifs, the vigour and life of the piece becomes

---

[26] ibid, p. 227.   [27] ibid, p. 231.   [28] ibid, p. 230.   [29] ibid, p. 233.

[30] ibid, p. 247, 255, 261.

[31] The three extant examples are printed in Th. Gérold, *La Musique au moyen âge*, p. 82, 83 86f.

[32] 26 are published in square medieval notes in A. Jeanroy, P. Aubry and L. Brandin, *Lais et descorts du XIIIe siècle* (1901).

[33] ibid, p. 113ff; cf. the modern transcription of the first section in *New Oxford History of Music* II, p. 247.

[34] *Lais et descorts*, p. 135.

apparent. The *Lai des Hermins*[35] may well contain actual Breton music, since the author mentions that he has put 'Romance reason' into the *Lai des Hermins*. These rather obscure words probably refer to the composition of a French text, since the *Lai des Amants*[36] starts with the sentence, 'Here begins the *Lai des Amants* all in Romance (language)'. Like the anonymous lays, the lays by known composers are mainly written in a fairly simple first mode rhythm with occasional use of the second or third mode, but they are less primitive melodically and have a wider compass. Such is Thibaut de Navarre's *Comencerai a faire un lay*,[37] whose rhythm is clearly defined in the valuable Chansonnier Cangé.[38]

The Trouvères

The lays have already brought the North French counterparts of the Troubadours into view, and indeed the importance of the Trouvères lies partly in the quantity of compositions we possess by them today. At a conservative estimate, there are certainly about 1,500 songs with melodies. As with the Troubadours, the Trouvères like to give their names in the song-books, so that we know a good many of them. They clearly followed in the steps of the Troubadours, since their musical forms very often employ the same names as Troubadour forms. Typical is the name rotrouenge for retroencha, a type of song whose characteristics have not been properly identified yet. The tenso becomes tenson (or *joc partit = jeu parti*) and the canso becomes chanson. While the Troubadours were active from the end of the eleventh century, the earliest Trouvères like Blondel de Nesles and the Chatelain de Coucy date from the end of the twelfth. Richard the Lion Heart himself was highly esteemed as a Trouvère, and his song *Ja nuns hons pris*[39] has a powerful melody belying its composer's temporary captivity. He is concerned that his friends are slow in arranging his ransom, and says it will be a scandal if he is not released before two winters are out. This may well date the piece in the year 1194 when the king was imprisoned by Emperor Henry VI of Germany. The melody is reminiscent of Troubadour song with its initial repeated lines and its repetition of the same note at the opening. It is also characteristic of medieval pieces which appear to be in C major, since they generally drop down to A at the end as this one does.

Blondel de Nesles, the friend of Richard according to a famous

---

[35] *Lais et descorts*, p. 147.   [36] ibid, p. 123.
[37] ibid, p. 100; modern transcription in J. Beck, *Le Chansonnier Cangé* II (1927), No. 57.
[38] Beck, ibid, I, f. 23.   [39] Apel and Davison, p. 16.

legend, is a more celebrated Trouvère, but in fact nothing certain is known of his life. He is probably of noble birth and has been identified with Jehan I, lord of Nesles and chastelain of Bruges, who died before 1202. One of his songs can be dated before 1179, because its melody was used for the Latin conductus *Ver pacis aperit*, written for the coronation of Philip Augustus.[40] His subject-matter is the courtly love of the Troubadours. Hence, like them, he often mentions his own name but conceals that of the beloved for fear of slanderers. The popularity of his songs can be gauged by the degree in which they were cited and borrowed by other writers. Apart from two more Latin pieces, we may mention four borrowings in Gautier de Coincy's *Miracles de Nostre Dame*,[41] written between 1218 and 1227, and one by the Minnesinger Ulrich von Gutenberg. *Tant ai en chantant proié*[42] is one of the best of his songs with its clear rhythm and cheerful melody. *L'amours dont sui espris*[43] is a second mode work for the most part, but the opening breaks up the mode a little and apparently even allows an occasional first mode bar among the rest.

It is probably by breaking up the second mode that the sixth mode came into being, equivalent in modern notation to a bar of three quavers in $\frac{3}{8}$ or six quavers in $\frac{6}{8}$. Each phrase is concluded by a longer note of course, for instance in two $\frac{6}{8}$ bars one might have nine quavers, a crotchet and a quaver rest. A fine example is Conon de Béthune's *L'autrier avint en cel païs*,[44] which has the simplest up-and-down movement within the narrow interval of a fourth. In spite of this, the overall aesthetic effect is perfectly satisfying. Nevertheless, it seems likely that the sixth mode may be a later transformation of the third mode into short values. And this particular melody may not be the original, since it is not the only one set to these words. The question is not simple, but at least one may say that such economy of material and such a small compass suggest an early date. Indeed, this melody actually consists of eight repetitions of one basic phrase.

Another example of a second mode song which is broken by ornamentation into something more like the sixth mode is the Chastelain de Coucy's famous *Quant li rossignol jolis*. The Parisian theorist Johannes de Grocheo, writing about 1300, quotes this piece as an example of a

[40] Both texts with the music in H. Besseler, *Die Musik des Mittelalters und der Renaissance* (1931–34), p. 107.
[41] Cf. article *Gautier de Coinci*, by F. Gennrich in *Die Musik in Geschichte und Gegenwart* IV (1955), col. 1493.
[42] Beck, II, No. 335.   [43] ibid, No. 196.
[44] *New Oxford History of Music* II, p. 234.

cantus coronatus,[45] i.e. the type of chanson for which the composer was crowned at the minstrel competitions of the Middle Ages (Ex. 5).

Ex. 5

Quant li— ros-sig - gnol jo - lis   chan-te seur la— flor de-sté,

Gui II, the Chastelain de Coucy (d. 1203) is another early Trouvère whose poems show considerable Troubadour influence, for instance in their predilection for decasyllabic lines of identical length throughout. An example is *La douce voiz dou rossignol sauvage*,[46] another simple but attractive nightingale song which is apparently again in the sixth rhythmic mode.

Gace Brulé (c. 1159–1215) has left no less than fifty-seven authentic songs with music and fifteen unauthentic pieces. He worked among the Trouvères who frequented Marie de France's half-brother Geoffrey, count of Brittany (d. 1186). After the count's death he wrote songs for many other nobles, including Marie herself. Gace's works tend to fall into the standard chanson form of Trouvère song, and of course the subject-matter is courtly love. He even attacks one Trouvère for neglecting and even abjuring this refined theme. *Je ne puis pas si loing fuir*[47] is a very cheerful composition in spite of its text, which deals with the lover's sadness at being dismissed by the lady to whom he has revealed his love. Another fine piece which breathes the air of springtime is *Quant voi la flour boutonner*,[48] a smooth second mode melody. *Quant noif et gief*[49] is a similar composition, but with noteworthy economy in thematic material.

Colin Muset and Colart li Boutellier belong to a slightly later period, flourishing about the middle of the thirteenth century. Colart belonged to the minstrel fraternity of Arras, which included such names as Moniot d'Arras and Adam de la Halle. Songs were dedicated to him by various local musicians, while he wrote pieces for Guillaume li Vinier (d. 1245) and Jehan Bretel (d. 1272). His music, however, seems less interesting than that of Colin Muset, another Trouvère of about the same time who seems to have worked in the neighbourhood of Chaumont. His work has a popular flavour which makes it of particular appeal for the modern listener, as for example in his egocentric *Volez*

[45] E. Rohloff, *Der Musiktraktat des Johannes de Grocheo* (1943), p. 50.
[46] Beck II, No. 184.
[47] *New Oxford History of Music* II, 238.
[48] Beck II, No. 267.
[49] ibid. No. 270.

oïr la muse Muset?[50] The tonality is clearly C major throughout and the melody itself is wonderfully alive. The same is true of *Sire cuens, j'ai vielé*,[51] another minstrel's melody, except that it is in the popular mode on G. In this piece the poet complains that he has not been rewarded properly for his services. Both songs mention the musician's viol.

This type of composition is actually a definite genre, which is not surprising, since the Trouvère was dependent on the generosity of his masters for his livelihood, and no doubt it was necessary to jog their memory occasionally to obtain payment due. Of Colin's eighteen extant songs, five are of this kind, but he also left a variety of other pieces, including love-songs, a lay, a *descort*, a tenso and four drinking songs. The *descort* is a similar form to the lay, but generally brings in some element which clashes with the rest. It may be simply that the words are sad and the music is gay, or the text itself may be concerned with some dispute, as in the tenso. The lay is not necessarily a *descort*, but often is, owing to the variety of poetic structure which in itself is a simple type of disagreement or discord.

Thibaut de Navarre (1201–53) was not only a king but also count of Champagne and the most prolific of the Trouvères. He has left sixty-eight songs with music in quite a variety of forms, of which the jeu parti seems to have particularly interested him. As in other cases however, nearly all the melodies of the jeux partis, seven out of nine, are certainly pre-existing ones. It is characteristic of songs in this form that they borrowed well-known melodies, since the main interest was clearly the dispute chosen as subject-matter. Here again the structure of the song might coincide with that of many love-songs which have an initial repeat, like Thibaut's *L'autre nuit*,[52] a dialogue between the king and the personification of love. On the other hand, it might not. Some jeux partis have been preserved with several different melodies in different manuscripts.

Thibaut took part in the Albigensian crusade, but soon left his allies in the lurch. Since he was obviously very much influenced by the Troubadours, one wonders whether he disliked the senseless attacks on Provence made by the northerners in the name of religion. He was apparently in love with Blanche of Castile, the wife of Louis VIII of France, and it is to her that many of his songs must have been addressed.

[50] F. Gennrich, article *Colin Muset*, in *Die Musik in Geschichte und Gegenwart* II (1952), col. 1550.

[51] ibid.

[52] Beck II, No. 173.

Tuit mi desir[53] is a fine piece in F major, a third mode melody which turns up again in a lay preserved in a fourteenth century source. Thibaut himself wrote the attractive lay *Comencerai a faire un lay*.[54] The melodic repetitions are typical of the lay, but they do not pall, owing to the lilting first mode rhythm which prevails throughout (at the beginning with anacrusis). *Pour conforter ma pesance*,[55] a ballade-like piece, is almost entirely based on the material of the first line, except for the unusual refrain in long notes to the vowel 'e'.

Adam de la Halle († c. 1287) is particularly representative of the middle class Trouvère, and is one of the first composers to leave a complete manuscript of his works. He was born in Arras and appears to have been very fond of it, since he wrote a farewell to it in song in 1269. The name Adam the Hunchback was not a nickname, but apparently his family had adopted the surname li Bossu to distinguish it from other de la Halles. Adam had a good education at the Cistercian abbey of Vaucelles and the University of Paris. After making signal contributions to the jeu parti literature at the Arras minstrel competitions, he followed his patron Robert of Artois to Naples and there became attached to the court of the king of Sicily.

He had already written a play, the *Jeu de la Feuillée*,[56] for the Arras musical festival in 1262, but at Naples he produced his most significant work, the *Jeu de Robin et de Marion* (c. 1285).[57] This attractive work is a pastoral comedy based on the subject-matter of the medieval Pastourelle. It might be described as an early comic opera, with its songs and dialogues interspersed between spoken parts. The best-known piece in it is undoubtedly the attractive *Bergeronette, douche baisselete*,[58] basically a rondeau. A similar piece, *Robins m'aime*,[59] has the same delightful vein of melody but is less lively. The popular element is very evident in this pastoral play, and there can be no doubt that it has preserved many popular refrains of medieval times. It has been said that Adam is musically of secondary importance, but such melodies as *Hélas, il n'est mais*[60] and *Je n'ai autre retenance*[61] are ample proof that he is a first-rate composer.

As with the Troubadours, the anonymous compositions of the Trouvères are quite up to the standard maintained by known composers. Indeed, they frequently lack the artificiality of the court atmos-

[53] *New Oxford History of Music* II, p. 231.
[54] See note 37. [55] Reese, p. 224. [56] Ed. E. Langlois (1923).
[57] G. Cohen, *Adam le Bossu, dit de la Halle, Le Jeu de Robin et de Marion* (1935).
[58] *New Oxford History of Music* II, p. 232 f.
[59] Reese, p. 223. [60] Beck II, No. 141. [61] ibid, No. 164.

phere and hence may be more immediately appealing. This is often the case with the many anonymous rondeaux which repeat two melodic phrases in the pattern ABaAabAB, the capital letters representing the text of the refrain. These pieces often move simply but effectively between a narrow compass such as the fifth, as in *Vous arez la druerie*.[62] Another charming work, *En ma dame ai mis mon cuer*,[63] appears to be based merely on the notes between the descending fifth on the keynote C. The rondeau already existed in the thirteenth century with a Latin text, though often without the initial refrain which became traditional in vernacular compositions. *Christo psallat ecclesia*,[64] which has a religious text, is a fine example whose melody may well have a secular origin. The basic form of the virelai is ABBAA, but this overall pattern has to fit many and varied poetic structures and line lengths. It would be hard to find a more pleasing virelai than *E, dame jolie*,[65] which, although it is in the Dorian mode, has a swinging first mode melody which is quite carefree. The Troubadour theme of service is still in evidence here, but the poet's love does not seem quite so hopeless. If he complains of the pains caused by love, this malady agrees with him and makes him sing.

The name *ballade*, which doubtless had some general dance significance in the thirteenth century, acquired structural importance about 1300 and was applied to the typical Trouvère song form with initial repeat. The ballade form became gradually more standardized till the time of Guillaume de Machaut (1300–77), so that it was usual to have three stanzas of seven or eight lines each, with a refrain. Although Machaut's ballades are all polyphonic with one exception, Jehannot de Lescurel (d. 1303) has left an important collection of thirty-two monodic ballades, rondeaux and virelais.[66] Their melodies show the influence of the late thirteenth-century motets, with their ornamented upper parts, and duple time occurs in several cases. In the works of Lescurel there is still a certain variety in poetic structure, e.g. in *Amour, voulés vous acorder*, a ballade with only a six-line stanza and a short initial repeated phrase more like the usual Trouvère song than the ballades of Machaut. The piece has a lovely melody which ends on D but is in F for the most part.

62 Gérold, p. 156.   63 Apel and Davison, p. 17.
64 ibid, p. 14.   65 ibid, p. 17.
66 F. Gennrich, *Rondeaux, Virelais und Balladen* I (1921), p. 307–72.

The same manuscript, which contains a large collection of motets and conductus as well as pieces of plainsong, also includes some further but anonymous secular songs in ballade and rondeau form.[67] This very important source of early fourteenth-century music was completed in 1316. It contains the *Roman de Fauvel*,[68] a verse fantasy with a moral about the adventures of a horse called Fauvel. Fauvel epitomizes vice and the letters of his name stand for seven deadly sins: flattery, avarice, usury, villainy and variability, envy and lowness. The music is intended as a commentary to the poem, and so the texts are often adapted to fit it, as in the rondeau *Fauvel est mal assené*.[69] The ballade *Douce dame debonnaire*[70] is an attractive second mode melody in F ending on the dominant C. The text is in the popular dialogue form in which the lover's pleas are promptly and firmly rejected.

Machaut himself wrote twenty-five one-line virelais[71] and sixteen monodic lays.[72] The *Roman de Fauvel* also contains four lays which are difficult to date. Their relative complexity and masterful composition suggest that they can hardly be earlier than the late thirteenth century. The poetic structure is less fixed than in Machaut, but two already have the twelve double strophes normally used by Machaut. The rhythmic modes from one to three are still employed too, while Machaut makes some use of duple time and prolation. Melodically these works are sheer masterpieces, particularly *Talant que j'ai* and *En ce dous temps d'esté*.[73] The latter is a sort of *jeu parti*, though the text actually defines the work as a *descort* too. The fact is that we are here right in the middle of a session of a court of love. In each stanza a new female character intervenes, be it countess, duchess or chatelaine.[74] In some of Machaut's lays the rhythmic element predominates, and these pieces are generally less interesting than such melodically smooth lays as *J'aim la flour*[75] and *Nuls ne doit avoir marveille*.[76] An exception is *Longuement me sui tenus*[77] with its drooping opening phrase.

From the standpoint of tonality, these lays are quite remarkable. Unlike the shorter songs, which tend to keep to a compass of just

[67] ibid, p. 290–306.
[68] Ed. A. Långfors (1914–19).
[69] Gennrich, *Rondeaux*, p. 294.
[70] Apel and Davison, p. 16.
[71] F. Ludwig, *Guillaume de Machaut: Musikalische Werke* I (1926); L. Schrade, *The Polyphonic Music of the Fourteenth Century* III (1956), p. 167 ff.
[72] Ludwig IV (1954), p. 24 ff.; Schrade II (1956), p. 1 ff.
[73] Cf. G. Reaney, *The Lais of Guillaume de Machaut and their Background*, in *Proceedings of the Royal Musical Association* LXXXII (1955), p. 22 f.
[74] Complete text in E. Dahnk, *L'hérésie de Fauvel* (1935), p. 187 ff.
[75] Ludwig IV and Schrade II, lay No. 2.
[76] Ludwig IV, lay No. 5; Schrade II, lay No. 4.
[77] Ludwig IV, lay No. 18; Schrade II, lay No. 13.

over an octave, these works modulate. Individual stanzas tend to stay within a certain range, but succeeding ones may move the whole compass up a fifth or down a fifth. The procedure is more like transposition, but, since there was no organized key system, it is clear that the idea of modulation was present against the modal background.[78] Like the lays, the monodic virelais were the last of their kind. They are akin to the lays in the variety of poetic structure and line length which they show. Short lines are common to both forms and moreover both reflect the length of the text lines in the musical phrases. Finally, in spite of Machaut's preoccupation with the ornamental rhythmic formulae which appear already in the works of Guiraut Riquier, the Virelais and lays reveal a melodic gift which tends to be subordinated to rhythm and harmony in the polyphonic works.

Quant je sui mis au retour[79] is a hybrid work with ballade characteristics, but its duple rhythms and happy melody mark it out musically. *Foy porter*[80] is a good example of the use of short lines of three and four syllables with equally crisp melodic phrases. *Aymi! dame de valour*[81] with its sigh on the first note is a remarkable work of more melancholy cast, which seems to be accentuated by the dragging second mode rhythms. In fact, the monodic virelais of Machaut bring the treasury of French medieval music written for a single voice with only improvised accompaniment to an admirable conclusion. He himself wrote music for the *complainte* and the *chanson royal* in his didactic poem *Le Remède de Fortune*,[82] but the development of polyphony in fourteenth-century song writing, which was furthered by Machaut in particular, put the ballade and rondeau in the forefront of contemporary interest.

The Minnesinger

It is customary to date the origin of German song in the Troubadour style from the year 1156 when Frederick Barbarossa married Beatrix of Burgundy.[83] As it happened, the Trouvère Guiot de Provins was at the Emperor's court in 1184, and certainly Friedrich von Hausen wrote his *Ich denke under wilen* to Guiot's *Ma joie premeraine*,[84] but the connection between Guiot and Beatrix is not established. To be sure, German song existed before this period. The *Petruslied* (tenth century) is written in staffless notation which precludes a transcription, and of

---

[78] See further in G. Reaney, .The Lais . . . , p. 29 f.
[79] Ludwig I and Schrade III, Virelai 13.
[80] Ludwig I, Virelai 25; Schrade III, Virelai 22.
[81] ibid, Virelai 3. [82] Ludwig I, p. 96, 97; Schrade II, p. 106, 107.
[83] Reese, p. 231. [84] Both texts with the music in Besseler, p. 108.

course Latin song existed in the monasteries, as we have seen. Still, the earliest extant songs set to German texts dealing with courtly love date from the end of the twelfth century. Friedrich von Hausen (d. 1190) also borrowed melodies from Bernart de Ventadorn, Folquet de Marseille and Conon de Béthune as well as Guiot. There are in fact far less melodies preserved by the Minnesinger than by the Troubadours or Trouvères, and even then the big manuscripts of Minnesinger song tend to be rather late. In the fourteenth century the Minnesinger tradition is superseded smoothly by the more bourgeois and somewhat decadent Mastersinger rules.

One of the earliest of the Minnesinger seems to have been Spervogel,[85] whose music has a square vigour like that to be found in early Troubadours like Marcabru. This is partly due to the heavier accents of German verse, which make it difficult to decide whether modal rhythm or simple duple time is to be applied to the music. Since the music is not in mensural notation, this is a very real problem. Editors have generally been very cautious, adopting one or the other solution according to the character of the verse and the music. Thus the folk-like summer and winter songs of Neidhart von Reuental (c. 1185–1236) with their dance associations have all been transcribed modally in a recent edition.[86] *Blozen wir den anger*,[87] a compact little Dorian melody, actually occurs in mensural notation in the first mode in one manuscript, so that there is some justification for this method. The form with initial repeat occurs frequently in these songs, as it does throughout the Minnesinger repertoire, and indeed has the special name of *Bar* form. There are many more songs attributable to Neidhart than the seventeen included in the above edition, but the others are unauthentic.[88] Works like *Der sumer kumpt*[89] and *Winder wie ist nu*[90] will, however, stand comparison with any of the genuine Neidhart compositions.

Pieces like these are rather the exception than the rule in Minnesinger writing, which tends to be more serious in general. The only complete song of Walther von der Vogelweide († c. 1230), *Nu alerst lebe ich* [91], which is generally associated with the crusade of 1228, illustrates this trait very well. He says that he only begins to appreciate

---

[85] Cf. his *Swa eyn vriund* in Apel and Davison, p. 18.
[86] A. T. Hatto and R. J. Taylor, *The Songs of Neidhart von Reuental* (1958).
[87] ibid, No. 2.
[88] Sixty-two authentic and unauthentic songs are published by W. Schmieder and E. Wiessner in *Denkmäler der Tonkunst in Österreich* (1930), Jahrgang XXXVII[1], Band 71.
[89] and [90]. Both printed in duple time in Apel and Davison, p. 18 f.
[91] Reese, p. 234; Apel and Davison, p. 18.

life as he should now that he has seen the Holy Land. The measured gait of the music, best transcribed in $\frac{4}{4}$ time, brilliantly heightens the prevailing mood of tranquil meditation. Such themes as this tend to distinguish German from Troubadour song, but both employ some of the same forms, such as the Tagelied, identical with the alba, and the Leich, very similar to the lay. The Spruch is a song with a moral content, like Frauenlob's *Myn vroud ist gar czugangyn*,[92] in which he laments his sins. This piece is said to be sung to the green melody, which was probably one of the standard melodic-types used by various composers. These colourful descriptions were used in particular by the later Mastersingers.

Frauenlob is a nickname for Heinrich von Meissen (d. 1318), because he used the word *Frau* and not *Weib* for woman. He has left a leich *Ey ich sach*[93] which clearly reveals the indebtedness of this form to the liturgical sequence, for it is written throughout in paired stanzas. This work has a religious text and is in fact entitled *Unser frauen leich*, ('The Leich of Our Lady'). The melody is serious and moving. Here we can already see the transition from Minne (courtly love) to Mastersong, whereby the adoration of woman is transferred definitely to the Virgin Mary and her son.

Witzlav von Rügen (d. 1325) stuck to the older type of song and wrote a number of masterpieces, of which *We, ich han gedacht*[94] may specially be mentioned. This is an example of the developed *Bar* form which not only has the initial repeat but also repeats all this first part of the music at the end of the stanza. The piece has a soaring melody which makes it outstanding among contemporary German songs. Between the period of Neidhart and Walther come masters like Tannhaüser, Alexander and Rumelant. Tannhaüser has left only two pieces with musical notation but his *Ez ist hiute eyn wunnychlicher tac*[95] has a splendid impetus when transcribed in modal rhythm. The theme of the poem is rather a contrast, with its prayer for God's grace, but the idea seems to be that the day of death is a joyous one, and Tannhaüser greets it with happiness if God will grant him atonement. Alexander is represented by five melodies and Rumelant by ten but Frauenlob is the most prolific of the Minnesinger with twenty-six compositions.

---

[92] H. Rietsch, 'Gesänge von Frauenlob, Reinmar von Zweter und Alexander' as Jahrgang XX², Band 41 of the *Denkmäler der Tonkunst in Österreich* (1913), p. 67; A. Schering, *Geschichte der Musik in Beispielen* (1931), No. 21.

[93] First two sections in *New Oxford History of Music* II, p. 258.

[94] Gérold, p. 218.

[95] *New Oxford History of Music* II, p. 254.

Of the later fourteenth-century masters, the Monk of Salzburg has left well over 100 monodic songs as well as half a dozen polyphonic examples. At least forty-seven of his works have religious texts and eighty-seven secular ones. It is possible that more than one composer contributed to the repertory attributable to the Monk, but certainly his work is extremely varied. There are sacred songs and drinking songs, love songs and Leiche, and particularly in his secular works the Monk borrows obvious folk elements. The court of Archbishop Pilgrim II of Salzburg (1365–1396) was very suited to secular production, and one can imagine the performance there of the Monk's *Untarn slaf*, whose melody imitates the sound of primitive alpine horns. Moreover, the initial fanfare melody is repeated with rhythmic variations, first in $\frac{6}{8}$ and then in the original $\frac{2}{4}$ (Ex. 7). More normal but equally simple is the

intimate *Ich han in ainem garten gesehen*[96] with its instrumental interlude and postlude. Such works reflect the Monk's conscious striving after the straightforward and unforced ease of folk music, so different from contemporary French music.

The music for the songs of Count Hugo von Montfort (1357–1423) was written by his minstrel Burg Mangolt, but few of the ten extant compositions seem to be of value.[97] Another member of the nobility, Oswald von Wolkenstein (1377–1445), is more important, for his complete output comprises at least 124 works,[98] of which the great majority are monodic. During his adventurous life he travelled a great deal throughout Europe, particularly with the emperor Sigismund, and hence came into contact with many different kinds of music. Nevertheless, his own melodies generally follow those of his German predecessors and his forms too are traditional. By way of the typical German

[96] F. A. Mayer and H. Rietsch, *Die Mondsee-Wiener Liederhandschrift und der Mönch von Salzburg* (1896), p. 362.

[97] P. Runge, *Die Lieder des Hugo von Montfort mit den Melodien des Burk Mangolt* (1906).

[98] Inventory in W. Salmen, *Werdegang und Lebensfülle des Oswald von Wolkenstein*, in *Musica Disciplina* VII (1953), p. 155 ff.

duple time song, however, he progresses to a more developed kind of song in $\frac{6}{8}$ and finally in $\frac{3}{4}$. Many songs were written to his beloved Margarete and quite a few others during his imprisonments. His earlier pieces seem to have often been less smooth than the later ones melodically, but nevertheless the leaps of such a work as *Es seust dort her*[99] are powerful, not awkward. In spite of frequent borrowings and remakes of known songs, Wolkenstein's production represents a remarkable unity of the most diverse tendencies in German song. As such, especially since all the music has been published,[100] this opus is most valuable, and moreover it brings to the fore a definite artistic personality, whether he is revelling in a tavern scene like *Und swig ich nu*,[101] discussing class matters in *Ain purger und ain hofman*[102] or pouring out his heart in *Herz, muet, leib, sel*.[103]

Song in Other Countries

Italy and Spain have left us two monuments of monodic song from the Middle Ages, and it is significant that both have religious texts. They are however in the vernacular and undoubtedly contain many popular elements. Indeed, the general impression is far more of secular than sacred song. It has to be remembered that the Troubadours were very active in both Spain and Italy, though recent discoveries have made known a number of Spanish songs from as early as the first half of the eleventh century,[104] i.e. before the earliest known Troubadours. Unfortunately, there is no music for them, and the same is true of the majority of early Portuguese songs. Actually there are in existence half a dozen love songs by Martin Codax, a Galician poet-musician of the early thirteenth century, and these have pleasing melodies of a folk-like cast.[105]

The really important medieval Spanish song collection is however the *Cantigas de Santa Maria*[106] compiled by Alfonso X the Wise, king of Castile and Leon (1252–84). It consists of 423 songs in the Galician-Portuguese language in praise of the Virgin or relating miracles done by her. Fortunately this music is not only written down in three large manuscripts but it is also written in a notation which makes the

---

[99] ibid, p. 161.
[100] *Oswald von Wolkenstein, geistliche und weltliche Lieder*, in *Denkmäler der Tonkunst in Österreich* (1902), ed. J. Schatz and O. Koller, Jahrgang IX¹, Band 18.
[101] ibid, Koller No. 66.   [102] ibid, Koller No. 3.   [103] ibid, Koller No. 31.
[104] Cf. Damaso Alonso, *Cancioncillas 'de amigo' mozarabes*, in *Revista de Filologia Espanola* XXXIII (1949), p. 297 ff.
[105] I. Pope, *Medieval Latin Background of the Thirteenth-Century Galician Lyric*, in *Speculum* IX (1934), pp. 18–20, 22–24.   [106] Complete edition by H. Anglès (1943).

rhythms clear. The rhythmic modes are evidently the basis of these songs as of other medieval songs, but in addition there is a tendency to mix the first and second modes, while duple rhythms are also to be found. *Quen na Virgen gloriosa*[107] is an attractive example of second mode rhythms with a simple melody moving in a narrow compass. Even in duple time the inverted rhythmic patterns of the mixed modes occur, as in *A que as cousas* (Ex. 8). This collection of songs contains

Ex. 8

A que as cou - sas ·coi - ta - das d'a - ju - dar muit' e' te - ū - da

some real masterpieces, sometimes astonishingly alive and gay, at other times more tranquil and meditative, though rarely sad. There is something definitely Spanish about the $\frac{6}{8}$ *Quen serve Santa Maria*,[108] even to modern ears, which might consider the melody too gay for a religious text. *Os sete dões*,[109] a Dorian piece in duple time from the Prologue to the *Cantigas*, is outstandingly beautiful. In common with much early Italian music, the *Cantigas* make use most often of a song-form with the basic design of the virelai.

In Italy, native poetry took as its starting point in the thirteenth century the songs of Troubadours, many of whom fled after the catastrophe of the Albigensian crusade. The court of Frederick II of Sicily was particularly welcoming, and Guilhem Figuiera, Gaucelm Faidit, Elias Carel, Albert de Sisteron and Nue de San Caro, to mention but a few, made their way there. In any case, the Provençal language was natural to the Italians at this time and most poetry was written in it till the early fourteenth century. The Italian Troubadours, like Lanfranco Cigala, Sordello of Mantua, Ferrari of Ferrara and Zorzi of Venice, became as famous as their teachers. Actual imitations of Provençal poetry soon became current in Italian, but by the time of Guido Cavalcanti, the friend of Dante and the founder of the *dolce stil nuovo* based on the work of Guinicelli (1240–76), the themes of Provençal literature had been idealized to such an extent that they were scarcely recognizable. Certainly woman was put on a pedestal by the Troubadours, but it was usually someone else's wife that was concerned. Her name was disguised so that the slanderers (and the husband) would not find out. However innocent such subjects may have been as a theme for the writing of poetry and music, they possess an underlying immorality.

[107] ibid, p. 285.
[108] ibid, p. 235.
[109] ibid, p. 445.

In Cavalcanti, however, everything is on the highest moral plane and a conscious desire for obscurity is evident.[110]

No music has been preserved for these poems. Instead, we find another large group of songs with religious texts in virelai form.[111] Whatever the origin of the Cantigas, the *laude*, as Italian sacred songs in the vernacular were called, must be associated with the religious companies of laymen named *laudesi*. The impact of St. Francis of Assisi (1182–1226), who was a fervent believer in singing to God, doubtless accounts for the large number of laude that were composed in the late thirteenth century and noted down in three important sources. Moreover, the flagellant movement was in full swing at this time, and this resulted in the composition of special songs in fourteenth-century Germany too.[112] St. Francis' own Canticle of the Sun has been preserved, but without music.[113] The laude are written in a notation devoid of mensural significance, but their melodies have the same strength and character as those to the *Cantigas*. Duple or triple time may be employed according to the character and the note-groupings of the music. Many pieces are relatively syllabic in setting, especially in the late thirteenth-century Cortona manuscript. The lively duple-time *Venite a laudare*[114] exemplifies this style admirably, while *Ave, dei genitrix*[115] has florid cadences reminiscent of the Italian Ars Nova pieces discussed below. Highly ornamented melodies like *Santo Lorenzo*[116] are less frequent, but this Dorian piece is full of Italianate descending scales over the full compass of a ninth.

The development of notation known as the Ars Nova in France had its counterpart in Italy, so that by the early fourteenth century both countries possessed notational techniques permitting us to transcribe their music without difficulty. Moreover, duple time gained a recognized footing in art-music, so that all the usual modern measures could be employed. These developments were mainly employed in part-music, but in Italy one secular form at least was originally monodic, namely the Ballata. Once again we find a basic form like the virelai, but the music is essentially Italian with its florid lines and coloraturas. It seems likely then that the ballata was a secular counterpart to the Lauda, but it only acquired artistic importance in the fourteenth

110 See further R. Briffault, *Les Troubadours et le sentiment romanesque* (1945), p. 136 ff.
111 F. Liuzzi, *La Lauda e i primordi della melodia italiana*, 2 vols, (1935).
112 P. Runge, *Die Lieder und Melodien der Geissler des Jahres 1349* (1900).
113 F. Ludwig in G. Adler, *Handbuch der Musikgeschichte*, I, (2nd ed. 1930), p. 207.
114 Liuzzi I, p. 257; or Reese, p. 238.   115 Liuzzi I, p. 301.
116 Liuzzi II, p. 259; or Apel and Davison, p. 19.

century. It was probably poetry written essentially to be set to music, and as such did not attract the attention of the *literati*, who preferred a more extended work like the *canzone*.

Apart from one or two early examples, there are a few monodic ballate by such mid-fourteenth-century composers as Gherardello and Lorenzo Masini, but even they have only left five each.[117] Those of Gherardello are relatively brief and straightforward, while Lorenzo constantly introduces coloratura passages at the beginning and end of refrain and verse and sometimes at other places too, as in *Donne, e fu credenza* (Ex. 9) or *Non vedi tu*.[118] Nicolo da Perugia's only monodic

Ex.9

Don - ne

ballata is not quite so elaborate but has an attractively ranging melody with occasional syncopations.[119] The history of the ballata would not be complete without mention of this handful of monodies, but the form was first and foremost polyphonic. Still, the presence of monodic ballate in the earliest Trecento manuscript shows that monody preceded polyphony as far as the ballata was concerned, even if there are so few examples left.

Since the Norman conquest the French language had been in use by the ruling classes in England, and so it is not surprising that few songs with English texts have been found before the fifteenth century. Those that do exist may be found side by side with Latin or French pieces, but at least they often have a character of their own. The problem of rhythm exists in England too, but modal rhythm certainly prevails in many cases. The songs of Godric,[120] a hermit who died in 1170, have religious words. They appear to be based on liturgical music, though it is unlikely that the music is as old as the texts. However that may be, the few other early English songs do not appear to antedate the thirteenth century. One of the earliest, *Mirie it is while sumer ilast*,[121] is typical of the rather melancholy mood prevailing in these works. *Man mei longe him lives wene*[122] is concerned with the eternal theme of repentance. Nevertheless, the C major melody is by no means conventional.

[117] All in J. Wolf, *Der Squarcialupi-Codex* (1955); those by Gherardello also in N. Pirrotta, *The Music of Fourteenth-Century Italy* (1954).
[118] Wolf, p. 80.
[119] ibid, p. 133.
[120] J. B. Trend, *The First English Songs*, in Music and Letters IX (1928), p. 120 ff.
[121] Unpublished, but a facsimile in J. Stainer, *Early Bodleian Music* I (1901), pl. 3.
[122] Reese, p. 243.

In spite of a pentatonic outline, this song is outstandingly powerful and sincere.

The often-quoted *Worldes blis*[123] is very similar but more equivocal rhythmically. A short piece preserved as the tenor of a Latin motet may well be a genuine lullaby (Ex. 10). *Bryd on brere*[124] is a love song

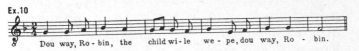

Ex.10

Dou way, Ro-bin, the   child wi-le   we-pe, dou way, Ro - bin.

with the most fascinating little repetitions in both text and music. Other early pieces tend to have more liturgical connections. Obviously it was common practice to use a known melody when composing new words, and *Stond wel moder under rode*[125] is little else but a new rendering of the sequence *Stabat iuxta Christi crucem*.[126] The famous *Angelus ad virginem*[127] quoted by Chaucer in *The Miller's Tale* is a hymn which soon acquired the English words *Gabriel from evene king*.

From works such as this, it was but a short step to the most popular English form of the fifteenth century, the carol. The words of these often polyphonic songs might also be in either Latin or English or a mixture of both languages. They too were usually religious, and the form was once again an ABA pattern like the virelai. There are fine monodic pieces such as *Nowell, this is the salutation*[128] and *Nova, nova, ave fit*[129] but also polyphonic works like *Abyde I hope*[130] with a monodic burden for solo voice which is taken up again in polyphony by a three-part chorus. Monody, however, soon disappeared and two- and three-part polyphony became the rule.

POLYPHONIC SONG

France

The advent of music in more than one part is probably more important to us than it was to the medieval musician. Part-music can in fact be traced from the ninth century, but it does not seem to have

---

123 Modal version in *New Oxford History of Music* II, p. 251.
124 J. Saltmarsh, *Two Medieval Love-Songs set to Music*, in *The Antiquaries Journal* XV (1935), p. 1ff.
125 Facsimile in *Early Bodleian Music* I, pl. 5.
126 C. A. Moberg, *Uber die schwedischen Sequenzen* II (1927), No. 20.
127 The original melody with both texts in Trend, p. 113.
128 J. Stevens, *Mediaeval Carols* (1952), p. 110.
129 ibid, p. 111.
130 ibid, p. 8 and p. 31.

attracted much attention at first. Moreover, as we have seen, early medieval secular song is written in the manuscripts for a single voice only, though minstrels and jongleurs did usually add an improvised accompaniment. The earliest important collections of part-music are for church use, and go back to the twelfth century. It is probably due to the diligence of monks that they still exist today. Secular song on the other hand was so often learned by heart that special circumstances were required before it was written down. For instance, the Troubadours were either nobles or at least artists convinced of their importance and hence considered their works to be worthy of preservation. Still, we shall be making a mistake if we consider that secular and sacred were such distinct categories as they are today. An example of this is the famous English canon *Sumer is icumen in*.[131] Probably it would never have come down to us had it not been used as a basis for new words in Latin of religious inspiration. Again, while it is true that the motet originally had Latin sacred texts, French texts of an amorous character often replaced the original words as the thirteenth century progressed. Even these pieces must have originated in monasteries and churches, for, apart from the evidence of the manuscripts, the lowest part or tenor nearly always comes from plainsong.

The medieval motet hardly enters into the pattern of this book except insofar as it can be called solo song. In every case where there are three or four parts the motet can be considered as a duet or trio accompanied by a presumably instrumental tenor. The assumption that these tenors are instrumental is gratuitous, but is confirmed by an absence of text, unvocal movement and awkward rhythms. A two-part motet may well be considered therefore as an accompanied song. Taking into account the lack of secular instruments in religious establishments, the accompanying instrument was probably often the organ. The upper part in any case is song-like enough and may be even a complete Rondeau, like *Ja n'iert nus bien assenés* with the tenor *Justus* (Ex. 11).[132] In other cases snatches of melody are borrowed from well-known songs and refrains, as in the charming *Huic main au doz mois de mai* on the tenor *Hec dies*.[133] Of course, as with the Gothic cathedrals, so with medieval part-music, an extra part might often be added or taken away from the already completed whole. Thus a two-part motet could become a three-part work by the composition of

[131] In triple rhythms in Apel and Davison, p. 44; in duple rhythms by M. Bukofzer, '*Sumer is icumen in*', *a Revision* (1944), appendix.

[132] F. Gennrich, *Rondeaux Virelais und Balladen* I (1921), p. 6.

[133] Apel and Davison, p. 32.

Ex.11

1.4.7. Ja n'iert nus bien as - se - nés, 2.8. s'A - mours ne li_ font a - i - - e.
3. C'est la_ jus ens mi_ les prés,
5. gieus et_ baus i a_ le - vés 6. quant la ro - se est es - pa - ni - - e:

Justus

another voice one stage higher than the other two, and a three-part motet could lose one of its voices if only two parts were required.

One thing, however, seems clear. During the thirteenth century the tenor retained its position as corner-stone of the composition and the idea of another similar voice was rarely considered. The reason, of course, was that it was not easy to combine two tenors, each derived from plainsong, with each other. The idea of adding a contratenor, i.e. an accompanying voice like the tenor but not derived from plainsong, did not apparently come to mind till the fourteenth century. An exception to the general rule that tenors had to be borrowed from plainsong does seem to be present in the two-part *Bien m'ont Amors entrepris*.[134]

Meanwhile, in the largest medieval motet manuscript,[135] which is available in a luxurious modern edition,[136] there are no less than seventy attractive two-part motets. And, of course, other sources have many other works of this kind, but they are often not to be found in modern transcription. The seventy easily available pieces are, however, as charming as the monodies, whose accompaniment has to be improvised while these two-part compositions have the advantage of a ready-made and genuinely medieval accompaniment. Like the monodies, many texts are concerned with the coming of spring and the delights or problems of love.

On the other hand, a delightful and popular work like *Ne sai que je die* with the tenor *Johanne*[137] has a text dealing with the vices of the times. One of the beauties of a work like this is the way the short lines are paralleled by exactly fitting brief musical phrases. Medieval musicians knew how to treat a melody which was superficially short-breathed due to this method of unifying poetry and music into a whole. The impetus given by even the smallest deviation from stepwise

[134] Beck II, No. 53.
[135] Montpellier, Faculté de Médecine, H 196.
[136] Y. Rokseth, *Les Polyphonies du XIIIe siècle*, 4 vols., (1935–39).
[137] ibid III, No. 185.

43

movement continually propels a piece like this forward. The accompaniment is simple enough and always falls on the beat. Not a single note of it is shorter than the dotted crotchet of the $\frac{6}{8}$ bar. Many tenors are like this. However, while some may have a rest every second bar, a cheerful work like *Au tans pascour meinent joie* with the tenor *Domino*[138] never has a break at all in the accompaniment. Continuous quaver movement with occasional breaks appears in *A la clarté qui tout enlumina* on the tenor *Et illuminare*.[139] The text of this piece is addressed to the Virgin Mary. Each quaver of the upper voice has a syllable of text, rather like the later operatic *parlando* or patter song, though here the movement is much more placid.

The first rhythmic mode is most prevalent in these pieces but the second mode also occurs. Usually it also finds a place in the tenors when the upper voice has it, and, providing it is performed smoothly, this mode will be found as satisfying as the first. An excellent example of medieval craftsmanship in this mode is *Qui laoiaument sert s'amie* with the tenor *Letabitur*.[140] There can be no denying the fascination of the ascending and descending sections of the scale which form the basis of the upper voice melody. The song nature of these works is perhaps most obvious in one of the rare pieces which has come down to us with a text in English. This is *Worldes blis*, and it has already been mentioned. In two sources there is only a melody for this work, but in another a new melody is set to a tenor based on the plainsong (*Benedicamus*) *domino*.[141]

Apart from these works which are called motets but are really accompanied songs, the only other thirteenth-century songs in more than one part are the Rondeaux of Adam de la Halle.[142] These cannot strictly be called solo songs, since all three voices sing the text in a fairly note-against-note manner and all are of equal importance. This trio form continued to be used sporadically in the fourteenth century, but was generally abandoned, doubtless due to its lack of independent part-writing rhythmically.

By the beginning of the fourteenth century the motet was still a flourishing form. Indeed the advent of more varied upper voice rhythms gave it a new lease of life. A change had already come about between the latter part of the thirteenth and the beginning of the

---

[138] Y. Rokseth, *Les Polyphonies du XIIIe siècle*, 4 vols. (1935–39), No. 190.
[139] ibid, No. 189.   [140] ibid, No. 209.
[141] M. F. Bukofzer, *The First Motet with English Words*, in *Music and Letters* XVII (1936), p. 225 ff.
[142] Gennrich, *Rondeaux* I, p. 54 ff.; J. Chailley, *Adam de la Halle, Rondeaux à trois voix égales* (1942).

fourteenth century, but it was Philippe de Vitry (1291–1361) who first codified the rules of what he called the Ars Nova, the new art of motet writing.[143] Already in the works of Jehannot de Lescurel, more short notes were introduced into a measure than before. At one time the breve (equal to our quaver) had been the shortest note-value, but occasional groups of two or three semibreves (equal to triplet semi-quavers) were used too. By slackening the tempo, it was possible to introduce more short notes and Petrus de Cruce, writing in the last quarter of the thirteenth century, made it clear that from two to nine semibreves might fill in the time of a single breve. Of course, all these variations in the value of a semibreve, which had the same appearance no matter how many of them there were to a breve, made it increasingly necessary to define the values of the shorter notes.

This was done by adding a tail to the semibreve and calling it a minim, a procedure which apparently originated in the College of Navarre in Paris, hence shortly after 1315. Philippe de Vitry's innovation seems to have been the codification of this system in his treatise *Ars Nova* and its practical application in the most noteworthy art-form of the period, the motet. Instead of a haphazard grouping of from two to nine short notes, he grouped the semibreves and minims into what he called the 'four prolations', which are the equivalents of our $\frac{6}{8}$, $\frac{9}{8}$, $\frac{3}{4}$, and $\frac{2}{4}$. This last, $\frac{2}{4}$, was of little importance at first, but Vitry can be credited with firmly establishing it theoretically as of equal importance with triple time. Instead of being a short note, the breve was now equal to a complete measure in each of the four prolations, so that the semi-breve and minim of the fourteenth century are transcribed most conveniently in modern editions as crotchet and quaver respectively. Other novelties of Vitry's system, which were not heeded much for fifty years or so but came to be generally employed later, were time signatures and the semiminim (equal to our semiquaver).

The high authority and standing of the motet in early fourteenth-century musical composition can easily be understood, but it is note-worthy that the two-part work went out of fashion quickly and we do not find it at all in France after the *Roman de Fauvel*. Even there most of the two-part works are older thirteenth-century pieces, though there is a hybrid work with the AAB form of the Ballade and the completely note-against-note counterpoint of the conductus.[144] This composition

[143] Ed. G. Reaney, A. Gilles and J. Maillard in *Musica Disciplina* X (1956), p. 13 ff; French translation ibid XI (1957), p. 12 ff.
[144] Schrade, *The Polyphonic Music of the Fourteenth Century* I, p. 4.

is listed among the two-part motets in the index of the manuscript but there is no indication that the tenor is derived from plainsong. Nor does the tenor have any text, which, together with the AAB form, may qualify it for a place among the accompanied songs. On the other hand the text is a Latin motet text and, owing to the note-against-note movement, could quite well be sung to the tenor in conductus style. The fourteenth-century motet as exemplified by the works of Philippe de Vitry,[145] Guillaume de Machaut[146] and anonymous works from the Ivrea and Chantilly manuscripts is predominantly a three-part work, with different texts in the two upper voices.

The four-part motets, apart from an isolated example in older style in the *Roman de Fauvel*,[147] are rarer but important. It may be that Vitry was again the instigator of an important innovation, in this case the textless contratenor. Moreover, he developed in his motets a principle of motet composition that was to be of far-reaching importance for over a hundred years. This was the so-called isorhythm, which existed in embryo in the thirteenth century. Then it was just a matter of employing short rhythmic motifs in the tenor which, once performed, were employed throughout a motet, the melody varying continually of course. But in the fourteenth century the lengthening of the longer note-values made it possible for Vitry to exemplify the principle on a far larger scale. Instead of short motifs he would take a rhythmic pattern of considerable length and repeat it several times, naturally less often than the short thirteenth-century patterns. Moreover, isorhythmic patterns were not built on the rigid rhythms of the rhythmic modes but could be in appearance quite free. These repeated patterns began in the tenor, soon appeared in the contratenor as well (in four-part works) and eventually dominated the entire composition.

All this is of considerable importance for the history of polyphonic song, because it is from this background that fourteenth-century accompanied solo song detached itself to become the most popular musical form of the age. The difficulty lies in the absence of sources containing early fourteenth-century polyphonic song. At first there is nothing, and then suddenly, as from nowhere, we are presented with a wealth of great works by Guillaume de Machaut in no less than six complete manuscripts. Probably what happened was that in many cases the motet itself was able to absorb creative activity in the early fourteenth century, whether in Latin or French.

[145] Schrade *The Polyphonic Music of the Fourteenth Century* I, p. 72 ff.
[146] ibid II-III and Ludwig, *Machaut* III.   [147] Schrade I, p. 18.

As we have seen, French was generally used for texts of an amorous character, and the number of motets using this language increased tremendously towards the end of the thirteenth century. Even the tenor was often derived from a monodic song in the vernacular, and it is clear that Machaut himself followed this trend, for two of his motets are built on rondeaux and one on a virelai in the tenor.[148] Moreover, seventeen out of twenty-three works have French texts in the upper voices. Comparison with Machaut's Ballades, which, like his other compositions, are generally in chronological order, suggests that he started out as a motet composer, probably writing a few two-part Ballades about the same time or slightly later. These are solo songs with textless accompanying tenors, the latter being freely composed.

The fact that a number of these pieces left room for a third voice called triplum in at least two manuscripts, though the triplum staves remained blank, is proof that the three-part polyphonic songs were originally planned on motet principles. The highest voice of the motet was called triplum, but existing song tripla have no text and are accompanying voices like the tenor. Two early three-part rondeaux have tripla, but these soon gave way to the standard fourteenth-century type of polyphonic song with a single voice part accompanied by two textless instrumental parts, the tenor and contratenor. The rarer four-part works had a triplum as well.

Although earlier monodic song had been very varied in poetic and musical form, fourteenth-century polyphonic song fell into only three main types, namely the ballade, rondeau and virelai. In the poetic field the rise of these forms can be traced more completely than in that of music. Such poets as Jehannot de Lescurel, Nicole de Margival, Jehan Acart de Hesdin and Jehans de Le Mote show the gradual transition from varied lines and metres to very standardized forms and versification. The subject-matter does not change much, but the idyllic love of many Trouvère songs and two-part motets becomes a conventional affair based on such personifications as Honte, Paour, Doux Penser, mainly drawn from the *Roman de la Rose*.

The courtly love of the Troubadours is still very much a feature of fourteenth-century verse. The poets themselves from Machaut onwards were called rhetoricians and the art itself rhetoric. The aim was prettiness and charm but not depth of feeling. Small wonder then that most thought went into the versification of the small lyric forms. The rondeau of course had not altered basically since the thirteenth century,

[148] ibid II-III and Ludwig III, motets 11, 20 and 16.

but the short eight-line form became mainly a vehicle for rhyme- and word-play. Puns were exploited and number anagrams concealed the name of the poet's lady. The ballade and virelai had greater length because of their three stanzas, although the single stanzas of the ballade have either seven or eight lines as a rule. The virelai however never had the settled form of the fourteenth-century ballade, and its short lines and varied line-lengths point back to the thirteenth century. The fourteenth-century tendency to standardization made itself felt particularly in the ballade, where the ten-syllable line predominated, the lines became equal in length and the general rule was to employ a one-line refrain at the end of each stanza.

The musical form of the ballade too was less repetitive than either rondeau or virelai. It was however often unified by musical rhyme in the first and second half of the stanza, a feature that became more popular with Machaut as his career proceeded. Here is the opening of a typical Machaut ballade. It does not show the musical rhyme, but the major character of the melody is clearly visible, together with the combining of the rhythms of first and second rhythmic modes which is such a feature of fourteenth-century song (Ex. 12). One of the prob-

Ex. 12

Nes que on   por-roit _____   les   es-toil - - les
et   les   gou-tes _____   de   pluie et _____ de

lems of performing these works is also apparent. Contrary to our present habits of singing, many notes have to be sung without text. Whether some of the textless passages were performed by instruments is a moot point. It may be that we are simply unfamiliar with this style. Much of Bach's vocal writing has been called instrumental, but we do not therefore substitute instruments for the voices. Moreover, Machaut himself describes the preceding ballade *Plourés, dames* as simple to sing, in spite of its textless arabesques. In any case, these are certainly solo songs, even if an instrument may possibly have helped the singer out with his florid lines occasionally. The actual instrumental parts are evidently the textless tenors and contratenors. They are never marked with the the names of definite instruments in the manuscripts, but this is not surprising, since the fourteenth century did not rigidly confine its music to one type of instrument. Good performers were rare birds, and their services were greatly valued. The more popular instruments were small Gothic harps, portable organs, shawms, viols, slide trumpets and bagpipes. The music-loving princes of the time were glad enough to get hold of a good performer, whatever his instrument.

Hence, even today, it is quite permissible to make use of many types of instruments for one and the same accompanying voice. The viol is an obvious choice, because, as Johannes de Grocheo, pointed out about 1300, one could play anything on it. It was one of the few instruments that went down below middle C, so that it could easily play Machaut's tenors and contratenors at the correct pitch. Other likely instruments are slide trumpets and bombards, which seem to have come into fashion at the time of Machaut. Admittedly, it is not always easy to imitate these sounds on modern instruments, but trombones may take the place of slide trumpets, bassoons can replace bombards, and the viola da gamba or the viola approximate the medieval viol well enough.[149]

Of course, not all the Machaut ballades,[150] and there are forty-two of them, fit into the category of solo songs accompanied by instrumental tenors and contratenors. Quite apart from the two-part pieces, there are two three-part works which must be considered entirely vocal.[151] They both have different ballade texts in all parts like the motets and so must be considered as trios. Even one of the two-part ballades shows motet influence, because it is an early attempt to incorporate isorhythm in the secular polyphonic song.[152] However, although the isorhythm is complete and the song quite attractive, this work remained an isolated experiment and composers after Machaut preferred to employ isorhythm in the rondeau, which was divided into two rhythmically identical halves. Machaut writes songs in all the four prolations, but those in $\frac{2}{4}$ and $\frac{3}{4}$ tend to be more accessible to the modern ear. Such is the attractive *Biauté qui toutes autres pere*[153] with its yearning melodic line and repeated melodic motifs at the end of each half of the composition.

The virelais, which are mostly monodic, perhaps form the best approach to Machaut's songs. Only eight out of thirty-three are polyphonic, and even these are, with one exception, two-part works. This however is probably an advantage, since the simple accompanying

---

[149] See further G. Reaney, *Voices and Instruments in the Music of Guillaume de Machaut*, in *Revue Belge de Musicologie* X (1956), p. 3–17, p. 93–104.

[150] Schrade III and Ludwig I.

[151] ibid, nos. 17 and 29.

[152] ibid, No. 1.   [153] ibid, No. 4.

tenors concentrate attention on the vocal soloist. Instead of the rhythmic complexities of some of the larger ballades, we are treated to delightful melodies such as the sighing flow of *Se je souspir parfondement*[154] and the quietly animated line of *De tout sui si confortée*,[155] both of which are in $\frac{2}{4}$. The accompanying tenors too are easy to play, quite unlike the excited syncopated contratenors of many ballades.

Nevertheless, it was the more complicated works which attracted the attention of musicians in the fourteenth century. The virelais were not imitated, whereas the ballades and rondeaux are found in numerous later manuscripts and these forms were developed by Machaut's contemporaries and successors. One may quote the example of F. Andrieu who wrote a ballade with two texts on Machaut's death.[156] Probably Machaut's four-part works were the most popular, but it is not always certain whether a song in four parts should be performed in three or four parts. A work like *De Fortune*,[157] for instance, started out as a three-part ballade with a triplum. The contratenor which occurs in later sources does not seem to fit at all well with the triplum.

On the other hand, the rondeau *Rose, liz*,[158] one of Machaut's most successful compositions, is in four parts from the outset. The rich harmonies of the opening and the striking movement from chords of C major to those of E flat and back are both delightful and fascinating. However, it remains true that the three-part songs with accompanying tenor and contratenor form the backbone of Machaut's output. And perhaps none of these is more charming than the final ballade, which only occurs in the very latest manuscripts. The unusual sixteen-line poetic stanza with no refrain is accommodated by repeating each half of the music, which is deceptively simple in appearance for Machaut. In fact the vocal part is tautly organized, though nothing could be more simply emotional than the music to the first line *Ma chiere dame, a vous mon cuer envoy*.[159]

After Machaut, the French polyphonic song did not develop structurally. The three-part solo work remained standard and creative activity was concentrated on the development of rhythmic and notational complexity. One exception to this development is the so-called realistic virelai, which tends to imitate the sounds of nature, bird calls and the like, or other striking noises such as battle scenes, fires, etc. These pieces have fresh, cheerful solo voice parts with relatively simple

[154] Schrade, No. 30; Ludwig, No. 36.
[156] Ludwig, No. 41.
[158] ibid, No. 10.
[155] Schrade, No. 32; Ludwig, No. 38.
[157] Schrade and Ludwig, No. 23.
[159] ibid, No. 40.

tenors and contratenors. None of these virelais is more attractive than the lark-song *Or sus, vous dormés trop*[160] which was so popular in fourteenth-century Italy. Its *lire, lire* and *ti-ti-ton* bird-calls have a charm which few could resist.

While Machaut represents French song of the early and mid-fourteenth century with a large output, scarcely any other composers of this period are now known. Quite the opposite is the case in the second half of the century, for, while most composers are represented by only a handful of compositions, many names have come down to us. Such are Jean Cesaris,[161] Solage,[162] Jean Galiot, Jacob de Senleches, Jean Vaillant, Jean Susay and many more. The case of Solage, of whom we know nothing, is typical. All his compositions are to be found in a luxurious manuscript at Chantilly, and he is one of the major composers in it with ten polyphonic songs. He represents the transition between the Machaut style and that of a man like Senleches, for, although a number of Solage's works are relatively simple in style, his ballade[163] for the art-loving maecenas John, duke of Berry, is full of the rhythmic complexities and syncopations of the late Ars Nova.

In certain cases the experimental nature of these rhythms is obvious and the musical result less satisfying, as in the isorhythmic rondeau *Loyauté me tient en espoir*[164] by Garinus, who is only known by this one work. Senleches however is a master in these matters, and, in spite of the extreme notational and rhythmic complexity of all but one of his five compositions, the results are quite remarkable musically. The combination of a large number of varied note-values and syncopations is a fluid melodic line, which, when mastered, is incomparable in its underlining of the emotional text in *En attendant esperance*.[165] Another composition which looks over-complicated on paper but is in fact remarkably moving is the ballade *Par les bons Gedeon et Sanson*[166] written by the Italian Philip of Caserta for the Avignon Pope Clement VII (1378–94). Many of these composers were employed by the music loving king John I of Aragon (1350–95), whose court was at Barcelona, while Gaston Phébus, count of Foix (1331–91), another member of the house of Aragon, is glorified in at least five ballades by this circle of composers.

The large-scale ballade, which allowed full scope for the display of

---

[160] W. Apel, *French Secular Music of the Late Fourteenth Century* (1950), No. 70.
[161] Complete works in G. Reaney, *Early Fifteenth Century Music* I (1955).
[162] Complete works in Apel, *French Secular Music*, Nos. 31–40.
[163] ibid, No. 34.   [164] ibid, No. 78.   [165] ibid, No. 49.
[166] J. Wolf, *Geschichte der Mensural-Notation* II–III (1904), No. 66.

rhythmic subtleties made possible by the development of notation consequent on Philippe de Vitry's *Ars Nova*, was the most popular musical form of the late fourteenth century. The motet, instead of being in the forefront of musical development, became somewhat conservative in general, and the ballade with a Latin text often took its place as the musical form dedicated to the glorification of worldly princes. It had already become apparent by this time however that the limit had been reached in the direction of rhythmic difficulty, and even Guido, one of the Chantilly composers, points this out in the text to a ballade which is by no means simple.

Johannes Cesaris and Baude Cordier[167] were two of the principal composers around 1400 who cleared the way for the new, simple song style of the early fifteenth century. Both of them started by writing in the fashionable esoteric manner, but they soon left the large-scale ballade behind and concentrated on rondeaux with charmingly refreshing melodies and simple accompaniments. In works like Cordier's *Ce jour de l'an*[168] and *Je suy celuy*,[169] we have the typical rondeau of the early Dufay period with its prevailing $\frac{6}{8}$ time, broken only by a few bars of $\frac{3}{4}$ on occasion to create variety. In both cases there is a textless introduction of about six bars, so that we may assume the voice part is doubled by an instrument. This does not always happen. For instance, Cordier's simple *Tant ay de plaisir* (Ex. 13)[170] in $\frac{2}{4}$ (really $\frac{4}{4}$) is vocal

Ex. 13

from start to finish. Nevertheless, most songs have a lead-in of a measure or two at least. One of Cordier's most attractive rondeaux, *Belle, bonne, sage*,[171] has an imitative opening, so that, before the voice enters, its initial motif is anticipated by instruments in contratenor and tenor respectively.

Cesaris, like Cordier, has left us one rondeau in $\frac{2}{4}$, but his *Je ris, je chante*[172] does have an instrumental introduction. Moreover, the contratenor looks back to the era of rhythmic complexity, for its triplets

167 As note 161.
168 ibid, p. 1.
169 ibid, p. 3.
170 ibid, p. 6.!
171 ibid, p. 9.
172 ibid, p. 20.

conflict with the prevailing duple time almost throughout. Compared with Machaut's rondeaux, many of the early fifteenth-century works had longer refrains and hence longer strophes, as far as the text was concerned. This often meant that, to avoid repetition, only the refrain was performed, so that the music was performed in its entirety once only. This tendency is already evident in such works of Cordier and Cesaris as possess only a couple of lines of text in addition to a four-line refrain.

The immediate predecessors of Dufay and Binchois followed the example of Cordier and Cesaris. Men like Richard Loqueville, Nicholas Grenon, Adam,[173] Jean Legrant[174] and Pierre Fontaine wrote the most delightful solo songs, mostly in rondeau form. Guillaume Legrant[175] stands apart from the rest because of his note-against-note writing, his liking for duple rhythms, his unusual accidentals and his ABB song form akin to the virelai. Quite a number of early fifteenth-century composers are known by only one work, but this may have been well worth preserving. Such is the amusing dialogue *J'aim. Qui? Vous. Moy?* by Paullet,[176] which is not a duet in spite of the text. At least, it could only be sung as one by dividing the vocal part between a lady and a gentleman. The rapid conversational exchanges between a lovelorn swain and his recalcitrant lady are skilfully mirrored in the music. Again, Raulin de Vaux's *Savés pour quoy suy sy gay?*[177] is a charming little rondeau whose individual lines of verse are carefully set off by rests in the music. Here is a clear case of the harmonious wedding of poetry and music which we have already met in the monodic *lais*. On the other hand, a composer like Guillaume Malbecque[178] with some five compositions to his name wrote in a more conventional style, which nevertheless has its charm. Indeed, in two rondeaux he apparently ends by repeating the words of the first line of the refrain at the end of the music, an apt and novel idea.

One could continue discussing the varied and attractive songs of this important school of secular composers for a long time, because there are plenty of composers and indeed a whole corpus of anonymous songs. With this example, there is no wonder that Dufay himself continued to write polyphonic songs throughout his life. To be a musician in the early fifteenth century meant to be a composer, if only in a small way, and so the names of men like Cardot de Bellengues,

[173] Complete works in G. Reaney, *Early Fifteenth Century Music* II (1959); also in Sir John J.F.R., and C. Stainer, *Dufay and his Contemporaries* (1898), pp. 52, 54, 57.
[174]–[178] Complete works in Reaney II.

Charité, Haucourt, Lebertoul, and Gautier Libert[179] turn up in both ecclesiastical records and at the head of secular songs. These are still men of the Middle Ages with their wandering minstrel instincts and their acceptance of the diminutive names Perrinet for Pierre, Paullet for Paul, Gilet for Giles, and so on. Only from this period can one date the Renaissance, though undoubtedly no hard and fast line can be drawn, particularly in the less advanced musical cultures. The polyphonic chanson of course continued to live on in Burgundy without much change till the end of the fifteenth century, but then Burgundy itself remained a kind of island of medieval culture which it only relinquished when the dukedom was incorporated into the kingdom of France in 1479.

Italy and Other Countries

The Italians have always had a reputation as singers and composers of songs, and so it seems only natural that they should have preserved a flourishing body of native medieval art-music of this kind. In fact, as we have seen, much depended on the activity of clerics in copying music down. Polyphonic song in any case seems to have been a new development in Italy in the fourteenth century. Obviously many of the Italian composers of secular music were clerics, like Provost Nicolo da Perugia, Abbot Vincenzo da Rimini, Fra Bartolino da Padua and Lorenzo the priest.[180] Under these circumstances, it is likely that such learned music as polyphony originated in ecclesiastical sources. This in fact seems to be the case, since no secular polyphony exists in Italian manuscripts before about 1330 at the earliest. On the other hand, what does exist in these manuscripts dating from the early part of the century mainly consists of a note-against-note duet polyphony set to the same text in both voices, like the conductus.

Particularly important in this respect are some processional works from Padua which were to be performed during great festivals of the church year in the sacred dramas.[181] A few similar pieces from Lauda manuscripts complete the picture.[182] It can scarcely be doubted that the earliest Italian secular polyphonic songs, the two-part madrigals, are

[179] Complete works of all five in Reaney II.

[180] J. Wolf, *Der Squarcialupi-Codex* contains all the works from the Squarcialupi manuscript by Giovanni da Cascia, Jacopo da Bologna, Gherardello, Vincenzo da Rimini, Lorenzo, Donato, Nicolo da Perugia, Bartolino da Padua, Francesco Landini, Egidius and Guilielmus de Francia, Zacharias and Andreas.

[181] G. Vecchi, *Uffici drammatici Padovani* (1954).

[182] E.g. *Nato nobis hodie*, in J. Wolf, *Handbuch der Notationskunde*, I (1913), p. 267 f.

based on such works. For one thing, they have the same tendency to employ harmonies of the third and sixth as well as the characteristically medieval fifths and octaves. The madrigals, however, as befits secular works, tend to employ more florid writing, which can be most effective in performance. The upper voice in particular is soloistic in character, and, for the modern performer, Italian music of this period is especially useful owing to its well-balanced phrases and emphasis on melody rather than rhythm.

It is true that the madrigals are essentially duets, but the characteristic fluidity of medieval performance practice suggests that these pieces were not only performed on instruments alone but also by a voice accompanied by an instrument. Indeed, there is actually a report of a singer accompanied on the lute at the end of the first day of Boccaccio's *Decameron*. Such a performance could well include chords as well as the tenor proper, but there is no harm in playing the tenor on a viol or a wind instrument. The position of three-part madrigals is not quite so clear, since these are really vocal trios. The textless performance of the tenors of two-part madrigals seems proved however by the London source of Trecento polyphony, which leaves out the text in tenors which have text in other sources. Cases in point are Donato's *L'aspido sordo*[183] and Lorenzo's *Povero çappator*[184] and *Ita se n'era star*.[185] Even Bartolino's three-part madrigal *La douce çere*[186] with a French text referring to the Visconti of Milan appears in the London source with a text in the Cantus part only.

As we have said, the madrigal was cultivated above all in the early part of the Trecento. The principal masters were Giovanni da Gascia,[187] Jacopo da Bologna,[188] Donato da Cascia and Gherardello.[189] Lorenzo Masini, Nicolo da Perugia, and Bartolino da Padua belong more to the intermediate generation who flourished after the middle of the century and gave more time to the new ballata form of polyphony. The first generation seem to have spent much of their time at Padua and Verona, though Jacopo later entered the service of the Visconti of Milan. Giovanni, Jacopo, and Piero seem to have been rivals, for they all wrote madrigals employing similar subject-matter popular at the court of Mastino II della Scala. This is conventional enough, with its setting in a garden near a river with a tree named *perlaro* and a lady called Anna.

[183] Wolf, *Der Squarcialupi-Codex*, p. 112.   [184] ibid, p. 95.
[185] ibid, p. 77.   [186] ibid, p. 159.
[187] Complete works in Pirrotta, *The Music of Fourteenth-Century Italy*.
[188] Complete edition by W. T. Marrocco, *The Music of Jacopo da Bologna* (1954).
[189] As note 187.

Mastino was lord of both Padua and Verona between 1328 and 1337, which helps to date these early madrigals.[190]

Generally speaking, Giovanni's style is more impersonal than Jacopo's and seems more synthetic. Nevertheless, all his two-part madrigals have great charm with their long coloraturas and fluctuating time signatures. The early madrigals employed many time signatures, so that the time might change from $\frac{4}{4}$ to $\frac{12}{8}$, $\frac{4}{4}$, $\frac{12}{8}$, and $\frac{3}{4}$ in the course of a single work.[191] Still, within each section the rhythms were generally simple with sequences of quavers, semiquavers or triplet quavers in the Cantus. The tenors make ideal accompaniments, because they move in minims and crotchets mainly, only making use of short values where the upper voice rests. Both Giovanni and Jacopo were fond of their art. The former describes music as his dear art and describes himself as *corda di tuo consonancia*.[192] Jacopo however is more concerned about the many composers who dabble in music and bring it into disrepute.[193] In contrast to Giovanni, whose madrigals are predominantly note-against-note in spite of the more highly ornamented upper part, Jacopo often introduces very effective imitative passages which may be of some length. Quite typical is *Di novo e giunt'un cavalier errante*,[194] in which the tenor only enters three measures after the Cantus and indeed with a rather different motif.

Jacopo is fond of the typically Italian triplet quaver motif introduced into a prevailing duple time section, and it certainly helps to give a work like *Non al suo amante*[195] much of its energy. This piece has a text by Petrarch, though the majority of madrigal poems seem to have been written by the composers of the music. Franco Sacchetti in particular is the author of *Come la gru*,[196] *Come selvaggia*,[197] *Nel meço gia del mar*[198] and *Povero pellegrin*[199] by Nicolo, which helps to date these works in the 1350s or '60s. Other madrigal poets are Nicolo Soldanieri, Steffano di Cino Merciaio, Cino da Pistoai and even Boccaccio. The madrigal form has something in common with the French ballade, though there is more variety of verse-form in the Italian works. The first and longer part of the madrigal is the strophe, which often consists of only three

[190] Cf. N. Pirrotta, *Marchettus de Padua and the Italian Ars Nova*, in *Musica Disciplina* IX (1955), p. 57 ff.

[191] As in Gherardello's *Cacciando un giorno*: Pirrotta, No. 24; Wolf, p. 57.

[192] In *O tu, cara scienza*: Pirrotta, No. 12; Wolf, p. 12.

[193] In *Uselletto selvaggio*: Marrocco, 78; Wolf, p. 26.

[194] Marrocco, p. 36; Reese, p. 363; Wolf, p. 26.

[195] Apel and Davison, p. 52 f.; Marrocco, p. 69; Wolf, p. 23.

[196] Wolf, p. 144.   [197] Wolf, p. 141.

[198] Wolf, p. 119.   [199] Wolf, p. 127.

lines of verse. Musically the strophe may be quite long and in any case several strophes will usually be repeated to the same music, followed by the ritornello after the last strophe. Unlike the French refrain, the Italian ritornello is not repeated, though it may be necessary to repeat its music in order to accommodate two lines of verse. Giovanni's *Quando la stella*[200] is rather exceptional in having a different ritornello after each of the two strophes.

Gherardello, who died c. 1364, wrote ten madrigals as well as two polyphonic mass pieces, his five monodic ballate and a caccia. If anything, these are more exciting than those of Giovanni. The measures of *Cacciand' un giorno*[201] are constantly changing and, when he starts a running passage of quavers or semiquavers, this often proceeds without a halt or a slower note at all. The imitative opening of *Intrand' ad abitar*,[202] a long canonic imitation, is breathtakingly thrilling.

But, after all has been said about the madrigal, it has to be admitted that the ballata is more of a solo form. Considering that it started out as monody, this is hardly surprising, and moreover it doubtless lent itself to comparison with the virelais of Machaut in this respect and with regard to its ABBAA form. At all events, the fact remains that a composer like Landini,[203] who wrote very few madrigals but 141 ballate, cultivated the three-part ballata with solo cantus and textless tenor and contratenor. Admittedly, ninety-two of his ballate are for two voices and the tenors nearly always have text, but even in these pieces there is a greater tendency for relatively central manuscripts to leave out the tenor texts by way of exception. With the three-part works however, there can be no quibbling. Two-thirds of these compositions are clearly accompanied vocal solos. And, till the end of the trecento, it is normal for two-part ballate to have text in both voices, while three-part pieces in this form are either accompanied vocal solos or accompanied duets. Probably the reason why there were more two-part than three-part works at first was greater familiarity with two-part writing, due to the madrigal. Nicolo da Perugia left no three-part works at all. All his twenty-one ballate are for two voices, with the exception of a monodic piece. Even Andreas, who died in 1415, and left no madrigals, left only twelve three-part ballate as against eighteen two-part works.

The solo ballate of Landini, with their emphasis on melody, stand out as the fourteenth-century Italian counterparts to the ballades of

---

[200] Pirrotta, No. 15.   [201] See note 191.   [202] Pirrotta, No. 26; Wolf, p. 61.
[203] Complete works by L. Ellinwood, *The Works of Francesco Landini* (1945).

Guillaume de Machaut. Perhaps the Machaut works are more appealing to the connoisseur, but there can be no doubt that the simpler rhythms and the smooth accompaniments of Landini's compositions are more immediately attractive. Take a piece like the popular *El gram disio* (Ex. 14).[204] It has the $\frac{6}{8}$ (here twice $\frac{6}{8} = \frac{12}{8}$) measure with trochaic

Ex. 14

El gram di - si - o e la dol - ce spe - ran - - - - za

movement typical of the fourteenth-century French motet, a conservative form, and the piece has none of the rhythmic variety of the French works. The tenor proceeds in plain dotted crotchets and dotted minims, while the only rhythmic spice is provided by hocketing quavers in the contratenor. Nevertheless, the vocal solo is a moving and controlled melody.

The similarity between tenor and contratenor suggests the use of similar instruments for these two parts rather than contrasting ones, as often in the French polyphonic songs. Thus one might have two viols or two bassoons. There are certain characteristic melodic idioms in this music, as one can see from a comparison between the opening of *El mie dolce sospir*[205] and *Amar si li alti*.[206] $\frac{6}{8}$ time is not the only one to be found in these pieces, in spite of French influence. $\frac{4}{4}$ is quite frequent, and $\frac{9}{8}$ occurs too, e.g. in the pleasant *Partesi con dolore*.[207] This particular work is in fact rather more French than many of Landini's compositions, owing to its use of a favourite motif of Machaut's and iambic rhythms. Perhaps the appeal of Landini's works is largely due to the smoothness of his melodies and the clarity of his polyphonic texture. It is unusual to find him experimenting with the use of the Italian triplet group in duple time in *Quel sol che raça*,[208] or introducing even a simple syncopated passage, as in the closing cadence of *Selvagia fera*,[209] a work in $\frac{3}{4}$ time.

Of course, Landini was by no means the only important composer of three-part ballate for solo voice, but he was the most prolific. In spite of the blindness which attacked him in early childhood, he became a virtuoso on many instruments, including the portative organ which

204 Ellinwood, No. 118; Wolf, p. 257.
205 Ellinwood, No. 119; Wolf, p. 259.
206 Ellinwood, No. 102; Wolf, p. 280.
207 Ellinwood, No. 139; Wolf, p. 276.
208 Ellinwood, No. 146; Wolf, p. 236.
209 Ellinwood, No. 148; Wolf, p. 232.

was so popular in the fourteenth century. He must have composed many items of church music as well as the corpus of secular compositions so fortunately preserved in the attractive codex once owned by the Florentine organist Antonio Squarcialupi (1417–80).[210] This manuscript has a portrait of each composer at the head of his compositions. Landini died in 1397, and his fame as an organist is proved by the tombstone which shows him holding his portative.[211] Obviously the centre of Trecento musical life at this time must have been Landini's home, Florence, and indeed this is proved by the delightful work of Giovanni da Prato entitled *Il Paradiso degli Alberti* and written in 1389. At the Alberti family's home, Landini performed so well that the very birds were quiet, but then sang louder in sympathy with him and approached him.[212]

Andrea dei Servi, whose name occurs in the account-books of Pistoia Cathedral in 1366 and again in 1380 and 1389,[213] has left some half-dozen accompanied solo ballate. At least, it seems likely that this Andrea is the same man as Frater Andreas Horghanista de Florentia, whose name stands at the head of the compositions in the Squarcialupi codex. *Dal traditor non si puo* (Ex.15)[214] bemoans man's inability to

Ex. 15

Dal _____ tra - di - tor non si puo l'uom guar - da - re _____ che mo - stri buo - na fac - ... - cia

gauge when a person is trustworthy or not. Musically it is interesting because both halves of the composition begin with the Cantus solo, the tenor only joining in at the end of the opening coloratura in each case. The tenor is the only accompaniment in this piece, and it is simple enough, for it contains no notes shorter than a crotchet in length. The three-part *Sotto candido vel dolce risguardo*[215] and *Deh! che faro*[216] are both

210 Florence, Biblioteca Laurenziana, Pal. 87.

211 Ellinwood, pl. II.

212 Ellinwood, xv.

213 R. Taucci, *Fra Andrea dei Servi*, in *Rivista di studi storici sull'Ordine dei Servi di Maria* II (1935), p. 32 ff.

214 Wolf, p. 329.   215 Wolf, p. 344.   216 Wolf, p. 355.

in $\frac{12}{8}$ time. The rhythm of the former piece is reminiscent of Machaut and the tenor and contratenor occasionally have groups of three crotchets across the beat. The opening of both pieces is very cheerful, and particularly the second work is remarkable, since it not only opens unaccompanied but soars up to top D[217] after the initial descent.

Two other composers of ballate, perhaps one was the poet and the other the musician, are Egidius and Guilielmus de Francia. These men were Augustinians from Santo Spirito in Florence, though Guilielmus seems to have been Parisian in origin. One feels that French influence was particularly in evidence in the five ballate which they composed. All are two-part works for cantus and instrumental tenor, and their brevity and predilection for $\frac{6}{8}$ time confirm the first impression. Their simplicity makes them easy to perform and they have at least a greater breadth of melody than similar French works. *Piacesse a dio*[218] in $\frac{4}{4}$ time is in C and tells the familiar story of a young woman who is married to an old man. *Mille merce*,[219] which has shorter phrases, is very jolly. The singer offers thanks to the God of love for making him happy and removing his sorrows.

In a similar style are the Ballate of Zacharias, a late Trecento composer who served under Pope Martin V when the schism ended in 1417. Only *Ferito gia d'un amoroso dardo*[220] is a duet. The textless tenors of the other pieces have the same simple accompaniments as may be found in Egidius and Guilielmus's compositions. *Benche lontan mi trovi*[221] in $\frac{3}{4}$ and *Movi t'a pietade*[222] in $\frac{4}{4}$ have attractive little imitative passages at the end of the refrain, the latter piece with a fanfare touch. *Sol mi trafigge'l cor*[223] is a little more complicated. Essentially in $\frac{9}{8}$, it has $\frac{3}{4}$ motifs, while triplet quavers overlap between cantus and tenor.

The late Trecento produced some interesting interrelationships between French and Italian music in Italy. Florence had always been open to French influences and Padua even adhered to the Avignon Pope during the schism. The influence of French and even Italian composers active at Avignon in the latter part of the fourteenth century seems to have been profound in early fifteenth-century Italy. Zacharias is just one example, for he wrote a very complex ballade with a Latin text completely in the French style.[224] It seems likely that he was associated with the Italian anti-pope John XXIII, who was active at Bologna from 1410 to 1414. Another member of this group was probably Bartholo-

[217] Bar 3.   [218] Wolf, p. 319.   [219] ibid.   [220] Wolf, p. 325.
[221] Wolf, p. 326.   [222] Wolf, p. 327.   [223] Wolf, p. 332.
[224] Wolf, *Geschichte der Mensural-Notation* II–III, No. 70.

meus de Bologna, a prior[225] whose seven works comprise a Latin ballade, an Italian rondeau, a Latin ballata, 2 Italian ballate and 2 Mass pieces. The two Latin pieces are again very complex works[226] but the two Italian ballate are much simpler and quite delightful compositions. Both are in three parts, but one is a vocal solo[227] and the other a vocal duet. Bartholomeus even used these two pieces as a basis for his Gloria and Credo,[228] like another Italian of the period, Antonio Zachara da Teramo.

Antonio certainly wrote mainly Italian ballate, but some of them have macaronic texts, whether they combine Latin with Italian, or Italian with French.[229] His melodies are most attractive, and he is fond of repeating words, a technique which seems to gain considerable favour in Italy at this period but is almost unknown elsewhere. Of his 9 ballate, 5 are for three and 4 for two parts. Johannes Ciconia (c. 1335–1411) belongs in this Italian group, for he was not only active in Padua but wrote many Italian secular pieces as well as Mass movements and motets. He was certainly a forward-looking composer and a man of genius into the bargain. The extent to which this musician from Liège assimilated the Italian style of composition can be judged from his ballata O rosa bella,[230] which would be a prize in any singer's repertory.

Ciconia wrote madrigals too, which may date well back into the fourteenth century, since he already had a prebend at Cesena in 1362.[231] A typical work of this kind in duple rhythms is Cacciando un giorno, vidi una cervetta,[232] a two-part work with textless tenor. It has the introductory prelude, the syllabic passages, the melodic sequences and the change of measure at the ritornello characteristic of the classic Italian form. It also contains the repeated passages which may be associated with Ciconia, like his three-part madrigal Una panthera in compagnia di Marte,[233] written for the ruler of Lucca. A remarkable two-part solo ballata also bears the stamp of Ciconia's genius. It is the anonymous Merce, merce, o morte[234] with its yearning repeated notes and

225 According to a manuscript at Oxford.
226 Arte psalentes and Que pena maijor, the latter in Wolf, Geschichte, No. 68.
227 Stainer, Dufay and his Contemporaries, p. 60.
228 Ch. van den Borren, Polyphonia Sacra (1932), pp. 37, 44.
229 Deus deorum Pluto in Italian Ars-Nova Music, supplement to Journal of Renaissance and Baroque Music I (1946), p. 14; and Je suy navrés tan fort in N. Pirrotta and E. Li Gotti, Il Codice di Lucca II, in Musica Disciplina IV (1950), p. 151.
230 Denkmäler der Tonkunst in Österreich VII (1900), p. 227.
231 S. Clercx-Lejeune, Johannes Ciconia de Leodio, in Kongress-Bericht, Internationale Gesellschaft für Musikwissenschaft, Utrecht 1952 (1953), p. 113.
232 Italian Ars-Nova Music, suppl. to Journal of Renaissance and Baroque Music, p. 3.
233 ibid, p. 6.   234 ibid, p. 17.

sequences at the words *o morte* and *ch'i moro*. These musical pictorialisms mark out Ciconia as one of the first if not the first genuine Renaissance figure in music.

Another musician who stands out among early fifteenth-century Italian composers because of his relatively large output is Matteo da Perugia, the Milanese singer and discanter. He is to be found at Milan Cathedral between 1402 and 1407 and again from 1414–16.[235] He quite probably served Pope John XXIII in the intervening years while he was absent from Milan. At least thirty compositions are certainly his work and six more may well be. There can be no doubt about his predilection for French texts, for twenty-two out of his thirty compositions are written in French, all except one of these being in ballade, rondeau or virelai form.[236] The French influence generally appears in the predominance of the composition with vocal cantus and instrumental tenor and contratenor. Three rondeaux and one virelai are two-part works, but even here only one rondeau has the text in both voices. By no means all of these works employ the complicated rhythms of the French Ars Nova, though a few do, but many of the songs are relatively straightforward rhythmically and have quite charming melodies, like *Pres du soloil*[237] and *Belle sans per*.[238] Matteo's heart was certainly not in Italian ballate, because he has only left two pieces of this type and both of them are musically uninteresting except from a technical point of view.[239]

Men like Petrus Rubeus, Bartholomeus Brollo, Antonius de Civitate and the Provost of Brescia continued to write their ballate, their rondeaux and their virelais till the 1430s, and indeed works by the late Trecentists turn up as far afield as Germany or Poland. In fact, native polyphony in Germany was very primitive until well into the fifteenth century. Secular polyphony was almost non-existent, and what sacred polyphonic music was available seems to have been divided into two classes: very archaic note-against-note conductus-like pieces and two-part motets. The latter were often enough either direct borrowings or rehashes of thirteenth-century French works. The monk of Salzburg, who has already been noticed as a composer of monody, also left a few polyphonic songs. These are harmonically very elementary,

[235] C. Sartori, *Matteo da Perugia e Bertrand Feragut i due primi Maestri di Cappella del Duomo di Milano*, in *Acta Musicologica* XXVIII (1956), pp. 12–23.
[236] All the French compositions in Apel, *French Secular Music*, nos. 1–22.
[237] ibid, No. 4.
[238] ibid, No. 11.
[239] G. Cesari and F. Fano, *La Cappella Musicale del Duomo di Milano* I (1956), pp. 323, 328.

with a tendency to what are little more than drone tenors. It goes without saying that there are no more than two parts.

A piece called the *Nachthorn*[240] has a tenor named *der pumhart*, which may actually be written for the bombard, since it is mostly restricted to the tonic and dominant. The bombard was the lowest member of the shawm family, the equivalent of the present-day oboe group. Of course, movement in thirds was a common feature of Minnesinger music, and so it is not surprising to find this type of progression adopted in tenors like the monk's *Tagelied*.[241] The whole piece is called 'the trumpet', so that it can obviously be performed by a solo voice supported by a trumpeter playing the tenor. This piece has an outspoken vigour which makes a satisfying change from the artificialities of contemporary French and even Italian music. Even the works of Oswald von Wolkenstein do not show much progress with respect to part-writing. The handful of polyphonic works which he has left are very often borrowings, for instance *Der may*[242] from Jean Vaillant's *Per moutes fois*,[243] and *Wolauff, gesell*[244] from *Fies de moy*.[245] Certainly *Der may* transforms Vaillant's triplets into duplets and rearranges the ornamentation, but it also makes a three-part piece into one with only a cantus and tenor. Musically the work is a success, which cannot be said of many of Wolkenstein's three-part compositions. His *Wach auff, myn hort*[246] is notated as a vocal duet, but sounds well as an accompanied solo.

Polyphonic song can hardly be said to exist in England before the time of Dunstable, except in the form of two-part vocal duets, of which there are in any case only a handful. 'Sumer is icumen in', a four-part vocal canon over two accompanying voices, is a unique work for its time (*c*. 1260–80), but hardly falls into the category of solo song. Pieces like *Foweles in the frith*[247] and *Edi beo*[248] could scarcely have been sung as accompanied solos, since the two parts move continuously note-against-note. A similar situation prevails in Spain, except at the court of Barcelona, which evidently continued to cultivate late Ars Nova secular music till it died a natural death in the early fifteenth

240 Mayer and Rietsch (see note 96), p. 387.
241 ibid, p. 328.
242 Apel and Davison, p. 64.
243 Apel, *French Secular Music*, No. 69.
244 Koller (see note 100), No. 113.
245 F. Kammerer, *Die Musikstücke des Prager Kodex XI.E.9* (1931), p. 134.
246 Reese, p. 379.
247 Handbook to the *History of Music in Sound* II (1953), p. 49.
248 *New Oxford History of Music* II, p. 342.

century. The Montserrat codex dating from *c.* 1400 contains simple two-part duets and canons, but also two religious songs of straight-forward early fifteenth century type.[249] They have Latin texts and one has an accompanying tenor, the other an accompanying contratenor too. Both are in duple rhythms and appear to be attractive little pieces. The same is true of simple two- and three-part Dutch pieces to be found without texts in the Prague codex XI.E.9,[250] for these too are evidently based on French principles. Outside France and Italy, polyphonic song was evidently a novelty and its flourishing period was to be the sixteenth century. But the impetus had been given. It came from France and its echoes are to be heard ringing down the fifteenth century.

[249] H. Angles, *El 'Llibre Vermell' de Montserrat*, in *Anuario Musical* X (1955), Nos. 2 and 8.
[250] Kammerer, pp. 159, 160, 162, 163.

The Renaissance

The Renaissance

DENIS STEVENS

IT was due in no small measure to the spirit of the Renaissance, whose humanizing and broadening influences can be detected in embryo as early as the beginning of the fifteenth century, that singing as an art and a science emerged from among the medieval arcana to which it had long been relegated. It emerged slowly, for the knowledge of singing and song-repertoire was restricted to a handful of highly capable practitioners, and they were understandably loth to give up secrets that provided them with secure, if not luxurious, appointments in the courts and castles of Europe. The art of these musical practitioners, who were often both singers and composers, was a subtle and refined one, and the notation they used displays the same characteristics, besides a strong element of complexity. Thus it was difficult for a musician of moderate accomplishment to come to terms with the kind of song which graces the handsomely-written manuscripts of the late middle ages.[1] A more direct and straightforward type of notation was needed, and though this did in time appear –

[1] I am thinking now not so much of the relatively sane complexities of the Chantilly and Reina manuscripts (excerpts from which may be seen in Apel, *French Secular Music of the Late Fourteenth Century*, and in Reaney, *Early Fifteenth Century Music*) but of the extraordinary rhythmic tumours of the Cyprus manuscript (Turin, Bibl. Naz. J II 9) which still awaits publication. Surely there can be few songs more difficult to perform than the ballade *Sur toute fleur*, with its proliferation of duple and triple hemiolas, duple sesquitertia (7 against 3) and even triple sesquitertia (10 against 9).

simplifying the reading of music besides its component parts, melody and part-writing – it was a relatively slow process, covering at least the first third of the fifteenth century.

As art-song became more supple, more ready a vehicle for the sister art of poetry (which, as in later ages, almost always antedated the music) it became simpler and more settled in texture. The vocal line favoured the alto or tenor ranges, while the two accompanying parts remained independent though prone to cross each other. Names or types of instruments were rarely specified, for it was left to the performer or the circumstance to dictate the instrumentation. Three-part texture held the field for more than a century as the most popular and suitable for song-form, yet there were numerous songs provided with only one accompanying line, or with as many as three. The song might contract or expand in harmonic depth according to who performed it: and it was not unknown for composers to take over songs by other writers, add an extra part, and so provide for a possibly more opulent musical establishment. When times changed and retrenchment was the order of the day, a part could just as easily be dropped without doing irreparable damage to the music. This feature of flexibility was one that distinguished Renaissance song from its predecessors.

In view of the general lack of specified instrumentation in the sources, we are obliged to fall back on the evidence offered by artists and writers. Finely illuminated copies of chronicles and romances often include a representation or two of a musical concert, either in or out of doors, and although there is always the possibility that certain instruments are depicted merely because the artist felt them to offer shapes and colours agreeable to the eye, or because certain groupings of instruments offer a pleasing symmetry, this important evidence must not be taken lightly. It is perfectly within reason to suppose that four, five or six instruments could share between them the polyphony of a three-part song, especially when we bear in mind the fact that most – whether string or wind – were monodic. A recorder might double the voice-part either in unison or at the upper octave; a lute and portable organ the middle part (tenor); a viol and harp the lowest part (contra-tenor). In this way the musicians could enter into the spirit of creative music-making, for if the art of composition eluded them, the science of orchestration – even on a diminutive scale – was theirs to experiment with and investigate.

Musicians learned to master individual instruments, and in course of time various kinds of bowed- and plucked-string instruments were developed as media for polyphony. After a century in which the harmonic hegemony of song-accompaniment was unquestionably interlinked with the ensemble, the lute came to be regarded as an ideal instrument for conveying the necessary structure and characteristics of any given accompaniment, so that at long last the singer could make himself, if need be, entirely independent of other musicians. The lute was not an easy instrument to learn or to maintain, but once its essential technique had been mastered a whole new realm of possibilities was opened up for professional and amateur musicians alike.[2]

One of the most obvious of these was the adaptation for lute and voice of polyphonic songs already in the repertory of larger ensembles. At first these were made by individual musicians and copied into personal manuscript collections; later on, publishers began to realize the vast possibilities of this new market for songs, and issued books of songs with the voice part in ordinary staff notation and the accompaniment in tablature, this tablature containing perhaps two out of three of the original parts. Thus, a four-part frottola arranged for the lute in Petrucci's collections would normally lose its alto line, for the average lute-player of the early sixteenth century could easily play two parts and sing the melody, though if he were expected to play three parts he might well stop singing from sheer concentration. Besides, song-publishers in the sixteenth century, as in the nineteenth, sought their largest clientele among the middle-class or well-to-do amateur, and an impossibly difficult accompaniment would seriously hinder sales.

Notwithstanding the tremendous popularity of the lute during the sixteenth century, and the infrequent use of keyboard instruments for song-accompaniment, the ensemble still remained an effective if cumbersome alternative. German and English composers especially made good use of the voice-and-viols combination, though published examples of this genre often mislead modern readers because the composer and publisher (with a business eye cast longingly in the direction of madrigal singers) have underlaid the instrumental parts with words. This fact should not obscure the true form and style of the original, for it will nearly always be found that the works are most effective when performed as songs with accompaniment, rather than as madrigals or part-songs for a group of soloists. There is, of course, some evidence of this identical technique in earlier years, when a chanson of Dufay or Ockeghem might appear in different guise

---

[2] The revival of interest in the lute, its construction, repertoire, and technique, has of late brought about the formation in England of a Lute Society, which has its own Journal.

depending on the manuscript source consulted. In one, there will be a song pure and simple, with the uppermost part only underlaid with text; in another source, the same music may appear with words written out beneath the tenor part as well as the cantus, so that to all intents and purposes the work is a duet with one independent accompanying instrumental part.

Music discussed in the following pages will, as far as possible, belong to the category of solo song. Certain compositions may, however, exist in quasi-duet versions as well, and the criterion here will be the internal evidence of manuscripts and the relative effectiveness of the underlay to the second voice-part. If the words have obviously been added later in an attempt to convert a song into a duet, the work will be counted as a song.[3] This is done, not in order to add at any cost to the already enormous song-repertory, but to help redress the unfortunate and widespread belief that most secular music of the Renaissance is for *a cappella* chorus. In fact the appeal and personality of a fine solo voice was as great in those early centuries as at any other time, and it is only when the songs are interpreted today by accomplished and sensitive artists that they take on some part of their former glory. As vehicles of perfectly matched musical and poetical expression, the best of these songs are unrivalled.

SPAIN

The Cancioneros

French, Flemish, and Italian musicians who visited Spain in the fifteenth century brought with them songs from their own countries, where style and method in setting poetry to music had deep roots. Even though the style grew more simple over the course of years, the method remained largely the same as far as solo song was concerned. A verse of the lyric was written beneath the uppermost voice-part, and the remaining verses (*residuum*) appeared as a separate section to be used by the singer in accordance with certain known rules. The accompanying parts were also written out separately, with word-cues here and there to guide the instrumentalists. This common physical aspect of a chansonnier is found also in the earlier *cancioneros*, and in some cases overlapping repertoire bears out the links between French and Spanish

---

[3] For example, *Je ne fait tousjours que penser*, by Binchois, has only the superius underlaid in the Escorial chansonniers (IV a 24 and V III 24) whereas a copy in the Vatican (Urb. lat. 1411) provides both tenor and superius with text. The obviously instrumental shape of the tenor is sufficient to prove the superiority of the Escorial versions.

musicians. Eventually there grew up in Spain a host of composers and singers who contributed to the great wealth of secular song at the court of Ferdinand and Isabella.

The oldest cancionero now extant is that forming part of the library of Ferdinand Columbus (son of the explorer) and preserved in Seville at the Biblioteca Colombina. Unfortunately, it has not yet been published in a modern edition, though some of its ninety-five pieces also appear in other sources. A smaller and later collection in the Biblioteca Públia Hortênsia (Elvas, in Portugal) bears not a single composer's name, though concordances prove that Encina and Escobar contributed some of the songs, even though they may have been subsequently rearranged.[4]

By far the largest single manuscript is the so-called *Cancionero de Palacio*, discovered on a musty top shelf of the library in the Royal Palace, Madrid, in 1870. It was first published by Francisco Barbieri in 1890 under the title *Cancionero Musical Español de los Siglos XV y XVI*, and a reprint appeared at Buenos Aires in 1945. A new modern edition by Higinio Anglés is in course of publication, the first and second volumes being available as Vols. V and X of *Monumentos de la Musica Española*. Although well over sixty composers are represented in this great anthology, Juan del Encina takes pride of place through both quality and quantity of his songs. Most of them are cast in the form of the *villancico*,[5] which had gradually become simplified during the fifteenth century so that the final aspect was akin to a symmetrical ABBA, with each A section having a common coda or refrain. The villancico could be extensive, like the anonymous *Harto, de tanta porfia* (100 bars) or brief and to the point, like this setting, again anonymous, of *Yo con vos, señora*:

Ex. 1

There were, even so, departures from this basic form and style, and it was probably due to the flexibility of the villancico that it survived

4 This manuscript has been edited by M. Joaquim as *O Cancionero Musical* (1940).

5 For a penetrating study of the development and influence of this important form, see Isabel Pope, *Musical and Metrical Form of the Villancico*, in *Annales Musicologiques* II (1954), p. 189.

up to and during the heyday of the vihuelistas. In common with these later composers, those of the cancioneros used material both musical and poetical that was the common property of court minstrels throughout Spain. Songs of wide currency such as *Durandarte* and *La bella mal maridada* are found in the Cancionero de Palacio, set by Millán and Gabriel respectively, and it is noteworthy that the tenor melody of Gabriel's setting agrees with the theme used by both Narváez and Valderrábano. Melodic links of an even more definite nature are found frequently, and the fact that the rhythm as well as the melody corresponds to the tiniest detail suggests that composers liked to use pre-existent material and try their hand at varying the harmony. Examples of this treatment are the settings by Cornago and Madrid of *Pués que Dios*, and those of Millán and Alonso de Mondéjar of *Mios fueron, mi corazon.*

Occasionally divergences of style and texture can be usefully compared when the text remains constant, as in the two anonymous settings of *Tristeza, quien á mi vos dió.* The three-part song is in predominantly homophonic style, all parts beginning at the same time. In the four-part setting, the uppermost voice-part and text are the same as before, except for two empty bars at the beginning which allow for the entries of the three instrumental parts in close imitation, foreshadowing the shape of the main theme. Most songs are in duple time, like these settings of *Tristeza*, though now and again sprightly rhythms in triple time are introduced, often with excellent effect. A particularly successful song in this manner is the slightly cynical *Ojos morenicos* by Escobar. In many instances, however, triple time is used for plaintive love-songs and sombre legends from Spanish history. The melodies derive their flavour and character from deep-hidden wells of sacred and secular song, from sinuous contours rather than clear-cut rhythms.

There is an uncanny depth of expression and intensity of feeling in Juan Urrede's *Muy triste será mi vida*, set for soprano voice and three accompanying instruments. Urrede, whose original Flemish name was Johannes Wreede, had come from Flanders to serve at the court of the Duke of Alba, and although he retained his mastery of northern polyphony he knew how to adapt its expressive possibilities to such texts as this one by Juan Rodríguez del Padron. The lower three parts of the song, with their flowing lines oddly interrupted by melodic leaps of a fifth or an octave, suggest that stringed instruments might well have been the composer's own choice as ideal vehicles for his subtle accompaniment. An even darker tone-colour is postulated by the almost morbid text of Badajoz's *Poco á poco me rodean las angustias de la muerte*, matched by a three-part texture of bass voice and two bass instruments. There are few songs for bass voice in this Cancionero: another song by Badajoz, *Malos adalides*, and Lope de Baena's *Todo cuanto yo serví* at least indicate that there were singers who cultivated the lower register. By far the greatest number of songs are for soprano or mezzo-soprano.

A dozen or so of the songs in the Barbieri Cancionero (as it is some-times called, after its first editor) seem to have been intended for the tenor voice. Once again they range from short three-part villancicos such as Francisco de la Torre's *No fié nadie en amor*, the anonymous *Otro bien si á vos no tengo*, and Mondejar's *Mios fueron mi corajon*, to extended settings of the calibre of Medina's *Es por vos si tengo vida* or the wonderfully expressive ¡ *Oh desdichado de mí!* by Badajoz, whom we have already found to be partial to darker tone-colours. The prevalence of songs for higher voices should not blind the reader to the fact that the male alto or countertenor voice was much cultivated in Spain, and textual bienséance demands that many of these villancicos be sung by a man. There are few examples of an exceptionally high range for male alto (though it is fairly certain that pitch was lower in the fifteenth century than today) and in these cases a treble clef is used. The popular song *La zorilla con el gallo*, which was turned into a carol at the express wish of Fray Juan de Tolosa, and another anonymous song *Lo que queda es lo seguro* both appear to require a top E.

A highly important song-type, represented by thirty-six examples in this Cancionero, is the *romance*,[6] whose musical form (often sym-metrical and regular) consists of four successive melodic phrases corre-sponding to four lines of each verse. Many of the romances dealt with historical subjects such as the campaigns of Ferdinand between 1486 and 1489. *Una sañosa porfia* tells with surging harmonies and burning intensity of one of the battles against the Moors, while Anchieta's *En memoria d'Alixandre* and the anonymous *Sobre Baza estaba el Rey* recount the sombre details of the campaigns at Baza and Malaga. The conquest of Granada in 1492 inspired the romance ¿ *Qu'es de tí, desconsolado?* by the prolific Juan del Encina, who – like many of his contemporaries in Spain – made considerable use of the interval of a diminished fourth, both as a leap and as a melodic progression.

---

[6] A succinct study, with useful appendices dividing the romances into their proper categories, may be found in *Musique et Poésie*, p. 299: Miguel Querol Gavalda, *Importance Historique et Nationale du Romance*.

The Vihuelistas

Although Spain was largely responsible for transmitting the lute from its eastern cradle to its western niche, via numerous generations of Arabian scholars and musicians who had made their first important impact on national culture during the reign of Alfonso the Wise, it is significant that the plucked-string instrument which eventually dominated musical life among the sixteenth-century amateurs was the *vihuela de mano*. This instrument had many of the physical and tonal characteristics of the guitar, which it resembled in shape and size, but it was tuned in the manner of the lute and had six or seven strings. It was undoubtedly easier to play than the lute, and easier to hold. As an instrument for accompanying solo song, it was ideal, and when instruction books and collections of graded pieces began to be published. songs that had long proved their worth appeared in settings for voice and vihuela or in arrangements for vihuela solo.[7]

Suitably enough, the first publication of all was intended for beginners – Luis Milán's *Libro de Música de Vihuela de Mano intitulado El Maestro*, which appeared in 1536. It was re-published in a modern transcription by Leo Schrade in *Publikationen älterer Musik* (Vol. II, 1927), and excerpts in less reliable form were given in *Les Luthistes espagnols du XVI siècle* edited by G. Morphy (1902). In Milán's original edition, the music for both voice and vihuela was printed in tablature, though red ink was used to show which part was to be sung. The player was probably expected to play both red and black ciphers, so that the voice part was doubled by the lute throughout the entire composition.

In his four *romances*, Milán draws on the vast reservoir of traditional song, but adds to these melodies with their four-line verses a development of his own. The second part of *Durandarte* (a song about Roland, the good, proven knight) is clearly built on a motive from the first part, yet is just as clearly separated from it by a florid vihuela interlude. Similarly constructed is the song referring to Don Gayferos, *Con pavor recordó il moro*. Milán's easy familiarity with the heroic vein may be seen in his fine setting of *Triste estaba muy quexosa*, inspired by the account of the death of Hecuba in the Trojan epic. A group of six *villancicos*, also in Castilian, display a fair variety of style within a short space, and several of them are provided with alternative settings in which the melody is broken up and the virtuoso element brought to the

---

[7] See Daniel Devoto, *Poésie et Musique dans l'Oeuvre des Vihuelistes* in *Annales Musicologiques*, IV (1956), p. 85.

fore in the accompaniment. In *Aquel caballero, madre* the first version has a simple though occasionally independent accompaniment; the second version is considerably more ornate, calling for accurate yet quasi-extempore performance of the vihuela part. *Amor, que tan bien sirviendo* recalls the homophonic style prevalent in the *cancioneros*, while the narrow compass of the melody (a minor sixth) suggests a popular origin. By way of exception, *Toda mi vida os amé* has something of the dance in its insistent hemiola rhythm:

Ex.2

To - da mi vi - da os a - mé Si me a - máis yo no lo___ sé.

Since Milán's book was dedicated to King John of Portugal it is not surprising to find a further group of villancicos in Portuguese, though the six examples printed follow, in general, the stylistic features of the Castilian compositions. *Quiem amores ten à fim* moves elegantly within the confines of a perfect fifth, yet its cadences are tame when compared with the baroque flourishes of *Falai miña amor*, supplied by the ever-ready hand of the vihuelista.

In 1538 Luis de Narváez published *Los seys libros del Delphin de música*,[8] and the six books referred to in the title are concerned with various aspects of the vihuela and its repertoire – scales, fantasies, intabulations, and songs. Book V, which consists of 'música para canto y vihuela', indicates that Narváez had slightly different ideas from those of Milán, although they were exact contemporaries, with regard to song setting and accompaniment. Narváez prints only four initial lines of the text of each romance, explaining that they are so well known that singers can add as many more quatrains as they wish. Most of the romances were very long indeed, as may be gathered from those contained in the *Romancero general* of Duran, where texts often show deviations from the versions set to music. Nevertheless it was part of a Spanish gentleman's education to know by heart some of the more famous romances, and it was thus easy for them to fit extra stanzas to the available music.

Ya se asienta el rey Ramiro is a song conerning the adventures of

[8] Edited by Emilio Pujol as Vol. III of *Monumentos de la Música Española*.

King Ramiro of Aragon, and its typically steady tread is rarely interrupted by notes of shorter value, though the vihuela part is more mobile by far. Often the plain and ornamented versions of a phrase are heard simultaneously, and it is possible that when the accompaniment becomes less florid the singer is expected to add embellishments of his own. The vihuela part is much more restrained in the setting of one of Spain's most popular romances, *Paseábase el rey moro*, which tells how the Moorish king was walking through the gardens of Granada, brooding on the news that Alhama had been captured. In common with other composers who set this melody (among them Fuenllana and Pisador) Narváez makes much of the king's impassioned cry which recurs as a refrain: 'Alas my Alhama!' A twist of a more unusual kind is to be found in the villancico *Si tantos halcones*, where concepts of love and falconry are momentarily turned heavenwards, a procedure known among poets as 'vuelta a lo divino'. This song has three alternative forms, with virtuoso passages for the vihuela and introductions of varying length and scope. The melody of another villancico, *Y la mi cinta dorada*, lies entirely within the compass of a perfect fourth, but Narváez offers one variation for each verse, and manages to sustain the interest right through the two five-line verses with their questioning refrain. The range of *Con qué la lavaré*, with its span of a tenth, is in complete contrast, suggesting the techniques of composed song rather than the psalmodic repetitions of traditional tunes.

Alonso Mudarra's *Tres Libros de Música en Cifra para Vihuela* (1546) is also available in an edition by Pujol.[9] It follows the general lines of the two previous books of tablature by Milán and Narváez, though certain innovations are introduced. The first of these concerns the melody, which appears for the first time on a stave of its own. The second concerns repertoire, which is enlarged to include several romances on biblical subjects, such as *Durmiendo iba el Señor* (Jesus causing the tempest to subside) and *Triste estaba el rey David* (the lament for Absalom). Mudarra also gives some examples of the *canción*, in one of which (*Claros y frescos rios*) there is a trace of written-out ornamentation in the voice part. There are seven *sonetos*, three in Spanish and four in Italian, two of the latter showing a penchant for extended construction in the use of a short prelude thematically related to the melody itself. An interesting group described by Mudarra as 'versos en latín' includes an occasional piece on the death of Princess Mary, *Regina qui mesto spectas*, and settings of famous passages from Virgil, Horace and

⁹ *Monumentos de la Música Española*, Vol. VII.

Ovid.[10] A final group of five villancicos includes a well-known song about an abbess and a knight (*Gentil caballero*) which was also set, with slight textual variants, by Pisador. Another song in this group, *Isabel, perdiste la tu faxa*, is notable for an extremely long and florid introduction on the vihuela.

The next important collection of songs is that of Enriquez de Valderrábano, whose *Libro de música de vihuela intitulado Silva de Sirenas* was published in 1547. Extracts are available in Morphy's edition referred to above, but it must be borne in mind that the edition is not scrupulously accurate. *Los brazos traigo cansados* is a romance based on a stanza from the *Romance de Don Beltran*, and Valderrábano heightens the pathos by prolonging the last syllable of each line to an unprecedented extent, and suffusing it with ornate cadential passages on the vihuela. Another romance tells the grim story of the Moor Calaynos, of his love for the Infanta and the subsequent demand for the heads of three French peers (*Ya cabalga Calaynos*). There are also echoes of Mudarra in a group of biblical romances: *Adormido se ha el buen viejo* describes the flight to the desert of the prophet Elijah; *Ay de mi, dice el buen padre* represents the lament of Mattathias on the destruction of Jerusalem; *En la ciudad de Betulia* concerns the story of Judith and Holofernes.

Diego Pisador's *Libro de música de vihuela*[11] appeared in 1552, and continued the tradition of intabulating both secular and sacred music of other composers. Yet there was room for a dozen compositions by Pisador, and he included not only romances and villancicos but also an elegy (*Endecha*). He set two songs which have been encountered previously in this chapter – *Paseábase el rey moro* and *Gentil caballero*, bringing to them his own highly sensitive and sympathetic feeling for traditional melody and text. His version of the historical romance *Guarte, guarte el rey don Sancho* is also successful. The events referred to in *A las armas, Moriscote* place the origin of the text, and perhaps the original melody too, at the close of the fifteenth century during the reign of King Ferdinand. *La mañana de San Juan* is a fine song on the subject of the Moorish king hearing about the loss of Antequera, and proves Pisador an adept in handling a keen dramatic situation.

Two years after Pisador's book, there appeared in Seville one of the richest collections of songs and instrumental music Spain has ever

---

10 These may be intabulations of vocal settings. Latin poetry was a medium with special attractions for the Renaissance composer.

11 See Morphy, *Les Luthistes Espagnols du XVIe Siècle*, Vol. II.

known. Its author was the blind virtuoso of the vihuela, Miguel de Fuenllana, and he called his book *Orphénica Lyra*.[12] In such a late anthology, it is not surprising to find several songs which had previously been set by other composers – *Paseábase el rey moro* (Narváez and Pisador), *A las armas* (Pisador) and *De Antequera sale el moro*, which is based on the same story as Pisador's *La mañana de San Juan*. The setting of *Paseábase* is typical of the high quality encountered in this publication, for the almost hypnotic repetition of overlapping phrases is perfectly set off by an accompaniment that stresses independent figures of imitation and ever-changing rhythms.

Ex. 3

Fuenllana has taken over six polyphonic vallancicos of Juan Vasquez and arranged them for voice and vihuela, thus adding to the song repertoire and demonstrating his interest in allied *a cappella* forms.

The widespread interest in the romance even penetrated works that were mainly theoretical in design and content. When Juan Bermudo published his *Declaración de instrumentos musicales* in 1555 he included the famous song *Mira Nero de Tarpeya*, cited time and time again in early Spanish literature – *Don Quijote* (Cervantes), *Don Florisel de Niquea* (Feliciano de Silva), and *Roma Abrasada* (Lope de Vega). Nero's alleged musical activities during the burning of Rome would appeal in more than one way to poets and musicians, and this song (which must have enjoyed considerable popularity, although it never appeared in any of the regular song-anthologies) demonstrates the continuing appeal of classical themes and the vihuelista's love of narrative.

Many years were to elapse before the publication of the last anthology for vihuela de mano. This was Esteban Daza's *El Parnaso* (1576) which included a few romances and villancicos, still set in the hallowed manner of the great school, and still dependent on traditional melodies and texts. One such romance, *Enfermo estaba el rey Antioco*, dates back to the last decade of the fifteenth century, as is proved by a similar composition in the *Cancionero del Palacio*. After Daza, the vihuela

---

[12] Morphy, op. cit., the song *Paseábase el rey moro* is reprinted in *Historical Anthology of Music*, I, p. 132.

78

seemed to decline in popularity, and its place was eventually taken by the five-course guitar. Nevertheless, the forty years that separated Milán's tablature from Daza's gave to Spain, and to the world, a rich and variegated repertoire of solo song.

ENGLAND

Ballades and Ballads

England had no song tradition corresponding to the music of troubadours, trouvères, and their German imitators. The English monarchy, with its frequently irksome French ties, preferred to regard secular music – like wine – as a necessarily imported product. One consequence of this reliance on foreign singers and foreign songs was the dearth of secular music in Britain during the later middle ages and the early years of the renaissance. English composers wrote their songs to French and Italian texts, and were influenced perhaps by the courtly elements in this type of poetry, which then seemed both fashionable and preferable.

Nevertheless there are a few examples of a happy marriage between the music and poetry of England, from this comparatively early period. Two songs in ballade style, that is with vocal line uppermost and two instrumental parts below, demonstrate the fluent and expressive writing of which composers were then capable. *Go, heart, hurt with adversity* is a musical jewel of small size yet great radiance in a poetical setting that was surely more extensive originally. Only the first verse is now extant, and as a result the song is over far too soon; we long to hear the same music again, with additional verses.[13] The other song, *Well were him that wist*, is suffused with a lively rhythm which might nowadays be considered oddly at variance with the moral, even philosophical, pointers of the text.[14]

Several English songs achieved wide currency in continental Europe, and although their texts were often translated or replaced, they can legitimately take their place among the minor masterpieces of the century. An anonymous song *Princess of youth* is found in a manuscript at the Escorial, and has been discussed by Manfred

[13] An easily accessible transcription of this anonymous song may be seen in John Harvey's *Gothic England*, p. 85, but the extent to which the parts cross each other is clearly shown only in the second volume of Stainer's *Early Bodleian Music*, p. 68.

[14] A facsimile and transcription appeared in *Music, Cantelenas and Songs*, edited by S. L. Meyer (1906).

Bukofzer.[15] There are also three English songs, two definitely by Walter Frye and the other by Bedingham, in the Mellon Chansonnier at Yale University. Easily the most famous of these was *So is imprinted in my remembrance*,[16] a song of great charm and melodic individuality, with a memorable opening phrase that falls and rises in its descent like the homeward flight of a seagull:

Frye's *Alas, Alas* and Bedingham's *Mine heart* are also preserved in the Mellon Chansonnier, and the former has been printed by way of supplement to an article on this important source.[17] The rondeau *Tout a par moi*[18] is ascribed in one manuscript to Binchois, but in two to Frye; we may thus assume a possible total of four songs by him.

Italian texts set by Englishmen include *Gentil madonna* by Bedingham and *O rosa bella* (on a text by the Venetian poet Giustiniani) attributed to Dunstable. *O rosa bella*, with its clearly-defined phrases and supple melody, was destined to become one of the most popular songs of the fifteenth century. It even served as a basis for Masses and motets, and eventually spread itself through manuscript sources all over Europe. Together with Dunstable's rondeau *Puisque m'amour*, it is printed in Bukofzer's edition of Dunstable's works.[19]

The advent of the Tudors, to whose court Welshmen as well as continental musicians were welcome, marked the decline of the chanson and the rise of the freemen's songs. This term may be a corruption of *three-men*, for most of the songs are in three parts and would require that number of singers, since all parts were underlaid with text. In spite of the musical riches of this repertory, it cannot be included under the heading of pure song, since it foreshadowed the part-song or the

[15] *Music and Letters*, XIX (1938), p. 119.

[16] Printed in full, with French and Latin contrafacta on p. 201 of Sylvia Kenney's article on Frye, in *Journal of the American Musicological Society*, VIII (1955), p. 201.

[17] See Manfred Bukofzer, *An Unknown Chansonnier of the Fifteenth Century*, in *The Musical Quarterly*, XXVIII (1942), p. 14; also Dragan Plamenac, *A Postscript to 'The "Second" Chansonnier of the Biblioteca Riccardiana'*, in *Annales Musicologiques*, IV (1956), p. 264.

[18] This delightful song, rich in rhythmical subtleties, is available in a transcription by Dragan Plamenac in *The Musical Quarterly*, XXXVII (1951), p. 530.

[19] *Música Británnica*, Vol. IX.

glee in regard to manner of performance. Although the lute song began to be cultivated during Henry VIII's reign, and was encouraged by the arrival of Venetian musical families such as the Bassanos, it relied for its material upon the intabulation of pre-existing vocal polyphony, usually liturgical. As in Italian tablatures, one or more of the inside parts was omitted, so that the performer had only to sing his part and play a fairly simple accompaniment. Very few lute songs with secular text can be traced back to the early sixteenth century, though poets as well as musicians practised the lute and must often have set their songs to music. Sir Thomas Wyatt, who called his poems 'songs', frequently mentions the lute:

> Blame not my lute for he must sound
> Of this and that as liketh me,
> For lack of wit the lute is bound
> To give such tunes as pleaseth me;
> Though my songs be somewhat strange,
> And speak such words as touch thy change,
> Blame not my lute.

A lute song by John Heywood (1497–1578) entitled *What heart can think* almost certainly goes back to pre-Elizabethan days, for he resigned his court appointment on religious grounds in 1558 and fled to the continent. Of two anonymous lute songs, probably written about the middle of the century, one is a setting of the poem by Lord Vaux, *I loathe that I did love*, exhibiting simple, four-square melodic features, while the other, *My little pretty one*, moves in a flowing triple measure.[20]

Songs for Voice and Viols

In the meantime, the viol consort reigned supreme in the field of domestic music-making, and it is not surprising to find that such consorts were used to accompany solo song from the middle of the sixteenth century. Compositions by Edwards, Parsons, Farrant, Nicholson, Patrick and Strogers demonstrate the excellence and variety of this basically simple combination of voice and string quartet, which was brought to its highest peak in the works of Byrd. Peter Warlock edited three volumes of these songs (Oxford University Press, 1926) and was the first to point out their wide range of subject-matter and

---

[20] Reprinted in Warlock and Wilson, *English Ayres*, Vol. IV.

technique. Most of them appear to be stage songs, taken perhaps from the repertory of the Chapel Royal children, and they share the same characteristics of textual assonance and music of a frankly melodramatic cast.[21] Panthea's heartfelt 'Alas, alas', rising slowly and inexorably through the space of a diminished octave in Farrant's *Abradad* is matched by the rising figure 'Let sobs, let sighs, let plaints, let tears' in Patrick's *Send forth thy sighs* and the long drawn-out death of the heroine in the anonymous but moving *Guichardo*. They were musical and literary conventions, yet their treatment of the pathetic vein was rarely to be equalled by madrigal or lute-song.

This same delightful collection contains the first song ever to be printed for voice and viols: a street cry, *Buy new broom*, set by Thomas Whythorne. There are Christmas songs of great beauty by unknown authors (*Sweet was the song the Virgin sung; Born is the Babe*) and there are songs full of delectable imitations of bird calls. Two of these, by Nicholson, give prominence to the cuckoo (*In a merry May morn; Cuckoo*) while another skilfully suggests the song of nightingale, sparrow and lark (*This merry pleasant spring*). Satire is represented by Wigthorp's *I am not, I, of such belief*, the refrain making clever use of aposiopesis.

William Byrd left far more songs for voice and strings than any other Elizabethan composer, yet this fine legacy has long been obscured by the fact that the 'Psalms, Sonnets and Songs'[22] of 1588 have text underlaid to every voice, even though the composer admits in his preface that the songs were 'originally made for instruments to express the harmonic, and one voice to pronounce the ditty'. Byrd probably knew, through his close connexion with music-publishing, of the impending issue of Yonge's 'Musica Transalpina'; and he hastily made ready a collection of his songs by adding text to the string parts so that they could be sung as if they were madrigals. He was ahead of Yonge by a few months, but the added texts are not all that satisfactory. When the 'first singing part' (Byrd's own designation) is compared with the others, it soon becomes evident that these songs shine with their pristine brilliance only when performed as accompanied songs. Byrd could imitate the Italian madrigal when he liked, but in this collection his fine setting of Ariosto's *La Virginella* remains stubbornly but delightfully English, in spite of the hint of a 'Ruggiero' bass:

[21] See the two articles *Early Elizabethan Stage Music*, in *The Musical Antiquary*, Vol. I (1909), p. 30; Vol. IV (1912), p. 112.
[22] *English Madrigal School*, Vol. XIV; William Byrd, *Complete Works* (edited by E. H. Fellowes), Vol. XII.

He often draws upon prominent poets of his own day – Sir Edward Dyer for *I joy not in no earthly bliss* and *My mind to me a kingdom is*, the Earl of Oxford for *If women could be fair*, which gains in impetus from its subtle hemiola rhythm, and may be compared to the similarly attractive *Though Amaryllis dance in green*. The 'first singing part' is by no means always the soprano: in the serious but splendidly-written *Care for thy soul* Byrd has entrusted the melody to the alto, so that the viol or violin part above takes on the character of a descant. Another fine song in serious vein is the memorial for Edmund Campion (d. 1581) *Why do I use my paper, ink and pen*, where once again we find an alto solo. The *Lullaby* in this set may be usefully compared with Byrd's shorter lullaby (*My sweet little darling*).[23] Sometimes Byrd chooses odd or peculiar texts for his songs. *An aged dame*, with its macabre satire and naïve madrigalisms, comes from one of his favourite poetical sources, Whitney's *Emblems*. Several of his songs are strophic, with extra verses printed not beneath the voice-parts but at the foot of the page, and in the case of some of the moralistic texts (*Sit hence that Death; What steps of strife*) it is as well to perform all three verses. In one instance at least the one available verse makes no sense on its own: *As Caesar wept* consists merely of a subordinate clause. Yet many of these songs were arranged for voice and lute in conformity with the fashion, and one example of such a song, reconstructed by E. H. Fellowes as *Truce for a time*[24] gives a fair idea of this type of transformation.

Songs to the Lute

Publication of lute songs began in earnest with Dowland's 'First Book of Songs or Airs',[25] and the appearance of this modest volume in 1597 touched off a splendid salvo of songs which lasted, in that particular form, until Attey's 'First Book of Airs' dated 1622. But it must not be

23 William Byrd, *Complete Works*, Vol. XV.
24 ibid., p. 129
25 The most complete collection of lute-songs is that of E. H. Fellowes, *The English School of Lutenist Song Writers* (32 vols.). A smaller collection, in six volumes, is available in Warlock and Wilson, *English Ayres*.

forgotten that Dowland and others were cautious about their ventures into a new field of musical activity: they arranged their airs in such a way that a group of singers could use the book for performance in madrigal fashion. The lute tablature was printed below the soprano part, while the three lower voice-parts appeared facing outwards, so that a quartet sitting round the book could easily read each part. Gradually however the solo song prevailed, and people began to realize the superiority of the lute as a supporting instrument. There is documentary evidence of a song or two accompanied by a keyboard instrument, but the music has not come down to us. Lute songs survive in profusion. Some composers advocated the bass viol as an additional instrument, doubling the bass line which the lute could ill sustain: some even recommended the viol as a replacement of the lute, preferably when played 'lyra-way' which afforded great scope in multiple stopping.[21] Whatever the instrument or instruments used, the essence of monody remained unchanged, and the solitary singer could accompany himself and enjoy the great variety of songs then in vogue.

The texts of the majority of lute songs indicate that they were intended for a baritone or tenor voice, though there are a few songs either composed for women or else suitable to be sung by them.[26] When John Danyel dedicated his song-book of 1606 to 'Mistress Anne Grene the worthy daughter of Sir William Grene of Milton, Knight' he ended *Coy Daphne* with a pun on Mistress Anne's name: 'She rests still green, and so wish I to be'. Another light-hearted song quite clearly destined for a soprano not too advanced in years is Robert Jones's *My father fain would have me take a man that hath a beard.*

Love-lyrics of a conventional nature form the backbone of the repertoire. Yet in spite of convention there is a marriage of music and poetry in the best of these songs that makes them shine like jewels. The uneven yet consistently repeated phrase-lengths of *Love me or not, love her I must or die* (Thomas Campian) are perfectly echoed in the phrases of the music, where two bars are regularly followed by three. The dance-like triple metre so often used for this kind of song is not so much a contradiction in emotive terms as a wistful but enchanting ingredient relieving the mock-seriousness of the situation. Elizabethan lovers were not alone in seeming happy only when they felt wretched. Fortunately the major mode appealed with equal strength, and brought forth such strophic successes as Michael

[26] For a detailed discussion of Elizabethan lyrics in a musical context, see Bruce Pattison, *Music and Poetry of the English Renaissance.*

Cavendish's *Love is not blind* and Jones's *Now what is love?* Some of Philip Rosseter's songs show a keen feeling for the music of poetry besides the subtle touches of declamation that grace *If she forsake me* and *Kind in unkindness*; others are four-square in their melodic plan, yet remain fresh through the cunning use of sequential skips, as in the second half of *And would you see my mistress' face?* In the music of John Dowland, there is an unparalleled virtuosity of technique and catholicity of taste, ensuring rapt attention as much for an apparently frothy song like *Daphne* (which turns contrapuntal as it proceeds) as for the striking *Time stands still*. The only disadvantage in a song where lyric and music are so wonderfully apt for each other is the inevitable anticlimax of the second verse, whose opening line alone suffices to prove that Dowland cared not a rap whether subsequent verses fitted the music as long as the first one hit the mark.

Second only to the love-songs are those quasi-philosophical conceits so beloved of Elizabethan poets and lutenists. Rosseter's setting of *Though far from joy*, a poem in praise of the golden mean, has a justifiable sobriety that is not without charm, and a lightly contrapuntal idiom that perfectly suits the moralizing text. In similar metre and mode is *The heart to rue the pleasure of the eye*, a memorable song with long, sweeping phrases by Cavendish. Far more epigrammatic, yet attractive by reason of its effective change of time for the refrain, Jones's *The sea hath many thousand sands* treats of love in the abstract and warns the ready victim of its snares. Dowland's sure grasp of the recitative-arioso idiom is apparent in his setting of Sir Henry Lea's poem *Far from triumphing court*, a near-autobiographical account of the former Queen's Champion in his retirement. Although Dowland was a brilliant soloist, he was clearly not averse from featuring the lute as a mere thoroughbass instrument, which could nevertheless assume, as it does in the latter part of this song, a rather more independent role. On occasion, a delightful tune was accorded a somewhat fatalistic lyric such as Campian's *What if a day or a month or a year*, based on the favourite 'sic transit gloria mundi' theme. The anonymous setting is found not in one of the printed collections of lute-songs, but in Giles Earle's manuscript dated about 1615.[27]

There was one other vein that the lutenists explored with unqualified success – the pathetic. In the plaints of Dowland and Danyel some of the most touching utterances in the whole realm of solo song are to be found. *In darkness let me dwell* is remarkable not only for

[27] See Warlock and Wilson, *English Ayres*, Vol. VI.

Dowland's unfailing sense of declamation and his powerful use of the more expressively pathetic intervals to heighten the meaning of the text, but for the essential and interdependent functions of lute and gamba. His most famous song, *Flow my tears*, is frankly an air with a finely-contrived though necessarily subordinate accompaniment. As *Lachrymae* it was borrowed and set by dozens of Dowland's contemporaries and successors. Danyel, in *Stay, cruel, stay* seems to hark back to the stage songs with viols in his treatment of the word 'farewell', while repetition of an even more poignant character is developed in the tearful triptych he wrote on the death of Mistress M.E.'s husband (*Grief, keep within*).

The plaint in Shakespeare's *Othello*, usually known as 'The Willow Song', is often presented in a more or less altered form, though the correct version established by John P. Cutts takes on a welcome freshness and beauty of design.[28]

Tendencies towards continuo song in the works of the lutenist songwriters grew as the seventeenth century progressed, and but for the Commonwealth these tendencies might have been reflected in printed sources as well as in manuscripts whose contents, alas, still remain unpublished. Collections of songs in the libraries of New York, Tenbury, Oxford, and London contain a wealth of unknown material that will some day fill in the cumbersome and tantalizing gap that stretches between the Elizabethan lutenists and the song-writers of the Restoration period. It is reassuring to know that Englishmen sang to the lute or viol, no matter what the political or religious situation.

GERMANY

The first stages of German song during the Renaissance closely parallel the development of song in Spain, for the various manuscript

---

[28] *Journal of the American Musicological Society*, X (1957), p. 21.

and printed *Liederbücher* consist mainly of songs for a solo voice accompanied by two or three instruments. But whereas in Spain the polyphonic cancioneros gave way to a flourishing school of lutenist song-writers, in Germany the lutenists went their own way, largely independent of singers, so that there never appeared a German counterpart of Fuenllana, Dowland, or even Gabriel Bataille. Song in Germany reached its peak in the first half of the sixteenth century, and its greatest exponents were Hofhaimer, Isaak, and Senfl.

Early songs, probably dating from the middle of the fifteenth century, are found in such widely scattered sources as the manuscripts of Trent, Madrid (Escorial), Basel, and Strasbourg. Although the last-mentioned source was destroyed in 1870, a quarter of the total number of pieces survive in a copy made by Coussemaker, and among them is a song by a presumably German composer, Egidius de Rhenis. It is a May song set for soprano and two instruments, with a possible third either doubling the vocal part or else taking care of the expressive codettas attached to the last three lines. *Wie lieblich ist der Mai*,[29] is typical of this early period in German song, when Franco-flemish influences were all-powerful. Anonymous songs such as *Der Tag ist so freudenreich* and *Dein Treu die ist noch wohl*, both from Trent, display similar characteristics.[30] Indeed, the hegemony of the treble-dominated style was severely shaken by the advent of the *Tenorlied* (which, in spite of its name, was sometimes well within the range of a baritone or even a bass voice) though it was never entirely banished. It must not be forgotten that the earliest lute-songs in Germany, those of Arnolt Schlick, anticipated the principle of accompanied monody as practised by the Italians, French, and English, by some ninety years.

Like many heterogeneous manuscript song-books of the time, the Lochamer (or Old Nuremberg) song-book is a mixture of self-contained pieces in two- or three-part harmony, and single melodic lines which may belong to polyphonic settings whose instrumental parts were copied in other books, now lost. The possibility of monophonic lieder must not, however, be entirely ruled out.[31] A decade after the copying of the Lochamer book (probably completed before 1460) came the Schedelsches Liederbuch, painstakingly written out by the historian Hartmann Schedel, who had brought back from his student days in Leipzig and Padua a varied corpus of secular song. Yet in spite of the

[29] *Deutsche Lieder des 15. Jahrhunderts aus fremden Quellen* (*Das Chorwerk*, Vol. 45).
[30] ibid.
[31] Konrad Ameln: *Locheimer Liederbuch und Fundamentum organisandi des Conrad Paumann* (facsimile edition); also *Das Locheimer Liederbuch. Teil I: Die mehrstimmigen Sätze.*

typically international nature of the collection, just over half are German songs, and the prevailing texture is three-part.[32] Sometimes the texts are present in one voice-part, sometimes they are written out at the end of the piece, even (in one or two instances) at the end of the book. In his invaluable though sometimes inaccurate edition, Eitner has given these unattached texts to what he calls the principal melodic line, and though this sometimes coincides with the tenor, it does occasionally fit the uppermost part in a far more satisfactory way. He admits that the text does not fit the ligatures of the tenor part in *Der winter sicht mich.* But it makes good sense when underlaid to the soprano part. Similarly the tenor part of *Bei wuniglichen scherzen* seems quite oblivious to the reasonable demands of a vocal, singable line, whereas the soprano accepts the text with ease, offering smooth contrast to the arpeggic, quasi-instrumental parts beneath. Perhaps the most successful of the two-part songs are *Herzlibstes lib* and *In hoffnung tu ich leben,* while a comparative rarity in that it demands three accompanying instruments is the pure tenorlied *Es taget vor dem walde,* a particularly beautiful setting of a first-rate melody much prized by later composers.

This tendency towards four-part texture may be seen in some of the pieces contained in the manuscript at Basel,[33] where three-part songs in the usual AAB form (*Ich scheid mit leid*; *Zart frau anschau mein kläglich leid*; *Artlicher hort du mein einigs ein*) very occasionally give way to four-part songs whose style and manner look forward to Senfl. Such a song is the charming *Nach grossem leid kommt gwöhnlich freud,* for tenor and three instruments, on a text dealing lightly with the idea that every cloud has its silver lining.

The Glogau Liederbuch, named after the town in which it was written in the 1480s, consists of three volumes, and thus ranks as an early example of the use of part-books. Three part-books must have seemed an ideal medium for the prevailing texture of late fifteenth-century German song, but even so there are a few pieces in four parts, with the extra one written out on a facing page. Thus the two upper parts of *Ich bins erfreut*[34] may both be found in the discant part-book. This piece may be a re-working of the three-part setting found in Schedel's song-book; certainly there are considerable differences in the musical texts, and the four-part setting is in many ways an improvement. As with many other songs in the Glogau book, a complete

---

[32] Printed in Vol. 2 of Eitner's *Das deutsche Lied des XV und XVI. Jahrhunderts.*

[33] *Das Chorwerk,* Vol. 45.

[34] *Das Erbe deutscher Musik* (Reichsdenkmale), Vol. IV: *Das Glogauer Liederbuch, Teil I. Deutsche Lieder und Spielstücke,* p. 18.

version of the lyric is lacking, and were it not for the Schedel text reconstruction of the song would be an impossibility. There is every likelihood that singers knew the poems by heart, and needed no more than an incipit to remind them of the first verse. Among the wealth of three-part songs offered by Glogau are such attractive pieces as the lilting *Auf rief ein hübsches freuelein*, a simple but effective setting of the favourite *Elslein, liebstes Elslein*, and two completely different ones of *Ich sachs eins mals*. Although the first-mentioned song has its tune in the tenor, the others keep to the older tradition and retain the melody in the soprano. In contrast to the predominantly simple non-imitative style of these songs, *Seh in mein herz* shows from the very beginning that contrapuntal skill can be effectively high-lighted by imitative entries:

Ex. 7

Manuscript song-books such as these remained in vogue until the invention of movable music-type enabled printers to set to work and produce anthologies of songs by the best composers of the era. The first of these song-books was that of the printer Erhard Öglin (1512), and his example was soon followed by Peter Schöffer's book (1513) and the undated publication of Arnt von Aich, almost certainly belonging to the same decade. Unfortunately the only available reprint of the Öglin song-book[35] somewhat obscures its true purpose by applying text to all four voice-parts. In his preface, the editor (Robert Eitner) draws attention to the great difficulty of underlaying texts, and of having to create voice-parts 'out of nothing'. It is however significant that he admits the comparative ease of applying text to the tenor part;

---

[35] *Publikation älterer praktischer und theoretischer Musikwerk*, Vol. IX: *Erhart Öglin: Liederbuch zu 4 Stimmen.*

a sure indication that these songs were meant for solo voice and an accompanying ensemble. No composers are named by Öglin, though several of the pieces can be traced to well-known authors such as Hofhaimer (*Herzliebstes bild*), Isaak (*Zwischen perg und tieffe tal*), and Senfl (*Könnt ich, schön reines werthes weib*). Other four-part songs of good quality are those by Malchinger (*Wer säh dich*) and Adam Rener (*Mein hochste frücht*).

Schöffer's book cannot boast such a high musical standard as Öglin's, for it relies on a group of lesser-known men (to whom he gives full credit) attached to princely courts, notably that of the Württembergs at Stuttgart. The composers named include Jörg Brack, Heinrich Eytelwein, Johann Fuchswild, Andreas Graw, Malchinger, Jörg Schönfelder, Johann Sies, Sebastian Virdung, and Martin Wolff.[36] Once again the texts, with one or two exceptions, are placed in the tenor part only. Pleasing as these songs are, they cannot avoid a certain impression of sameness, since their melodic formulae savour of an almost mechanically stereotyped formula. This consists of a long note, followed usually by four or six notes of half the length, a brief shift of accent to give the impression of cadential hemiola, and then the same pattern is repeated for the next line. The entire section is then repeated, and though the second half of the song has fresh music the tendency to rely on the same formulae is still very strong. The opening phrase of three songs by Fuchswild, Brack, and an unknown composer displays the formal symmetry that characterizes not only these but many other songs in the same collection:

Ex.8

a) Kein trost auf erd ich ha - - - - - - - ben mag

b) Ich hoff es sei fast wohl _____ mög - - - - lich

c) Ohn alls ge - fähr sich viel _____ be - geit

To be fair, there are certain songs which appear to strive for a different, perhaps more personal utterance, as in Brack's *Mein dienst und will*, where he may have been inspired to write an unusually fine melody by the high moral tone of the lyric, which deals with the pledges of a faithful lover. The soloist's part ranges freely and comfort-

---

[36] *Fünfzehn deutsche Lieder aus Peter Schöffers Liederbuch* (*Das Chorwerk*, Vol. 29).

ably over a tenth, from *D* to *f*, and the accompanying part adds ample support without overloading the texture with too much detail. Unusual by reason of its imitative entries is a cleverly constructed song by Graw about an ardent lover: *Die brinnet lieb bringt mich dahin*. The melody rises naturally to its climax on a high *a*, which remarkably enough coincides with a word needing stress in each of the three verses ('gmüt', 'lieb', 'wollt'). Technically these songs published by Schöffer display a high degree of technical competence, but this is counteracted to some extent by their lack of imagination and enterprise. It was left to the great masters of the German school of secular song to give the world those typically warm expressions of German sensibility which remain veritable miniature masterpieces even though they are seldom sung and played in modern times.

The seventy-five anonymous songs in Arnt von Aich's book inculde a good proportion of first-class works by Hofhaimer and Isaak, as well as songs by lesser-known masters of the calibre of Adam Rener and Adam von Fulda. The latter, like Sebastian Virdung (who is represented in Schöffer's book) is known to posterity largely by his fame as a theorist, yet the music he composed for the song *Ach Jupiter*, with its twelve verses crammed with classical allusions, shows him to be a capable, even tuneful craftsman.[37] As might be expected, the main content of this song-book deals with love in its many aspects, from the high-flown, courtly declarations that distinguish Hofhaimer's lyrics to the bucolic coarseness of *Ein Bauer sucht sei'm sohn ein weib*, which has thoughtfully been provided with a more decorous text by the modern editors, Moser and Bernouilli. The most amusing feature of this particular song is not so much its original text as the fact that its music, like that of Mozart's *Musikalischer Spass*, makes fun of the musical idiom associated with peasant gatherings immortalized on canvas by Isaac van Ostade, de Bry, and Jan Molenaer.

Stylistically the songs show more variety than either of the two undoubtedly earlier song-books. Although many of the songs begin homophonically, and with all the parts sounding together, quite a few afford evidence of the growing preference for imitation: *Der welte lauf*; *Was ich durch glück*; *Ich klag und reu* (Hofhaimer); *Freundliches bild*. The contrapuntal strands are for the most part smoothly woven, and the tenor melodies constructed with a real feeling for growth of phrase and progress towards a peak. The instrumental parts are active and interesting, though occasionally they seem to begin tamely (as in the song

[37] Moser, H. J. and Bernouilli, E. (eds.): *Das Liederbuch des Arnt von Aich*.

Rosina) before running into genuine animation. A few of the songs include a 'personalized' touch in that the singer can fill in the name of his beloved where the composer has left an initial. Hofhaimer's *Mein einigs A* is a case in point; another is the smoothly-flowing *Mein M ich hab*.

Side by side with these printed and manuscript collections of lieder there ran a parallel movement which was concerned not so much with solo song as with part-songs, designed for a group of singers with or without instrumental support. The music of Heinrich Finck (a contemporary of Hofhaimer) is carefully underlaid with text in every voice-part, so too are most of the lieder of Isaac, who must be mentioned here on account of his successful internationalism even though he was a native of Flanders. Of course, it would have been possible to perform the songs of Finck in the same way as those of Hofhaimer and the many other contributors to the early song-books, for the melody remained in the tenor and the surrounding parts are perfectly suitable for instrumental performance. In the case of Isaak's songs, some of the sources present his works as part-songs, others as solo songs. His fresh, lyrical setting of the poem *Freundlich und mild* appears in Öglin's collection as a tenorlied, and the rather more venturesome *Was frewet mich*[38] is also given in this form. The latter song, in which the lover compares his riches to those of King Croesus, exultantly stresses the wealthy monarch's name by giving an upward run, traversing an octave, to the solo voice.

Hofhaimer's achievement bestrides a peak of its own, and is over-topped by Senfl only because of the vast quantity of the later master's songs. One does not usually think of an organist as a potentially great song-writer, but Hofhaimer was an organist of wide culture and sympathies, and his feeling for vocal contour is always lively and sensitive. He writes mostly for voice and three instruments. A fifth part, however, was added to *Ich habs in sinn* by his friend Kugelmann,[39] and it is noteworthy that the second, third and fourth words of the title become in turn the opening words of the second, third, and fourth verses respectively. Tricks of this kind, together with occasional acrostics, were by no means foreign to the high-flown and courtly literary style of the time. Although the typically epigrammatic effect of Hofhaimer's sectional method of construction classes him as a traditionalist, he so often succeeds in imparting a true musical conception of the poem's content that recurring cadences come to be accepted as a valid and not entirely

[38] *Denkmäler der Tonkunst in Osterreich*, Jahrgang XIV[1] (Vol. 28): *Heinrich Isaac: Weltliche Werke*, ed. by Johannes Wolf.

[39] Reprinted, together with all other available songs by Hofhaimer, in H. J. Moser: *Paul Hofhaimer*.

unpleasing aspect of his style. The intimacy of *Ich hab heimlich ergeben mich*, the sorrow at parting in *Ade mit leid*, the humour of *Greyner zanner* all testify to a mastery of the idiom of solo song, and a sympathy with the claims of poetry.

The generally high quality and great quantity of Senfl's songs are almost sufficient to bestow on him the title of 'the Schubert of the sixteenth century'. His compositions, fortunately available and well edited,[40] were sung throughout German-speaking countries and circulated in numerous manuscript sets of part-books as well as in publications by Egenolff and Formschneider. Senfl's greatest gift is his instinct for melodic construction, whether old tunes were to be re-set and reshaped, or new ones composed. Even in an early work, like *Könnt ich, schön reines werthes weib*, which first appeared in Öglin's song-book, the tenor melody and the additional parts blend flowing lines with admirable control. Better still is *Allein dein huld*, with its resourceful harmonic pointing of the melody climax ('was möglich mir'), a feature which is recalled in *Geduld und huld*, which Gustave Reese refers to, with every justification, as 'one of his loveliest songs'.[41] *Hoch wohlgefallen ist in mir* reverts to the sectional type of tune with frequent cadences, whereas the melody of the expressive *Gross weh ich leid* rises slowly and inexorably to its splendid climax on a high F. An unusual song in triple metre and boasting eleven verses is *Wiewohl vier herter örden sind*, an attack on the greed and prejudices of corrupt courtiers. Unusual for another reason – because its melody is in the soprano instead of the tenor – is *Jetz scheiden bringt mir schwer*; it is only when we realize that the song is that of a girl bidding farewell to her lover that the change in register becomes truly significant. In *Lust hab ich ghabt zuer musica* Senfl avails himself of the richest possible vein of polyphony, for the poem bears as an acrostic 'Ludwig S' and mentions in verse five the name of Senfl's teacher:

> Isaac, das was der name sein
> halt' wohl, es werd' vergessen nit,
> wie er sein kompositz so fein
> und klar hat gsetzt, darzue auch mit
> mensur geziert.

In the eighty-one songs that Senfl contributed to Ott's '121 neue Lieder' (1534) one finds the same spontaneous, lightly-woven counterpoint and

(40) *Das Erbe deutscher Musik (Reichsdenkmale)*,Vols. X and XV; also *Senfl: Sämtliche Werke*, Vols. II, IV, V.
41 *Music in the Renaissance*, p. 708.

a mine of melody old and new. With such a profusion of first-class solo songs, there is little wonder that the lutenists turned their talents mainly in the direction of arrangement and ornamentation.

The German Lutenists

In spite of the thorough work that has been done on the flourishing school of German lutenists, the existence of lute-song as it was known in England and France from the 1590s onward has never been postulated. True, the example of Schlick's *Tabulaturen* of 1512 has been cited as a foreshadowing of monody, yet his principles of transcription are identical with those of Francis of Bosnia, whose arrangements of frottole were first published by Petrucci in 1509. The principle was to have the soprano melody sung, the alto omitted, and the tenor and bass played on the lute. The soprano part, given in mensural notation opposite the lute tablature, was probably sung quite frequently by a tenor voice transposing the melody to a lower octave, so that the original tenor of the tenorlied would remain in the lute, and a new tenor would be created in the middle of the arranged lute-part. The important corollary of all this is that two-part arrangements of songs in the lute-books of Gerle, Newsidler, and others may also be intended for performance with a solo voice. Presenting as they do only the two lower parts of a song in four-part harmony the effect is bleak in the extreme, and its artistic value almost nil. It may well be asked why the melody of each song was not printed in these later books, as it had been in the Schlick publication. Surely the answer is that the simultaneous printing of mensural notation and tablature was extremely difficult even for Petrucci, and apart from their one early attempt German publishers did not care to follow it up.

For the performers, the situation was entirely different. The songbooks they owned were the fount and origin of the lute arrangements, and it was an easy matter to write the text beneath the soprano part and sing it along with the lute. Even when the lute arrangement has undergone an upward transposition in order to avoid notes that are too low, and to ensure the sounding of the tenor melody in a sonorous register, the vocal compass is still perfectly well suited to the soprano or tenor voice. Newsidler's two-part arrangement of Thomas Stolzer's *Ich klag den tag*[42] could thus be reconstructed in the following manner as a lute-song:

[42] See Radecke, E., *Das deutsche weltliche Lied in der Lautenmusik des 16. Jahrhunderts*, in *Vierteljahrsschrift für Musikwissenschaft*, VII (1891), p. 285.

In three-part arrangements, the soprano part always appears in the lute tablature, either in its original form or ornamented. When the original form is preferred, the possibility of a lute song is still not ruled out, since the Spanish vihuelistas sometimes make a point of doubling the vocal line with an instrument, and this would be a perfectly acceptable method of performance. It was the method adopted by Sebastian Ochsenkuhn in his tablature of 1558, as is shown by the songs *Sieh bauernknecht* and *Ich schwing mein horn*.[43] The Cologne printer Adrian Denss, in his 'Florilegium' of 1594, printed the lute tablature on one page and the vocal line (facing outwards) on the opposite page, thus reverting to the early example of Schlick; in this manner he presents transcriptions of numerous songs by Lechner and others who were not really concerned with monody at all, and in some cases the result is quite successful. Of especial interest are the intabulations of Lechner's arrangements from the villanelle ('Kurtzweilige teutsche Lieder') by Regnart. The original three-part lieder have been augmented by two extra voices and additional counterpoint, and then reduced again in the lute version of Denss, sometimes with a choice of either soprano or bass part for singing.

There was no great vogue for monody in Germany until as late as 1623, when Nauwach's 'Arie passegiate' appeared, and although this volume doubtless introduced many German singers to the new methods of vocal ornament as set forth by Caccini and others, it did very little to encourage a genuine German school of continuo song. The villanella craze that had begun with Regnart in 1576 was continued by Nauwach in his 'Teutsche Villanellen' of 1627. Once again there was no real incentive to begin a national counterpart to foreign forms and

---

[43] *Denkmäler der Tonkunst in Österreich*, Jahrgang XXXVII[2] (Vol. 72): *Das deutsche Gesellschaftslied in Österreich 1480–1550*.

styles, and nearly a decade passed before one of Schütz's pupils, Caspar Kittel, produced a volume of cantatas (some of which were for solo voice and continuo) purporting to train juvenile voices in the art of vocal ornamentation. It was left to Heinrich Albert and his contemporaries to provide a genuine and lasting resurgence of the lyrical song which had set Germany on a high plane at the beginning of the sixteenth century, and which was to lead, albeit by diffuse and devious routes, to the wealth of fine songs in the romantic era.

ITALY

Compared with the rich and abundant artistic activity in fifteenth-century Italy, music, at least among her native composers, seems to have been less intensely cultivated. The Italian genius lay fallow, but not idle, during the half-century from 1440, during which time music and musicians from other parts of Europe (but especially from France and Burgundy) served to please the rulers of court and cloister. The results of this artistic invasion may be seen in the extant manuscripts of the time. They bulge with French, Flemish, and even English names, whereas Italian composers are conspicuous by their sparse representation or quasi-anonymity. It would be tempting to hazard the guess that secular songs with Italian texts, unattributed and unclaimed amongst this great mass of material, might be the work of native Italian composers; but we know too well that the northerners were quick to learn both the language and the poetry of their southern hosts, so that many a ballata unsigned in the manuscripts may be a work of Dufay or Ciconia.

The few songs that survive from the middle years of the century show a definite leaning towards French models, with both tune and text in the uppermost voice-part and subsidiary instrumental parts, liable to cross frequently, below. In the famous manuscript at Oxford,[44] half a dozen songs by Italian composers afford adequate proof of the powerful influence of northern nations in the matter of musical style: yet the fact remains that Italian song-writing had not entirely ceased, as some historians have reluctantly admitted in the past. The Provost of Brescia (which provost we may never completely ascertain) has left two quite well-written *ballate* for solo voice and instruments: *Or*

[44] Bodleian Library, Canonici misc. 213. See Gilbert Reaney's article and inventory in *Musica Disciplina*, IX (1955), p. 73.

s'avanta omay chi vol amor, and *I ochi d'una ancolleta*, while a contemporary of his from Bologna is the author of *Vince con lena çascun aspro orgoglio*, a song which was so well received that it was turned into a *Gloria in excelsis*.[45]

Two more *ballate* from this same source are the macaronic *Vivere et recte reminiscere* of Bartlomeo Brollo[46] and *O stella chi a respiender* by Pietro Rosso (Petrus Rubeus).[47] Brollo's song is full of imitative phrases running through all three parts, and there is a sudden and effective change from major to minor as soon as the Italian text ('gia che la nera lingua . . .') begins. Nevertheless it is strange to find only a handful of genuinely Italian pieces in a manuscript copied – in all probability – in Venice, and containing well over three hundred pieces. It is only when we look at similar, if later sources that we realize that this picture is reproduced time and time again. Even in the later chansonniers there are generally very few Italian compositions in comparison with the superabundance of French ones. In the French chansonnier of the Biblioteca Colombina, Seville, less than ten per cent of the contents makes use of Italian texts, and it is not possible to say with certainty that the anonymous items were composed in Italy, even though the manuscript was undoubtedly copied there.[48]

It is interesting to note that several of the *strambotti* were sung also to devotional but non-liturgical texts known as *laude*. For example, *So stato nel inferno* became *So stato in peccato*, and *La morte che spavento de felice* became *L'amor ch'i' porto a te, Imperatrice*.[49] Thus did the preaching of Savonarola make itself felt in musical circles, and although laude continued to be published well into the sixteenth century, the return of carnivals and other manifestations of carefree enjoyment may have helped to spur on the next great stage of Italian song – the epoch of the frottolists. They did not burst upon the musical scene fully armed. Many were the examples of solo song which they might have heard or helped to perform in some noble household of northern Italy. A Florentine chansonnier, again almost certainly copied in Italy, contains among its few Italian pieces a pair of genuinely original and

---

[45] Bartolomeo da Bologna's song is reprinted in Stainer, *Dufay and his Contemporaries*, p. 60. Other songs from this manuscript are due to appear in *Unpublished Music from the Oxford Manuscript*, by Gilbert Reaney.

[46] *Polyphonia Sacra* (ed. C. van den Borren), p. 293.

[47] Reaney, *Unpublished Music from the Oxford Manuscript*.

[48] Dragan Plamenac, *A Reconstruction of the French Chansonnier in the Biblioteca Colombina, Seville*, in *The Musical Quarterly*, XXXVII (1951), p. 501; XXXVIII (1952), pp. 85, 245.

[49] For further examples, see Ghisi, *Strambotti e Laude nel travestimento spirituale della poesia musicale del Quattrocento*, in *Collectanea Historiae Musicae*, I (1953), p. 45.

beautiful songs. *Le bionde treçe*, for soprano and two instruments, combines flowing and expressive phrases with shorter, almost epigrammatic statements that are underlined by the more melodic of the accompanying parts.[50] The other song, *Vergine sola*, is for alto and three instruments, and its predominantly chordal style assists the careful declamation of the uppermost part. As Dragan Plamenac has said, 'the composition is a noble rendering of Petrarch's great canzona, in a musical idiom that is genuinely Italian and of popular appeal; of all musical settings of the poem the present may easily be the one most consistent with the spirit and the atmosphere that gave birth to the verses.'[51]

In nine cases out of ten, the starting point for Italian secular music was popular poetry. The versifiers of the court of Isabella d'Este were for the most part shameless imitators of Petrarch, yet even they could at times put forth some strambotto or barzelletta with a vein of true originality and charm running through it. This was, after all, light poetry, and the musicians were left to heighten its emotional content or tone down its exaggerations as best they could. For this purpose they used the musical style called *frottola*, the old term for street songs or music sung in a crowd of people. Many of these frottole have been re-published in recent years, though oddly enough they are never performed, perhaps because the correct manner of performing them has never been grasped or understood, or because our ideas of solo song are in some way limited.

The best of these frottole are really delightful, well-made compositions; not too complex as regards part-writing, and tuneful enough to sustain the lyric without overpowering it. Early in the year 1500, a noble poet wrote to Isabella d'Este: 'Your Excellency knows that at the time of my departure from Mantua, you promised to send me some of Tromboncino's songs set to my verses, but I have never received them.' Then he goes on to name specific titles, and several of these can be traced even today. Tromboncino's songs were also in great demand whenever there were celebrations or courtly festivities, and his music for the marriage of Lucrezia Borgia and Alfonso d'Este in 1502 shows yet another aspect of his versatile nature.[52] Among other frottolists mentioned in contemporary literature is Marco Cara, who set a sonnet of Baldassare Castiglione, *Cantai mentre nel cor lieto fioria*,[53] and was

[50] This together with *Vergine sola* is reprinted in the supplement to Dragan Plamenac's article and inventory, *The "Second" Chansonnier of the Biblioteca Riccardiana*, in *Annales Musicologiques*, II (1954), p. 105.   [51] Plamenac, loc. cit., p. 122.
[52] Einstein, *The Italian Madrigal*, I, p. 46.
[53] *Smith College Music Archives*, IV, p. 61.

rewarded by an honourable and endearing mention in *The Book of the Courtier*: 'And no less [than Bidon] move in his singing, but with a more soft harmony, that by a delectable way and full of mourning sweetness maketh tender and pierceth the mind, and sweetly imprinteth in it a passion full of great delight.'[54]

Between 1504 and 1514 Ottaviano Petrucci issued no less than eleven books of frottole, of which ten have been preserved.[55] Besides Tromboncino and Cara, there was an active group of lesser-known composers including Giovanni Brocco, Antonio Caprioli, Filippo da Lurano, Francesco d'Ana, Lodovico Fogliano, and Michele Pesenti. Some of the best frottole of these composers appeared in publications of Petrucci's rival, Andrea Antico, who nevertheless discovered a few good contributors in Italy and nearby France.[56] In contradistinction to the German tenorlied, the text of the frottola was normally applied to the topmost part only, and although the simple harmonic style invites performance by a group of singers it is much more likely that frottole were given as solo songs with a broken consort of lute, voice, and viol, as in the picture by Bonifazio di Pitati in the Venice Accademia.[57]

Tromboncino possessed the gift of expressing simply and directly the ethos of a poem without indulgence in detailed illumination of single words and phrases. His skilled and sensitive treatment of Petrarch's *Hor che'l ciel et la terra*,[58] evokes the atmosphere and formulae of extemporized chant, an impression that is strengthened by the narrow range of the voice-part. In a setting of the same poet's *S'il dissi mai*, Tromboncino allows the soloist more scope while retaining a firm

Ex.10

a) Hor che'l ciel et la ter - ra_el _____ ven-to ta - ce

b) S'il dis - si mai ch'i ven-ga_in o - dio_a quel - la

c) Se per col-pa del vos-tro_al - tie - ro sde-gno

hold on tonality through his opening melodic gambit. The latter part of his *Se per colpa del vostro altiero sdegno* even affords a rare flight of

---

[54] *The Book of the Courtier* (Everyman edition), p. 61.

[55] A reprint of Books I–III, appeared in *Le Frottole*, ed. Cesari, Monterosso, and Disertori.

[56] *Smith College Music Archives, IV: Andrea Antico.*

[57] Pirro, *Histoire de la Musique de la fin du XIVe siècle à la fin du XVIe*, plate XXVIII.

[58] This and the four next mentioned songs appear in volume III of Einstein's *The Italian Madrigal.*

melodic fancy recalling the methods of the trecento madrigalists, though Sannazaro's innocuous ballata calls for no noticeable element of virtuosity. As with the melodies of the German tenorlieder, those of the frottole tends to begin in a stereotyped manner. The French chanson had its key-rhythm, too, and it would be wrong to deny a sister nation its well-deserved musical footprint, however obvious and apparently repetitious.

Ariosto's ottava rima *Queste non son piu lachryme* and the anonymous *Aqua non e'l humor* show us Tromboncino's mastery of the flexible cadence, for however isorhythmic (if one may borrow a term from the fifteenth century) the beginnings of each phrase, the endings are deliciously varied and anything but monotonous. His part-writing tends now·towards homophony, in Galeotto del Caretto's *Se gran festa*,[59] now toward the brilliance of a quasi-obligato tenor part, in *Pregovi fronde, fiori, acque*, an anonymous capitolo from Petrucci's Book VII. There is even greater contrast between the busy inner parts of a setting (from Petrucci's Book I) of Horace's *Integer vitae*, and the steady, cantus-firmus-like progression of the voice-part.[60]

In the frottole of Marco Cara there is plentiful evidence of a desire to experiment with unusual combinations of musical and poetic metre. Often these experiments are successful and rewarding, as with the sprightly bantering of Poliziano's *Io non l'ho* which is in triple metre throughout,[61] and loses no chance to play with a hemiola. In *Sonno che gli animali*,[62] we have another example of the dexterous use of tripla, here caused by black notation which is in turn inspired, as eye-music, by the word 'morte' in the fifth line of the sonnet. Something of the 'mourning sweetness' mentioned by Castiglione as one of Cara's main attributes may be sensed in the beautiful setting of Andrea Navagera's madrigal *Fiamma amorosa e bella*. Like Tromboncino, Cara attempted to set Latin verse and was fairly successful, though he usually chose, as in the elegy *Quicunque ille fuit* by Propertius, to adopt a simpler polyphonic style than that employed in the frottole. In his treatment of sonnets, he allows himself to be swayed by the general emotion of the lyric rather than by any particular detail. The frank confession of *Se alcun tempo* finds its counterpart in the utterly straightforward melody and *stile familiare* of the accompanying parts, whereas *Di piu*

[59] Walter H. Rubsamen, *Literary Sources of Secular Music in Italy.*

[60] *Smith College Music Archives*, IV, p. 37.

[61] Rubsamen, op. cit., p. 139; note that the metrical scheme is more subtle than would appear at first sight.

[62] *Smith College Music Archives*, IV, p. 3.

varii pensier derives its restlessness from a constant movement and syncopation.

Ex. 11

Di più va - rii pen-sier me pas-se_a - mo - re

Other composers display at least as much variety of mood and style, and now and then reach comparable heights of lyrical expression. There is more than a slight reminiscence of folk-music in the tuneful vocal line of the setting of Bembo's canzona *Non si vedrà giamai*,[63] by Antonio Caprioli, and his bass part, which cheerfully limits itself to only three or four notes, suggests the amiable obligato of a bucolic bassoon player. Particularly happy with the carefree and amusing *villotta* are such men as Don Michele Vicentino, whose *So ben che lei non sa* was immensely popular, and Alessandro Mantovano, the composer of one of the most amusing of all frottole, *Tintinami la brocha*.[64] In his sonnet *Quest'e quel locho* Francesco d'Ana affects something of the simplicity of Tromboncino, without however attaining quite the same intensity of feeling. In the paired frottole of Filippo de Lurano, *Donna contra la mia voglia* and *Donna questa e la mia voglia*,[65] the voice has by far the most ornate of the four lines, and the similarity between the tenor parts helps to throw into relief the closely related subject matter of the lyrics.

As soon as the frottole enjoyed widespread popularity, an attempt was made to bring them within reach of a single performer. It was a southern Slav lutenist, Francis of Bosnia (Francesco Bossinensis) who persuaded Petrucci to publish arrangements for voice and lute of all the best frottole of the time. The first book of Francis's transcriptions came out in 1509, and contained seventy frottole, while the second book (with only fifty-six frottole) followed in 1511.[66] The seventeen composers represented in the two books include those previously named in our discussion as well as Francesco Varoter, Piero Zanin Bisan, Josquin des Pres, Nicolò Pifaro, Nico Craen, Giovan Batista Zesso, Piero da Lodi, Alessandro Demofon, Giovan Piero Mantovan, Don

---

[63] Rubsamen, op. cit., p. 63.

[64] *Smith College Music Archives*, IV, p. 18.

[65] Ernst T. Ferand, *Two Unknown Frottole*, in *The Musical Quarterly*, XXVII (1941), p. 319.

[66] Sartori, *A Little Known Petrucci Publication: The Second Book of Lute Tablatures by Francesco Bossinensis*, in *The Musical Quarterly*, XXXIV (1948), p. 234.

Pellegrino Cesena, Ludovico Milanese, and Antonio Padovano. Music and text of the uppermost part was printed in mensural notation on five lines, and below this the lute tablature (on six lines) presented the tenor and bass parts of the original. Thus, although the alto part was missing, a lutenist-singer could enjoy this wide and varied' repertory without too much difficulty.

The tremendous vogue of the madrigal in all its forms and aspects soon banished the humble frottola from the musical scene in Italy. Banished too was the hope of an Italian school of lutenist song-writers, for the only material available for lutenists during the middle years of the century was the kind of publication that Francis had started in 1509: intabulations of polyphonic compositions with one or more parts missing. Exceptionally keen lutenists like Cosimo Bottegari wrote simple songs for voice and lute in the 1570s, and in Cosimo's manuscript collection of songs – 107 secular songs all told – there are more than thirty of his own compositions and six by Hippolito Tromboncino, perhaps a descendant of Bartolomeo.[67] These songs, slight as they are, nevertheless help to move back the usually accepted date for the beginnings of Italian monody, and it is of especial interest to note that Cosimo includes two verses from Caccini's *Fere selvaggie*, which was not published until 1602. Since the manuscript was compiled from 1574 onwards, and Caccini's song appears a quarter of the way from the beginning, it may not be unreasonable to assume that certain of the early monodies were known and sung from twenty to twenty-five years before publication.

Cosimo Bottegari was a Florentine, and served the court of the Grand Dukes of Tuscany for many years. Among his musical colleagues there were Peri and Caccini, both of whom played an important part in the development of Italian song in the early years of the baroque. It was in Florence that the two principal forms of monody were culti-vated side by side: madrigal and aria. The madrigal had much in common with its polyphonic predecessor; and the elaborate word-painting, wide range of keys, indulgence in occasional harmonic asperities all reappeared now in solo guise, with a bass line to be realized in simple chordal style by theorbo, double harp, chitarrone, or harpsi-chord. Madrigal texts were usually chosen from the works of the finest poets – Guarini, Marino, and older poets such as Bembo, Ariosto, and Sannazaro. The test of a good composer of solo madrigals

[67] Carol McClintock, *A Court Musician's Songbook, Modena Ms C 311*, in *Journal of the American Musicological Society*, IX (1956), p. 177.

lies in his ability to avoid perfect cadences at the end of each and every line of the lyric: unfortunately some of the best composers occasionally lack this ability.

The aria was primarily a setting of a strophic poem, but there were two different ways of approaching this apparently straightforward task. One was to retain the instrumental bass almost intact throughout all the verses, varying only the voice-part; the other was to let the bass and melody move in similar rhythm, thus giving the effect of a more popular style akin to the scherzo or balletto. The former style is well represented by Caccini's *Fere selvaggie*,[68] the latter by Calestani's delightful *Damigella tutta bella*.[69]

Monodies appeared in great spate from the presses of Venice and Rome during the first third of the seventeenth century, and the composers were mainly Venetians, Romans, or Florentines. At first the Venetian composers seemed uninterested in monody, and when in 1611 Marc' Antonio Negri published a book of songs it was plain that his penchant was towards the aria rather than the madrigal. Negri's style was much influenced by that of his more illustrious colleague Monteverdi, whose Seventh Book of Madrigals (1619) included four remarkable monodies. *Tempro la cetra* is a magnificent setting of Marini's poem for tenor and continuo, the stanzas being separated by ritornelli for five-part string ensemble. Instrumental elaboration is carried to a glorious extreme in the variety and combination of timbre to be found in *Con che soavità*, in which a solo soprano declaims Guarini's cunning conceit against a sonorous triptych of plucked strings, viols, and violins. Equally moving, though simpler in outward form, are the paired songs 'in genere rapresentativo', *Se i languidi* (a musical love-letter) and *Se pur destina* (a lover's farewell).[70]

In the same year as Monteverdi's book came a volume of songs by Falconieri, whose slighter stature is nevertheless occasionally redeemed by an exceptionally good song such as *Deh', dolc' anima mia*, with its delightful, if pointless, changes of metre.[71] Grandi's songs of 1620 continue the story of the strophic aria in Venice, the true point of departure for Italian song of later epochs, and a peak is reached in those of Valentini, whose collection appeared in 1622 but has so far not been reprinted. Two years later, Giovanni Pietro Berti provided singers with

[68] *La Flora*, ed. Knud Jeppesen, Vol. I, No. 3.
[69] The melody quoted by Nigel Fortune, in his *Italian Secular Monody from 1600 to 1635, an Introductory Survey*, in *The Musical Quarterly*, XXXIX (1953), p. 171.
[70] Monteverdi, Complete Works, vol. VII.
[71] Quoted in Suzanne Clercx, *Le Baroque et la Musique*, p. 106.

an attractively varied book of songs which included the charming *Dove sei gita*[72] and one of the earliest examples of the solo cantata, *O con quanta vaghezza*. Noteworthy also are the songs of the blind musician Martino Pesenti: his *O biondetta lascivetta* is a typical Venetian patter-song based on a light but trivial lyric.[73]

In Florence the initial lead of Caccini was modified in due course by a succession of monodists among whom the Pisan, Antonio Brunelli, the Sienese, Claudio Saracini, and – greatest of all – Sigismondo d' India, must be counted. The style of these men closely approaches that of the native Florentine group, and though Sigismondo lived and worked in Turin for many years his music reflects the basic principles of the early monodists while improving vastly on their over-epigram-matic phrasing and their too frequent indulgence in ornamentation. 'I discovered', said Sigismondo, 'that you could compose in the true manner with intervals that are out of the ordinary, passing with the utmost novelty from one consonance to another according to the changing sense of the words.'[74] Indeed, one of his most endearing traits is his flexible yet logical melodic line, florid and chromatic in *Là tra le selve in solitario orrore*, gay but never trite in *Se bel rio*, and baroque in the truest sense of the word (though expressive and highly original) in *Pianget' occhi miei lassi*.[75] One of the great tragedies of music is the non-availability of most of his eighty or more monodies.

In his 'Seconde Musiche' of 1620 Saracini mixes madrigals and arias in the usual manner, but his harmonic vocabulary is even more intrepid than that of Sigismondo d'India. *Udite, lagrimosi spirti* and *Se la doglia e'l martire* (dedicated respectively to Monteverdi and to Cesare Saracini, the composer's brother) afford numerous instances of strikingly original turns of phrase. In complete contrast, an aria like *Vezzosa pargoletta* marks Saracini as an agreeable writer of lightly floating melodies, full of charm, to be sure, but no more substantial than the verse which they sustained so easily.[76]

Ex. 12

Vez - zo-sa par-go-let-ta ch'ai del mio cor___ l'im. pe - ro, vol - gi quel lu-sin-ghie-ro

[72] *La Flora*, II, 14.   [73] *La Flora*, II, 13.

[74] Quoted by Nigel Fortune, *Sigismondo d'India*, in *Proceedings of the Royal Musical Association*, 81 (1954–5), p. 29.

[75] Reprinted in the article by Federico Mompellio, *Sigismondo d'India e il suo primo libro di Musiche da cantar solo*, in *Collectanea Historiae Musicae*, I (1953), p. 113.

[76] Facsimile reprint of *Le Seconde Musiche*, Siena (1933).

Another genius of the Florentine school was Marco da Gagliano, whose *Valli profonde* alone is sufficient to stamp him as a writer of more than unusual skill and originality, and a sympathetic interpreter of the Tansillo sonnet which inspired his sombre and powerful music.[77] Monodies by Peri, Rasi, Brunelli, and Benedetti follow the accepted outlook of the greater masters, while even lesser lights occasionally produced songs of great beauty and melodic interest. Vincenzo Calestani was such a composer, and in addition to his *Damigella* already mentioned there are at least two more songs worthy of praise – *Accorta lusinghiera*, and *Ferma, Dorinda mia*.[78]

The music of Caccini and of Sigismondo d'India was highly regarded in the best Roman social circles, but the songs of native Romans displayed none of the infectious lilt of Venetian arias, and little of the adventurous madrigalisms of the Florentines. Stefano Landi, who published a book of arias in 1620, possesses solid musical virtues but little in the way of inspiration. Rather better in this field are the songs of Paolo Quagliati (1623) and Antonio Cifra, whose 'Scherzi ed Arie' of 1614 contains many examples of songs based on well-known ground basses such as *ruggiero* and *romanesca*. *La violetta* and *Del mio sol* are typical specimens of Cifra's fragile yet forthright vein of musica' lyricism.[79] Similarly the songs of Filippo Vitali display an able melodic touch, notably in *O bei lumi* and *S'el sol si scosta*, and a feeling of light-hearted spontaneity in *Pastorella*.[80] The sixteen songs in Frescobaldi's collection of 1630 reveal, as one would expect, a high degree of technical competence allied with a firm sense of linear growth; yet there is nothing remarkable or adventurous as in the best of Saracini and d'India. Nevertheless, arias of the calibre of *Dunque dovrò* (on a *romanesca* variant) and *Entro nave dorata* together with a sonnet such as *Donna siam rei di morte*, for bass, afford ample proof of Frescobaldi's versatility and craftsmanship.[81] It was from these beginnings that the future greatness of the solo cantata sprang.

FRANCE AND BURGUNDY

Music in the reign of the four Dukes of Valois

During the fifteenth century, the rise to fame and power of the State of Burgundy was a northern counterpart of the rapid growth, in north-

[77] *La Flora*, I, 7.   [78] *La Flora*, I, 8; III, 10.   [79] *La Flora*, III, 6; III, 32.
[80] *La Flora*, II, 9; III, 11; III, 33.
[81] Frescobaldi, *Primo Libro d'Arie Musicali*, ed. Felice Boghen.

east Italy, of the Venetian Republic. Bruges was the Venice of the north in more than one sense, and the wealth of trade and facilities for travel gave most musicians of French or Flemish birth the opportunity to visit Italy and imbibe her stylistic traditions in song and dance, mass and motet. It is neither fair nor possible to isolate the northern masters of song, for they left behind them the complexities of the schools of Paris and Avignon because they were able to appreciate the clarity of the Italians, and they knew how to instil that clarity into their music through the extra-musical influence of those advocates of the *devotio moderna* who made oases of peace and tranquillity in the often violent times of political expansion. By the time Charles the Bold succeeded to the Burgundian State in 1467, its political boundaries were sufficiently far-flung to embrace Amiens and Amsterdam, Liège and Nancy, Auxerre, Macon, and the borders of Alsace.

Musicians thrived under the lavish ducal patronage that went hand-in-hand with an appreciation, if only for their material worth, of all that was precious and beautiful in the arts. Composers and singers were employed to provide music for court as well as chapel, and in many cases a far greater proportion of secular music in the surviving manu-scripts may well indicate the constant demand for a composer's rondeaux and ballades. Nicole Grenon and Pierre Fontaine were certainly known and appreciated in Italy, for Matteo da Perugia arranged their four-part songs for three-part ensembles, on the *solus contratenor* principle. His added part to the smoothly-flowing lines of *Je ne requier de ma dame*, by Grenon,[82] undoubtedly serves the purpose, though in rather baroque manner; as with Bach's arrangements of Vivaldi, we have no great difficulty in penetrating the revision and admiring the felicities of the original, albeit in a new light. Grenon, still in a mood of unencumbered lyricism, endows *La plus belle et doulce figure* with a vocal line of slender and appealing beauty such as few singers would wish to resist. The accompaniment likewise remains simple, and with no hint of imitation. Pierre Fontaine uses the hemiola to carry along his lengthy spans of melody both in *Mon cuer pleure* and in the remarkable *Sans faire de vous departie*.[83] This latter song appears to be written on a cantus firmus, an excellent melody in its own right, and one that was later used as a basse-dance. The composer brings his own name into the quaintly amusing *Fontaine a vous dire le voir*.[84]

[82] Marix, *Les Musiciens de la Cour de Bourgogne*, pp. 1, 4.
[83] ibid., pp. 10, 14.
[84] ibid., p. 16. Note that the musical phrase set to the third line of the poem is foreshadowed in the accompaniment.

Four songs by Jacques Vide, apparently a *valet de chambre* and secretary rather than a singer, show considerable skill allied with a tendency to begin the voice-part with an identical rhythmical figure, as in *Espoir m'est venu conforter*, *Puisque je n'ay plus de maystresse*, and *Vit encore ce faux dangier*.[85] His *Las j'ay perdu mon espincel*,[86] is a kind of musical joke, since the lady complains of losing the pen given by her lover; sure enough the contratenor part is not written down, although there is plenty of room for it on the page. Duple time is fairly rare in secular songs of the Burgundian composers, yet Gilles Joye uses it convincingly in his song *Non pas que je veuille penser*.[87] The Englishman, Robert Morton, who is mentioned in company with Hayne van Ghizeghem in the anonymous *La plus grant chiere*,[88] wrote at least two highly successful songs, found in manuscripts all over Europe: *N'aray je jamais mieulx*, and *Le souvenir de vous*.[89] Hayne was an important figure and a prolific composer, whose works were incorporated into the galaxy of masterpieces chosen by Petrucci for his 'Harmonice Musices Odhecaton A', published at Venice in 1501. Although some of his songs looked forward to the newer style of the imitative *a cappella* chanson, others are quite firmly embedded in the Burgundian song-tradition, with its prevailing three-part texture and non-imitative style. A song that gained wide currency in the late fifteenth century was *De tous biens plaine*.[90] It was frequently taken over by other composers and used as a basis for contrafacta, both sacred and secular, so there must have been good reason for its popularity. The range of the song lies perfectly within the average compass of a counter-tenor (or, allowing for a lower standard pitch, possibly a high tenor) and the accompanying parts are rich in rhythmic interest, especially in the four-part version of the Odhecaton, without ever becoming fussy. The melody is formed of long, sweeping paragraphs, with a climactic high note twice in the last phrase of all.

Like *De tous biens plaine*, many of Hayne's other songs are in duple time rather than compound duple, which tended to be used with less frequency as time went on. Songs like *Ce n'est pas jeu* and *Les grans regretz*[91] are in a sense transitional works, for they are found sometimes with text in all three voices and sometimes with only the uppermost voice underlaid. *Se une fois*[92] begins with the same kind of quasi-

[85] ibid., pp. 20, 24, 26.   [86] ibid., p. 23.   [87] ibid., p. 87.   [88] ibid., p. 86.
[89] Jeppesen, *Der Kopenhagener Chansonnier*, pp. 4, 37.
[90] Droz, Thibault and Rokseth, *Trois Chansonniers Français du XVe siècle*, p. 20; Jeppesen, p. 7; Hewitt, *Harmonice Musices Odhecaton A*, p. 263 (four-part version).
[91] Marix, pp. 103, 118   [92] ibid., p. 127.

canonic imitation found already in *Ce n'est pas jeu*, yet apart from the opening there is little difference – even making allowance for verse-form – between it and *De vous amer*.[93] In both songs the lower voice-parts are active not only contrapuntally but also in pressing forward the harmonic rhythm. The same is true, generally speaking, of the four-part songs in the Odhecaton: *Amours, amours,* and *A la audienche*,[94] both of which again favour duple metre.

Towering above these figures were two composers whose lives led them on widely different courses although their music is in many respects similar. Binchois was a loyal servant of the Dukes of Burgundy, and achieved wide renown as a song-writer although he may never have travelled far outside the ducal domain. Dufay, on the other hand, was constantly moving between Dijon, Laon, Paris, and Cambrai, with frequent and productive visits to Rome, Ferrara and the Court of Savoy. He was a truly international figure, and though he knew Binchois well he never served the Dukes of Burgundy as Binchois did. Fifty songs of Binchois have come down to us, and nearly all of them are in the old style with text and melody uppermost, and two accompanying parts below.[95] They display considerable artistry and a deep sympathy with the poetry of the time, and among the lyrics set are some of the finest of Christine de Pisan, Alain Chartier, and Charles d'Orléans. Soprano and alto voices are the ones favoured mainly by Binchois, though a few songs are suitable for the tenor or baritone range.

The musical superiority of Binchois is evident in many aspects of his work, yet none is perhaps more striking than the variety of motives he employs for the beginnings of his songs. These opening motives, whether in French, Italian, or German music, settle down into stereotyped patterns even with the best composers, but Binchois refuses to fall into easy fluency of this kind. Five of his songs, all beginning with the word 'Adieu',[96] choose five motives distinct in both melody and rhythm to accompany an identical word and idea. It is this variety of approach that sets Binchois apart from the host of lesser Burgundian composers, and his sensitive feeling for melodic line combined with the lively, and definitely 'instrumental' nature of his acompanying parts lend his songs an air of distinction without any suspicion of learnedness.

[93] ibid., p. 106.
[94] Hewitt, p. 237, 411.
[95] Rehm, *Die Chansons von Gilles Binchois.* There are four doubtful attributions, and other songs without text.
[96] Rehm, pp. 1–4.

Notable among his rondeaux are *De plus en plus, Jamais tant* (found in two related versions using different metres), *Joyeux penser, Mes yeux,* and *Qui veut mesdire.* For all their amorous parley, these songs have a refreshing pastoral lilt, their melodies contasting strongly and effectively with the arpeggic motives of the lower lines. Songs of a more serious nature are often, though not invariably, set in the elegiac triple metre, as with *Je ne pouroye estre joyeux, La merchi, Liesse m'a mandé,* and *Plains de pours.* An exception is *Margarite, fleur de valeur,* which breathes the purest of pastoral air while yet retaining some of the features of courtly sophistication.

Of the handful of ballades by far the most popular were *Dueil angoisseus,* with its striking F-major triad at the very beginning, and *Je loe amours,* which appears to have been especially liked in Germany, for there are copies of it in the Lochamer Liederbuch as well as in the Buxheim organ-book. This song also begins with an F-major triad, this time in descent, and the static lower voice-parts allow the melody to stand out clearly and with emphasis:

Ex. 13

Je loe a-mours et ma da-me mer - cy - - - - - - - e

One of Binchois's most attractive ballades has hitherto not been recognized as such. It is the well-known *Filles à marier,* usually printed (and performed) after a unique copy in Rome. Unfortunately the text there is incomplete, but a different composition on the same poem, preserved in the Seville Chansonnier, allows us to complete the missing words. This may well be a song for voice and three instruments, yet the imitative second voice may possibly have been meant for singing, even though no words were underlaid.[97]

More progressive than Binchois, though still partaking of common stylistic features, was Guillaume Dufay, whose contribution to song literature of the fifteenth century is of the very highest order. In Dufay's work there is a larger proportion of duets, trios, and even an occasional quartet, already an indication of the freer, less restricted outlook of a composer not bound to the service of a single prince or potentate. By his visits to Italy and his knowledge of the Italian language he was able

[97] The repeat of the first section should carry the text: 'Si bien ne vous savez quel mari vous prendra'. For the last 'joie n'ara, n'ara' in the superius, substitute 'et pour ce pensez, pensez-y'.

to attain such musical felicities as the setting of Petrarch's *Vergine bella*, a masterpiece of expression and fine declamation.[98] The pathetic vein is successfully exploited in *Je languis en piteux martire*, a ballade which has been skilfully reconstructed by Besseler from a textless manuscript source and a copy of the poem in 'Le Jardin de Plaisance'. *Craindre vous vueil* was also sung to the text *Quel fronte signorille* (one source even preserves a Latin contrafactum), while *Malheureux coeur* enjoys the distinction of a change of metre for its middle verses. *Adieu ces bons vins de Lannoy* is a song of great charm, in which we seem to hear the composer himself bidding farewell to the wines of the Laon district (he held a benefice at Nouvion-le-Vineux), and to his friends there.[99] Some songs by Dufay, like those of Grenon, have at least one accompanying part that suggests the use of a wind instrument. *Helas, madame*[100] has a contratenor rich in arpeggic movement and in rests, though the tenor is absolutely continuous and would be especially suitable for a stringed instrument.

Further examples of Dufay's art at its very best may be seen in the New Year's song *Pouray-je avoir vostre mercy* and in *Las, que feray?*[101] Even in his songs written for an occasion he is always spontaneous, never studied or stilted. *Seigneur Léon*, in all probability written to celebrate the appointment of Leonard of Chios to the archbishopric of Mitylene in 1444 (as suggested in a brilliantly reasoned article by Dragan Plamenac)[102] achieved great popularity and was even made into a lauda with the words *Signor Iesu*. *Resveillés vous* is an epithalamium for Carlo Malatesta (who is mentioned in the text as 'Charle gentil qu'on dit de Malateste') and Vittoria Colonna, a niece of Pope Martin V.[103] Lyricism of the purest kind is, as so often in Dufay's works, here combined with sonorous but simple harmonies that set him apart as a musician who creates art by concealing it.

There is a hint of his influence in the music of the three composers from the Liége district, Hugo and Arnold de Lantins, and Jean François de Gembloux.[104] The first two were presumably related, and from the available stylistic evidence it seems that Arnold was the elder and Hugo the more progressive. *Quant je mire* and *Puisque je voys* are

---

[98] This and the next three songs are contained in *Das Chorwerk*, Heft 19.
[99] Pirro, *Histoire de la Musique de la fin du XIVe siècle à la fin du XVIe*, p. 62. When completed, this song is a rondeau.
[100] Besseler, *Bourdon und Fauxbourdon*, p. 261.
[101] Stainer, *Dufay and his Contemporaries*, pp. 152, 146.
[102] Plamenac, *An unknown composition by Dufay?*, in *The Musical Quarterly*, XL (1954), p. 190.
[103] Pirro, op. cit., p. 59.
[104] Van den Borren, *Pièces polyphoniques profanes de provenance liégoise*.

both three-part songs suitable for a mezzo-soprano voice, and thanks to a copyist's note in one of the manuscripts containing the first song, we know that it was composed in Venice in March 1428. Hugo de Lantins, in his sole surviving song *Je suy exent*, affects a partial return to the complexities of the late fourteenth-century composers, though most of his work looks forward to the generation of Busnois and Ockeghem. Jean François proves himself a neat craftsman in his rondeau *Sans oublyer*, and the song was considered good enough to form the basis of a keyboard arrangement, now preserved in the Buxheim organ book.

Of the later group of composers in the service of Charles the Bold, Antoine Busnois was one of the most prolific and most adaptable. Equally at home (to judge by his music) in church or at court, he re-united in his brilliant and resourceful style some of the most endearing features of the earlier generation, while foreshadowing to some extent the technical devices and ideas usually associated with Obrecht or Josquin.[105] The name of his innamorata was enshrined in several chansons, acrostically in *A vous sans autre*[106] ('A Jacqueline') and *Je ne puis vivre* ('Jacqueline'), and as the first word of the poem in *Ja que lui ne s'i attende*[107] and *Ha que ville et abhominable*[108] (Hacqueville was her surname). Many of his best rondeaux are written in the variable triple metre so beloved in the fifteenth century, and there is no question of the high quality of *Quant ce vendra*, *Ma demoiselle*, and *Bel acueil*.[109] In spite of the repeated 'C'est vous' in *C'est vous en qui j'ay esperance*, Busnois shapes each paragraph anew without ever seeming at a loss for new and appropriate motives.[110] The four-part *Je ne demande* displays a typically flowing Burgundian line, the voice being as it were prompted by themes from one of the accompanying parts.[111] The Copenhagen chansonnier preserves two of Busnois's most delightful songs in bergerette form – the *Ja que lui ne* mentioned above, and *M'a vostre coeur*,[112] in which imitative phrases link the three voices in close fellowship. Yet another, hardly less fine and appealing, is *Ma plus qu'assez*, about a lady chosen among fifty, and perhaps referring again to the ubiquitous Jacqueline.

[105] The chansons of Busnois have been studied recently by Perle, in *The Music Review*, XI (1950), p. 89; and Brooks, in *Journal of the American Musicological Society*, VI (1953), p. 111.

[106] Droz, op. cit., pp. 34, 64. [107] Jeppesen, op. cit., p. 60. [108] Droz, op. cit., p. 28.
[109] ibid., pp. 5, 22, 36. [110] ibid., p. 78. [111] Hewitt, op. cit., p. 311.

[112] This and the following bergerettes are from Jeppesen, *op. cit.*, pp. 16, 24. Two further bergerettes are published as a supplement to the article by Brooks cited in note 105. See also Linker and McPeek, *The Bergerette form in the Laborde chansonnier*, in *Journal of the American Musicological Society*, VII (1954), p. 113.

Although Ockeghem's songs are less characteristic of his genius than are the liturgical works, the few that have come down to us display a marked movement in the direction of a continuous web of polyphony instead of arpeggic instrumental parts primarily designed for filling in the harmony, beneath a vocal line shaped according to the lyric. A particularly happy example of his art (and much of it is serious or sad rather than happy) is the song referred to by the theorist Tinctoris: *Ma maistresse*. Each of the first seven bars of this song contains a different rhythmical disposition of the notes, so that the effect to the listener is one of constantly renewing life and pulse.[113] Another fine song is *Ma bouche rit*, with its wonderful turn of phrase at the word 'pleure', and its sidelong glances at compound duple metre even though the basic duple time remains unchanged.[114]

Ex. 14

Ma bou-che rit et ma pen-sé-e pleu - - - - re

Duple time exercised evident attraction for Ockeghem, for it is found also in *Les desleaulx ont la saison*, the famous *Fors seulement* (much used as a parody), *Quant de vous seul*, and *D'un aultre amer*.[115] All of these songs embody a simplicity that is at one and the same time deceptive and enchanting. Only those who sing and play these songs can appreciate their beauty at its true worth. Ockeghem's polyphony is not basically of the imitative kind that draws attention to contrapuntal felicities; it possesses rather a balanced, flowing character that carries the listener forward by the sheer strength of its inevitability.

Song-writing was so much a part of musical life in the fifteenth century that very few composers abstained from it; even a theorist like Tinctoris could find time to pen an elegant trifle from time to time. His *Vostre regart*, though obviously influenced by Ockeghem, is not unsuccessful.[116] Similarly, the poet-musician Molinet may have composed the four-part *Tart ara mon coeur* which is ascribed to him in two sources.[117] Michelet, Convert, Baziron, Prioris, and Caron also wrote songs that are well turned and pleasing if not always very inspired. As the century drew to its close there appeared more and more traces of

[113] Davison & Apel, *Historical Anthology of Music*, Vol. I, p. 78.
[114] Droz, op. cit., p. 9.   [115] ibid., pp. 16, 48, 62, 72.   [116] ibid., p. 46.
[117] Jeppesen, op. cit., p. 12.   [118] Hewitt, pp. 319, 329, 343, 381.

the prototype *a cappella* chanson, though the earliest publications of the sixteenth century still exhibit a transitional mood rather than a clear-cut adoption of new principles.

The Sixteenth Century

Petrucci's *Odhecaton* contains a small but significant number of three- and four-part songs by some of the most important composers of the time. Loyset Compère is represented by several particularly fine specimens of his style: *Male bouche* and *Se mieux ne vient* show him in a comparatively straightforward melodic mood, while *Guerrisés moi* and *Le renvoy* are more florid and rhythmically somewhat more complex.[118] Jean Japart sets his songs for preference in four parts, and their slow-moving, elegantly curved melodies suspended above an active trio of instrumental parts are rewarding for both singers and players. *J'ay pris amours* is a rondeau of exceptionally fine proportions, with a vocal range perfectly suitable for a soprano or alto. A ballade of considerable scope and quality is *Se congie pris*, its transparent texture contrasting strongly with *J'ay pris amours* and *Hélas qu'elle est à mon gré*.[119] The two rondeaux by Alexander Agricola, *Allez mon coeur* and *J'ay beau huer*, show how easily a simple three-part song can be beautified by subtle and discreet melodic imitation.[120] Even Josquin is not entirely allied to the new style of chanson. His *Bergerette savoysienne* is epigrammatic in the best early Burgundian manner, while the close canon between the two lower parts of *De tous biens playne* (also in four parts) suggests a medieval method even though the guise is new. Josquin's extensive travels and wide contacts in the musical world enabled him to contrive the flowing ornamental lines of *La plus des plus* as well as the almost teutonic *tenorlied* type of song seen at its best in *O venus bant*, originally a Flemish poem of no less than eighteen stanzas.[121]

After the first decade or so of the sixteenth century the French chanson led the way in continental Europe towards a new conception of polyphonic song, rich in imitation, deft in counterpoint, and admirably set forth for a small group of skilled singers. Song in its basic form disappeared except for the lute intabulations that were occasionally published from the 1530s onwards. An important step forward was made in 1571 when Adrien Le Roy brought out his 'Livre

---

[119] ibid., pp. 265, 267, 284.   [120] ibid., pp. 357, 392.
[121] ibid., pp. 240, 418, 355, 383. See also the article by Sartori, *Josquin des Prés, cantore del Duomo di Milano*, in *Annales Musicologiques*, IV (1956), p. 55.

d'airs de Cour miz sur le Luth', but this was not followed up until Adriaensen's 'Novum pratum musicus' (1592) which contained one song among numerous purely instrumental transcriptions, *La rousée du joly mois de May*, expressly transcribed for voice and lute. In the introduction to his 'Airs mis en musique à quatre parties' (1599) Pierre Cerveau pointed out that the most learned musicians of the day admitted that songs could be sung in two distinct ways; either unaccompanied, or with the lower parts arranged for an instrument, or group of instruments. There was in this remark the tacit assumption that the 'song' would be nothing more nor less than the uppermost part of the four-part version. In fact for years the air de cour and its predecessor the *vaux-de-vire*, or *voix-de-ville*, had presented the melody in the superius rather than in the tenor, and the way was thus paved for the advent of the fully-fledged air de cour.

This air, later to influence the English ayre, was also in a sense a by-product of the 'musique mesurée à l'antique' which enjoyed such a vogue during the latter half of the sixteenth century. The principle whereby accuracy of declamation and apparent authenticity of style could be ensured was closely bound up with the obligatory use of long and short notes (corresponding to our minim and crotchet) as musical vehicles for long and short syllables. But there was no one indivisible class of songs into which the entire repertory of the early seventeenth century could conveniently fit. Broadly speaking, there were two; and while both shared common characteristics such as a very free rhythm and an almost meaningless time-signature, the one pointed up the metre of the text by using long notes at the *coupe* and at the end of a line, whereas the other was completely free. When a book of French airs, duly translated, was published in London in 1629, the editor (whose name was Filmer) explained in his preface that 'the *French* when they compose to a ditty in their owne Language being led rather by their free Fant'sie of Aire (wherein many of them do naturally excell) then by any strict and artificiall scanning of the Line, by which they build, doe often, by diproportion'd Musicall Quantities, invert the naturall Stroke of a Verse, applying to the place of an *Iambicke* Foot, such modulation as Iumps rather with a Trochay'.

As might be expected, the principle of *musique mesurée* had been lost sight of by some of the smaller musical practitioners of the time. For there were many who were little more than amateurs, and they joined forces with poets who were on roughly the same, or possibly even a lower level. Yet there are many reputable names among the musicians and the poets of this generation: de la Grotte, Bonnet, Tessier, Cerveau, and La Tour were the men who supplied music for the verses of Baïf, Ronsard, du Bellay, Desportes, Bertaut and Malherbe. There were new songs composed in profusion, while old chansons were rearranged for the medium of voice and lute. Frequently the usual order was reversed, and a successful lute-song found itself hastily arranged for four voices. The complete poem did not always appear in the musical publications devoted to the airs de cour, since it was understood that the singer would adapt further stanzas to the music on the same basis as the stanza underlaid.

In style and general outlook the air de cour was far removed from the English lute-songs of Dowland and the Italian monodies of Caccini. French composers favoured melodies with a small compass, using conjunct motion or small intervals, admirable for expressing the languor of a lyric in the Petrarch style. Decoration of a given melody was supplied either by the composer himself, as in *Beautés vivants portraits de la divinité*,[122] or by some fashionable singer with a more than usually flexible organ.[123] Unfortunately, relatively few of the many lute songs published by Gabriel Bataille between 1608 and 1620 have been made available in good modern editions. The spontaneous charm of the best of these songs deserves to become more widely known, not only because of its own unique flavour but because a much-neglected chapter of musical history might be profitably re-read. This first phrase of an anonymous setting of Desportes *Lieux de moy tant aimez* will suffice to indicate the simplicity of both tune and accompaniment of a typical song of the period; yet in spite of this simplicity there is an impression of great care and devotion in the shaping of the melody:[124]

Ex.15

Lieux — de moi tant ay - mez,   si   doux à   ma nais-san - ce.

122 Verchaly. *Poésie et Air de Cour en France jusqu'à 1620*, in *Musique et Poésie*, p. 221.
123 Bukofzer. *Music in the Baroque Era*, p. 146. See also Walker, *The influence of musique mesurée àl'antique, particularly on the Airs de Cour of the early seventeenth century*, in *Musica Disciplina*, II (1948), p. 162.
124 Verchaly, *Desportes et la Musique*, in *Annales Musicologiques*, II (1954), p. 340.

At its best, the air de cour provided an untrammelled framework for the poem, allowing its metre and form to be heard, allowing its sense to come through (a bitter test for the lesser versifiers), and providing both singer and lutenist – sometimes reunited in one – with material of considerable appeal though of no great difficulty. Little wonder that the air de cour became so popular, and spread its musical balm as far as Italy, England, and Germany.

The Modern Period

Belgium

DAVID COX

THERE are no important Belgian composers of the seventeenth century; and in the eighteenth the composers of talent emigrated (such as Gossec and Grétry). It always seems to have been the case: in Belgium there has been no adequate field for the full expression of musical talent. The most important of all Belgian composers, César Franck (see p. 206), was born at Liége in 1822, but passed his life in France and was a naturalized Frenchman.

At the end of the eighteenth and the beginning of the nineteenth century the stirring historical events gave rise to the expression of strong national feelings. Flanders was incorporated in France; then, in 1815, Belgium – including the Walloon regions and most of Flanders – was united with Holland, leading to the revolution of 1830, which brought freedom to Belgium.

The name of the tenor singer and composer François van Campenhout is associated with the 1830 revolution. It was for this that he composed what is now the Belgian national anthem, *La Brabançonne*, to words by a French actor who was then in Belgium and who was known as 'Jenneval'. The title is derived from Brabant – and the fact that the Brabançons were fierce fighters in the twelfth century.

In Albert Lavignac's *Encyclopédie de la Musique*, the chapter devoted to Belgium is written by René Lyr and Paul Gilson, the latter a composer of distinction. We are told that at the beginning of the nineteenth century an individualism began to express itself in Belgian music. The Flemish composers, akin to the Dutch – as distinct from the Walloons, akin to the French – tried to throw off the foreign yoke and express themselves in their own way. In folk-song and Flemish literature they hoped to find the inspiration that was lacking. Peter Benoit, founder of the École Flamande de Musique at Anvers in the nineteenth century, and a strong advocate of a national Flemish art, set Flemish words in a lively, quasi-popular but personal style in his 'De Liefde in het Leven' ('Love in Life'), composed 1868–70, and another set of songs called 'Liefdedrama' – ('Love-drama') composed 1872. He also wrote charming and simple *romance*-like songs in a very French style – such as, *Mon amour*, *À toi*, and *Écoute-moi*, comprising 'Trois Mélodies', Op. 10 (Paris, 1865). Later, he developed a strong German-influenced style in his compositions, not without considerable personality.

Henri Waelput (born in Gand in 1845) also was inspired by the poems of his own country, and was considered in his day to be a fine song-writer. But his songs are very difficult to obtain – as are also the songs (for one and two voices) of Christian Urhan, who was, incidentally, one of the first to make known the songs of Schubert in Belgium.

The four 'Chansons de Printemps' (Paris, 1867) by Adolph Samuel are pleasant and Gounod-like, but nothing special. There are also some good examples of the simple, *romance* type of song in the 'Douze Mélodies' (Schott, no date) by Jan van den Eeden – and with well-written accompaniments. In *La Neige*, for example, the fall of snow-flakes is well suggested. And we find a pleasant mixture of French and German elements in the two books, of twenty songs each, by Jean-Théodore Radoux, published in Gand in 1875. In the second book a charming setting is found of Gautier's famous poem *Le Spectre de la Rose*.

Jan Blockx was a pupil of Peter Benoit at the École de Musique in Anvers, and the most important of his disciples in the establishing of a Flemish national school of composers. In his numerous songs Blockx displays lyrical gifts, and an individual harmonic style which is somewhat anti-Wagnerian. Most are with piano accompaniment, but there is a set of five (under the title 'Liederalbum') accompanied by violin. There is also a delightful set of nine 'Kinderliederen', Op. 50 (Faes, Antwerp, no date), for medium voice and piano, with Flemish words – dedicated to the composer's own children – the subjects of the songs ranging from howling wind to cat and mouse.

There is 'A Cycle of Fourteen Old Flemish Love-Songs', Op. 12 (Schott, 1877), simply set, in clear Mendelssohn-like texture, by Edgar Tinel; and there is also the same composer's excellent set of 'Four Old Flemish Drinking Songs', Op. 13 (Schott, 1877), which deserves special mention. Tinel was a gifted and influential composer, whose style showed German and French qualities. Of the two early Lenau song-cycles (Schott, no dates), the 'Schilf-lieder', Op. 10, show the strong influence of Schumann, and the 'Fünf Gesänge' from Lenau's 'Lieder der Sehnsucht' are all short, attractive and simple. The influence of Schumann is also very evident in his other sets of songs – Op. 38, Op. 40, Op. 42. The most personal of these is Op. 42 – 'Sechs Lieder' (Breitkopf, 1894) – which contains the excellent song *Am Strande*, serious in purpose, but light in texture and of great elegant charm.

Fernand Le Borne was a pupil of Franck and Massenet. The influence of these French composers is shown in Le Borne's well-written 'Cinq Lieder', Op. 7 (Leipzig and Brussels, 1884). Of these five love-songs, the most extended, and perhaps the best, is *Nuit d'amour*. His 'Six Mélodies', Op. 12 (Schott, 1887) are simpler, more *romance*-like in style. But No. 5 (*Méditation religieuse*), with cello obbligato, is sentimental and cloying – rather like the religious songs of Gounod.

The songs of Guillaume Lekeu deserve to be better known. His music had a lyrical and strongly personal quality about it, and he followed in the Franck tradition. His extended song *Chanson de Mai* (Rouart, Lerolle, 1909) reminds one very much of Franck with its particular use of arpeggios and rich harmonic texture. *Les Pavots* (Rouart, Lerolle, 1909), with words by Lamartine, has a good vocal line and makes effective use of *ostinato* in the accompaniment.

Like Lekeu, Joseph Jongen was also strongly influenced by Franck. There are a number of fine songs of Jongen: *Après un rêve* (Chester, composed 1902) has a distinctive lyrical quality; and *Bal des Fleurs* (Chester; no date) – very different in character – is a light, graceful waltz-song of simplicity and charm. In spirit it is akin to the work of Emiel Hullebroeck, a pianist, singer, and composer, who has written a large number of songs to Flemish words, in a very popular style. In Joseph Jongen's songs, the style is perhaps most akin to Chausson at his best and clearest. Specially to be recommended is the beautiful song *Calmes, aux quais déserts*, Op. 54 (Chester, no date), for voice, string quartet and piano – the poem by Albert Samain, with an English version by Rosa Newmarch. This meditation amid the beauties of an autumn evening has inspired music of considerable atmospheric subtlety: music and words are at one.

Ex. 1

(Calme – très modéré)

Calmes, aux quais dé-serts s'en-dor-ment les ba-teaux!

meno dolce

Les be - so - gnes du jour ru - de sont ter-mi-

- né - es

One of the most famous of twentieth-century Belgian composers is Jean Absil, whose music shows a freedom of spirit, but at the same time has its roots in tradition. Songs do not form a particularly important part of his output: there are some with piano, and some with orchestra – and there is a set of 'Cinq Mélodies', Op. 12, for voice and string quartet, which is particularly worth noting. Three of the poems are by Maeterlinck, and the unreal quality of these is well portrayed in the music; another is a setting of Victor Hugo's poem *Guitare*, in which the strings have a brilliantly effective pizzicato accompaniment.

There are a good many other Belgian song-composers; but I think the ones I have dealt with – albeit briefly – are the most interesting. I have not mentioned Paul Gilson, an important teacher of Belgian musicians, who showed Russian and oriental influences in his own compositions, including songs. One of his pupils to have achieved wide recognition is Marcel Poot, whose music has been described as expressing genuine emotion touched with irony, like Prokofiev. Among Poot's songs are 'Three Negro Poems' (composed 1925).

Among the songs of Fernand Quinet are 'Trois chansons hebraïques';
and Marcel Quinet has set poems by Apollinaire and Jean Cocteau.
Victor Vreuls was a viola-player, conductor and composer, who in
his songs – for example, *Pour toi* (Chester, 1921) and *Le Soir* (Rouart,
Lerolle; no date) – shows a decided sympathy for the idiom of Fauré.
And both these songs are highly effective.

As a link between the songs of Belgium and those of Holland, I
should like to mention a song-arrangement by Bernard van Dieren
(the Dutch-born composer who made England his home) – a setting of
the sixteenth-century Belgian-born composer Orlande de Lassus's
song *Mon coeur se recommande à vous* (O.U.P.). On the face of it van
Dieren's accompaniment is so elaborate and contrapuntal that one
feels it to be out of keeping with the simplicity of the melody. And yet,
in performance, it is highly effective and somehow quite appropriate.

The British Isles

ARTHUR JACOBS

THE collection which Francis Turner Palgrave called *The Golden Treasury of the Best Songs and Lyrical Poems in the English Language* first came out in 1861, thereafter to undergo many reprints and new editions. It is significant that in England a book nominally of 'songs', like this, was a book of poems, without music. And Palgrave, while surprisingly claiming that he had modelled the arrangement of the poems in his anthology on 'the development of the symphonies of Mozart and Beethoven', said nothing about such music as might be intended for the poems themselves. Similarly a book of 1772, John Aikin's *Essays in Song-Writing*, is a book about poetry, without a note of music.

England has indeed been more generally celebrated for literary than for musical achievement. Cultivated English musicians have themselves sometimes felt their native traditions a second-best. It was Harry Plunket Greene, that distinguished singer, who wrote in 1934: 'The "song" was born 113 years ago with Schubert's Opus 1' (meaning *The Erl King*). In the nineteenth century, the British (and the Americans) curiously adopted the German word *Lied* for any song – not necessarily German – designed to fulfil a high artistic aim and to be suited to a recital, as though the English word 'song' were debased. 'Sullivan . . .

has written songs too,' declared the American writer Henry T. Finck in 1901, '. . . but the real *Lied* was as much beyond him as Italian opera.'

The idea that music – vocal music especially – is mainly to be sought abroad is older than that. 'Music is a manufacture in Italy,' wrote Burney in 1789, 'that feeds and enriches a large portion of the people; and it is no more disgraceful to a mercantile country to import it, than wine, tea, or any other production of remote parts of the world.' In the time of Queen Elizabeth I, Thomas Morley had deplored Englishmen's tendency to prefer a foreign composer's work to an equally good English product.

We need not, by reaction, be provoked into insular boasts. It would be absurd to claim for Britain a body of classic solo song comparable to that achieved by German and Austrian composers from Schubert to Richard Strauss. That was dependent on a unique historical combination: great composers, capable poets (either living or only recently dead), and a public susceptible to the subtle matching of verse and music as the representation of an individual emotion. Such conditions have been lacking in Britain. Apart from church music, English song for about two centuries before 1840 was predominantly either vulgar (in the best sense – that is, broad enough in treatment for the crowd to sing) or linked to the theatre, or both. Then, in the Victorian 'ballad', English song freed itself from the domination of the theatre only to be almost crushed by the prevailing over-sentimentality of the drawing-room.

Almost crushed, but not quite; and in the late nineteenth and early twentieth centuries, English song grew in artistic seriousness, so much so that certain composers could achieve distinction primarily by song-writing. Even so, their work penetrated little beyond English-speaking countries. At the present time, admittedly, British composers are more widely known; but the present time is also (for good reasons, as we shall see) one in which songs no longer hold their former importance for most composers.

This is in part, perhaps, a reflection of the sad gap that has grown in this century between 'serious' and 'popular' song. But in considering previous times, we shall not be inhibited from praising a song just because many people liked to sing it; and indeed we shall find not a few songs in which public usage altered the composer's original melody (not always to its disadvantage). If the circumstances of musical and social history do not promise us the discovery of a great, magnificently cultivated garden of English song, we shall still find some choice individual blooms – and not all in the expected places.

From Lawes to Purcell

In May, 1660, Charles II was proclaimed king and the Civil War was over. John Milton, who had held public office under Cromwell, settled down in the Restoration to leisure and poetry. But already, in 1646, he had inscribed to Henry Lawes the famous sonnet beginning:[1]

> Harry, whose tuneful and well measur'd song
> First taught our English music how to span
> Words with just note and accent, not to scan
> With Midas' ears, committing short and long. . . .

Henry Lawes (1596–1662) had set the songs in Milton's *Comus* (and had performed the part of the Attendant Spirit in it at its original production at Ludlow Castle, 1634). The verse-setting in the lute-songs of John Dowland (1563–1626), not to mention that in Elizabethan madrigals, makes Milton's tribute seem to us grossly exaggerated. Yet Lawes's special attention to the sense of the words in his songs would quite naturally have appealed to a poet, and occasionally may still appeal today. There is something almost modern about this, from *A lady to a young courtier*:[2]

Ex. 1

Nor was Milton's praise unique. Lawes was similarly commended by other poets including Edmund Waller (the author of 'Go, lovely rose') and, perhaps more remarkably, by his fellow-composer, John Wilson, in the preface to the second book (1669) of the *Ayres and Dialogues* issued by John Playford, the leading London music-publisher of the time. Wilson first praised Lawes's choice of texts and then went on to compare his straightforward settings with those of other (unnamed) composers:

> These with their brave Chromatics bring
> Noise to the ear, but mean No-thing.

[1] Spelling and punctuation in this and subsequent quotations have been modernized where convenient. Convenience has similarly dictated the display of the musical examples. Where the harmonization in the accompaniment was left for the performer to 'realize' at a keyboard from a bass-line (see next page), a simple keyboard harmonization has been provided. Where the original accompaniment was orchestral, a condensed version has been provided which may be played on a keyboard for the purposes of study.

[2] Reprinted in *Ten Ayres by Henry Lawes*, edited by Thurston Dart (Stainer and Bell, 1956).

(Strange how little the terminology of musical abuse changes through the centuries!) John Wilson himself is thought to be identical with the 'Jack Wilson' mentioned as an actor in the First Folio edition (1623) of Shakespeare's plays. His long life (1595–1674) spans from Shakespeare's day to Defoe's, and his own settings of Shakespeare's *Take, O take those lips away* and *Lawn as white as driven snow* have a simple charm still.

The form generally favoured by Lawes and Wilson was the 'strophic' song: that is, a song of which the music is complete for the first stanza of the verse and is then repeated for each successive stanza. Their song-melodies, moreover, generally follow (at any rate for the first stanza) the natural rhythm and melody of speech – tamed, as it were, to regular musical metre. But with Matthew Locke (1630–77) we encounter either this regular strophic pattern or a freer declamatory style which contemporaries referred to as 'recitative music'. The strophic style is seen for instance in *Vulcan's song*, the declamatory style in *To a lady singing to herself by the Thames' side*. Both are reprinted in *Three Songs of Matthew Locke*, edited by Anthony Lewis (Lyrebird, 1938) – the third song being taken from the stage music to *Macbeth*, which, after long giving Locke his chief fame, is now thought not to be by him.

In the songs of Pelham Humfrey (1647–74) and John Blow (1649–1708) the use and contrast of the regularly-patterned style and the free, declamatory style is also characteristic. Humfrey's remarkable *Hymn to God the Father*, to John Donne's poem, consists of three stanzas musically not identical but varied, with the mastery of a Schubert. (This is available in a good modern edition by Michael Tippett and Walter Bergmann – Schott, 1947.) Blow's bass song, *Rise, mighty monarch*, sets the words 'headlong down' with a descent of a third from G sharp to E and then a descent to the E below: a typical example of that musical 'word-painting' which, like many other general traits of the whole age, we too readily count as a particular characteristic of the figure in it we know best – Purcell.

Playford's *Ayres and Dialogues*, to which we referred above, were stated on the title-page to be written for accompaniment of 'theorbo-lute or bass viol'. (This is a large-sized lute or a viola da gamba.) In these and other songs so far discussed, the accompanist's written part consisted merely of a simple line of bass notes. From these and from the consideration of the singer's part, the accompanist filled in the harmonies on his instrument. During the second half of the seventeenth century it became general in England for him to receive extra help in harmonization through the printing of a figured bass.

In Playford's third book (1676) a significant line appears which was not in the second book of seven years before. The music was described as 'being most of the newest ayres and songs, sung at court and at the public theatres'. The dominance of the court and the theatre over musical taste could not be more sharply indicated. Music had its place in social and ceremonial life at the court of Charles II (who reigned until 1685), to which French, Italian, and Portuguese musicians were attached. A string orchestra, modelled on that of Louis XIV, played at the Chapel Royal. The fashionable theatrical entertainment of the time took the form of a spectacular play with music and dances; and English opera, though formally dated from Commonwealth days with *The Siege of Rhodes* (1658), now began properly to develop. On a more modest scale, it was at court itself that John Blow's *Venus and Adonis* was performed, about 1684. It was described as a masque, but in effect it is an intimate short opera – irredeemably quaint, it is to be feared, for modern taste, despite several well-intentioned revivals.

Such was the musical environment in which Henry Purcell (1659–95) worked. A pupil of Humfrey and Blow, he succeeded Blow as organist of Westminster Abbey in 1679; and after Purcell's early death, Blow resumed the post. Purcell was also officially a composer to the king and organist of the Chapel Royal, and among his works are a number of 'Welcome Songs' (short choral works) for Charles II and James II.

But in considering Purcell as a song-writer, it is with his five operas, his music to more than forty plays, and his occasional isolated songs that we are concerned. Only in *Dido and Aeneas* (produced in 1689), composed not for a public theatre but for a girls' school, does the music run continuously. The other operas are now sometimes called semi-operas: the music has a large but not always preponderant share in the drama, and some of the characters do not sing. These semi-operas are *The Prophetess, or the History of Dioclesian* (more often known just as *Dioclesian*), 1690; *King Arthur, or the British Worthy* (1691) with text by Dryden; *The Fairy Queen* (1692) adapted from Shakespeare's 'A Midsummer Night's Dream'; *The Indian Queen* (1695) with text by Dryden and Robert Howard; and *The Tempest* (composed about 1695), a version taken from a previous adaptation by Dryden and Davenant from Shakespeare's play. Dryden was also the author or part-author of six of the plays to which Purcell wrote songs or other music.

Dido and Aeneas – its songs ranging from the pathetic *When I am laid in earth* to the cheery solo-and-chorus pattern of *Come away, fellow-sailors* – is too well known to need comment here. But of Purcell's other songs, though all are published (some with texts slightly expurgated) in the Purcell Society's many-volumed edition, it is hard to see a good reason for the present division into those which are well known and those which are hardly known at all. *Fairest Isle*, from *King Arthur*, is admittedly a gem; but no less so is the unfamiliar *How blest are shepherds* from the same work.

A masterpiece of song (yet, it is almost fair to say, totally unknown) is *Anacreon's Defeat*, which begins humorously about poets and their 'rattling numbers', continuing:

> Not fleets at sea have vanquish'd me,
> Nor brigadiers nor cavalry,
> Nor ranks and files of infantry

– and then suddenly becomes serious about the really wounding weapon:

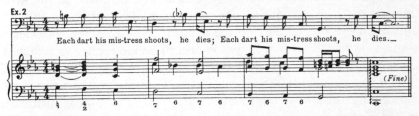

The pathetic fall on 'dies' is a characteristic not merely of Purcell but of his period of song-writing: what is really notable in Purcell is that he seems to handle such effects of the declamatory style more tellingly than anyone else. And yet he could also set forth the 'plain man's' four-square style with a liveliness which seems to forecast the best Vauxhall Gardens songs of almost a century later. Indeed, one of his songs anticipates a famous title of James Hook:

Many of Purcell's songs are available in good modern individual reprints. There are many others which would thoroughly repay performance but which must be sought in the Purcell Society's collected volumes. Among them are: *Wake, Quivera, wake* from *The Indian Queen*; *Dear pretty youth, My dear, my Amphitrite,* and *Your awful voice I hear* from *The Tempest*; *Still I'm wishing* and *Since from my dear* from *Dioclesian*; *Take not a woman's anger ill* from *The Rival Sisters* and *There's not a Swain on the plain* from *Rule a Wife and Have a Wife*; and (individual songs), *Cupid, the slyest rogue alive, I take no pleasure, Pious Celinda goes to prayers,* and *What can we poor females do?* It is possible that the big, 'impressive' Purcell songs like *Bess O'Bedlam* and *Let the dreadful engines,* which formed the first approach to Purcell for many singers of a former generation, have been allowed to obscure his songs of a more gentle charm. It is to be noted that recitative in Purcell, as in his English contemporaries, is written so as to be sung in strict time.

It must be admitted that there is often an unsatisfactory 'shape' in other songs of Purcell – that the climaxes are not fully achieved or that the ending lacks impact. A problem also arises, for all music of this period, in the matter of accompaniment. The piano is, in the great majority of cases, unavoidably the accompanying instrument, but it is not the most suitable; nor do the piano parts of the Purcell Society's edition (in which the bass had of course to be interpreted or 'realized' by an editor) always make the best of the job. A harpsichord, if available, gives a desirably lucid as well as an historically authentic sound: but an instrument for which many of the song-accompaniments are suited is more easily come by, namely, the guitar.

Purcell wrote his songs to fit the taste of the town, whether in the context of the theatre or not. We may guess that he sometimes became as bored as we with his lovesick swains and cruel nymphs, and that he was glad to cater sometimes for the drinking-party instead:

> Since the pox or the plague of inconstancy reigns
> On most of the women o' the town,
> What ridiculous fop would trouble his brains
> To make the lewd devils lie down?

We need not dissent from the view that ranks Purcell as among the greatest English composers. In his total achievement, moreover, song writing ranks high. The English language seems still to have splendid life through his music. Yet Italian operatic airs were then already beginning to have a vogue. Purcell himself must have been amused when he came to set incidental music to Southerne's play *The Wives' Excuse* (1691) and found after an Italian song the lines:

Springane: The music's extremely fine—
Wellvile: —Especially the vocal part,
    for I did not understand a word on't.

Henry Purcell died at the age of thirty-six. Other musicians rank as his 'contemporaries' but lived until the eighteenth century had begun: among them Jeremiah Clarke (born about 1659, died 1707), John Eccles (1650–1735), John Weldon (1676–1736), Purcell's brother Daniel (1663–1717), and Richard Leveridge (1670–1758). When their careers began, the expansive, declamatory manner of recitative was at its height; but the eighteenth century brought a less fantastic, more regularly ordered style to English song. In the century's first decade, Italian opera in Italian began its occupation of the London theatre, and the ground was ready for Handel.

Jeremiah Clarke has achieved a twentieth-century fame because the work known as 'Purcell's Trumpet Voluntary' has been found to be his. His songs, which follow the taste of the time without particular distinction, are unlikely to win him further renown. It is amusing, however, to recognize in one of his comic songs a strain which might have come from the nineteenth-century music hall:

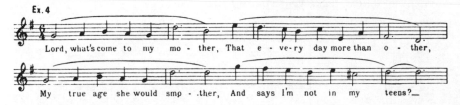

Ex. 4

Lord, what's come to my mo-ther, That e-ve-ry day more than o-ther,
My true age she would smo-.ther, And says I'm not in my teens?

This indeed suggests, like the *Harvest home* song from Purcell's *King Arthur*, that the 'underground' tradition of popular song has a remarkable strength.

The songs of John Eccles come mainly from plays. In Eccles – a highly popular song-composer of his day, now hardly known even by name – may perhaps be most clearly seen the bridge between Purcell's day and Handel's. At one moment (as in *Silvia how could you*) he will shoot forth Purcell's drooping, pathetic sevenths; then, in the patriotic *While Anna with victorious arms*, he will anticipate Handel's best flag-wagging vein. ('Anna', of course, is Queen Anne.) Eccles perhaps deserves less than his present neglect. In *If I hear Orinda swear*, he enhances the music's charm with 'imitation' between the melody and

131

the bass: in *A dialogue between two sleepy chairmen* (i.e. sedan-chair men) *waiting at a tavern door* he displays a rich comic gift, with an amusing imitation of a drunk; and in *Nature fram'd thee sure for loving* (from *The Judgement of Paris*) he has a charming 3–4 lilt before, typically, changing to a faster two-beat concluding section.

The Judgement of Paris, with words by Congreve, was the text set for a competition in musical composition in 1700; the first, second, third, and fourth prizes were respectively gained by Weldon, Eccles, Daniel Purcell, and Godfrey Finger (or Gottfried Finger, a German-speaking composer from what is now Czechoslovakia). Weldon's winning score has not been preserved, and a few songs of his do not seem to indicate any particular distinction. Of Daniel Purcell, however, it is possible to feel that a little more fame would have come to him but for his brother's towering position. Daniel Purcell completed Henry Purcell's music to *The Indian Queen*, and is the actual composer of several pieces formerly ascribed to his brother.

Daniel Purcell favours the regular-patterned (rather than the free declamatory) song, but characteristically 'extends' by an extra bar what would otherwise be a rather plain four-bar phrase. The result is often to convey an appealing freshness, as in such songs as *Lovely charmer, Let not love on me bestow,* and (see the following musical example) *Cupid, make your virgins tender.*

Richard Leveridge was a noted bass singer, active in the theatre until 1751. As a composer, he is still known by *Oh, the roast beef of old England,* of which the tune sung today slightly alters the original; and another song which long held favour was his setting of John Gay's

All in the downs the fleet was moored. These appear to have been lucky hits by a not too distinguished composer.

The lute, which had been on the decline in the second half of the seventeenth century, had almost fallen out of use by 1700. In his play, *The Funeral* (1701), Steele[3] emphasized the comic old-fashionedness of Mrs. Fardingale by making her decline the accompaniments of a spinet for her singing:

> No! Who wants those? Pray bring me my lute out of the next room. (*Enter servant with lute.*) You must know I conned this song before I came in, and find it will go to an excellent air of old Mr. Lawes's who was my mother's intimate acquaintance. My mother's?—I mean my grandmother's. Oh, here's the lute. (*Sings and squalls.*)

From Handel to Thomas Arne

Never was the art of music more international than when Handel, a Saxon, came to England to try his fortune by writing Italian opera. Later he plagiarized from Stradella (and possibly other Italian composers) and from another German, Kerl, to effect a major English oratorio, *Israel in Egypt*. It was, admittedly, a common and indeed regular practice of composers of that period to travel internationally and to take up court or operatic appointments wherever they might be offered, from London to St. Petersburg. But the case of Georg Friedrich Händel, who became George Frideric Handel, was exceptional. He made England his permanent home, took British nationality (in 1726) and came to dominate the London musical scene.

Handel wrote few separate songs in English. Yet to consider him as anything but a major figure in the history of English song would be misleading. In his first twenty and more years in London, from 1710, his major attention was given to Italian opera; but it was not long before the 'easier' songs from these operas were fitted with English words for home use – and moreover, words were fitted to instrumental movements from his opera overtures too. So when, in 1728, the highwaymen of *The Beggar's Opera* sang *Let us take the road* to the tune of a march from Handel's *Rinaldo* (his first London opera, produced 1711), the procedure was not altogether novel.

Moreover, Handel was interested in the dramatic musical setting of English texts – we might say, in the idea of English opera. 'A Pastoral Opera' was one of several designations given to Handel's *Acis and Galatea*, to words by John Gay, performed in 1720 at the estate of

---

[3] Quoted by J. S. Manifold, *The Music in English Drama from Shakespeare to Purcell*, 1956.

Handel's patron, the Duke of Chandos. At the same place and time a work called *Haman and Mordecai* was also performed, as a dramatic representation with action and costumes. Twelve years later Handel gave the latter work (which had acquired a new title, *Esther*) in London with additional music and without action – that is, as a concert performance. Thus, quite suddenly on May 2, 1732, English oratorio was born. It is usually said that Handel was compelled to this new method of performance by the Bishop of London, who, as Dean of the Chapel Royal, refused to permit his choristers to participate in anything so profane as enacting a biblical story on the public theatrical stage. But this story is very doubtfully substantiated, as the present author has endeavoured to show elsewhere (in the magazine *Opera*, June 1959). It is more probable that Handel decided on concert performance as financially more economic, and artistically perhaps more suited to the looser dramatic structure of the newly inflated score.

For twenty years afterwards Handel continued to write oratorios on biblical or other religious texts (up to *Jephtha*, 1752), and there is no evidence that he ever tried to have one theatrically staged in London or even expressed a regret that he could not. We need not, therefore, fall into the fashionable twentiety-century error of considering these oratorios – and their secular relations, *Semele* (1744) and *Hercules* (1745) – as, in some way, would-be operas. They are *sui generis*; their structure is apt to be too loose for the visual stage. But it is a kind of dramatic structure none the less, involving the participation of named characters in defined incidents. (*Israel in Egypt*, 1739, and *Messiah*, 1742, are exceptions.) Some of the songs in the oratorios depend for their full effect on dramatic context, occasionally being musically linked to a succeeding chorus. Yet other songs, and likewise the songs in Handel's smaller concerted works like *Alexander's Feast* (1746) can be considered as satisfying in themselves.

The norm of a Handel song is the 'da capo aria', in which there is presented a first strain, a contrasting middle strain, and then a resumption of the music from the beginning (da capo) until the point where the first strain ends. All this, the air proper, is usually (not always) preceded by a recitative – to be declaimed fairly freely, not in the strict time appropriate to Purcell. But Handel does not always keep even to the *da capo* form; he is less strict about doing so in his English oratorios than in his Italian operas. He brought a distinctive 'grand style' to English song, but he could strike the simpler note too. His work thus ranges from a song conveying the most formidable of vocal heroics in strict *da capo* form (like the bass air, *Revenge, Timotheus cries* in *Alexander's Feast*) to the simple pastoral charm of *Straight my eye hath caught new pleasure* (from *L'Allegro, il Penseroso, ed il Moderato*, adapted from Milton, 1740) which is not in *da capo* form at all.

From this last-named aria we can see an example of Handel's favourite playing-off of two-beat against three-beat rhythm:

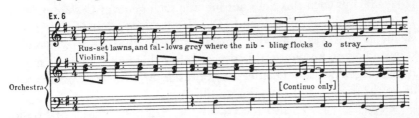

(The effect is more familiar in *And the glory of the Lord shall be revealed* from *Messiah*.) There is nothing in the extract quoted here that is not, so to speak, 'formula'; but it is often in the handling of such things, in quite square two-bar or four-bar rhythm, that Handel proves himself the master. At other times his boldness still speaks vividly to us – and how much more vividly to those accustomed to the conventions of his own time! – as in these two extracts from *Belshazzar*:

It is to be feared that over-familiarity with *Messiah* is balanced by the public's ignorance of Handel's other oratorios. Admittedly such characters as Achsah, Asenath and Josabeth do not sound so inviting as they would have been to our Bible-reading grandparents, but the musical loss is a great one. The best collection of individual songs from Handel's oratorios is that made by Walter Ford and Rupert Erlebach (1927–8); but even this does not include such gems as *O sleep, why dost thou leave me?* from *Semele* and *How blest the maid* from *Hercules*; and it deliberately leaves out what it claims to be the really well-known songs. (Today, however, thirty years after this publication, it may be doubted whether *any* Handel songs outside *Messiah* are well known at all to the greater concert-going public.)

Handel's era was also the era of the pleasure gardens of London, where the citizens found diversions in the summer months. The principal gardens were those of Marylebone (1659–1776), Vauxhall (1660–1835, known until 1786 as Spring Garden), and Ranelagh (1742–1805). At the last-named, in Chelsea, the eight-year-old Mozart performed on the harpsichord in 1764. A statue of Handel by Roubiliac (it now stands in Messrs. Novello's premises in London) was erected in Vauxhall Gardens in the composer's own lifetime – a rare honour. Handel's music itself was performed in the London gardens, and every composer in London was naturally drawn to write light songs suitable for the concerts there. Published song-sheets of the period carry inscriptions such as 'Sung by Miss Chambers at Marybon-Gardens', indicating no less a recommendation than, at a later age, would be conveyed by the name of a Bing Crosby and of a Hollywood film.

Such light songs were the current taste, and not only at the Gardens. They were songs with an easy, catchy charm, in which neither woe nor jollity was allowed too deep expression. Impassioned declamatory song, such as had been sometimes cultivated by Purcell, would have doubtless been thought extravagant. Elegance of melody was the aim, and we can see a growing distaste for the old idea that the music should 'paint' the words. The composer Charles Avison (1709–90) wrote in his *Essay on Musical Expression* (second edition, 1753):

'The musical composer who catches at every particular epithet* or metaphor that the part affords him to show his imitative power, will never

---

* To give but one instance, how many composers hath the single epithet 'warbling' misled from the true road of expression, like an *ignis fatuus*, and bemired them with a pun?

fail to hurt the true aim of his composition, and will always prove the more deficient as his author [i.e. the author of the words] is more pathetic or sublime.'

But Charles Avison, notable for his instrumental works in *concerto grosso* style, is perhaps unique among his contemporaries in having apparently published no songs. A composer who had particular success in hitting the popular taste in song (in both the amorous and convivial veins) was Henry Carey (1685–1743). He rarely departed from a four-square musical framework (there is an exception in *Sad Musidora* with its curious seven-bar phrasing); but within this framework displayed a lively knack, as in the jovial *Once for all*, delightfully subtitled 'Henry Carey's general reply to the libelling gentry, who are angry at his welfare'. Carey also wrote both the words and the original tune of *Sally in our Alley* (quoted in *The Beggar's Opera* to the words 'Of all the friends in time of grief') but the tune to which Carey's words later became fixed was an earlier one whose composer is unknown.

Anthony Young, also born about 1685 (his exact dates are not ascertainable), numbered among his successful songs *The Shy Shepherdess* ('Shepherd, when thou seest me fly'). In 1899, H. Lane Wilson brought out this song with the tune altered and with different words ('Phillis has such charming graces', originally set to a different tune by Daniel Purcell). Young's own charming song now deserves an authentic modern edition. George Monro (or Monroe or Munro), also born about this time, showed a similar easy melodic gift in such a song as *Gold a Receipt for Love*.

The Flemish-born Willem Defesch (or De Fesch), who came to London in 1731 and died there about 1758, published various English songs in the conventional vein of the time. More important is Maurice Greene (1695–1755). Though best known for his church music, he was also a popular composer of songs: of real individuality is *Fair Sally* (a modern edition by Roger Fiske appeared in 1957) which has a clever mixture of the amorous and the comic. (For a comparison, see page 145 under Hook.)

William Croft (1678–1727), also best known as a church composer, likewise composed some pleasing songs, among them *How severe is my fate* with its expressive harmonies. His extended song in several movements with the title of *By purling streams* remained in manuscript until brought out in an edition by Fritz Spiegl in 1957 (Schott): within the convention of the time it still makes an appeal, and has an obbligato for oboe or violin interplaying with the voice. Like other such extended songs, popular among composers from Purcell's day onward, it was styled a 'cantata'.

In January 1728, at Lincoln's Inn Theatre, *The Beggar's Opera* was produced. The manager of the theatre was named John Rich; and, irresistibly, the punning verdict was that the success of the work 'made Gay rich and Rich gay'. John Gay wrote the words of all but five of the sixty-nine songs, setting them to popular tunes of the day. There is every reason to credit Gay with the choice of music; the share of John Christopher Pepusch (who was born in Berlin in 1672, settled in London and died there in 1752) was presumably limited to the musical arranging of the songs and to the composition of the overture from some of the songs themselves.

The Beggar's Opera presents a tale of low life – of whores, highwaymen, a fence, a corrupt jailer. There are plenty of whip-cracks against 'respectable' people. Peachum, the fence, sings:

> The priest calls the lawyer a cheat,
> The lawyer beknaves the divine;
> While the statesman, because he's so great,
> Thinks his trade as honest as mine.

The airs are separated by spoken dialogue. Yet if the work was thus not exactly a parody of current Italian opera (in which speech was replaced by recitative), it to some extent made fun of it.

The Beggar's Opera enjoyed success not only at the time but also later. In 1920, with the music arranged by Frederic Austin (1872–1952), it began a run at the Lyric Theatre, Hammersmith, London, which lasted for 1,463 performances; Benjamin Britten, with a very free adaptation of the music, made a version which was first produced in 1948; and Kurt Weill used the dramatic idea (though with his own original music) in *Die Dreigroschenoper*, 'The Threepenny Opera', produced in Berlin, 1928. Moreover in its own time *The Beggar's Opera* inspired other works in the same 'ballad opera' form, setting new words to currently popular tunes.

The actual music of *The Beggar's Opera* was chiefly such songs as were available in the standard collections of the time – principally the early eighteenth-century editions of John Playford's *The Dancing Master* and of Thomas Durfey's *Pills to Purge Melancholy*; some other traditional airs, and some by known composers such as Purcell and Eccles, are also included. There is nothing musically new about *The*

Beggar's Opera, and indeed the whole point about it was that there was not. But its lowbrow success in the face of the fashionable Italian opera was highly significant. Dr. Johnson, who disapproved of *The Beggar's Opera*, described the Italian opera in London as 'an exotic and irrational entertainment'. He did *not* define opera itself in this way.[4]

Thomas Augustine Arne (1710–78) also grew up in the shadow of Italian opera; of his own operas, *L'Olimpiade* is the setting of an Italian text (by Metastasio, whose librettos were set by Handel and countless others), and *Artaxerxes* is an English translation of a Metastasio original. Arne was himself attached as composer to Drury Lane Theatre, and the provision of music for English operas and plays largely occupied him. The justly famous songs to verses from Shakespeare's *As You Like It – Under the greenwood tree, When daisies pied* and *Blow, blow thou winter wind* – were written for a Drury Lane production of the play in 1740.

The work which chiefly established Arne was *Comus*, and it has some claim to be considered his best work. (It has been most usefully reprinted in the 'Musica Britannica' series, 1951.) This work, produced at Drury Lane in 1738, was an adaptation by John Dalton of the masque by Milton which Henry Lawes had originally set. It sustains a high musical level, a serious composer's craft going even into the light-hearted songs.

In contrasting serious mood, Arne gives us the long sweep of this melody and the suspended harmonies beneath:

Ex. 9

So from the first did Jove or-dain E-ter-nal bliss for trans-ient pain, E-ter-nal bliss_____ for trans-ient pain.

[4] The misattribution of this phrase to Johnson's Dictionary as a definition of opera occurs in the first edition of E. J. Dent's Penguin book, *Opera* (1940). Professor Dent withdrew the misattribution in later editions, but the damage was done. The actual quotation, in the more limited sense, is to be found in Johnson's *Lives of the Poets: Hughes*.

Arne sometimes used the da capo aria, sometimes the plain strophic form (repeating the music for each stanza, with or without a refrain or chorus). In this popular strophic form he threw off dozens of songs catering for the entertainment of pleasure-going Londoners at Vauxhall, Ranelagh and Marylebone Gardens (at each of which he enjoyed an official status as composer). Some of these songs still have special charm or a special musical 'knack' to display – like *Tell me, pride of this creation*, with its imitation between melody and bass (a trait of an earlier age, as we have noticed with John Eccles); but many are no more than the pleasant small change of that day's musical currency. It is in such works as *Comus* or the oratorio *Judith* that we must seek his real musical strength.

It was neither of these, however, that won him particular immortality, but *Alfred* – produced privately at Cliveden, Bucks, in 1740, and described as a masque (like *Comus*). We shall not go far wrong in considering it as somewhere between a pageant and an opera. It ends with *Rule, Britannia*, sung by King Alfred himself, with chorus. The tune quickly won fame. Less than a year after *Alfred* reached the London stage, in 1745, Handel quoted a characteristic phrase from the song in his *Occasional Oratorio* with the words 'War shall cease, welcome peace'. Musical detectives who have pointed this out might also have remarked a coincidence in words between *Rule, Britannia* ('with matchless beauty crowned') and Handel's *Joseph* ('with such matchless beauty crowned') of 1744.

A curious point is that, as with many other songs which have achieved enormous popularity, the version of *Rule, Britannia* which posterity has acquired differs significantly from what the composer really wrote. Nearly all standard song books print the words 'Britannia rule the waves' in steady, even crotchets – a nineteenth-century corruption, it seems – though Arne wrote the notes in dotted, jerky rhythm. There are other differences equally radical. The composer's own version is much the better; and now that it is again in print (edited by Humphrey Searle, published by Joseph Williams), and is enthusiastically performed at the annual 'last night of the Proms', the other corrupt form should be firmly dropped.

Thomas Augustine Arne has somewhat oddly gone down to posterity as 'Dr. Arne'. To distinguish him from his son, Michael Arne (see page 143) it would be better to refer to him by his first names or initials than by a title which has also been the right of hundreds of musicians, eminent and otherwise.

From Boyce to Bishop

Those who were the contemporaries and immediate successors of Thomas Arne – that is, composers born between 1710 and 1740 – lived at a time when music was undergoing notable changes, not least in England. The senior of these composers saw above them the dominating figure of the living Handel; they saw, too, the dominance of Italian opera in its formal, mid-eighteenth-century shape. The later composers, living until 1800 or just after, inhaled something of the spirit of Haydn (whose works were well known even before he visited London in 1791–2 and 1794–5) and of Mozart.

A bridge between the Handel era and the Haydn era (as we may call them) was provided by such figures as Johann Christian Bach, Johann Sebastian Bach's youngest son (1735–82) who settled in London and wrote both Italian operas and English songs for London music-lovers. In England he was known as John Christian Bach. His song *Cruel Strephon, will you leave me* is significantly headed 'Rondeau'. The form of the rondo (to use the Italian spelling which later ousted the French in English usage) was happily adopted in many later English songs. As distinct from the verse-and-refrain pattern (ABABAB . . .) or the da capo aria (ABA) the rondo gives ABACA . . . : that is, the 'episode' that separates the occurrences of the main theme is different each time.

The eighteenth century was indeed a time when English musical taste was swayed by fashionable Continental visitors; but specifically English tradition was maintained in church music. Not the least service rendered by William Boyce (1710–79) was his editing of three large volumes entitled *Cathedral Music* (a collection of composers going back to the days of Henry VIII). He himself was a prodigious composer of church music. But as a song-composer Boyce worked, like so many other composers of the time, primarily in the theatre. The sole song by which he is now known, *Heart of Oak* (*not* 'Hearts of Oak'), comes from a Christmas entertainment called *Harlequin's Invasion* (1759, with text by David Garrick) and has topical reference to the victories over the French at Minden and Quebec.

But an examination of Boyce's song as originally printed shows a clear difference from that now in circulation:

Ex. 10
[a. 'Accepted' version

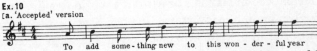

To add some-thing new to this won-der-ful year

Boyce wrote even quavers, not a dotted, jerky rhythm; and he failed

141

to achieve a melodic climax (as our current version does) at 'this wonderful year' Boyce's original is plainly less effective than the song as shaped by usage, and makes us think less of his gifts as a melodist:

[b. Boyce's original

To add some-thing new to this won - der-ful year

That impression is confirmed by such a work as *The Chaplet*, another stage entertainment, in which conventional pastoral verses are matched by the insipidity of the music.

Samuel Howard (1710–82) also composed songs which now convey little distinction, though very popular in their day. His *The nut brown maid* has a curious and almost literal quotation from the popular *Love in her eyes sits playing* from Handel's *Acis and Galatea*.

Thomas Linley, senior (1733–95), is a composer of peculiar historical interest, both musical and literary. Two of his stage works (*Selima and Azor*, and *Richard Cœur de Lion*) are adaptations from Grétry; and Sheridan, who was Linley's son-in-law, was the librettist of his opera *The Duenna* (1773, and several times since revived). For Sheridan's *The School for Scandal*, Linley wrote his most famous song, *Here's to the maiden*. Linley's son, also Thomas (1756–78), an intimate friend of the young Mozart, also contributed to *The Duenna*; cut off at twenty-two by drowning, he was a figure of rare promise. The achievement of the Linleys is in simple, graceful songs.

But with Samuel Arnold (1740–82) a flavour comes to us of a different world. Arnold at one time took the lease of Marylebone Gardens, but was not content to compose for it the simple strophic songs which had been chiefly in favour there. His song *The tender heart*, with accompaniment for flutes, horns, and strings is worth consideration as an example. It starts with a long (eighteen-bar) introduction. Then the first section of its vocal part ends in the dominant key, the next section goes to another related key, and the concluding section is a varied repeat of the first but turns round to conclude in the tonic. Here we have, indeed, something like the key-scheme of sonata form. Another song, *If love can melt the frozen heart*, presents a similarly striking formal scheme; and when, in such a context, we have a pathetic diminished-seventh chord, agitated violins, and a suddenly rising flute part, then we feel indeed in Haydn's or Mozart's world (see Ex. 11 opposite).

An English pupil of Mozart was Stephen Storace (1763–96), a gifted composer of Italian descent who died young. He cultivated the fashionable English opera of his day – usually incorporating items from

celebrated Continental operas. Storace's *The Pirates* contains not only the charming and half-comic *Oh, the pretty, pretty creature* but also a real approach to a Mozartian dramatic aria, *Some device my aid to cover.* (It was written for Michael Kelly, the tenor, another personal friend of Mozart.) Also a man of the theatre was Jonathan Battishill (1738–1801), singer, harpsichordist, and composer. Among the songs he wrote for the London public gardens was *Kate of Aberdeen* – once well known, and published with the rich accompaniment of three violins (instead of the usual two) and bass.

Among the other minor composers of the time one fact alone gives fame to John Stafford Smith (1750–1836): he published, and probably himself composed, a song called *To Anacreon in Heaven*, the tune of which was adapted for 'The Star-Spangled Banner'. The sharpened fourth of the tune as it is now known (at the words 'our flag was *still* there') is unsharpened in the original, as shown in the early editions. This and *Rule, Britannia* are remarkable examples of how a song which has a very complex poetic and musical scheme of lines can nevertheless achieve popularity.

Michael Arne (1741–86) was the son of Thomas Arne – according to Burney, the illegitimate son. It was as 'Master Arne' that his name appeared as a composer of a collection of 'English Songs sung at the

Public Gardens' in 1750. Changing fashions may be observed in the contrast between these songs, in which there is nearly always a correspondence of one syllable to one note, and his later songs with more decorative runs. There is a justly famous example of such decoration in *The lass with the delicate air* – though it is amusing to note, as with so many other eighteenth-century songs which have retained their popularity, that there is a considerable difference between Michael Arne's original tune (published anonymously in *The Universal Magazine*, 1762) and the tune now sung:

About this time the guitar was becoming popular in the home. The vocal score of Michael Arne's opera *The Fairy Tale* (after Shakespeare's *A Midsummer Night's Dream*) carries on its title page the inscription 'Those airs which are not in proper keys for the guitar are added at the end of the book'; and in another song called *The tinkling guitar* ('my strumming, my thrumming, my tinkling guitar') he pays direct attention to the new vogue. The keyboard instrument in general use was still the harpsichord, but from the 1780s pianos came gradually into general use in Britain. They were all 'grand' (horizontally strung) pianos until 1821 when the first practical upright piano was patented, leading to the universal Victorian popularity of the instrument.

Another instrument in domestic favour was the harp. Samuel Webbe (1740–1816), for instance, specifies it as an alternative to the piano in 'Star of Beauty', and William Shield (1748–1829) has a song entitled *An address to Lady Cadogan's harp* subtitled 'a canzonet for voice, harp, harpsichord, or piano forte'. The song-copy also contains an arrangement for guitar. From the accompaniment to this very conventional song, one surmises that Lady Cadogan's harp technique was not advanced.

Shield has been given twentieth-century fame by Benjamin Britten, who includes 'The Ploughboy' in his arrangements of English folksongs. Shield composed this song for an opera, *The Farmer* (1787). The original does not contain the sharpened fourth at the end of the first half of the song (as in Britten's version); but, curiously, it does contain an obbligato for a 'small flute' (presumably a recorder, not a piccolo) which performs a similar function to the imitation-whistling in Britten's piano part. There are other songs in the opera which could well be heard today, including the patter-song, *Gad a mercy* and the pathetic *Winds, softly tell my love*, in which a soprano voice is initially accompanied only by pizzicato violins.

Charles Dibdin (1745–1814) also wrote operas, but was associated particularly with 'table entertainments' – one-man shows in which he was author, composer, narrator, singer, and accompanist. It was for these entertainments that Dibdin wrote nearly all of the sea-songs (*Ben Backstay*, *The lass that loves a sailor*, *Tom Bowling*, etc.), which remained popular throughout the nineteenth century, and beyond.[5] They have a well-shaped, simple charm as well as a topical patriotism. But only topicality could justify the set of songs written for a cele-bration at Stratford-on-Avon. The tunes are no better than the words, and both today seem made for Miss Anna Russell:

> Let Beauty with the sun arise,
> To Shakespeare, Shakespeare tribute pay,
> To Shakespeare tribute pay,
> To Shakespeare, Shakespeare, Shakespeare, Shakespeare,
> To Shakespeare, Shakespeare tribute pay.

Among the songs of James Hook (1746–1827) is *Sweet Nancy loved a gallant sailor*, of which the poem is a version of that set by Greene as *Fair Sally* (see page 137); Hook's is more ornate, but less boldly effective. Hook's other songs range from *The sooner the better*, in a popular comic vein which survived into the Victorian music-hall, to his great success *The lass of Richmond Hill*,[6] with the pretty elegance typical of the songs sung at Vauxhall and the other public gardens.

It was rather odd of Britten to call *The Ploughboy* a folk-song – a term implying, normally, an anonymous, popular origin for a song – since he acknowledged in his publication that the tune is William Shield's. Yet a similar carefree confusion between 'popular' and 'com-

---

[5] *Tom Bowling* is included in the surviving part of Henry J. Wood's 'Fantasia on British Sea Songs' given annually at the last night of the London 'Proms'. It is ironic that a song which was originally orchestrated because it was well known as a simple vocal melody is now hardly to be encountered except in its dressed-up orchestral form.

[6] The supposition that this refers to Richmond, Yorkshire – in support of which it is alleged that Leonard McNally, the author of the verse, was married to a girl of that town – is patently absurd. The song was only one of several aimed at pleasing a London audience by mentioning its favourite spots. See Purcell's example on page 129.

posed' music may be said to be characteristic of Shield's own time. Composers of English operas incorporated traditional airs as they wished. The tune of the delightful half-Latin song, *Amo, amas, I love a lass,*[7] is usually ascribed to Samuel Arnold because it comes in his opera *The Agreeable Surprise*; but in an early vocal score of the opera Arnold acknowledges that the tune is a traditional one, *The mouse and the frog*.

Composers could make such borrowings without artistic violence because their own style was near enough to the style of the traditional popular airs. An example is Arnold's own song beginning *A clerk I was in London gay, Jemmy-Jemmy-Linkum-Feedle,* in the opera *Inkle and Yarico*. Thus, too, the elder Linley could enliven *The Spanish Rivals* with two tunes stated to be borrowed from Cumberland dances, *When I was in Cumberland*, and the splendid *Last Martinmas gone a year* (in dashing 9–8 metre). It is doubtless because they themselves were still so near to the English popular tradition that the composers of the time did not make a special point of collecting what we should now call English folk-songs (the term was not then used) though they often arranged popular airs of Scotland and Ireland.

Traditional Scottish tunes had long enjoyed wide circulation in English song-books, and throughout the eighteenth century there seems to have been no English composer who did not seek to cash in on the vogue by writing his own 'Scotch song' – usually with a prominent use of the little rhythmical figure called the Scotch snap: and usually with verses about Jockey and Jenny (or Maggie, or even Moggy). But towards the end of the eighteenth century the interest in gathering authentic Scottish tunes seems to have had a new impetus, of chiefly literary inspiration. Both Sir Walter Scott and Robert Burns wrote new verses to these old tunes, and both were associated with George Thomson (1757–1851), song-collector and antiquary, who, having decided to publish such songs in voice-and-piano form, commissioned musical arrangements from Haydn and Beethoven as well as from lesser composers.

Irish songs, similarly, were not new to the English scene. Purcell has a harpsichord piece headed 'A New Irish Tune' which is an arrangement by him of 'Lilliburlero' (sometimes mistakenly said to be a composition of Purcell's own). George Thomson set Haydn and Beethoven on to arranging Irish songs too – and also Welsh ones. But,

---

[7] This song has earned an unlooked-for twentieth-century distinction by its entirely happy incorporation in Rolf Liebermann's opera *School for Wives* (1955).

although some traditional Irish harpers had penetrated to London, Welsh traditional music was much less well known outside its homeland than Scottish or Irish.

Haydn's and Beethoven's arrangements of these airs do not deserve their almost total oblivion – though today they would have to justify their place on a recital programme as pieces by Haydn or Beethoven, since they do not now seem what an audience expects folk-song arrangements to be like. It is to be noted that Beethoven's arrangements have optional violin and cello parts, in addition to the piano, and that, in some of Haydn's, the violin and cello parts are obligatory.

Thomson's enterprise provided the stimulation for that of a Dublin publisher, William Power, who enlisted Thomas Moore (1779–1852) to write new words for what became a famous collection called *Irish Melodies* (issued serially between 1808 and 1834). Sir John Stevenson (1761–1833) and later Sir Henry Bishop did the musical arrangements. The collection contained such deservedly famous songs as *The minstrel boy* and *The Harp that once through Tara's halls*, with words by Moore. It did not include *The Londonderry Air*, now possibly the most famous of all Irish traditional tunes: this was published in the Petrie Collection of the Ancient Music of Ireland (1855), without words. It is presumably vocal in origin and has had various words set to it since – of which the sentimental 'Danny Boy' is at least better than the school-room inanity of 'In Derry Vale'.

Thomas Moore was occasionally composer as well as poet, and the music of 'The Last Rose of Summer' is his, as well as the words. It was borrowed by Flotow in *Martha* (1847) to represent a traditional air sung by one of the characters, and is very effectively re-quoted at various parts in the opera.[8]

Besides his folk-song arrangements, Haydn wrote fourteen original song-settings of English words. Twelve of these fell into two sets of six 'canzonets' (a term which some English composers of the time had also used). Easily the best known is *My mother bids me bind my hair* (original title, *A Pastoral Song*); but its elegance is somewhat insipid, and the words do not help. It is difficult to imagine anything sillier than 'Alas, I scarce can *go or creep* while Lubin is away' (my italics), though one must add that the seemingly absurd name Lubin is also to be found in other English songs of the period. The setting which Haydn gave to

---

[8] Incredibly, the song is not mentioned in the fairly long article on Moore in Grove's Dictionary of Music (1954); and under *Flotow*, it is mentioned simply as an 'Irish Tune', without acknowledgement to Moore.

Shakespeare's words *She never told her love* (from *Twelfth Night*) is not really suited to the words, and the otherwise agreeable *Sailor's Song* is marred because Haydn seems to have thought the words 'hurly-burly' (which he repeats many times over) were a mere equivalent of fa-la-la.

The Spirit's Song, however (published separately, not among the sets of canzonets), is a masterpiece of atmosphere. The voice enters commandingly on a chord which is not that of the tonic, and then there is an effect of mystery from the repeated notes. The author of the poem is unknown but it is certainly not Shakespeare (as Haydn thought). There is slight awkwardness in the words of one line: we do not immediately grasp that in 'nor sorrow o'er the tomb' the word 'sorrow' is a verb. But the impact of the song is striking. Dr. Karl Geiringer, a great authority on Haydn, suggests that Haydn's piano accompaniments to these English songs were really thought of in terms of the orchestra; and certainly there can be little objection to an orchestral arrangement of them.

But the point of great historical importance was that Haydn set down these piano accompaniments with fully-written-out right-hand parts: and these must have been among the first songs published in England to do so. Previously, composers wrote songs on only two staves, not three. The upper stave could accommodate an accompanist's right-hand part only in what were then called the 'symphonies' – that is, the introduction, postlude, and any intermediate bars where the singer was silent. At other points the lower stave held the bass-line and the upper the vocal line; to devise a right-hand accompaniment, the player had to work out his own correct harmony, aided sometimes by figured bass and very exceptionally by an odd note or two inserted in the upper stave beneath the singer's part.

The change from this two-stave song-writing to the three-stave plan, with full right-hand parts for the accompanist, was a necessary condition for the development of song as we understand it in its expressive nineteenth- and twentieth-century sense. Among the composers who followed Haydn's example was Thomas Attwood (1765–1838) who had been a pupil of Mozart in Vienna. Attwood's settings of verses from Sir Walter Scott's 'The Lady of the Lake' constitute perhaps the first important songs in this new sense by an English composer. Particular interest lies in his setting of *Ellen's Song* or *Ave Maria,* since this anticipates Schubert's by some fifteen years. Attwood gave this song a really pianistic accompaniment, fairly bold harmonies, and a setting which varied the melody according to the changed poetic meaning of each verse—a device now almost inevitably labelled Schubertian. A few bars from this remarkable song must suffice for a sample:

Ex.13

Safe may we sleep— be - neath thy care, Thou ban-ished, out-cast, and re-viled;

Mai - den, hear a mai - den's pray'r, Mo - ther, hear— a sup - pliant child,—

Mai - den, hear a mai - den's pray'r, Mo - ther, hear a sup - pliant child.

Another English composer set *The Erl King* (so entitled) before Schubert did: John Wall Callcott (1766–1821). But Callcott's setting is a three-part glee, one voice representing the child, one the voice of Death, and all three singing the father's part as well as the narration. This kind of concerted song-setting remained popular, and likewise the humorous 'catch' for several voices. Callcott's own 'Ah, how Sophia', for instance, has the double meaning throughout of 'A house afire'. But the pieces written by Callcott as solo songs are of lesser importance, though their evolution through his life shows the expected change from two-stave to three-stave form. Callcott's 'To all you ladies now at hand', which achieved considerable life as a song with chorus, is really arranged from a glee.

Despite such steps as Attwood's in establishing English 'recital songs',[9]

[9] Not that this term would then have been used. 'Recital' dates in British usage apparently from Liszt's appearances in 1840 as pianist; song-recitals, that is concerts entirely of songs (solo and duets), did not appear in London till the 1880s. Songs with either orchestral or piano accompaniment, however, figured earlier in orchestral and miscellaneous concerts.

the stage remained the chief way in which new songs were presented to the public. Samuel Wesley (1766–1837) and John Field
(1782–1837), concentrating respectively on music for the church and
for the piano, are two British composers who do not affect our present
narrative. But Sir Henry Bishop (1786–1855) wrote prolifically for the
stage: and his *Home, sweet home*, which we may think of as a domestic
ballad *par excellence*, comes in fact from his opera *Clari, or the Maid of
Milan* (1823). But we may take the origins of this song back a little
further: it is an improved version, with new words, of a song which
Bishop had written a few years earlier and had passed off as a Sicilian
traditional melody.

Bishop's well-known songs, *Should he upbraid* and *Bid me discourse*,
composed respectively for productions of *The Two Gentlemen of
Verona* and *Twelfth Night*, are written with orchestral accompaniment;
the even more famous *Lo, here* [not 'hear'] *the gentle lark* presumably
has a theatrical origin too, and includes a 'contest' of soprano with
a flute (like that in Donizetti's *Lucia di Lammermoor* of 1835). Bishop
has a liking for long, formal roulades which links him with Handel's
era, and his elegant construction has kept such songs as these alive.
He was apparently the first composer to be knighted at the hands of
a British sovereign (by Queen Victoria in 1842). Social historians may
remark that, a century afterwards, a distinguished senior composer
became more conspicuous by *not* having a knighthood.

John Braham (1777–1856) was a distinguished tenor (he sang the
leading part in the first performance of Weber's *Oberon*, given in
London in 1826) and a theatrical composer of conspicuous but
ephemeral success. Long-lasting favour, however, was won by his song
The Death of Nelson, which is itself in the operatic form of recitative-
and-aria. Even now it may be recognized as free from the gross over-
sentimentality of so many later 'patriotic ballads cut and dried'. It is,
incidentally, in *The Death of Nelson* that the famous words 'England,
home, and beauty' are originally to be found.

C. E. Horn (1786–1849) was likewise a man of the theatre – not only
a composer, but a singer whose extensive voice enabled him to under-
take both tenor and baritone parts. There is no essential difference
between the style of *The deep, deep sea*, a song which came from a stage
work, and the pretty *Cherry ripe*, which did not. Both look back to the
eighteenth century rather than forward to the Victorian ballad; the
former song is a rondo, the second a modified rondo.

J. L. Hatton (1809–86) has a well-thought-out application of the rondo in *The Maid I Love*: the recurring rondo-theme is in 3–4, and the interpolated episodes in 4–4 take the form of different addresses to a mariner, a cavalier, and a shepherd-boy. But in actual musical effect the song is dull. Hatton wrote many songs, some in stage works; but we probably do not wrong him in thinking of him only as the composer of *To Anthea* (a remarkable song, with an impetus that carries the music through a continuously unfolding structure without repetitions) and of the character song, *Simon the Cellarer*. Both these would inevitably figure in any musical depiction of the Victorian era in music.

The Victorians and after

'Whirr! whirr! all by wheels! – whiz! whiz! all by steam!' said the Pasha in Kinglake's *Eothen*, marvelling at the achievements of Victorian England. The new industrial and social organization of the country (though in truth it antedates Victoria's accession in 1837) was not without an early effect on musical life. An album of up to twenty songs by a serious but fashionable composer (Mendelssohn, Hatton, Donizetti) could be bought for 1s. and (in 1854) the vocal score of Handel's *Messiah* for 1s. 4d. Small choral societies all over the country called modest cantatas into existence (the word 'cantata', which in English had previously meant chiefly an extended solo song, now took on its modern meaning). The writing of cantatas on sacred subjects, of anthems and services, and of hymn tunes took up much of the zeal of English musicians: H. J. Gauntlett (1805–76) is said to have written literally thousands of hymns besides the familiar 'Once in Royal David's City'. Such hymns formed in effect one kind of repertory of universal popular song: it was to such tunes as 'The church's one foundation' (by S. S. Wesley, 1810–76) or 'Onward Christian Soldiers' (by Sullivan) that the British soldier fitted his un-hymn-like verses in 1914–18, and even in 1939–45.

English serious composers, who had tended to choose Italy for overseas study during the opera-minded eighteenth century, now turned more to Germany. Henry Hugh Pearson (1815–73), after writing some unremarkable English songs, settled in Germany as Heinrich Hugo Pierson. William Sterndale Bennett (1816–75), whose visits to Germany resulted in his friendship with Mendelssohn and Schumann, set both German and English texts: dullness generally prevails, but is absent from the charming *Winter's Gone* (poem by John Clare).

Mid-century opera provided a few songs of lasting popular success in the drawing-room. *I dreamt that I dwelt in marble halls* comes from

The Bohemian Girl by Michael William Balfe (1808–70); and *Yes! let me like a soldier fall* from *Maritana* by William Vincent Wallace (1812–65). But in general the drawing-room had its own repertory, specially written and not borrowed from the stage. Longfellow was fallen on by many composers. Balfe had much success with *I shot an arrow into the air*, but the version of *The Village Blacksmith* which became popular was not his but that of W. H. Weiss, a singer (1820–67).

Weiss's setting brings in the hymn-tune known as the 'Old Hundredth' in the piano accompaniment when the singer reaches the words about being in church; it is one of the more pretentious of ballads. The class of ballads as a whole, usually with a portentous and wooden declamation of words and a feeble accompaniment, has come in for some well-deserved abuse in the last fifty years. (Still, it is to be wondered if they are any worse than those Neapolitan trivialities with which Italian singers are still permitted to end their recitals.) Conventional love (with death optionally thrown in, providing it was romantically achieved), conventional heroics, and conventional piety were the favoured subject-matter. Humour was a rare visitor: one surmises that G. Berthold's 'Duetto for Two Cats' (to a text of repeated *miaows* plus the instruction 'at the points marked *, imitate the spitting of the cats') did not achieve wide popularity.

With the taste for conventional ballads, however, went a taste for things a good deal better. Schubert's *To music* and Haydn's *The Spirit's Song* are side by side in a popular song album of the late-Victorian era with *She wore a wreath of roses* by J. P. Knight (1812–87) which plumbs the depth in obviousness. Such a coexistence could also be found within a single composer. The trivial portentousness of *The Diver* comes from the pen of Edward Loder (1813–65), but Loder was also the composer of *The Brooklet* (on Longfellow's translation of the poem which Schubert set as *Wohin?* in 'Die schöne Müllerin'), the delicacy of which has earned justifiable praise.[10]

There are songs by other composers which, though well within the 'Victorian ballad' category, have a certain individuality that deserves to save them from oblivion. Charles Kingsley's verse, *Three fishers went sailing out of the west* was set with subtle avoidance of pathetic exaggeration by J. P. Hullah (1812–84). *She is far from the land*, composed nearly at the end of the century by Frank Lambert (d. 1925), derives a curiously impelling swing from harmony and bass-line as well as from its melody:

[10] Reprinted as *I heard a brooklet gushing* (O.U.P., 1936).

Ex.14

She is far from the land____ where her young he-ro sleeps, And lo-vers a-round her are sigh-ing

Ballads naturally sold much more readily if leading singers could be persuaded to perform them in public. From the 1860s, publishing firms found it worth while to promote ballad concerts in which leading artists of opera and oratorio sang a programme all or nearly all compiled from the firm's publications. Moreover, the system grew of paying to a singer, as a reward for 'pushing' the song at concerts, a money royalty on every copy sold to the public. Such songs came to be known as 'royalty ballads', and the direct commercialization of the field of song must have contributed to holding down the level of public taste. The biography of a highly artistic tenor, Gervase Elwes (1866–1921),[11] tells of his successful defiance of this system: but he was exceptional. In mitigation of the system it should perhaps be said that composers and publishers were, in those days, honestly dependent entirely on the number of copies sold: there were no performing rights.

A composer who, exceptionally, was able to carry on the one-man style of performance established by Dibdin was Henry Russell (1812–1900) – singer, pianist, author, and composer. Like Dibdin, he had a pleasing line in nautical patriotism (as in *A life on the ocean wave*) but he was also adept at a more emotional appeal. His famous *Woodman, spare that tree* is the source of many good anecdotes in his own memoirs, but he omits to say that he evidently borrowed his dramatic theme from a song called *The Oak* by the now forgotten composer Charles Stokes (1784–1839) which ends:

> Oh! spoil the shades on every side,
> But, Woodman, spare that sacred tree.

[11] W. and R. Elwes, *Gervase Elwes*, 1935.

A son of Russell's was Landon Ronald (see page 164).

The 'ballad' type of Victorian song was usually composed as a single entity for the drawing-room market, but not invariably. Frederic Clay (1838–89) achieved fame equally by *She wandered down the mountain-side* (a separate song) and *I'll sing thee songs of Araby*, which comes from his cantata, *Lalla Rookh*. Clay also composed for the light musical theatre; he introduced Sullivan to Gilbert, and his theatrical talent is overshadowed by Sullivan's own.

The double standard of composing is no less observable with Sir Arthur Sullivan (1842–1900) than with Loder. On the one hand stands a song like *Were I thy bride*, from *The Yeomen of the Guard* (produced in 1888, the last success but one of the so-called 'Savoy Operas', with W. S. Gilbert as librettist): here there is a sprightliness and subtlety of melody, harmony, and rhythm alike (and of orchestration too). On the other hand, *The lost chord* stands for many as the epitome of all that is worst in the Victorian ballad. Even if one discounts in fairness the associations arising from mere over-familiarity, it seems to combine the maximum of solemnity in its manner with the maximum of triviality in its content. The song is, incidentally, written for the accompaniment not merely of a piano but harmonium *ad lib.* as well – gaining an extra succulence from the Victorians' domestic 'Sunday instrument'.

Yet Sullivan's 'ballad' and 'Savoy' styles were not entirely separate. Just because it is sung by the ridiculous Lady Jane, *Silver'd is the raven hair* becomes a comic, mock-pathetic song in *Patience*; but, when fitted with new words as *In the twilight of our love*, the tune was issued as a drawing-room ballad with seriously pathetic intent. In general, however, the theatre gave Sullivan a kind of musical freedom by allowing him a detachment – sometimes an ironic detachment – from the emotions of his texts, to which otherwise he might have been too ready to respond with clichés. Thus, outside the 'Savoy Operas' (or operettas, as they are more properly called) Sullivan's songs are generally sunk by conventional sentimentality. *Orpheus with his lute* is a welcome exception: and this, significantly, was also originally written for the theatre.

Edward German (real name Edward German Jones, 1862–1936) completed the operetta which Sullivan left unfinished, *The Emerald Isle*; and like Sullivan had less success with serious than with lighter music. His was a less distinctive artistic personality than Sullivan's. *The Yeomen of England* and *The English Rose* (both from the operetta

154

Merrie England), the Waltz Song from *Tom Jones*, and the ballad *Glorious Devon* – these exemplify his minor but mellifluous gift.

Other stage entertainments which followed Sullivan's in providing popular songs up to the 1914–18 war were such operettas as *The Geisha* by Sidney Jones (1861–1946), *Floradora* by Leslie Stuart (real name Thomas Barrett, 1866–1928), and *The Arcadians* by Lionel Monckton (1861–1924) and Howard Talbot (real name Richard Lansdale Munkittrick, 1865–1928). Within their convention, such songs often had real individuality. A link with the music-hall is directly provided by Leslie Stuart, who also wrote *The Lily of Laguna* and *Soldiers of the Queen*; and indeed songs of the music-hall overlapped slightly with those of the operetta and the ballad concert. But music-hall tunes also had other, and sometimes surprising, affiliations. The swinging 6–4 of *Two lovely black eyes* (it is written in three-beat time but its pulse is really of six beats) links Charles Coborn (1852–1945) with a type of popular song as old as Purcell's *Harvest Home*; and the chorus of *A little bit off the top* is derived from the American Civil War song, *When Johnnie comes marching home*, which in turn suggests a folk-song original.

With Parry and Stanford we arrive at what English musical histories used to call 'the English Renaissance'. That may now seem a comic over-statement. Viewed from today, Hubert Parry (1848–1918) is a man who composed four symphonies and three oratorios (besides a great deal else) now not performed at all; Charles Villiers Stanford (1852–1924) composed seven symphonies and seven major operas, now not performed at all. It is something, of course, to have given one's country almost another national anthem, as Parry did in 'Jerusalem';[12] and there are part-songs and motets of Stanford still rightly cherished by choirs. But 'renaissance' would seem to imply a more substantial staying-power than that.

Yet in the field of song theirs is a real achievement. They were fully conscious of nineteenth-century German style in song-writing (Stanford indeed set Heine in the original) and frequently adapted the character-istically German structure of successively varied stanzas. Parry's songs include seventy-four 'English Lyrics' grouped in twelve sets (the last two sets posthumously published), many of them to words of Shakespeare, Herrick, and other major poets. These songs display an extraordinary care for the natural inflexions of English words, as in this example from the fine song to Julian Sturgis's poem *Through the Ivory Gate*:

12 The orchestration is by Elgar.

Ex. 15

I had a dream last night   Dream of a friend that is dead

In his setting of Lovelace's well-known *To Althea, from prison* Parry carefully and correctly accents 'Know no such *liberty*' – instead of obviously accenting the last syllable, on which the rhyme falls. Yet this song, like many of Parry's, strikes us as slightly too 'comfortable' – too predictable in mood and line, too ready in its accompaniment to use only the easiest and warmest notes of the piano. Elsewhere, in leaving the harmonic sense of the last line incomplete, so that the piano postlude is structurally necessary and not merely a conventional rounding-off, Parry sometimes reminds us of Schumann; but more of his music is distinctively Brahmsian. Such a song as *A lover's garland* might deceive many people if sung in German translation – and would indeed justify its place in a Brahms group. What Parry appears generally to lack are the qualities of energy, surprise, and irony: it is notable that *Love is a bable*, which is exceptional among his songs in that respect, is also exceptional in keeping some hold on singers. At the other extreme, even Parry could be un-self-critical enough to turn out *When lovers meet again*, no better than a thousand contemporary drawing-room effusions.

Stanford's voice-and-piano texture is, like Parry's, close to that of Brahms; but Stanford had a notable gift (greater than Parry's) for evoking atmosphere. This quality, best known in such songs as *A soft day* and *The fairy lough*, is evident also in the lesser-known but equally fine setting of Tennyson's *The Vision*, with its range through many keys and its rapt return to the opening strain: the short conventional piano postlude presents the sole disappointment. Stanford was fond of the Schubertian effect of the sudden switch from minor into major: a particular example is in his remarkable setting of Keats's *La belle dame sans merci*, a rare example of an extended English narrative poem successfully fitted to the technique of modern solo song. Stanford's work has also a distinctive Irish side. He was born in Dublin, and made many able voice-and-piano arrangements of Irish folk-songs; and moreover there was still enough of a link in his day between the serious and popular style for him to adopt the Irish folk-song vein in his own *Rose of Killarney*, and to fit the traditional *Father O'Flynn* into his opera *Shamus O'Brien*.

The demand for drawing-room songs gave composers the opportunity of making money quickly from the craftsmanlike application of ready-made formulas. We need not blame them for accepting the temptation to do so, any more than one blames a mid-twentieth-century composer for writing film music. We may rather admire a constant endeavour to write, also, songs of a more serious kind. Thus it was, for instance, with Sir Frederic Cowen (1852–1935). A song like *Golden Glories* (from the eleventh of his twelve series of six songs each) shows a real individuality and shapeliness in its cunning setting of a five-line stanza; and *The nautch girl's song* (from the same set) has an application of pseudo-oriental touches which is by no means overdone: the song is, incidentally, composed straight through with only irregular suggestions of recapitulation.

The example of German song-writing was constantly before English composers, but the German cultivation of song-cycles seems to have awakened only a tardy response – naturally enough, considering how rarely the opportunity would come of occupying an audience's attention with such a sustained exposition of voice and piano. But Liza Lehmann (1862–1918) won a remarkable success with her cycle 'In a Persian Garden' (on the 'Rubáiyát' of Omar Khayyám, in selected verses from Fitzgerald's translation). This, however, written not for solo voice but for four voices and piano (the voices being used both separately and together, in short sections), approaches a cantata. But she wrote other cycles for solo voice in more conventional form, and the song-cycle in England is said to have been firmly set awheel by her.

Maude Valérie White (1855–1937) was the first woman composer to become established in England, and song was her chief field. *The devout lover* was her most famous, and is a not inoffensive drawing-room ballad; her setting of Browning's 'King Charles', which musically incorporates the tune of 'Lilliburlero'[13] is dashingly effective. She made a striking, if not totally successful, approach to musical modernity in *On the fields of France* (1919), with its bold harmonic clashes and its intense expression.

Dame Ethel Smyth (1858–1944), still the most distinguished woman composer this country has produced, published few English solo songs

---

[13] Miss White's political sense was weak. She incorporated into a song glorifying the Stuarts the tune which was said to have driven them out of three kingdoms.

(a few more in German). But in *Chrysilla*, with accompaniment either for instrumental ensemble or piano, she gave a fluent romantic setting to a sonnet by Henri de Régnier (in French and in a metrical English translation); and a different kind of skill in vocal expression is evident in her comic opera, *The Boatswain's Mate*.

Like Liza Lehmann, Sir Arthur Somervell (1863–1937) made his mark in song-cycles, of which 'Maud' (Tennyson) and 'A Shropshire Lad' (Housman) may particularly be mentioned. At a time when (both in ballads and serious songs) others felt it almost essential to vary the melody in successive stanzas to suit changed poetic emotion, Somervell frequently dared to write a simple strophic song: *Loveliest of trees*, the first of the Housman cycle, is one, and its melody is so strong and individual that it fully bears repetition. Moreover, it is recapitulated (first in the piano, then in the voice) in the last-but-one song of the cycle: *not* the last, a clever unconventional touch. Housman's verse, the prey of dozens of hungry composers of that period, has perhaps never been set better. The restraint of Somervell suits the poet much better than does Vaughan Williams's treatment in the cycle 'On Wenlock Edge', in which a string quartet in addition to the piano emphasizes the over-emotional approach to the texts.

Somervell's isolated songs include a curiosity:

Ex. 16

As I went forth one sum-mer morn-ing to take a walk a-mong the hills

Here, plainly, is the exemplar of Vaughan Williams's *Linden Lea*. Evidently thinking of Brahms's examples, and not liking the implications of the English word 'popular', Somervell on his title-page described the song as *in Volksweise*[14] (in popular style). When Frank Howes in his book on Vaughan Williams (1954) came to consider *Linden Lea*, he was similarly driven to German: 'It is, is it not? the only true *volkstümliches Lied*[15] in the corpus of English song'. The answer is no, it is not, though it remains incomparable.

Before considering Vaughan Williams further, we are confronted by two other commanding figures: Elgar and Delius. Yet Sir Edward Elgar (1857–1934), a major figure in orchestral and choral music, is something much less in song-writing. We cannot say (with his biogra-

[14,15] The actual words used by Somervell and Howes were '*Im* Volksweise' and 'Volkstümlichelied': such inaccuracies are not the best argument for the use of German terms in English contexts.

pher Percy M. Young) that he was not interested in the combination of voice and piano, since he continued to turn out occasional songs until 1931; but it seems that the restricted dimensions simply did not give room for the expression of his expansive gifts. It is not without significance that the cycle 'Sea Pictures' (five songs with orchestra) has had the most staying power, since its accompaniment evidently stimulated Elgar to greater subtleties than a piano could. In the fourth song of the set, *Where corals lie*, the voice ends in D major but the orchestra carries on to B minor – a process curiously paralleled in one of the better of Elgar's other songs, the sardonic *Inside the bar*. Also gaining much from their orchestral accompaniment are Elgar's charming contributions to the children's play 'The Starlight Express'.

It might be thought that the man who wrote the *Pomp and Circumstance* marches could beat the ballad-writers at their own game; but in fact Elgar's ballads have no particular distinction even within their own undistinguished class. Between *Pleading* by Elgar and *Homing* by Teresa del Riego (both with words by the same writer, Arthur L. Salmon) one might well choose del Riego's. Standing rather outside Elgar's other songs are the two called *The Torch* and *The River*, which would be worth reviving with the orchestral accompaniment which Elgar afterwards provided. They are subtitled 'Folk-songs: Eastern Europe' but this must evidently be a joke unnoticed by Elgar's biographers, for the place where they are supposed to have been arranged, 'Leyrich-Turasp', is non-existent (is it an anagram, a familiar Elgarian diversion?). Elgar gives a clue that he is joking by ascribing the paraphrase of the 'folk-song's' words to 'Pietro d'Alba and E. E.': 'Pietro d'Alba', an italianization of 'Peter Rabbit', i.e. a white rabbit, no more existed than Leyrich-Turasp.

Frederick Delius (1862–1934) is to be considered an English composer only by courtesy, so to speak. Though born in Bradford his musical affiliations were less with England than with Scandinavia (through the influence of Grieg) and with Germany, where he at first received more attention than in England. He dedicated to Nina Grieg (the wife of the composer and, as a soprano, the most famous interpreter of her husband's songs) his twelve early songs (1888–90) on Norwegian texts. These songs, with their drooping chromatic harmonies and their frequent echoing of the voice by the piano, bear Grieg's definite influence; yet they manage to be among Delius's best and most characteristic. That is equally true of the songs in Danish (1897) – in which are to be noted certain modal cadences, a technical feature which is more

159

conspicuous later with Vaughan Williams and others. It is our loss that the published versions give the songs in German (not the original language) and in an English which is often silly: retranslation is badly needed of such a song as *Sweet Venevil* (Norwegian text by Bjørnson).

From another of the Bjørnson songs, *Twilight Fancies*, comes an example of falling chromatic harmonies set to a tune which is itself diatonic and which earlier composers would never have harmonized otherwise than diatonically:

When the sun goes down, When the sun goes down.—

This, a characteristic of all Delius's work, left a lasting impression on the next generation of song composers – among them Peter Warlock (see page 169). Delius's three settings of Shelley (1891) represent an approach to the English ballad style: they show no particular musical merit and sometimes a lack of feeling for poetic scansion. A set of 'Old English lyrics' (well-known poems by Shakespeare, Nashe, Herrick and Jonson), composed in 1916, jettisons the ballad style and jettisons also some of the sentimental tenderness of the early works, but is hardly remarkable.

Much more remarkable are the settings of Dowson's *Cynara* for tenor and orchestra (1907) and of Henley's *A late lark* for baritone and orchestra (1925). Dowson's poem now reads like a treasury of quotations ('gone with the wind', 'I cried for madder music', 'I have been faithful to thee, Cynara, in my fashion'); but Delius, in Dowson's own day, admirably caught its dark nostalgia. (The accenting of *Cynara* on the first syllable is an oddity, possibly indicating that Delius first set the poem in the German translation made by his wife.) The setting, with the orchestral instruments standing out as soloists, and with its ending on a chord of the added sixth, should be compared with Mahler's *Das Lied von der Erde*, first performed in 1911. Like *Cynara*, the Henley setting carries a characteristically individual Delius orchestration, and a performance with piano would be no reasonable substitute.

Delius thus brings a master's use of 'modern harmony' to English song, and a new era is reached.

Into the twentieth century

Tonality; rhythm; melodic shape; the texture and instrumentation of accompaniment – in all these, English song underwent marked changes in the first half of the twentieth century. The changes were of course part of those which overtook English music in general during a period when so many major experiments were being carried on elsewhere. What is called 'the rediscovery of English folk-song' also occurred then, but it acted on the composition of new songs less as a direct influence than as a catalyst. Ralph Vaughan Williams (1872–1958) made dozens of arrangements of English folk-songs, some for voice and piano and some for chorus, but none of his own songs sounds like a folk-song. (From that generalization we may perhaps except *Back and side go bare*, from the opera *Sir John in Love*.)

Cecil Sharp (1859–1924), reckoned the chief though not the first of the folk-song revivalists, noted down his first song in 1903; and it was then that Vaughan Williams also began his quest in the English countryside for songs which, handed down orally for generations, still remained to be notated and published. For him, the discovery that many of the songs still used the old modes and that a few of them freely used an 'irregular' $\frac{5}{4}$ time, must have acted as a partial liberator. But it is significant that Gustav Holst (1874–1935) never cultivated folk music in this way, yet enjoyed the same kind of liberation as Vaughan Williams did: and indeed the two men shared a musical association no less intimate than their personal friendship.

Of the two men, Holst had the more radical mind. His interest in Indian religion, which led him to study Sanskrit and to produce that remarkable opera *Sāvitri*, also bore fruit in nine 'Vedic Hymns' for voice and piano (1907–8). Here are to be found the use of 5–4 and 7–4 metres, of the sharpened fourth and the whole-tone scale, and of a free declamatory vocal utterance – all features of Holst's most characteristic later work. The eighth hymn, *Creation*, starts with a subdued and almost monotonous stanza for voice alone, followed by the words *Then there was One*: and at the word 'One', sung softly, the piano sounds its low octave C's, also softly. It is a tremendous effect, no less so by comparison with Haydn's way of illustrating the creation of light a century before.

Austerity (let us use the word without implying praise or blame) clothes Holst's 'Four Songs for Voice and Violin' (1920), in which the absence of a piano shows a new and significant attitude towards song-accompaniment. The second of these songs, which are all to medieval religious texts, is only eight bars long; in it the violin supplies inter-jections between the singer's declamatory phrases, but in the fourth song the instrument accompanies in almost parallel fashion the steady march of crotchets and minims in the singer's voice. In 1929 Holst returned to the piano in a set of twelve songs to words by Humbert Wolfe which constitute as close a marriage between verse and music as can be imagined: moreover it is intellectual verse, far from conven-tional song-fodder. If the bare *Journey's End*, with its scale-climbing melody and its stark fourths, just fails to be a great song, it does so because (as often with Holst) its total intended effect seems to be implied rather than conveyed. The final song of the set, *The floral bandit*, is happy astonishment: it follows the poet in quoting Shakespeare's and Schubert's *Who is Sylvia?* (artistically, not in parody) and, at the con-cluding line 'breaks off her music in the middle', Holst's music does almost that.

Vaughan Williams followed Holst in using voice and violin for a set of songs to words by Housman: they were not published until 1954 (with the title 'Along the Field'), but were written more than twenty-five years before. Kinship with Holst is such matters as free-rhythmed declamation, changing bar-lengths, modal melody, and consecutive triads is shown by Vaughan Williams in *The new ghost* (1925). And yet it is not kinship that is most evident in this finely effective song, but individuality – comparable to that of such contem-porary works of Vaughan Williams as A Pastoral Symphony and the opera *The Shepherds of the Delectable Mountains* (both of which appeared in 1922).

From the same set of songs as 'The New Ghost' (to poems by Fredegond Shove) comes 'The Water Mill': deservedly famous, it shows that even if Vaughan Williams supposedly disliked the piano, he knew all about how to accompany a song with it. From an even earlier period – before 1910 – come not only *Linden Lea*, but the settings of R. L. Stevenson's 'Songs of Travel' (including *The roadside fire*) and of six sonnets from D. G. Rossetti's 'The House of Life' (including *Silent Noon*) – songs which were little prophetic of the later Vaughan Williams, yet which had and still have a freshness of their own. From the years before the 1914–18 war come also 'A Shropshire Lad' with accompaniment for string quartet and piano (see page 158) and two sets in which Vaughan Williams's music rises to a mature beauty in a vein which he associates with religious subjects. These two sets are the 'Five Mystical Songs', with optional chorus, and the 'Four

Hymns', for tenor, viola and either piano or strings. From the latter we may quote a typical phrase of this religious vein:

Ex.18

When this dry soul those eyes___ shall see And drink the un-seal'd source of Thee.

Rather curiously – though not without precedent in various other composers – Vaughan Williams gave Shakespeare's *Orpheus with his lute* two different settings, in about 1902 and again some twenty years later. Songs were thus an important part of Vaughan Williams's output till about 1930. They became much less so later on, perhaps partly because, as public interest in performances of solo song apparently waned, so Vaughan Williams seemed to prefer the opportunity of displaying his skill in song-writing within the larger forms of choral works (particularly happily in 'Five Tudor Portraits', 1936) and opera.

It was only later that the idiom of Vaughan Williams gathered many followers. Meanwhile, other song-composers continued to develop a tradition in which the Victorian ballad and the German art-song still formed the principal and partially opposite points of reference. Samuel Coleridge-Taylor (1875–1912), son of a West African father and an English mother, chiefly famous as the composer of the cantata *Hiawatha*, was less successful in his more deliberately artistic essays in song than in *Eleanore*, a piece of distinction within the ballad type.

Sir Granville Bantock (1868–1948) numbered among his works six volumes of 'Songs of the East', to verses written by his wife on subjects referring respectively to Arabia, Japan, Egypt, Persia, India and China. The oriental touches in these and other songs have been dismissed as mere 'Brummagem ware' (Bantock succeeded Elgar as professor of music at Birmingham University) – yet, after all, such things in Western music *must* be synthetic and formalized, and we do not hold Mozart or Verdi at less worth on that account. The trouble is rather that, with the occasional exception such as the strophic *Lament* in the Arabian set, Bantock's musical inspiration is not memorable. It is worth noting, however, that he was among the first English composers to write accompaniments demanding on occasion a really skilled modern pianist – as in *The nautch girl*, in the Indian set.

Sir Hamilton Harty (1879–1941) was an Irish Protestant like Stanford; and, like Stanford, he both arranged Irish folk-tunes and occasionally adopted elements of their style in his own songs. His song *The Sea Wrack* is strong and dramatic. Rutland Boughton (1878–1960) made one of the most famous contributions to the British singer's repertory in *The Fairy Song*, that delicately individual piece from the opera *The Immortal Hour* (1914). Boughton's isolated songs are sometimes marred by a certain stiffness in word-setting – as in the otherwise attractive *Immanence* (1914) with figurations and harmonies somewhat resembling Debussy's. Sir Landon Ronald (1873–1938), a son of Henry Russell, was a distinguished conductor who also composed many songs in the accepted taste of his time: *Down in the Forest* won extreme popularity. Charles Wood (1866–1926), notable as a university teacher and church musician, wrote many songs including *Ethiopia saluting the colours*: his poet here was Walt Whitman, whose great appeal to the English composers of that period (including Vaughan Williams) testifies to the new interest in song as conceived rhapsodically rather than in regular stanzas.

Sir Walford Davies (1869–1941) effected a charming semi-pastiche of seventeenth-century style in *An uncouth love-song*, of which the air is duly preceded by recitative; but his more ordinary songs are somewhat lacking in character, like those of Thomas F. Dunhill (1877–1946). There is more individuality and more dash in Frank Bridge (1879–1941), whose songs chiefly date from before the more modern style which stamps his later instrumental works. Of these songs, *Love went a-riding* is perhaps over-rated; but *Go not, happy day* (on the Tennyson poem which attracted so many composers, including Liszt[16]) is a masterpiece: the use in song of a perpetual-motion type of piano accompaniment was never bettered, even by Schubert.

In many songs of this period, however (and earlier), one may get the impression that the accompaniment is little more than comfortable padding, supplying harmonies that are implied anyway, and providing a routine overture to the song. An attempt to bypass this was made by Liza Lehmann's husband, Herbert Bedford (1867–1945), in writing songs which dispensed with accompaniment altogether. The first were issued in 1922. In these the voice must carry the whole weight of the

---

[16] Liszt's setting was contributed (in the year after that in which Bridge was born) to an English collection of songs on Tennyson's poems.

song, and the singer is instructed to announce the full title and author-ship of the song to replace the instrumental introduction: 'This requires to be rehearsed no less than the song.' The songs are short (some only about two dozen bars) but not easy to sing nor simple in their harmonic implications. Some of them, such as *The hay sings*, would do admirably as a so-called encore at the end of a group of normally accompanied songs.

Josef Holbrooke (1878–1958) wrote many songs, in a predominantly romantic vein. In the first of 'Six Landscapes' (1907) there is a curious apparent discrepancy between such old-fashioned touches as a 'turn' (musical ornament) and such a technical innovation as ending in a different key from that in which the song began. This same innovation is present in Holbrooke's *My Jean* (1910), and is also used by Cyril Scott (not very convincingly) in the song rather oddly called *Arietta* (1910).

Cyril Scott (b. 1879) is, as Holbrooke is not, a major composer of English songs. The *Arietta* bore (with an advertisement for other songs and piano pieces by Scott) a 'testimonial' by Debussy which described him as 'one of the rarest artists of the present time. . . . [His] music unfolds itself somewhat after the manner of those Javanese rhapsodies which, instead of being confined to traditional forms, are the outcome of imagination developing itself in innumerable arabesques.' There were those, indeed, who labelled Scott as 'the English Debussy'; and though the label is as imprecise as such things must always be, one can see the reason for it in Scott's *A song of wine*:

In the tritone in the melody (the intervals from E up to B flat and from B flat to E), in the consecutive fifths and consecutive sevenths in the harmony, in the passing use of the whole-tone scale, and in the use of vocal *glissando*, we can sense Scott's venturesome approach to song-writing: and this in a song dated 1909, from the set 'Song of Old Cathay', after Chinese poems. The same song incorporates a piano *glissando* on the black keys, and some other songs in the set end on a chord of the seventh or the added sixth. But such things do not only constitute technical innovation: they helped Scott to create some remarkably effective songs, whose latter-day neglect is rather more astonishing than the supposedly exaggerated vogue which the composer once enjoyed.

Among Scott's other notable songs, using the added-note chords and the harmony of fourths which were his characteristic, are *Lilac Time* (to words of Whitman, composed for Maggie Teyte, 1914), and *Sorrow*, written as early as 1904 with words by Ernest Dowson. A weakness of Scott's is his occasional heavy accent on an unimportant word; it is this insensitivity, as well as a conventional postlude, which prevents *The Huckster* (1921, with words by Edward Thomas) from being ranked with the songs of Hugo Wolf – with which, in its sense of character and its mixed sardonic and affectionate touch, it might otherwise be compared. Scott also took Mendelssohn's old label 'Songs without words' and used it literally – that is, for two wordless vocal pieces with piano. Partly with words, partly without, are an *Idyllic Fantasy* for voice with oboe and cello, and an *Idyll* for voice with a brilliantly written flute accompaniment.

Both Cyril Scott and Roger Quilter (1877–1953) studied at Frankfurt-on-Main with Iwan Knorr, but their paths diverged. The contrast is most clearly seen in the arrangements by Scott of old English songs with deliberately obtrusive, new harmonies, as compared with Quilter's arrangement of traditional nursery tunes in *A Children's Overture*, where the harmonies are occasionally enriched but are always faithful and never obtrusive. Quilter's songs may be regarded as a peak in that English tradition of decorous romanticism which is also to be found in Parry. Such a song as *Now sleeps the crimson petal* (Tennyson) showed how Quilter shared with Parry a particular sensitivity to the accentuation of words as well as a high standard in choice of verse.

Quilter's *To Daisies*, one of the songs which his melodic gift and his enriched harmonies combine to most haunting effect, is not of involved construction. In fact the plan of its three stanzas – basically similar, but with the note of climax going higher from one stanza to the next – is exactly paralleled in the popular ballad *I hear you calling me* (a good song by an otherwise unknown composer, Charles Marshall, published 1908). Quilter's excellence consists in doing the same kind of thing as so many other English song-composers but with surer taste.

To Daisies comes from a set of 1906 called 'To Julia' (poems by Herrick) which has a melodic link between the songs and also includes two not very striking piano solos as an introduction and an interlude between two of the songs.

Quilter composed many settings of Shakespeare, beginning in 1905 with three which include *O Mistress mine*. If this now seems rather marred by the sentimental effect of the final repeated line and the 'juicy' concluding chords, it is none the less effective in hitting on a strophic form which will do for the very different poetic meanings of the stanzas of the poem – a point in which Quilter excelled. Some of his songs are available also with the composer's own orchestral accompaniment, but the important thing is that Quilter was able to make his name chiefly through performances of his songs by voice and piano. That is, he was able to make a serious reputation. This was something new: it testified to a new readiness on the part of the public to receive this kind of song (as distinct from conventional ballads), and to the readiness of such singers as Harry Plunket Greene (1865–1936), Gervase Elwes (1866–1921), and John Goss (1894–1953) to pour their gifts into the interpretation of such music.

Among Goss's friends was Bernard van Dieren (1884–1936), who was born in Holland but settled in London in 1909. In 1921 he wrote a setting of the seventh sonnet of Spenser's 'Amoretti' for tenor and eleven instruments (including cornet and basset-horn) in contrapuntal chamber-music style and with a complex chromatic harmony. Here was a link with the world of Mahler and early Schoenberg: and van Dieren encountered much the same kind of resistance as Schoenberg – only, being polite and English, the resistance took the form of indifference rather than hostility. When Eric Blom (in Grove's Dictionary) speaks of van Dieren's 'tortuous' and 'unvocal' setting of words, he is not reflecting the standards of a more modern generation of singers. Today, indeed, such songs as *Take, O take those lips away* and *Weep you no more, sad fountains* (both published in 1925) would be found not only singable but finely effective for singing.

The two songs display two sharply different techniques, both typical of van Dieren. *Take, O take those lips away* has an accompaniment in which the acute discords arrive by contrapuntal processes; additionally, there are meticulous, almost note-by-note instructions as to dynamics (with exclamation marks, as in Mahler). In the other song the voice has a sustained melody, with pauses between each line of verse, while the piano pursues a steady movement of thick, homophonic chords (almost entirely in even crotchets) without bar-lines and with freely chromatic, sometimes nearly atonal harmony, *sempre pianissimo*. Strange as this effect is, it is yet more convincing than van Dieren's approach in *She I love* to a more conventionally conceived song.

Songs, together with piano music, also formed a major activity of John Ireland (born, like Quilter, Scott, Bridge, and Harty, in 1879). Ireland's *Sea Fever* (1913) is the last really well-known English song by a leading serious composer. Allowing even for the particular appeal to British audiences in John Masefield's words, it is still possible to realize the great musical skill in this song: its economy, in particular, becomes obvious by a comparison with *Bells of San Marie* (also by Masefield and Ireland, 1919). Both songs give prominence to the use of the major sixth in the minor key. But these easily assimilable tunes, like *Hope the hornblower*, *When lights go rolling round the sky*, and *I have twelve oxen* (to mention three more early songs), are only one side of Ireland's song-writing: he has also a more involved, more contemplative, and sometimes more darkly brooding side.

In his song-cycle 'The Land of Lost Content' (1921) he, like so many of his contemporaries, set Housman. But the fifth song, *The Encounter*, is entirely distinctive and gripping in its effect. The singer's melody is in what appears to be D minor, with not a single accidental, but includes neither F sharp nor F natural; yet the piano accompaniment, after having set up various contradictions between sharps and naturals and after making use of an ascending *ostinato* bass on the notes F, G, A, B (a tritone, confusing the idea of key), finally pulls the song round to C major. One has the feeling here, as in a few later songs of similarly dark mood, that Ireland is not far from atonality. An equally remarkable but quite different kind of song is *My fair* (poem by Esther Meynell) in the 'Songs Sacred and Profane' of 1934, which has the same tenderness (may we say the nostalgic tenderness?) that showed itself at this period in the slow movement of the piano concerto. In another Housman set, 'We'll to the woods no more', Ireland makes the remarkable gesture of following two songs with a piece for piano alone which ends the cycle.

That the piano should not be ranked lower than the voice was obviously also desired by Sir Arnold Bax (1883–1953) in such an early song as *Golden Guendolen*, composed in 1905 to a poem by William Morris. Here the stormy piano part (with Lisztian double thirds and perhaps a look towards Richard Strauss) is more imposing than the rather plain vocal line. More than twenty years later, setting *Out and away* (1926, to a poem by James Stephens), Bax was still pursuing harmonic complexity to an extent that seems to smother rather than illuminate the singer's message: at one point the piano part ascends the diminished-seventh line E, G, B flat, etc., with a changing chord alternately of the fourth or the sixth beneath each of these, all above the sustained bass notes F sharp and C sharp.

On this account Bax is not in the front rank of English song-writers, though his occasional works of simpler texture carry an appeal – among them *I heard a piper piping* and, in imitation-traditional Irish vein, *A rann of wandering*. It should be mentioned that Bax was not Irish, despite the association of his music with Irish subjects. Perhaps Celt-dom in general rather than Ireland in particular was his never-never land: some of his earliest songs (1904–5) were to poems on Scottish Gaelic subjects by 'Fiona Macleod' (William Sharp).

Before ever these were written, a young Australian studying in Germany had struck an extraordinary experimental note. Percy Aldridge Grainger (b. 1882) did not publish his song *The Men of the Sea* (one of several Kipling settings) until much later, but it bears a date which shows he composed it at seventeen. It has the curves and the downright simplicity of a folk-song, with the basis of one note to one syllable; its accompaniment, too, is simple, with no introduction; its harmonization is bold, not merely by beginning in A flat and ending in C minor, and not merely by its chains of consecutive fifths, but by its deliberate confusion at one point of tonic and dominant – an effect which today suggests a link with Britten. Grainger's capacity for experiment, it is true, does not seem matched by a like measure of genuine artistic creativeness; yet this and other early songs deserve to ensure that he is not remembered merely by his eccentric musical anglicisms ('louden lots' for *molto crescendo*, and so on). His folk-song arrangements, including the song *Six Dukes Went A-Fishing* as well as the instrumental version of the 'Londonderry Air', are notably fine.

Another but entirely different eccentric was Lord Berners (1883–1950) whose taste for humour led him to set Heine's *Du bist wie eine Blume* on the assumption that the poet was thinking of a pig. No mere joke, however, is *The Lady Visitor in the Pauper Ward*, with harsh bitonal chords which match the sharp attack of Robert Graves's poem.

These, however, were by-roads. On the main highway of English song the next milestone was set in place by 'Peter Warlock' (the pseudonym of Philip Heseltine, 1894–1930). Song-writing was his chief work, and his gift is distinguished by its absorption of so many

169

musically enriching elements – modern harmony, modal scales, free declamation, irregular barring – together with a contrapuntal ease, a felicitous treatment of words, and a taste for an occasional popular swinging tune. Or perhaps we had better call it not 'popular' (because this suggests the Victorian ballad type) but 'vulgar' in its good sense. There is something in songs like *Captain Stratton's Fancy*, *Good Ale*, and *The Countryman*, with their strong suggestions of solo-and-chorus (though the songs are in fact for solo only) which link them alike with folk-song, with the convivial songs of the seventeenth century, and with the music-hall of Warlock's own day. A curiosity is Warlock's *Johnnie wi' the lye*, of which the tune is a kind of cross between *Charlie is my darling* and *The keel row*.

Warlock keenly admired both van Dieren and Delius. The former's influence is seen in the contrapuntal chromaticism of Warlock's *Sleep*; while in his *Balulalow*, Delius's drooping chromatic harmonies are blended with modal scales and with cross-relations whose inspiration came from sixteenth- and seventeenth-century music. (He himself brought out able modern editions of various English compositions of that period.) But he had also, as Delius had not, a gift for brilliant piano writing: it is this which makes *Consider* a song as splendid a duet for voice and piano as any of Wolf's. Warlock issued some of his song-accompaniments in scoring for string quartet as an alternative for piano.

Warlock's *The Fox* is an intense, sardonic, declamatory song; *The Frostbound wood* is (though it will probably not be recognized in performance) a melodic *tour de force* which draws a wealth of tender expression while confining the singer to four notes, D, E, G, and A (with a final top E). When such songs as these are put alongside the jollity of the 'vulgar' songs and the bitter nostalgia of *The Curlew* (a cycle with accompaniment for flute, English horn, and string quartet), Warlock justifies by his range as well as by his individual works the title of a great composer of songs.

Warlock died of gas poisoning, presumably self-inflicted. Another premature loss was that of Ivor Gurney (1890–1937), who was wounded, gassed, and shell-shocked while serving in the 1914–18 War, and became insane in 1922. What he might have later become as a composer we do not know; the songs he did write show a fine sensitivity to words and a delicate matching of voice and accompaniment, in a somewhat restrictedly lyrical vein which forbids us to rank him with Warlock. Gurney's harmony is romantic but diatonic, and he modulates deliberately with 'rich' transitions like the change from C major to A flat or E flat; in general, his style is more related to Parry and to Schumann than to the moderns and the Elizabethans who stood to Warlock as joint sources.

Gurney, a poet himself, rarely set his own words: but he did so with distinction in *Severn Meadows*. In setting the words of other poets he occasionally (apparently by an unconscious trick of memory) made slight alterations in the words. He set Housman and the so-called 'Georgian poets' (Edward Thomas, J. C. Squire, etc.) and their contemporaries as well as Elizabethan verse. In such a song as *Nine of the clock* (Robert Graves) the effect is perhaps rather 'precious'. But in setting *Sleep* by John Fletcher (1579–1625) he wrote a masterpiece, as did Warlock. It is instructive to compare the two songs on this poem, which are entirely typical of their composers. It should be noted that Warlock specifically instructs the singer to treat the music as unbarred, and not to accent the first beat of the bar unless the sense demands it:

George Butterworth (born 1885, killed in action in 1916) was an early colleague of Vaughan Williams; his apposite settings of poems by A. E. Housman (including, notably, *Is My Team Ploughing?*) also furnished material for his orchestral rhapsody, 'A Shropshire Lad'. In the 1920s, such living poets as Housman, Walter de la Mare, and (among several Irish writers) Seamus O'Sullivan stimulated a number of composers to songs which are often intimate and craftsmanlike but not exciting. C. Armstrong Gibbs (b. 1889) found de la Mare particularly attractive: among his best settings are *Nod* and *Silver*. C. W. Orr (b. 1893) has set Housman almost exclusively, and less memorably than some other composers. Norman Peterkin (b. 1886) numbers among his many agreeable songs *Advice to girls* and *The garden of bamboos*, to texts adapted respectively from Chinese and Annamese: perhaps because he had actually lived in the Far East, he was able to set these without hackneyed westernized orientalisms.

Herbert Howells (b. 1892) carefully and mellifluously avoids the obvious, but rarely permits in his songs the harmonic complexity of some of his larger works. E. J. Moeran (1894–1951) was a friend of Warlock's, and the two were joint composers of *Maltworms*, a convivial drinking song with optional chorus. Some of Moeran's songs indeed resemble Warlock's, but there is a fine individuality in 'Six Poems by· Seamus O'Sullivan' (1944), with its strong 'architectural' contrast between songs composed straight through and those with a marked recapitulation or refrain. Moeran showed a certain Irishness in his music and his choice of verses, but (like Bax) was English-born. The deliberate attempt of Francis George Scott (1880–1958) to create an idiom of modern Scottish song, related both to folk-music and to the rhythms and inflections of popular Scottish poetry, resulted in his publishing six volumes of songs to Scottish texts ranging from William Dunbar to the present day. Only in the years since the 1939–45 War have these songs become fairly well known in Scottish musical circles, and they have yet to make their mark elsewhere.

Unlike these composers, Sir Arthur Bliss (b. 1891) was considered in his early career as a 'rebel' (the term 'Angry Young Man' being then in the future). His *Madam Noy* (1918), a song for voice and six instruments, and *Rout* (1919) for wordless soprano and ten instruments[17] show an influence of Stravinsky. In 1951 he ventured with some success on the apparently obsolete form of an extended dramatic 'scena' for solo voice and orchestra – with *The Enchantress* (words adapted from Theocritus). In the intervening period, from which come Bliss's best-known works, songs are not prominent; but his 'Seven American Poems' (1940) display a notable combination of disciplined modern harmonic resource with the traditional appeal of English song.

Arthur Benjamin (born in Sydney, 1893) came to London and studied with Stanford. His easy handling of the voice, and the fitness of his

---

[17] The accompaniment was later arranged for full orchestra.

generally romantic style to vocal writing, are demonstrated in his operas *Prima Donna* and *A Tale of Two Cities*. In isolated solo song, he is perhaps most notable for having introduced into English serious music the characteristic syncopation of the West Indies, as in *Linstead Market* (1948).

Benjamin indeed spans successfully and with integrity the increased gap between the serious and the popular spheres of music. There were others whose serious work won little attention but who successfully cultivated a few blooms in the still lingering drawing-room tradition. Examples are Wilfred Sanderson (1878–1935) with *Drake goes west*; Haydn Wood (1882–1959) with *Roses of Picardy* and *A brown bird singing*; Eric Coates (1886–1957) with *Bird songs at eventide*; and Montague Phillips (b. 1885) with *The fishermen of England* (from the operetta *The Rebel Maid*). The pseudonym 'J. P. McCall', as composer of a setting of Kipling's *Boots*, concealed the identity of a popular baritone, Peter Dawson (b. 1882). The actor, singer, and playwright Ivor Novello (1893–1951) composed not only music for his own stage shows but also *Keep the home fires burning*, immensely successful in the 1914–18 War.

But English light music, thus politely stagnating for the most part, gradually came to be vanquished in public favour by the livelier American songs of jazz and its derivatives. The distribution of popular song to its consumers was meanwhile revolutionized by the universal advent of the radio and the gramophone. (The British Broadcasting Company, as it then was, was set up in 1922; record sales rose until reaching a pre-slump peak in 1929.) Just about this time, the English folk-song revival penetrated the schools. So English city children sang in class about English milkmaids dabbling in the dew, but they sang for pleasure about a home in Wyomin'.

The Present Prospect

The composers who remain to be considered – all born in 1900 or after – were affected by these new circumstances. With the decline of drawing-room singing and the coming of mechanical reproduction, song-writing no longer offered composers one of the quickest ways of earning money: the film score and (if successful) the brief, breezy concert overture did that better. With the increased following for the symphony orchestra, the combination of voice and piano was no longer necessarily the medium through which the composer reached the widest audience: Benjamin Britten's *Serenade* and Lennox Berkeley's

'Four Poems of St. Teresa of Avila', both with stringed orchestral accompaniment, became better known than any contemporary songs with piano.

Nor was this all. The taste of recital audiences became generally fossilized round Schubert, Schumann and Wolf, especially as sung by picked German and Austrian singers with heavy commercial backing. Before seeking to capture such audiences, the living composer had to consider public reluctance to come to terms not only with modern music but with modern poetry – poetry which, from the 1930's, was often satiric, didactic, anti-romantic, and which no longer called sympathetically for music as Housman's or Bridges's had done.

Some of the older composers managed, nevertheless, to carry on more or less within existing traditions. Despite the reputation among his contemporaries which Gerald Finzi (1901–56) won for his seriousness, history is unlikely to see him except as an offshoot of Vaughan Williams – at his best in 'Dies Natalis', a song-cycle with religious texts and string accompaniment. (The fact that Finzi's posthumous song *At a lunar eclipse* was written entirely without bar-lines represents only a superficial novelty.) With other composers, the influence of Quilter or Warlock was more powerful. These and others exercised an apparent influence on Michael Head (b. 1900), who also became a successful recitalist as a singer at the piano. Warlock's influence shows obviously in the work of his friend, Elizabeth Poston (b. 1905), for instance in the modified archaism of *Sweet Suffolk Owl*. Even a younger composer might shut his eyes, pretend that nothing had changed, and write the 2,000th setting of *Sigh no more, ladies* in a jolly, neo-Warlock style. Geoffrey Bush (b. 1920) appears to have done just that, and to have done it quite well.

But for others, new challenges called forth new responses. A sturdy yet fanciful song, eminently individual, called *Tritons* was published in 1920 by a composer who was styled W. T. Walton on the title page: he was not yet nineteen. Yet, despite the gift for song-writing this revealed, Sir William Walton (b. 1902) thereafter left this activity almost entirely alone, as if irrelevant to a composer's relation with his public. Or rather, he found a new relevance for song with a new twist: for what is 'Façade', in its original form, but a set of 'Songs Without Tunes'? A similar lack of apparent interest in song-writing was shown by Alan Rawsthorne (b. 1905), although his tender song *Carol* shows that he could make a success of it.

If English song could be revivified, it needed a new kind of language, as distinct from the old as W. H. Auden's was from Walter de la Mare's. It needed a composer who thought vocally, was thoroughly modern, and was (above all) a major composer. And so it happened. It is hardly too much to say that with Benjamin Britten (b. 1913) English song has been born again. He developed an expressive musical language which looked to the expansive, declamatory utterance of Purcell (which may be called 'baroque' in its proper architectural sense of 'twisted and heavily ornate') as Warlock had looked to the composers of 1600; yet it was a language also enriched by the influence of two of the most individual of modern Continental masters, Mahler and Stravinsky. Moreover Britten, as a pianist, as a conductor, and as founder-director of the English Opera Group, was in constant practical association with singers and their art. Such singers, particularly Peter Pears (b. 1910) and Kathleen Ferrier (1912–53) in their turn greatly stimulated other composers.

'Let the *florid* music praise': it was an apt line for Britten to set in his early song-cycle, 'On This Island', to poems by W. H. Auden (1938). He then undertook cycles in French and Italian ('Les Illuminations', to poems by Rimbaud, and 'Seven Sonnets of Michelangelo') before arriving in 1943 at the now famous *Serenade* for tenor, horn, and strings. 'The Holy Sonnets of John Donne' and 'A Charm of Lullabies' were among the cycles that followed, and the fine *Nocturne* (1958), with orchestra, matches the *Serenade*. Britten also gave to the word 'Canticle' the peculiar personal meaning of an extended song for solo voice or voices, with piano, on religious or quasi-religious texts. The third Canticle (1954) on a poem by Edith Sitwell, is like the *Serenade* in using a solo horn as equal partner to a tenor voice – a procedure which owed its inspiration to the virtuosity of the horn-player Dennis Brain (1921–57). In this work, exceptionally, Britten makes a passing use of 'speech-song' (a device of Schoenberg's, according to which the stated pitch of a note is just touched, not sustained). This Canticle was written in memory of the gifted pianist Noel Mewton-Wood (1924–53), who committed suicide.

Britten's general musical style was brilliantly analysed and illustrated in a symposium published in 1952 (*Benjamin Britten*, edited by Donald Mitchell and Hans Keller). Here we may pick out three characteristics by which he enriched song in particular. First, by an enlargement of harmonic resource, particularly by a simultaneous combination of tonic and dominant harmony; second, by the florid, expansive, 'Purcellian' treatment of melody, especially the extension of a single syllable (not necessarily in an emotional word) over a long run of notes; third, by the building of accompaniments not through the extension of chords into continuous flowing lines, but through the use of short melodic motives often contrapuntally used and having both thematic and expressive value. Of the following two quotations, the first (from the *Serenade*) illustrates the first of the above points, and the second quotation (from *Canticle I*) illustrates the other two:

Important in Britten, moreover, is a definite flair for the popular, easy, swinging tune. This is most obviously seen in the audience-songs from *Let's Make An Opera!* (was there ever before a 'community song' in 5–4 time?) but is also present for example in *Albert Herring* (*Bounce me high, bounce me low*) and *Noye's Fludde* (the *Kyrie Eleison*). It is here, even more than in his folk-song arrangements, that Britten shows what it is now old-fashioned to call 'the common touch'.

That Britten has exerted a liberating influence on many composers, even those older than himself, need not be doubted. It is instructive to compare, for instance, two works of Edmund Rubbra (b. 1901). In

1928 he set *A duan of Barra* (duan means 'little song') very skilfully, but adhering to the fairly common formula of a folk-song-like tune with an accompaniment of added-note chordal harmonies. Quite different are the 'Three Psalms', published in 1947, significantly with a dedication to Kathleen Ferrier. The first Psalm, especially, is based on a florid voice-line and the repetition in the accompaniment of short, thematic patterns of notes. Rubbra has here achieved individual, fine music in which the newer elements are blended with those of an older lineage, perhaps stemming chiefly from Vaughan Williams.

Mátyás Seiber, who was born in Hungary in 1905 and came to live in England in 1935, dedicated to Peter Pears his song-cycle 'To Poetry' (1953). While standing successfully on its own feet, it carries a definite reminder of Britten's *Serenade*. It begins with an *Invocation* and ends identically with it, as Britten's work begins and ends with parallel (not identical) horn-calls, and Seiber's setting of William Dunbar's *Timor mortis* recalls the atmosphere of the Dirge in Britten's set.

That Britten should also join so many of his songs in sets or cycles, or extend them into 'Canticles' is also notable. It is as if the short, isolated song, suitable for musically echoing the gently romantic poetry of former days, was no longer apt for the musical expression of the different poetic ideas to which composers of lively minds were now attracted. This was indeed a general phenomenon of the 1940s and 1950s – a tendency to make the song into more than a song, and even the song-cycle into more than a song-cycle. Thus Alan Bush (b. 1900), writing the work which he called 'Voices of the Prophets' (1953), made of it something of a sonata in four movements for piano and voice (one may deliberately choose that order of mention). It was dedicated jointly to Noel Mewton-Wood and Peter Pears. Bush's music, closely interwoven and predominantly diatonic, follows a somewhat austere style entirely his own. In this work the voice delivers its utterance in a somewhat impersonal and uninteresting way, rather as the vehicle for a kind of 'pure music': were it not for this, one might tolerate even the banal neo-Whitmanesque political verse with which Bush chose to follow up his selections from Isaiah, Milton, and Blake.

Michael Tippett (b. 1905) shares with Britten a devotion to Purcell, and he dedicated to Britten and Pears his cantata for tenor and piano, 'Boyhood's End'. Like Bush's cycle, this has something of the character of a sonata in several movements. Its onward flow is emphasized by Tippett's striking choice of text – not a poem, not anything divided into regular lines of stanzas, but a prose passage by W. H. Hudson. As in Britten, we notice the characteristic florid vocal line and the thematic value of the accompaniment: they are blended with that pronounced use of chords of the fourth which, with certain methods of contrapuntal progression, Tippett owes to Hindemith. It is an effective work; and equally so is Tippett's song-cycle 'The Heart's Assurance'. Especially fine, perhaps, is the matching of words, music, and mood in the fourth song, *The Dancer*.

Of Lennox Berkeley (b. 1903) we have already noted the 'Four Poems of St. Teresa of Avila' for contralto – with which, again, Kathleen Ferrier was especially associated. A pupil of Nadia Boulanger, Berkeley has developed an idiom poised between a modern tendency to concise expression and an older romantic feeling. If the 'Four Poems' show the result at its best, Berkeley's setting of a *Spring Song* by the Greek poet Antipater (in 'Three Greek Songs', 1953) is also thoroughly happy. Although at one time closely associated with Britten, Berkeley has maintained a distinct independence from Britten's style.

Another pupil of Nadia Boulanger was the South African woman composer, Priaulx Rainier (b. 1903), who has lived in Britain since student days. Her 'Cycle for Declamation' – yet another work dedicated to Peter Pears – uses the word 'declamation' in a different sense from the usual: this is an unaccompanied work, a setting of lines from John Donne (including the now over-quoted *For whom the bell tolls*). Its handling of the solo voice, whose part is notated in exact rhythm, is remarkably assured and varied: whether the work can be called a success appears to depend solely on the acceptability of the medium.

Howard Ferguson (b. 1908) took five poems by Denton Welch for his song-cycle 'Discovery', for voice and piano. All the songs but the final one are very short, the whole cycle lasting barely seven minutes. The effect, somewhat epigrammatic and didactic rather than emotional, is pleasantly distinctive, and is emphasized by the transparent musical texture and the almost entirely syllabic treatment (one note, one syllable). Benjamin Frankel (b. 1906) also favoured syllabic treatment in his song-cycle 'The Aftermath' (1947), on a text by Robert Nichols, though the harmony is thick compared to Ferguson's. Frankel's vocal line may seem to be somewhat monotonous, though strikingly accompanied by strings, an off-stage trumpet, and kettle-drums. (Pedal drums are needed, as is also a gong, though it is not specified on the title page.)

The artistry of the young guitarist and lutenist, Julian Bream (b. 1933) led Britten to compose a set of 'Songs from the Chinese' (1958, not a major work) for voice and guitar. The guitar was also inventively used by Humphrey Searle (b. 1915), together with flute and cello, as accompanying instruments to a speaker in a setting of Edward Lear's 'The Owl and the Pussycat': the speaker's part is notated only in approximate pitch, and the accompaniment is written according to the twelve-note method. (The mating of Schoenberg and Edward Lear is unexpected but not ineffective.) Searle also used the twelve-note method in setting W. R. Rodgers's *Put Away the Flutes* for voice and six instruments – emotionally telling music, dedicated to Peter Pears.

Britten's re-editing of Purcell's Latin elegy on the death of Queen Mary (*The Queen's Epicedium*), together with the success of Alfred Deller (b. 1912) in resuscitating the counter-tenor or male alto voice for secular use, doubtless stimulated the composition of *The Tomb of Saint Eulalia* by Peter Racine Fricker (b. 1920). This is a setting for counter-tenor (or contralto), viola da gamba (or cello) and harpsichord (the piano *not* given as an alternative) of a Latin text by Prudentius. Published in ultra-Third-Programme manner, without a translation for singing or otherwise, it deliberately evokes seventeenth-century style (with many ornaments, usually written out in full); but it is disappointing in its lack of florid expansiveness in the vocal part.

In general, however, Fricker – like Richard Arnell (b. 1917), Malcolm Arnold (b. 1921) and Iain Hamilton (b. 1922) – achieved post-war prominence through music other than songs. A rarity, indeed, is a young, lively-minded composer who *has* cultivated song with some success: John Joubert (b. 1927). He borrowed from jazz the trick of an accented syllable falling half a beat before the expected strong beat. Not that the result is anything like jazz: rather might one say, on the strength of such short and successful songs as *Stay, O sweet, and do not rise*, and *My love in her attire*, that here are the makings of a modern Quilter.

Not, of course, that there can be another Quilter, any more than that Britten is another Purcell. Reasons have already been given why songs for the conventional recital are not likely to occupy a major part of an English composer's output today. A composer inclined to song may feel more impelled to put his gifts into opera or – following the admirable example of Antony Hopkins (b. 1921) in *Three's Company* – into satiric operetta. Or he may find that, despite the dominance of

179

America in the field of commercialized entertainment, the revue stage still offers to the serious composer an opportunity to display his craft lightly – as Donald Swann (b. 1923) has done. One may indeed envisage the possibility that the stage may become, as it was in pre-Victorian times, the main avenue through which (apart from Tin Pan Alley) new songs are presented to the public.

The prospect of English song in the traditional sense is, accordingly, not bright. But the number of good English songs in the past still awaiting their proper exploitation in the present is considerable.

Czechoslovakia

GERALD ABRAHAM

UNLIKE the music of Russia, that of the lands that constitute the modern republic of Czechoslovakia has always formed part of the main stream of European music, strongly influenced by it and valuably contributing to it. Indeed, so many 'Czech' composers – among whom we commonly, if wrongly, include Moravians and Slovaks as well as true Czechs – have settled in Germany, England, France, Italy and Russia that it is not always easy to decide whether they belong to the history of Czechoslovak music. Only if Handel's oratorios are to be classed as 'German' can we consider the songs of Reicha 'Czech'. Even the language test is not decisive, for Smetana composed German poems before he turned to Czech ones. The history of Czech music is further complicated by political events – above all, the Thirty Years War – which seriously interrupted the natural development of native art, so that the rich heritage of the Middle Ages – the songs of the wandering scholars, Hussite song, the secular songs of the early fifteenth century – was not directly handed on as the basis for a deep-rooted specifically Czech tradition.

In the eighteenth century we find Czech composers employing the favourite European vocal forms without marked individuality or national flavour: e.g. J. A. Plánický (c. 1691–1732) in his collection of solo motets 'Opella ecclesiastica seu Ariae duodecim' (Augsburg, 1723)[1], which are stronger in the recitatives than in the arias, and J. L. Dukát (1684–1717) who wrote Italianate solo cantatas with two violins ('Cithara nova', 1707). (The earliest known Czech piece of solo church music is the *Concertus de resurrectione* (1691) of Ferdinand Bernard Artophaeus, for soprano, two violins, two violas and organ.) Music with Czech words is rare at this period, but there is a setting of the Czech translation of the 150th Psalm as an aria for bass and orchestra by the leading baroque master J. D. Zelenka (1679–1745), probably composed for the Bohemian Brethren at Dresden. A younger composer, František Xaver Brixi (1732–71), a member of one of the famous Czech musical families, composed both arias in Neapolitan style and Christmas *pastorely*. These pastorals, solos or for several voices, usually accompanied by a little orchestra and organ, were performed all over the country in the village churches and very often composed in the eighteenth century by the village *kantoři*: curious fusions of the style of Czech popular song with that of the Viennese classics. They played an important part in the evolution of the Czech national idiom and lasted into the middle of the nineteenth century.[2]

It was the simple, popular songs of the village cantors, schoolmasters and organists, to whose musicianship in the 1770s J. F. Reichardt paid generous tribute in his *Briefe eines aufmerksamen Reisenden*, which set the pattern for the later development of the Czech solo song as surely as the *romances* of the aristocratic dilettanti did for the later development of the Russian art-song. The consequence was natural; Czech song has been generally unpretentious and – lacking the stimulus of poets of the rank of Pushkin – less sophisticated than that of Russia. Famous 'emigrants' such as Jiří (Georg) Benda and Josef Mysliveček wrote solo cantatas and numerous arias and ariettas, and Leopold Koželuh, who went no farther from home than Vienna, published sets of 'Ariette italiane', 'XV Lieder beym Clavier zum Singen' and 'XII Lieder mit Melodien beym Clavier'[3] (both Vienna, 1785), and Masonic *Lieder* (Berlin, c. 1800). (There was a good deal of Masonic song-composition by Czechs at this period.) But Koželuh did not altogether neglect his native language; his *Číhání* ('Lying in wait') was printed posthumously in K.S. Macháček's first collection of 'Zpěvy

---

[1] One specimen reprinted in Jaroslav Pohanka, *Dějiny české hudby v příkladech* (Prague, 1958), No. 112. See also the study by Camillo Schoenbaum in *Acta Musicologica*, XXV (1953), p. 39.
[2] A solo *pastorela*, dated 1859, by Jan Michalička is printed in *Musica antiqua bohemica*, No. 23.
[3] No. 11 of the *XII Lieder*, *Liebeserklärung eines Mädchens*, is reprinted in *Studien zur Musikwissenschaft*, V (Leipzig and Vienna, 1918), p. 141.

české' ('Czech Songs') (Prague, 1825). Jirovec (Gyrowetz) also set Czech words occasionally.

Tomášek and his Contemporaries

The real founders of the Czech art-song bear names much less familiar. The most important was Koželuh's pupil, Jakub Jan Ryba (1765–1815). Despite their German titles, Ryba's 'Zwölf böhmische Lieder' (1800)[4] and 'Neue böhmische Lieder' (1808) are settings of Czech poems mostly by Šebestián Hněvkovský and the Nejedlýs – the music as naïve as the words. In 1808 he also published 'Dar pilné mládeži' ('A Gift for Industrious Youth'), a book of children's songs, a field in which he had been preceded by Mozart's friend F. X. Dušek. Ryba was also the composer of the earliest ballad in Czech, a setting of Vojtěch Nejedlý's *Lenka*, modelled on Zumsteeg (1808), and the earliest Czech romance, *Průvod od dobré Bětolinky*, on the same poet's translation of some verses attributed to Hölty, Jan Doležálek's Czeské Písně v hudbu uvedené' ('Czech Songs set to music')[5] came out in Vienna in 1812.

It was perhaps the success of these publications which induced the greatest Czech composer of the day, Václav Tomášek (1774–1850), to turn to his native language. From 1800 onward Tomášek had been a fairly prolific composer of *Lieder* by Hölty, Voss, Tiedge and others: sets of songs Opp. 2, 6, 33, 34, 37 and 44, Bürger's *Lenore*, Op. 12, Schiller's *Leichenphantasie*, Op. 25, to say nothing of four Italian canzonets, Op. 28. Then in 1813, 'lest I should quite forget my mother-tongue' (as he says in his autobiography), he composed 'Šestero písní' (Six Songs) to Czech words, which he published in Prague, four of them to poems by Václav Hanka: they are very naïve but not without charm; the set is prefaced by a 'Word to Patriots' concerning the special suitability of the Czech language for musical treatment. Tomášek did not abandon German; indeed he composed a great many more *Lieder*, including a series of seven Goethe sets, Opp. 53–59 and four Schiller sets, Opp. 85–88. But he returned in Opp. 50 and 71[6] to Hanka, set five poems by K. E. Ebert, Op. 69, and five excerpts from his 'Czech national epic' *Vlasta*, Op. 74, and – most interesting of all – six 'Starožitné písné' ('Ancient Songs') Op. 82 (1823), on words from the notorious Kralové Dvůr manuscript, then generally believed to be a

---

[4] Example in Pohanka, op. cit., No. 155.
[5] ibid., No. 160.
[6] Op. 71, No. 2, in Pohanka, op. cit., No. 158.

specimen of ancient Czech literature, actually a forgery by Hanka and others. To Tomášek himself, and to Hanka and his friends, it seemed that the unusual texts had opened a new vein for him in music, and it is true that the 'Starožitné písné' have novel touches. Consider No. 5, *Žežhulice* ('The Cuckoo'):

'In the broad field stands an oak tree, in the oak a cuckoo; it cuckoos and laments that it is not always spring.'

Some of Tomášek's songs were published in the first volume of 'Věnec ze zpěvů vlastenských uvitý a obětovaný divkám vlastenským' ('A garland woven of patriotic songs and offered to patriotic young ladies'), a collection edited by the poet Josef Krasoslav Chmelenský (not to be confused with his contemporary, the composer Jan Chmelenský). Macháček's collections of Czech songs have already been mentioned, but Chmelenský's 'Věnec' is much more important. It was an annual publication and appeared for five years, 1835–39[7]. Despite the title, the first volume contained a few opera-songs by Mozart and other non-Czech composers. Nor are all the Czech songs original songs-with-piano; Chmelenský's co-editor František Škroup (1801–62) printed a number of songs from his stage works – including the one which eighty years later was adopted as the Czech national anthem, *Kde domov muj?* ('Where is my home?') from *Fidlovačka*. All the same, 'Věnec' presents an interesting cross-section of Czech song during the period of Smetana's youth, from Doležálek and Tomášek to such younger composers as Josef Vorel (1801–1874); many of the songs are

[7] Complete list of contents in Zdeněk Nejedlý, *Bedřich Smetana*, II (Prague, 1925), pp. 438–41.

settings of Chmelensky's own words, obviously written 'for music';
but the musical level is generally low.[8] A few years later Škroup tried
to revive 'Věnec', but only one volume appeared – in 1844.

Smetana and Dvořák

The non-existence of a strong tradition of Czech solo song is
curious, considering the intense musicality of the Czechoslovak peoples,
especially their love of song. The explanation is perhaps to be found in
two circumstances: the country was bilingual and many patriotic
Czechs, including Smetana, felt themselves more at home in German
than in their mother-tongue so that the better composers tended to
compose *Lieder* in the styles of the German masters; on the other hand,
genuine Czech song – as represented in 'Věnec' and other collections –
was apt to be weak and sentimentalized imitation of folk-music,
inferior to the comparable work of Varlamov or even Gurilev in
Russia. Czech song never had a Glinka or Moniuszko to crystallize tradition, and the solo song with piano has never occupied a
central or near-central place in the work of any important Czech
composer.

The case of Smetana (1824–84) is typical. At sixteen he made his
first – never completed – essay in song-writing: a setting of Schiller's
Der Pilgrim. And all but one of his handful of earlier songs are to
German texts: *Liebchens Blick* and *Lebe wohl* (which are headed 'Gesang-
komposition 1. Lied. – 2. Das durchkomponierte Lied', i.e. they are
composition exercises), the Wieland *Schmerz der Trennung* and Jacobi
Einladung (all four written in 1846), and the much finer *Liebesfrühling*
(*Dieses Saitenspiel der Brust* from Rückert's famous cycle) of 1853, which
might be a rejected number from Schumann's Op. 37. The one early
Czech song is a setting of Kollár's *Píseň svobody* ('Song of Freedom')[9]
written during the patriotic excitement of 1848. Then a quarter of a
century passed before Smetana returned to solo song. But for his
'jubilee concert' in Prague on 4 January 1880 he composed five of
Vítězslav Hálek's 'Večerní písně' ('Evening Songs'), a collection of rather
feebly romantic lyrics which had already attracted Dvořák and Fibich.
The 'Večerní písně' are Smetana's best songs, but by no means his best
music. The choice of words was obviously meant very personally: e.g.
the first two, *Kdo v zlaté struny zahrat zná* ('Give honour to him who

[8] Examples by Vorel and J. N. Škroup (1811–92), František's brother, in Pohanka, op. cit.,
Nos. 165 and 166.
[9] In Pohanka, op. cit., No. 175.

knows how to sound the golden strings') and *Ne kamenujte proróky*
('Do not stone prophets. For singers are like birds, for ever fleeing him
who throws a stone at them.') But the music hardly suits the theme and
both these songs seem pianistic in origin, the words to have been fitted
later:

Ex. 2

The third song – *Mně zdálo se* ('It seemed to me that pain had already
grown old') – is declamatory, the fourth a polka (with a twist), while
the fifth and best and most extended – *Z svých písní* ('Out of my songs
I'll build a throne for you') – returns to the exultant mood and the
pulsing triplet accompanying chords of *Liebesfrühling*.

The songs of Dvořák (1841–1904) are a different matter. He was
hardly one of the world's great song-writers, but, like Tchaïkovsky, he
was a great composer who wrote songs throughout his creative life –
some of them very fine indeed. His earliest essay in this field was the
cycle of eighteen 'Cypřiše '('Cypresses') to poems by Gustav Pfleger-
Moravský, composed in July 1865 under the immediate influence of
his passion for the actress Josefa Čermáková, whose sister he afterwards
married. 'Cypřiše' in their original form are naïve and awkward compositions and were never published, but they were always peculiarly
dear to Dvořák and he used their material in operas and piano pieces;
as late as 1887 he turned twelve of them into movements for string
quartet. But twelve also appeared later in revised forms as songs:
Nos. 1, 5, 11, and 13, were published in 1882 as Op. 2;[10] Nos. 8, 3, 9,
6, 17, 14, 2, and 4 were revised the following year and published as
'Pisně milostné' ('Love Songs'), Op. 83, in 1888. The extreme simplicity of Op. 2 has suggested to some critics that in this case revision
was slight. This is not true; on the contrary, the simplicity of
(for instance) No. 4 represents a great improvement on the fussy
original:

[10] Opp. 2, 5, 17 and 31 are published complete, but with English and German words only,
as 'Sixteen Songs' by Novello. Most of Dvořák's other songs were published by Simrock; they
have not yet appeared in the Czech 'complete edition' of his works.

'Quiet on the hills, quiet in the valley.'

And four and a half $\frac{4}{4}$ bars of piano introduction have been reduced to two of $\frac{3}{8}$. The workmanship of Op. 83 is finer but even here Dvořák sometimes left the original voice-part unchanged, as in No. 8, O, *duše drahá, jedinká* ('Thou only dear one'); the song was put up a semitone, the clumsy accompaniment totally rewritten, but the original voice-part remains except for the final cadence and a magic modification in bars 10–11 (and 12–13):

'Oh, would I were a singing swan.'

Even in their revised forms, most of these songs of Op. 2 and Op. 83 are essentially *Lieder* in the veins of Schubert, Schumann or (once or twice) Mendelssohn, though with many individual touches. And some of them – *Mé srdce často* ('My heart often in sadness'), Op. 2, No. 3, *O, naší lásce nekvěte* ('Our love will never blossom') Op. 83, No. 1, *Já vím, že v sladké naději* ('I know that in sweet hope'), Op. 83, No. 4, and – a special favourite of the composer's – *Zde v lese u potoka* ('Here in the forest by the stream'), Op. 83, No. 6 – are things that no one but Dvořák could have created.

During 1871–2, stirred by Ludevít Procházka's public appeal for the creation of a Czech national music, Dvořák composed a whole group of songs: four poems from a book by Smetana's friend and librettist Eliška Krásnohorská, the ballad *Sirotek* ('The Orphan') by K. J. Erben, four translations of Serbian folk-songs, and six poems from the Kralové Dvůr manuscript – the same six that Tomášek had set as his Op. 82 half a century earlier. The Kralové Dvůr songs were published complete in 1873 as Op. 17; in 1879 Simrock published the first four, with *German* texts, as Op. 7. Simrock also issued Nos. 2 and 4 of the Krásnohorská songs with German texts as Op. 9, Nos. 1 and 2, in 1879, and the Serbian songs with German texts as Op. 6 the following year. *Sirotek* belatedly found a Czech publisher in 1883 and appeared with its original words as Op. 5. The Kralové Dvůr songs are the best of this group; the Serbian songs are feeble and the Schubertian ballad, *Sirotek*, is a failure. One of the Krásnohorská songs, *Proto* ('Because'), Op. 9, No. 1, is specially characteristic of a type of song with which Dvořák experimented at this period presumably in an attempt to break away from German models: the melody is broad and hymn-like but flows in asymmetrical phrases. However, *Proto* is earthbound by its dull chordal accompaniment. A similar style is employed more successfully in No. 5 of the Kralové Dvůr songs, *Opuščená* ('The Deserted Girl'), but the two most original songs of this set are *Róže* ('The Rose') and *Žežhulice* ('The Cuckoo'); neither is wholly successful yet Dvořák must have been pleased with the opening of *Žežhulice* for he used it again ten years later in the first movement of the great F minor Trio. Some of the other songs of Op. 17 are charming in a vein that suggests folk-song or, rather, Schubert at his most *volksliedartig*.

Next, in 1876, came twelve settings of Hálek's 'Večerní písně', from which Dvořák had set two (never published) as early as 1865. Instead of being published together, two appeared in 1880 (with German texts only) as Op. 9, Nos. 3 and 4, four came out in 1881 as Op. 3[11], five were revised in 1882 and published the following year as Op. 31, and one – condemned on the autograph copy as 'weak' – never appeared at all. For the German versions of the 'Večerní písně' Dvořák used an existing translation of Hálek's poems, altering his vocal line to fit it: an apparently sensible idea which, as we shall see in connexion with the 'Biblické písně', sometimes had unfortunate results. Op. 3, No. 1 (*Ty hvězdičky tam na nebi*, 'Thou art like the little stars'), with its asymmetrical phrases and its simple chordal accompaniment, is a more successful essay in the style of *Proto*, and the mature fruit of this line of experiment appears in Op. 31, No. 4, *Vy všichni, kdož jste stísněi* ('All ye that labour') with its free and original declamation in five-bar phrases. But Op. 31 contains all the best of the 'Večerní písně': the sweeping and powerful *Když jsem se díval do nebe* ('When I looked up to the heavens'), the delightful *Jsem jako lípa košatá* ('I am like a spreading lime-tree'), and two charming, light-handed songs in the lighter *Lied* style.

Of the 'Tři novořecké básně', Op. 50[12] ('Three Modern Greek Poems', i.e. Czech translations of Greek folk-poems), the best is the third – originally the second – *Žalozpěv Pargy* ('Lament for Parga'), another piece of free declamation. All three are dramatic ballads and were originally composed with orchestral accompaniment for the baritone Josef Lev to sing at the concert of Dvořák's works at Prague on 17 November, 1878. But full mastery appears, though even then not always, in the songs of the 1880s: the 'Zigeunermelodien' Op. 55, of 1880, the settings of folk-poems (1885–6), and the 'Vier Lieder', Op. 82 (1887). The pressure on Dvořák to produce songs with German texts is revealed here, above all in the fact that although Adolf Heyduk's poems which inspired the 'Zigeunermelodien' are Czech, the music was actually written to German versions prepared by the poet himself. Again, the two songs without opus-number composed at Sydenham in May 1885 – of which the first, *Schlaf' mein Kind in Ruh'*, is quite enchanting – are settings of German translations of Czech folk-poems. The 'Zigeunermelodien' are too well known for their real merit to be properly appreciated; the first and last, *Mein Lied ertönt* and *Darf des Falken Schwinge*, are full-blooded masterpieces – as in its different way is the hopelessly hackneyed *Als die alte Mutter* – while the three dance-songs and the deeply felt, if slightly Brahmsian, *Rings ist der Wald* are worthy foils. The whole cycle, except No. 3, is completely Dvořákian

---

11 Dvořák scored the accompaniments of Op. 3, Nos. 2 and 3, for small orchestra a little later.
12 An edition with English words is published by Hinrichsen.

and completely Czech. The same may be said of the four songs 'Ve slohu prostonárodním' ('In Folk-Style'), Op. 73, settings of three Slovak folk-poems and one Czech; the first, *Dobrú noc* ('Good night') is a masterpiece of an unusual kind, a *passionate* serenade, and at least the second and third are hardly inferior. Op. 73 was provided with German translations by Otilie Malybrok-Stieler and in gratitude to this undistinguished poetess Dvořák composed four of her poems as Op. 82, though he had them translated into Czech and 'made the music to both texts at the same time, only hoping that the declamation is good'.[13] (Declamation was never his strongest point.) The best is No. 3, *Frühling*, but the others contain some very beautiful passages.

The problem of Czech and German texts is raised in its most acute form in Dvořák's last cycle, the ten 'Biblické pisně', ('Biblical Songs') Op. 99, written in New York in 1894.[14] He originally set these excerpts from the Psalms in the seventeenth-century Czech version of the so-called 'Kralice Bible', but realizing the impossibility of fitting a tolerable German translation to his music, he completely rewrote the voice-parts and, in doing so, destroyed much of their rhythmic life. (The familiar English text is wretchedly cobbled on to the German vocal line.) Again and again characteristic triplets and syncopations are obliterated. Yet even in their true forms, the *Biblické pisně* are very unequal and often disappointing. As in other of Dvořák's works of the 'American' period, the workmanship is apt to be facile and slipshod. The exquisite simplicity of No. 4, *Hospodin jest můj pastýř* ('The Lord is my shepherd'), is one thing, the embarrassing naïveté of some of its companions quite another. One would be sorry to lose *Při řekách babylonských* ('By the waters of Babylon'), but several of the songs remind one too effectively that the composer enjoyed playing the organ in the village church at Spillville, Iowa.

Fibich and the Epigones

The composer whom Czech critics tend to bracket with, if a little below, Smetana and Dvořák is Zdeněk Fibich (1850–1900). Fibich was a very fine miniaturist and a copious song-composer, though the greater part of his output in this field remains unpublished. He leans toward Schumann and Franz, and appears to have composed more German than Czech poems; Heine attracted him above all and one of his very earliest songs, *Dämmernd liegt der Sommerabend*, Op. 3, No. 2, written

---

[13] Covering letter to Simrock, January 21, 1888.
[14] Nos. 1–5 orchestrated by the composer the following year.

at sixteen, supplied him years later with the chief theme of the wood-spirit in his symphonic poem *Toman*. His Op. 5, composed in 1871, consists of five of Hálek's 'Večerní písně' but of the four ballads that constitute Op. 7 (1872–3), the best are the two Heine pieces, *Loreley* and *Tragödie*, the latter a real masterpiece. Nearly all Fibich's best songs date from the 1870s: the cycles 'Jarní paprsky' ('Gleams of Spring') Op. 36, and 'Šestero písní' ('Half-a-dozen Songs'), Op. 12, and a number of separate songs, including *Kytice* and *Žežhulice*, from the Kralové Dvůr manuscript. The late opus-number of *Jarní paprsky* is due to the fact that it was withheld from publication until No. 1, Vrchlický's *Předtucha jara* ('Presentiment of Spring'), was added in 1891 – a song which epitomizes Fibich's double allegiance, for the first nine bars are pure Schumann while what follows is unmistakably Czech. Among his last works are five delightful children's songs, 'Poupata' ('Buds'), Op. 45.

Another composer of this period who was attracted by the Hálek 'Večerní písně' was the rather older Karel Bendl (1838–97); like his friend Dvořák, Bendl also set a cycle of Heyduk's 'Cigánské melodie' ('Gypsy Melodies').

As in Russia at the same period, a host of talented epigones came to the fore during the late nineteenth and early twentieth centuries, most of them pupils or disciples of Dvořák or Fibich. Among those who distinguished themselves as song-writers are J. B. Foerster (1859–1951) – particularly in the two Falke cycles 'Noční violy' ('Night Violets'), Op. 43, and 'Láska' (Love), Op. 46 (1899–1900), Rudolf Karel (1880–1945), and Vitězslav Novák (1870–1949). Novák was one of the few Czechoslovak composers who have written a considerable corpus of solo song (including a number of pieces, mostly to words by Jan Neruda, for voice with orchestra). In his nonage he was content to follow more or less closely in the footsteps of his master Dvořák, even venturing to rival him by setting some of Heyduk's 'Cigánské melodie' (Op. 14) (1897). A slightly earlier cycle 'Pohádka srdce', Op. 8 ('A Fable of the Heart'), was one of the first compositions with which Novák attracted attention and during the pre-1918 period he produced several other notable cycles – 'Melancholie', Op. 25, 'Údolí nového království' ('The Valley of the New Kingdom'), Op. 31, 'Melancholické písně o lásce' ('Melancholy Songs concerning Love') with orchestra, Op. 38, 'Notturna', Op. 39, and 'Erotikon', Op. 46 (the last two to German words originally) – in which he revealed a highly passionate nature and employed a more modern harmonic vocabulary. Then, except for 'Jaro' ('Spring'), Op. 52, two sets of children's songs – one to be sung *to* children, the other *by* children – came a hiatus in his song-writing which lasted until 1944 when he took up an old idea. At the end of the last century he had published three sets of 'Písničky na slova lidové poesie moravské' ('Little Songs on Moravian Folk-Poems'), Opp. 16, 17, and 21; now he produced two more, Opp. 74 and 75, which are comparable with similar things by Bartók and contain some of Novák's most delightful music. The cowherd's song, *Pasu krávy, pasu*, Op. 74, No. 1, for instance, is quite enchanting. A few other songs date from this last period.

Janáček and the younger generation

The Moravian Leoš Janáček (1854–1928), though older than Novák or even Foerster, emerged from relative obscurity much later than they – in fact, only during the First World War. He is a far more original figure but he owes his place in the history of the Czech art-song to only one work: the famous 'Zápisník zmizéleho' ('Diary of One who Vanished'), a setting of a sequence of short poems that had been found by the police in an exercise-book belonging to a young Moravian peasant of good character whose mysterious disappearance they were investigating. The poems, which were evidently autobiographical – outlining the story of the young man's seduction by a gypsy woman, his shame, and his resolve to leave home and parents and run away with her – were published in a Brno newspaper and deeply interested Janáček. During 1916–19 he made a novel semi-dramatic setting in which the tenor takes the part of the hero, Janik, singing on a half-darkened stage; in the ninth, tenth, and eleventh numbers a contralto, representing Zefka the gypsy, comes on unobtrusively and a trio of female voices comments off-stage; No. 13 is for piano solo. If the general idea is novel, the music is equally so, as far as Czech music is concerned. Whereas most Czech composers have tended to think instrumentally, or at any rate to put pure melodic line before word-setting, Janáček's ear for verbal intonation was exceptionally acute; not only does his voice-part carry the words very subtly and sensitively; his verbally inspired motives sometimes provide the thematic germs of instrumental texture – as they do in the piano-part of 'Zápisník zmizelého.'

Two other Moravians, both pupils of Janáček – Vilem Petrželka (b. 1889) and Jaroslav Kvapil (b. 1892) – have been far more prolific song-composers than their teacher but far less gifted. Of Novák's older disciples, among whom also Petrželka must be reckoned, Vycpálek (b. 1882), Křička (b. 1882), Axman (1887–1949) and Jirák (b. 1891) have

been the most notable song-composers, of his younger ones Alexander
Moyzes (b. 1906), Eugen Suchoň (b. 1908) and Ján Cikker (b. 1911), all
three Slovaks. A much more individual composer who also studied
with Novák for a time (as well as with Křička and Foerster) is Alois
Hába (b. 1898), protagonist of quarter-tone and sixth-tone composition;
he has written two sets of songs in the quarter-tone system – 'Dětské
nálady' ('Children's Moods'), Op. 51, and 'Poesie života' ('Poetry of
Life'), Op. 53 – as well as others in the more normal one, using the
guitar as accompanying instrument in both Op. 51 and Op. 53. A more
moderate, eclectic modernist is the expatriate Bohuslav Martinů
(1890–1959); he too has written songs, including settings of Czech folk-
poems (his 'New "Špalíček"' of 1942), but as with so many Czech
composers his solo songs with piano have only been relatively unimportant footnotes to his *oeuvre* in general.

France

DAVID COX

Votre âme est un paysage choisi
Que vont charmant masques et bergamasques
Jouant du luth et dansant et quasi
Tristes sous leurs déguisements fantasques.

Tout en chantant sur le mode mineur
L'amour vainqueur et la vie opportune,
Ils n'ont pas l'air de croire à leur bonheur
Et leur chanson se mêle au clair de lune. . . .

HERE, in Verlaine's famous *Clair de Lune*, is enshrined the spirit of French song, from the early *airs de cour* to Debussy's 'Fêtes galantes' and beyond. Fastidious beauty of line (*paysage choisi*), direct sensuous enjoyment of sounds, often under fantastic disguises. A spirit which comments intelligently and wittily, never taking the passing show too seriously, and seeming to believe neither in its own happiness nor in its sorrow. There is a lack of anything suggesting morbid introspection or moral high-mindedness. French song is a completely different world from German song; and in spite of strong foreign influences at various times during the last three hundred years – Italian, German, Spanish, oriental – it has managed, all in all, to maintain its characteristically French qualities through everything that has happened. Francis Poulenc, one of the most sophisticated of French song-writers, has said: 'You will find sobriety and sadness in French music, as in German or Russian music. But the French have a finer sense of proportion. We realize that sombreness and good humour are not mutually exclusive. French composers, too, write profound music; but when they do, it is leavened with that lightness of spirit without which life would be unendurable.'

In the history of solo song, France's heritage is rich and important. From the middle of the sixteenth century we find many polyphonic compositions being arranged and published for solo voice with lute accompaniment. By the seventeenth century the reign of the solo song was established. The monodic character (as distinct from the poly-phonic, with several voices on equal terms) asserted itself more and more, the form became more flexible, and the accompaniments for lute, guitar, or harpsichord, instead of being mere figured basses, were often carefully written out.

The poetry of the songs reflected the over-precious tastes of the society for which it was written: pastoral affectations; the unhappy lover sighing and complaining; the beauty of his mistress's eyes; and so on. The songs were of many varieties: the *air de cour*, courtly, refined and amorous; the simple *pastourelles* and *bergerettes*, about shepherd and shepherdess, or the like; the *romance*, descendant of the Troubadour songs; *chansons narratives*; *vaudeville*, from *voix de ville*, or popular tunes heard in the street; dance songs and drinking songs (*chansons à boire*, *chansons à danser*); the *brunette*, simple, unaffected, tender, lighthearted, named from the dark-haired girl to whom it was often addressed. The *chanson à voix seule* could take any of these forms, and many others.

In seventeenth-century society everyone from the king downwards showed an interest in vocal music. Louis XIII showed such an interest that he composed songs and sang them himself. The number of dis-tinguished singers, male and female, was immense. In many cases, the singers were the composers, and they accompanied themselves as they sang.

French songs and singers, in the early seventeenth century, found great favour at the English Court. As early as 1597 Charles Tessier, who was a *musicien de la chambre du roi*, came to London, and published there his collection of *Chansons et airs de cour*. And his earlier collection of *Airs* (1582) was dedicated to Elizabeth I.

One of the most important composers of this time was Pierre

Guédron, who was said to surpass all others in talent, fertility, and reputation. His songs were known in many countries besides France. They are extremely varied, mature, and (for their time) highly developed and showing a fine dramatic sense. The lute parts, instead of slavishly following the voice, often show signs of achieving independence – as in the excellent song *Quel espoir de guarir*.

The above version, which follows very closely the original accompaniment, is taken from Peter Warlock's admirable collection, 'French Airs' (O.U.P., 1926), which includes also another of Guédron's best songs, *Aux plaisirs, aux délices, bergères*.

Other famous names were Antoine Boesset, whose fame outlived that of Guédron; and Gabriel Bataille, an excellent lutenist, who made and published several collections of songs. Later in the century came Michel Lambert, many of whose songs are highly developed – *Vous ne sauriez, mes yeux* and *Ombre de mon amant* (two of his best) being in rondo form. Sébastien Le Camus often began his songs with an instrumental introduction. Michel de la Barre was adventurous and a good craftsman, sometimes trying unusual forms. One of his airs is entitled *Rondeau sur le mouvement de la chaconne*. (But the theme of the chaconne is not strictly maintained.)

Most of the early collections of songs are called *Airs* or *Airs de cour* –
a term of very wide meaning, including not only solo songs but songs
for several voices – not only serious, gallant, refined songs, but popular,
vulgar, bawdy and drinking songs. By *air de cour*, however, was
usually meant the gallant and somewhat over-precious *musique courtoise*.
In form, these were short and strophic – the quatrain and sizain being
the most commonly used. The rhythm of the words was followed
without contrapuntal complications of treatment. The first stanza acted
as pattern for those which followed. But often variants of the stanzas
(*doubles*, as they were called) were found in solo songs. Normally the
melody divides into two sections, each of which can be repeated.
Variations in mood and embellishments were generally left to the
singer.

The *récit* sought to heighten expression by greater liberty, by declamation, descriptive passages, richer ornamentation. And as a reaction to
the somewhat mannered *airs de cour*, there were the *airs bachiques*, trivial
and burlesque forms of song, gay and dance-like, celebrating the
pleasures of wine and of the flesh. They were not spurned by the most
refined society. Molière liked to use them in his plays, and Louis XIV
liked to hear them sung by young girls.

The vocal music of the *ballets de cour* is of considerable importance
in the history both of song and of early opera. This was of three kinds:
récits which explained and commented on the subject of the spectacle;
chansons mesurées, or rhythmic songs (for one or several voices) which
accompanied certain dances; and songs of varied kinds inserted episo-
dically, having no bearing on the action. All these became increasingly
interesting as they departed from the normal couplet form.

Early song collections

An immense number of song collections were published in the late-
sixteenth, seventeenth, and eighteenth centuries – among the most
notable being 'Airs de cour et de différents auteurs', five books published
between 1615 and 1623 in Paris by Pierre Ballard, 'imprimeur de la
musique du Roi' (for more than two hundred years the Ballard family
held the monopoly of music-printing in France, similar to the
monopoly which was held in England by Tallis and Byrd). Another
was 'Brunettes ou petits airs tendres', including also a large number of
chansons à danser, collected and arranged by Christophe Ballard
and published in 1704 and 1711. A very interesting collection
covering five centuries was entitled 'Anthologie Française ou chansons

choisies depuis le treizième siècle jusqu'à présent', published by Monnet in 1765.

A good idea of the range and scope of these collections – of the kinds of song that preceded the birth of the *mélodie* (as the accompanied art-song since Berlioz's day has come to be called) – can be gathered from a useful collection published in recent years (Durand), edited and (considerably) arranged by J. B. Weckerlin, under the title 'Echos du Temps Passé' (three volumes), a collection of *chansons, Noëls, madrigaux, brunettes, musettes, airs à boire et à danser, menuets, chansons populaires*, etc., from the twelfth to the eighteenth century. Here the enterprising singer will find, for example, a song attributed to Henri IV, *Charmante Gabrielle*; a *chanson à boire* from Marc-Antoine Charpentier's music for Molière's *Le Médecin malgré lui*; and – besides songs by Jannequin, Guédron, Boesset, Michel Lambert, Pierre Ballard, and many others – a song and psalm-setting by Clément Marot, one of the great poets of the early sixteenth century. Marot's song (*Plus ne suis ce que j'ai été*) is charming, and very characteristic of its time.

Another collection published in recent years is 'Chants de la Vieille France', twenty *mélodies* and *chansons*, ranging from the thirteenth to the eighteenth centuries, transcribed and harmonized by Julien Tiersot (Heugel). In the introduction Tiersot says: 'We find one feature common to most of these songs – a melancholy, which, though taking on many guises, casts a veil over everything and thus confirms what Schopenhauer said about French music: "The *allegro* in the minor key is common and very characteristic; it is as though somebody started to dance with shoes that hurt him." ' This collection includes a *pastourelle* of the King of Navarre (*La bergère et le roi*) from the thirteenth century; the wonderful melody *L'Amour de moi*, noted in different forms in many song-books from the fifteenth to the seventeenth centuries; the famous ode of Ronsard, *Mignonne*; the *musette, Clairs Ruisseaux*, which Tiersot calls 'one of the best examples of what one might call the *genre Watteau* in music'; a touching setting by the Swiss-born Jean-Jacques Rousseau of the Willow Song from Shakespeare's *Othello*

Ex. 2

A - le - xis de - puis deux ans A - do - rait Gly - cè - re

(called *Romance du Saule*), and another song by Rousseau, *Romance d'Alexis* (see Ex. 2) a favourite poem of this composer (three different settings of it are found in the collection of his *romances* published after his death under the title 'Les Consolations des Misères de ma Vie').

From 1700 onwards

The seventeenth century, as we have seen, was a rich period in the history of French solo song, with a range and variety that was immense – though it would be difficult to discover any vocal composition displaying such rhythmic and melodic flexibility combined with depth of expression as we find in some of the songs of John Dowland. In the eighteenth century the musical stress was on opera; and the principal opera composers (such as Monsigny, Philidor, and the Belgian-born Grétry) did not trouble much about solo song, except to write a few *bergerettes* and *romances* here and there. At the beginning of the eighteenth century, however, certain French composers produced chamber-cantatas, a form which had developed in Italy. Jean-Philippe Rameau wrote a small number of these, mostly for one solo voice with *basso continuo* (harpsichord with viola da gamba), and usually a violin. These were published in 1728, and form a volume of Rameau's complete works (Durand). One of the most gracious and attractive of these is *Orphée*, which in form is typical of all these cantatas of Rameau. Three arias interspersed with recitatives tell the familiar Orpheus story.

The four books of cantatas by Louis Nicholas Clérambault, also, contain fine, ornate examples, in a style which combines French and Italian elements – such as we find in the charming extended work *L'Amour piqué par une Abeille* (1710) for high voice and figured bass.

Among François Couperin's vocal music are to be found some airs for solo voice and *basso continuo* – a sombre, impressive *Air sérieux* of 1697 (*Qu'on ne me dise plus*), and a *Brunette* of 1711, each of the five couplets of which is ornamented in a different way – being in fact an instructive exercise in eighteenth-century ornamentation.

Before discussing the *mélodie*, of the special kind which developed in the nineteenth century, mention should be made of the many patriotic songs produced by the troubled period of the French Revolution. The most famous, of course, is *La Marseillaise* by Rouget de Lisle. It is probably the most loosely-constructed song ever to achieve popularity: there is no form about the tune whatever, yet it is one of the most stirring ever written. It cheered the Marseilles volunteers of 1792 and it has cheered the French on other occasions of national stress. Other songs of Rouget de Lisle (*Hymne à la Raison, Hymne à la Liberté*) are now only of historic interest – as are the patriotic songs of François-Joseph Gossec, who was also an official composer of the Revolution.

From Romance to Mélodie

The *romance* was the descendant of the Troubadour songs. In his *Dictionnaire de Musique*, 1767, Jean-Jacques Rousseau describes the *romance* as divided into strophes in accordance with the poem, the subjects being mostly 'quelque histoire amoureuse et souvent tragique'. He adds: 'As the *romance* is written in a simple, touching style, with a somewhat antiquated flavour, the tune should be in keeping with the words: no ornaments, nothing mannered – a simple, natural, rustic (*champêtre*) melody, which makes its effect of its own accord, without depending on the way it is sung. . . . For the singing of *romances* one needs no more than a clear, carefully-tuned voice, which pronounces the words well, and sings simply.' In the words of one who favoured the return to nature and the simple life, such was the *romance* – the form which was to provide the point of departure for so many song-writers that came after – including Berlioz, Gounod, Bizet, Fauré. In a way, the *romance* was to the French song-writers what the German folk-song was to the great *Lieder*-composers.

In his book *La Mélodie Française de Berlioz à Duparc*, Frits Noske points specially to *Plaisirs d'amour*, the famous *romance* of Martini, published in 1784, as being of particular interest in that it is in rondo form, with a specially designed piano part, and with prelude, interlude and postlude. The artistic level of the *romance*, he says, then developed in a way that distinguished it from the simple *romances* of Rousseau, Monsigny, and others. He goes on to distinguish two types of *romance*: the first is where expression has first place, structure is freer, and the piano part, showing German influence, underlines the meaning of the words. Such were the *romances* of Adrien, Méhul, and d'Ennery. The other type, more Italian, is where the melodic line has a purely musical character, not contradicting the text, but not specially underlining its meaning – and with a simple harmonic or arpeggio accompaniment. Such were the *romances* of Plantade, Boïeldieu, d'Almivare, Pradher, Carbonel. And examples of both types are found in the work of Doche, Lemoine, and Gail. After about 1815, the romance declined and broke up into many forms – barcarolle, tyrolienne, chansonnette (humorous or anecdotal), nocturne, tarantelle, boléro, and so on. The *scène*, also – with its free structure, its combination of *récit* and *chanson* (*arioso*) –

came much into favour; and about 1825, the *romance dialoguée* appeared, created by Auguste Panseron, with voice and piano on equal terms, and often another instrument descriptively introduced, as in his *Le Cor* and *Le Songe de Tartini*. Thereafter, as regards the *romance*, the rot set in, with the bourgeois, inelegant effusions of Loïsa Puget, so popular in their day, and the immense number of albums of *romances* published during the nineteenth century, becoming more and more banal and cliché-ridden. Francesco Masini was 'the Bellini of the Romance', and the enormous popularity of the countless *romances* by Antoine-Louis Clapisson spread to Victorian England.

From about the time of Berlioz the term *mélodie* has been used to signify the French *pièce vocale* (piece for the voice), with its combination of rhythmic flexibility, melodic subtlety, and harmonic richness, as we find on such a high level of perfection in the mature songs of such composers as Fauré, Duparc and Debussy. It is thus distinguished from the songs in which melodic line is everything. Why the word *mélodie* came to be established is not clear. '*Mélodies*', however, was used as a French title for Schubert's *Lieder*; and Berlioz seems to have been the first composer to call his short vocal works *mélodies* with any consistency.

The main forerunners of the *mélodie* were the Swiss-born Niedermeyer (see p. 400) and Hippolyte Monpou. Strongly attracted to romantic poetry, Monpou set many poems by Alfred de Musset and Victor Hugo. The publication of *L'Andalouse* in 1830 (Lemoine) made him famous. But although the exotic and bizarre qualities in his songs are arresting, he was not a musically interesting composer.

What is of special interest about the setting of romantic verse is that it led naturally to greater freedom of melodic structure. The lines of uneven length meant the abandonment of the stereotyped *phrase carrée* of the *romance*. In this, Monpou, Halévy and Clapisson, minor composers, were pioneers. And something of the harmonic experimentation of Berlioz is foreshadowed in a song like Adolf Vogel's *Satan*.

In Berlioz's youth, the *mélodie* had not developed far. His earliest songs, such as *Le Dépit de la Bergère* (Leduc), are in conventional *romance* form. But by the age of twenty-seven, we find him writing a work of great originality – the 'Neuf Mélodies Irlandaises', Op. 2 (1830), to words adapted from poems by Thomas Moore, in which the formal symmetry and expected cadences of the *romance* are no longer to be found. *Le Coucher du Soleil*, from this set, is particularly impressive; and the *Élégie en prose* (No. 9), which Berlioz described as extremely difficult to sing and to accompany, is already an expression of extravagant romanticism; and it is not without significance that it is dedicated to Harriet Smithson, the object of the composer's passion. The poetry of Gautier inspired Berlioz in his great song-cycle 'Les Nuits d'Été' (1841). The accompaniments, originally for piano, are perhaps more effective in their orchestral version, for Berlioz was never happy when writing for the piano. Nevertheless, the remarkable imagination of these songs —besides great depth and beauty—comes through in their original form. There is something special about each of the songs, but probably the most moving is *Sur les lagunes*, with its mournful refrain (underlined by the accompaniment): '*Ah! sans amour s'en aller sur la mer!*'

After 'Les Nuits d'Été' Berlioz returns to a more *romance*-like style in his songs (which are not numerous) – and with less satisfying results. *La Captive*, Op. 12 (c. 1832), to a poem by Victor Hugo, became very popular, however; and *La Mort d'Ophélie* (1848) vividly expresses Berlioz's disillusionment on re-encountering *Hamlet* and his 'Ophelia de jadis' – his Harriet.

Very different are the songs of Meyerbeer. A collection of forty of them, published in Paris in 1849, show a wide variety of types, but not specially French. Nor are Liszt's settings of French poems (Hugo, Musset, Dumas, and others) French in style, but directly influenced by German *Lieder*. During the Second Empire and the beginning of the Third Republic the German influence was felt, but it never seriously affected the blossoming of a typically French school of song-writers.

Of these, Charles Gounod is important and had considerable

influence – though Ravel surely went too far when he called him 'le véritable instaurateur de la mélodie en France'. He wrote about two hundred songs, basing them on the strophic, *romance*-like form, but influenced by Schubert, Chopin, and Mendelssohn, elements of whose styles were transplanted and acclimatized. The best, with but few exceptions, are the early ones, written before 1870 – and most of these are to be found in the two volumes published by Choudens. After 1870 there was a deterioration in quality, the early charm and freshness departed, the successful composer pandered to the tastes of the masses, and we have the crude sentimentality of the religious songs, and the banality of the English songs (including *Maid of Athens*). But, here and there, one finds in Gounod something of real excellence – a combination of melodic freshness, gracious simplicity, and many harmonic touches of a personal kind – as, for example, in the famous *Sérénade*; the settings of old poems, such as *Le Premier Jour de Mai* (Passerat) and *O ma belle rebelle* (Baïf); *Viens, les gazons sont verts* (Barbier); his second setting of *Ma belle amie est morte* (poem by Gautier, set also by Berlioz). *L'Absent* with its subtly changing harmonies might almost be by Fauré:

According to Saint-Saëns, Gounod saved French verse and prosody from the careless way in which it had been handled by foreigners – in the settings of Offenbach and Flotow, for example. Gounod was always scrupulously careful in his word-settings. But just how subtle a matter the compromise between tonic accent and melodic accent is, in French song, has been made very clear by Frits Noske in *La Mélodie Française*. The musical accent normally falls on the last sounded syllable of a French word. But this is certainly not a hard and fast rule. In the phrase 'bois jolis' the stress would fall on the second syllable of 'jolis'; but in the phrase 'jolis bois', the first syllable of 'jolis' would have the stress. Why? It is difficult even for a French musician to give a convincing reason. But there is no doubt that foreigners commit many barbarisms when they set French words to music – and in our own day, no more glaring example of this could be found than Benjamin Britten's settings of Rimbaud, *Les Illuminations* (Boosey, 1940), in which there are many 'howlers', including such things as stressing the first and third syllables of 'après-midi', instead of the second and fourth.

To return to the nineteenth century – Félicien David, composer of sixty songs, had great success in his day. Within the framework of the *romance* he showed the influence of Schubert particularly. There is charm and freshness in *Les Hirondelles*; exotic variety in the collection 'Les Perles d'Orient' (dated 1845); and a fine example of the extended *pièce vocale* in *Le Jour des Morts* (composed 1837).

There is nothing particularly striking about the songs of Victor Massé, Henri Reber, and Ernest Reyer. Neither Bizet nor Delibes seems to have been particularly interested in the writing of songs; but nevertheless both these composers left some charming examples. Bizet wrote about forty-eight songs in all, most of which are in the two volumes published by Choudens and Heugel. Among the best are those in which the dramatic element is present, as in *Adieux de l'Hôtesse arabe* (Victor Hugo). But also, the *sicilienne* rhythm of the *Sonnet* (Ronsard) is charming; and *Guitare*, *Pastorale*, and the *Berceuse* (based on an old tune) are near-perfect in their way.

Similarly, Léo Delibes wrote some colourful and dramatic songs. *Départ* ('Partons, mes amis; j'ai soif de courir') is a sort of *scène* and strongly dramatic. The grace and attractive rhythms of *Myrto*, *Avril*, and *Les Filles de Cadiz*, bring these songs vividly to life. Though Delibes's songs are often exotic in content, he was always essentially a French composer. (Collections of his songs were published by Hartmann and by Heugel.)

A picture by Aublet, 'Autour d'une partition', shows Jules Massenet seated at the piano surrounded by beautiful and enraptured young ladies – which is some indication of his immense popularity. Although Massenet was an important composer for the stage, he shows in his 200-odd songs that he understood perfectly the rôle of the voice in the drawing-room. In style he is a follower of Gounod, but with a greater refinement and sensibility. The acclimatized influence of Schumann is felt; and his output includes song-cycles, a form which Massenet might be said to have established in France. There is always a sensitive feeling for the words; and the musical interest is usually divided equally between voice and accompaniment, as with Schumann. As a professor of composition at the Paris Conservatoire for the last thirty-four years of his life, he had an influence on the younger composers rather similar to that of Stanford in England. From Massenet's large output of songs, some of the most impressive should be mentioned: the 'Poème d'Avril' (Hartmann; composed 1866) consisting of a prelude and seven pieces (words by Armand Silvestre); the fresh and charming 'Poème pastoral' (Hartmann; composed 1872) also divided into several sections (the words by Florian and Silvestre); and, one of the most interesting, the collection 'Expressions lyriques' (Heugel, 1913), one of the vocal works in which he used rhythmic declamation as a contrast to singing – a procedure which became rather a mannerism, (see Ex. 5.)

Although remembered chiefly for his *Symphonie Espagnole* for violin and orchestra, Edouard Lalo wrote some remarkably fine songs. Apart from the words, however, there is nothing particularly French about them. The German influence is very strong. Parts of the song

Ex.5 (Modéré)

Où donc al-lez-vous, Ma-da-me, Sans pos-til-lon ni pi-queur?

Oh, quand je dors, one of his best, might have come straight out of Brahms. So fine is the craftsmanship of a song such as *Guitare,* or the *Ballade à la lune,* and so well did he know how to catch the atmosphere and meaning of the poems he set, that he deserves a fairly important place in the history of French song. He wrote one really astonishing song, *Amis, vive l'Orgie,* which appeared in the first edition of the 'Six Mélodies', Op. 17 (Maho, 1856 – now Hamelle) but in subsequent editions was replaced by a more moderate setting of the same words under the title *Chanson à boire.* The first version is far more original and striking.

César Franck, Belgian-born, wrote comparatively few songs. The heavy romantic quality in his music, with its strong German influences, make him one of the most un-French of composers who made France their home. But his highly personal idiom, and his *père séraphique* personality, led to the founding of a school of composers, of which Vincent d'Indy was one of the leading spirits.

Two of Franck's early songs are notable for their Schubertian freshness and charm: *Souvenance* (dated 1846; poem by Chateaubriand) and *Robin Gray* (poem by Florian). Later, in his maturity, we feel the shadow of Gounod in the background (Gounod, who also was German-inspired) in the fine song *Le Mariage des Roses* (composed 1871; Enoch) which deserves to be heard more often; while in his setting of L. de Fourcaud's poem *Nocturne* (1885; now Enoch) there is drama, nobility, and depth of feeling, making it one of his best. The famous *Panis*

Angelicus, however, is a sentimental effusion of no particular musical interest. Undoubtedly the finest is *La Procession* (composed 1888; Leduc) which is published with orchestral and also with piano, or organ, accompaniment. The subject is the blessing of the crops – the procession of the Host through the fields – and very effective use is made of the plainsong melody *Lauda Sion* in the accompaniment.

Compared to Franck, Camille Saint-Saëns seems a very superficial composer who wrote too much too quickly in too many different styles. He was indeed a remarkable mixture: a fine pianist, a forceful master of prose, and a disquietingly fluent composer. In some of his early songs he even set German words in a purely German style – and the German influence was always strong in his work, without ever being really assimilated (for he was the most styleless of composers). And later in life, he, of all people, was to attack Wagner for his teutonizing effect on French music! The qualities that can save Saint-Saëns's music, including some of his songs, are a spontaneous lyrical gift, a colourful imagination, craftsmanship, and a sense of humour. *La Cigale et la Fourmi* (poem by La Fontaine) is cleverly effective. *Le Pas d'armes du Roi Jean* (Richault, 1855 – now Billaudot), to a poem by Victor Hugo, is remarkable, especially for a boy of seventeen. There is a solemn beauty about *Plainte* (Richault, 1855), and a bogus oriental quality about the 'Mélodies persanes' (Durand, 1872). We can find pretty well everything in Saint-Saëns, but nothing in particular.

The one collection of songs by Alexis de Castillon, 'Six Poésies d'Armand Silvestre' (Heugel), composed between 1868 and 1873, show the remarkable promise of a composer who died at the age of thirty-four, before reaching artistic maturity. In spite of many faults, these songs show great originality and an ability to realize musically the inner meaning of a poem in a way that we never find in the songs of Saint-Saëns.

Vincent d'Indy's large output includes comparatively few songs. He was a pupil and follower of César Franck and a great admirer of Wagner; his music has a seriousness of purpose and a sombre beauty. A fine example of his song-writing is the *Lied Maritime*, Op. 43 (Rouart, Lerolle, 1910 – now Salabert) – to the composer's own words – with its effective portrayal of distant storm at sea.

Most of Emmanuel Chabrier's songs are in *romance*-like form, but expressed with wit, brilliance and a considerable imagination. The *Villanelle des petits canards* (Enoch) and other amusing animal songs (such as *Ballade des gros dindons* and *Pastorale des cochons roses*) are particularly attractive.

Fauré, Duparc and Debussy

The three great masters of French song were undoubtedly Fauré, Duparc and Debussy. In each case, we find a superb achievement that is highly personal, and in each case a temperament and mentality essentially French.

The composer Charles Koechlin has summed up the characteristics of Gabriel Fauré's songs as follows: '. . . No "popular" inspiration; also, he quickly freed himself from the couplet form – ever since the *Lamento* [written at about the age of twenty]. In short, externally and inwardly, he shows a subtlety – French and quite special (indefinable in a few words) – which stems from the musical language, the nature of personal taste, a certain restraint in expression, an imagination rich, varied and precise. There is no comparison between his *mélodie* and the German *Lied*.'

The musical language, in the early songs of Fauré, is perhaps akin to that of Gounod. But very soon many personal touches are found, such as the characteristic melodic rising through the intervals of a tritone, found at the beginning of *Lydia* (1871), one of the best of the early songs.

In Fauré it is usual to find a lyrical vocal line combined with subtly changing harmonies in the accompaniment. The rhythms are remarkably varied, and his method of compromise between melodic stresses and verbal stresses – one of the major problems of French word-setting – is highly personal, as the flowing line of *Au bord de l'eau*, with its gentle syncopations, proves. For a combination of elegance and sensibility it would be difficult to find a more satisfying example than *Mandoline*, or, in a different way, the *Sérénade toscane*. When a descriptive element is introduced – such as the swaying figures of the accompaniment in *Les Berceaux* representing the rocking of boat and cradle – the musical integration of such an idea is achieved with wonderful restraint and artistry. On the other hand the three Baudelaire songs are not satisfactory, because there are elements in Baudelaire which temperamentally Fauré was incapable of expressing. For more convincing musical setting of this poet we have to wait for Debussy. There are other things, however, which Fauré could express to perfection: *Clair de Lune* (Verlaine), for example, with its archaic evocation of *masques et bergamasques* of a bygone age; or the luscious, exotic perfumes of the Leconte de Lisle settings – *Les Roses d'Ispahan* and *Le Parfum Impérissable*. (The latter was said to be Fauré's favourite amongst all his *mélodies*.) The four volumes of Fauré's collected songs (Hamelle and Durand) are an invaluable possession.

Besides, there are the song-cycles. Of supreme importance is 'La Bonne Chanson' (Hamelle; composed 1891–2) – nine poems from a collection of the same title by Verlaine, expressing the poet's love for the young Mathilde, who was to become his wife. Fauré has expressed the various moods of the poems, ranging from fear to hope, with a marvellous instinctive musical perception, and for all their diversity the nine movements have a unity which binds them into a perfectly satisfying whole. The passionate lyricism culminates in the radiant song *L'Hiver a cessé* (in which the themes from the other songs are brought together).

The original version of 'La Bonne Chanson' is for voice and piano, but Fauré also made an arrangement of the accompaniment for string orchestra and piano. The work is often sung, inappropriately, by a woman; but the composer certainly gave this his sanction, so there is a justification.

Fauré wrote nothing better than 'La Bonne Chanson'. The song-cycles that follow are simpler in style, more austere, more intensely personal in a way that is not always grateful. In both 'La Chanson d'Ève' (Heugel; composed 1906–10) and 'Le Jardin Clos' (Durand, 1915), the words are by the Belgian poet Charles van Lerberghe, the subject being the Age of Gold, the dawn of creation. And in the last vocal work of Fauré – 'L'Horizon Chimérique' (Durand, 1922) – the composer, aged seventy-seven, has set poems about the sea by Jean de la Ville de Mirmont, a young man killed in the First World War.

In contrast to Fauré's large output as a song-writer, the handful of fourteen songs (published by Salabert), on which the reputation of Henri Duparc rests, seems very tiny. Although he lived on until 1933, these songs were all composed between 1868 and 1884, for the following year a mental breakdown caused him to give up composition. The remarkable quality of this handful of *mélodies* places him among the great song-writers. Sydney Northcote's book, *The Songs of Henri Duparc* (Dobson, 1949) should be read by all who are interested in this composer.

Certain elements of Duparc's style were inherited from his master César Franck – a chromatic richness of texture and depth of expression. Combined with this was a very personal melodic gift, and a musical instinct which enabled him to reflect so sensitively the meaning and spirit of the fine poems he chose to set. There is the nostalgic *Chanson triste* with its undulating arpeggio accompaniment and beautiful sustained vocal line; the passionate lament of *Soupir*; the restrained intensity of *Extase*, which is said to have been deliberately Wagnerian in its harmonic texture; the dramatic and highly effective *Manoir de Rosemonde*. One of the most perfect of his songs is *L'Invitation au Voyage*, in which Baudelaire's imagery is matched by an impassioned lyricism bordering on the ecstatic. This was originally composed for voice and piano, and in the orchestral version of the accompaniment the peculiar radiance of the piano part is somewhat lost. On the other hand, in the magnificent setting of Leconte de Lisle's *Phidylé*, the orchestral version of the piano part is more satisfying, especially near the end where the tremendous climax needs something which the piano cannot give – and the texture is not pianistic. Outstanding also is *Au pays où se fait la guerre*, which is a wonderful realization, in simple but intense musical language, of the mood of lonely, anxious expectation which the poem expresses – the anxiety of a girl whose lover is away fighting in another country.

Duparc's achievement was a highly individual one – a self-contained little world of remarkable richness. The individuality of Claude Debussy (one of the great innovators of music) found expression in the gradual emergence of a highly personal idiom, far-ranging, closely related to the literary and pictorial movements of the day, and strongly influenced by them – the impressionist painters, the symbolist poets, the over-refined, sensual prose of Pierre Louÿs – and with musical influences ranging from Massenet and Wagner to Russian and (possibly) Javanese music. The early songs of Debussy (before 1887) say little that is new or particularly interesting. The best of these is perhaps the well-known *Mandoline* (Durand). It is not till we come to the 'Cinq Poèmes de Baudelaire' (Durand, 1902; composed 1887–9) and the 'Ariettes oubliées' (Jobert, 1903), to poems by Verlaine, that the highly personal voice of Debussy is heard. The 'Ariettes oubliées' (written in 1888 and originally published in that year under the title 'Ariettes, Paysages belges et Aquarelles') are elegant and charming; while the Baudelaire songs are sombre and introspective, charged with passionate hope and despair – in a style which is astonishingly original and a superb musical counterpart to the poems from *Les Fleurs du Mal*.

From *Mandoline* onwards, many of Debussy's most satisfying songs are settings of Verlaine. *L'Échelonnement des Haies*, from the 'Trois Mélodies' (Hamelle, 1901), is especially vivid: the poem depicts an English country scene with its spaced-out hedgerows. And there are the two sets of 'Fêtes galantes' (Jobert, 1903, and Durand, 1904), which range from the brilliant imagination of *Fantoches* to the quiet, subtle intimacy of the *Colloque sentimental*, in which the ghosts of two lovers evoke the past.

The 'Proses lyriques' (Jobert, 1895), the poems of which Debussy wrote himself, are an unsatisfactory mixture: passages of genuine beauty are found in what is mainly a collection of clumsy, affected, over-precious experiments in words and music. The last of the four songs, *De Soir*, however, is a vivid ironic picture of a Parisian Sunday.

In the three 'Chansons de Bilitis' (Jobert, 1899) Debussy found the exact musical equivalent of the delicate, sensual paganism of Pierre Louÿs's famous collection of prose-poems about the loves of a girl of ancient Greece. The beauty, simplicity and tenderness of *La Flûte de*

Pan, in which the girl's lover teaches her to play the flute; the passionate restraint of *La Chevelure* – a vivid portrayal of an erotic dream; and the exquisite depicting of an icy landscape in *Le Tombeau des Naïades*: these are something unique in the whole literature of song.

In a completely different way, the 'Trois Ballades de François Villon' (Durand, 1911) with their stark, dramatic quality, are also among the finest of Debussy's songs – especially the moving *Ballade que feit Villon à la requeste de sa mère pour prier Nostre-Dame*, with its medieval flavour and its combination of restraint and intensity.

The 'Trois Poèmes de Stéphane Mallarmé' (Durand), which Debussy composed in 1913, five years before his death, are experiments in transposing into music 'cette préciosité pleine de profondeur si spéciale de Mallarmé' – in the words of Ravel, who also set three of his poems.

Ravel

As a song-writer Maurice Ravel is far less important than Debussy, but his less extensive list of vocal works is of very great interest. In the early published songs of Ravel, the individuality of the composer is already much in evidence: the clarity, fastidiousness, wit, harmonic richness, melodic subtlety, can already be discerned in the 'Deux Épigrammes de Clément Marot' (Schott, 1898) – two charming miniatures about a girl called Anne 'who threw snow at me' and 'playing the spinet' – and in the delightful *Noël des Jouets* (Salabert), to words by Ravel himself, with its guitar-like piano accompaniment and its vivid, childlike impressions of the crèche and the toy animals. Ravel's finest and most satisfying song-cycle, 'Shéhérazade' (Durand, 1911), requires the orchestral accompaniment for its full effect. But the three songs, 'Don Quichotte à Dulcinée' (Durand, 1934), his last work, can sound splendid in the version for voice and piano (as the recording by Pierre Bernac and Francis Poulenc proves). They were written for Chaliapin to sing in a film of Don Quixote – but were never used. There is a Spanish flavour about the first (*Chanson romantique*) with its alternating $\frac{3}{4}$ and $\frac{6}{8}$ rhythms and guitar-like accompaniment, and there is a Rabelaisian gaiety, a highly-coloured booziness, about the final *Chanson à boire*. They deserve to be heard more often.

The 'Histoires Naturelles' (Durand, 1907), which caused such a scandal when first performed, are settings of ironic animal poems of Jules Renard. Ravel illustrates these texts with a biting humour and sarcasm which is most telling. Completely different in every way are the three 'Chansons Madécasses' (Durand, 1926), for voice, flute, cello, and piano. These settings of Madagascan poems (translated into French by Evariste Parny) show Ravel at his most lyrically imaginative, with primitive and exotic accompaniments, the patterns of which are often intoxicating.

Tes bai-sers pé-nè - trent jus-qu'à l'â me; tes ca-res-ses brû-lent tous mes sens

Other Composers Born before 1900

Charles-Marie Widor was principally an organ composer, but wrote many songs, most of which are published in two volumes (Durand) under the title '54 Mélodies'. He was a pupil of Rossini, and his style is wide-ranging and always extremely practical. The second volume includes the 'Soirs d'Été', Op. 63 – one of his most imaginative works.

The songs of Ernest Chausson show first the influence of Franck and the German song-writers, and later the influence of Debussy. He was a very unequal composer. A collection of fourteen 'Mélodies', published by Hamelle, includes two of his early songs, both of which are well known: *Les Papillons* has freshness and charm, and *Le Colibri* (in $\frac{5}{4}$ time) is Fauré-like in its harmonic richness. (Both these are from Op. 2.) Chausson's Maeterlinck song-cycle 'Serres chaudes' (Salabert) shows individuality, but the texture is over-thick and further obscures the hothouse unreality of the poems. Better are the musically suggestive settings of somewhat obscure poems of Camille Mauclair – the 'Trois Lieder', Op. 27 (Rouart, Lerolle – now Salabert; composed 1896): *Les Heures, Ballade*, and *Les Couronnes*. And as an interpreter of Verlaine – 'Deux Poèmes', Op. 34 (Rouart, Lerolle; composed 1898) – he shows a poetic insight and delicacy in *La Chanson bien douce*, which has a remarkable beauty of vocal line and texture. The deservedly famous *Chanson perpétuelle*, Op. 37 (Durand), on verses by Charles Cros, was written in 1898, less than a year before his death. (The accompaniment can be for piano, or for orchestra, or for piano and string quartet.) The mood of sadness and despair is splendidly realized in this short work, and it has a haunting and extremely moving quality about it.

André Caplet is surely a very under-estimated composer. His work always showed great sensitivity, a fine craftsmanship, and a sure and personal manner of expression. His three 'Fables de La Fontaine' (Durand, 1920) portray the crow and the fox, the cicada and the ant, the wolf and the sheep, interestingly and imaginatively, in a capricious, declamatory style recalling Ravel's 'Histoires naturelles'. And under the title of 'Cinq Ballades Françaises de Paul Fort' (Durand, 1921) we find some complex and highly imaginative impressions of la vie française. The following year, 1922, he published the remarkable work, 'Le Pain Quotidien' (Durand). The 'daily bread' in question consists of 'intimités vocals en 15 exercises' – a teaching work, written to train soundly interpreters of modern vocal music and familiarize them with the perils of the new technique. They must be the most interesting vocal exercises ever written!

Benjamin Godard started as a conscientious and thoughtful composer, but with success took the easy course of writing pleasant, superficial music of no particular character. His six 'Fables de La Fontaine' (Hartmann) are ordinary and miss the ironic spirit of the words altogether. He was best in the *romance* type of song, volumes of which are published by Durand and Choudens, and in the collection of 'Six Villanelles' (Durand), which are simple, unpretentious. Cécile Chaminade also wrote agreeable drawing-room music, and her songs have enjoyed popularity in England (a collection of her 'Mélodies' is in fact published by Joseph Williams). And a collection of 'Douze Chants' by Louis Albert includes his attractive 'Rimes tendres', Op. 4 (Duand, 1909), the poems (love songs) by Armand Silvestre. These are simple and *romance*-like in style.

On a higher artistic level are the songs of Reynaldo Hahn (who was Venezuelan by birth, but came to Paris as a child). As a boy of eighteen he set some of Verlaine's poems in an admirably appropriate style, albeit very simple. This was the collection 'Chansons grises' (Heugel). Shortly after came his ten settings of Leconte de Lisle – 'Études Latines' (Heugel), some of which are for mixed voices, but most are solo songs. A representative selection of songs by this many-sided but innocuous composer can be found in the two volumes of his 'Mélodies' published by Heugel. And of the same generation as Hahn was Gabriel Pierné, who seems fated to be remembered mainly by his orchestral trifle, *The Entry of the Little Fauns*. But his output, in many branches of composition, including song, is very large. His miscellaneous songs and song-cycles are extremely varied, and show an agreeable lightness of touch. The 'Trois Mélodies' (1904), to poems of Tristan Klingsor, and his 'Six Ballades françaises de Paul Fort' (Chappell, 1923) – the latter published with both French and English words – deserve specially to be mentioned. The 'Ballades' range from the medieval romance flavour of *Les Baleines* to the joyous simplicity of *La Ronde autour du Monde*.

The French conductor and composer Manuel Rosenthal has written, in a most accomplished manner, twelve 'Chansons du Monsieur Bleu' (Jobert, 1934), to lighthearted poems by Nino. Of these, the satirical cradle-song *Le Marabout* is memorable, and the stylised barrel-organ effects in the accompaniment of *L'Orgue de Barbarie* are skilfully handled.

The twelve 'Rondels de Charles d'Orléans' (Rouart, Lerolle, 1931 – now Salabert) – six for high voice, and six for medium voice, with piano – are good examples of the refined, lyrical quality of Pierre de Bréville's songs. The melodic lines, over an appropriately simple harmonic basis, are ornamented in characteristic and attractive ways. Attractive, too, are some of the songs of Paul Ladmirault: the chromatic richness of *Mélodieux Automne* (Jobert, 1913) and the more traditional but highly personal *Triolets à Catherine* (Salabert, 1928).

The songs of Gustave Charpentier, composer of the successful opera *Louise*, are superficial in style and lacking poetic insight. This is especially unfortunate, because the composer chose to set, for example, five poems from Baudelaire's *Fleurs du Mal*. The 'Poèmes chantés' (Heugel; composed 1894–5) – one set for voice and piano, the other set for voice and orchestra – also include unsatisfying settings of Verlaine and Baudelaire.

There was nothing very individual about the style of Georges Hüe, but he wrote two unpretentious and charming sets of 'Croquis d'Orient' ('Oriental Sketches') (Heugel, 1904 and 1905) to poems of Tristan Klingsor, of which *L'Âne blanc* and *La Barbe blanche* are particularly agreeable in a pseudo-oriental way.

The strange and unique personality of Erik Satie, and the influence he had on many of the younger composers of his time, is of considerable significance in the history of French music. His songs are not numerous, and (like everything else he did) they are anti-pretentious and direct. The 'Trois Poèmes d'Amour' (Salabert, 1914) have ironic words by the composer himself and a melodic line suggesting plainsong. According to Rollo Myers (in his study of the composer) the 'Trois Mélodies' (Salabert, 1916) – consisting of *La Statue de Bronze*, *Daphénéo*, and *Le Chapelier* – contain the essence of Satie the ironist, the wit, and the skilful parodist. This is also true of 'Ludions' (Salabert, 1923), in which he collaborates with Léon-Paul Fargue in a literary-musical joke that is personal and unique. We have here also a glimpse of Satie's music-hall style. But in the 'Quatre Petites Mélodies' (Eschig, 1920) when he sets poems by Lamartine, Cocteau and Raymond Radiguet, the results seem forced and unconvincing.

The songs of Jean Rivier display fine craftsmanship and an easy-going, positive style which varies considerably according to the poems he sets. In the 'Huit Poèmes de Guillaume Apollinaire' (Salabert, 1929) the texture is simple and the moods of the songs are highly varied. A really excellent song-cyle is his 'Quatre Poèmes' (Salabert, 1947) for baritone or mezzo-soprano and piano. The sixteenth-century poems by Ronsard and Clément Marot are set in a style of our own day which is nevertheless perfectly in keeping with the spirit of the words; they are beautifully singable, and the accompaniments are particularly satisfying. The spirit of an earlier century, seen through present-day eyes, is also to be found in songs of Roland-Manuel – for example, his 'Trois Romances de P. J. Toulet' (Heugel, 1923), the moods ranging from the violence of the song *Géronte* to the limpid beauty of *Le Temps d'Adonis*.

Albert Roussel evolved a style which was a happy synthesis of many different influences: impressionism, neo-classicism, d'Indy, German composers, oriental music. The results are quite unlike any other French composer's work, as we see in his highly interesting songs. These include three sets of Chinese poems – Op. 12 (1921), Op. 35 (1927), and Op. 47 (1934). In the first of these sets Roussel uses the pentatonic scale; but in the others there is no obvious *chinoiserie*, and the right atmosphere is created by a fragmentary lightness of texture and unusual melodic procedures. The 'Odes Anacréontiques', Op. 31 and 32 (Durand, 1927) – settings of translations from the Greek by Leconte de Lisle – are a highly personal utterance, remarkably economical in texture. The 'Deux Poèmes de Ronsard', Op. 26 (Durand, 1924), for voice and flute, are unusual and perfectly convincing – as is also Roussel's setting of an English poem, *A Flower given to my Daughter* (O.U.P.), of James Joyce. But his parody on jazz of the 'twenties – *Jazz dans la Nuit*, Op. 38 (Durand, 1929) – is heavy-going. 'Deux Mélodies', Op. 50 (Durand, 1934), to words by René Chalupt (*L'Heure du Retour* and *Coeur en péril*), could be singled out as specially effective among Roussel's songs; and the amusing song *O bon vin, où as-tu crû* would be a sure winner at any concert.

The thick texture of Florent Schmitt's music suggests teutonic sympathies rather than French. The 'Trois Mélodies', Op. 4 (Durand, 1911) for medium voice, include a somewhat artificial setting of Verlaine's *Il pleure dans mon coeur*. In his later songs we find a highly personal style and a depth of utterance, sombre and impressive. The 'Quatre Poèmes de Ronsard', Op. 100 (Durand, 1942) – which were later orchestrated – are certainly not neo-classical: the atmosphere of the sixteenth-century poetry is expressed in the composer's own personal way. An intense individuality is found in the 'Monocantes', Op. 115 (composed 1949) for voice and five instruments; and the 'Trois Poèmes de Robert Granzo', Op. 118 (also composed in 1949) are anguished and dissonant to the point of atonality.

There is a personal quality, too, of a more direct sort, in the music of Déodat de Séverac, expressing as it sometimes does the spirit of certain parts of southern France. His best-known song is *Chanson de la Nuit durable* (Rouart, Lerolle, 1911 – now Salabert); but in a collection of 'Douze Mélodies' (Rouart, Lerolle) of Séverac, we find an effective, atmospheric setting of Baudelaire's poem *Les Hiboux* (1913) and a straightforward, gracious *Chant de Noël* (1917).

Another composer of individuality is Georges Migot. So individual is he, in fact, that he has been nicknamed 'The Group of One'. He has also been called 'the spiritual brother of Guillaume de Machaut' because of certain affinities in his polyphonic style – several independent strands of melody freely combined and creating unusual harmonic progressions. His enormous output includes 'vocal chamber music', in which the composer favours unusual combinations of instruments. His 'Deux Stèles' (Leduc, 1934) are for voice, harp, celesta, double bass, and percussion – setting of two poems by Victor Ségalen (a *stèle* being a stone slab bearing a sculptured design or inscription on it). Simpler in texture, his seventeen songs on poems by Tristan Klingsor, 'Les Poèmes du Brugnon' (Leduc, 1934), are a noteworthy achievement. The individual harmonic twists of the 'Trois Berceuses Chantées' (Leduc, 1936) are attractive and convincing.

The early twentieth century is certainly a rich period in French song, and to do full justice to it would need a book in itself. From the richness I am endeavouring to pick out what seems to me the most significant – and in this, personal taste, of course, plays a large part.

Jean Cras was an officer in the French Navy besides being a successful composer (which reminds one of Rimsky-Korsakov). Cras's 'L'Offrande lyrique' (Salabert, 1920; later orchestrated) consists of settings of

Rabindranath Tagore as translated into French by André Gide: the musical style is rich and intense, avoiding any kind of obvious orientalism. Roger Delage wrote an interesting cycle of 'Trois Chants de la Jungle' (Salabert, 1935) – translations of Rudyard Kipling – including a good deal of rhythmic recitation in place of singing. The final section, *Themmangu* (song and dance of the Tiger) is vivid and exciting, and it calls for a singer with a good technique. And *État de Veille* (Eschig, 1946) by Marcel Delannoy is impressive – four songs on poems by Robert Desnos; the last, *Terezin 45*, bears the inscription: '8 June 1945: The poet, deported, prostrated by typhus, is dying in a hut at the camp of Terezin (Czechoslovakia).'

The life of Lili Boulanger (sister of the famous Nadia) was cut short at the age of twenty-five; but her musical personality had already strongly developed, as can be seen from her lengthy and extremely interesting song-cycle for high voice and piano, 'Clairières dans le Ciel' (Ricordi, 1919), to poems by Francis Jammes, which is original without being at all far-fetched in style.

The pleasant, fanciful, childlike spirit of Gabriel Grovlez is something very different, and finds a most attractive form of expression in the two volumes of 'Chansons enfantines' (Eschig, 1924) – poems about children by Tristan Klingsor, set often in a folk-song-like style.

Songs of 'Les Six'

All the members of the Parisian group that was arbitrarily known as 'Les Six' (Georges Auric, Louis Durey, Arthur Honegger, Darius Milhaud, Francis Poulenc, and Germaine Tailleferre) wrote vocal music – much of which is now deservedly forgotten. In the early days, under the influence of Stravinsky, Satie, and the writer Jean Cocteau, the alleged aims of the group were simplicity, conciseness and clarity; but in the case of Auric and Poulenc, at least, this spirit became too easily an anything-will-do-so-long-as-it's-not-serious attitude: a reaction partly to the war and partly to impressionism and over-serious romanticism. Looking again at the early songs of Auric – the three 'Interludes' (Demets, 1918 – now Eschig); or the 'Huit Poèmes de Jean Cocteau' (Demets, 1920), which includes a *Hommage à Erik Satie* – the banality is depressing. But by 1925 a more serious purpose is discernible in Auric's 'Cinq Poèmes de Gérard de Nerval' (Heugel, 1925). The 'Cinq Chansons de Lise Hirtz' (Heugel, 1930) are short, amusing songs about animals, and they are well written and effective. Like Satie, Auric has found inspiration in popular music; he shows also a fine intelligence and a Gallic scepticism. More recently, 'Quatre Chants de la France malheureuse' (Heugel, 1947) – to poems by Aragon, Supervielle and Éluard – have a real depth of feeling; and in the 'Six Poèmes de Paul Éluard' (Heugel, 1948), the complicated disquiet of the poems is well expressed in the music. On the whole, Auric is an under-rated song-writer.

Louis Durey did not remain long with 'Les Six', but went his own way, often in contradiction to the avowed aims of the group. (Much later, after the Second World War, he was to become so-called 'Progressist' and write communist mass-appeal music.) His 'Images à Crusoé' (Chester, 1922) for voice, string quartet, flute, clarinet, and celesta, is an outstanding song-cycle. The poems of Saint-Léger Léger, which express Robinson Crusoe's disillusionment after returning from his desert island to the world of men, are set with imagination, simplicity, and great sensitivity. In 'Le Bestiaire' (poems by Guillaume Apollinaire) Durey showed himself a master of irony and a very neat craftsman.

The songs of Francis Poulenc extend over forty years and are as varied in style and quality as the texts he has chosen. As Edward Lockspeiser has written, 'despite the variety of the texts which he has drawn upon, Poulenc is essentially the illustrator of the surréaliste poets: he is the musician of Guillaume Apollinaire, Max Jacob and Paul Éluard, as Debussy was the musician of Verlaine and Mallarmé'. For Martin Cooper (in his book French Music) he is 'a musical clown of the first order, a brilliant musical mimic and an adroit craftsman, who pieces together the most heterogeneous collection of musical styles to form an unmistakable personal style of his own'. It is no doubt this personal synthesis of seemingly contradictory elements that makes him so successfully the 'illustrator of the surréaliste poets'. That he is capable of writing serious and beautiful music is proved by much of 'Tel Jour Telle Nuit' (Durand, 1937), settings of surrealist verses by the great French poet Paul Éluard – perhaps his finest song-cycle. (In this work the influence of Schumann is often apparent.) And as early as 1919, when Poulenc was twenty years old, we find him writing with remarkable polish and sophistication in 'Le Bestiaire, ou Le Cortège d'Orphée' (La Sirène Musicale – now Eschig), to Apollinaire's delightful little animal poems (of which a set was also made by Louis Durey) – amusing and vivid thumbnail sketches of the dromedary, the Tibetan goat, the grasshopper, the dolphin, the crab, and the carp. The accompaniment is either for piano or for flute, clarinet, bassoon and string quartet: both versions are very effective.

But it is the poetry of Paul Éluard which seems to have inspired the most interesting song-settings of Poulenc: the 'Cinq Poèmes' (Durand, 1935), 'La Fraicheur et le Feu' (Eschig, 1951), and 'Le Travail de Peintre' (Eschig, 1957) – the last-named being poems about seven modern painters (Picasso, Chagall, Braque, Juan Gris, Paul Klee, Joan Miró, Jacques Villon). On the other hand, in the five 'Poèmes de Ronsard' (Heugel, 1925) for mezzo-soprano, the spirit of the poems is missed completely, because Poulenc in his portrayal of 'classical' styles is always slapdash.

A representative selection of Poulenc's songs can be found in the two volumes, each of twelve songs – 'Douze Mélodies' – one for high voice, the other for medium (published by Rouart, Lerolle).

Darius Milhaud is the most uneven of composers. Traditional patterns, polytonality, jazz, folklore, everything is mixed together and poured out with a dreadful fertility. Whatever its quality, however, it is always *musical* outpouring – even if the music means very little. Amongst the many songs we find some of the composer's best compositions. 'Alissa' (Heugel), written in 1913, is a lyrical work of beauty and simplicity – a setting of passages from André Gide's *La Porte Étroite*, in the form of a lengthy lament for voice and piano. It was revised, but not substantially altered, by the composer in 1931.

The 'Quatre Poèmes de Léo Latil' (Durand, 1920) is another good early work of Milhaud, and dates from 1914. Latil, the poet, like Milhaud, was born in Provence; these poems, about a forsaken lover, are set in a rich, expressive style, harmonically and contrapuntally very free. Two years later, 1916, with the 'Poèmes Juifs' (Demets, 1920 – now Eschig) an intimate subjective side of the composer's nature finds expression. Milhaud comes of an old Provençal Jewish family, and these settings of translations of Hebrew texts are a personal expression of faith.

Two humorous works of Milhaud have achieved fame: 'Catalogue de Fleurs' (Durand, 1923) and 'Machines agricoles' (Universal, 1926), both for voice and seven instruments. The 'Catalogue de Fleurs' consists of seven tiny fragments by Lucien Daudet, each describing a flower, and the work ends with the words 'Price-list will be sent by post'. Similarly, 'Machines agricoles' sets, in pastoral style, passages from a catalogue of agricultural machinery – such as 'La déchau-meuse-semeuse-enfouisseuse est avec étançons et certaines parties renforcées pour pouvoir supporter convenablement la caisse semoir' ('The plougher-sower-burier is reinforced with props and certain attachments so as to give proper support to the sower-case'); or the following (*La Faneuse*):

Ex. 10

Among the most interesting of Milhaud's more recent works are the 'Quatre Chansons de Ronsard' (Boosey, 1941) for high soprano, written in California in 1941, and 'Rêves' (Heugel) which date from 1942. The former are sixteenth-century poems, set with a beautifully expressive, flexible vocal line; the latter are anonymous poems of the twentieth century, very diverse in character. The 'Chants de Misère' (Heugel, 1946), settings of poems by Camille Paliard, are simple and very deeply felt and reflect something of the misery of occupied France.

> Tant de vagabonds sur les routes,
> Tant d'enfants dans les hôpitaux,
> Tant de soldats, tant de déroute,
> Tant de prisons et de barreaux.

Very recently there have appeared Milhaud's twenty-four 'Tristesses' (Heugel, 1957) to poems by Francis Jammes – a 'suite' for baritone and piano of great variety and interest. This is published with French and English words – the translations being by Rollo Myers. (Another interesting song-cycle on ten of the same collection of poems, 'Tristesses', set by O. d'Estrade Guerra, had been published (Durand) in Paris the year before – 1956.)

'Les Six' did not remain a group – in fact, right from the start there was little they had in common beside friendship and mutual interest. Arthur Honegger (born of Swiss parents) was always an essentially serious-minded composer. Perhaps in the 'Six Poésies de Jean Cocteau' (Senart, 1924 – now Salabert) he approached to some extent the spirit of the early Poulenc and Auric. But on the whole he went his own highly individual way; and his name is probably the most important of those who were once called 'Les Six'. His songs, however, were not the most significant part of his output. Of his early songs worth remembering are the 'Six Poèmes' (Mathot, 1921 – now Salabert) from Apollinaire's *Alcools*, and the 'Trois Poèmes' (Senart, 1922 – now Salabert) from Paul Fort's *Complaintes et Dits*. Honegger's style stemmed from Bach and d'Indy – strongly flavoured with dissonance; the melodic element was always of great importance. One of his finest later sets of songs is 'Trois Poèmes de Claudel' (Salabert, 1942) – of which the last, *Le Rendez-vous* is a characteristic, serious song of great beauty. In a more straightforward style, the 'Trois Psaumes' (Salabert, 1943) recall psalm sections of the composer's oratorio *King David*. They are settings of passages from the French metrical versions of Psalms 34, 140 and 138. And in a very different and lighthearted mood, there is the 'Petit cours de morale' (Salabert, 1957) composed in 1941 – five *mélodies minutes* – settings of amusing 'moral' rhymes from Jean Giraudoux's novel *Susanne et la Pacifique*.

Composers Born since 1900

Henri Sauguet, like Erik Satie, has a new and original outlook on traditional procedures. The direct influence of Satie is evident in his song-cycle 'Cirque' (Rouart, Lerolle, 1926 – now Salabert), to five poems of Adrien Copperie. Sauguet's free and expressive style, based on tonality, is perfectly convincing for the setting of Baudelaire, Mallarmé and Laforgue in his 'Six Mélodies sur des poèmes symbolistes' (Amphion, 1944), and for setting the poetry of Max Jacob in 'Les Pénitants en maillots roses' (Heugel, 1949) and 'Visions infernales' (Heugel, 1950) – the latter, for bass-baritone, being imaginative and exciting (and quite restrainedly infernal!).

The eclectic Henry Barraud is very mixed in style. His 'Chansons de Gramadoch' (Amphion, 1944) – poems by Victor Hugo – are simple, neo–classical, and effective; and in 'Quatre Poèmes de Lanza del Vasto' (Amphion, 1945), a rich web of sound surrounds the *Prière du Soir*, and *Dieu sanglant* is strikingly dramatic and violent. There are neo–classical elements, also, in the well-written songs of Claude Arrieu. Her choice of Mallarmé as a poet seems out of keeping with her style, but the set of 'Poèmes de Louise de Vilmorin' (Amphion, 1946) is very different and far more convincing, with fanciful, elaborate accompaniments and a strong feeling for atmosphere.

Jean Cartan, born in 1906, died at the age of twenty-four – a highly gifted composer. His rich, imaginative settings of Klingsor and Mallarmé are far more than just promising – especially the 'Cinq Poèmes de Tristan Klingsor' (Heugel, 1927), the accompaniment of which is either for piano or for flute, harp, and string quartet. Two other song-composers, also born in 1906 – neither of them very well known – deserve not to be overlooked. One is Jacques Leguerney, whose 'Sept Poèmes de François Maynard' (1951), for medium voice and piano, are short, epigrammatic songs written in a clear, interesting style. But 'La Solitude' (1951) – four songs to poems by Théophile de Viau, dedicated to Pierre Bernac – are more searching and elaborate, and highly effective. The other composer is the versatile Maurice Thiriet, who has written about fifty songs. His cycle 'Fleurs' (1951) – to six poems by Blanche Pierre-Biez – is a fine work, with a colourfully-written piano part.

There are some delightful songs of Jean Françaix – who seems to be the personification of the Gallic spirit in music. In 'L'Adolescence clémentine' (Eschig, 1948) everything is lighthearted and beautifully polished: a spontaneous quality in the music catches to perfection the atmosphere of these fresh sixteenth-century poems by Clément Marot. The 'Cinq Poésies de Charles d'Orléans' (Schott, 1950) seem to go back in spirit to the courtly music of the seventeenth century – but at the same time the songs are very much of our own day. Two more songs (Schott, 1950) with guitar (or piano) accompaniment, are also highly effective: the expressive *Prière du Soir* (poem by Agrippa d'Aubigné) and the scintillating *Chanson* (poem by Clément Marot).

La Jeune France and after

In 1936, a group was formed of the four composers Yves Baudrier, Daniel Lesur, André Jolivet, and Olivier Messiaen – which became known as *La Jeune France*. They asserted the right of the young composer to write music of a lyrical kind with a personal message – the reinstatement of certain values which French music at the time seemed to have lost. One would expect this credo to find its most spontaneous realization in song.

The songs of Messiaen are strongly personal in idiom – a disquieting mixture of many stylistic elements, including impressionism, elaborately experimental rhythms, both juicily naïve and highly sophisticated harmonic procedures, and much that seems rather tasteless and pretentious, however original. The influence he has had on the younger composers is immense. An organist and a fervent Catholic, he has given many of his works religious titles, as for example his 'Chants de Terre et de Ciel' (Durand, 1939) – one of his most important song-cycles (the words being the composer's own). There are also two books of 'Poèmes pour Mi' (Durand, 1937) – 'Mi' being his wife's nickname. 'Poèmes pour Mi' and 'Chants de Terre et de Ciel' are, according to the composer, specially 'true' in sentiment and representative of his musical manner, with its carefully devised modes, chordal polyphony, and rhythmic fluidity. Here is an example from 'Poèmes pour Mi' – part of the song *Les Deux Guerriers*, from the second book:

The influence of Indian music is shown in the difficult song-cycle 'Harawi' (Leduc, 1948), songs of love and of death, for *grand soprano dramatique*, the words, again, being by the composer.

The songs of Daniel Lesur are notable for the lyrical, singable quality of the vocal writing – to which is added a strongly personal piano part, often showing unusual harmonic invention. His 'Trois Poèmes de Cécile Sauvage' (Amphion, 1944) and 'Clair comme le jour' (Amphion, 1946) are experimental and of considerable interest: the former containing a sensitive, polytonal *Nocturne*; the latter containing the simple, exuberant *Jeunes filles*. There are lyrical qualities also – and imagination – in the songs of Yves Baudrier, which include the 'Trois Poèmes de Tristan Corbière' (composed 1939–40). But the most interesting and important side of this composer's work is his experimental film music.

With André Jolivet, the spirit of *La Jeune France* found expression in a magical, incantatory style, related to the practices of primitive religion – not to Catholicism (as with Messiaen). For the spell of the rich and highly personal music to have its full effect on the listener, orchestral colour seems to be necessary; and the two principal song-cycles of Jolivet are published 'for voice and piano' and 'for voice and orchestra'. These are 'Les trois Complaintes du Soldat' (Durand, 1942), the words of which are anonymous, and 'Poèmes intimes' (Heugel, 1949), with words by Louis Emié. In strong contrast to these concentrated, Priapean evocations, the 'Trois Poèmes galants' (Heugel, 1954) are far simpler in texture – spirited and effective settings of sixteenth- and seventeenth-century love poems: the irony of the sonnet to a whimsical woman (*Sonnet à une lunaticque*) contrasts strongly with an exciting, violent imprecation (*Épître imprécatoire*).

In the songs of Henri Dutilleux we find a cultivated eclecticism. His 'Quatre Mélodies' (Durand, 1943) is a characteristic and varied set: a fantastic scherzo, *Féerie au clair de lune*, is followed by a lugubrious lament *Pour une amie perdue*, with a gradually rising chordal accompaniment; then, after a deeply-felt setting of a poem by the Comtesse de Noailles, *Regards sur l'Infini*, the final song, *Fantasio*, is of lively festivity masking a deep sorrow.

What will be the future of *la mélodie française*? What effect will the a-thematic serialism of Boulez have on it, and the work of the other twelve-note composers? André Casanova has set poems by Tristan Tzara in a naïvely Schoenbergian style; Serge Nigg, restless and questing in style, has made some complex settings of Paul Éluard. But whatever forms French song may take, we may be fairly sure that it will always (in Poulenc's words) be 'leavened with that lightness of spirit without which life would be unendurable'.

Germany and Austria

PHILIP RADCLIFFE

OF the development of the solo song in Germany during the seventeenth century some idea may be formed by comparing it with similar movements in other countries. The monodic movement in Italy was a reaction against a polyphonic tradition which had produced magnificent music, but was to a considerable extent due to the impact of Netherland composers upon a country whose national inclinations tended towards solo rather than to choral singing. It would have led to more abiding results if opera had not soon become the main outlet for Italian composers of vocal music. In England, on the other hand, the growth of the great lutenist school certainly was not due to any conscious reaction against the past. It was a short step from Byrd's songs, 'apt for voices or viols', to Dowland's first book of Airs, that could be sung either as part-songs or by a solo voice with lute accompaniment, and, though in the Airs of the younger composers the rhythms were more regular and the texture more homophonic, there was no sudden, revolutionary change of style.

In Germany the parallel development was more similar to its English than to its Italian equivalent, the link between the two centuries being the music of Schütz. He was deeply interested in Italian music, but it was not so much the monodic experiments of the Florentine Camerata, as the massive polychoral style of the Venetians that influenced him most. The texture of his polyphony is often derived from vigorous rhythmic figures and broad harmonic sequences that look, not back to the smooth, flowing lines of Palestrina, but onward to the incisive counterpoint of Bach. And in his *Symphoniae Sacrae* this is intensified by the fact that voices and instruments are treated on equal terms, sharing the same melodic material, and not pursuing independent paths, as in Monteverdi's *Sonata sopra Sancta Maria*.

It was against this background that German song developed in the seventeenth century, first as a kind of modest undergrowth, and it is appropriate that one of its composers, Heinrich Albert, should have been a nephew and pupil of Schütz. He was born in 1606 and his eight volumes of 'Arien'[1] contain an interesting variety of pieces, some choral and some for solo voice, which reflect in various ways the style of his uncle, but always on a much smaller scale. In some of the choral pieces the texture is contrapuntal, and in some of the solo songs the words are set to a free recitative, as in the remarkable *Letzte Rede*, in which there is some striking word-painting, but most commonly his melodic idiom is simple and homely. Sometimes there are rhythmic twists that look back to the sixteenth century, as in the *Abendlied* in Vol. 5.

Ex. 1

O Chris - te Schutz - herr dei - ner Glie - der.

More often his rhythms are flowing and straightforward, as in the melody of the choral *Morgenlied* in the same volume, of which both words and music, the latter heavily disguised, appear as the Bach Chorale, *Gott des Himmels und der Erden*. There is no attempt to differentiate between a secular and an ecclesiastical style; the tune of the *Morgenlied* just mentioned is no more hymn-like than that of a song entitled *Spes lectat amantes* that is to be found in the previous volume. Some of the tunes are described as *aria gallica*, and many of the others may well have been inspired by, if not borrowed from, popular songs.

The first volume of Albert's songs appeared in 1638 and the last in 1650; between these came the 'Weltliche Oden oder Liebesgesänge' of Hammerschmidt (1642–3) and, later, collections by J. E. Kindermann (1652), Adam Krieger (published posthumously in 1676), and many others; the songs of the last two have instrumental ritornelli, which are not, however, thematically connected with the songs themselves.

(1) Denkmäler Deutscher Tonkunst, 12–13.

The rhythmic flexibility of the sixteenth century has by now become a thing of the past, and the phraseology of the songs written in the latter half of the seventeenth century shows the squareness and simplicity characteristic of the Chorale and the German *Studentenlied;* the following tune by Kindermann,[2] (Ex. 2), is a good example. And

with this increase of rhythmic regularity comes an equal increase of tonal clarity; the modulations are precise and well balanced, stabilizing the classical major and minor key system which was to remain a controlling feature of European music throughout the eighteenth and nineteenth centuries.

The eighteenth century

Throughout the eighteenth century an enormous amount of music was written, both in Germany and in other European countries, but it was not until the last decades of the century that the solo song began to emerge to a position of importance. The continued existence of the continuo was a hindrance to the development of an independent accompaniment, and until that could happen, the separate solo song was for the most part a pale reflection of things that were said with more vitality in larger works. J. S. Bach and Handel wrote their greatest songs as parts of choral or dramatic works, and it is significant that, outside these, Handel's best songs are the nine 'Deutsche Arien' which are for voice, continuo and violin obbligato, and are in a generally operatic style. They contain some beautiful music, especially *Süsse Stille, sanfte Quelle,* which is in Handel's serenest E major vein. For a composer like J. S. Bach, who was concerned so much with richness and subtlety of detail, it could hardly be expected that song for solo voice and continuo would offer much attraction, though the well-known *Bist du bei mir* is very characteristic in its intimate tenderness.

The songs of C. P. E. Bach are very varied in both size and quality, but are of considerable interest. The contrapuntal style of his father's music had little attraction for him, and the texture of his songs is always

(2) Denkmäler der Tonkunst in Bayern, 23.

230

simple. Sometimes the vocal part is supported by nothing but a bass; more often the piano part is fully harmonized, but includes the vocal line and has no independent figuration of its own, though occasionally, as in *Wider der Übermuth*, it has interludes of some importance. One or two, such as *Selma* and *An Doris*, are on a large scale, with contrasted sections, but for the most part they are highly compressed. Some are thoroughly trivial, but often, even in the most unpretentious, there are unexpected and attractive harmonic turns, and in some there is remarkable depth of feeling. The set of *Geistliche Gesänge* contains two very striking songs, *Der Tag des Weltgerichts*, in which the hammering repeated notes in the bass give place, in the last line, to a simple and very impressive setting of the words 'embarme dich unser', and *Über die Finsterniss kurz vor dem Tode Jesu*, which ends on a half-close, and has a strange, almost Schumannesque intimacy. The set of 'Geistliche Oden und Lieder' to the words by Gellert include several that were later set by Beethoven; of these the best is *Bitten*, and *Die Ehre Gottes aus der Natur* has something of the energy, though not the broad simplicity of Beethoven's setting. But in *Vom Tode* Bach's pleasantly flowing tune seems superficial beside Beethoven's sombre music.

Varied influences are to be found in the songs of C. P. E. Bach; his love of rich harmonic colour is characteristically German, and his melodic decoration is often Italianate, though it is liable to suggest an instrument rather than the human voice. In the many songs of Johann Christian Bach Italian traits are more predominant; this is not surprising in a composer who spent most of his life outside Germany and wrote a large number of operas. But for the most part German songs written in the central decades of the eighteenth century were homely and unassuming in style: those, for instance, by Marpurg and Kirnberger are far simpler than might be expected from men who were best known as theoreticians. On the other hand, those by J. A. Hiller have the direct and popular character of his *Singspielen*, and in Gluck's settings of Odes by Klopstock the style is certainly related to that of his operas, but far paler and more impersonal (Ex. 3); the rather stilted open-

Ex. 3 *Feurig*

Ich bin ein deutsch-es Mäd - chen, Mein Aug ist blau und sanft mein Blick

ing of the first song, *Vaterlandslied*, is nothing like as effective as C. P. E.

Bach's commonplace but more direct setting of the same words (Ex. 4).

Ex.4

Ich bin ein deutsch-es Mäd-chen, Mein Aug ist blau und sanft mein Blick

Of the German song-writers of this period, C. P. E. Bach is by far the most interesting and individual, but in the work of his less distinguished contemporaries we can already see the musical inflexions that were eventually to be raised to a sublime level by Mozart in *The Magic Flute* and Haydn in *The Creation*.

The songs of Haydn, however, though they contain much admirable music, do not on the whole show him at his most completely individual; for this, the problems of instrumental composition were necessary. In his vocal music, even at its greatest, the style differs less from that of his contemporaries, and an unlearned listener might be forgiven for supposing the melodies of *With Verdure Clad* and the duet for Pamina and Papageno in Act I of *The Magic Flute* to be the work of the same composer. In many of the songs the piano part doubles the vocal line in a rather pedestrian manner, and sometimes, as in the curiously inappropriate setting of *She never told her love*, he uses a rather floridly operatic idiom, of the kind into which Mozart could infuse the greatest beauty, but which never became so integral a part of Haydn's style. Some of the smaller, homelier songs are more characteristic, such as *Gegenliebe*, afterwards used in Symphony No. 73 (La Chasse), *An die Freundschaft*, used later in the 75th Symphony, and *Liebes Mädchen, hör' mich zu*. More independence in the piano accompaniments can be found in the songs written in England. The two volumes of Canzonets contain familiar favourites such as *My mother bids me bind my hair* and *The Mermaid's Song*, but there are others less well known, but fully worthy of attention: especially *The Wanderer* and *Despair*, both richly emotional in the manner of some of his later instrumental slow movements, and *Fidelity*, which is more extended and has a striking foretaste of the first movement of Beethoven's Sonata in F minor from Op. 2. Finer still, however, are two separate songs, *O Tuneful Voice* and *The Spirit's Song*. These are both broadly designed and very original, the first entry of the voice in both of them being particularly striking. In *O Tuneful Voice* the wide range of the modulations points to Schubert, and *The Spirit's Song* foreshadows Beethoven in its general mood and especially in its treatment of a menacing repeated-note figure.

Mozart, like Handel, was a composer of supreme lyrical gifts whose greatest songs were parts of larger works. Of his separate songs many are slight and unimportant, and in the earlier ones the piano part is very simple, usually doubling the vocal line; the only exception, *Ridente la calma*, is thought to have been originally written with orchestral accompaniment. The French Arietta *Dans un Bois solitaire*, written in 1778, is far more interesting in this respect; both this and the delightful *An Chloe*, composed nine years later, are gaily operatic in feeling. Equally operatic, but in a very different mood, is *Erzeugt von heisser Phantasie*, in which a young woman burns the letters of her faithless lover. This is the most dramatic of the songs: it covers much in a small space, the structure being held together by a defiant phrase of the kind so frequently used by Mozart when writing in the key of C minor. Apart from this unifying factor the shape of the song is guided entirely by the words, a moment of deep pathos being introduced by a descending chromatic passage just before the end. In a very different mood a similar freedom of form is achieved in the well-known setting of Goethe's *Das Veilchen*; here again the music is guided by the words, Mozart achieving in the final bars a touch of thematic unity by a manipulation of the text that in a modern composer might be regarded as slightly sharp practice. In *Abendempfindung*, certainly the most beautiful of Mozart's songs, the design is broader and the texture more continuous. A few of the opening bars return towards the end, and a very attractive cadential phrase recurs several times in the piano part, in various keys; the quiet modulation to E flat is a moment of extraordinary beauty. These five songs all, in their different ways, illustrate the earlier stages of the *durchkomponiert* type of song, and the freedom and continuity of some of Haydn's late songs, such as *The Spirit's Song* and *O Tuneful Voice*, may well be due to their influence. And in them Mozart shows that to him, as to most great writers of vocal music, the setting of metrical words made his rhythms not less but more flexible than usual. The small strophic songs, in their unpretentious way, often have great charm; one of the best is the elegiac *Lied von der Trennung*, in which two of the many stanzas are set to different music.

Growth of the Lied

It is tantalizing that, while a man of Mozart's lyrical powers regarded the writing of separate songs as no more than a pleasant by-path, those of his contemporaries who were most interested in the development of the song were composers of so much smaller calibre. But there is no doubt that towards the end of the eighteenth century there was a deep and widespread interest in the Lied, resulting largely from the stimulus provided by the lyric poetry of Goethe. For the most part the songs were simple and unpretentious, following on the lines of Hiller and his contemporary J. A. P. Schulz, without the individuality of C. P. E. Bach, or Haydn, or Mozart. Reichardt, slightly senior to Mozart, and Zelter, slightly his junior, both set many poems by Goethe; Zelter was a friend of the poet, who preferred his settings to those of any other composer. Reichardt was also a prolific writer of opera, and some of his larger songs are in the style of a scena, containing a large amount of recitative. These include settings of two celebrated Goethe poems, the *Rhapsodie Harzreise im Winter* and *Prometheus*. In both of these, especially the latter, he is obviously straining his utmost to be dramatic, but he had not the personality that could deal successfully with poetry of this kind. When aiming less high his music has a pleasantly homely and intimate character that still has considerable charm; *Freudvoll und leidvoll* is a very characteristic specimen. Zelter is also at his best when writing on a small scale; sometimes, as in his second setting of *Nur wer die Sehnsucht kennt*, he shows more emotional depth than Reichardt. Neither composer was very successful with *Der Erlkönig*; Zelter's is the more imaginative, and makes some attempt to convey the tragedy of the final stanza. Reichardt's setting is strophic, except that for the words of the Erlkönig himself the tune is transferred to the piano, the voice singing on a monotone, an idea carried out more convincingly in a later setting by Bernhard Klein. Zumsteeg, two years younger than Zelter, was a song-writer of a different kind who excelled in the setting of narrative ballads. He had not a very distinguished melodic gift, and in his ballads there is no attempt at musical unity except where this is demanded by the poem, as in *Des Pfarrers Tochter von Taubenhayn*, but sometimes there is an harmonic imaginativeness that must have made a special appeal to Schubert. He, like Reichardt, was also a composer of opera. And when looking back at the development of German song in the eighteenth century, it is particularly important to see it against the background of opera; in Germany, as in other European countries, opera was the medium to which a composer of vocal music turned most readily. The solo Cantata, so popular in the late seventeenth and early eighteenth centuries, gradually disappeared because it had become a pale reflection of what was being said with more vitality

in opera; similarly, solo song could not become a really important branch of composition until it ceased to be a poor relation of
opera, and it is significant that none of the great song-writers of the
nineteenth century was particularly successful as a composer for the
stage.

Beethoven and his contemporaries

The songs of Beethoven hold a curious position in his output, and
offer certain parallels with Haydn. Both composers originally
approached music from an instrumental rather than from a vocal
angle, though they both excelled in choral writing at the end of their
lives. In writing vocal music Beethoven was far slower to find his
individuality than in his instrumental works. The flowing and leisurely
operatic idiom of the early song *Adelaide* can still be found, with
subtler details and a wider harmonic range, in the second of his two
settings of Tiedge's *An die Hoffnung*, composed about twenty years later.
Equally operatic is *Der Wachtelgesang*, which is an elaborate scena;
the mere mention of bad weather produces an outburst of recitative
at a moment where Schubert, in his simpler but far more effective
setting of the same words, was content with a quiet modulation to the
tonic minor. The Arietta *In questa tomba oscura* also shows traces of
operatic influence, but is far more terse and individual; the modulation to the flat submediant in the middle has a strong foretaste
of Schubert and Schumann. Many of the shorter and simpler songs
have great charm, though they often sound earlier than they actually
are.

There are four settings of Goethe's *Nur wer die Sehnsucht kennt*, all
apparently written in 1808; the fourth is the most interesting, but
there is little in their style to distinguish them from many much earlier
songs. And in the early *Mailied* and the little Arietta *Der Kuss*, written
in 1822, there is the same simple geniality, a quality that is perhaps
more characteristic of Beethoven than his more pontifical admirers
have sometimes imagined. The Goethe settings include a considerable
variety; *Mit einem gemalten Band* is notable for its lighthearted anticipation of the theme of the Ninth Symphony, and *Wonne der Wehmuth*,
in a more serious vein, is a song of great beauty. The setting of *The
Song of the Flea* from *Faust* is a rather self-conscious attempt at realism.
On the whole Beethoven's finest song-writing is to be found in the set
of six religious songs, to words by Gellert, and in the song-cycle
'An die ferne Geliebte'. The former, composed in 1803 are, with the

exception of the final *Busslied*, on a very small scale, but they contain music of great power and dignity, and *Vom Tode* is one of Beethoven's most impressive miniatures. 'An die ferne Geliebte' is more lyrical. It was written in 1816, but, as is liable to happen even in quite late works of Beethoven, there are individual phrases that might belong to an earlier date. But this could not be said of the work as a whole; the unceremonious modulations between the first and second, and between the second and third songs, and the abrupt end, are very character-istic of Beethoven's last period. The return of the opening melody towards the end is beautifully contrived, and there is much that is prophetic of later composers; the opening phrase of the sixth song finds several echoes in the music of Mendelssohn and Schumann. In Beethoven's own music the closest parallel to its intimate and some-times enigmatic tone is to be found in some of the late Bagatelles. His career as a song writer reached its climax in this work, and none of his later songs rise to the same level.

Of Beethoven's junior contemporaries, Spohr and Weber both wrote songs, the former being the more fastidious and the latter the more vital. Those of Spohr, like most of his music, suffer from pro-nounced mannerisms, notably in his harmony, in which the chromati-cism handled so delicately by Mozart in his later works reappears in a more cloying and concentrated form. His rhythms also tend to be rather square and complacent, and when, as in his curious setting of *Kennst du das Land*, he aims at greater flexibility, the result is rather self-conscious. A comparison of his setting of Müller's *Ungeduld* with that of Schubert is revealing; Spohr's approach to the poem, though somewhat demure, has moments of genuine feeling, especially at the words 'dein ist mein Herz', but it can be seen at once that Schubert's impulsive ardour was totally beyond his reach. The songs in minor keys tend to be more vital than the others; one or two of them, such as *Lied der Harfnerin*, have considerable breadth. The style of Spohr's songs is unified to a fault; in those of Weber, on the other hand, there is more variety. As a composer of opera he was influenced, probably more than he would have liked to admit, by some of his Italian con-temporaries, and at the same time he was much attracted by the simple German *volkstümliches Lied*. And despite his predominant interest in opera, his melodic idiom was often of an instrumental rather than a vocal kind, with frequent arpeggio phrases that sometimes suggest a clarinet rather than a voice; the opening of *Das Veilchen in Thale* (Ex. 5) is a good example. Frequently he shows a naïve delight in very

Ex. 5 Andante con moto

Ein Veil - chen blüht in_ Tha - le er wacht am Mor - gen - strah - le

simple and obvious tonic and dominant harmonies, and his handling of remote and unexpected modulations is sometimes clumsy. But, although, compared to opera, song-writing was obviously a sideline for him, he wrote a number of very attractive specimens that might well be worth reviving. Of the more serious ones, *Der Schwermütige* and *Das Mädchen an das erste Schneeglöckchen* are among the most sensitive. One of the most frequently set poems of the period is Matthisson's *Ich denke dein*, in which the first three stanzas all end with a question. Zumsteeg's simple strophic setting is attractive musically, but makes no attempt to portray the question; Beethoven does it by a rather perfunctory modulation to the dominant. Weber's setting is far more operatic; it is continuous, the question being set with increasing intensity each time. But, with all its richly expressive character, his treatment seems over-emphatic compared with the simple intimacy with which the question is conveyed by Schubert.

Schubert

Of all the qualities most generally associated with Schubert's songs, the most obvious is that of lyrical beauty; it is therefore surprising to find how little of this there is in his earliest songs. Most of them are settings of long, melodramatic ballads, of the kind that might well have attracted a boy of fourteen. They are clearly modelled upon those of Zumsteeg, and the individual touches are harmonic rather than melodic. In the earliest of them all, *Hagar's Klage*, the word 'Jehovah' evokes an impressive modulation strongly prophetic of his later work. A slightly later song, with the promising title of *Der Vatermörder*, opens with a passage that might be the introduction to almost any operatic scena of the period, except for one unexpected harmonic turn. These songs date from 1811; the next year produced hardly any, but in 1813 there are signs of increasing maturity. In *Die Schatten* a more individual lyricism can be felt: the six-bar phrases of the opening and the modulations that come later are thoroughly characteristic. In *Verklärung*, the words of which are a translation of Pope's *Vital Spark of heavenly Flame*, the semi-operatic manner of the earliest songs appears in a more concise form; for so short a song the contrasts are perhaps over-emphasized, but the quieter sections are of great beauty and individuality. In the best songs of 1814, Schubert is able to combine

237

variety of mood with continuity of texture. It happens on a comparatively small scale in his setting of Goethe's *Schäfers Klagelied*, and,
with supreme results, in *Gretchen am Spinnrade*. This, his first Goethe
setting, is by far the finest thing that he had yet written; the spinning-
wheel figure in the piano accompaniment gives the song unity, and
the varying moods of the poem are portrayed with astonishing
vividness, with a kind of controlled and graded intensity most remarkable for so young a composer. Already can be seen the wide and
imaginative range of modulation that was to become so marked a
characteristic of his later work.

The composition of this masterpiece seemed to loosen the flood-
gates, and the following year, 1815, saw the production of an enormous
mass of songs. Goethe had obviously made a deep impact upon him
which was to continue for many years, and there are many settings of
his poems among the 1815 songs. Schubert was far from discriminating
in his choice of words, but he hardly ever failed to respond to great
poetry. One Goethe poem, *An den Mond*, was set twice during this
year, the second version being far more distinguished than the first;
several of the shorter settings, such as *Meeresstille* and *Freudvoll und
leidvoll* are astonishingly mature and might well have been written
some years later; the latter is as simple and direct in its treatment of
the poem as Reichardt's setting, but harmonically and melodically
belongs to an entirely different world. *Kennst du das Land*, one of the
most immediately appealing of all Goethe's poems, has attracted
innumerable German composers; Schubert's setting has points in
common with that of Beethoven, and both are attractive, though
neither quite conveys the nostalgia of the words, the refrain in
Schubert's song being almost hilarious. At about the same time he
wrote the first of his many settings of *Nur wer die Sehnsucht kennt*;
this is more sensitive, though the harmonic scheme is not carried out
with quite the supreme sense of inevitability of his maturer work.

These songs are all on quite a small scale; the longer ones are more
apt to wander, but they include two masterpieces, both to words by
Goethe. In *Der Erlkönig*, as in *Gretchen am Spinnrade*, the song is unified
by a figure in the piano part suggested by the poem, the galloping of
the horse serving the same purpose in the one song as the spinning-
wheel in the other. And against this there is a variety of melodic
material, and again, as in *Gretchen*, the tension is superbly graded. The
words of the Erlkönig himself are at first cajoling and then increasingly
insistent, and behind all the drama there is a feeling of immense

spaciousness that no earlier setting of the poem had achieved. Equally impressive is *Rastlose Liebe*; here no contrasts are needed, but an unbroken flow of passionately impulsive music.

Looking back for a moment at the enormous mass of songs that Schubert had already written, we can see at once how wide a variety he had achieved, ranging from long, rambling narrative ballads such as *Die Burgschaft*, to delicate strophic settings of poems by Hölty. And the rhythmic variety so characteristic of his work as a whole can already be seen; a comparison between the two settings of *An den Mond*, just mentioned, shows that in the later setting he could use phrases of three bars as convincingly as the more usual two- or four-bar periods. This flexibility of phrase probably arose in the first place from the stimulus provided by the setting of metrical words; it was not till later that it became equally characteristic of his instrumental music.

The instrumental works of 1815, which include the third Symphony, the Quartet in G minor and two unfinished Piano Sonatas, are of small importance compared with the enormous mass of songs produced in that year. In 1816 the instrumental music shows an advance both in quantity and quality, especially in such works as the Fifth Symphony and the five-movement Piano Sonata in E, but the songs are far more individual than any of the other works. They are not quite as numerous as those of the previous year, but the general level is higher, with a wider emotional range, and far less that is derivative. There are still a few ballads of the rambling episodic type, and some of the other longer ones, such as *Der Wanderer*, are somewhat uneven, though they almost always contain fine passages. Many of the best songs are settings of Goethe, the most remarkable being *An Schwager Kronos*; this has the dramatic power of *Der Erlkönig* presented with far greater concentration, and is equally convincing when employing the boldest modulations or the simplest diatonic harmony. There are several settings of the Harper's songs from *Mignon*; the finest of them is the third version of *Wer nie sein Brot*, with its startlingly dramatic end, though it is thought by some to be too long-drawn a setting of the words. He began to be attracted by the poems of Mayrhofer, who was a close friend. Many of these dealt with ancient Greek mythology, which often inspired Schubert to write music of great dignity and breadth. Among the songs of 1816 the most familiar instance is *Lied eines Schiffers an die Dioskuren*, but there are some finer ones written in the following year, such as *Memnon* and *Der entsühnte Orest*.

239

All through 1816 there was a continuous stream of shorter songs, including many of delightful quality; one of them, *In's stille Land*, was, perhaps unconsciously, rewritten ten years later, as Schubert's last solo setting of *Nur wer die Sehnsucht kennt*. His harmonic idiom had by this time become far maturer and more subtle; sometimes, as in *Stimme der Liebe*, the chains of remote modulations sound almost breathless. He had also become aware of the charm of floating quietly from tonic minor to tonic major; this device can be found at its simplest in the cadence of *Der Sänger am Felsen*.

In the year 1817 Schubert's instrumental music began to show far greater individuality, especially in piano sonatas, and the output of songs is considerably smaller. There are a number of fine settings of Mayrhofer, including the two just mentioned, and those of other poets include two extraordinarily dissimilar masterpieces. The one, *Ganymed*, is notable for the beautiful interweaving of the vocal line with the piano part in the opening section, and the increasing rapture of the final pages; the other, *Gruppe aus dem Tartarus* is one of the wildest and most powerful songs that he ever wrote. And at the same period, he could write a simple and homely song like *An die Musik*, the words of which were by his friend Schober; it illustrates well the distinction with which he could use an unpretentious, repeated-chord accompaniment figure. The same kind of inspired simplicity and directness can be felt in the slightly earlier *Litanei*, and all through his life Schubert, like Brahms, never lost interest in the strophic song.

The next two years are comparatively unproductive all round, though the increasing interest in instrumental work continues, culminating with the delightful Piano Sonata in A, Op. 120, which is thought to have been composed in 1819. But the songs, though not very numerous, are remarkably varied, ranging from the delicately austere *Vom Mitleiden Mariae* to the setting of Goethe's *Prometheus*, which has not the sweep and continuity of Wolf's song, but contains some magnificent music. By this time Schubert had become less and less interested in the rambling sectional song. In 1818 he wrote two, *Elysium* and *Der Kampf*, both to words by Schiller; *Prometheus* is equally sectional, but more concise. The only remaining specimens are *Einsamkeit* and *Viola*, written in 1823, which are more lyrical in character. But of the extended songs written by Schubert during the last eight years of his life, the most successful are those in which the texture is unbroken throughout; one of the finest is *Im Walde*, which was composed in 1820, and has a splendid sweep and continuity. A similar spaciousness is achieved on a less enormous scale in the two beautiful *Suleika* songs, and the strangely ecstatic setting of Mayrhofer's *Auflösung*. In all of these songs the piano supplies a continuous background, and the design is free but admirably balanced.

In considering Schubert's songs it is always important not to lose sight of his instrumental works. It was not until 1817 that they began to show real individuality, and even then it was some time before they could reach the same level as the songs written at the same period; such a deeply characteristic mood as the dignified solemnity of some of the Mayrhofer songs, written in 1816 and 1817, does not appear in the instrumental music until the Andante of the A minor Piano Sonata of 1823. But, once he had really found himself in instrumental writing, his interest in it undoubtedly affected certain aspects of his song-writing. Strong contrasts of mood within a single song are not common in his later years, such things being reserved for instrumental music; the two central movements of the String Quintet in C and the Andantino of the posthumous Piano Sonata in A are very remarkable instances. And just as the scale of his later instrumental works tended to become more luxuriant and leisurely, so the designs of the songs became generally more concise.

A detailed account of the development of Schubert's style in the songs of his last eight or nine years is hardly necessary, so individual is his music in every way. His love for chains of remote modulations, sometimes too concentrated in his earlier songs, is indulged with equal boldness but greater breadth in the later ones; his setting of Goethe's *An die Entfernte*, written in 1822, is a particularly lovely instance. He is also fond of going to a comparatively remote key in a single leap without any intervening stages; one of the most wonderful instances is the quiet transition from B major to G major in *Nacht und Träume*. And at the same time he can remain within a very narrow harmonic range with supremely beautiful results, as in *Im Abendrot*, in which a brief glance at the key of the subdominant is done with profoundly moving effect (Ex. 6). He is as endlessly inventive of

Ex. 6 Langsam feierlich

Nein, ich will im Bu sen tra - gen dein- en Him- mel schon all-hier accompaniment figures as of melodies; in the innumerable songs in which the words demand a watery background, he never repeats himself, and is particularly happy when using a simple keyboard figuration that has an implied melodic outline of its own, as in the opening bars of *Der Jüngling an der Quelle* and *Du bist die Ruh*. His melodic ideas are infinitely varied, and are by no means always of the familiar lyrical kind. Sometimes the tune flows in an almost unbroken sweep, as in *Ave Maria*; sometimes, as in *Pause*, it is built of short phrases of varying lengths. Schubert, like Beethoven, was fully aware of the possibilities of varying harmonic movement; in *Das Lied im Grünen* and *Frühlingsbotschaft* there are moments where the background continues unabated, but the melodic line and the harmony move at half the pace, producing a wonderful effect of mystery. And there are several instances of songs that grow almost entirely from a single short phrase in a manner prophetic of Hugo Wolf; in their very different ways *Geheimes, Freiwilliges Versinken* and the remarkably beautiful *Dass sie hier gewesen* all illustrate this, and in the very impressive setting of Goethe's *Grenzen der Menschheit* there is something almost Wagnerian in the development of the opening phrase.

The settings of Goethe, so numerous in Schubert's earlier years, become far less common towards the end of his life, the last being the duet version of *Nur wer die Sehnsucht kennt* and the richly emotional second settings of *Heiss mich nicht reden* and *So lasst mich scheinen*, written in 1826. No other poet inspired him to write so great a variety of songs, and when the same poem was set more than once, the results were often startlingly dissimilar; perhaps the most remarkable instance is *Am Flusse*, of which the earlier setting, composed in 1815, is restless and agitated, and the second, dating from 1822, serene and rippling. And *Nur wer die Sehnsucht kennt* also produced an extraordinary variety of settings, a tribute both to Schubert's versatility and to the fascination of the poem. His connexion with the poetry of Müller began in the summer of 1823, when he started 'Die Schöne Müllerin'; 'Die Winterreise' was completed in 1827. These two cycles give between them a very complete picture of Schubert as a composer of comparatively short songs. Many of those in 'Die Schöne Müllerin' are strophic, but often their idyllic charm may be combined with an extraordinary depth of feeling, particularly in the simple but very subtle *Des Baches Wiegenlied* with which the cycle ends. The restraint with which the gradually unfolding tragedy of the story is depicted in the music shows Schubert's power of saying much in an essentially simple and unrhetorical manner; in 'Die Winterreise' this same power can be felt in a far more generally sombre atmosphere. Here the songs are freer in form, the only strophic one being *Gute Nacht*, with its wonderful change to the major key in its last stanza. Some of them have great warmth, especially *Der Lindenbaum* and *Im Dorfe*, but the prevailing mood is of a grey resignation more impersonal than the pathos of the earlier cycle. It is expressed with great depth in *Der Wegweiser* and with a strange, remote bleakness in *Der Leiermann*, which in some ways is prophetic of Mussorgsky. But, great though these cycles are, it is important, as Maurice J. E. Brown has said in his biography, that they should not be allowed to overshadow the larger songs written at the same time, such as the magnificent *Die junge Nonne*. The posthumously published collection of songs known as 'Schwanengesang' consist mainly of settings of Rellstab and Heine, and those of the latter poet include three of the boldest songs that Schubert ever wrote; *Der Atlas*, with its extraordinary final cadence, *Die Stadt*, in which the diminished seventh is used in a purely impressionistic way, far removed from the sentimentality often associated with it, and *Der Doppelgänger*, the grimmest of them all, in which the few harmonic highlights shine out with immense power against their sombre background. And it is perhaps in character with the strangely fascinating mixture of imaginativeness and homeliness in Schubert that, after writing the most prophetic of all his songs, he should conclude his career as a song-writer with the amiable geniality of *Die Taubenpost*, and, finally, with the charming *Der Hirt auf dem Felsen*, with accompaniment for piano and clarinet.

The emotional range in Schubert's songs is astonishingly wide, but, despite the magnificence of his *Erlkönig*, he was on the whole least successful with the narrative ballad, which he hardly attempted at all in his last years. And it was this branch of song-writing that Carl Loewe, his senior by a few months, found most congenial. He has nothing like Schubert's lyrical gifts, and in such songs as *Die Mutter an der Wiege* or *Süsse Begräbnis*, where there is no narrative interest, he is usually dull, sometimes with rather incongruous patches of coloratura, but some of the dramatic ballads are remarkably powerful and original, especially those that were written in his youth. One of the earliest is *Edward*, which has great dramatic force, and holds together an unusual tonal scheme with complete success; particularly impressive is the variety with which the frequently recurring 'O!' is set. Equally fine is his *Erlkönig*, though it has not quite the spaciousness and melodic invention of Schubert's setting. But there are some wonderfully imaginative touches, such as the use of the notes of a major triad for the Erlkönig's speeches, and the harmony on which the last word of the poem is sung, and the tension of the final page has almost a foretaste of the *Walkürenritt*.

Loewe is not always so successful in maintaining the interest throughout a whole ballad; sometimes, as in *Die Leiche zu St. Just*, an impressive opening is followed by music of a far more conventional kind. Harmonically he could be quite bold when the words demanded it, as when depicting the barbaric trumpets and drums in *Der Mohrenfürst auf der Messe*; more often he contrives to infuse great brilliance and gusto into very simple tonic-and-dominant formulae; the passages that describe the dancing goblins in *Hochzeitlied* and *Herr Oluf* and the picturesque vivacity of *Tom der Reimer* are reminiscent of Weber in their ebullience. But Loewe's melodic gift was not of great distinction, and, although he lived for many years after Schubert's death, he never developed to anything like the same extent. Fine though the best of his ballads are, his inspiration was always liable to falter without the stimulus of a dramatic story or situation.

Mendelssohn, Schumann, and others

Of the German song-writers born in the nineteenth century, Mendelssohn is the oldest and the most conservative, and his songs, though often very pleasant, only occasionally show him at his most distinguished. Compared with the *Songs without Words* for piano, they move within a narrower range, neither rising so high nor sinking so low. On the whole the earlier ones are the best; *Hexenlied* and *Neue Liebe* combine the usual brilliance of his Scherzo-like moods with exceptional fire and energy; the setting of Heine's *Reiselied* also has considerable power. Some of the more lyrical songs suffer, as so often, from complacently ambling rhythms, but *Scheidend* has an appealing pathos, and there are one or two, such as *Das erste Veilchen* and *Die Liebende schreibt* where the phraseology is more varied than usual: indeed the latter is rhythmically more flexible than Brahms's setting of the same words. *Nachtlied*, one of his last songs, achieves on a small scale a dignity and solemnity at which he often aimed far less successfully in more ambitious slow movements. He was not in sympathy with Schubert's music, and the only song of his that might almost be by Schubert is the simple but very charming setting of Heine's *Gruss*. Something of the same homely quality is to be found in *Volkslied* ('Es ist bestimmt'), but there the music could be by no one but Mendelssohn. Although his piano accompaniments are always pleasing both to the ear and to the fingers, they do not show the endless variety of figuration so characteristic of Schubert, nor are they allotted so rich a share of thematic interest as those of Schumann. It was probably a lack of vivid response to words that prevented Mendelssohn from becoming a greater song-writer; in general he was more stirred by scenery and by a picturesquely dramatic situation than by poetry.

Schumann's approach to song, on the other hand, was strongly coloured by the literary background of his youth. Equally important is the fact that he originally intended to be a pianist, not a composer. His early response to poetry made him more fastidious than any of his predecessors in the details of word-setting, especially in connexion with repetition, and his love for the piano made him particularly eager to give it a generous share of musical material. In both of these matters he stands about half-way between Schubert and Wolf. His melodic gift was more distinctive than that of Mendelssohn, and far more so than that of Loewe. His tunes have not quite the variety and flexibility of those of Schubert; they are usually squarer and more short-breathed but they have a strongly personal character of their own; Schumann had a peculiar power, characteristic of the nineteenth rather than the eighteenth century, of compressing a world of emotion into a few bars, as in this passage from *Er, der Herrlichste von Allen* (Ex. 7).

Apart from a few very early songs, some of which were afterwards used in piano works, his career as a song-writer began in 1840, the year at the end of which he married. By this time he had written the greater part of his piano music, and his style had broadened from the mercurial, capricious manner of such works as the *Papillons*, to the more sustained lyricism of the *Humoreske* and the great C major Fantasia. And the impact of the poetry and the excitement of writing for the human voice made that lyricism even warmer and more impulsive than before. An extraordinarily high proportion of his output of songs was written in 1840, including a large number of master-pieces.

He was particularly successful when setting Heine; his own rich sentiment and Heine's biting terseness seemed to act as correctives to each other, and often produced results of unique quality, most of all in the 'Dichterliebe' cycle. Here a great variety of mood is expressed, as in so much of Schumann's finest work, in an essentially intimate and informal manner; even in *Ich grolle nicht* the passion of the music is terse and unrhetorical. Here the balance of interest between the voice and piano is perfectly maintained, and after the bitterness of the last song the pathos of the epilogue is overwhelming. Outside the 'Dichterliebe', Schumann's other Heine settings of this year include a great variety of songs; his two most successful ballads, *Belsatzar* and *Die beiden Grenadiere*, richly lyrical songs, such as *Schöne Wiege* and *Die Lotosblume*, and some of impressive reticence, as *Lieb Liebchen, leg's Händchen auf's Herze mein*. The Eichendorff settings are for the most part softer and gentler: in their different moods *Mondnacht* and *Frühlingsnacht* are supremely beautiful instances; impressive in a very different way is the strangely austere and archaic *Auf einer Burg*. The far less distinguished poetry of Chamisso sometimes proved a greater inspiration to Schumann than might have been expected; the 'Frauen-liebe und -leben' cycle, though it has not the variety of the dramatic intensity of the 'Dichterliebe', contains much beautiful music and, again, the piano epilogue, though less subtle than that of the other cycle, is very moving.

Schumann's harmony is very individual; he does not employ chromatic colouring to a very great extent, but is fond of sudden modulations to comparatively remote keys, and diatonic dissonances and sequences that may well have resulted from his love for the music of J. S. Bach. Sometimes there are technical weaknesses, such as the enormous range of the vocal parts of *Ich grolle nicht* and *Stille Tränen*, in which a singer whose voice is not of exceptional compass is compelled to follow a less interesting alternative. But the finest of the songs written in 1840 are full of a warmth and vitality that appeared more fitfully in the later ones. In 1841 came the songs from Rückert's *Liebes-frühling*, which are on the whole less interesting; the following years were devoted to the composition of orchestral and chamber music, and it was not till 1849 that Schumann returned to song-writing. The album of children's songs is the vocal equivalent of the *Album für die Jugend* for piano written during the previous year; the settings of songs from Goethe's 'Wilhelm Meister' are more ambitious but very uneven in quality. *Kennst du das Land* is a finely passionate song, emotionally somewhere between the pleasant but comparatively slight settings of Beethoven and Schubert on the one hand, and the very rich and elaborate ones by Liszt and Wolf on the other. *Heiss mich nicht reden* has a central section of almost Wagnerian intensity, but in several of the others there is a sense of strain and weariness; the slackening of the old lyrical impulse results in rather self-conscious attempts to achieve greater rhythmic variety, and a curiously restless figuration in the piano parts. The songs of 1850 and 1851 include one or two of great beauty, such as *Ihre Stimme* and *Requiem*, and some charming ones in a lighter vein such as *Aufträge*, but the general standard is uneven, and the settings of poems by Mary Stuart, written in 1852, are dull and colourless.

Considering Schumann's songs as a whole, their strongly individual character is more easily felt than defined. It owes much to the interweaving of the vocal and piano parts, seen at its simplest in *Der Nussbaum*. Often it occurs more subtly, the voice entering in the middle of a phrase or, more frequently, ceasing before the end, and leaving the piano to finish it. Sometimes, as in *Aufträge* and *Du bist wie eine Blume*, the piano steals the climactic note of a phrase in a way that might well be galling to the singer, and would probably have been avoided by Schubert or Brahms. All these procedures have the effect of softening the obvious formal and harmonic landmarks, giving to the music an intimate, confiding character. There is a limit to its range of emotion; the impersonal calm of Schubert at his serenest or the inhuman grimness of a song like *Der Doppelgänger* were beyond its reach, but within its limits Schumann's music has considerable variety of mood, and, despite its strongly Teutonic character, it has had a surprisingly wide influence in other countries, especially France and Russia.

His influence was of course felt in Germany as well, and in various ways. He himself was aware of dissimilar elements in his personality. His own differentiation between Florestan the impulsive, and Eusebius the contemplative, may not always seem as clear-cut to us now as it did to him, and the two are sometimes inextricably blended in his finest work. But it is possible for us now to see how his passionate enthusiasm could be tempered by something more homely and domestic – the side of him that was repelled by much of the operatic work of his contemporaries. The German song-writer most influenced by this aspect of Schumann's personality was Robert Franz. In some of his earlier songs he is surprisingly bold: *Ja, du bist elend*, from Op. 7, is an interesting though not entirely successful experiment in constant modulation built round a single phrase, and *Da sind die bleichen Geister wieder* has considerable power, with a surprising final cadence. But the prevailing tone of his songs as a whole is quiet and demure; many of them are Schumannesque, not only in their intimacy but in their tendency to end inconclusively on a half-cadence, as in the first of Schumann's 'Dichterliebe'. Rhythmically he is usually very simple, though in *Wird er wohl noch meiner gedenken* he uses septuple time rather cautiously. His best songs are gently elegiac in mood; one of the best is a setting of a German translation of Mrs. Hemans's *Mother, oh sing me to rest*. Quite often he will make a song end out of its key in a manner decidedly unusual for the time, and his harmony often has unexpected touches, sometimes gently astringent and sometimes archaic; the opening bars of *In meinem Garten die Nelken* (Ex. 8) are very charac-

teristic. But, attractive though Franz's style can be, its limitations are clearly seen on the occasions when he comes into competition with other and greater composers, especially in his settings of Goethe's *Rastlose Liebe*, and of the poems by Heine treated by Schumann in the 'Dichterliebe'.

The songs of Cornelius show the influence of the more impulsive Schumann, and also those of Liszt and the earlier works of Wagner. For Wagner song-writing was a by-path, and the only point of interest in his early French songs is the way in which his setting of a translation of *Die beiden Grenadiere* anticipates Schumann in its use of the *Marseillaise*. But the settings of five poems by Mathilde Wesendonck, composed in 1857 and 1858, are very characteristic, and the two best, *Im Treibhaus* and *Träume*, contain material used later in *Tristan*. It is not surprising that Wagner wrote so few songs; the very deliberate harmonic movement so characteristic of his mature idiom fitted far more easily into large than into small designs, and his thematic invention was not, generally speaking, of a lyrical nature. Liszt's style, harmonically, has a good deal in common with that of Wagner, but it is less broad, and his melodic ideas are far more varied, both in character and in quality. Though he set many German poems to music he can hardly be included as a German song-writer: his musical style, like his career, was essentially cosmopolitan. His settings of Italian words, including the three Petrarch sonnets, are early in date, but the language of Italian opera affected him deeply, and its influence can be found in a large proportion of his songs, in whatever language the words were written; the result is usually more grandiose and less delicate than in the music of Chopin, where the same influence is equally strong.

On the whole, Liszt's most completely successful songs are purely lyrical, such as *Oh, quand je dors* and *Es muss ein Wunderbares sein*. In the finest of his big instrumental works, such as the Sonata in B minor, the structure is entirely convincing, but in the larger songs, such as *Ich möchte hingehn* vivid word-painting is apt to result in incoherence. His settings of Goethe contain beautiful and characteristic music, though the gestures are apt to be over-emphatic. The poetry of Heine was more akin temperamentally, and some of his settings are very remarkable, such as *Ein Fichtenbaum steht einsam*, but here again, individual details are sometimes overstressed; in *Am Rhein, am schönen Strom* the sudden burst of rhetoric at the words 'das grosse, das heilige Köln' spoils an otherwise beautiful song, and puts it on a lower level than Schumann's very impressive setting. And, despite his intense interest in the words, his stressing of the syllables sometimes shows that German was not his native language; the opening of his *Kennst du das Land* is a well-known instance. But harmonically his songs are of the greatest interest. In many of the early ones he uses a chromaticism more advanced than anything that Wagner was doing at the time; occasionally, as in *Die drei Zigeuner*, the colouring is vividly Hungarian, and in the latest songs, such as *Gebet* and *Ihr Glocken von Marling*, harmony is used in a strange, almost impressionistic way, with no idea of tonal unity. Throughout Liszt's songs there is far less suggestion of the piano virtuoso than might have been expected, and in the later ones there is no trace of it whatever.

Cornelius was a close friend of Liszt and a keen student of Wagner's music; some of his larger songs, such as *Auf eine Unbekannte*, come near to Liszt's rhapsodical manner, though with more restraint, and often he uses a pleasantly flowing lyricism that seems to be half-way between *Lohengrin* and *Die Meistersinger*. But the fierier and more provocative aspects of these two composers had little effect on Cornelius, to whom the more intimate warmth of Schumann's music was obviously more congenial. It can be felt particularly in his most familiar songs, the charming 'Weihnachtslieder'. But the simple friendliness of these songs is only one facet of his personality; the other song-cycles (for most of which he wrote his own words) have more variety. The third of the 'Rheinische Lieder' experiments very successfully with irregular rhythms; *An Bertha* and the 'Brautlieder' have great warmth and harmonic richness; the latter is one of his best works. The nine songs on the Lord's Prayer use plainsong themes with much unobtrusive ingenuity; among the other songs, *Auftrag* is notable for its harmonic originality, and the setting of Heine's *Warum sind denn die Rosen so blass* for its sombre breadth. Cornelius's songs are certainly the work of a personality stronger and more vital than is often imagined, and deserve to be better known. Those of Adolf Jensen, also influenced by Schumann, are pleasant but on the whole less significant, and more limited emotionally; now and then, however, they show more distinctive traits, as in the setting of Eichendorff's *Waldesgespräch*, which is completely unlike that of Schumann, and has considerable dramatic fire.

Brahms

Brahms was younger than Cornelius, older than Jensen, and in his general approach to composition very unlike either. They both, in their different ways, wrote in what was definitely a contemporary idiom, while that of Brahms, though very individual, was more firmly rooted in the past. It shows traces of Schumann's influence, especially in some of the earlier works, but it was far more deeply affected by Schubert. Both composers approached the composition of songs from a predominantly musical standpoint, and had not Schumann's literary background. But Schubert, the more instinctive and impulsive of the two, could respond more vividly to poetry, though he was liable to be careless in the details of word setting. Brahms could not command so wide a range of emotional expression and the words of his songs were not often taken from the greatest poetry. Beauty of melody, of rhythm, and of musical texture were his chief concerns, and all can be found in profusion throughout his songs. His word-setting, like that of Schubert, was sometimes careless, but his musical sensitiveness often enabled him to transcend words that were in themselves of no great distinction. The early songs are unequal: the best, such as *Liebestreu*, are very individual, but some are pleasantly Schumannesque with no marked character of their own, and one of the very earliest, *Heimkehr*, is original, but in a curiously clumsy way.

As his style develops, it is possible to discover various distinctive traits, which sometimes seem to point in conflicting directions. He was deeply attached to the folk-music of Germany, but at the same time he inherited from Schubert a love for phrases of unusual length, which give many of his tunes a rhythmic variety far removed from the squarely regular periods of Teutonic folk-song. In his personality there were contradictory features; a streak of dourness resulting probably from his very grim early youth, and another of kindness and sympathy that found easier expression in his later years. All these have left their mark on his songs. The influence of folk-song is found more in the earlier than in the later ones, but all through his life he retained his interest in the simple strophic song, and he could write such things as *Der Schmied*, which has all the simplicity and directness of a folk-song, though its idiom is purely personal, and could come from nobody but Brahms. The early songs are on the whole less consistently individual than the early piano works, but Op. 32, a set of nine songs published in 1864, gives a thoroughly clear picture of Brahms's musical personality. But it is still the sombre, north German side of him that is most prominent; it is expressed with particular power in the first two, *Wie rafft ich mich auf in der Nacht* and *Nicht mehr zu dir zu gehen*; only in the last song, the famous *Wie bist du, meine Königin*, is his more genial, lyrical side allowed to assert itself fully. In the next set, however, the fifteen songs to words from Tiecke's 'Magelone', it luxuriates almost to excess and the effect of the cycle as a whole is somewhat cloying, though some of the individual songs are of very high quality, such as *Ruhe, Süssliebchen* and *Wie froh und frisch*.

In the 'Magelonelieder' there is a leisurely expansiveness that can be found in some of the earlier instrumental slow movements, such as those of the F minor Piano Sonata and the A major Piano Quartet, but is not on the whole characteristic of his later work. A large number of songs appeared in 1868, mostly on a comparatively small scale, but in their different ways very characteristic. There are a number of small strophic ones, sometimes archaic in style, such as the severely modal *Vergangen ist mir Glück und Heil*. In one of the largest and finest, *Von ewiger Liebe*, the sombre and more genial aspects of Brahms appear in juxtaposition: in one of the smallest and most charming, *Wiegenlied*, a traditional Austrian *ländler* is woven ingeniously into the accompaniment. The piano writing becomes increasingly sensitive in these songs;

it is particularly delightful in *An ein Veilchen*. The only one that approaches the scale of the 'Mageloneelieder' is *Abenddämmerung*, which is in a spacious but closely-knit rondo form; the opening of what might be called the second episode is peculiarly characteristic in its texture (Ex. 9). The deeply thoughtful mood of this song is one that became

increasingly prominent in Brahms's later songs; but the next set, Op. 57, look back rather to the earlier and more exuberant emotions, especially in the magnificent *Unbewegte laue Luft*. These appeared in 1871, and for the rest of Brahms's life his output of songs continued steadily.

There is not the slightest trace of slackening vitality, as there certainly is in the last songs of Schumann; on the other hand there is not the astonishing adventurousness of some of Schubert's latest songs. Brahms is concerned more with an ever-increasing perfection of technique and concentration of emotion. Sometimes his touch is exquisitely light, as in *O komme, holde Sommernacht* and *Das Mädchen spricht*; in some, such as *Meine Liebe ist grün* and *Willst du das ich geh* there is a passionate exuberance. Some of them have affinities with the more lyrical instrumental works; the melody of *Regenlied* is used in the Finale of the Violin Sonata in G, and both *Minnelied* and *Wie Melodien* have thematic resemblances to the first movement of the Violin Sonata in A. Many of the finest are deeply thoughtful, in a mood that is sombrely resigned rather than tragic. His setting of Heine's *Der Tod, das ist die kühle Nacht* is peculiarly characteristic, not only in its general tone, but also in its extraordinary concentration and continuity. *Auf dem Kirchhofe*, concerned also with the peace of death, has something of the same atmosphere, and it finds still more majestic expression in the first three of the 'Vier ernste Gesänge' written in 1896. But at the end of the third the pessimism melts into a deep tenderness that is equally characteristic of Brahms, and is again felt at the end of the exultant fourth song.

Considering Brahms's songs as a whole, it is, more than anything else, their melodic invention that impresses. It has not quite the supreme spontaneity and variety of Schubert but it is beautifully fashioned, spacious in line, and flexible in rhythm. The influence of folk-song can be found in some of them, *Sonntag* being a pleasant example, but songs of this kind usually sound slightly archaic compared with the others. In general Brahms's tunes are more far-flung melodically and more varied rhythmically than the average German folk-song. Harmonically he makes no attempt to break new ground, but can use a traditional idiom in a thoroughly independent and individual way. His use of chromatic colour is nothing like as concentrated as that of Chopin, or even Schumann; plain diatonic harmony and the simple, traditional modulations he could always use with distinction. Earlier in this chapter attention was drawn to the serene profundity of Schubert's *Im Abendroth*; the song of Brahms that comes nearest to its mood is *Feldeinsamkeit*. Brahms's music is of very great beauty, but it has not quite the simplicity and directness of Schubert's, and depends more upon details. But in the latter half of the nineteenth century it was not easy for a composer to write at the same time in so conservative and in so independent a style, and it was Brahms's sense of detail, warmed by his great melodic gift, that enabled him to continue in the classical tradition with such success; the emotional range and the literary sensitiveness of his songs may have been limited, but their musical value is of the highest, and few song-writers have maintained so consistent a standard.

Wolf, Mahler, Strauss

But, in general, literary considerations preponderated more and more in the developments of German song towards the end of the nineteenth century. Brahms died in 1897, and in the same year Hugo Wolf, his junior by twenty-seven years, wrote his last songs, the three settings of translations from Michelangelo, before going out of his mind. His earliest were written in 1875, and, with his very literary approach to song-writing, it is not surprising to find the influence of Schumann strongly imprinted on these. At this stage Wolf was more successful when writing in a lyrical and comparatively traditional manner than when attempting something more ambitious; *Morgentau*, *Ernst ist der Frühling*, and some others of this kind still sound fresh and charming, while such songs as *Nächtliche Wanderung*, though more prophetic of his later style, seem to aim at more than they can achieve. On the other hand in *Zur Ruh', zur Ruh'*, written in 1883, the style, though still simple compared with many of the later songs, is very individual. He was an enthusiastic Wagnerian, and, as was almost inevitable at that time, a proportionately violent anti-Brahmsian. He disapproved strongly of Brahms's predominantly musical approach to words, and his sometimes insensitive declamation; quite apart from technical considerations he was far removed temperamentally from what would have seemed to be cold and archaic in Brahms's music. He was attracted to Wagner by his harmonic adventurousness, and also by his handling of words; scrupulously careful about declamation and at the same time treating the vocal line as part of an ensemble, and not as the unopposed master of the situation. But his musical thought was more concentrated and less spacious than that of Wagner, and in the more restrained of his mature songs the texture is as intimate and delicate as that of chamber music.

Throughout the productive part of his life bouts of intense activity would be followed by periods in which he was unable to write a note. When in the vein, however, he would work with formidable concentration, and the collection of Mörike songs, which contains many of the best known, were all written in 1888. Some of the most popular, such as *Der Gärtner* and *Fussreise*, are comparatively conventional, though very delightful. But there is great variety in this volume, both of mood and of texture. *In der Frühe* shows Wolf at his most concentrated, a freely flowing vocal part being woven over a piano part in which a single short phrase is taken through a variety of keys with a feeling of complete inevitability. Something of the same idea, but with lighter texture and on a larger scale, is carried out in the delightful *Auf einer Wanderung*, where the piano part has two contrasted themes. There are some intensely dramatic songs, such as *Der Feuerreiter*, some that are sardonically humorous, and some, such as *Gesang Weylas*, *Auf ein altes Bild* and *Schlafendes Jesuskind*, that use a very simple language in a wholly individual manner. The Eichendorff songs were for the most part written in the same year, though a few of them were of earlier date. They are fewer in number, and on the whole less interesting than the Mörike settings, but *Verschwiegene Liebe* has great delicacy and tenderness, and *Das Ständchen* is a beautiful instance of Wolf's skilful interweaving of vocal and piano parts.

Close on the heels of these come the Goethe settings, which cover a wider range than any of the other collections. The more lyrical ones are all of the greatest beauty; *Anakreons Grab*, *Frühling übers Jahr*, *Blumengruss* and *Gleich und Gleich*, show Wolf at his simplest and most sympathetic. On the other hand some of the settings of poems from the 'West-östlicher Divan' are unattractively turgid and rhetorical. Most of the moods in this volume had been foreshadowed to some extent in the earlier collections; what is new, however, is the spaciousness of some of the songs. Wolf was well acquainted with Schubert's numerous Goethe settings and he himself never set poems to which he felt that Schubert had done complete justice.

It is particularly interesting to compare the two composers' treatment of *Prometheus, Ganymed,* and *Grenzen der Menschheit.* The two settings of the third poem have something of the same solemnity, though Wolf's is the more sombre. In the others, the composers differ more markedly, and in both cases Wolf has produced the more continuous and closely knit structure. In his *Prometheus* the piano part is almost too massive for so long a song, but in *Ganymed* the texture is beautifully woven and produces an atmosphere of extraordinary serenity. In his settings of poems from *Wilhelm Meister,* Wolf competes with both Schubert and Schumann. In *Wer sich der Einsamkeit, Wer nie sein Brot,* and *An die Türen,* Wolf, if not more beautiful musically than Schubert, sets the words with more concentrated emotion, the first being especially fine; Schumann is impressive in *An die Türen* but rather laboured in the others. Of Mignon's songs, Wolf's *So lass mich scheinen* is of strange beauty, with a haunting, rather Grieg-like phrase recurring in the piano part; his *Nur wer die Sehnsucht kennt* has a tenser and more tortured atmosphere than any earlier setting, and his *Kennst du das Land* contains some magnificent music, though it might be thought almost too rich and grandiloquent for the words. Among the other Goethe songs there are many of a very different kind that should be mentioned; *Der Rattenfänger, Die Spröde,* and *Die Bekehrte* are vivid character portraits, *Epiphanias* is charmingly gay, and the first *Cophtisches Lied* reflects perfectly the sardonic geniality of the words. With all his dramatic power, Wolf, like Schubert, was not generally at his best in the narrative ballad; none of those that appear among the Goethe songs are as successful as the earlier *Feuerreiter.*

Wolf never visited either Spain or Italy but was deeply attracted by the atmosphere of both countries; the fact that he never saw either of them may have enhanced this attraction. The Goethe songs were finished in 1889, and he then began his 'Spanisches Liederbuch', to translations from the Spanish by Paul Heyse and Emanuel Geibel. These are for the most part on a smaller scale than the Goethe settings, and can be divided more easily into categories; the religious and the secular, which in their turn can be subdivided into the serene and the intense. The gentler of the religious songs have a wonderful serenity and simplicity of texture; *Nun wandre, Maria* and *Ach, des Knaben Augen* are beautiful instances, and the rather more spacious *Die ihr schwebet* has a strange, ecstatic atmosphere. In all three songs the piano provides an unbroken background to the vocal line. Others are in a far more tortured mood, and in these the accompaniment is often built on a single rhythmic figure, repeated with a kind of relentless persistence, against sombrely chromatic harmony; *Herr, was trägt der Boden hier* and *Mühvoll komm' ich* are fine examples. In these is no suggestion of a Spanish background; it can be felt more in some of the secular songs, though it does not amount to more than imitations of a guitar in the piano part. Sometimes in the religious songs the chromaticism suggests *Parsifal*, and in the secular, *Tristan*, but the proportions are so much smaller, with the result that the details are more concentrated, and the harmonic movement less deliberate. Of the more hectic love-songs, the finest is *Geh', Geliebter*, which has an immense sweep and passion, and makes a magnificent climax to the volume. There are other secular songs of gentler character, such as the delightful lyrics *Auf dem grünen Balkon* and *Wenn du zu den Blumen gehst*, both of which contain some of Wolf's most delicate part-writing, and *In dem Schatten meiner Locken*, which was afterwards used in *Der Corregidor*. There are others in the same playful vein, and, in a completely different mood, the sombre and magnificent *Alle gingen, Herz, zur Ruh*.

The first part of the 'Italienisches Liederbuch' was written in 1890 and 1891; the second in 1896, the year after the composition of *Der Corregidor*. But the songs are very unified in style and it could never be guessed that between the two parts there had been a period of complete inactivity. They are nearly all on a small scale and, though there are many moods, they are always expressed in a delicate and intimate way. The violent emotions that were liable to appear in the earlier books have no place here; the humorous songs are gentler, and the love-songs, of which there are still many, are tender rather than vehement; *Heb' auf dein blondes Haupt* and *Und willst du deinen Liebsten sterben sehen* are two particularly lovely instances. The texture is more economical than formerly, and there is never any suggestion, as there sometimes is among the earlier songs, that the accompaniment is excessively orchestral in feeling. Wolf's lyrical counterpoint is particularly prominent; a very simple and moving instance comes near the end of *Wenn du mich mit den Augen streifst* (Ex. 10), where first the voice and then the

Ex.10 Langsam doch leidenschaftlich

Wenn es aus-bre-chen will vor gros - ser Lust

rinforzando

ff

piano rise to a climax within two beats of each other. The simplicity of these songs conceals an extraordinary depth and subtlety, and their clarity and economy of notes does not involve the sacrifice of any of Wolf's individuality

After the 'Italienisches Liederbuch' he wrote very few more songs; translations of two poems by Byron and three by Michelangelo. The two Byron songs, *Sun of the Sleepless* and *There be none of Beauty's Daughters* contain fine and characteristic music, but the Michelangelo songs, his last, are more remarkable. The first, *Wohl denk' ich oft*, has immense power and dignity, and is followed by *Alles endet, was entstehet*, which is bleak and sombre beyond words. The third, *Fühlt meine Seele*, is less forbidding and has something of the warmth of the love-songs written in earlier years. These songs were written in March 1897; before the end of the year his mind had gone. Of his German predecessors, Schumann is probably the one to whom he owed most, and it is strange that the lives of both composers should have ended in the same sad way. It was Schumann who had led the way towards a more sensitive accentuation of words and a more subtle blend between voice and piano; Wolf developed both of these things, and his treatment of the voice was also influenced by Wagner. But the result has been something wholly individual, and not to be judged by the standards of earlier song-writers, but of the greatest value, both for its own interest and for ways in which it pointed to the future.

Wolf and Mahler were born in the same year, and in their youth they were friends and fellow-students; both tense and highly strung personalities, sharing a warm admiration for the music of Wagner and Bruckner. But a comparison between the early songs of the two composers at once shows striking differences. With all his wide emotional range, Wolf had little feeling for melody of a simple popular type; even in his early works it plays only a small part and, in later years, he bitterly resented the success of Humperdinck's *Hansel and Gretel*. But in Mahler's 'Lieder und Gesänge aus der Jugendzeit', which

257

were written between 1880 and 1892, the music is steeped in the idiom of Austrian popular melody; some of them are commonplace, but often the familiar turns of phrase are given odd and unexpected twists. One of the best and most characteristic is *Nicht Wiedersehn*, where, under the very simple tune, the strange harmonic touches are curiously moving, and the haunting setting of the word 'Ade' looks ahead to the last song of 'Das Lied von der Erde'. In the 'Lieder eines fahrenden Gesellen', completed in 1885, there is the same melodic simplicity, with far more flexibility of rhythm and subtlety of texture. Already there are signs of the contrapuntal tendency that was so pronounced in Mahler's later work; the melody of the second song, later used in the First Symphony, is treated canonically with delightful ease. The words of this set of songs are by the composer; for most of the earlier ones he draws upon 'Des Knaben Wunderhorn', a collection of traditional German poems. He returned to this for his next set, begun in 1888 and finished in 1899.

These are on a larger scale and more dramatic in character; they illustrate well the odd, almost tragic significance with which Mahler could surround the street music that he had heard in his youth. They are far removed in atmosphere from the songs that Brahms and Wolf were writing at the same period; there is nothing like the intricate chromaticism of Wolf, and Brahms, even in his most *volkstümlich* mood, would not have written tunes as frankly popular as those that appear, with strangely nostalgic effect, in *Wo die schönen Trompeten blasen*. These 'Knaben Wunderhorn' songs have more in common with Schubert, especially the delightful *Rheinlegendchen* which is the most lyrical of the set. Like the 'Lieder eines fahrenden Gesellen', they exist with both piano and orchestral accompaniment. *Urlicht* and *Es sungen drei Engel* were taken respectively from the Second and Third Symphonies, and *Des Antonius von Padua Fischpredigt* was expanded into the third movement of the Second Symphony. And apart from this transference of material, these songs have much in common with the Second, Third and Fourth Symphonies, all of which employ voices.

The rest of Mahler's songs were written after 1900, and are subtler and more rarified in style. *Revelge* and *Der Tambourg'sell*, which are both settings of 'Knaben Wunderhorn' poems, were written in 1901, though not published till 1905, and are in his pre-1900 manner, on a very large scale. But the five settings of poems by Rückert and the 'Kindertoten-lieder', also by Rückert, show hardly any trace of popular influence. The orchestral accompaniments are most fastidiously scored, and the suggestion of a street band, though it is still sometimes felt in the later Symphonies, has no place in these songs. There is much melodic beauty in the vocal parts, but rhythmically they are very flexible. An oversentimental setting of the words of the 'Kindertotenlieder' would be unbearable, but Mahler has handled them with a delicacy and restraint that is deeply moving. Among the other Rückert songs, *Liebst du um Schönheit* and *Ich atmet' einen linden Duft* have a similar lyrical tenderness: *Um Mitternacht* ends with a massive climax achieved by great economy of means, and *Ich bin der Welt abhanden gekommen*, perhaps Mahler's finest song, has an extraordinary depth and serenity (Ex. 11). These songs show Mahler in a far more intimate mood than the enormous Symphonies written at the same period; it was not until 'Das Lied von der Erde' that the oddly dissimilar elements in his personality could be combined in what was certainly his masterpiece. In many ways his music is very characteristic of the latter half of the nineteenth

Ex.11 Molto lento e ritenuto

Ich bin der Welt ab - han-den ge - kom - men

century, especially in its romantic nostalgia; but the increasingly contrapuntal texture of his later work, sometimes at the expense of euphony, looks strongly ahead to various developments of the present century.

Richard Strauss was born four years later than Mahler, but, although he could on occasion use dissonances of considerable pungency, his work as a whole is decidedly less prophetic than that of Mahler, and became more and more conservative in his later years. The majority of his songs were written before 1900; the more declamatory of them show the influence of Wagner, and the more lyrical, that of Schumann in his most impulsive moods, the Schumann of *Widmung* and *Er, der Herrlichste von Allen*. But compared with these, the lyricism of Strauss, though often broad and exhilarating, is more rhetorical and less sensitive; the subtle delicacy of a song like *Mondnacht* was beyond his grasp, though his very attractive setting of *Traum durch die Dämmerung* is not very far removed. The early song *Allerseelen*, with its rich and full-blooded sentiment, is highly characteristic; many of the later songs use what is basically the same idiom, but with a greater harmonic elaboration resulting sometimes from dissonances but more often from remote modulations. The success of the songs often depends on the skill with which these are handled; sometimes, as in *Mein Auge*, or *Glückes genug*, the results are fidgety and pointless, and sometimes as in *Befreit* or *Freundliche Vision*, they are of great beauty. The piano writing is often rich to a fault, but it is very varied; sometimes, as in *Morgen* and *Stiller Gang*, the texture, in very different ways, is more contrapuntal than usual, with beautiful results. On the whole the more lyrical songs are the most successful, and some of the most lightly built, such as *Ständchen*, have an enduring freshness and charm. The more declamatory are more unequal; some are impressive, such as *Ruhe, meine Seele*, but many are rather ponderously turgid. All through his life Strauss retained a characteristically German love for very simple diatonic harmony. One of his most elaborate songs is *Frühlingsfeier*, the words of which had previously been set in a gently sedate manner by Franz. Strauss's song is in his most grandiose vein but the most characteristic moment is the following phrase (Ex. 12), with its combination

of simple harmony and widely curving melody. On the whole Strauss's musical personality was simpler and more forthright than that of either Mahler or Wolf, and his style did not develop to the same extent as theirs. But the 'Vier letzte Lieder', written in his last years, are, especially perhaps the last two, full of a wonderfully rich, nostalgic beauty, and make a touchingly valedictory end to his career as a song-writer; gentler and less poignant than Mahler's 'Lied von der Erde', with which it has something in common.

In the songs of both Mahler and Strauss diatonic melody plays an important part; in Strauss it is more florid and Italianate than in Mahler. But after them the melodic idiom of German song tended to become more and more chromatic. Pfitzner and Reger both derive to some extent from Schumann and Brahms, but neither had any outstanding lyrical gift; both were fundamentally conservative composers, but with a restlessness that affected details more than general questions of style. Pfitzner, the older composer of the two, is musically the more austere and the more traditional; sometimes he looks back to some of the less obvious and more withdrawn of Schumann, such as *Zwielicht* and *Auf einer Burg*. But there are also signs of a rather uneasy striving for something more adventurous. In the 'Alte Weisen', for instance, which were written in 1923, there is considerable difference of style between *Tretet ein, hoher Krieger*, which is very much in the Schumann-Mahler tradition, and *Wie glänzt der helle Mond*, which is much freer in idiom.

In the former, though it may seem rather square and ultra-Teutonic, Pfitzner seems more at his ease than in the somewhat tentatively impressionistic style of the latter. Reger's style is more opulent, with immense wealth of harmonic detail; as a song writer he is most attractive when writing on a small scale, as in the 'Schlichte Weisen', where the intimate tone acts as a corrective to Reger's exuberance, and saves the music from becoming turgid. In the larger and more ambitious songs the very thick texture and the perpetually shifting chromatic harmony give the impression of a constant striving to break new ground which results, however, merely in an unsatisfying restlessness that often seems to get nowhere in particular. This is especially the case in the quicker and more energetic songs; when the tempo is slower there is more time for the harmonies to make their point and the vocal line has greater breadth; some of the more reflective songs such as *Der Bote* and *Schlafliedchen* have considerable beauty. But even at its best, Reger's chromaticism seems ponderous beside the subtle and sensitive harmonic colour that Fauré, a composer nearly thirty years his senior, was able to achieve with so much less ado. Joseph Marx, born in 1882, has written many songs; the earlier ones, such as *Japanisches Regenlied*, *Barcarolle*, and many others, are in a pleasantly rich, late-Romantic vein, somewhere between the subtle intricacy of Wolf and the more direct impulsiveness of Strauss. Later, as in his 'Italienisches Liederbuch', the harmony is more impressionistic, with suggestions of Debussy, but fundamentally Marx's style has remained conservative.

The Twentieth Century

Meanwhile in the works of some other German song-writers, chromaticism leads to more far-reaching results. In the early songs of

Schoenberg the style is an extension of that of Wagner's last works, the general intensity being emphasized by very wide leaps in the vocal line; the same characteristic can be found in the early songs of Alban Berg, probably the most gifted of Schoenberg's pupils. In his *Sieben frühe Lieder*, completed in 1908, the tonality, though very fluid, can still be felt; in the slightly later songs, Op. 2, it is more tenuous, the last song being atonal. And in 1908 Schoenberg himself took a similar step; his Second String Quartet, though very chromatic, could just be described as being in F sharp minor, but the three piano pieces, Op. 11, and the fifteen songs from 'Das Buch der hängenden Gärten' by Stefan George are definitely atonal. The songs are mostly on a small scale and the manner is mysteriously epigrammatic; despite the absence of tonality the style is not markedly different from the works written shortly before. It is still possible for an occasional common chord to appear without seeming out of place, and sometimes, as in the opening bars of the tenth song, the influence of Wagner can be strongly felt.

During the following years Schoenberg's style became increasingly provocative, and in 'Pierrot Lunaire', a song-cycle for voice and a small combination of instruments, the vocal part is throughout written for 'Sprechgesang' in which the singer is concerned with rhythm and interval but not with exactitude of pitch. The songs are highly concentrated, and melodically angular and fragmentary, but the style is entirely suited to the words, and the whole work shows an amazing sense of colour and atmosphere of a macabre kind. But it was not the kind of thing that could be done more than once; in a few years' time Schoenberg began to develop a style that was to be less concentrated, less colourful, and more consciously concerned with problems of form, and with the systematic use of twelve notes of the chromatic scale on equal terms. This led to an even more rigid avoidance of traditional harmony, and an even more consistent melodic angularity, of the kind that took little account of the convenience of any instrument, and still less of the human voice. Once Schoenberg had evolved the twelve-note system, he wrote a large amount of instrumental music, and also some choral and dramatic works, but only one set of three songs.

Berg wrote no more songs after his early sets, but several sets were written by Anton von Webern, who was one of the most uncompromising of Schoenberg's pupils. Even the earliest of these, dating from 1909, are completely atonal, and at least as advanced in idiom as Schoenberg's 'Buch der hängenden Gärten' songs. His adoption of the twelve-note system in 1924 led to an extreme sparseness of texture, and a strangely disembodied type of melody, often highly fragmentary. (Ex. 13). It shows, as it were, the bare bones of twelve-note system at its

bleakest, and appreciation of it will probably always be a matter of individual temperament. The complete absence of tonality inevitably brings with it a danger of monotony, and the idiom of Webern's songs is essentially one for work on a very small scale; in his Cantatas the vocal line, though very difficult to sing, is slightly more sustained. In all his work the economy and consistency of texture show him to be a highly finished and fastidious stylist; this fact cannot be denied even by those to whom his idiom is unsympathetic. Other German composers have made a more eclectic and less thorough-going use of the twelve-note system, such as Krenek and Henze, both of whom have written songs, though they have been more concerned with instrumental and dramatic music. The enormous output of Hindemith does not include many songs, and his idiom is more naturally instrumental than vocal.

But he has a very individual melodic idiom, which has gradually become more genial and approachable; he has always been a very practical composer, and even in a comparatively early work like *Die junge Magd* he could write a vocal line far more straightforward than in the very angular instrumental music that he was writing at the time. And, although his approach to composition has always been instinctively contrapuntal, he has obviously realized that in a song, however contrapuntal the texture, the voice must, sometimes at least, sing something that is broader and more obviously melodic than anything in the accompaniment. Hindemith's most important work for voice and piano is the cycle 'Das Marienleben', originally written in 1922, and drastically revised in 1948, receiving treatment not unlike that applied by Brahms to his Piano Trio in B major. In 1944 appeared some settings of English words. Hindemith's music, even during its most provocative period, has never been atonal, and in his later work there has been not only a greater smoothness of melodic line, but also a clearer sense of tonality and a less constant reliance on counterpoint. It is possible that, in the long run, his songs may reach a wider section of the musical public than those of the atonalists.

The future developments of German song depend on various very uncertain considerations. Although the twelve-note system is now being used by a number of composers in several European countries, it still seems more likely that it will continue as an interesting and provocative tributary rather than a part of the mainstream of European music. But if, in its most uncompromising form, it were to acquire a more dominating position, it might lead to the end not only of solo song but of all vocal music. Earlier in this chapter stress was laid on the importance of seeing the development of song side by side with that of opera. Despite his overwhelming interest in dramatic music, Wagner's music was in many ways written with more sympathy for instruments than for voices, and the great German song-writers of the nineteenth century had little success with opera. It is significant that during the latter part of his life Richard Strauss concentrated more and more on opera and wrote proportionately fewer songs. And among the younger German composers of vocal music, many, such as Carl Orff, Werner Egk and Boris Blacher show far more interest in choral and dramatic music than in song. Howard Hartog, writing about contemporary German music, has said that 'in Germany a composer who does not compose an opera is regarded as in some degree impotent', and it may be that for the time being the more retiring lyric Muse will be thrust into the shade by her more self-assertive operatic sister. Nor are the electronic experiments of such composers as Stockhausen likely to encourage the progress of song. But the great outpouring of lyrical song in Germany throughout the nineteenth century is one of the great glories of her musical past, and it is hard to believe that a similar movement will not one day come to light in the future.

Holland

DAVID COX

IN an article on music in Holland in the periodical *Music Survey*,
Marius Flothuis, the distinguished Dutch composer, wrote: 'I have
often noticed that my British colleagues are astonished that so few
Dutch compositions are available in printed editions . . . After the long
gap in musical creation in Holland, Dutch composing did not have a
good reputation and publishers did not expect a large market for works
by Dutch composers . . . Since 1946 Dutch composers have had an
institute which is unique in the whole world, the Foundation Donemus
(short for 'Documentation in the Netherlands for Music'). This
institute replaces the work of publishers by making photo-copies of the
scores . . . Every composer who associates with Donemus keeps the
right to publish a work as soon as a publisher is ready to handle it.'

That was written in 1949, and the situation is much the same
today.

For examples of early solo song, the first composer to be noted is
Constantijn Huygens. Besides writing poems in several languages, and
other literary works, Huygens was the composer of twelve Italian airs,
seven French airs, and twenty Latin psalms, all for solo voice accompanied by *basso continuo* (harpsichord and string bass). These were
published all together under the title *Partodia sacra et profana* in Paris in
1647, and again in 1882 – and again in 1957 (Bärenreiter), this time

edited by Frits Noske. The Italian and French airs show considerable mastery of quite a wide range of expression, and (as Frits Noske says) are of historical interest as a rare example of true solo song (pure monody) at that time in the Netherlands. The words were probably all by the composer. Here is an example of one of the Italian airs: it might almost be by Monteverdi.

Ex. 1

Que fe-rons-nous? que fe-rons-nous, mon— pau-vre coeur? A qui — s'en faut - il pren - dre? Clo-ris — est sourde à — la fu-reur Des cris, — des cris que sans cri-er el - le sou-lait en-ten - dre.

Very different in style, a collection of *Four-and-twenty Songs from the fifteenth and sixteenth centuries*, arranged for voice and piano by J. C. M. van Riemsdijk, was published in Amsterdam in 1890. Half of these are with secular words and half with sacred. They are simple, unpretentious melodies simply and attractively arranged. Arrangements of old Dutch songs and dances have also been made by Julius Röntgen. And Willem Pijper has published two collections of old Dutch songs (Wagenaar, 1924 and 1935) and a collection of old Dutch love-songs (Wagenaar, 1920).

The eighteenth century produced nothing worth noting in the way of Dutch solo song. Johannes Verhulst, in the early nineteenth century, set Dutch words to music and tried hard to cultivate a truly Dutch style, but his songs are conservative and dull. An exception, however, is his 'Kinderleven' Op. 30 (Amsterdam, 1860?), forty-one songs – some solo, some for mixed voices – attractively portraying various aspects of child life. This composer was a friend of Schumann, whose *Scenes of Childhood* were obviously a strong influence.

Richard Hol and Willem Nicolai followed Verhulst and did much for the emancipation of Dutch music from the German yoke under

266

which it was then labouring. The more interesting of the two was Nicolai; and in some of his settings of German words he uses the German musical idiom with a certain individuality. His 'Drei Gesänge' (Leipzig, 1859) for low voice and piano, include *Nachtlied*, an exciting and dramatic setting of Uhland's poem 'Ich reit' ins finstre Land hinein' – a sort of *Erl-King*. The other two, *Herbstklage* and *Trost*, are Schumann-ish, slow and sad. Nicolai's 'Fünf Lieder', Op. 8 (Leipzig, 1859) are all short, well varied in expression, and technically accomplished. No. 3, Geibel's poem *Vöglein, wohin so schnell?* is charmingly set, with an effective change from minor to major half-way through. No. 4, *Gondoliera* (the poem also by Geibel) has a fine Mendelssohn-like melody over a rocking semiquaver accompaniment. Much less good is his song *Bleib' bei mir* – published in London in the mid-nineteenth century under the title *Now the blooming flow'rets tremble* – the style of which suggests Victorian sentimentality.

Alphons Diepenbrock was a friend of Mahler, and developed a personal and richly chromatic style. He left quite a number of songs – settings of poems ranging from Goethe to Baudelaire. His setting of the latter's *L'Invitation au voyage* is quite unsatisfactory; but he is more successful in his *Due Canzone* (Alsbach, 1917). The first is for tenor – *Preghiera alla Madonna* – with a straightforward vocal line and a rich diatonic accompaniment; the second, for soprano – *Come raggio di sol* – has a florid, Italianate vocal line and a highly chromatic piano part.

It was mainly as an opera composer that Jan Brandts-Buys made a mark. Of his numerous songs, the 'Drei Lieder', Op. 33 (Weinberger, Leipzig, 1916) for voice and string quartet, are varied and effective in a nineteenth-century Mahlerish style. No. 3, *Sturmlied*, is strongly dramatic, working up to a fine climax with the words: 'In Sturm und Wetter, der Herr er ist nah. Hallelujah!' A later song-cycle, 'Vier Lieder', Op. 42 (Doplinger, 1925), for bass voice and piano, is equally well written, and the energetic setting of Goethe's *Prometheus* is particularly memorable.

Willem Landré was of French descent, and nineteenth-century French influences can be found in his music. His 'Drei Liebeslieder' (Alsbach, 1910) are straightforward, but with attractive personal touches.

An important and influential figure in Dutch music, Sem Dresden has developed a highly personal style of composition – but songs are not a particularly important part of his output. Some show French influence; and of the ones set to Dutch words, the 'Vier liederen'

(Donemus 1942), to poems by Anthonie Donker, are individual in style and atmosphere, ending with a song called O *Merel* ('O blackbird'), the accompaniment of which is a successful exercise in stylized chirpings.

Jan van Gilse was a prolific composer, very varied in style. His 'Two Songs on German texts' – *Die Eigensinnige* and *Ein kleines Lied* – composed in 1908 (Donemus), could not be more contrasted: the first is diatonic, simple, and strong; the other, thickly chromatic.

Often somewhat uncouth in style, Daniel Ruyneman has written quite a large number of songs, experimental and unusual in many ways. His choice of words frequently shows a taste for the exotic – for example, in his 'Chinese Songs' (Alsbach, 1917), and the 'Three Persian Lyrics' (Donemus, 1951). The latter are from Omar Khayyam (in a German version) and Mohamet Hafiz, set in a simple but rather meandering musical style, without bar-lines. More consistent in style and more musically imaginative are the earlier 'Twee Wijzangen' – ('Two Sacred Songs') (van der Meer; composed 1915) – which are settings of Dutch translations of the great Indian poet Rabindranath Tagore. One of Ruyneman's most interesting sets of songs is the 'Quatre Poèmes' (Chester, 1925), extracts from Guillaume Apollinaire's 'Alcools'. The musical style is rhythmically and harmonically very free – somewhat elusive. Again, there are no bar lines.

The songs of Henri Zagwijn have considerable originality, showing influences ranging from Debussy to Schoenberg. 'Die Stille Stadt' (Donemus, 1950; composed 1915), for mezzo-soprano, flute, string trio and harp, has atmosphere and freshness, an impressionistic flavour, and good craftsmanship. A later set 'Eenzame Wake' ('Lonely Vigil') (Donemus 1948), is in a mature, evocative style, and the vocal line is not at all easy.

Willem Andriessen, one of a distinguished family of Dutch musicians, has not composed a great deal, but there are some effective songs to Dutch words in which the influence of the folk-music of his country is discernible. His brother Hendrik has written far more songs, in a more adventurous style, showing both German and French influence in his 'Trois Pastorales' (van Rossum, 1935), to poems by Rimbaud.

An extensive tour of the East and a close friendship with Reint van Santen – a poet, orientalist, painter and musician – gave colour to the works of Bernard van den Sigtenhorst Meyer, who otherwise tried to cultivate a Dutch style in his compositions. He set a number of poems by van Santen, including 'Stemmingen', Op. 6 (Alsbach, 1918) – three songs, one of which is a colourful *Morning in the Tanger*. The three 'Fluisteringen', Op. 5 (Alsbach, 1917) – 'Whisperings' – are in a straightforward, intimate style.

The songs of Rudolf Mengelberg, a Dutch musicologist and composer of German birth, include some settings of poems from *Chamber Music* by James Joyce (Broekmans). The two books of 'Lieder nach Verlaine', Op. 10 and Op. 11 (Rozsavölgyi) – to German translations – established him as a song-composer of some importance. They show refinement and a certain originality.

Bernard Wagenaar, the violinist, conductor and composer, settled in the U.S.A. in 1920, at the age of thirty-six. His best-known song-cycle is 'From a very little Sphinx' (Schirmer, 1926) – seven short, charming, effective settings of words by the American poet Edna St. Vincent Millay. They are not difficult, but need a singer who can convincingly put across the many moods in a recitative-like style. Wagenaar's 'Three Songs' (Schirmer, 1926) for medium voice and piano, are in a rich diatonic style with interesting modulations: the first, an atmospheric setting of Verlaine's *Calmes, dans le demi-jour*; the third, a deeply-felt interpretation of Heine's *Ich stand in dunklen Träumen*. The second, *May-night*, has Dutch words – and all three of them have English versions.

One of the most important of Dutch composers, Willem Pijper, published quite a number of songs. We have already mentioned his collections of old Dutch melodies. He was strongly influenced by French literature and French music, and set some of Verlaine's *Fêtes galantes* (Donemus, 1947) for voice and orchestra. The uninhibited and somewhat rugged inventiveness of Pijper's style is better suited to the Dutch poems of Bertha de Bruijn – 'Four Songs' (Donemus 1950) for high voice and piano. Of these, the sweetly joyful *Meiliedje* ('Song of May') is the most memorable. (See Ex. 2)

There is a lightness of touch in Alexander Voormolen's songs which is most attractive. He sets Dutch, German, French, and English poems. The 'Four Old-Dutch Poems' (Alsbach, 1932) are published with per-

Ex. 2   Rustig (*dolce*)

'kZit   voor mijn   ven - ster   op een

forming versions in all those four languages – for high voice and piano –
and they are wholly agreeable in every way. But 'Three Poems of
Rilke' (Donemus, 1946) show that the composer can capture difficult
moods and feelings with a fine musical instinct.

Johannes Röntgen, one of the five sons of Julius Röntgen (all of
whom were successful musicians), made in 1956 a song-cycle of 'Eleven
Zoological Exercises in Poetry' by Trijntje Fop from Pennewip's
inheritance gathered by Kees Stip (Donemus, 1956). They are for
mezzo-soprano or contralto and piano – lighthearted and without
sophistication. A more serious contribution of the same composer is
'Two Songs from Stefan Zweig' – *Die frühen Kränze* and *Graues Land*
(Alsbach) for soprano, flute and viola.

Composers born since 1900

The pianist and composer Piet Ketting was a pupil of Pijper; in his
compositions he shows also that the influence of Schoenberg has been
strong. Among his songs are 'Three Sonnets of Shakespeare' (Broekmans, 1938) set in a style hardly suited to the words. More personal and
convincing is his 'Minnedeuntjes' – 'Love-songs' (Donemus, 1939).

There is an adventurousness also about the style of Robert de Roos,
who shows what an influence French music and literature have had on
him – as they had on Pijper. Of the two sets of 'Cinq Quatrains de
Francis Jammes' (Donemus), composed respectively in 1932 and 1941,
the texture tends to be thick and heavy – though in the second set
there is greater economy and a stronger musical characterizing of the
poems.

Henk Badings is certainly one of Holland's most interesting and versatile composers. His music is eclectic, with contrapuntal elements, and highly enterprising. Most of what he writes is difficult to perform; but adventurous singers should be encouraged to look at his 'Chansons orientales' (Jeannette, Bilthoven, 1943) or the 'Three Songs from Rilke' (Donemus, 1932). The former are highly original in form and content.

The Dutch pianist and composer, Hans Henkemans, has written an imaginative and extremely difficult set of five songs for tenor and piano under the title 'De Toverfluit' (Donemus, 1946) – ('The Magic Flute'). Both vocal line and piano part are of considerable virtuosity. Between the raucous night musicians of No. 3 and the tender regret of the final song (*The Unfaithful Lover*) a wide range of expression is encompassed.

The composer Marius Flothuis was one of the founders of Donemus (see p. 265). He has written an imaginative work entitled *Love and Strife*, Op. 34 (Donemus 1943), to words by Kathleen Raine, set convincingly in English, in a very free modern style, not twelve-note. It is described in the score as 'a serious cantata' for contralto, flute, oboe d'amore (also oboe), viola, and cello, and it is dedicated to the famous British contralto, the late Kathleen Ferrier, and the ensemble Alma Musica. The work consists of reflections on love and war – in very impressionistic verse. There is also a 'Kleine Suite', Op. 47 (Donemus, 1952) by Flothuis, a set of *vocalises* for high soprano and piano. What vowel-sounds are used in the voice part is left to the singer's discretion. It is a varied, interesting and effective suite.

There is also a *Vocalise* (Donemus, 1951) by Lex van Delden, for mezzo-soprano and piano, bitter in harmony, but with a singable vocal line. The two songs for mezzo-soprano and piano, 'De Goede Dood', Op. 47 (Donemus, 1956), a mature work of the same composer – who was born in 1919 – have a similar astringent harmonic flavour, but the texture is clearer. 'The Good Death' is an important contribution to Dutch song – not at all easy, but well worth consideration by an enterprising singer. The song-cycle 'L'Amour' (Donemus, 1937) by van Delden, for soprano, flute, clarinet, and string trio, is a very early work and not representative of this composer – from whom much may be expected in the future.

Hungary

HANS NATHAN

Béla Bartók*

BARTÓK'S earliest compositions were written for the piano. They were followed by a quartet for piano and strings and, in 1898, by 'Drei Lieder' to German texts.[1] The first, based on Heine's 'Im wunderschönen Monat Mai', gives no inkling of the composer's later stature; for it is heavily indebted to Schumann's setting of the same text though more so to *Der Nussbaum*, and in general to his harmony and basses. Furthermore, the ending of Bartók's vocal part, with its melodic and textual repetition, is entirely Schubertian, while the brief piano postlude turns out to be a romantic stereotype and practically identical with the conclusion of Chopin's Nocturne, Op. 32, No. 2. The song is obviously a piece of juvenilia – Bartók was then seventeen years old – and merely of documentary value.

Shortly after 1900, responding to an upsurge of nationalist trends, he became interested in Hungarian folk music but, like his contemporaries, he had misconceptions about it, as he himself admitted later:[2]

* Grateful acknowledgement is made to Peter Bartók and Dr. Victor Bátor (Béla Bartók Archives, New York) for photostats of Bartók's Op. 15 and to Béla L. De Pottyondy and Dr. Stephen Foltiny for translations from the Hungarian.

[1] None of these works is published. A facsimile of the first of the 'Drei Lieder' in János Demény, *Bartók Béla-Levelek, fényképek, kéziratok kották* (a collection of documents), Budapest, 1948.

[2] See Bartók's Autobiography in Bence Szabolcsi, *Béla Bartók* (German edition), Budapest, 1957, p. 145.

272

he took its urban representative for the real thing. For instance, he called a part of a symphony by Dohnányi 'distinctly Hungarian (gypsy!)'; and he occupied himself with a popular, composed song, trying to work it into a canon, in the belief that it was primitive.[3]

His 'Négy Dal' ('Four Songs') of 1902, published two years later, reveal the type of national flavour that he sought. For his texts he had chosen verses of the poet Lajos Pósa, which resembled folk poetry. But melodically (as one would expect) he follows the Hungarian pseudo-folk-style of the late nineteenth century and in his harmony and the manner of his accompaniment the 'Hungarian' tradition of Liszt and Brahms, as this extract from the first song clearly shows:

Ex.1 Andante non troppo

Tüs - ke bo - kor meg-fog-ja a le - ve - let, U - gyan, u-gyan

mért bán - tod a szi - ve - met?

His first notations of peasant tunes occurred in 1904.[4] About this time, and under their influence (which, as is well known, was to imbue his work up to the end of his career), he wrote the three songs *Esti Dal* ('Evening Song'; text by Sándor Peres), *A jótevők* ('The Benefactors'; text by István Havas), and *Harangszó* ('Ringing Bells'; text by Béla Sztankó).[5] Their tunes, though not consistent in style, are nevertheless significant in Bartók's development. Not only are they almost entirely free of Hungarian nineteenth-century elements, but they are related to real peasant music, if in a restricted sense. That is to

[3] Bartók in a letter of November 12, 1902, and Kodály in his article on 'Bartók as a folk-lorist'; see Szabolcsi, *op. cit.*, p. 217 and p. 68.

[4] See Kodály's article mentioned above.

[5] See No. 24 in Bartók's bibliography in Szabolcsi, *op. cit.*, p. 325. The tunes were published in Ödön Geszler, 'Énekiskola' (a collection of songs for the use in public schools), the first two in Vol. I, the third in Vol. II, both Budapest, 1928. The facsimile of an arrangement of 'Á jótevők' (slightly varied in melody and text), for voice and piano, dated 1905, was published in Demény, *op. cit.*

say, they contain passages from such music without resembling any specific example of it.

In 1905 Bartók published *Székely Népdal* ('Székely Folk-song') in the magazine *Magyar Lant*, the setting of a tune which he only later recognized as 'probably an art-song in the folk-character.[6] Perhaps more revealing than this error is his piano accompaniment. It has much in common with nineteenth-century art-song, especially with the type cultivated by Liszt: the instrumental introduction, also reminiscent of Wagner,[7] anticipating the opening of the tune but finally obscuring its rhythmic pattern with quickened repetitions as in Liszt's *Die Schlüssel-blumen*, the doubling of notes throughout, with octaves in the left hand, and above all the alternation of phrases of the melody with ascending arpeggios in the piano part. Towards the end of the song we are even reminded of a passage in the second of Brahms's 'Hungarian Dances'.

'Magyar Népdalok' *(Bartók-Kodály)*

In 1906 appeared 'Magyar Népdalok' ('Hungarian Folk-songs'), a volume of twenty (or, counting the actual settings, of twenty-two) peasant songs. These were undoctored versions, all but five of them taken down in the field by Bartók and Kodály; each had arranged his own selection. As stated in its preface, the publication was intended to show Hungarians the purity and artistic value of a neglected fruit of their culture, and to replace the cheap popular music which was in general favour. Although the composers did not explicitly say so, they no doubt referred also to what was then considered Hungarian folk music but was only a faint echo of it. 'Magyar Népdalok' was the very first edition of some of the best Hungarian folk-songs (in the truest sense of the word) in professional and tasteful arrangements.[8]

[6] Béla Bartók, *Hungarian Folk Music*, London, 1931, commentary, p. 77 (original edition, Budapest, 1924). Kodály's article, mentioned above, in Szabolcsi, op. cit., pp. 68–9.

[7] A relation to the beginning of the *Tannhäuser Overture* does not occur by chance in view of Bartók's interest in Wagner around 1900.

[8] Note, however, that only 1,500 copies of this edition were sold between 1906 and 1938 (see 'Postscript 1938'). Liszt, Brahms and other composers of their time, even when they used peasant tunes, wrote settings in the gypsy style which, in their confusion about the origin of the tunes, they took for the original one. Since then Bartók has proved this totally erroneous. That his distinction between the gypsy manner of performance on the one hand and Hungarian song (urban, composed in the folk-vein, and rural) on the other was already known earlier, though perhaps not widely, is shown by the following quotation from the preface (dated 1890) of Francis Korbay, 'Hungarian Melodies', for voice and piano, Vol. I, London and Leipzig, copyrighted in Washington [D.C.], 1891: '—it is . . . astonishing that the hypothesis, that Hungarian music is of Gypsy origin, should ever have become the subject of any serious discussion. The Gypsies play our songs and dances at dinners, balls, or weddings, with a dash and fire, and with that instinctive rhythmical verve, which is imperatively demanded by our music. As composers, they have no more claim to it than a German street band has to 'Norma', or 'Trovatore', to 'Home, sweet Home', or 'Robin Adair'.'

Bartók and Kodály published the tunes as they had perceived them at that time, that is without their characteristic embellishments, but this was corrected in the edition of 1938 wherever it was typographically possible. In the matter of dynamic markings they did not strictly imitate the rigidity of primitive singing as they had observed it. Although conscious of the need for editorial restraint, they found a small number of crescendi and decrescendi indispensable, and this indeed was in keeping with their harmonization.

In order to transfer these melodies from country to city, they recognized the need for piano arrangements, and they endeavoured (to use their own words) not to make the new 'city-clothes' so tight as to impede the 'breathing' of their tunes.

Thus their accompaniments serve merely as a support, with just enough sonority to suggest a natural, though by no means truly primitive, vocal timbre, and without additional motives or solo passages. Usually they made their piano arrangements duplicate the melody, as in the second song (Bartók):

Hungarian folk tunes used to be harmonized as if they were in a major or minor tonality. This produced flabby phrasing and weakened distinctive intervals such as the fourth and the major second. Bartók and Kodály avoided this mistake. Conscious of the frequent modal and pentatonic features of their tunes, they used more than merely tonic, dominant, and subdominant chords. Sometimes their harmonization, consisting in the main of traditional chords, is truly modal. But more often it is varied, as when certain phrase endings, concluding with two or three repeated notes, are strengthened by authentic cadences.[9]

[9] However, in a lecture of 1931 on 'The Influence of Peasant Music on the Music of Our Time' (see Szabolcsi, op. cit., p. 162), Bartók emphasized the fact that Hungarian folk tunes contain no suggestion of authentic cadences. This reference is omitted in a translation of the lecture in *Tempo*, No. 14, 1949–50.

Moreover, the composers, trying to give each individual phrase its due, follow almost every one of its harmonic implications and underline them with a V^7–I progression.

Although the settings of the two composers are quite similar (compare, for example, No. 2 with No. 15), they nevertheless differ in a few subtle details. In contradistinction to Kodály, Bartók, preferring a sparse texture, more often puts nothing but the tune into the right-hand part. Rarely does he use parallel sixths, the trademarks of nineteenth-century 'Hungarian Dances'; he has hardly any ninth chords, and fewer seventh chords than Kodály, and he avoids both passing notes and appoggiaturas, while his harmony changes less frequently within a melodic phrase.

But his settings are not without flaws,[10] and he recognized this in later years. In 1931, when reviewing an anthology which included two of his early arrangements (No. 1 and No. 6 of 'Magyar Népdalok'), he seized the opportunity of criticizing them severely and of declaring them inferior to Kodály's.[11] 'I must confess,' he wrote, 'that they are not above reproach. They are perhaps better, technically, than the ones discussed so far, but from the point of view of art they are so imperfect that I would never have permitted their resurrection and their inclusion in the anthology had I known about it and had my permission been asked. The only absolutely unimpeachable piece in the whole volume is No. 9 [No. 15 in 'Magyar Népdalok], which is the only arrangement by Kodály.' Finally, in 1939 or so, he undertook a revision of his early settings.[12]

1907–1929 (Folk Songs)

Bartók's 'Nyolc Magyar Népdal' ('Eight Hungarian Folk-Songs'), published in 1922, contains arrangements written between 1907 and 1917. Because of the length of this time-span more specific dates would be revealing but unfortunately they do not exist. One would like to know, for example, which arrangements originated in 1907, the

[10] To quote only two examples. At the end of No. 4b (No. 5 in the second, revised edition), the sudden regard for the modality of the tune is inconsistent within a harmonic interpretation tending towards a major tonality. So is bar 9 in song No. 8 where the only chromatic passage in the tune is singled out through an altered ninth chord, with the additional result that the dissonance and its resolution practically sound like a quotation from Strauss's *Till Eulenspiegel* (bars 47–49) – an echo of Bartók's previous admiration of that composer.

[11] A review of H. Möller's *Lied der Völker*, Vol. XII, in *Ethnographia*, Budapest, 1931, Vol. XLII, No. 2, translated by Paul Henry Lang in *The Musical Quarterly*, April, 1947 ('Gypsy Music or Hungarian Music?').

[12] See Szabolcsi, op. cit., p. 326. The whereabouts of the manuscript are not known at present.

tail-end of the composer's youthful, tentative period. Perhaps it was No. 8, the most traditional and even conventional piece. It may also be significant that the ritornello of song No. 5 shares its tune and several harmonic aspects with the third of 'Három Csíkmegyei Népdal' ('Three Folk-Songs From the Csík District' for piano) of 1907, but the greater aptness and sophistication of its setting suggests a later date.[13] Finally, the first two songs are harmonically rather close to Bartók's 1906 collection, while Nos. 6 and 7 are far removed from it. The latter are the most mature arrangements in the volume, their sparseness of means fully matching the taut perfection of their tunes and texts. More attention is paid to melodic lines and the common-place basses in 'Magyar Népdalok' are superseded by inventive examples like this one from the fourth song:

Notice that the tune here, with telling effect, has become a middle voice as in No. 2. There is, further, the semi-linearity of Nos. 6 (second half) and 7, but, aside from the basses, movement is frequently stepwise. With many additional notes sustained, Bartók is thus able to do justice to tunes consisting of a small number of adjacent notes – a problem that always intrigued him[14] although he had previously failed to solve it.

His harmony remains essentially tertian. Its numerous seventh chords (not all of them resolved), he tells us,[15] are the ones which the gapped scales of Hungarian folk tunes had suggested to him and Kodály.

He is conscious of the possibility, particularly useful for repetitions of the tune, of underpinning it with chord progressions that gravitate now to this, now to that centre.[16]

Dissonances are used with moderation and always meaningfully,

[13] See Halsey Stevens, *The Life and Music of Béla Bartók*, New York, 1953, p. 150. The rondo-form of No. V and the wide spacing of its instrumental ritornello also relate to No. 5 of 'Tíz Könnyű Zongoradarab' ('Ten Easy Piano Pieces') of 1908.

[14] 'The Influence of Peasant Music on the Music of Our Time', see above.

[15] *ibid.*   [16] *ibid.*

277

both as to music and text. There are those that look like the head-on clashes of Bartók's art-songs (a minor second between the tune and the right-hand part of the accompaniment), except that one of their notes is sustained; several striking ones that occur in passing (No. 7); and finally, those on accented beats that are brought about by sounding a major and minor third, within a larger chord, simultaneously. Widely spaced, the latter dissonance has a mildly poignant effect and thus, like the rest, matches the subdued melancholy occasionally displayed by the text.

None of the repetitions of the tunes are transposed. However, at one place (No. 3, bars 14 to 17), the composer creates the opposite impression by shifting the accompaniment from E flat minor to E major. The tune keeps to its original pitch but, since it remains a part of the underlying harmony (now slightly more opaque than before) it seems to have risen along with it. This anticipates a kindred passage in 'Husz Magyar Népdal' of 1929 (Vol. II, No. 5, bars 34 to 36).

'Falun' ('Tót Népdalok'), usually translated 'Village Scenes' ('Slovakian Folk-Songs'), a cycle of five songs for female voice and piano written in 1924,[17] is more than a mere arrangement. What the composer has added to his tunes is not only apt but so strikingly novel as to make his work almost an original composition. This is confirmed by certain liberties he has taken such as the insertion of instrumental interludes of his own invention, the use of two folk-tunes within the same movement (in No. 3 which is rondo form, and in No. 4), extensions of the tunes and frequent transpositions, and finally the planned order of the songs.

The style of the score may be called 'primitive', in the sense of hard contrasts and of a highly restricted, repetitive vocabulary. But since Bartók works with a multitude of variants, simplicity is an effect rather than a method.

He selected Slovakian tunes for his artistic purpose instead of Hungarian ones because of their non-cantabile progression in seconds, their repetition of phrases (most of which quickly return to their starting-point) and of single notes, and their use of the tritone which appears literally or outlined within the melody. Though not primitive by itself, it is far removed from the usual Central European folk idioms.

Just as the pentatonic scale of Hungarian folk tunes had induced him to compress it into a chord, so he considers it now appropriate to utilize simultaneous seconds and, in accompaniments, tritones, the

[17] In 1926 Bartók arranged the three last songs for women's voices and chamber orchestra.

latter more often in succession. Here is a passage from the first
song:

The harmony tends towards the lean sonority of intervals, which are
audibly displayed in a manner that is not merely shrill but bright like
the colours of peasant costumes.

Taking another hint from his tunes, Bartók also applies ostinati
and quasi-ostinati to his accompaniment. Apart from their rhythmic
effect, they support his interest in bitonal chord combinations.

Song No. 2 contains none of these devices. What relates it to the
preceding song (Ex. 4) and to the character of the entire work is the
bareness of the parallel motion of intervals. But from the combination
of accompaniment and voice there emerges a severely linear setting –
a remarkable example of polyphony in folk vein:

It does not detract from the originality of 'Falun' to state that to
some extent it shares the aesthetics of Stravinsky's *Les Noces*.[18] Certainly
the text, in both cases descriptive of a peasant wedding, is not sufficient
evidence for that. More convincing, however, is the raw exuberance
of Songs 3 and 5 (also the realistic shrieks in one and the imitation of
bagpipe music in the other), the obsessiveness of recurrent figures and

[18] Stevens, op. cit., p. 51, denies this relation.

the irregularity of their accentuations, the sudden and extreme changes in volume and tempo, and the clangorous, percussive sound of the piano.

'Húsz Magyar Népdal' ('Twenty Hungarian Folk-Songs') of 1929 are of particular artistic and historical significance. Preceded by the *String Quartet No. 4* and followed by the *Cantata Profana*, they are the product of a densely creative period of three years. In it Bartók summarized, so to speak, all of his previous experiences with folk material and established folk-song arrangement as a major type of musical composition.

Three of the four volumes are organized under specific headings, such as 'Songs of Sorrow', 'Dance Songs', and 'Songs of Youth'. Volume III is merely entitled 'Diverse Songs', but by way of relation and contrast in tunes and texts it is just as suitable for consecutive performance as Volume IV, whose movements are interconnected.

The tunes, which were collected by the composer himself between 1906 and 1918,[19] are quoted essentially without modifications, except for a coda in Song No. 6 in Volume II. Additional changes of a minor character chiefly involve rests between phrases as well as repetitions of the last phrase or (as in IV) of the entire second half of the tunes. Rests are always motivated by the text: they stress the reflection of a lover (I, No. 3, and the second song, actually No. 17, in IV), the humorous hesitation in telling an embarrassing point of a story (III, No. 12, where the repetition of a few phrases acts like a stammer), and the tongue-tied speech of a tipsy peasant (III, No. 15). Here too the presentation of sections of the tune alternately by piano and voice, each time on a different pitch, is justified by the contents.

In Volume IV each tune is stated in full once only. Where repetitions occur in other songs, they do not always adhere to their initial pitch as in earlier arrangements.

It was perhaps a regard for the identity of his tunes that persuaded Bartók to avoid the bold, non-tertian idiom of his piano pieces *Out of Doors* of 1926 and his *Fourth String Quartet* of 1928. Though he drew various elements from these works as well as from his *Piano Sonata*, Op. 26, he preferred to fuse contemporary with traditional concepts. This accounts for the occasional appearance of functional harmony and such older types of accompaniment, including tremolos, as we find them in Kodály's arrangements. At one place he even utilizes a

---

[19] They are published in Bartók's book on *Hungarian Folk Music*, see above, and listed in John S. Weissmann, 'Notes Concerning Bartók's Solo Vocal Music (II)', *Tempo*, No. 38, Winter 1955–56. In 1933 Bartók arranged Nos. 1, 2, 11, 12 and 14 of *Magyar Népdalok* for voice and orchestra; this version is still in manuscript.

passage of a nineteenth-century arranger for whose style he otherwise had little respect.[20]

Bartók[21] saw similarities in principles of structure between his ideal of folk-song arrangements and Bach's arrangements of chorales. With regard to 'Húsz Magyar Népdal' the relation is more specifically to chorale variations. In both cases a pre-existent melody is set into a series of musical patterns each of which is at once valid by itself and meaningful in its relation to a text. Bartók's folk tunes have, of course, none of the sturdiness and spiritual detachment of Protestant chorales, but they certainly possess elements of solidity, namely, allegiance to a tonal centre and melodic coherence. These assert themselves against the ambiguous tonality of the accompaniment and its different and complex articulation of individual voice-parts.

The piano part is very active, difficult of execution and sometimes highly elaborate (perhaps too much so in Vol. III, No. 11), but it avoids a concertante manner. Even where it displays solo passages, it confirms the genre in continuing the motivic pattern of the preceding accompaniment or anticipating what is to follow. And since Bartók postulated that settings should be 'derived from the musical qualities of the melody, from such characteristics as are contained in it openly or covertly',[22] they never repeat themselves but reveal all the differences that the composer's subtle ear can detect between one tune and another. This method of composition also makes it possible for the settings to be intricate and yet remain as genuine and direct as their source.

The tremolos of the accompaniment are not merely relics of the romantic past. They belong in fact to a system of repetitive devices such as extensive trills, repeated and sustained notes as well as ostinati and quasi-ostinati. Often these devices appear simultaneously and give rise to such patterns as these, from I, No. 4, and No. 2, respectively:

Ex. 6

Mi-kor gu-la's le-gény vol-tam,

[20] Eight bars from *piu allegro* onwards in Vol. IV, No. 5 are related to a passage in Korbay ('Look into my eye . . .'), op. cit. See Bartók's highly negative reference to Korbay in 'Gypsy Music or Hungarian Music?' mentioned above.   [21] The Influence of Peasant Music . . .'

[22] From the translation of 'The Influence of Peasant Music . . .' in *Tempo*, No. 14, Winter 1949–50.

while a more uniform combination of ostinati is rarer. In all cases the distinct levels that are established in the harmonic fabric strengthen the linear aspect of the arrangement.

In his attempt to vary the harmonic interpretations of his tunes, Bartók moves back and forth – with many intermediary stages – between confirming their scalar structure and contradicting it. For the latter effect, he frequently changes the tonal centres of his chord progressions (and recurrent patterns as well), as he did in 'Nyolc Magyar Népdal' but now in such a way that they disagree with that of the tunes. Consequently he arrives at polytonality, though less often than one would expect. He usually limits himself to two planes which merge into a unit in spite of their disparateness, as in I, No. 4:

Bartók's interest in part-writing, which was restricted in earlier arrangements, is in keeping with his emphasis on linear features by way of recurring notes and motives. In several songs it develops into imitations in the accompaniment, and in one case (the beginning of No. 13, III) it leads even to real polyphony.

1915–1916 (Art Songs)

In the opera *Duke Bluebeard's Castle* (1911) there appears for the first time a characteristic vocal style of the composer's own making. Faithful to the accents and inflections of Hungarian speech, syllabic and replete with note-repetitions, it seemed to Kodály[23] like recitative,

---

[23] See Kodály's articles on 'Béla Bartók's Opera' (1918) and 'Béla Bartók' (1921), reprinted in a German translation in Szabolcsi, op. cit., pp. 62 and 56.

but it is generally close to an arioso. Almost entirely fashioned after phrases of Hungarian folk-song, it has a cantabile quality. On the other hand, the vocal line is divided into very brief phrases which lack coherence. The composer knew that this melodic style distinguished by many equal unhurried note-values, though wholly appropriate to the statuesque, legendary figures of his opera, would not fit to the small dimensions of song nor lend itself to the required detailed interpretation of its text.

'Öt Dal' ('Five Songs'), Op. 15, written between 1915 and 1916, have never been published, and they came to light only recently in a recording.[24] Their texts are anonymous but it is assumed that the last two are by Béla Balázs.[25] It was impossible to elicit from Bartók any specific information about them. He merely spoke of a single author and one of little reputation, which would exclude Balázs. He also expressed his low opinion of the literary quality of the texts.[26] Was he afraid to admit that he (or a friend) had penned them? Bartók feared difficulties arising from publication since the poems are conspicuously erotic, though they are no more so than the plots of his ballets *A Fából Faragott Királyfi* (*The Wooden Prince*, 1914-16) and *A Csodálatos Mandarín* (*The WonderfulMandarin*, 1918-19), and the words of Op. 16. Even the song *Az Ágyam Hívogat* ('My Bed is Calling') in the latter work, the most risqué of all, is no less frank than song No. I (containing such lines as 'In a passion I fling open my naked arms, The coverlet falls away from my body') in Op. 15. Since Baudelaire, such subjects had been common in European literature, though of course the general public accepted them reluctantly.

The melodic style of Op. 15 again borrows from Hungarian folk music, above all its main element, the combination of a fourth and a major second. Nevertheless, in spite of additional rhythmical relations,

---

[24] No. 927, *Bartók Records Inc.*, New York (Magda László, soprano, and Leonid Hambro, piano). The accompanying pamphlet contains the texts of Op. 15 and English translations by Peter Bartók and Howard Sachler as well as an introduction by Edward Jablonski, copyright 1958. Photostats of the manuscript of Op. 15 were obtained from the *Béla Bartók Archives*, New York (Dr. Victor Bátor, executor Béla Bartók Estate).

[25] Szabolsci, op. cit., No. 61 of Bartók's bibliography.

[26] Jablonski (*Bartók Records*, see above), p. 4: 'Bartók admitted that he did not like the texts and later explained to the publisher (when in 1923 the question of publication came up again) that the author's name was not generally known, and further "I don't want to name him".' In this connexion it may perhaps be of interest that song No. 4 (beginning with 'Szomjasan vágyva várom aszellőt') has the following German translation: 'Harre vor Durst verschmachtender Brise / Blau die Himmelsglock' hoch oben blendet, / Nirgends Schatten wohin man sich wendet / Vor der Sonnengluth schwebt hin die Wolke, / Offnen Mundes trink ich Sonnenfluthen, / Der flammende Himmel niederstürzen will, / Unter dichtem Grün hält für Minuten,/ Hinstürmend der Sommer ein Weilchen still.'

the vocal line remains a liberal variant of its model, particularly since it admits the third (sometimes as many as three in succession) and, in passing, other intervals alien to the folk-idiom.

While Bartók reiterates rhythmical patterns in the manner of folk-song, he avoids large-scale repetitions. Instead he goes from one passage to another following the text as it proceeds to ever-new images. This is in keeping with contemporary Austrian art-song (not to mention Richard Strauss's stage works) and the gradual shifting of phrases to higher and higher pitch levels, for moments of excitement, reaffirms its late romantic heritage. At the tragic climax near the end of his opera he had done the same thing, but by orchestral means only. Finally there is, in Op. 15, the influence of Debussy and Ravel, which manifests itself in unaccented triplets, in phrase openings with repeated notes and a cantabile ending, usually in downward motion. More than anything else it affects Bartók's piano part, but often he is harmonically

quite independent. Even then, it sometimes happens that the fleeting figuration of his accompaniment, essentially tertian, fuses disparate harmonic elements through the use of the sustaining pedal into the filmy, oscilating sonority that convention dubs 'Impressionist'. In no other work does Bartók approach the two French masters more closely than in this one, though, compared with Kodály, he is still at a distance from them.

At the same time Bartók points towards new horizons – the octaves in song No. 5 thickened by clusters of notes, and the dissonant minor second resulting from overlapping imitations, as in the bitonal clash between the last note on the higher level and the first on the lower, at the end of song No. 3.

With 'Öt Dal' ('Five Songs'), Op. 16, composed in 1916 to words by Endre Ady[27] (whose name does not appear in the published edition), Bartók detaches himself further from folk-music. His aim is to project the text with a poignancy bordering on psychological realism: its

[27] See No. 63 of Bartók's bibliography in Szabolcsi, op. cit.

moments of resignation, of foreboding, of erotic abandon. In consequence, the harmony assumes major significance, while the vocal part
tends to assimilate itself with the high-strung poetry with disjointed,
recitative-like phrases consisting of nothing more than repeated or
adjacent notes in speech rhythm. The formal organization of the songs
is ambivalent. It is partly additive, as in Op. 15, but it is also marked
by several brief sectional restatements.

Everywhere, even at passages of greater coherence or cantabile style
(songs Nos. 1 and 5), the frequency of two intervals in the vocal part is
noticeable. One is the descending third, usually accented on the first
note. Conspicuous at phrase endings or standing in isolation, it is like
a declamatory nuance rather than an ordinary interval. The other is
the minor second, appearing in appoggiatura fashion, which, in view
of its harmonic context, was probably suggested by early Schoenberg.[28]

The emotionalism of the music is intensified by constant dynamic
changes. Thus a crescendo combined with a chromatically ascending
sequence both in the voice and the piano part becomes as violent
(especially in association with an erotic situation in the text) as the
convulsions of Tristan, and – with its phrases shrinking into gasps –
even more insinuating.

Within a few measures, Bartók touches on a multitude of notes.
Some of them are fleeting and, by means of the sustaining pedal,
they become harmonic elements. The more stable of them, however,
contribute to a high degree of tonal ambiguity. Because of repeated
figurations and cadence-like chord progressions, this does not develop
into atonality, though at times it is not far removed from it. Indeed a
passage in song No. 2, aside from the tenths in the bass, seems to have
been inspired directly by one in Schoenberg's Op. 11, No. 1:

Ex. 10

[28] Bartók knew Schoenberg's 'Drei Klavier-Stuecke', Op. 11, since 1912 (they were, as he
said, 'the first Schoenbergian music with which I became acquainted . . .'; see his report on 'Arnold
Schoenbergs Musik In Ungarn' in *Musikblätter des Anbruch*, Vienna, 1920, pp. 647–48) and probably
a few of his other works, such as the second string quartet, also (see Szabolcsi, op. cit., p. 29).

As in Bartók's later works, tonal instability is also suspended for a moment. This happens intermittently in song No. 4 and with particular firmness at a place where both voice and accompaniment are involved. While it serves here to symbolize a lyrical climax of the

poetry, it operates more abstractly in the first movement of the String Quartet No. 6, for example, as a sort of temporary anchorage. The quoted example is further noteworthy because of its bitonality, suggested rather than carried out and an early instance of one of the composer's typical devices.

What sets off the harmony of Op. 16 against the rest of Bartók's compositions is chiefly the parallel motion of fourths and tritones in the accompaniment, of superimpositions of two fourths or two tritones, or else of a fourth and a tritone, again reminiscent of Schoenberg.

Except in songs No. 1 and 5, much of the former colouristic filigree accompaniment (now highly chromaticized) is retained, and even the parallel fourths occasionally become a part of it. Viewing the total style of the work, one might say[29] that it unites aspects of German or Austrian music of about 1910, which had grown out of Wagner, with Debussyste trends. However, the latter are strongly qualified by pungent chords and dissonances, among them a piercing minor second between the voice and the right-hand part of the accompaniment.[30]

Zoltan Kodály

The period of Kodály's song writing began and ended, for all

[29] Weissmann, in his 'Notes Concerning Bartók's Solo Vocal Music (I)' in *Tempo*, No. 36, Summer, 1955, speaks of Bartók's 'conscious attempt to combine Wagnerian usage with impressionist principles'.

[30] The following songs for voice and piano have not been discussed. *Unpublished:* 'Drei Lieder' (Nos. 2 and 3), 1898; 'A Kicsi "Tót"-Nak' (To the Little Slovak), 'Five songs', 1905 (one is mentioned in footnote 5); 'Nine Rumanian Folk-Songs', 1915 (see Nos. 10, 32 and 59 of the Bartók bibliography in Szabolcsi, op. cit.). *Published:* Nos. 65, 74b, 95b and 127 in *Mikrokosmos*, 1926–37; 'A Ferj Keserve' (Ukrainian Folk-song Arrangement), 1945 (facsimile; see Szabolcsi, op. cit., p. 291, and bibliography, No. 118); a few piano pieces with added text.

practical purposes,[31] with folk-song arrangements: it is thus delimited by 'Magyar Népdalok' of 1906, prepared in collaboration with Bartók, and several volumes of 'Magyar Népzene' of 1932. In between, his interest shifted to the composition of art-songs.

Guided by his expert knowledge of Hungarian folk-lore, from which even Bartók's earliest ethno-musicological activities profited, he almost entirely escaped the spell of the pseudo-Hungarianism of the late nineteenth century. From the very beginning of his career he oriented himself towards the ancient style of peasant music, but it took him many years to translate his enthusiasm and scholarly vision into artistic terms of his own.

His songs of 1907 (the first three of 'Négy Dal' ('Four Songs')) are distinguished by such folk-song characteristics as modality and the use of an incomplete scale, the cadential formula of a descending fourth with its repeated ending, the rhythmic pattern of an accented short note followed by an unaccented long one, and (except for a few modifications in song No. 3) by strophic form. That the result is Gallic rather than Hungarian is due partly to the third within the melodic line which retains some of its triadic function, and partly to the powerful influence of Debussy and his own method of pentatonic harmonization, as in *Haja, haja*:

The vocal parts of songs written between 1907 and 1909, published as Op. 1 under the title 'Énekszó' ('Dalok Népi Versekre'), or 'Song

[31] See his 'Epigrams' of 1954 which consist of nine pieces for voice (or solo instrument) and piano.

Album' ('Songs on Hungarian Folk Poetry'), are still absorbed into the delicate sounds of their piano accompaniment and thus into an atmosphere alien to their own. Nevertheless, several of them approach the composer's ideal more closely than 'Négy Dal' did.

Between 1909 and 1915–16, in 'Két Ének' ('Two Songs'), Op. 5,[32] and 'Megkésett Melodiák' ('Belated Melodies'), Op. 6, the French element persists but becomes retrospective. Influenced by the romantic texts, it reverts to the style of French art-song of the late nineteenth century and its Germanic ingredients, as this extract from *Elfojtódás* ('Sobbing') shows:

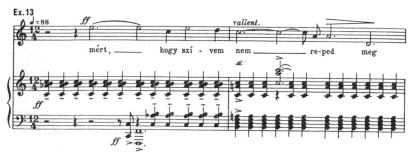

The accompaniment is now hypersonorous and sometimes rhetorical, and even when folk-song-like passages appear in the vocal part, they cannot be appreciated as such since the chords obscure their modality.

With 'Öt Dal' ('Four Songs'), Op. 9, written between 1915 and 1918 to poems of Endre Ady and Bélá Balázs, Kodály allows himself to be guided not only by the harmony of the mature Debussy and Ravel, but also by their sophisticated use of piano registers, their spacing of chords, and their manner of placing the vocal part within the accompaniment. Having thus adopted a genre of song originally inspired by symbolist poetry, Kodály found it appropriate to modify his melody. Though he makes its folk-song contours (where they are preserved) more audible than in Op. 5 and Op. 6, he suggests a declamatory element with recurring notes – mainly those that appear intermittently within a phrase – and brief sequences.

In spite of the consistency of his style, it nevertheless seems to be true that the most original moment in Op. 9 is that in which a genuine Hungarian folk-song quality in the melody is paralleled by a congruent chordal progression. This occurs in song No. 4, *Kicsi Virágom* ('My Little Flower'), composed in 1916:

[32] Their original version is for low male voice and orchestra.

A year later, in *Fáj A Szivem*[33] ('My Heart Aches', No. 4 in 'Négy Dal') Kodály proceeds to write a melody, strophic in form, resembling a real peasant tune without being a copy of it. Its piano part, however, features the tremolo and the figuration of the gypsy cimbalom.

Finally in 'Három Enek' ('Three Songs'), Op. 14 (1924–29), based on Hungarian poems of the sixteenth and seventeenth centuries, he attained the style he had aimed at since 1907. Again his melodies are no mere quotations. Distinguished by the characteristics of peasant music, they are underpinned by an accompaniment that confirms and enhances them, as in the second song of the set:

But the composer offers more than stylized folk-lore. By using melodic and harmonic variants and, at climactic moments (chiefly in middle sections) melodic transformations, he also aligns himself with the traditional concepts of European art-song.

Between 1925 and 1932 Kodály arranged fifty-seven Hungarian folk-songs and published them in ten volumes under the title 'Magyar

[33] Also for voice and orchestra.

Népzene' ('Hungarian Folk-Music'). One of the songs appeared separately, with orchestral accompaniment,[34] and several others too as parts of the opera *Székely Fonó* (*Székely Spinning Room*).

Kodály's aims are no longer those of his collection of 1906. At that time he made his arrangements so simple that they were playable by amateurs. Now, however, he addresses himself to the professional pianist and even the professional singer. His settings are worked out in great detail and sometimes so lavishly as to become concert versions. Since he is less anxious to break with the romantic past than Bartók was at that time, although he retained a distaste for the 'mammoth works'[35] of its late period, he does not hesitate to borrow some of its stylistic means. For about half of his tunes – tragic ballads, laments (mainly of lovers), soldiers' songs, patriotic songs – he avails himself of throbbing, syncopated chords, of chords repeated in triplets, of quick, arpeggio-like figurations, tremolos (also trills and sometimes both together), frequent crescendi and decrescendi, and a very specific, descriptive interpretation of the text. Some passages, totally based on harmonic effects, look like transcribed orchestral sonorities (such as Vol. I, 1; Ex. 16), others have the massiveness and

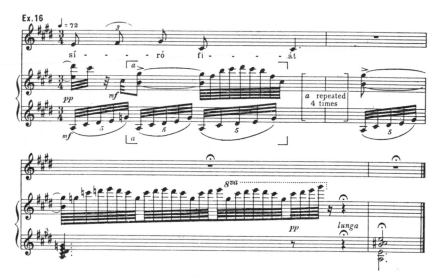

virtuosity of Liszt, to say nothing of the presence of Brahms in song

[34] *Kádár Kata*, Vol. IV, No. 18. The opera was completed in 1932.
[35] Zoltan Kodály, 'What is Hungarian in Music?', *Hungarian Quarterly*, Vol. 5, New York 1939.

No. 39 of Vol. VII and even of a few traces of gypsy music elsewhere. As long as these features, most of them associated with the Lied and the romantic opera, are highly appropriate to the rhythm and the phrasing of the tune, one overlooks their historical derivation. This is impossible, however, where they are crowded and where they magnify the song into a dramatic scene.

Kodály is at his best in gay, lively, and ingenuously lyrical tunes, as in kindred passages in the above-mentioned categories. It is here that one can agree with Bartók when he speaks of 'wonderful melodies in impeccable arrangements'.[36] In type they draw on nineteenth-century conventions of the genre, and they essentially perpetuate and elaborate, as in Vol. III, No. 14, the composer's harmonic vocabulary of 1906:

But he always succeeds in asserting his own personality within self-imposed limitations. Moreover, fully aware of the contemporary idiom, he deviates from traditional harmony, briefly and without effort, to lend bite to nuances in the text. In a few cases he adopts a new harmonic texture with very original results – not so much by relying on striking dissonances as on recurring patterns, parallel motion of chords, and a greater degree of linearity. This happens, for example, in *Zold Erdöben* ('In the Green Woods'), *Elmenyek, Elmenyek* ('Shall I Go, Shall I Go'):

[36] Translation of 'Gypsy Music or Hungarian Music?' in *The Musical Quarterly*, April 1947. Bartók's reference was actually to the first three volumes only.

El-më-nyëk, el - më-nyëk, hosz-szú út - ra më-nyëk,—

and two spirited songs, *Ludaim, Ludaim* ('My Geese, My Geese') and *Most Jöttem Erdélyből* ('I've Just Arrived from Transylvania'),[37] both characterized by a restless combination of 3+3+2 beats with which Kodály ordinarily did not concern himself. That all these arrangements thoroughly differ from each other proves how inventive he could be within this particular stylistic area, and it is a cause for regret that he did not cultivate it more extensively.

In many of the fifty-seven songs of Kodály's collection we find that the descriptiveness of their arrangements, which has no parallel in ethnic practice, is counteracted by two realistic features: the melody, when it is repeated with additional stanzas, frequently retains its initial pitch; and sections of the melody are left unaccompanied. The latter device serves equally to reinforce the folk-lore aspects of the composer's art-songs.

[37] Vol. IV, No. 21; Vol. VIII, Nos. 46 and 47; Vol. IV, No. 23.

Italy

ANTHONY MILNER

T HE new forms of solo song that developed in seventeenth-
century Italy were strongly influenced by those of the rising
opera. The early chamber cantata, like the first operas, had its
roots in the monodies written at the end of the previous century. These
had two main styles: the first tending towards recitative, the second
towards that of the early type of operatic aria. The latter were from the
first organized in short sections with frequent repetitions, being built
over sequential bass patterns or ground-basses. A favourite form was
strophic variation, in which the bass remained constant for each stanza
of the poem while the melody of the opening stanza was varied,
ornamented, or elaborated in subsequent stanzas. Some of Monteverdi's
later madrigals are really monodies of this sort. It would seem that the
first composer to call such compositions cantatas was Alessandro Grandi
(d. 1630) who in 1610 published a collection entitled 'Cantade et arie
a voce sola'.

The first examples of the typical solo (or chamber) cantata[1] were
written in the new *bel-canto* style which appeared simultaneously in
opera and cantata in the fourth decade of the century. It represented not
only a logical development of the monodic style but also a reaction

---

[1] The term *cantata* includes compositions for solo voice with orchestral accompaniment as
well as those for chorus, solo voices, and orchestra. Neither of these groups is discussed in this
chapter.

from its intensive concern with problems of word-setting and its consequent rapid changes of mood and rhythm. In so far as opera was concerned, the stylistic change was partly prompted by the influence of popular taste, for with the opening of the first public opera house at Venice in 1637 (which was rapidly followed by similar erections in other important Italian cities) opera ceased to be a purely aristocratic art. Whereas solo-singing in the first operas involved the use of a good deal of coloratura, mingled arioso and recitative, and chromatic harmonies to emphasize the meanings of individual words, the *belcanto* preferred a more obviously tuneful vocal line, simple rhythms (generally in triple time), the separation of aria and recitative, and a concentration on harmonies of the primary triads. The same characteristics are found in the cantatas (most of them written by opera composers) which offered the cultured music-lover a means of enjoying in private the same sort of music that he heard in the opera house. But since the cantata (unlike the opera) was designed for small groups of connoisseurs it could include subtleties which would have been lost on the opera-house public. Moreover, the cantata in Italy soon took the place of the older madrigal as a social art-form; composers often vied with one another in setting the same texts, just as they had in the madrigalian era; and these contests were frequently held in the *Accademie* or musical societies that had previously sponsored the madrigal. The cantata was also valuable as a training ground for composers: experiments with new formal, melodic and harmonic features were often tried out in cantatas before being used in the operatic arias and recitatives. The great popularity of the form may be judged from the thousands of examples that survive in manuscripts, many of which are still unpublished and even uncatalogued.

The first prominent cantata composers, Giacomo Carissimi (1605–74) and Luigi Rossi (1598–1653) wrote for the ecclesiastical and aristocratic élite of Rome. Since opera was banned in Rome for most of the seventeenth century, the cantata and the oratorio were assiduously cultivated as substitutes. Rossi and Carissimi gave the cantata its characteristic form as a setting of a dramatic or pastoral narrative poem to a mixture of aria, arioso, and recitative, generally for solo voice, though duet and trio cantatas are by no means uncommon. The accompaniment consists of a continuo bass: a stringed instrument (viola da gamba or cello) plays the bass line over which the harpsichordist fills in the implied harmonies, extemporizing rhythm and texture to suit the melodic contours of the vocal part and to underline the emotions expressed in the text. In some cantatas the continuo is joined by one or two violins. Most of Rossi's 250-odd cantatas show the influence of the earlier monodies in their use of a species of rondo form: repetitions of an aria separated by arioso and recitative sections. Some are merely single arias, either in simple ternary form ABA (the first example of the da-capo aria)[2] or expanded binary form AB, B_2. Long poems are divided into as many as ten separate sections: thus *Del Silentio* has triple-time arias interspersed with duple-time recitatives.[3] Several cantatas have short instrumental ritornelli between the vocal sections, either for continuo alone or with the addition of one or two violins.

Carissimi's cantatas have longer sections than Rossi's and consequently tend to make each section more of a self-contained formal unit. Thus the continuo frequently emphasizes the unity of a section by ground-bass technique, repetition of a rhythmic pattern, or melodic rhythmic sequences. Internal unity is strengthened by the frequent use of the same thematic material by melody and bass so that a contrapuntal relationship between the two lines results. This device became a fundamental feature of all later cantatas. The dramatic character of many of Carissimi's cantatas shows the increasing influence of the opera, also to be seen in the employment of sequential coloraturas supported by a steady rhythm moving to a cadence (the famous *Vittoria* contains fine examples of this technique). *I Filosofi* paints the contrasting moods of rival philosophers by sudden changes from major to minor: other humorous devices are found in *The Testament of the Ass* and *The Charlatan*. The long soaring melodic lines so typical of his work are another feature shared in common with the *bel-canto* opera.

From Cesti (1623–69), Carissimi's pupil and one of the greatest opera composers of the baroque, to Alessandro Scarlatti (1659–1725) and Handel (1685–1759) the development of the cantata parallels very closely that of the operatic recitative and aria. Legrenzi (1625–90) and Stradella (1645–82) established a sequence of two contrasted arias preceded by recitatives as the pattern for future cantata composers.[4] Within this framework the utmost variety could prevail, as may be seen from the following brief summary of the chief formal and stylistic techniques characteristic of cantata-composition *c.* 1660–1750.

(i) The recitative could be accompanied either by the continuo instruments alone (*recitativo secco*) or with the addition of violins

---

[2] See Apel and Davison *Historical Anthology of Music*, Vol. (II), No. 203, for a typical example.
[3] The last six sections are recorded in *The History of Music in Sound*, Vol. (VI), No. 3.
[4] For a typical piece by A. Scarlatti, see *Historical Anthology of Music*, Vol. II, No. 258.

(*recitativo accompagnato*). Recitatives frequently included phrases in arioso style.

(ii) In the aria the da-capo form was more frequently used than any other, though the earlier ABB forms were still used by Scarlatti and Handel. The da-capo form was enlarged by later baroque composers by means of the extended resources of harmonic organization developed towards the end of the seventeenth century. Consequently the separation of first and middle sections tended to be more strongly marked, and by the first decades of the eighteenth century there was seldom any thematic connexion between the two.

(iii) Legrenzi and Stradella regularly commenced their arias with an instrumental ritornello which anticipated briefly the motif or phrase sung by the voice on its first entry. Subsequent composers enlarged the opening ritornello till it came to present nearly all the material of the aria's first section which the voice then repeated and expanded. If one or two violins were required in addition to the continuo, their use was no longer restricted to the ritornelli: they participated in the aria proper by imitating the vocal line and thus provided an elaborately polyphonic texture.

(iv) Cantatas were written either in the style of the *opera seria* or in that of the *opera buffa*. Some were obviously intended for professional singers, others for skilful amateurs. While the lighter *buffa* type of cantata might include humorous elements such as rapid word-repetition and even nonsense refrains, the *seria* type would have arias designed mainly for display (as in the operatic *aria di bravura*) or expression (*aria cantabile*) or, more rarely, for pictorial illustration (the so-called 'simile' aria, in which the singer compares his mood to some such subject as 'an army going into battle' or 'a storm at sea' and then proceeds to describe this).

So few cantatas of this period are available in modern publications that it is unprofitable here to discuss details of individual works. When (to mention but two composers) by far the greater part of Legrenzi's and Scarlatti's output (190 and 600 respectively) are to be found only in manuscript it is impossible to give any adequate picture of this field of copious production. A noteworthy feature of many of Scarlatti's cantatas is the elaborate quasi-virtuoso writing for the continuo bass which thus becomes the equal partner of the voice. Though Scarlatti does not employ obbligato instruments, nearly all the other Italian composers of his time delighted in the delicate accompaniments for arias that obbligato instruments could provide. The following quotation from a cantata by Antonio Caldara (1670–1736) is typical in the way the violin subtly underlines and supports the vocal melody without ever intruding upon the voice's chief rôle:

Handel's seventy-two solo cantatas (which, since they are printed in the complete edition of the Handel Society, form the only group of such works readily available) provide a representative cross-section of cantata composition at its height. Their style is closely modelled on that of Scarlatti, whose treatment of the continuo bass and avoidance of obbligato instruments they follow exactly. Most of them are for soprano: the rest for alto and bass. The variety exhibited in these works is remarkable, ranging from light airs with a popular ring (e.g. the siciliana in No. 20, *Filli adorata e cara*) to the extraordinary demands made upon the bass voice in *Nell'Africane selve*, including a compass of nearly three octaves. Comedy in the buffa style appears in *Dalla guerra amorosa* (No. 8): a warning against the dangers of falling in love. A good example of a 'simile' aria occurs in the middle of No. 25 *Lungi dal mio bel nume*, which describes a shipwreck in a storm. One of the finest, *O Numi eterni!* (No. 46), portrays the last hours of Lucretia in the manner of *opera seria*.

There is little of importance or interest in the Italian songs of the nineteenth century. Composers ceased to cultivate the solo cantata (which became obsolete concurrently with the continuo) turning to a sentimental type of song utilizing the clichés of the new operatic styles which for the most part appealed to a very low level of taste. Of the numerous works of Donaudy, Arditi, Tosti, and Denza, only a few of Tosti's are still heard occasionally today, and these are fairly representative of the genre. The few good songs of the period were the productions of opera composers. Though a great many of Rossini's songs are drawing-room trifles (often written for autograph albums) several bear comparison with the best of his opera arias which they closely resemble in style, being obviously designed for the amateur singer with operatic pretensions. The abrupt, sometimes jerky modulations so characteristic of his operas appear also in the songs. Example 2

provides a typical instance, not only of this feature, but also of Rossini's two favourite methods of accompaniment: broken chord patterns and 'oom-pah' rhythms. Some songs were intended for virtuoso performers: the coloratura ornamentation of *La fioraia fiorentina* and the sequential arpeggios of *Aragonese* demand the utmost refinement of vocal technique. Towards the end of his life Rossini composed six settings of a poem by Metastasio, two for soprano, one each for mezzo-soprano and contralto, and two for baritone. He entitled the group 'Musique anodine . . . J'offre ces modestes Mélodies à ma chere femme Olimpe comme Simple temoignage de reconnaissance pour les soins affectueux intelligents qu'elle me prodigue dans ma trop longue et terrible maladie (Opprobre de la vacuité).' The contrasts exhibited by the different settings are both clever and amusing, but this sort of *tour de force* presented him with no difficulties. He set another of Metastasio's poems over one hundred times for insertion in admirers' albums.

Verdi (1813–1901) composed the greater part of his small output of songs comparatively early in his career. They reveal a quasi-operatic approach to song-writing similar to Rossini's without ever descending to the facile inanities of the older man's album pieces. *L'esule*, written in 1839, is almost a cantata: cast in the form of a *scena* opening with an extensive introduction for piano, it consists of alternating sections of recitative and arioso leading to a conventional *strepitoso* ending. The accompaniment to this finale sounds exactly like a pianoforte reduction of an orchestral score. Apart from a few songs written for albums in later years, the rest of Verdi's songs are to be found in the twelve *Romanze* published in two books of six in 1838 and 1845. The majority are cast in regular four-bar phrases similar to those of the arias of his early operas. Of the first set, *Deh, pietoso, o Addolorate* (a translation of a poem from Goethe's 'Faust') is the most interesting for the instructive comparison it affords between Italian and German attitudes to song composition. Whereas Schubert's setting of the same poem has all the chamber-music intimacy so fundamental to the German conception of the *lied*, Verdi's treatment immediately suggests stage performance and the presence of an audience at a spectacle: everything is slightly 'larger than life' and the details of emotional portrayal are submerged in rhetorical gesture. The second set of *Romanze* makes larger demands on the singer: *La zingara* (in Spanish style) requires a virtuoso to do it justice. The same is true for *Lo spazzo camino* with its high coloratura and trills and interesting mixture of 3–8 and 3–4 metres.

Throughout the nineteenth century the dominance of opera had effectively prevented the development of a body of Italian song comparable to that of other nations. But the generation of composers born between 1880 and 1890 strove against this dominance, turning their attention to the problems of instrumental and non-dramatic vocal music. In their search for new paths (which met with considerable opposition from the public) they studied the older Italian music of the late medieval and early renaissance which was then coming to light through the research of the first Italian musicologists. The poet D'Annunzio founded the National Music Collection to rediscover the riches of the past and thus provided support for the 'musical renaissance'. Ottorino Respighi (1879–1936) was deeply attached to the Italian musical forms of the past and strove to aid their revival by transcriptions and editions, even though he interpreted them in what can only be regarded today as an intensely subjective and romantic manner. His songs are of slight importance in relation to the rest of his works, but they nevertheless represent the first attempts to break away entirely from the 'operatic' style of previous song composers. Thus he set medieval and renaissance poems in 'Cinque canti all'antica' (1906), and Armenian poems in the collections of 1921 and 1924. One of his last works 'Tre vocalizzi' (1933) consists of experiments in wordless song. His vocal lines are always pleasantly lyrical, if sometimes lacking rhythmic impulse, and his accompaniments for the greater part avoid the mechanical broken-chord patterns of the previous century.

If Respighi be regarded as heralding the new outlook in Italian song, Alfredo Casella (1883–1947) may fairly be considered as its leader. He was the first to state unequivocally the aims of the new composers: 'We are in the presence of a total reaction against immediate and superficial sentiments, in place of which we are trying to substitute the return to the contemplative feelings of the greater classicism. Therefore it is not "neo-classicism", as it is improperly called by certain critics, but a true and right return to the pure classicism of our ancestors.' Casella's neo-classicism was at first largely the result of a cosmopolitan education: between the ages of thirteen and thirty-two he was away from Italy, studying in France and later travelling in Europe, thus meeting all the most prominent musicians of his time. His earlier works were stylistically eclectic, displaying the half-digested influence and mannerisms of most of the new idioms appearing in the first years of the century. It is significant in this connexion that six of his first seven groups of songs are to French texts (Op. 26, 'L'Adieu à la vie', is a setting of French translations of poems by Rabindranath Tagore). Not until the end of the First World War did he achieve a consistent personal style. The first songs to show this were the 'Tre Canzoni trecentesche' (1923), whose melodies reveal a free diatonicism that can embrace all the notes of the chromatic scale. Example 3, from the first

Ex. 3

of the group, *Giovane bella*, shows an abrupt modulation in the piano accompaniment softened by the simple stepwise movement of the voice. *Fuor de la bella garda* has a vocal line which mingles recitative-like phrases and *arioso*, breaking out into occasional coloratura. Towards the end of his life Casella turned to religious subjects for his vocal music: the 'Tre Canti Sacri' (1943) for baritone and organ on Latin texts have long recitative-like lines reminiscent of Gregorian chant accompanied by chromatic harmonies. This mingling of diatonic lines with the utmost freedom of harmonic movement is typical of Casella's attempt to synthesize elements from the remoter musical past with the panchromaticism of a new age.

Ildebrando Pizzetti (b. 1880) avoids lyricism for its own sake, using it only when he considers it justified by the meaning or mood of the words. His vocal lines mingle a supple (if at times almost mono-tonic) recitative with *arioso* at significant moments. This characteristic style is well exemplified by 'Tre Sonnetti del Petrarca' (1922). The sensitive opening of *Quel rosignuol che sì soave piagne* (Example 4)

suggests the call of the lark, which the voice adopts as its 'recitative' pattern, departing from and returning to it in short scale-motifs that precede important words or stresses. The complete dependence of the accompaniment on the vocal line is typical of most of Petrassi's songs. Later songs are more chromatic. In *Bebro e il suo Cavallo*, the first of *Tre liriche* (1944), a translation of a Greek folk poem is set to a quasi-folky melody moving in speech rhythm but which includes a great deal of incidental chromatic alteration. *Vorrei voler, signor, quel ch'io non voglio* is unusual in that its melody contains frequent wide leaps contrasted with modulatory scale-passages: this vivid emotional display is called forth by Michelangelo's poem. The last of the group, *In questa notte*, has a melody composed of triad formations which are mixed to produce a wide-ranging chromaticism. This technique affords an effective solution of the problems that panchromatic melody and harmony can raise in vocal settings, and one which younger Italian composers have used with great success in serial composition.

Gian-Francesco Malipiero (b. 1882) has perhaps had more influence as a musicologist than as a composer. His studies of the seventeenth- and eighteenth-century Venetian composers, especially of Monteverdi, have profoundly affected his musical development: his melodic style derives from elements of the earlier operatic recitative as does his free treatment of rhythm. His few songs show the nobility of expression and delicate declamation, to be found in his choral music. G. F. Ghedini (b. 1892), like Malipiero, has prepared practical editions of baroque Italian music, though their influence on his compositions is not so noticeable. His few songs display firmly diatonic melodies often disposed in variable metre: the second of the 'Quattro Strambotti di Guistiani' (1925), for example, alternates $\frac{7}{4}$, $\frac{8}{4}$, and $\frac{6}{4}$. Castelnuovo-Tedesco (b. 1895) has written far more songs than any of his contemporaries or juniors. The majority are settings of English poems (in the original language) including twelve books containing songs for all the poems in Shakespeare's dramatic works (1922–24), three sonnets by E. B. Browning (1926) and twenty-seven sonnets by Shakespeare (1945). In these he avoids underlining the imagery of the poetry, preferring to suggest what may be called the general mood of each poem by the impulse of the melodic line and the texture of the accompaniment. For the cycle of 'Coplas' (1915) on Spanish folk poems, he adopts the unusual course of what can only be described as commenting on the texts in the accompaniment: there is no trace of the word-painting or 'folky' modalism that most composers would have used. His treatment of every language he sets is impeccable, and, although he rarely reaches the heights, his songs must be accounted some of the most effective and successful of the present century.

The seeming reluctance of Italian composers born since 1900 to embark on song composition has both social and musical causes. Nowhere in the contemporary world does the song have the part in domestic life that it had in the nineteenth century, and even if it had, most contemporary songs are too difficult to be performed adequately by amateurs. Rightly or wrongly, songs written today are thought of as concert pieces: they are heard only at recitals, and there infrequently, because the singer knows that they will not be a main attraction for the audience. Also, many composers feel that the combination of voice and piano has romantic associations that are better avoided today and have consequently experimented with accompaniment of various types of chamber ensemble. These lie outside the scope of this article; nevertheless, in estimating the scanty songs of Petrassi and Dallapiccola (both born 1904), it should be remembered that their works for voice and chamber orchestra (or small ensemble) provide a better picture of their attitude to music for solo voice.

Like those of so many recent Italian composers, Petrassi's first songs ('Tre liriche', 1929) are settings of medieval poems. Influenced by Casella, they exhibit the older man's technique of freely modulating diatonic lines accompanied by chromatic harmonies. Later songs show an approach to panchromaticism, a style which in his choral and orchestral writing has led him to the serial technique but which so far he has not employed in songs. Dallapiccola turned to dodecaphonic methods more quickly and decisively than did his contemporary. His 'Quattro liriche' (1948) on poems by the Spaniard Antonio Machado employs a twelve-note row arranged in two scale-formations that permit quasi-diatonic vocal movement. The first two bars of Example 5, the beginning of the vocal entry in the first of the group,

Ex. 5

present this series in melodic order, while the accompaniment selects notes from the patterns for an impressionistic texture. This typically Italian use of the series to obtain a flowing vocal line is to be found also in Dallapiccola's opera *Il Prigioniero*. Younger composers, such as Riccardo Malipiero (b. 1914), and Mario Peragallo (b. 1910), tend increasingly to imitate the wide leaps and angular intervals of Webern's last works; neither has written any songs of importance though both have used the voice in chamber ensemble and choral music.

Latin America

GILBERT CHASE

THE area loosely called 'Latin America' is a vast region extending from the Rio Grande on the continent of North America to Tierra del Fuego, where the tapered end of South America points toward the Antarctic Cirle. In climate and topography it is a region of extremes and contrasts, containing immense mountain ranges (the massive Cordillera of the Andes), coastal deserts, vast grassy plains (such as the Argentine *pampa*), tropical forests, and quasi-impenetrable jungles. Once the seat of ancient and mighty empires – dominated by the Aztecs in Mexico, the Maya in Central America, and the Incas in South America – rich in treasures of silver and gold, these far-flung territories were conquered and colonized, in their largest extent, by the Spaniards and the Portuguese, with some smaller enclaves remaining to the British, the Dutch, and the French (chiefly in the Caribbean area).

Thus, while Spanish became the language of the majority, the largest country of all, Brazil, is Portuguese-speaking, and French is the official language of Haiti as well as of the French West Indies. Nor should we forget that various Indian tongues, such as *quechua* and *aymara* in the Andean highlands, are still spoken by millions of the Indian population of 'Latin America' (which some writers would prefer to call 'Indo-America'). Ethnically, there are marked differences in the racial composition of the various countries of this area. Generally speaking, there are some countries in which the Indian element is preponderant – such as Bolivia and Guatemala – others in which the mixture of Indian and Spanish predominates (Mexico is the outstanding example), others in which the Negro element is either dominant, as in Haiti, or widely prevalent, as in Brazil and Panama; and finally, there are those countries in which the population, formed largely by European immigration since the nineteenth century, has very few traces of indigenous or Negro elements. Prominent in this group are Argentina and Uruguay. These are generalizations, of course, and one finds, here and there, significant exceptions, such as the large influx of Italian immigrants in the region of São Paulo, Brazil, which not only increase the complexity of the picture but also (and São Paulo is certainly a case in point) exert a direct influence on the cultural 'climate' of a particular region or city. The rise of an internationally important school of virtuosity in São Paulo, for example, is due mainly to the strong Italian influence in that city.

Obviously, to deal consecutively and succinctly with an area so vast in extent and so varied in its cultural components, is by no means an easy task. To attempt to trace the history of song in each of the twenty Latin American countries would require at least one long chapter, if not a whole volume to itself. Furthermore, some of this material would be of only local interest, since not all of these countries have as yet attained to international significance in their musical production. The problem, however, is somewhat mitigated by the fact that, when it comes to solo art-song, there is little to deal with, historically, in Latin America.

During the period of Spanish and Portuguese domination, composition was confined chiefly to polyphonic music for the church. Secular music was mostly either instrumental or theatrical. The traditional types of Iberian folk-song, such as the *romance* (which became the *corrido* in Mexico) and the *décima* (widely used from the Rio Grande to the Rio de la Plata), were transplanted to American soil and became the basis of what is known as *música criolla* – music of Hispanic origin acclimatized in the New World. The whole domain of folk and popular music, in its many ramifications – including indigenous and negroid influences – is of fundamental importance for the history of art-song in Latin America, because the composers who wrote the latter have drawn extensively on the folk-popular traditional material. While we cannot here go into the details of this historical process, it will be evident, even in this brief survey, that a very large portion

K—HOS

of Latin American art-song is inextricably intertwined with the folk and popular idioms of this region. So inextricably, indeed, that it is often difficult to make a clear-cut distinction between what is art-song and what is merely an arrangement of a folk-song.

The point can be illustrated by reference to the most celebrated songs that have come out of Latin America: *La Paloma* and *Estrellita*. These songs are doubtless known to millions of persons who never heard of their composers. The former was written by the Spanish composer Sebastián Yradier (1809–1865), who spent some time in Cuba and later published two collections of 'Spanish' songs, *Echos d'Espagne* and *Fleurs d'Espagne*, which were widely popular in their day. This was the source from which Bizet, while working on the score of *Carmen*, got the theme for his famous *Habañera*, taking it from a song called *El Arreglito*. His excuse for this 'borrowing' was that he thought it was a genuine folk-song. But in these matters, as we have intimated, it is not easy to determine what is 'genuine', either as a folk-song or an art-song. One is forced to admit a sort of intermediate or hybrid type. Certainly the *habañera* (named from the city of Habana in Cuba) existed as a generic type long before Yradier published *La Paloma*. But if he had not given a particular musical setting to this *habañera*, it might have disappeared with the passing of time or remained as a strictly local product, instead of going around the world, transmitted from generation to generation even by those who have never seen the music or heard of the composer. Something similar was accomplished a couple of generations later by the Cuban composer Eduardo Sánchez de Fuentes (1874–1944), whose habanera entitled *Tú*, written at the age of eighteen and published in 1894, became so universally popular that it is generally regarded as the paradigm of this type of song.

As for *Estrellita*, it was first published in 1914 in a collection of Mexican songs by the composer Manuel Ponce (1886–1948), and was simply one of numerous such 'arrangements' that he made (about sixty in all). One reason for the special popularity of *Estrellita* is that it was not protected by copyright – an added inducement for publishers to reprint it and for singers to record it. For the rest, Ponce was a prolific writer of songs, of whom we shall have more to say later.

The earliest known collection of Mexican typical songs was published around 1830 by J. A. Bohme of Hamburg, with the title 'Colección de 24 Canciones y Jarabes Mexicanos', arranged for voice and piano by a certain Juan Dupré. It contains arrangements of some of the best-known traditional songs of Mexico, such as *La Petenera*,

La Morenita, La Tapatía, and *La Indita.* Of special interest is the song called *El Butaquito,* which has the pattern of the Spanish *seguidilla* and includes the traditional refrain *Ay, ay, ay! cielito lindo,* subsequently incorporated in the well-known song *Ay, ay, ay!* by the Chilean composer Osman Pérez Freire.

Outside the field of folk and popular music, the history of song in Latin America during the nineteenth century is mainly of antiquarian interest. In Argentina, for instance, numerous songs were composed by the three 'precursors' of Argentine music: Amancio Alcorta (1805–1862), Juan Pedro Esnaola (1808–1878) and Juan Bautista Alberdi (1810–1884). Of these, only Esnaola had professional training in music, while the others were prominent political figures who cultivated music as amateurs. Their songs are sentimental and salonesque, with such titles as *To a Flower, Absence, The Angel,* and *The Troubadour* – faded flowers of a bygone epoch, but still capable of exhaling a nostalgic aroma if treated tenderly.

In Brazil the type of sentimental song *par excellence* was the *modinha,* strongly Italianate and apt for the salon, but with its erotic content enhanced by a tropical voluptuousness. Throughout the nineteenth century it was the type of Brazilian song most in vogue among all classes of society. The famous Brazilian operatic composer Carlos Gomes (1836–1896), whose opera *Il Guarany* was acclaimed at La Scala of Milan, wrote a number of *modinhas,* including *As Bahianas* and *Tão longe de mim distante* ('So far away from me'), which are more Brazilian in character than his operatic works. The *modinha,* deeply embedded in the Brazilian character, has left its impress upon the modern art-song of Brazil.

Although most of the Latin American countries acquired their political independence early in the nineteenth century, artistic independence was more difficult to achieve. Hence in nearly all these countries we find, toward the beginning of the present century, strong movements toward musical nationalism which strive to give characteristic musical expression to the cultural traits of each nation. In some cases these national movements were linked to profound social, economic and political upheavals that sought to transform the entire structure of the nation. This was the case, notably, in Mexico, where music and all the arts were profoundly involved in the 'Mexican Revolution' that began with the overthrow of Porfirio Díaz in 1910.

The precursor of musical nationalism in Mexico was Manuel Ponce (1886–1948), who, in spite of having studied in Bologna and

Berlin, and of being influenced by Chopin and other Romantic composers, very early in his career began to inject Mexican elements into his music. We have already mentioned his numerous arrangements of Mexican songs, of which *Estrellita* is the most famous. He wrote in addition a considerable number of art-songs, among which those that have been published include Six Archaic Poems, Three Poems by González Martínez, Three Poems by Mariano Brull, Three Poems by Lermontov, and Three Poems by Rabindranath Tagore. The Lermontov songs are typical of his post-Romantic tendency.

Mexico's leading contemporary composer, Carlos Chávez (b. 1899), has written relatively few songs. In early life he wrote some romantic lieder to texts by Heine, Hugo, J. A. Silva and Ronald de Carvalho, and in 1923 he began a more characteristic style of vocal composition with 'Three Hexagons' for voice and piano, on poems by Carlos Pellicer, a poet whose verse he was to set again in 1924 ('Three More Hexagons', for voice, flute, oboe, bassoon, viola and piano) and in 1938 ('Three Poems' for voice and piano). In 1941 he made a setting for voice and piano of García Lorca's *La Casada Infiel* ('The Faithless Wife'), and the following year he wrote *North Carolina Blues*, with text by Xavier Villaurrutia. Of these, only the 'Three Poems' of Carlos Pellicer have been published, with Spanish and English text.[1]

Silvestre Revueltas (1899–1945) was one of the most original composers, not only of Mexico, but of all Latin America. His music is thoroughly 'Mexican', in the sense that it is permeated with the colours, landscapes, sounds and rhythms of the land and its people; but it is never merely picturesque or descriptive. It is above all highly personal and new. Although Revueltas did not write many songs, they are very characteristic and deserve the attention of singers looking for unusual programme material. They include *Ranas y el tecolote* ('Frogs and the Tecolote'), 'Two Songs' on texts by Nicolás Guillén for voice and various instruments, 'Seven Songs' on texts by García Lorca for voice and piano (1938), and *Canto a una muchacha negra* ('Song for a Negro Girl'), text by the American Negro poet Langston Hughes.

Among the Mexican composers most closely associated with Chávez and Revueltas are Luis Sandi (b. 1905) and Blas Galindo (b. 1911). The former, specializing in choral music, is the founder and director of the excellent 'Coro de Madrigalistas' of Mexico City. Galindo is Director of the National Conservatory of Music of Mexico. Sandi's published songs include 'Cuatro Canciones de Amor' and

[1] G. Schirmer, Inc., New York.

'Diez Haikais', based on poems by José Juan Tablada, with English translations by Noel Lindsay. Galindo has published 'Dos Canciones', of which the first is a *Lullaby for the child in the picture* (text by Alfonso del Río, English translation by Noel Lindsay), the second a sad song translated from the *nahuatl*, one of the native Indian languages of Mexico, entitled *When I Die, My Mother*.[2] The alternation of $\frac{3}{8}$ and $\frac{5}{8}$ metre is typical of much Latin American music.

'When I die, my mother, then lay me to rest beneath the hearthstone, mother of mine.'

Among Mexican women composers, María Teresa Prieto has published 'Celestial Odes' for voice and piano, four songs with texts by various poets (including one in French by Charles le Goffic, *Les Peupliers de Kéranroux*).

After the Spanish Civil War of 1936–39, a number of Spanish musicians settled in Mexico and identified themselves with the musical life of that country. Among them are Jesús Bal y Gay and Rodolfo Halffter. The former has written 'Four Pieces' for voice and piano, on texts by Emilio Prados, Juan Ramón Jiménez, and Rafael Alberti. Halffter's songs include admirable settings of 'Two Sonnets' by Sor Juana Inés de la Cruz, *Celia, spying the roses* ... and *Feliciano adores me* (English versions by Noel Lindsay).

In Cuba, the *criollo* element prodominated in musical composition during the nineteenth century and the early years of the twentieth, producing many kinds of typical song, such as the *bolero*, the *guajira*, the *guaracha*, the *punto*, and the *habañera* (already mentioned). Numerous

2 English version by Noel Lindsay.

composers have cultivated these types of Cuban song, which are not 'art-songs' in the strict sense of the term, yet are neither folk nor popular, but a hybrid product born of the tropics. The songs and their composers are too numerous to list, but we might mention at least such composers as Eduardo Sánchez de Fuentes (1874–1944), Gonzalo Roig (b. 1890), composer of *Quiéreme Mucho*; Jorge Anckermann, Sindo Garay, Eliseo Grenet, Moisés Simons, and Ernesto Lecuona[3].

Beginning with the important composers Amadeo Roldán(1900–1939) and Alejandro García Caturla (1905–1940), the emphasis began to shift toward the Afro-Cuban element, and an attempt was made by these composers to combine musical modernism with a primitive quality derived from the Afro-American dances and rituals, including the utilization of African-type drums and other primitive instruments. In this they were aided and encouraged by a simultaneous 'Africanist' movement in Cuban poetry, whose leading exponents were Nicolás Guillén and Alejo Carpentier.

Developing this Afro-Cuban trend, García Caturla wrote 'Two Afro-Cuban Poems' for voice and piano (also orchestrated by Américo Rojas), to texts by Alejo Carpentier,[4] *Bito Manué* to text by Nicolás Guillén, and *Yambambó*, text by the same, for voice and piano. As the Spanish critic Adolfo Salazar remarked: 'The typical musical inflexion of Caturla is the limited melodic ambitus, and his avoidance of the intervals of the minor second.' And Carpentier adds that: 'His themes always carry the freshness of a primitive song.'

Roldán's contribution to Afro-Cuban music consists of *Danza Negra* for voice and seven instruments (1928) and *Motivos de Son*, eight pieces for voice and seven instruments, text by Nicolás Guillén (1934).[5]

After the deaths of Caturla and Roldán, the 'advanced' movement in Cuban music was led by José Ardévol (b. 1911), a musician of Spanish origin who settled in Habana in 1930. His tendency is strongly neo-classical, but he also encouraged his pupils to deal with Cuban themes, as he did himself in several of his compositions. In 1953 he won the Cuban National Prize for his settings of six poems by the great Cuban writer José Martí, for soprano voice and piano (also orchestrated).[6] This song-cycle was composed in 1949 under the title 'Versos sencillos'. He also composed a song for soprano and pianoforte to a text by Nicolás Guillén, *Ay Señora mi vecina!* (1950).

---

[3] See the collection edited by Emilio Grenet, *Popular Cuban Music; eighty revised and corrected compositions* . . . (Habana, 1939). [4] M. Sénart, Paris, 1929.

[5] Score and reduction for piano published in 'New Music', 1934.

[6] Published by Ricordi Americana, Buenos Aires.

Ardévol and some of his followers formed the 'Grupo Renovación', whose members included Hilario González, Gisela Hernández, Harold Gramatges, Argeliers León, Virginia Fleites, Serafín Pro, Edgardo Martín, and Julián Orbón. Notable songs are those by León, 'Dos Canciones' for tenor and piano (1944), G. Hernández, 'Dos Cantos al Mar', soprano and piano (1943), Martín, *Sonnet by Petrarch*, soprano and piano (1942).

Two of the most prominent of the younger Cuban composers are Aurelio de la Vega and Julián Orbón, both born in 1925. The former studied composition with Ernst Toch in California. He has written the song cycle 'La Fuente Infinita' ('The Infinite Fountain', 1944), 'Two Songs' on poems by Tagore (1945), and 'El Encuentro' ('The Encounter') for contralto and piano (1950). Orbón has written 'Dos Canciones' ('Two Songs') on poems by Neruda, for contralto and piano (1946).

In a more popular vein, Ernesto Lecuona has had many songs published in the United States, of which the best-known is probably 'Siboney'.

BRAZIL

The musicologist Luiz Heitor Correa de Azevedo is of the opinion that 'in its song literature, Brazilian music finds its moments of most intimate and effective lyricism, and at times of strongest national affirmation'. Certainly, 'national affirmation' is at the heart of Brazilian art-song, as it is of most Brazilian music composed during the present century. The main preoccupation of each composer has been to express some aspect of the national character as reflected through his own personality.

Throughout the nineteenth century, Italian was the dominant language of art-song in Brazil. Therefore the first battle on behalf of a national song literature in Brazil had to be fought on the language front. The composer Alberto Nepomuceno (1864–1920) was the pioneer in developing the Brazilian *lied* along national lines. Although trained in Rome, Berlin and Paris, he showed a strong interest in everything that pertained to his native country, including its popular traditions. At first he composed songs with foreign texts, somewhat in the manner of Grieg, but soon he launched a vigorous campaign on behalf of the Portuguese language, which he used for most of his songs after 1902. As Director of the National Institute of Music he stopped short of making Portuguese obligatory for the classes in singing, but outside of the Institute he insisted on the use of the vernacular as the proper medium of art-song, in spite of strong opposition from some influential critics. At various times Nepomuceno set to music texts in German, French, Italian, Latin, and Portuguese. His prevailing musical idiom is Impressionistic. He published about forty songs, of which the most important were issued by Artur Napoleão in Rio de Janeiro. Of these songs, one of the best is also the one that has the most marked Brazilian character. It is titled *Xácara* and is based on a type of narrative folk-song sung with guitar accompaniment (which Nepomuceno evokes in his accompaniment for piano). His last song, *Jangada*, based on a theme of the northern province of Ceará, has a characteristic syncopated rhythm in the accompaniment. Left unfinished at the composer's death, it was completed by Octavio Bevilaqua.

Francisco Braga (1868–1945), pupil of Massenet in Paris and a frequent visitor to the Wagnerian shrine of Bayreuth, reflects Brazilian traits only in a very limited and superficial manner. His music is essentially eclectic. His best-known song is *Vírgenes mortas* (text by Bilac), in which a declamatory style alternates with expressive melody.

Barroso Neto (1881–1941) is known especially for his *Canção da Felicidade* ('Song of Happiness'), which has been widely sung by Bidu Sayão. It is somewhat in the style of a *modinha*, with a delicate melodic line. Another typical song by Barroso Neto is *Olhos tristes* ('Sorrowful Eyes').

Glauco Velasquez (1883–1914), lived and wrote entirely apart from the national movement in Brazilian music, although he did use the Portuguese language in most of his songs. Completely introspective, it has been said that his music 'reveals a morbid and tortured soul'. He set to music poems by Antero de Quental, Leopardi, Stechetti, etc. One of his best-known songs is *Cantique de Soeur Béatrice*.

Luciano Gallet (1893–1931) has a special place in the history of Brazilian song, not only because of his thirty-one published songs, but also because of the enthusiasm and insight that he brought to the study and diffusion of the folk-music of Brazil. His arrangements of Brazilian folk-songs are both artistic and authentic, and entirely suitable for concert use. His important work, *Estudos de Folclore*, published posthumously in 1934 with a preface by Mario de Andrade, contains nineteen folk-songs that Gallet collected from various regions of Brazil. Probably his best-known song is *Foi numa Noite Calmosa* ('It

Was a Night So Calm'), described as a *modinha carioca*. 'Carioca' is the term applied to the inhabitants of Rio de Janeiro, and by extension to their music. Typical of Gallet's folk-song arrangements is *Moréna, morena* ('Brunette, Brunette'), from the region of Paraná.[7]

With Oscar Lorenzo Fernândez (1897–1948) we reach one of the most outstanding figures in the contemporary song literature of Brazil, who was also a culminating figure in the movement for musical nationalism. Beginning under the influence of French Impressionism in his first period (1918–1922), he subsequently devoted himself to the systematic exploration and exploitation of Brazilian folk-music, pursuing this activity with uninterrupted intensity until about 1938. During the last years of his life he was less concerned with national elements, tending more towards the ideal of 'universalism'.

Lorenzo Fernândez's first important song, which enjoyed a sensational success and instantly established his reputation, was *Toada para Você* ('A Song for You'), composed in 1928 on a text by Mario de Andrade, the poet and musicologist who was a leader of the 'modernist' movement in Brazil. Considered by critics as one of the most perfect creations of Brazilian art-song, the *Toada para Você* also initiated a trend in Brazilian song-writing known as *voceísmo*, whose adherents included Francisco Mignone and Camargo Guarnieri.

Likewise from the year 1928 is the *Berceuse da Onda*, originally written for voice and orchestra (later transcribed for piano accompaniment), which is one of the few compositions in which Lorenzo Fernândez drew upon Amerindian rather than Afro-Brazilian elements. The accompaniment is polytonal. The song called *Notturno* (1934) is regarded by some critics as the best of this composer's songs. Others, however, would give the palm to *Essa Negra Fulô* ('Fulô, that Negress'), on a text by Jorge de Lima, published in 1939, which Vasco Mariz, in his excellent little book *A Canção de Câmara no Brasil* (Porto, 1948), characterizes as being 'one of the great moments of the Brazilian *lied*'. In this very effective song, for soprano, the composer makes direct use of folk-lore, but in such a creative manner that the result is a genuine art-song. The poem evokes, with both humour and realism, the jealous anger of an indignant wife, in the times of slavery, who is furious at the handsome Negro slave girl who has stolen many things from her mistress, including her husband's affection. The melodic line is full of

[7] This song, together with others by Villa-Lobos, Lorenzo Fernândez, Francisco Mignone, and Camargo Guarnieri, may be found in the collection *Musique Brésilienne Moderne* (Rio de Janeiro, 1937).

glissandi, while the accompaniment, percussive and dissonant, relent-lessly underlines the barbaric implications of the situation. This is the way it begins:

Ex. 2

The most famous Brazilian composer is, of course, Heitor Villa-Lobos (1887–1959), the extraordinarily prolific and remarkably original musician whose many-sided production epitomises all the tendencies of contemporary music in Brazil, but more especially the strong national movement to which he has given the greatest impulse.

During his first phase (roughly, from 1908 to 1918), Villa-Lobos was not particularly concerned with national factors in his music. To this period belong such songs as *Fleur fanée*, *Les Mères* (Victor Hugo), *Il Bove* (Carducci), and *Il Nome de Maria* (Stecchetti), the first two for baritone, the third and fourth for mezzo-soprano. The most interesting songs of this period are six 'Miniatures' on texts by various Brazilian poets, written in 1916–17, for voice with piano or orchestra.[8] The most successful number of this set is *Sino da Aldeia*, with its 'audaciously dissonant' accompaniment.

With the 'Canções Tipicas Brasilieiras' of 1919, Villa-Lobos began a new and important phase of his vocal production, initiating the trend towards overt nationalism. These songs are extremely effective arrange-ments of Brazilian folk-songs of many different types and regions, including Amerindian and Afro-Brazilian. Two of the latter type, *Xangô* (ritualistic song of the *macumba*) and *Estrela é lua nova* (fetish song), are probably the most frequently sung of this collection (pub-lished by Editions Max Eschig, Paris). The original collection consisted of thirteen songs; three more were added in 1935.

In his next 'nationalist' phase, represented by the 'Serestas' (1925–26) – fourteen songs for voice with piano (or orchestra) to texts by various Brazilian poets – Villa-Lobos ceases to make direct use of folk-lore,

[8] Published by Casa Napole o, Rio de Janeiro.

except in No. 5 (*Modinha*), writing instead original melodies and accompaniments in the style of Brazilian traditional music. This collection marks a high-point in the vocal production of Villa-Lobos. Among the most successful songs in the set are *Na paz do outono* ('In the Peace of Autumn'), text by Ronald de Carvalho; and *Canção do carreiro* ('Song of the Driver'), text by Ribeiro Couto.

With the three 'Poemas Indígenas' (1926), Villa-Lobos turned to Amerindian themes. The first song, *Canide-ioune* ('Yellow Bird'), is based on a theme noted by Jean de Léry among the Indians on a voyage to Brazil in 1553. The second, *Teiru* (a song for the death of an Indian chief), uses a melody transcribed by Roquete-Pinto in 1912 among the Parecís Indians; while the third song, *Iara*, has a text by Mario de Andrade.

The first volume of 'Modinhas e Canções', for voice with piano or orchestra, assembles seven songs in popular style written between 1933 and 1942; while the second volume (1943) contains harmonizations of six traditional children's songs of Brazil.

The *Bachiana Brasileira No. 5*, for soprano and orchestra of violoncelli, is in two sections, the first of which is an Aria (*Cantilena*) composed in 1938, the second a Dance (*Martelo*), written in 1945. The first is essentially lyrical, the second strongly rhythmic, based on a popular type of Brazilian dance-song called *martelo*. Widely sung by Bidu Sayão, this is one of the composer's most successful vocal works.

In 1941, Villa-Lobos composed what is perhaps his most ambitious and original work for solo voice with piano or with orchestra, entitled *Poema da Itabira*, on a text by Carlos Drummond de Andrade, dedicated to Marian Anderson. In this work the composer has endeavoured to use the human voice as a musical instrument, making it in effect the soloist in a kind of concerto for voice and orchestra. The music has no overt Brazilian elements, but may be regarded as impregnated with Brazilian 'atmosphere'.[9]

Later songs by Villa-Lobos include the 'Canções de cordialidade' ('Songs of Cordiality'), a cycle of five songs for voice with piano or orchestra (1945) on texts by Manuel Bandeira: *Canção de Cristal* and *Samba classica* (both 1950), *Coração Fanado* (1953), *Eu te amo* ('I Love You') composed in 1956, for voice with piano or orchestra,[10] *Canção das aguas claras* ('Song of the clear waters') and *Big Ben*, for solo voice and orchestra, dedicated to Frederick Fuller, which is the composer's 'salute' to London.

---

[9] Published by Max Eschig, Paris.   [10] Published by Eschig.

According to Vasco Mariz, Francisco Mignone (b. 1897) is the most frequently performed composer of vocal music in Brazil. Among his better-known songs are *Dentro da Noite* ('Within the Night'), *Dona Janaina*, *O Doce Nome de Você*, and 'Quatro Liricas' (1942) on texts by Manuel Bandeira, which includes the popular *Pousa a mão na minha testa* ('Place your hand upon my head').

The most prolific contemporary song writer of Brazil is without doubt Camargo Guarnieri of São Paulo (b. 1907), who has written over two hundred songs (many of these have been published by the composer himself in São Paulo). He has set to music lyrics by Mario de Andrade and other contemporary Brazilian poets. Especially noteworthy are his thirteen 'Canções de Amor' (1936–37), warmly lyrical and tenderly sentimental songs of love, with texts by various poets. In folkloristic vein, his *Quebra o Côco, Menina* (1939) became widely popular, especially in the United States, through the interpretation by Olga Coelho. One of Guarnieri's most characteristic songs is *O Impossivel Carinho* ('Impossible Love'), text by Manuel Bandeira (1930), with its chromatic inflexions and its simple but effective accompaniment suggesting a guitar-like background.

There are many other composers writing art-songs in Brazil today. Among them may be mentioned Radamés Gnattali (b. 1906), José Siqueira (b. 1907), Luis Cosme (b. 1908), César Guerra-Peixe (b. 1914), H. J. Koellreutter (b. 1916; composer of 'Nocturnes' for contralto and string quartet, 1945), and Claudio Santoro (b. 1919), whose songs include one with a text in French by Aragon, *Marguerite*, for bass voice with piano (1947). And there is Jaime Ovalle (b. 1894), who became celebrated through the popularity of one song, titled *Azulão* (of which, incidentally, other versions have also been composed by Gnattali, Guarnieri, and Hekel Tavares).

ARGENTINA

The contemporary musical movement of Argentina, like that of Brazil, has been strongly nationalistic, but with this important difference, that there is a conspicuous absence of the more exotic elements (such as the Afro-Brazilian cult songs) that give its peculiar non-European flavour to much of Brazilian art-music. Argentina, as indicated in the introduction to this section, is very markedly oriented towards European influences, particularly Italian and French. Although there are some Indian vestiges in the north, the main cultural tradition of the natives stems from the *pampa*, the vast grassy plains where cattle herding has been the main occupation since colonial times, and which produced the most characteristic type of Argentine folk-lore, the *gaucho*, the hard-riding herdsman with his picturesque costume, his guitar, and his songs and dances.

The precursor of the contemporary movement in Argentine music was Alberto Williams (1862–1952), who was trained in Paris and somewhat influenced by César Franck. After returning from years of study in France he devoted himself to musical evocations of the folk-lore and the landscapes of his native land. His most important collection of songs is 'Canciones de la Pampa y de las Sierras', Op. 82 ('Songs of the Pampa and of the Mountains'), ten songs for voice and piano, on texts written by himself. The folk-lore element in these conventionally written songs is extremely attenuated, being indeed scarcely discernible save in one or two designated as being 'In popular style', such as the humorous *Milonga calabacera* (No. 10). The *milonga* is a type of Argentine popular dance-song that employs the familiar *habañera* rhythm so extensively found in Latin-American music, from the Antilles to the River Plate. The expression 'dar las calabazas' is the Spanish equivalent of 'to jilt', hence the words of this song concern the woes of a jilted lover.

Williams also wrote a number of songs based on Indian melodies of northern Argentina, notably two sets of 'Canciones Incaicas' (Op. 45 and Op. 57), the first containing three songs (*Quena, Yaraví, Vidalita*), the second consisting of three *Huaynos*. Another typical song is the *Milonga del Arbol* (Op. 67, No. 17).[11]

The trend initiated by Williams was continued by other Argentine composers, among them Julián Aguirre (1868–1924), Carlos López Buchardo (1881–1948), Pascual de Rogatis (b. 1881), Felipe Boero (1884–1958), Gilardo Gilardi (b. 1889), Florio M. Ugarte (b. 1884), and others. López Buchardo is especially notable for his songs, of which two albums have been published.[12]

Among the older Argentine composers writing at the present time, those particularly noteworthy as song-writers include Luis Gianneo (b. 1897), whose 'Coplas' for voice and piano, have texts taken from Argentine folk-lore; Juan José Castro (b. 1895), who has made an impres-

[11] The music of Alberto Williams is published by Gurina & Co. of Buenos Aires, and is also obtainable through Breitkof & Härtel, Leipzig.

[12] By Ricordi Americana of Buenos Aires (who have also published a quantity of other vocal music by contemporary Argentine composers).

sive setting for voice and piano of García Lorca's *La Casada Infiel* ('The Faithless Wife'); Jacobo Ficher (b. 1896), composer of six attractive 'Canciones del Paraná' (Op. 77), on texts by Rafael Alberti; Carlos Suffern (b. 1905); and J. F. Giacobbe, whose 'Pajaritos Criollos' ('Little Creole Birds') is a set of three songs, brilliantly but perhaps somewhat over-elaborately developed, evoking the characteristics of three birds found in Argentina (*La Viudita, La Paloma Torcaza, El Siriri*).

Among the younger composers, Carlos Guastavino (b. 1914) has cultivated stylizations of folk and popular songs, as in his four 'Canciones Argentinas'; but most of his songs are settings of verses by well-known Spanish-American poets, such as Gabriela Mistral ('Seis Canciones de Cuna'), Rafael Alberti ('Siete Canciones'), and Juana de Ibarbourou ('Por los campos verdes'). Some of Guastavino's songs have been published with English versions, notably *La Rosa y el Sauce* ('The Rose and the Willow').[13] An English version might well be made of one of his most attractive songs, *Se Equivocó la Paloma* ('The Dove was Mistaken'), on a poem by Rafael Alberti. Somewhat in the same vein are the 'Canciones Argentinas' of Angel E. Lasala (which won the Muncipal Prize of Buenos Aires in 1938).

Alberto Ginastera (b. 1916), the most important Argentine composer of the mid-twentieth century, has written a number of admirable songs, particularly the 'Cino Canciones Populares Argentinas' ('Five Argentine Popular Songs'), which are to Argentine music what Manuel de Falla's 'Seven Spanish Popular Songs' are to the folk music of Spain. Taking anonymous traditional texts, Ginastera has made stylized settings of five types of Argentine folk-song: *Chacarera, Triste, Zamba, Arrorró* (Lullaby), and *Gato*. The melodies have been kept essentially faithful to the traditional models, while the accompaniments, although preserving characteristic rhythmic and harmonic traits, are written with excep-

Ex. 3

El ga-to de mi ca-sa___ es muy gau-chi-to___

---

[13] Spanish text by Francisco Silva, English version by S. Borton (Ricordi Americana, Buenos Aires).

pe - ro cuan-do lo bai - lan_   za - pa - tea - di - to_

tional artistry, and even, as in the case of the 'Gato' (an energetic dance of the 'Gauchos') with real bravura.[14]

Another notable collection of songs by Ginastera is 'Las Horas de una Estancia' ('The Hours of a Cattle Ranch'), on texts by Silvina Ocampo, a set of five songs evoking the daily cycle of life on an Argentine *estancia*, from morning till night. These are definitely art-songs, although, as in most of Ginastera's music, there are 'vibrations' (as it were) of popular feeling.[15] One of Ginastera's finest songs is *Canción al Arbol del Olvido* ('Song to the Tree of Forgetfulness'), on a text by Fernán Silva Valdés, in which he achieves that unique combination of personal and traditional elements, of artistry and folk-lore, which gives his music its particular fascination. The same remarks apply to another song by Ginastera, *Canción a la Luna Lunática* ('Song to the Lunatic Moon'), again with text by Silva Valdés, in which the accompaniment employs a typical pattern of Argentine folk-music.

Roberto Caamaño (b. 1923) has moved entirely away from the national trend towards folk-lore in Argentine music. His Opus 1 (1944) is a setting for voice and piano of the 'Baladas Amarillas' ('Yellow Ballads') of García Lorca. Two years later he made settings for voice and piano of 'Tres Cantos de Navidad' ('Three Christmas Carols'), on texts by Lope de Vega[16], and in 1952 he wrote *A Lament for the Tomb of Manuel de Falla* for voice and piano.[17] His 'Three Sonnets' by F. L. Bernérdez were written in 1954 for baritone voice with piano. Two of his best songs are the 'Dos Cantos Gallegos' (Two Galician Songs, Op. 3), on texts in the Galician language by Rosalia de Castro.[18]

OTHER COUNTRIES

In the neighbouring country of Uruguay, the chief composers of art-songs are Alfronso Broqua (1876–1946), Eduardo Fabini (1883–

[14] These songs are published by Ricordi Americana of Buenos Aires.
[15] This collection is published by Editorial Argentina de Música, Buenos Aires.
[16] Published by Barry & Co., Buenos Aires.   [17] Ricordi, Buenos Aires.   [18] *Idem.*

1950), Luis Cluzeau Mortet (1893–1957), Carlos Pedrell (1878–1941), Vicente Ascone (b. 1897), Carlos Estrada (b. 1909). Broqua and Pedrell lived in Paris most of their lives, which did not, however, prevent them from writing nostalgic evocations of their native land. Fabini is considered the leader of the 'national' movement in Uruguayan music. Among his art-songs are *El Tala* and *La Gueya*, the latter being his most powerful composition for voice and piano. The vein of art-song with folk-lore influences, so characteristic of Latin American music, was continued by Vicente Ascone, a good example of this kind being his *Como las frutas del monte* ('As the Fruits of the Mountain'), text by Fernán Silva Valdés, written in the style of a *chacarera* ($\frac{6}{8}$ metre).

Modern music in Chile is considered to have begun with Pedro Humberto Allende (b. 1885), whose art-songs include three settings of poems by Gabriela Mistral (*Mientras Baja la Nieve, El Surtidor, A las Nubes*), composed in 1925 and published by the composer in Santiago. Carlos Isamitt (b. 1885) has utilized the folk-lore of the Araucanian Indians in his collection of ten songs titled 'Friso Araucano'. Enrique Soro (b. 1884), trained in Italy, has set to music mostly Italian texts by Bignotti. The late René Amengual (1911–53), of post-Impressionist tendency, wrote songs to words by Gabriela Mistral, Pablo Neruda, and Arturo Torres Rioseco (contemporary Chilean poets). His most interesting vocal work is probably the song titled *El Vaso* ('The Urn'), with text by Gabriela Mistral, for contralto voice, flute, clarinet, bassoon, harp, and string quintet (completed in 1942).

Domingo Santa Cruz (b. 1899), the leading Chilean composer of the present day, has cultivated the art-song in a sophisticated and expressive style showing little influence from native sources. His songs for voice and piano include 'Four Poems' on texts by Gabriela Mistral (1927),[19] and 11 'Canciones de la Mar' ('Songs of the Sea'), with texts by the composer himself, written in 1952. His earlier songs include settings of verses by Tagore, Sully Prudhomme, and Verhaeren. Among younger Chilean composers, Juan Orrega Salas (b. 1919) and Alfonso Montecino (b. 1924) have written interesting songs for solo voice and piano. The former has also written 'Canciones en Tres Movimientos' ('Songs in Three Movements') for soprano and string quartet (Op. 12, 1945), 'Canciones Castellanas' ('Castillian Songs') for soprano and chamber orchestra (Op. 20, 1947), and 'Cantos de Advenimiento' ('Songs of Advent') for soprano, cello, and piano (Op. 25, 1948). Among his more recent songs are the cycle for soprano and

[19] Published by Institute of Musical Extension, Santiago de Chile.

piano entitled 'El Alba del Alelí' ('The Dawn of the Gilliflower'), recently published[20] with text in Spanish and English. Noteworthy also are the 'Cuatro Canciones' ('Four Songs') of Montecino, who has written, in addition, five songs on poems by García Lorca.

In Peru, Andrés Sas, who was born in Paris in 1900 and musically trained in Brussels, has written beautifully harmonized versions of native Peruvian Indian melodies, as in his 'Seis Cantos Indios del Peru', which contains the lovely melody *Suray Surita*.[21] The following example will serve to illustrate his skill and taste in setting this kind of melody:

Ex. 4

In another vein, nearer to that of the traditional art-song, Sas has written 'Canciones Románticas Peruanas' ('Peruvian Romantic Songs'), on texts by contemporary poets of Peru, and three 'Canciones Simbólicas' ('Symbolic Songs') on texts by the Mexican poet Daniel Castañeda. Carlos Sánchez Málaga (b. 1904) has written a number of attractive songs for voice and piano, including 'Cinco Canciones'[22] and 'Dos Lieder' on texts by the Peruvian poet Luis Fabio Xammar. The first of these collections contains one of his most successful songs, the delightfully evocative *Huayno*, with its typically Indian contrasts of gaiety and melancholy. Rodolfo Holzmann (b. 1910), a German-born composer who settled in Peru, has written, among other songs, 'Three Madrigals' for voice and piano on poems by Pablo Neruda.[23] These

[20] By the Pan American Union in Washington, D.C.
[21] These songs are published by Ricordi Americana, Buenos Aires.
[22] Editorial Tritono, Lima, 1950.
[23] Published by Editorial Argentina de Música, Buenos Aires, 1946.

are highly developed and 'through-composed' songs that reveal the composer's technical mastery.

In Venezuela, some of the finest Latin American art-songs have been written by Juan B. Plaza (b. 1898), whose 'Seven Venezuelan Songs' for medium voice and piano are settings of texts by Luis Barrios Cruz.[24] These songs are mostly evocations of Venezuelan landscapes, or rather of emotional moods suggested by certain places and images. They are gratefully written for the voice, the piano accompaniments are interesting without being over elaborate, and the varying moods are skilfully and sensitively established:[25]

'Look there, north, south, east, and westward, four birds brightly plumed
are flying.'

In Colombia the leading contemporary composer is Guillermo Uribe Holguín (b. 1880), trained at the Schola Cantorum in Paris, many of whose songs are settings of French texts. From his Opus 36 onwards, however, he turned to poems by Colombian writers, many of them in a pastoral or folk-like style. These include 'Seis Canciones' on texts by Vicente Medina, 'Quince Canciones' on texts by Rafael Pombo, and 'Cuatro Canciones' on texts by various authors. One of his best songs is *Hay un instante en el crepúsculo* ('There is a moment at dusk'), on a poem by Guillermo Valencia (Op. 80, No. 2).

The foregoing sketch, attempting as it does to cover a vast area comprising twenty different countries, is necessarily incomplete and doubtless omits to mention many composers whose music might be of interest to the reader. The number of composers in Latin America whose music deserves serious attention is steadily increasing.[25]

[24] English versions by Herbert Weinstock and Harvey Officer in the two-volume publication by Associated Music Publishers, New York.

[25] Readers who wish to explore the subject further should consult the very useful publications (bio-bibliographical monographs, complete catalogues, periodic bulletins, and musical scores) issued by the Music Division of the Pan American Union, Washington 6, D.C. (U.S.A.).

Poland

GERALD ABRAHAM

THE history of the art-song in Poland[1] in some respects is parallel to that of the Czech lands. Here again is an age-old musical culture closely related to that of the rest of Europe – though not confused by wholesale emigration and the intrusion of a foreign tongue – and here again the secular solo song, apart from folk-song, seems to be a relatively modern phenomenon inheriting little or nothing from the rich past. All through the seventeenth and early eighteenth centuries we find aria-concertos for church use. Mikołaj Zieleński's 'Communiones totius anni' (Venice, 1611) include fifteen solos for soprano, tenor or bass with organ and this type of work continued to be written by such composers as Mielczewski (d. 1651), Szarzyński (d. *c.* 1700), Kaszczewski (late seventeenth century) and Damian (d. 1729).[2] But no secular vocal solos, other than the melodies of vocal mazurkas,[3] have been preserved from before the last two decades of the eighteenth century, when the history of Polish opera opened with Kamieński's *Nędza uszczęśliwiona* ('Misery Made Happy') in 1778. At this period French songs predominated – at first *bergerettes* and *opéra-comique*

[1] I have been unable to consult Seweryn Barbag, 'Polska pieśń artystyczna', *Muzyka* (1927), which is said to be an important study.

[2] Examples by Mielczewski, Szarzyński and Damian in *Wydawnictwo dawnej muzyki polskiej*, ed. Chybinski, II, V, X and XIII. Such works are usually described as 'Concerto a 4' or 'a 3', the other solo parts being taken by specified instruments.

[3] See Jan Prosnak, *Kultura muzyczna warszawy XVIII wieku* (Cracow, 1955), pp. 67–72.

romances with Polish words, later revolutionary songs with patriotic texts – and the native patriotic pieces tended to imitate them, though the Constitution of 1791 and Kosciuszko's rebellion evoked a number of vocal mazurkas and polonaises. The broader foundations of a consciously Polish vocal style were laid in 1794 by another opera, Jan Stefani's *Krakowiacy i górale* ('Cracovians and Mountaineers'). (Incidentally Kamienski was of Slovak origin and Stefani a Czech of Italian descent.) But, although Stefani wrote some songs with piano, it was left to another opera-composer, the Silesian Józef Elsner (1769–1854), to become the real founder of the Polish art-song.

Elsner was a fairly prolific composer of songs with piano,[4] of which twenty-five of the earliest appeared in the periodical publication 'Wybór pięknych dziel muzycznych i pieśni polskich' ('Selection of Fine Musical Works and Polish Songs') for 1803 and 1805, side by side with piano polonaises by Ogiński and Polish dances by Stefani. They are rather weak and sentimental essays in the style of the lyrical songs of Zumsteeg and J. F. Reichardt.[5] In 1811 Elsner published nearly a score of Masonic songs. Though his songs seem artless, he gave a good deal of thought to the problems of Polish prosody and in 1818 published a *Rozprawa o metryczności i rytmiczności języka polskiego* ('Treatise on the Metrical and Rhythmical Treatment of the Polish Language, with special reference to Polish verse from the point of view of music'); in 1830 he returned to the subject in a second treatise of which only a fragment was ever published. By way of illustration to the *Rozprawa* Elsner published six songs, to words by Kazimierz Brodziński, of which the first, *Pasterka* ('The Shepherdess'), must be quoted since it 'points directly to the style of Moniuszko's songs':[6]

'Who tells my heart . . .'

The last of these 'Szesc pieśni', *Muza wiejska* ('The Rustic Muse'), is one of the best of Elsner's vocal polonaises.

[4] Complete list in Alina Nowak-Romanowicz, *Józef Elsner* (Cracow, 1957), p. 302.
[5] Two songs in the supplementary volume of musical examples to Nowak-Romanowicz's book, pp. 5 and 7.
[6] Nowak-Romanowicz, op. cit., p. 140; printed complete in the supplementary volume, p. 9.

Elsner's later compositions include German *Lieder* – one or two Schiller settings among them – and 'Tre Arie ed un Duettino' for soprano. But his songs, and those of his contemporaries Kurpiński, Lessel, and Kaszewski, were thrown into the shade by some of those of his pupil Józef Nowakowski (1800–65). Nowakowski was no master of the song: like Elsner's his melodies tend to be sentimental, his accompaniments to be stereotyped and conventional, but when he touches the life of the people he becomes really attractive and thoroughly Polish (e.g. in the mazurka song *Cóz ja winna*) and he set the pattern for a good many of the most popular Polish songs of later times.[7] In many respects his position is comparable with that of his Russian contemporaries Varlamov and Gurilev.

Chopin as Song-Composer

Like his friend Nowakowski, Chopin (1810–49) also was a pupil of Elsner, and the earliest of his songs to be preserved are those which he copied into Elsner's daughter's album at some time before he finally left Poland in November 1830; of all Chopin's works of this date, these are the only ones that still show anything of his master's influence. They are *Życzenie* (' The Wish'), *Gdzie lubi* ('Where she loves'), *Poseł* ('The Messenger'), *Wojak* ('The Warrior'), *Hulanka* ('The Carouse') and *Czary* ('Charms') – all from the 'Piosnki sielskie' ('Country Songs') of the composer's friend Stefan Witwicki – and *Precz z moich oczu!* ('Away from my sight!') by Poland's greatest poet, Adam Mickiewicz. With the exception of *Czary*, they were published posthumously as Op. 74, Nos. 1, 5, 7, 10, 4, and 6. Two other Witwicki songs, *Smutna rzeka* ('The Mournful River'), Op. 74, No. 3, and *Narzeczony* ('The Bridegroom'), Op. 74, No. 15, and a setting of a translated Lithuanian folk-poem, *Piosnka litewska* ('Lithuanian Song'), Op. 74, No. 16, were composed in 1831. Thus more than half of Chopin's nineteen songs[8] are comparatively early works. Two of these early songs, the familiar *Życzenie* and *Hulanka* are mazurkas; the first part of *Precz z moich oczu!* is a sort of dramatized slow mazurka (though the ensuing *andantino espressivo* is Bellinian) and there is a curious little mazurka interlude for piano in the *Lithuanian Song. Wojak* and *Narzeczony*, the former undistinguished, the latter really dramatic, are in ballad vein and might have been written by Loewe. Of the others, *Poseł* is notable for the sharpened fourths in its melody (a feature of Polish folk-music

---

[7] Zdzisław Jachimecki, *Historja muzyki polskiej* (Warsaw, 1920), p. 134.
[8] Published complete in the *Dziela wszystkie Fryderyka Chopina*, XVII (Warsaw).

which appears in other of Chopin's songs), *Smutna rzeka* – beautifully plaintive – for its three-bar phrases.

Four more songs came during 1836–8, two of them Chopin's best vocal mazurkas, Op. 74, Nos. 12 and 14. And the mazurka rhythm plays an important part in *Śpiew grobowy* ('Grave Song'), Op. 74, No. 17, the most complex in structure of all Chopin's songs and perhaps the finest; his country's tragic fate moved him deeply and the middle section of the song, beginning with the words 'Bili zimę całą' ('They fought the whole winter'), first sixteen bars of monotone on E flat, then a chromatically ornamented E flat ('Some rot in the ground and others are captive'), with the release of the tension in the outburst 'O Polska kraino!' is most impressive. The four settings of the Ukrainian poet Bohdan Zaleski, spread over the years 1840–5, are unimpressive; the earlier of the two *dumky* is a scrap of only eight bars and was not included in Op. 74, where the three others figure as Nos. 8, 11, and 13. Chopin's last song, *Melodya*, Op. 74, No. 9, composed in 1847, is a curious and striking piece in arioso style, quite different from the rest of his songs.

Although Chopin's pieces rise above the level of earlier Polish song, they are markedly inferior to most of his piano compositions and are much more closely related to the style of contemporary Polish song than to his personal style; most surprisingly, the accompaniments show little evidence of his skill in writing for the instrument. According to his friend Fontana, who contributed a preface to the posthumous collection of sixteen songs which he published as 'Zbior śpiewow polskich' ('Collection of Polish Songs'), Op. 74, in 1857,[9] Chopin simply improvised his songs at the piano, singing the words and accompanying himself.

Stanisław Moniuszko

By 1857, however, a better song-writer if lesser composer had emerged in the person of Stanisław Moniuszko (1819–72). As early as 1838 Moniuszko – then a pupil of K. F. Rungenhagen, Zelter's successor at the Berlin Singakademie – published in Berlin three settings of Mickiewicz: *Sen* ('Dream'), *Niepewność* ('Uncertainty') and *Moja pieszczotka* ('My darling') (which Chopin had composed the year before, Op. 74, No. 12).[10] All three appeared first with German words only, though

[9] Not 1855 as is commonly asserted: see M. J. E. Brown, 'The Posthumous Publication of Chopin's Songs', *Musical Quarterly*, XLII (1956), p. 51. The seventeenth song, *Śpiew grobowy*, was added to the set only in 1872 when Fontana himself was dead.

[10] The poem was later set by Cui (Op. 11, No. 2) and numerous Polish musicians, and in different Russian translations by Glinka and Rimsky-Korsakov (Op. 42, No. 4).

they were re-issued with the original texts in the 'Śpiewniki domowe' ('Song-Books for the Home') in which Moniuszko published his later songs, more than three hundred in number if we include those issued posthumously.[11]

The first 'Śpiewniki domowy', containing eighteen songs, appeared in 1843;[12] Moniuszko published five more volumes in his lifetime and six came out posthumously – a corpus of work which established him as the classic master of Polish song. It is difficult, if not impossible, to establish anything like a chronological order, for Moniuszko seldom dated his manuscripts or mentioned his songs in his correspondence; even the publication dates of the first six 'Śpiewniki' give us only *termini ad quem*, for songs originally intended for one book were published in a later one or even transferred after publication. (The ballad *Czaty* ('The Ambush'), for instance, was published in the third book but omitted from its third edition and transferred to the sixth 'Śpiewniki'.[13]) However this matters less in Moniuszko's case than it would with most composers, for even his early songs are mature. 'In the first three songs of 1838 and those of the first "Śpiewniki",' as Jachimecki says,[14] 'Moniuszko's talent as a song-writer makes its début in forms already crystallized'. The best way, therefore, to begin to convey some idea of the wealth and variety of his output[15] is to examine this early group.

They may be roughly divided into four categories: narrative, more or less dramatic ballads; lyrical pieces sometimes showing the parentage of the *Lied*, less often of the French *romance*; light, often playful songs; and short songs with a specifically Polish flavour, mazurkas, krakowiaks and the like. Naturally no firm lines can be drawn between the categories.

Two of the four ballads in this group are settings of Mickiewicz: *Świtezianka* ('The Nymph of the Świtez'–a Loreley story) and *Panicz i dziewczyna* ('The Lord and the Girl') (though that is only partly by

[11] See the thematic catalogue compiled by Erwin Nowaczyk, *Pieśni solowe Moniuszki* (Cracow, 1954).

[12] Moniuszko published an interesting prospectus in the Petersburg Polish paper, *Tygodnik Petersburski* (No. 72, 1842): reprinted in Witold Rudziński, *Stanisław Moniuszko, I* (Cracow, 1955) pp. 94–6.

[13] The contents of all twelve 'Śpiewniki' are listed in Jachimecki, *Stanisław Moniuszko* (Warsaw, 1921), pp. 47–57.

[14] *Historja*, p. 176.

[15] In 1862 the Paris publisher Flaxland issued thirty-seven of Moniuszko's songs, under the title 'Échos de Pologne', with French translations and titles that make them sometimes hardly recognizable. Otherwise, with a few exceptions, his works are – for Western musicians – locked behind the barrier of an unknown tongue. The most useful, easily accessible selection is the two-volume 'Wybór Pieśni' edited by Bronisław Romaniszyn and published by the Polskie Wydawnictwo Muzyczne (Cracow, 1951), but it has only Polish words.

Mickiewicz). The ballads of Mickiewicz inspired the ballades of Chopin; translated, they have inspired the song-composers of both Germany and Russia. In 1835, two years before Moniuszko went to Berlin, Loewe had published there two sets of Mickiewicz ballads, Opp. 49 and 50, including both *Świtezianka* and *Panicz*, and, while the extent of Loewe's influence on the earlier Russian ballad is doubtful, there can be little doubt that it stirred the young Moniuszko to emulation and it is clear that emulation first took the form of imitation – though of general style, not of specific models. Moniuszko's *Świtezianka* far surpasses Loewe's; it is the first masterpiece of Polish song. In *Panicz i dziewczyna*, however, as elsewhere in Moniuszko's early songs, his declamation has been criticized. The other two ballads illustrate other aspects of his work: humour in *Dziad i baba* ('Grandpa and Grandma'), which anticipates a genre cultivated by Mussorgsky, and even faintly his style; essential Polishness in *Żal dziewczyny* ('A Girl's Lament') with its mazurka opening, not really a ballad but ballad-like in structure.

All three of the songs published in Berlin show affinities with Loewe's more lyrical songs: *Sen* might be a companion-piece to Loewe's Goethe *Canzonetta*; *Niepewność* and *Pieszczotka* are in the vein, though not in the style, of *Niemand hat's geseh'n* and *Mädchen sind wie der Wind*. The once-popular *Barcarolle* in the first 'Śpiewnik' is naturally rather Italianate; *Triolet*, with a harmonic surprise which is characteristic, and *Kukułka* ('The Cuckoo': not to be confused with the vocal mazurka with the same title but different words in the fifth 'Śpiewnik') are essentially *romances*. More in the style of the *Lied*, robust, naïve or lyrical, are *Pielgrzym* ('The Pilgrim'), *Pieśń żeglarzy* ('Sailor's Song'), *Przyczyna* ('The Reason') *Zawod* ('Deception'), and *Morel* ('The Apricot') with its beautifully integrated voice and piano parts and (again) a harmonic surprise.

In lighter mood the delightful *Dalibóg* ('Upon my life!') stands beside *Niepewność* and surpasses *Pieszczotka*. *Kochać* ('Make haste to love') has a more markedly Polish flavour, and the first and third of 'Trzy piosnki' ('Three Country Songs from across the Niemen', from Jan Czeczot's volume of that name) are mazurkas, while the second might be a nursery-rhyme. These frankly national songs are generally, and of course appropriately, very lightly accompanied. But, although there is plenty of conventional figuration, Moniuszko's piano parts are extremely varied and generally well wrought; they are far superior to those of any earlier Polish song-composer, even (astonishingly) to Chopin's.

To consider the bulk of Moniuszko's songs at all closely is of course impossible; one can only glance at a few noteworthy examples in each category. Two of the best of the other ballads are the grim and dramatic masterpiece *Czaty* which, in Pushkin's translation, inspired Tchaïkovsky's 'symphonic ballad' *Wojewoda*, Op. 78, and the happier tale of the *Trzech Budrysów* ('The Three Budrys'), three Lithuanian heroes who are ordered by their father to bring back, respectively, plunder from the Germans, plunder from the Russians and a daughter-in-law from Poland, but who actually return with three Polish brides. Both of these, and most of the others, are settings of Mickiewicz but the Lenartowicz *Maciek* and the Béranger-Syrokomla *Stary kapral* ('Le vieux caporal')[16] are hardly inferior. To illustrate the ballads adequately one would need a host of musical examples, which would still not convey their real power. But one can give some idea of Moniuszko's lyrical work by quoting the opening of *Do oddalonej* (Grzymałowski's translation of Goethe's *An die Entfernte*):

Ex. 2

'So hab' ich wirklich dich verloren,
Bist du, o Schöne, mir entflohn?'

As for his setting of Mickiewicz's translation of *Kennst du das Land?*, Jachimecki has made out a reasonable case for preferring it to the versions by Beethoven, Schubert, and Schumann;[17] it certainly deserves a place among the finest compositions of Mignon's song. There are some other Goethe songs, including a pleasantly Schubertian *Heidenröslein* – though the words (*Polna różyczka*) are commonly attributed to

---

[16] Published in 1857, several years before Dargomïzhsky's not altogether deservedly more famous Russian setting.   [17] *Moniuszko*, pp. 40–2.

the translator, Józef Grajnert, as an original poem. (Rather similarly, *Wieczorny dzwon* is acknowledged as a translation of Kozlov's *Vecherniy zvon*, but nothing is said of Moore's 'Evening Bells' though as a matter of fact Moniuszko's music is better suited to Moore than to Kozlov.)[18] Schubertian influences also show themselves in the composition of original Polish poems, especially slighter pieces such as *Kotek sie myje* ('Pussy is washing') and *Wiosna* ('Spring') which outclasses Chopin's setting (Op. 74, No. 2). More individual, though also in the *Lied* tradition, are *Krásna góra* ('The Beautiful Mountain'), *Księżyc i rzeczka* ('The Moon and the Rivulet'), with its *Rheingold*-like suggestion of flowing water (though its date is not later than 1846), and the lullaby *Luli.*

Some of the best of the lighter songs are compositions of poems by Jan Czeczot, probably the most popular of all being *Prząśniczka* ('The Spinner'), with its effective, though conventional, humming-semi-quaver accompaniment. (Another spinning song, *Prządka*, seems to have been an attempt to repeat this success.) But the most delightful of the songs in this category is *Wybór* ('The Choice'). (The pianist's left hand continues its descent for two more octaves.)

'There are three young men who'd like to marry me: one
counts his money . . .'

As for the mazurkas and krakowiaks, they are innumerable and one can only draw attention to a few specially interesting or attractive ones:

[18] Moniuszko's other 'English' songs, settings of direct Polish translations, are *How should I your true love know*, from *Hamlet*, Medora's song from Byron's *Corsair*, three songs from *The Lady of the Lake* and one from *The Lay of the Last Minstrel*.

among the krakowiaks, *Nigdy serca krakowiaka* with its one-sharp signature yet largely poised on, and ending on, a dominant seventh in C, *Kłosek* ('The Little Ear of Rye'), *Sołtys* ('The Bailiff'), *Kozak* ('The Cossack') (a sort of slow krakowiak); among the mazurkas, the delicious E major *Mazurek*, *Hulanka* ('The Carousal') which again challenges a comparison with Chopin (Op. 74, No. 4), the brilliant *Stary hulaka* ('The Old Rake'). And then there is the most striking *Mogiła* ('The Tomb'), a painfully expressive slow krakowiak composed in June 1862: sounding like a premonition of the insurrection of the following year. Another song dating from the same year, the lament *Macierzanka* ('The Dead Mother'), sounds the same note and is more explicit in its expression of passionate patriotism, though the music is less specifically Polish than that of the very beautiful setting of Czeczot's *Dąbrowa* ('The Oak Wood'), which has the quality of an elegiac folk-song.

Moniuszko's Contemporaries and Successors

The titles of Moniuszko's publications – 'Song-Books for the Home' – indicate that he had the needs of amateurs foremost in his mind, and his example in this respect as in others was followed by his contemporaries and successors. Among the first of these were Ignazy Komorowski (1824–57) and Kazimierz Kratzer (1844–1890). Neither had anything like Moniuszko's talent; like Nowakowski, they were sentimentalists. But their melancholy strains harmonized with the prevailing mood of the Polish people and such songs as Komorowski's *Kalina* ('Guelder Rose') (1846) and Kratzer's *Skrzypki swaty* ('The Matchmaking Fiddle') and *Piosnka o piosence* ('A Song about Song') were, as Jachimecki said of the first, 'taken to the hearts of nearly three generations'. Less popular but musically superior are the songs of Ignacy Krzyżanowski (1826–1905).

The songs of Władysław Żeleński (1837–1921) and Moniuszko's pupil Zygmunt Noskowski (1846–1909) are on an altogether higher artistic plane. Żeleński is at his best in his songs, which are much more markedly Polish than the bulk of his work, while Noskowski's are essentially the songs of a good all-round craftsman. One of Noskowski's most successful songs, the krakowiak *Skowroneczek śpiewa* ('The Lark sings'), is said to have been sketched out in a few minutes when he needed money from a publisher;[19] his 'Śpiewnik dla dzieci' ('Song-Book for Children'), Op. 34 (1890), contains some of his most delightful

[19] Józef Reiss, 'Zygmunt Noskowski w stulecie urodzin', *Ruch muzyczny*, II (1946), p. 26.

music. But both Żeleński and Noskowski were also important as teachers; between them they trained nearly all the next generation of Polish composers, passing on to them the tradition of Moniuszko. Żeleński's pupils include Felicjan Szopski (1865–1939(?)) and the musicologist Henryk Opieński (1870–1942), who was also a song-writer, while Noskowski was the teacher of Szymanowski (1882–1937), Karłowicz (1876–1909) and Różycki (1884–1953).

Before we consider their work, however, something must be said about three late nineteenth-century song-composers: Jan Gall (1856–1912), Stanisław Niewiadomski (1859–1936) and Eugeniusz Pankiewicz (1857–98). Of this trio, Gall was the least important; he has little to offer beyond copious melodic invention but, as Jachimecki says,[20] 'the charm of his ideas, the smoothness of his phrases, the really Italian sweetness of his melody, and the light and skilful accompaniments earned for Gall's songs enormous popularity'. Similar in character and equally popular, but wider in range and more substantial in achieve-ment, are the songs of Niewiadomski. Niewiadomski was a very prolific but very unequal song-composer. His workmanship is impec-cable: prosody and general handling of words, well-written, light-handed accompaniments testify to his craftsmanship. He had a genuine lyrical gift; but his taste was unsure, so that he sometimes lapses into the amiably Mendelssohnian, as in the eleventh song of the cycle 'Piosnki z różnych stron' ('Songs from Different Regions'), or into the downright commonplace, as in *Dziewczę z buzią jak malina* (a trans-lation of Heine's *Mädchen mit dem roten Mündchen*), the first song of 'Z wiosennych tchnień' ('From Breaths of Spring'), and the name-song of the Mickiewicz cycle 'Kurhanek Maryli' ('Maryla's Grave'). Even the delightful mazurka *Otwórz, Janku!* ('Open, Janek!') comes peri-lously near banality in the – admittedly catchy – refrain lines, which would have been the making of an Edwardian drawing-room ballad. But on the whole Niewiadomski's salon vein is more perceptible in the quiet songs than in the livelier ones, which often have a more markedly Polish flavour. Such songs as *Zosia* (quite a different concep-tion from Moniuszko's popular setting) and *Grzeczna dziewczyna* ('The Sinful Maiden'), both from 'Kurhanek Maryli' or the breathless mazurka *Malowany wazonik* ('The Painted Vase'), from 'Piosnki starodawne' ('Old-time Songs'), are delightful. One of Niewiadomski's most attractive sets is the 'Humoreski', which contains a worthy counterpart of Moniuszko's *Wybór* (Ex. 3) in *Między nami nic nie*

[20] *Historja*, p. 211.

było ('There was nothing between us'), the charming *quasi parlato Rezeda*, and *Wiem ja coś* . . . ('I know something . . .') where the archness is of the *Lied*, not of the Edwardian ballad:

Ex. 4

Whereas Niewiadomski may be said to have slightly debased the Moniuszko tradition, Pankiewicz refined it – with the result that he was sometimes accused of over-intellectualism. Of his forty-odd songs,[21] only eight had been published at the time of his tragic death in a mental hospital in 1898: the four of Op. 5 (1887), the two Adam Asnyk 'Sonnets', Op. 6 (1887), and in 1888 Nos. 2 and 8 of the 'Osiem pieśni ludowych polskich' ('Eight Polish Folk-Songs') posthumously issued as Op. 14. (They consist of slightly sophisticated settings of melodies and words from Oskar Kolberg's various collections.) His most important set, the cycle 'Z miłosnych dziejów' ('From Love Stories'), Op. 19, to poems by Michał Bałucki, composed in 1888 for the singer Maria Bohte, whom he afterwards married, was not published until 1930.[22]

Pankiewicz's very first song, Op. 5, No. 1, is marked by the harmonic asperities which annoyed contemporary critics, and No. 2 shows a distinctly unusual approach to *Du bist wie eine Blume* (marked *allegretto giocoso*); but the other two songs of the set, another setting of translated Heine and a cradle-song for the infant Jesus, are very beautiful in their different ways. The second of the 'Sonnets' shows what Pankiewicz could achieve in very simple terms. But his masterpiece is undoubtedly *Poranek* ('Dawn'), Op. 19, No. 2. He sometimes reminds one of Chopin, the Chopin of the piano music (e.g. in Op. 19, No. 6, in the Rejnsztejn *Kołysanka* ('Lullaby'), and the *Mazurek* in C sharp minor). Harmonically and by his finely-wrought piano parts, he may be said to have paved the way for the generation of which Szymanowski is the outstanding figure.

[21] Thematic catalogue in Włodzimierz Poźniak, *Eugeniusz Pankiewicz* (Cracow, 1958), pp. 76–100.

[22] By Gebethner and Wolff (Warsaw), with German translations; the reprint in the Polskie Wydawnictwo Muzyczne edition of the 'Pieśni zebrane' (Cracow, 1956) has only the Polish text.

Szymanowski and his Contemporaries

With Szymanowski we at last reach a Polish song-composer of European importance, whose work can no longer be measured by the partly 'domestic' standards of the Moniuszko tradition.[23] Not that his earliest songs, dating from 1901–2, the six Tetmajer songs, Op. 2, are very successful; they depend overmuch on the harmonic basis; but the '3 Fragmenty', Op. 5 (three fragments from poems by J. Kasprowicz) and *Łabędź* ('The Swan'), Op. 7, show an advance in the handling of the poetic texts although the declamatory element is still over-important. The style is still not very individual but by 1907 in the sets Opp. 11, 13 and 17 Szymanowski had already achieved some real successes. He was then living in Germany and most of the songs of this period are settings of contemporary German poets: Dehmel in particular, Bodenstedt, Birnbaum, Mombert, and others. Op. 13, Nos. 2 and 4 – *Kołysanka Dziecątka Jezus* ('The Christ Child's Lullaby') and the Bodenstedt *Suleika* – and *Verkündigung* and *Liebesnacht* (Op. 17, Nos. 6 and 12) are outstanding lyrical pieces. (Two compositions for voice and orchestra from this early period, *Salome*, Op. 6, and *Penthesilea*, Op. 18, have never been published.) The Polish set, Op. 20, and the 'Bunte Lieder', Op. 22, of *c.* 1910, are also more vocal – and more individual in style. Szymanowski at the time considered the 'Bunte Lieder' 'the favourites out of all my songs. Their intelligibility depends entirely on the (only now) complete mastery of the song-form from the point of view of declamation and the style of the voice- and piano-parts – which one could hardly say of Op. 17, which is good music rather than good songs. They are tremendously decided and unambiguous in expression. . . .'[24]

This was the period when Szymanowski was finding his true creative self in all directions. Hitherto he had been a typical late-romantic, an admirer of Reger and Richard Strauss; now more advanced harmonic idioms and new techniques fascinated him increasingly – French impressionism, Skryabin above all, later Schoenberg and Stravinsky – fertilizing his art without smothering his creative personality. Already in such songs as Op. 17, No. 9, and Op. 20, No. 3, Szymanowski had stood on the brink of atonality, and now in the poetry of other cultures he suddenly found a catalyst which precipitated a new style. The first impulse came from Hans Bethge's German

[23] His songs are much more easily accessible than those of most Polish composers, being mostly published by Universal Edition with German translations.

[24] Letter to Stefan Spiess: quoted in Stefania Lobaczewska, *Karol Szymanowski* (Cracow, 1950), p. 230.

translations of Hafiz and the first fruits were the first set of 'Des Hafis Liebeslieder', Op. 24 (1911). (The second set of Hafiz songs, Op. 26, includes orchestral versions of three of these, together with five new settings for soprano and orchestra.[25]) Then, in turn, came 'Pieśni księżniczki z baśni' ('Songs of a Princess of Legend'), Op. 31 (to quasi-oriental verses by the composer's sister) (1915), four settings of Rabindranath Tagore, Op. 41 (1918), and 'Pieśni Muezzina Szalonego' ('Songs of the Crazy Muezzin'), Op. 42 (1918). These are songs of extreme difficulty for both singer and pianist: works of infinite delicacy and polished detail. The piano 'breathes and flutters' as in late Skryabin, and the singer has to perform similar feats, with much coloratura vocalization. The Fairy-Tale Princess begins most of her songs and ends her cycle with vocalizes on 'Ah!'; the Muezzin keeps on vocalizing on 'Allah' and 'olali' and 'olio'. The final vocalize of the Princess's second song, Słowik ('The Nightingale'), (see Ex. 5)

Ex. 5

is typical. It is highly artificial art, but exquisite of its kind.

This idiom is still more deeply but less exuberantly exploited in the five 'Slopiewnie', Op. 46 bis,[26] of 1921, but fresh aspects of Szyman-

[25] Only two of these have been published, No. 1, Das Grab des Hafis, only in a piano version as a posthumous work.

[26] A good deal of close analysis has been devoted to this remarkable cycle: see J. M. Chomiński, 'Studja nad twórczością K. Szymanowskiego. Cz. I: Problem tonalny w 'Słopiew-

owski's art are revealed in the three sets of 'Rymy dziecięce' ('Children's Rhymes'), Op. 49 (1923), and the four settings of James Joyce, from 'Chamber Music', Op. 54 (1926). Here the technical difficulties are much less for both voice and piano; the accompaniment of *Sleep now*, Op. 54, No. 2, is even rather heavy-footed in a curiously Mussorgskian way; but the Joyce songs are very singable – and well worth singing. Yet the 'Children's Rhymes' are much better. Here again one is sometimes reminded of Mussorgsky, e.g. in No. 8, *Święta Krystyna* ('St. Christine'), and No. 18, *Zły Lejba* ('Naughty Lejba'); but much more often one is reminded of Bartók, the Bartók of the miniatures. Here everything is economical and, while the harmony is as pungent as one could wish, the voice-parts – indeed the textures generally – are essentially diatonic, with the sharpened fourths and other characteristics of Polish folk-song. (Szymanowski's last work for voice and piano, the three sets of 'Piesni kurpiowskie', Op. 58, are actually folk-song arrangements.) The subjects of the 'Rhymes' are what one expects in pieces for or about children – lullabies (for Christine herself, for her dolls, 'for the brown horse'), games, visits to the cowshed, 'The Little Pig' whose adventure is narrated in a slow mazurka, 'Bumble-bee and Beetle', and so on – but they are treated with freshness and originality, with astringent objectivity and absence of sentimentality.

Compared with Szymanowski's songs, those of his contemporaries are rather tame. The early songs of Mieczysław Karłowicz, Opp. 1, 3 and 4, show that their composer could have become a notable song-writer, but Karłowicz turned to the orchestra and the larger forms and, in any case, died young. The songs were written in Berlin, where he finished his musical education after studying with Noskowski, so it is hardly surprising that some of them, e.g. Op. 1, Nos. 1, 4 and 5 (settings of Kazimierz Tetmajer, who also inspired Szymanowski's Op. 2), are *Lied*-like. On the other hand, the mazurka *Na śniegu* ('On the snow'), Op. 1, No. 3, and *Najpiękniejsze piosnki* ('The best of my songs'), Op. 4, might have been written by Moniuszko himself. Most characteristic are three melancholy songs in $\frac{4}{4}$ time – *Skąd pierwsze gwiazdy* ('From where the first stars'), Op. 1, No. 2, *Nie płacz nademna* ('Do not weep in vain'), Op. 3, No. 7, and *Pod jaworem* ('Under the sycamore') – but they are manifestly immature.

It would be unjust to omit mention of the names of Feliks Nowo-wiejski (1877–1946), Ludomir Różycki (1884–1953), Stanisław Lipski

niach', *Polski rocznik muzykologiczny*, II (1936), p. 53; S. Łobaczewska, op. cit, p. 464 ff. and 'O "Słopiewniach" Karola Szymanowskiego', *Ruch muzyczny* (February 1948), p. 2; S. Golachowski, 'W sprawie "Słopiewni" K. Szymanowskiego', *Ruch muzyczny* (March 1948), p. 15.

(1880–1937), and Adam Sołtys (b. 1890). The mild influence of French impressionistic harmony is apparent in their songs; several of those by Nowowiejski – notably *Sobótka w czarnym lesie* ('St. John's Eve in the Enchanted Wood'), Op. 40, and the three charming ones that make up his Op. 59 – echo the sonorities of early Ravel. Różycki produced four or five sets of songs, including some Nietzsche and Ibsen settings, about 1906, and here again one can detect French influence, e.g. in the translucent *Akwarela*, Op. 16, No. 6; the two best pieces in his later cycle 'Zerotyków', Op. 51 (1923), are the first, *Baśń* ('A Tale'), and third *Pieśń weselna* ('Bridal Song'), the words of which appear to be a very long way after Hymen's song in *As You Like It*. But Różycki was essentially an operatic and instrumental composer; indeed most of the Polish composers now living appear to belong to the class with whom song-writing is a rather marginal activity, though between them they have given us some notable things: Szeligowski's 'Pieśni zielone' ('Green songs') (1921), Maklakiewicz's 'Pieśni japońskie' for soprano and orchestra (1930), based not only on Japanese poems but on Japanese scales and employing a somewhat Debussyish orchestral technique,[27] Panufnik's 'Suita polska' ('Hommage à Chopin') (1949) for soprano and piano, based on folk-tunes but wordless. But, as with all contemporary or near-contemporary art, one is too near the picture to see it clearly. The music of one's age is a proper subject for the critic; the historian does wisely to leave it alone.

[27] See Z. Mycielski, 'Pieśni japońskie J. A. Maklakiewicz', *Ruch muzyczny*, October 1947, p. 13.

Russia

GERALD ABRAHAM

WHEN César Cui published 'an outline of the development of the Russian art-song'[1] in 1896, he began with Glinka. Nine years later, Findeisen declared that 'the Russian art-song came into being at the same time as the first attempts in the field of Russian opera – in the epoch of Catherine the Great'.[2] But in 1916 Bulich revealed the existence of a 'great-grandfather' of Russian song,[3] to wit the courtier and writer Grigory Nikolaevich Teplov (1711–79), tutor of Kirill Razumovsky (the father of Beethoven's Razumovsky), and so far Teplov's claim has not been disputed. Not that he made any claim himself. When he published his volume 'Mezhdu delom bezdel'e ili Sobranie pesen s prilozhennïmi tonami na tri golosa' ((Idleness amid Work, or A Collection of songs with music added in three parts),[4] he modestly appended only the initials 'G. T.' 'Mezhdu delom bezdel'e' consists of seventeen songs, settings of feeble lyrics by Sumarokov and

[1] *Russkiy romans: ocherk evo razvitiya* (St. Petersburg, 1896).

[2] *Russkaya khudozhestvennaya pesnya* (Moscow, 1905), p. 7.

[3] S. K. Bulich, ' "Pradedushka" russkavo romansa', *Muzïkal'nïy Sovremennik*, II (1916), 1, p. 11.

[4] Published by the Academy of Sciences, St. Petersburg, during the 1750s; second edition 1759, third edition (of 45 copies!), 1776; detailed discussion by A. N. Rimsky-Korsakov in *Muzïka i muzïkal'nïy bït Staroy Rossii* (Leningrad, 1927), p. 30; complete reprint in T. Livanova, *Russkaya muzïkal'naya kultura XVIII veka*, I (Leningrad and Moscow, 1952), pp. 189–245. The reprints in the volume *Nachalo russkovo romansa* (ed. Trofimova and Drozdov, Moscow 1936) are too heavily edited to be acceptable.

others, laid out on three staves with no indication of the manner of performance; but the lowest part is an obviously instrumental bass and the two upper parts, proceeding mostly in parallel thirds or sixths, with the words printed between, were doubtless to be played too, with voice or voices doubling one or both. One song has only one upper part; No. 13 is undoubtedly a duet. The three-part layout follows the Russian tradition of the *kantï* (three-part vocal pieces) popular during the first half of the eighteenth century, but there is nothing else particularly Russian about them. They have reminded more than one critic of the weaker songs in Sperontes' 'Singende Muse' by their artlessness, their simple sentiment, and the occasional suggestion of instrumental melodic origin. Four are marked 'Menuet', two 'Siciliana'; all but one of the others bears a slow tempo-marking, but the opening of the one exception, No. 10, is worth quoting since it is perhaps the most attractive of all. It may be of interest to give it in the original orthography:

'Why am I captivated by you so that, ardently loving,
I lament hourly?'

The second part of each stanza is an *andantino* in $\frac{3}{4}$ time.

Individual songs from Teplov's volume crop up in various Russian song-collections all through the rest of the century. They were evidently popular; indeed they are primitive examples of a type of song that persisted right up to Glinka's day: the sentimental products of cultured dilettanti whose limited musical technique restricted them to the simplest types of texture and structure. But the development of Russian song soon came under two influences less widely separated than one might suppose: folk-song and opera. Folk-song arrangements had figured among the earlier *kantï* but it was the introduction of 'Russian songs' in the operas of Catherine II's reign – in the Russian operas of the visiting foreigners, Paisiello, Cimarosa, Sarti and the rest, to say nothing of the native operas – that made the native idiom really fashionable. These 'Russian songs', both genuine folk-songs forced into Western European dress and imitations of folk-song, some even Western compositions with Russian words, were arranged for domestic performance and are preserved in almanacks and journals, in various manuscript collections, and in such printed ones as the 'Sobranie nailuchskikh rossiyskikh pesen' (Collection of the best Russian songs) issued by the bookseller Meyer at Petersburg in 1781, in five parts each containing six songs, all anonymous. Such songs were always printed on two staves, sometimes tune and figured or unfigured bass only, sometimes with meagre harmonic filling-in. In 1776, 1778, and 1779, V. F. Trutovsky had brought out the first three parts of his 'Sobranie prostïkh russkikh pesen s notami' (Collection of simple Russian songs with music)[5] in which he attempted to set down genuine folk-tunes accurately, and provided them with basses; when he published his fourth part in 1795 and the third edition of Part I the following year, he went further and printed full harmonies in small type. But by that time he had to compete with the much more famous 'Sobranie narodnïkh russkikh pesen' (Collection of Russian folk-songs – here for the first time actually called *narodnïe*: folk, popular, national) published by Ivan Prach in 1790. Prach – he was really a Czech, Johann Gottfried Pratsch or Prač – printed the voice-part on a separate stave and composed genuine keyboard accompaniments, sometimes surprisingly sympathetic, usually conventionally Western in harmony and figuration; these are Russian parallels to Haydn's almost exactly contemporary harmonizations of Scottish songs. But Prach included, beside his genuine *narodnïe* songs, others – such as the once very popular setting of Sumarokov's *Chem tebya ya ogorchila?* ('How have I grieved you?') printed in the second edition (1806) – which are evidently attempts by dilettanti to affect a national accent.

Most of these *romances* and pseudo-folk-songs are anonymous, often signed with initials, but in the case of the six anonymous 'Russian songs' in the 'Karmannaya kniga dlya lyubiteley muzïki na 1795 god' (Pocket book for music-lovers, for 1795'), published by the Petersburg bookseller Gerstenberg, the composer has been identified as Fedor Mikhaylovich Dubyansky (1760–96), a Petersburg banker and amateur violinist who usually took refuge behind the pseudonyms 'Brigadier D.'

[5] A modern edition, edited by M. V. Belyaev, was published by Muzgiz in 1953.

and 'F. M. D$_{* * *}$.' The opening of his best known song *Golubok* ('The Little Dove') may be quoted:[6]

Ex.2 Andante espressivo

Sto - net si - zïy go - lu - bo - chek, Sto - net on i den' i noch';

'The grey dove moans, moans day and night.'

both because the vein is characteristic and because the three-part lay-out belatedly continues the *kantï* tradition. But Dubyansky usually wrote an independent right-hand part for the accompanist. The poem, by his friend I. I. Dmitriev, one of the 'sentimental' poets, was a great favourite for many years and was set by several composers;[7] Dubyansky repeats each of its seven stanzas to the same ten bars of music.

Gerstenberg's 'Karmannaya kniga' for 1796 contains four songs by Józef Kozłowski (1757–1831), a Pole in the Russian service who is credited with the introduction of the polonaise into Russia. (His polonaises include not only piano and orchestral but also vocal polo-naises, sometimes based on Italian opera arias.) French songs and French titles were becoming more fashionable in the 1790s and we find Kozłowski publishing 'Six romances de Florian avec l'accompagnement de fortepiano'. He set French, Italian and Russian texts. Kozłowski styled himself amateur', but his compositions include an opera and a quantity of Catholic church music and, although most of his songs are modest enough, he sometimes shows real dramatic ability. For instance, his *Prezhestokaya sud'bina* ('Most cruel destiny')[8] has considerable, though conventional, expressive power; each of the two strophes is framed by a 12-bar prelude and 12-bar postlude in which the piano writing, unremarkable in itself, is strikingly superior to that of Kozłowski's dilettante contemporaries. Moreover he has a wider range; he can

[6] Reprinted by Findeisen, op. cit., p. 13, where it is misattributed to the Austrian, Ferdinand Titz; by Ginsburg, *Istoriya russkoy muzïki v notnïkh obraztsakh*, I (Leningrad and Moscow, 1940), p. 360, with two other songs by Dubyansky; and elsewhere.

[7] See, for example, the anonymous setting in the musical appendix to Findeisen, *Ocherki po istorii muzïki v Rossii*, II (Moscow, 1929), No. 115.

[8] Reprinted, with one other song, by Findeisen, *Russkaya khudozhestvennaya pesnya*, p. 16; in the *Istoriya russkoy muzïki* edited by M. S. Pekelis, I (Leningrad and Moscow, 1940), p. 181; and in Ginsburg, op. cit. II (Leningrad and Moscow, 1949), p. 15, with three other 'Russian songs'. On Kozłowski's life and work generally, see in particular the chapter by P. V. Grachev in the volume *Ocherki po istorii russkoy muzïki: 1790–1825*, edited by Druskin and Keldïsh (Leningrad, 1956).

write the simple 'Russian song' (*Vïydu l' v temnïy ya lesochek*), a *Lied* such as Zumsteeg might have composed (*Ya tebya moy svet teryayu*), and the pathetic or dramatic monologue (*Prezhestokaya sud'bina*) in which he is at his most characteristic.

The same dramatic note is sounded with much less technical competence in *K ravnodushnoy* (1819)[9] by a naval officer, A. S. Kozlyaninov (1777–1831), while a fresh one – that of satire, later very important in Russian song – was struck by A. Shaposhnikov in a setting of Derzhavin's *Filosofï p'yanïy i trezvïy* ('The intoxicated and sober philosophers') published in a set of 'Anacreontic songs' in 1816. Shaposhnikov also set Derzhavin's elegy *Potoplenie* ('Drowning')[10] on Dubyansky who, was drowned in the Neva. But the two most notable contemporaries of Dubyansky and Kozłowski were the blind composer Aleksey Dmitrievich Zhilin (*c.* 1767–*c.* 1848) and the Muscovite Daniil Nikitich Kashin (1769–1841), serf for most of his life, pupil of Sarti, all-round professional musician, and notable composer of patriotic songs of the 1812 period.[11] Zhilin won considerable contemporary popularity with his *Malyutka* ('A little boy') – or, to give it its correct title, *Belizariy* (1806);[12] he commands both grace (e.g. the setting of Neledinsky's *Tï velish' mne ravnodushnïm*, also composed by Kozłowski) and gloomy power (e.g. *Udaril chas*, 'The hour has struck', one of those songs of parting always popular in time of war). There is nothing particularly Russian in many of his songs, which lean rather to the style of the contemporary *romances* of Boieldieu, Isouard and Paër; on the other hand, Kashin's numerous songs – he left more than 250, as well as a collection of folk-songs with piano accompaniment (1833–4) – are decidedly Russian in flavour though technically feeble.[13]

Glinka's Elder Contemporaries

These two strains – the sentimental *romance* (Russian: *romans* – the word was at first applied in Russia only to songs with French words, e.g. in Bortnyansky's French operas, with simple, strophic structure) and the *russkaya pesnya* (the 'Russian song' imitating folk-song, often

[9] Reprinted in Ginsburg, op. cit. II, p. 344.

[10] The two songs by Shaposhnikov are reprinted in Ginsburg, op. cit. II, pp. 340 and 337 respectively.

[11] On Zhilin and Kashin see particularly the chapter by O. E. Levasheva in *Ocherki poistorii russkoy muzïki: 1790–1825.*

[12] Reprinted in the Pekelis *Istoriya russkoy muzïki*, I, p. 235, and in Y. Keldïsh, *Istoriya russkoy muzïki*, i (Moscow and Leningrad, 1948), p. 288; a different, obviously later, version is given by Ginsburg, op. cit. II, p. 330. The words of *Malyutka* are a translation of a song by Lemercier: 'Un jeune enfant, un casque en main'.

[13] One *romance* and six folk-song arrangements in Ginsburg, op. cit. II, pp. 218 ff.

with varied repetitions) – are clearly distinguishable throughout the second and third decades of the nineteenth century, though mutual influence often softens the distinction between the two styles; *romances* were sometimes based on genuine, if re-styled folk-tunes, and conversely some passed into the popular repertory of the cities. The composers of this generation, the older contemporaries of Glinka, were almost all essentially amateurs though their amateurishness was of varying degrees, from the pure dilettantism of the Titovs and A. P. Esaulov to the near-professionalism of Alyabiev.[14] They were luckier than their predecessors in that they had better lyrics to set; instead of the stiff pseudo-classicism of Sumarokov and Derzhavin, and the feeble pastorals and love-poems of the 'sentimentalists' (I. I. Dmitriev, Neledinsky-Meletsky, Kapnist, Merzlyakov and the rest), they had Zhukovsky – whose narrative ballads, first set by his friend, the dilettante A. A. Pleshcheev (1775–1827),[15] inspired a new genre of Russian song – they had Delvig and above all they had Pushkin. Poets and composers alike were Byronic romantics; the typical romantic themes of loneliness, dissatisfaction with oneself and the world, longing for some far-off land (Italy or some ideal country), were all too easy to cultivate under the autocracy of Nicholas I; but the composers for the most part lacked the ability to express all this fully. Even in his school-days Pushkin's juvenilia were composed by his friend Yakovlev (1798–1868), one of the dilettanti,[16] but his fertilizing and stimulating influence was not fully felt until later; yet from the first the composers recognized the challenge of fresh rhythms and metres.

Yakovlev is typical of the aristocratic, widely cultured dilettanti who copiously wrote *romances* at this period. Another was Count Mikhail Vielgorsky (1788–1856), who played an important part in Russian musical life generally and appears in every biography of Liszt, Berlioz and the Schumanns. But the technical weakness of these composers has left their songs with more social than musical interest. The best of them was undoubtedly Nikolay Alekseevich Titov (1800–75) – not to be confused with his brother Mikhail (1804–53) or his cousin Nikolay Sergeevich Titov (1798–1843), both of whom composed songs occasionally reprinted under his name.[17] Nikolay Alekseevich

[14] Russian scholars will observe that in transliteration I have allowed myself more latitude with proper names than with titles and texts.

[15] One of them was composed at least as early as 1814, though they were not published until 1832.

[16] Yakovlev's setting of *Zimnïy vecher* ('Winter evening') is printed in Keldïsh, op. cit. I, p. 286.

[17] e.g. N.S. Titov's *Talisman*, reprinted – correctly – in Ginsburg, op. cit. II, p. 394.

was actually christened 'the grandfather of Russian song'[18] – so that
when Teplov was rediscovered, he had to be the 'great-grandfather'.
Titov, on his own confession, began by modelling his *romances* on 'those
of Boieldieu, Lafont, and others'; his first composition was on a French
text, *Rendez-la moi, cette femme chérie*. His first published song, *Sosna*
('The pine-tree'),[19] appeared in 1820, and Bulich lists about sixty. They
are simple and the keynote is gentle melancholy, for which reasons they
enjoyed vast popularity throughout Russia, not merely (like those of
his predecessors) in St. Petersburg and Moscow. Bulich says that 'old
men . . . will tell you that in the '40s there was no musical young lady
who would not sing Titov's *romance, Kovarnïy drug, no serdtsu milïy*'.
It is worth while to quote the opening of this song,[20] not only because
it is characteristic but because the melodic line is a foretaste of a typically
Tchaïkovskian cast of melody:

'Insidious friend, but dear to my heart. I vowed I would
forget thy wiles.'

Bars 1–3 curiously echo an aria in an opera by the composer's father
(prod. 1805).[21]

Modern Russian critics sometimes speak of the 'Triad' of song-
composers, Alyabiev – Varlamov – Gurilev, a judgement perhaps
coloured by over-valuation of the folk element in Varlamov and
Gurilev. They were contemporaries of the Titovs but more accomplished technically. This is particularly marked in the case of Alyabiev
(1787–1851). Like the Titovs, he was an aristocratic amateur but, unlike
them, a semi-professional amateur who worked seriously at music
particularly during and after his years of imprisonment (on a trumped-
up charge of murder) and Siberian exile (1825–32). It was in his hands
that the Russian art-song began to rise toward the artistic level of the
contemporary German *Lied*. His wider range of harmony, his musi-

[18] S. K. Bulich, *Dedushka russkavo romansa: N. A. Titov* (St. Petersburg, 1900).
[19] Ginsburg, op. cit. II, p. 381.
[20] Reprinted in Ginsburg, op. cit. II, p. 383, and Keldïsh, op. cit. I, p. 282.
[21] Printed in Ginsburg, op. cit. II, p. 85.

cianly and imaginative accompaniments, his varied and extended forms, his greatly extended choice of subjects, place him above all his predecessors. It is unfortunate that he is best known by his setting of Delvig's *Solovey* ('The Nightingale'), which Liszt transcribed for piano and on which Glinka wrote piano variations (as well as orchestrating the accompaniment); *Solovey* is a beautiful example of a *romance* influenced by 'Russian song', but it is a relatively early work (composed about 1826–28 and published in 1831) and far from characteristic of Alyabiev at his best. (He quoted it himself in a much later song, *Chto poesh', krasa devitsa*, where he contrasts the nightingale's song with a barca-rolle-like 'song of golden Italy'; he also wrote two 'farewells to the nightingale'.)

Alyabiev was a romantic in that his art is one of personal expression and experience. Both temperament and experience combined to make him a Byronist and it is not surprising to find that some of his best songs, particularly his lyrical ones, were inspired by Pushkin: *Dva vorona* ('The two crows'), *Zimnyaya doroga* ('The winter road'). *Probuzhdenie* ('Awakening' – 'Dreams, dreams, where is your sweetness?'), an extended *durchkomponiert* song in three sections contrasted in key and tempo, *Sasha* (in which 'Russian song' seems to be crossed with Schubert, who was just beginning to be known in Russia), *Ya perezhil svoi zhelan'ya* ('I have outlived my desires'), and a dozen others. The first two of these alone would suffice to show Alyabiev's ability to 'set a scene or mood with the piano's opening bars – the harsh dissonances suggesting the cries of the evil birds, the tinkle of sleighbells on the winter road – though perhaps his most striking piano-part is that of his setting of Kozlov's *Vecherniy zvon* – based on Moore's 'Those evening bells', where the leaden sounds at once create the mood of the poem, which is gloomier than Moore's original.

Ex. 4 Andante sostenuto

Ve-cher - niy zvon, ve-cher - niy zvon! Kak mno-go   dum na - vo - dit_ on

fp

'The evening bell! How many a thought it calls to mind!'

'Pedals' like this are a favourite device of Alyabiev's.

Another Kozlov setting – of the famous *Lyubovnik rozï, solovey*

('Lover of the rose, the nightingale' – a free rendering of Byron's 'This rose to calm my brother's cares', *The Bride of Abydos, I, X*) now sounds rather conventionally pseudo-oriental, with its chromatic neighbour-notes, though it must have been charming in the early 1830s. But much of Alyabiev's oriental, or at least Caucasian, music is copied 'from life'; after his Siberian exile he lived for a time in the Caucasus and at Orenburg, and noted down and arranged Bashkir and Kirgiz (as well as Ukrainian) songs. His two 'Circassian songs' – to Pushkin's *V reke bezhit gremuchiy val* and Lermontov's *Mnogo dev u nas v gorakh* – particularly the latter with the augmented seconds in the melody, his 'Georgian song' *Plachet deva gor* (which might have suggested the third movement of *Scheherazade*), and the fine 'Kabardinian song' *Na Kazbek* (from Bestuzhev-Marlinsky's *Ammalet-Bek*, on which Alyabiev based an opera): these, with Glinka's *Ruslan*, are the foundations of the Russian oriental convention in music. Another outstanding song, the dramatic *Irtïsh* with its tone-painting and its sharp distinction between narrative and direct speech, though not oriental, has an Asiatic setting.

In the 1840s Alyabiev opened yet another new vein – the realistic song of peasant life, anticipating Dargomïzhsky and Mussorgsky – with settings of three poems by Ogarev: *Kabak, Derevenskiy storozh*, and *Izba*. Related to these and from the same period is the powerful *Nishchaya*, a setting of Dmitry Lensky's translation of Béranger's *La pauvre femme*, the effect of which depends largely on an *ostinato* figure in the left-hand of the accompaniment. And in very different mood Alyabiev could throw off such light-hearted things as *Sovet* ('Advice' – to a hussar about to marry).[22]

Neither Varlamov (1801–48) nor Gurilev (1803–58) possessed anything like Alyabiev's range or ability, yet they too contributed notably to the store of Russian song at this period when, as Professor Pekelis has put it,[23] it was 'a laboratory in which the elements of the Russian national musical style crystallized'. Love of minor keys, appearance of certain characteristic melodic cadences, fertilization from folk-music, gradual elimination of Italianisms and Gallicisms: all these traits and developments were 'crystallizing' not only in opera but, perhaps even more effectively, in song.

Varlamov's most striking quality is his rich fund of melody, a

[22] A complete edition of Alyabiev's songs was published in four volumes by Jurgenson in 1898. There is a chronological list in Grigory Timofeev's *A.A. Alyabiev* (Moscow 1912).
[23] Op. cit. I, p. 232.

melody saturated in the folk-style, so that his best known song, *Krasnïy sarafan* ('The Red Sarafan'),[24] has often been taken for a genuine folk-song. His favourite poets were Koltsov, like himself a 'man of the people' who cultivated the popular vein with great skill, and Tsïganov, the author of *The Red Sarafan*, an actor and poetaster probably of gypsy origin. Varlamov himself was influenced by the gypsy musicians of the Moscow restaurants; his more impassioned songs often suggest something of their manner of performance. He was not entirely free from Western influences; he sometimes writes in the measure of the waltz (*Tyazhelo, ne stalo silï*), the barcarolle (*Paduchaya zvezda*), or the bolero or polonaise (*Molodaya ptashechka, Grustno zhit'* and the setting of Lermontov's *Beleet parus odinokiy*). (Alyabiev wrote vocal mazurkas.) And these foreign rhythms are not always introduced as local colour, as the bolero rhythm is in Esaulov's *Ispanskaya pesnya*. He also essayed the ballad with success in *Pesnya razboynika* ('Brigand's Song'), *Pesnya starika* ('Old Man's Song' – 'I saddle my horse'), *Mechta ob Italii* ('Dream of Italy') and other pieces. But when all is said, it is by his long-drawn and melancholy melodies that one remembers Varlamov, melodies such as that of *Akh tï, vremya, vremyachko* ('Ah, dear time, golden time'), so near to the folk-melodies which he also arranged with sympathy and skill. But his poverty-stricken, conventional accompaniments – that of *Akh tï, vremya*, though better than most, doubles the voice much of the time – are unworthy settings for his gems.[25]

Conventional accompaniments also mar the work of Gurilev, who may be not unfairly described as a minor Varlamov; they fall into the idioms of guitar-strumming even more often than Varlamov's. Like Varlamov, to whose memory he dedicated a song entitled *Vospominanie* ('Remembrance'), he was attracted to Koltsov who provided him with the text of what is probably his best song, *Razluka* ('Parting') – which ends with a dozen bars of dramatic recitative. Like Varlamov, he was attracted by the music of the gypsies and his *Matushka-golubushka* (1845) within five years achieved the distinction of re-publication as a genuine gypsy song in the album *Tsiganskiy tabor* (St. Petersburg, 1850). Yet, given a lyric such as Lermontov's *I skuchno, i grustno* ('It's boring and sad'), Gurilev would turn out a *romance* that sounds like an anticipation of Tchaïkovsky.

Alyabiev, Varlamov and Gurilev were all essentially, though not

---

[24] Published with eight other songs in *Muzïkal'ny al'bom na 1833 god*, Varlamov's first opus (Moscow, 1833).

[25] On Varlamov, see S. K. Bulich, *A. K. Varlamov* (St. Petersburg, 1902); a 12-volume edition of his songs was published by Gutheil.

exclusively, song-writers. Their contemporary Verstovsky (1799–1862) was essentially an opera-composer who also wrote *romances* (such as the setting of Zhukovsky's *Dubrava shumit* ('The oak-trees rustle') (1827) which he used again, with different words, in Nadezhda's aria in the Third Act of *Askold's Grave*)[26] and 'Russian songs' and gypsy songs (such as his setting of Pushkin's *Starïy muzh, groznïy muzh* ('Old husband, cruel husband')). But Verstovsky's speciality was the ballad. Even Alyabiev wrote little in this genre; Verstovsky, with his dramatic gift, excelled in it. It is true that his *Nochnoy smotr* ('Midnight Review') – Zhukovksy's translation of Zedlitz's *Die nächtliche Heerschau*[27] – has been completely eclipsed by Glinka's, but he was the real founder of the Russian ballad (which he sometimes at first called 'cantata'). Two of his finest ballads, also Zhukovsky settings, the heroic *Tre pesni skal'da* (after Uhland's *Die drei Lieder*)[28] and *Bednïy pevets* ('The Poor Singer'), date from as early as 1832. In the same year his setting of Pushkin's 'Moldavian song' *Chernaya shal!* ('The Black Shawl'), one of his most popular songs, was performed in Moscow in costume and with scenery.

Chernaya shal! was also sung with orchestral accompaniment – as indeed had been A. A. Pleshcheev's *Svetlana*, as early as 1814 – but one of the most important contributions of the ballad in general to Russian song was that its dramatic and picturesque features encouraged composers to write more adventurous piano-parts, with descriptive or at least suggestive figuration and more expressive harmony. The form also offered them the challenge of a bigger canvas; the technique of the opera monologue was applied to the song-with-piano and it is probable that the emancipation of the *romance* after the 1820s was largely due to the example of the ballad.

Glinka and Dargomïzhsky

Glinka and Dargomïzhsky are regarded by almost all Russians as their first 'classic' song-composers.[29] Much of their work was, of course,

[26] Nadezhda's very first song in the opera, 'Gde tï, zhenikh moy', was also adapted from an earlier *romance*. Glinka followed suit in *Life for the Tsar*, borrowing the music for Antonida's song in Act III from his setting of Delvig's *Ne osenniy chastïy dozhdichek* (1829).

[27] Loewe's fine composition of the original poem, his Op. 23, was composed in 1832 and published the following year. Schubert had declined to tackle it: cf. O. E. Deutsch, *Schubert: die Erinnerungen seiner Freunde* (Leipzig, 1957), p. 87.

[28] Loewe also set this (Op. 3, No. 3) but his version was not published until 1825.

[29] On the 'classical' Russian song, see, in addition to general histories and works on individual composers, particularly B. V. Asafiev (ed.), *Russkiy romans* (Moscow, 1930) and V. A. Vasina–Grossman, *Russkiy klassicheskiy romans XIX veka* (Moscow, 1956).

contemporary with that of the musicians whose songs we have just been considering but their best songs came a little later; whereas Alyabiev reached maturity in the 1830s, Glinka's most characteristic songs were written only at the end of that decade and in the 1840s, Dargomïzhsky's later still. Both belonged to the same milieu and we can measure their achievement best by seeing them in relation to it. One at once recognizes Glinka's superiority and Dargomïzhsky's innovations.

One might almost say that Glinka (1804–57) contributed little to the *evolution* of Russian song; he was not, for instance, more many-sided than Alyabiev; he was simply a very much better composer. His earliest songs, those written before he went to Italy in 1830, hardly show him as that. The earliest of all, *Moya arfa* ('My harp'), composed in 1824, is preserved only in the form in which Glinka wrote it down from memory thirty years later, and the second, *Ne iskushay* ('Do not tempt me needlessly') was revised in 1851; it is a typical sentimental *romance* of the period with a typically conventional accompaniment. It has a number of similar companions; indeed Glinka went on writing this kind of song all his life, though a late example, such as *Lyublyu tebya, milaya roza* ('I love thee, dear rose'), composed in 1843, is likely to be given distinction by touches of characteristic Russian harmony (here, the free use of sharpened fifth/flattened sixth). The early songs also include 'Russian songs' (e.g. *Akh, tï dushechka* ('Ah, you darling') and the Delvig *Akh, tï noch' li* ('Ah, night')), a couple of *romances* with French words by Prince S. G. Golitsïn which were republished with Russian texts for Stellovsky's edition in 1854, and seven or eight arias and *canzonette* to Italian words, which were also published posthumously with Russian words. More interesting is the 'Georgian song' *Ne poy krasavitsa* ('Do not sing thy songs of Georgia') in which Glinka used not only Pushkin's words but the genuine Georgian melody, perhaps a little modified, to which he wrote them.

Glinka spent the years 1830–33 in Italy, and the winter of 1833–34 in Berlin studying composition with Siegfried Dehn. In Italy he wrote one or two more Italian songs of which the best – published post-humously with Russian words as *Zhelanie* – is a beautifully Bellinian setting of Felice Romani's *Il desiderio* ('Ah se tu fossi'). But his composi-tion of Zhukovsky's *Pobeditel'* ('The Conqueror'– 'A hundred bright-eyed beauties') is also Italianate, in the style of an opera polonaise, and the setting of Kozlov's *Venetsianskaya noch'* ('Venetian Night') – actually conceived in Milan – is appropriately a barcarolle. As we have seen,

the siciliana and barcarolle were nothing new in Russian music, but
Glinka's barcarolles sound a little more authentic; he returned to the
barcarolle in one of the 'Farewell to Petersburg' songs of 1840, *Usnuli
golubïya* ('The pigeons have gone to rest'), and in one of his last songs,
Palermo (published as *Finskiy zaliv* – 'The Gulf of Finland'). On the
other hand, the Zhukovsky song *Dubrava shumit* was composed in
Berlin (rewritten in 1843), which clearly accounts for its Schubertian
flavour. And the words of Pushkin's *Ya zdes'*, *Inezil'ya* (Barry Corn-
wall's 'Inesilla! I am here') demanded a Spanish idiom, though they
received only the conventional 'Spanish' treatment of the time; indeed,
it is rather ironical that all but one of Glinka's Spanish songs – and they
include the beautiful Pushkin *Nochnoy zefir* ('Nocturnal Zephyr')[30] and
two in the 'Farewell to Petersburg' – were written before he visited
Spain; the exception is *Milochka* ('Darling'), based in 1847 on a genuine
jota melody.

  With his newly strengthened technique and his new resolution to
'write music in Russian', Glinka was now poised for higher flights.
At first he was occupied with the search for an opera-subject and then
with the composition of *Life for the Tsar*, but most of his best songs date
from the years 1837–40, that is, from the period between the production
of the first opera and the composition of *Ruslan*: the famous *Nochnoy
smotr* ('Midnight Review'), the 'wedding song' *Severnaya zvezda* ('North
Star' – introducing the slow folk-melody later used in *Kamarinskaya*),
four outstanding Pushkin songs – *Nochnoy zefir*, *Gde nasha roza?*
('Where is our rose?'), *V krovi gorit* ('Fire of longing in my blood' – but
originally written to different words), and *Ya pomnyu chudnoe mgnoven'e*
('I remember the wonderful moment'), and the twelve songs published
by Gurskalin under the title *Proshchaniya s Peterburgom* ('Farewell to
Petersburg'). The entirely declamatory *fantaziya* or ballad *Nochnoy
smotr* is tremendously effective but, as with most songs of this kind, the
effect depends largely on the words and the manner of performance;
the song occupies a curiously isolated place in Glinka's output. Utterly
different, though also consisting of music that simply carries the words,
is *Gde nasha roza*, a tiny gem which was to have enormous influence on
the next generation of Russian musicians, suggesting the technique of
Mussorgsky's *Savishna* and *Ozornik* ('Ragamuffin') and the manner of
Borodin's epigrammatic songs. The whole piece is only seventeen bars
long, ten in $\frac{5}{4}$ time, seven in $\frac{3}{4}$, and almost the only note-value used
in the voice-part is the crotchet:

[30] Also set in Pushkin's lifetime by Verstovsky, N. S. Titov and Esaulov.

'Where is our rose, my friends? Has it wilted, that child
of the dawn? Do not say: "Thus youth fades".'

More conventionally beautiful, an idealized *romance*, is *Ya pomnyu
chudnoe mgnoven'e*. The poem is one of the most perfect love-lyrics in
the Russian language and has tempted a number of composers, from
N. S. Titov and Alyabiev onward, yet Russian critics seem to agree that
no other setting matches it as perfectly as Glinka's. It is not one of those
compositions that overwhelm the poem with superb music; as Serov
put it, it 'follows the poet's every thought' – and not only the shades of
his thought but the subtleties of his rhythms. It is in the ternary form
common in the *romance* of this period but the form is transfigured in
accordance with the sense of the poem, the six stanzas of which also fall
into three parts: the enchanted recollection of the first sight of beauty,
the passing of years and forgetfulness, and now the fresh meeting and
the renewal of passion – so that the music of the third part is first
harmonically, then melodically, changed, grows and rises to a climax,
and – with a sigh – sinks to rest.

In the songs of 'Farewell to Petersburg' there was no question of
matching immortal verse. The poet, Glinka's friend Kukolnik, was no
master – and Glinka knew it. In at least two cases, *K Molli* ('To Molly')
and *Poputnaya pesnya* ('Song of Travel'), the words were written to pre-
existent music. (The *Poputnaya pesnya* must be one of the earliest of
railway songs.) The best that can be said for Kukolnik is that he knew
how to provide a wide range of ideas and verses suited to music. The
best known song of the set is *Zhavoronok* ('The Lark'), an idealized
'Russian song'. Others are almost operatic. The variety is obviously
deliberate; there are theatrical pieces – David Rizzio's song from
Kukolnik's *Mary Stuart*, a 'Hebrew song' afterwards orchestrated for
his *Prince Kholmsky*,[31] the Crusader's *Virtus antiqua* – and there are a

---

[31] In 1855 Glinka orchestrated the accompaniments of *Nochnoy smotr* and one or two other
songs.

bolero, a cavatina, a cradle song, a barcarolle, and a fine *fantaziya* (ballad), *Stoy, moy vernïy burnïy kon'* ('Stand, my trusty, fiery steed') of which the subject – but not the music – is Spanish. The set ends with a *Proshchal'naya pesnya* ('Song of Farewell'), an idealization of the *zastol'naya pesnya* (drinking song with chorus). The idea of parting, of travel, is suggested in other of the songs but there is no real connecting thread; the set is not a cycle; the title refers only to Glinka's intention of leaving St. Petersburg at that time.

Dargomïzhsky (1813–69)[32] began song-composing, in the early 1830s, in the familiar contemporary styles: *romances* with French words (*Au bal* in waltz rhythm, Hugo's *O ma charmante*, and others) or Russian ones, 'Russian songs', a pseudo-oriental song or two. A little later he was attracted by Spanish subjects. He often chooses poems set by Glinka, by whom he was influenced for a time, only to show his marked inferiority as a lyrical composer; the melodies of his *romances* tend to be rather colourless and sentimental even in his more mature work, the accompaniments to be conventional. One or two of the early songs, however – notably *Baba staraya* ('The Old Woman') – hint at the directions in which his real strength lay: the comic, the dramatic (or, at least, the assumption of a character), the 'realistic' approach to peasant life. But at first his technique was too weak to do justice to his ideas. In the setting of Delvig's *Shestnadtsat let* ('Sixteen years old'), for instance, the girl's calf-love is charmingly sketched in a mazurka melody but the harmony and the accompaniment are naïve without suggesting naïveté.

The later *romances* are naturally more imaginative, harmonically more adventurous. There is real passion in the setting of Pushkin's *V krovi gorit*. But the best of Dargomïzhsky's straightforward *romances* are two Lermontov songs dating from 1847–8: *I skuchno, i grustno* ('It's boring and sad') and *Mne grustno* ('I'm sad because I love you'). Here the melodic utterance becomes more laconic, more fragmentary, closer to the intonation of the words; the lyricism is modified by character, as in opera. Yet in both, and in the later, rather similar setting of Kuroch-kin's *Rasstalis' gordo mï* ('We parted proudly, without a word or tear'), the piano-figuration is very conventional. Later still, in the late 1850s, Dargomïzhsky achieved a little masterpiece in this genre of lyrical monologue: *Mne vse ravno*. Here the Byronic hero, speaking through the lips of a poet far inferior to Lermontov, has outlived all passion.

---

[32] The best edition of his songs is the *Polnoe sobranie romansov i pesen*, edited by Pekelis (Moscow, 1947).

The vocal line, more laconic than ever, is perfectly in character and perfect in its verbal intonation, and the piano merely supports it without distracting the listener by inept arpeggio-figuration:

Ex. 6 Moderato assai

Mne vse rav-no, stra-dat' il' na-slazh-dat'sya K stra-dan yam ya pri - vï- kla uzh dav - no.

'It's all the same to me – come pain or pleasure. To suffering I'm long accustomed.'

It might be the very voice of Evgeny Onegin.

Dargomïzhsky's 'Russian songs' show a similar development, though his interest in the genre was later in growing; they became numerous only in the 1850s. One of the most beautiful – a typical crossing of *romance* with 'Russian song', with a great deal of gypsy bravura in both slow and fast sections – is the setting of Lermontov's *Tuchki nebesnïya* ('Heavenly Clouds'). And Dargomïzhsky could throw off a straightforward racy piece such as the Koltsov *Okh, tikh, tikh, tikh, ti!* But in this field, too, he is at his best when he makes himself the mouthpiece of a dramatic character: for instance, the drunken miller coming home late at night and his scolding wife in Pushkin's *Mel'nik* ('The Miller'). That is straightforward comedy, but *Likhora-dushka* – a folk-poem on the theme of the old and unloved husband – is bitter and subtle, despite its simple strophic form, and perhaps suggested Mussorgsky's *Gathering Mushrooms*.

Dargomïzhsky's more and more deliberate striving toward 'realism' and dramatic truth – in which he was completely in tune with contemporary tendencies in Russian thought and literature[33] – naturally found its fullest scope in the ballad or *fantaziya*. Even his earliest essay, the Delvig *Moy suzhenïy, moy ryazhenïy,* is more interesting than most of his songs of the same period, weak as it is. And his *Svad'ba* ('The Marriage'), a glorification of free love ('It was not in church we married, with crowns and candles . . . . but at midnight in the dark forest') published as early as 1843, justly maintained its popularity for half a century; the piano writing in the very Russian *andante* section, which

[33] Chernïshevsky's *Aesthetic Relationship of Art and Reality*, the 'bible' of the truth-in-art movement, was published in 1855.

353

alternates with more commonplace quick ones, again anticipates Mussorgsky. The later *Paladin* (Zhukovsky) is a worthy companion-piece to Glinka's *Virtus antiqua*. But the most famous of all Dargomï-zhsky's ballads – he calls it 'dramatic song' – is *Starïy kapral*, Kurochkin's translation of Béranger's *Le vieux caporal*, the ballad of the old soldier, condemned to death for insulting a young officer, who encourages the reluctant execution squad as they march him along: 'In step, lads . . . one, two!' (At the end, after the fatal shot, Dargomïzhsky oddly writes four bars of two-part chorus echoing the old man's refrain.)

Starïy kapral was written in the early 1860s (perhaps prompted by Moniuszko's setting of a Polish version), after the composer had made his often quoted assertion, 'I want the sound directly to express the word. I want truth' (letter to Lyubov Karmalina, 9 December 1857). Two other songs from the same late period of his life are usually considered his masterpieces of satirical comedy: *Chervyak* ('The Worm'), another of Kurochkin's translations of Béranger (*Le Sénateur*), and *Titulyarnïy sovetnik* ('The Titular Councillor').[34] They are very amusing, and no doubt stimulated Mussorgsky's satirical pieces, but the music of *Titulyarnïy sovetnik*, at any rate, is feeble; the fun lies less in it than in the words. Similarly, *Starïy kapral* – like Glinka's *Nochnoy smotr*, to which it stands in very close relationship – is essentially a vehicle for the words and for a dramatic performer. In *Chervyak* Dargomizhsky even gives 'stage' directions: 'very humbly', 'with profound respect', 'smiling and hesitating', 'screwing up the eyes'. But in this song, a self-portrait of a humble gentleman who is 'a mere worm' by comparison with the Count for whose friendship he is indebted to his own dear wife, the music itself is comic; here indeed are novelty and dramatic truth, for the vocal line – a sort of arioso mostly in even quavers – crawls and cringes with the inflexion of each sentence.

Finally two other declamatory songs must be mentioned, if only because of their influence on the next generation: *Tï vsya polna ochar-ovan'ya* ('Thou art all full of charm') and *Vostochnïy romans* ('Oriental Song'). Unlike *Paladin* and *Starïy kapral*, they are not dramatic in content. The setting of Yazïkov's address to a ballerina is actually styled 'recitative' though some phrases are melodious enough: the conception is orchestral, the pianist's right hand keeping up an almost uninterrupted demisemiquaver tremolo while the bass – suggesting pizzicato strings – interjects motives in the rhythm ꞏ𝄾𝅘𝅥𝅮𝅘𝅥𝅮𝅘𝅥𝅮𝄽𝅘𝅥ꞏ A bass motive (*x*):

---

[34] A rank in the Tsarist civil service. The words are by Peter Weinberg who was first and foremost a translator, so there may again be some Western original – by Béranger or Heine?

plays an even more important part in the *Vostochnïy romans* (a setting of Pushkin's *Tï rozhdena vosplamenyat'*) where the augmented-triad harmony and the fragment of whole-tone scale in the bars quoted, which open and close the song, are derived from Glinka's *Ruslan*, although the falling semitones of the voice-part – which never spreads melodious wings – and the diminished-seventh harmonies are nearer to the orientalism of Spohr's *Jessonda*. All the same, the *Vostochnïy romans* and *Paladin* were at first the only songs of Dargomïzhsky's that were thought anything of by the group of young musicians who gathered around Glinka's protégé Balakirev in the 1860s. At least, that is what Rimsky-Korsakov tells us in his memoirs.

The 'New Russian School'

The outstanding event in the history of Russian song in the 1860s was, of course, the advent of a strikingly original genius: Modest Mussorgsky. Yet, even apart from Mussorgsky, Russian song underwent notable changes in the hands of his friends, the group known as the 'mighty handful': Balakirev, Cui, Borodin, Rimsky-Korsakov – and an almost unknown composer, one of the last and most technically gifted of the dilettanti, Nikolay Nikolaevich Lodïzhensky (1843–1916), a diplomat who as a young man produced a handful of beautiful and sensitive songs, six of which were published by Bessel in 1873. During the period 1855–65, Balakirev (1837–1910) produced a couple of dozen songs. Cui (1835–1918) composed about the same number between 1856 and 1870, mostly grouped in his Opp. 3, 5, and 7, with a few in Opp. 9 and 10. Beginning with a pseudo-Italian barcarolle in 1861, Rimsky-Korsakov (1844–1908) turned to song-writing more seriously in 1865 and in five years produced more than a score of pieces (his Opp. 2, 3, 4, 7, 8, and Op. 25, No. 1). Borodin (1833–87) also made a 'false start' with some early *romances* with 'cello obbligato, but composed the first of his tiny group of masterpieces, *Spyashchaya knyazhna* ('The Sleeping Princess' – written, like most of his songs, to his own words) in 1867. In this considerable corpus of song one can detect a good many common tendencies.

Perhaps the most striking novelty is the treatment of the piano parts.

355

Not, of course, that even conventional arpeggio-figuration or repeated chords completely disappear. We find them whenever the composer – for instance, Cui in *Ya uvidel tebya* ('I saw thee') or *Prosti* ('Forgive'), Op. 5, Nos. 1 and 5 – falls into the old *romance* style in the voice-part. But the piano-parts are not only well wrought or mood-enhancing as in the best songs of Alyabiev, Glinka and Dargomïzhsky; they are more important, sometimes even seeming to outweigh the voice-part, often to equal it in interest (e.g. Balakirev's *Pesnya zolotoy rïbki* ('Song of the Golden Fish') and Rimsky-Korsakov's *Plenivshis' rozoy, solovey* ('Enslaving the rose, the nightingale')[35] Op. 2, No. 2, and *V temnoy roshche* (' In the dark grove') Op. 4, No. 3. And the voice-parts are apt to be correspondingly less vocal. For this there are two explanations. The Balakirev circle was very much under the influence of Schumann and Liszt, both exponents of the 'pianistic' *Lied*. And whereas Alyabiev, Varlamov, Glinka, and Dargomïzhsky had all been more than competent singers, even teachers of singing, and had composed songs primarily for themselves (like all the dilettanti) or for women-friends,[36] Mussorgsky was the only member of the 'mighty handful' with any vocal ability. Consequently, even the finest of their songs – Borodin's *Sleeping Princess*, for instance – are apt to have somewhat instrumental melodies.

Another consequence of this tendency is that voice-part and piano-part often seem to alternate: the picturesque or figurative piano-part changes to mere chordal accompaniment, or even stops altogether, when the voice enters (Balakirev's *Pesnya Selima* ('Selim's Song'), Rimsky-Korsakov's *Plenivshis' rozoy* and *Tikho vecher* ('Quietly the Evening') Op. 4, No. 4), or voice and piano seem to proceed simultaneously on different planes (as in Balakirev's *Golden Fish*). The young Rimsky-Korsakov, in particular, is all too ready to take refuge in recitative or quasi-recitative over a striking piano-part: hardly the best solution of the problem of 'making the sound directly express the word'. Some of these piano-parts are finely wrought and beautifully congruous – for instance, Balakirev's *Gruzinskaya pesnya* ('Georgian Song': another setting of Pushkin's *Ne poy, krasavitsa*) – but it is comparatively rare to find really close musical integration of voice and accompaniment, as in Lodïzhensky's *Da ya vnov' s toboy* ('Yes, I am with you again' – a setting of his own words):

[35] By Koltsov. Not to be confused with the Byron-Kozlov *Lyubovnik rozï, solovey*, which Rimsky-Korsakov set sixteen years later (Op. 26, No. 4).

[36] Dargomïzhsky gave lessons gratis to ladies but would take no male pupils. He often said, 'But for the existence of women-singers, I should never have been a composer. They have inspired me all my life'.

'Yes, I am with you again; in my breast my heart beats so
quietly; in my spirit all is light.'

Balakirev generally developed familiar genres, breathing new life
into them: the 'Russian song' (e.g. the Koltsov *Pesnya razboynika* –
'Brigand's Song'), a barcarolle (with a translated Heine text), *romances*
(sometimes in waltz or mazurka rhythm), and above all the 'oriental
song', a vein in which he early produced three masterpieces: the already
mentioned *Georgian Song* (not using the original melody, like Glinka,
but with an even more authentic-sounding one – Balakirev had visited
the Caucasus – and an accompaniment, afterwards orchestrated,
brilliantly suggesting an ensemble of native instruments), the virile
setting of Lermontov's *Selim's Song*, and the fantastic one of his *Golden
Fish* (so very different from Dargomïzhsky's). While Balakirev continues the Glinka tradition, even in the straightforward *romance* (e.g.
Pridi ko mne, 'Come to me', by Koltsov), Cui tends to follow Dargomïzhsky. His *Lyubov mertvetsa* ('A dead man's love'), Op. 5, No. 2, is
modelled on *Paladin, Nedavno obol'shchen* ('Lately beguiled'), No. 3 of
the same set, on the older man's *Ti vsya polna ocharovan'ya*. Both in his
critical writings and in his compositions, Cui laid stress on 'truth to the
words' and he makes extensive use of arioso, though his declamation is
by no means always faultless. His detailed treatment of poems is heard
at its best in such songs as the Maykov song *Lyublyu, esli tikho* ('I love,
though quietly') Op. 7, No. 6, and in the Heine settings. It was at this

357

period that Heine made his full impact on Russian song, partly of
course because of the Schumann settings but even more as a result of
the publication of Mikhaylov's volume of translations in 1858; all the
members of the 'handful', as well as Tchaïkovsky, composed Heine
poems during the 1860s, most of them in Mikhaylov's versions though
Borodin preferred to make his own. The musical influence of Schumann is also apparent sometimes in Cui, for instance in the Maykov
song *Istomlennaya gorem* ('Weary with sorrow'), Op. 7, No. 5.

Rimsky-Korsakov, being a little younger, often shows the influence
of Balakirev or Cui. His beautiful setting of the lullaby from Mey's
play *The Maid of Pskov*, Op. 2, No. 3, later incorporated in the opera
Vera Sheloga (which is based on the first part of the play) is a close companion to Balakirev's *Kolïbel'naya pesnya* ('Cradle Song'), and the
Lermontov *Kak nebesa tvoy vzor blistaet* ('Thy glance is radiant as the
sky'), Op. 7, No. 4, is a pale reflection of the *Georgian Song*, while the
arioso, half-declamatory element in others sometimes suggests Cui.
Yet these early songs of Rimsky-Korsakov's include some beautiful
and individual things, notably the Pushkin *Na kholmakh Gruzii* ('On
the hills of Georgia'), Op. 3, No. 4. Even the best of them, however,
are surpassed in power and originality by some of the songs which
Borodin began to produce towards the end of the 1860s.[37] First came
the already mentioned *Sleeping Princess*, with the famous incessant
syncopated seconds in the accompaniment which contribute so much
to the fantastic, dreamlike quality of the music, and the tremendous
descending whole-tone scale when the 'noisy swarm of wood-spirits
flew over the princess'. Next came a companion-piece, *Morskaya
tsarevna* ('The Sea King's Daughter') and the tremendous *Pesnya
temnavo lesa* ('Song of the Dark Forest') which deserves much more than
Cui's *Menisk* (Op. 7, No. 4) the description 'epic fragment'; the words,
again the composer's own, are an imitation of the *bïlini*, the old folk-
epics; they are set to a repetitive, metrically free melody which is
doubled by the piano in bare powerful octaves; the 'harmony' is for
the greater part of the song produced only by the sustaining of some
notes for two or three beats against the movement of the rest. In
strongest contrast are the two highly civilized, finely polished miniatures which followed: *Fal'shivaya nota* ('The false note') and *Otravoy
polnï moi pesni* (a translation of Heine's *Vergiftet sind meine Lieder*); in
these there is a superficial, stylistic affinity with Cui but both are

[37] They are all published, together with Borodin's juvenilia (of which the most striking
feature is the use of cello obbligato), in a volume edited by Lamm (Moscow, 1947).

inspired by a creative power far superior to Cui's; they have the gem-like hardness of great epigrams. Then, again, in *More* ('The Sea') Borodin gave Russian song-literature one of its great descriptive ballads, the piece which Stassov acclaimed as 'supreme among all Borodin's songs' – adding with typically Stassovian enthusiasm 'and, in my opinion, the greatest in creative strength and depth of all songs that have been written up to this time'. Without endorsing Stassov's judgement, one can agree that *More* is a very fine piece which, unlike so many things in this genre, does not depend largely on the words to make its effect. Borodin later orchestrated the tempestuous piano-part.

In 1873 Borodin wrote another Heine song, setting his own trans-lation of *Aus meinen Tränen*, and in the 1880s another little group of songs, including his only Pushkin piece, *Dlya beregov ˈotchizni dal'noy* ('For the shores of thy distant fatherland'), an *Arabskaya melodiya* employing a genuine Arab tune, an elaborated 'Russian song' (Nekras-sov's *U lyudey-to v domu*, 'In those people's house') and a companion-piece to Dargomïzhsky's *Worm* and *Titular Councillor*: on Aleksey Tolstoy's *Spes'* ('Pride'). These show the extent of Borodin's reach rather than add to his stature.

Mussorgsky's range as a song-writer was, of course, wider still, his originality more profound, his output vastly larger. But before con-sidering it, it may be as well to glance at the later songs of the three longer lived members of the group: Balakirev, Rimsky-Korsakov and Cui. Balakirev had two later bursts of song-writing: in 1895–6 and 1903–4. Like most of his later work, this score or so of later songs shows little stylistic advance on the early ones; one can only say that they include some beautiful things in the old manner, such as *Zapevka*, to words by Mey, in the purest folk-song idiom and treated like his own wonderful folk-song arrangements (of which he published two collec-tions, in 1866 and 1898). *Videnie* ('A Vision'), inspired by a poem by the Slavophile Khomyakov, is diffuse and sectional but extremely im-pressive; the vision is a typical Pan-Slav one, of Orthodox ceremonial and 'Slavonic prayers' resounding in the cathedral on the Petřín at Prague. In the Mey drunkard's song *Kak naladili, durak* ('As they kept on saying, "You fool" '), Balakirev successfully ventures on to Mussorgsky's special ground, the comic-pitiful character-study; bitter, tragic words are set ironically to a gay folk-like tune.

Rimsky-Korsakov's later songs were also conceived at two widely separated periods: 1877–83 (Op. 25, No. 2, Op. 26, and Op. 27) and

1897–8 (Opp. 39–43, 45, 46, 49, 50, 51, 55, and 56). Of these, the earlier group are much more technically assured than the songs of the 1860s but mostly follow the same lines. However, in *V porïve nezhnosti serdechnoy* (Op. 26, No. 1: a translation of Byron's 'In moments to delight devoted') and the Aleksey Tolstoy *Gornïmi tikho letela dusha nebesami* ('Softly the spirit flew up to heaven') Op. 27, No. 1, both in D flat as it happens, we at last find real lyrical warmth and expansive vocal melody in Rimsky-Korsakov's songs. *V porïve* reminds one a little of Schumann but still more of the 'kiss' scene in *Snowmaiden*, which had been written a year or two before; the A. K. Tolstoy song is weaker but still attractive. And it was this new 'vocal' approach to song that predominated in the nearly fifty songs of 1897–8. The composer was quite conscious of this; he tells us in his memoirs:

> It was long since I had written any songs. Turning to the poems of Aleksey Tolstoy, I wrote four songs and felt that I was composing them differently from before. The melody, following the turns of the text, poured out from me in a purely vocal form, i.e. it was so in its very origin, accompanied only by hints at harmony and key-plan. The accompaniment was devised and worked out after the composition of the melody, whereas formerly—with few exceptions—the melody was conceived as it were instrumentally, i.e. apart from the text and only harmonising with its general content, or evoked by the harmonic basis which sometimes preceded the melody. Feeling that the new way of composing produced true vocal music, and being satisfied with my first attempts in this direction, I composed one song after another to words by A. Tolstoy, Maykov, Pushkin and others.

The very choice of poets is significant; Aleksey Tolstoy and Maykov – with Tyutchev, Fet and Polonsky – were the later nineteenth-century champions of art for art's sake, not for truth's; they represent the retreat from 'realism'. And Rimsky-Korsakov, like the other composers of this period, now wished to compose essentially lyrical music.

The four Aleksey Tolstoy songs were published as Op. 39 and, although the new style is not fully developed in them, they point to most of its characteristics. No. 1, *O, eslib tï mogla* ('Oh, if thou couldst for one moment'), melancholy, with an undercurrent of passion, suggests Tchaïkovsky; the shadow of Tchaïkovsky – of his moods, sometimes even of his style – falls from time to time over this last crop of songs. No. 2, *Zapad gasnet* ('The west dies out in pallid rose'), is a beautiful lyrical piece in the vein of the *romances* of half-a-century earlier. In No. 3, *Na nivï zheltïe* ('Silence descends on the golden cornfields') a shapely melodic phrase is answered by an arioso one, *a piacere*. No. 4, *Usni, pechal'nïy drug* ('Sleep, my poor friend') similarly alternates arioso with snatches of a lullaby which is the twin sister of the one from *The Maid of Pskov*. The best of the lyrical songs of this period – Russian critics seem to agree in giving the palm to Op. 42, No. 3 (Pushkin's *Redeet oblakov letuchaya gryada*, 'The clouds begin to scatter') – are beautiful indeed, but too often the lyricism seems a little facile, the harmony and piano-figuration commonplace. The simple workmanship is sometimes highly effective, as in Op. 40, No. 1 (Lermontov's *Kogda volnuetsya zhelteyushchaya niva*, 'When the golden cornfield waves'), where the left-hand piano melody accompanying the singer's first phrase then passes to the voice, sometimes rather slipshod. The three cycles, 'Vesnoy' ('In Spring'), Op. 43, 'Poetu' ('To the Poet'), Op. 45, and 'U morya' ('By the Sea'), Op. 46, are disappointingly uneven, and the new 'Eastern songs', such as Op. 41, No. 4 (the Maykov *Posmotri v svoy vertograd*, 'Look in thy garden') and Op. 51, No. 2 (Pushkin's *Georgian Song* once more), lack the savour of the old. Op. 50, settings of Maykov's translations of modern Greek poems, contains two or three of the better songs. Everywhere arioso is liable to intrude. Op. 55, No. 3 (Pushkin's *Snoviden'e* ('Dream')) even begins by returning to the lay-out of Dargomïzhsky's *Tï vsya polna ocharovan'ya*. Several songs are actually styled 'arioso', notably the two bass pieces, Op. 49, settings of Pushkin's *Anchar* ('The Upas-Tree') (the first version of which dates from 1882) and *Prorok* ('The Prophet'), both orchestrated later; they can only be described as noble failures; neither poem needs music or is suitable for music, and the subjects are outside Rimsky-Korsakov's reach.

Surprisingly, the later Cui has a wider range than either the later Rimsky-Korsakov or the later Balakirev. He attempted everything from the tiny six-bar *Epitafiya* of Op. 57 to the big dramatic ballad on Richepin's *Les deux ménétriers*, Op. 42, which he afterwards orchestrated. During the late 1870s and the 1880s he set a number of French poems by Hugo, Musset, Richepin, and others; he composed German and Polish poems in the original languages and his Mickiewicz songs are among his best. (He was half Lithuanian and he had studied with Moniuszko.) He sometimes threw back to the simple *romance* of earlier days; in the '21 Stikhotvoreniy Nekrasova' ('21 Poems by Nekrassov', Op. 62) (1902) he unexpectedly turned towards Mussorgsky though tamely conventional harmony replaces Mussorgsky's expressive empiricism; and in *Sozhzhennoe pis'mo* ('The Burned Letter') Op. 33, No. 4, produced at least one outstandingly successful dramatic song. But Cui's natural gift was for the lyrical arioso and the polished miniature, and in the '25 Stikhotvoreniy Pushkina' ('25 Poems by Pushkin', Op. 57) (1899) he produced a real masterpiece of this kind, *Tsarskosel'skaya statuya* ('The Statue at Tsarskoe Selo'), a perfect synthesis of poem and music, deceptively simple and as subtly delicate as a scent. 'A girl has dropped her jar of water[38] and smashed it'; and there, oh miracle, the water still flows and she sits for ever sadly watching . . . . The temptation to quote must be resisted; one would have to quote the entire song to show how perfect it is.

Mussorgsky

It would be difficult to find a greater contrast with Cui's polished but generally insipid art than the rough-hewn songs of his comrade Mussorgsky (1839–81). He too began as a cultivated amateur, but whereas Cui always belonged in spirit to the tradition of the dilettanti – anaemic, impersonal in style, and conventional – these adjectives are the last one would apply to most of Mussorgsky's work. Even his very first song, *Gde tï, zvezdochka?* ('Where art thou, little star?'), dated 1857, has a certain tang.[39] A number of his early songs are in the old *romance* vein – one of the feeblest *Akh, zachem tvoi glazki poroyu* ('Why are your eyes sometimes so cold?') dates from as late as 1866 – but most of them have some touch – boldly empirical harmony, a striking 'last word' on the piano – which shows that the mind behind them was no ordinary one. Real creative individuality begins to reveal itself in the songs written in 1863–4: the two Koltsov songs, *Mnogo est' u menya teremov i sadov* ('I have many palaces and gardens') and *Duyut vetrï* ('The wild winds blow'), *Tsar' Saul* (adapted from Kozlov's translation of Byron's *Song of Saul before his Last Battle*), the Nekrassov *Kalistratushka*, and the *fantaziya*, *Noch'* ('Night'). The last of these exists in two versions so different that they must almost be considered separate songs: the first, and better, is a beautiful and fairly faithful setting of a Pushkin poem which Rimsky-Korsakov composed a little later as his Op. 7, No. 1, the second a composition of a text largely rewritten by the

[38] The statue, by P. I. Sokolov, really depicts La Fontaine's 'La laitière et le pot au lait'.

[39] Like other of Mussorgsky's early songs, it exists in two versions; in this case, the second is orchestral. Both versions are printed in the complete edition of Mussorgsky's works, edited by Pavel Lamm, V, 1–2 (Moscow, 1931), which should always be used where possible. The original editions of many of Mussorgsky's songs were more or less drastically 'revised' by Rimsky-Korsakov, who also published what he called a 'free musical rendering' of the first of the Nursery songs. There is a separate monograph on Mussorgsky's songs by Keldïsh: *Romansovaya lirika Musorgskovo* (Moscow, 1933).

composer himself;[40] the passage at the words 'vo t'me nochnoy tvoi glaza blistayut predo mnoy' ('your eyes shine before me in the dark night'), substantially identical in both versions, is in every respect characteristic of the mature Mussorgsky. So is practically everything in *Kalistratushka*, the first version of which is headed 'study in folk-style': Kalistratushka, a peasant remembering his mother's lullaby (a folk-lullaby heard on the piano), sings in that flexible, unsymmetrically melodious cantilena which was later to flow through so many pages of *Boris* and *Khovanshchina*.

Most of Mussorgsky's best and best-known songs were written soon afterwards, during the years 1866–68. The lyrical vein continued in such songs as *Na Dnepre* ('On the Dnieper', first version), *Evreyskaya pesnya* ('Hebrew Song'), *Detskaya pesenka* ('Child's Song'), all by Mey, and the Koltsov *Po nad Donom* ('Down by the Don'), but it is a fresh and unconventional lyricism no longer owing anything at all to the *romance* type and far more sophisticated musically, even in the simplest examples, than any of the old 'Russian songs'. However, it was not the lyrical songs that created such landmarks in the history of Russian music, but the realistic, half-comic, half-tragic ones written to the composer's own words. The first, epoch-making example was *Svetik Savishna*, inspired in 1866 by an incident Mussorgsky had seen in the country, the previous summer:

> an unhappy idiot . . . declaring his love to a young woman who had attracted him; he was pleading with her, though ashamed of his unseemliness and his unhappy condition; he himself understood he could have nothing in the world – least of all the happiness of love.[41]

He set the idiot's courtship to an uninterrupted, unvaried stream of even crotchets in $\frac{5}{4}$ time; the technique is that of Glinka's *Gde nasha roza* (see Ex. 5) but here it is applied to a very different subject. It was the choice of subjects quite as much as the musical technique that made such songs so shockingly novel. *Savishna* was the first of a series: *Akh tï, p'yanaya teterya* ('Ah, you drunken sot'), *Seminarist*, *Ozornik* ('The Ragamuffin'), *Kozel* ('The He-Goat'), *Klassik* ('The Classicist'), *Sirotka* ('The Orphan'). They are a gallery of realistic portraits: comic, pitiful, satirical, sardonic by turns. The convention of even note-values is by no means always preserved, but, without being at all like recitative,

---

40 Both versions were later orchestrated: the first by the composer in 1868, the second by Rimsky-Korsakov in 1908.
41 Stassov, 'M.P. Mussorgsky', *Vestnik Evropï*, III (1881), p. 506.

the vocal line is always controlled, if not dictated, by the inflexions of prose speech; the infusion of a lyrical element may be greater or less according to the subject. Closely related to these are the Mey *Hopak* (which, like *Na Dnepre*, is a translation from the Ukrainian Shevchenko's *Haydamaky*), *Po gribï* ('Gathering Mushrooms' – also by Mey), the Koltsov *Pirushka* ('The Little Feast'), and *Strekotun'ya beloboka* ('Chattering Magpie' – based on two unconnected poems by Pushkin, described as 'a joke', and in fact a delightful piece of nonsense).

Mussorgsky's 'realism' culminated, so far as his songs are concerned, in the cycle 'Detskaya' ('The Nursery'). This consisted originally of five songs, composed 1868–70 and published in 1872; two more were composed in 1872 and published posthumously. In this series of musical transcriptions of a child's speech, caught with extraordinary truth and total absence of adult sentiment, all existing musical conventions were thrown overboard; the voice part is often the purest musical prose – *S nyaney* ('With Nurse'), the first piece, is an extreme example – and though *S kukloy* ('With the doll') borders on the lyrical, even here the child's crooning never lapses into a near-conventional lullaby. From the same period dates an elaborate musical lampoon, *Rayok* ('The Peepshow'), in which Mussorgsky mocks a number of his musical enemies or supposed enemies; in the closed circle for which it was written this must have seemed extremely funny, but its musical allusions and parodies are lost on all modern hearers.

After *The Nursery*, Mussorgsky changed direction. The cycle *Bez solntsa* ('Sunless'), to words by his friend Golenishchev-Kutuzov (composed in 1874), abandons the objective image. These are songs of subjective, pessimistic emotion; the musical technique is the same but Mussorgsky now speaks in his own person, not as village idiot, sex-tormented theological student, or little boy, and his utterance is touched by almost lyrical melancholy – which becomes quite lyrical in the last song, *Nad rekoy* ('On the River').[42] Another Golenishchev-Kutuzov poem *Zabïtïy* ('Forgotten' – inspired by Vereshchagin's painting of a soldier's abandoned body) was set as a 'ballad' in the Glinka-Dargomïzhsky tradition, the same year, and probably suggested the cycle of 'Pesni i plyaski smerti' ('Songs and Dances of Death' – again to Golenishchev's words) composed in 1875. Each of these songs is a grim dramatic scene – the child dying in its mother's arms, Death serenading the sick girl, Death dancing with the drunken peasant who is lost in the snowstorm at night, Death riding over the moonlit battlefield – and

---

[42] A poem which Balakirev set twenty years later as *Nad ozerom* ('On the Lake').

these images evoked from Mussorgsky some of his most masterly and subtle music: perfect fusion of verbal sense and musical sense in the vocal line, supported by the most vividly expressive empirical harmony. Last of all, if we except a few unimportant oddments, in 1877 came a group of songs of which one – *Viden'e* ('The Vision') – is by Golenishchev-Kutuzov, the remaining five by Aleksey Tolstoy; they show an astonishing falling-off in creative power. Lyrical arioso predominates, but even the equal-crotchet declamation is stiff and insensitive; the piano parts consist largely of common chords *tremolo*, or even in triplet repetition or broken into simple 'harp' arpeggios. Even *Spes'* ('Pride'), afterwards set by Borodin, failed to produce anything comparable with the earlier comic pieces. In *Gornimi tikho letela dusha nebesami* ('Softly the spirit flew up to heaven') Mussorgsky placed himself in the – for him – very unusual position of inferiority to both Rimsky-Korsakov (Op. 27, No. 1) and Tchaïkovsky (Op. 47, No. 2).

Rubinstein and Tchaïkovsky

Mussorgsky and his friends were, through Glinka and Dargo-mïzhsky, the musical descendants of the dilettanti. In the 1860s a new force began to make itself felt, that of the 'sound professional educa-tion' offered by the newly founded conservatoires of Petersburg and Moscow; yet even the best representatives of the 'conservatoire move-ment' – Anton Rubinstein (1829–94), its head, and Tchaïkovsky (1840–93), its first distinguished product – were notably inferior to the heirs of the dilettanti as song-writers. All too many of Rubinstein's 200 songs show him as merely a highly competent imitator of Mendelssohn or Schumann, with little personality; he set German words with at least as much facility as Russian; indeed his best-known song, *Der Asra*, comes from a collection of Heine pieces, Op. 32. But one set is outstanding in each language: the so-called 'Persian Songs' – 'Zwölf Lieder des Mirza Schaffy aus dem persischen von F. Bodenstedt',[43] Op. 34, surprisingly successful essays in the field of *Ruslan*-like orientalism – and the six 'Basni Krïlova' ('Fables by Krïlov'), an early work, dating from 1851, showing unexpected, if rather heavy-handed, humour.

Tchaïkovsky – whose name it would be both sensible and logical to spell Chaykovsky – cuts a much more important figure, yet only a small proportion of his songs shows him at his best. He possessed a gift invaluable to a song-writer – natural lyricism – but was defective

[43] The later Russian translation was made by Tchaïkovsky.

in an essential one: the sense of the miniature. He tends to be heavy-handed and to inflate; for instance, far too many of his songs are marred by over-long piano preludes and postludes which make no particular point and are often rather clumsily written. (A classic instance is the Apukhtin song, *Den' li tsarit* ('Does the day reign?'), Op. 47, No. 6, which must be much better in its orchestral version of 1888). He was more sensitive to the general mood of a poem than to its details; a key phrase in the words would give him a melodic idea and this would dominate the whole or the greater part of the song (e.g. the Apukhtin *Zabït' tak skoro* ('To forget so soon'), an inflated companion-piece to Dargomïzhsky's *Mne vse ravno*, the Mey *Zachem zhe tï prisnilasya* ('Why did I dream of you?'), Op. 28, No. 3, or the Khomyakov *Vcherashnyaya noch'* ('Last night'), Op. 60, No. 1). Most of his songs are essentially *romances*. He wrote straightforward, melodious *romances* all his life, from the Heine-Mey *Otchego* ('Warum sind dann die Rosen so blass?'), Op. 6, No. 5, of 1869, to *V etu lunnuyu noch'* ('On this moonlit night'), No. 3 of the six D. M. Rathaus songs, Op. 73 (1893); but, as with the later Dargomïzhsky, declamation keeps breaking in, in one form or another, and the majority of Tchaïkovsky's songs might be described as arioso-*romances*. There are several examples of these in the very first published set, Op. 6, notably No. 6, the familiar *Net, tol'ko tot, kto znal* (Mey's version of *Nur wer die Sehnsucht kennt*). *Zabït' tak skoro* is another early example. The Grekov *Ne dolgo nam gulyat'* ('We have not far to walk') (1875), with its curious anticipation of Tatyana's letter song, is a finer one. (Relationships with this central scene of *Onegin* may be detected in several songs of that period, e.g. Op. 38, Nos. 2 and 4 (1878), the D flat passage in the middle of Op. 47, No. 3 (1880).) The well-known *Blagoslovlyayu vas, lesa* ('I bless you, forests'), Op. 47, No. 5, from Aleksey Tolstoy's poem *John of Damascus*, again belongs to this class. In some of the last songs, the Rathaus group, Op. 73, the balance is tipped more than ever on the declamatory side; in No. 6, Tchaïkovsky's last song, the principle of the verbally inspired motto is also carried to an extreme. On the lighter side, the more melodious songs seem to throw back to the serenades and waltz-songs of the 1840s: *Serenada Don Zhuana*, Op. 38, No. 1, *Prostïe slova* ('Simple words'), Op. 60, No. 5, *O, ditya, pod tvoim oknom* ('O child, beneath thy window'), Op. 63, No. 6.

Yet, however much Tchaïkovsky's corpus of song is dominated by the *romance* tradition – and naturally it is nowhere more marked than in the six French songs, Op. 65 (written as late as 1888) – there are many exceptions. The specifically Russian note is sounded in *Kak naladili, durak* ('As they kept on saying, "You fool" '), Op. 25, No. 6; but while Tchaïkovsky anticipates Balakirev in setting Mey's poem *giocoso*, he fails to convey a sense of irony as Balakirev does; it is as if he had read the poem as a straightforward drinking-song. In another Mey song, *Vecher* ('Evening'), Op. 27, No. 4 – one of his translations from the Ukrainian of Shevchenko – the piano part is 'Russian' and pictorial (it is a picture of peasant life) while the voice part is declamatory; the separated planes remind one of the earlier Rimsky-Korsakov. A later Shevchenko poem, this time translated by Surikov, *Ya li v pole da ne travushka* ('Was I not a little blade of grass in the field?'), Op. 47, No. 7, moved Tchaïkovsky as far as he was capable of being moved in the direction of Mussorgsky. Yet, when all is said, his most beautiful song in purely Russian vein is the exquisitely simple *Legenda*, Op. 54, No. 5 ('The Christ-child had a garden').[44]

Legenda is one of a set of '16 Pesen dlya detey' ('Songs for Children'), nearly all composed in 1883 and nearly all with words – original or translated – by A. N. Pleschcheev. Unlike Mussorgsky's *Nursery*, they are intended to be sung to children, some of them by children; as with Schumann's similar pieces, the degree of childishness varies considerably. The Russian note is sounded in several other of the songs: No. 8, *Kukushka* ('The Cuckoo' – one of the best), No. 10, *Kolïbel'naya v buryu* ('Lullaby in a Storm'), No. 16, *Moy Lizochek* ('My Lizzie').

Tchaikovsky seldom shows interest in non-Russian themes; the Mey *Kanareyka* ('The Canary'), Op. 25, No. 4, is one of his few oriental compositions, but *Pimpinella*, Op. 38, No. 6, is a charming Italian song based on one that he had heard sung by an urchin in the streets of Florence.[45] Another unusual type of song is *V temnom ade* ('In dark Hell'), Op. 16, No. 6, one of Maykov's translations from the modern Greek, which is based from beginning to end on the *Dies irae* in either voice or accompaniment. Another powerfully gloomy song, though of quite a different kind, is *Korol'ki* ('The Corals'), Op. 28, No. 2, Mey's translation of a dramatic Polish poem by Syrokomla, the story of a Cossack who brings back from the wars a string of corals for his sweetheart, only to find her dead. It is curious that Tchaïkovsky was so little attracted to the dramatic ballad – though some of his songs, for instance *Blagoslovlyayu vas, lesa*, have the feeling of opera numbers –

---

44 This was the original form of the piece; the popular *a cappella* version was made six years later, in 1889. Tchaïkovsky also orchestrated the accompaniment of the original version.

45 *Perepiska s N. F. von Mekk*, I (Moscow and Leningrad, 1934), p. 222, where the original tune is given.

but in *Korol'ki* he produced one of the finest of all Russian specimens of the genre.

Epigones and Modernists

During the thirty years or so before the Revolution of 1917 a great number of songs were produced by the pupils of Rimsky-Korsakov and Tchaïkovsky, and in turn by their pupils. Confronted by this vast corpus of work by Taneev, Arensky, Lyadov, Glazunov, N. N. Cherepnin,[46] Myaskovsky, Rebikov, Vasilenko, Grechaninov, Rakhmaninov, Medtner and others, one is struck by a certain sameness. Consider the six songs of Glazunov's Op. 59, Taneev's Op. 17, Nos. 8 and 9, Grechaninov's *Na nivï zheltïe* ('Over the yellow cornfields') and *Krinitsa* ('The Well'), Op. 73, No. 2, Rakhmaninov's popular *Siren'* ('Lilac'), Op. 21, No. 5, or his *Son* ('Dream'), Op. 38, No. 5, Medtner's *Den' i noch'* ('Day and Night'), Op. 24, No. 1: they might all be late Rimsky-Korsakov. Despite occasional influences from the contemporary *Lied*, the central place in Russian song was still held by the passionate or elegiac *romance*, the direct descendant through Glinka and Dargomïzhsky, Rimsky-Korsakov and Tchaïkovsky, of the *romances* of the dilettanti – though the arioso variety was by this time predominant. Nor did the other favourite genres lose their popularity: there are still successful lullabies (Cherepnin's Op. 7, No. 6, and Op. 33, No. 9; Grechaninov's Op. 1, No. 5, which laid the foundation of his popularity – like Cherepnin's earlier effort, a setting of the favourite Lermontov words), barcarolles (Glazunov's Op. 60, No. 6; Taneev's Op. 9, No. 1), dance-*romances* (Arensky's *Davno-li pod volshebnïe zvuki* ('Magic sounds'), Glazunov's Op. 60, No. 1, Taneev's Op. 34, No. 3, Medtner's Op. 32, No.5), oriental songs (Glazunov's *V krovi gorit*, Op. 27, No. 2 – a languorous setting instead of the usual passionate treatment – Cherepnin's Hafiz-Fet songs, Op.25, Rakhmaninov's *Ne poy, krasavitsa*, Op. 4, No. 4), and of course many deliberately 'Russian-flavoured songs' even by such composers as Rakhmaninov (Op. 26, Nos. 4 and 14) and Medtner (Op. 24, No. 3; Op. 29, No. 2) whom one does not commonly associate with national tendencies. The ballad or ballad-like song survives in Arensky's *Volki* ('Wolves'), Op. 58, and *Kubok* ('Goblet'), Op. 61, Cherepnin's *Trubnïy glas* (Merezhkovsky's 'Last Trumpet'), Taneev's *Zimniy put'*, Op. 32, No. 4, Medtner's *Vor Gericht* and *Der untreue Knabe* (both settings of Goethe in the original), Op. 15, Nos. 6 and 10, and his fine music for

---

[46] Whose son, A. N. Cherepnin, is also a song-composer.

Pushkin's *Kon'* ('The Horse'), Op. 29, No. 4. Among the later writers of children's songs – Arensky, Cherepnin and the rest – Lyadov and Grechaninov are outstanding. And at the other end of the scale we have Grechaninov's cultivation of the concert aria with orchestra, beginning with his 'musical picture' *Na rasput'i* (a bass setting of Bunin's 'At the Cross-Roads'), Op. 21 (1901). However, one also notes occasional experiments such as Rebikov's 'vocal scenes' for voice and piano, intended to be performed with simple scenery (a study with writing-table, a Chinese room, a snow-covered meadow in the moonlight) usually with another actor who remains mute, or (as in Op. 20, No. 5) speaks, or wordless song in Rakhmaninov's familiar *Vokaliz*, Op. 34, No. 14, Medtner's *Sonata-Vokaliz* and *Suite-Vokaliz*, Op. 41, and Grechaninov's *Polka-Vokaliz* (though the last three are later in date – 1921 and 1933 – than the period we are considering).

The technical level of most of these songs – especially of those specifically mentioned – is generally very high. The highly polished workmanship of the musicians matches that of their favourite poets: at first Pushkin and the 'Parnassians' (Fet, Tyutchev, Aleksey Tolstoy, Polonsky), later the 'Decadents' and Symbolists, Merezhkovsky, his wife Zinaida Hippius, Sollogub, Bryusov, Balmont (particularly his – very free – translations from Shelley), and Vyacheslav Ivanov, later still Bely and Blok. The workmanship may take the form of greater elaboration of detail, as with Medtner and Rakhmaninov, or refinement to bare essentials, as in Lyadov's children's songs and Grechaninov's 'Musulmanskiya pesni', Op. 25 (settings of Tatar and Bashkir melodies); the harmony may be luscious or reduced to a limpid sketch. There is considerable variety and much beautiful music within the framework of inherited conventions, but little genuine freshness and no really strong creative personality. The essential conservatism of the harmonic idiom is remarkable. Rebikov's experiments with mildly 'impressionistic' harmony at the beginning of the century do not conceal the poverty of his invention. It is only in the decade immediately preceding the Revolution that we find Myaskovsky employing impressionistic harmonies in his Hippius songs, Op. 4, or Grechaninov turning to the idiom of Skryabin in his cycle 'Ad astra', Op. 54 (1911), only to drop it again soon afterwards.

The 'real song-writers' who stand out from the crowd of those who 'also wrote songs' are Grechaninov (1864–1956), Rakhmaninov (1873–1943), and Medtner (1880–1951). (Perhaps one should add Taneev.) Grechaninov's songs were undoubtedly the most important part of his work and they cover a wide range: the already mentioned children's songs (from Op. 31 in 1903 to Op. 122 in 1929) and concert arias, settings of four Krïlov fables, Op. 33 (done with delightful humour) and five of Baudelaire's *Fleurs du mal*, Op. 48, arrangements of Scottish songs, Belo-Russian songs, Tatar and Bashkir songs. But the majority are *romances*.

The *romance* completely predominates in the work of Rakhmaninov and Medtner. Both were first and foremost piano-composers; like Tchaïkovsky – from whom they derive, through Taneev – they usually write heavily overloaded piano parts, with protracted epilogues, though their piano writing is far more beautifully polished (and far more difficult) than Tchaïkovsky's and their epilogues are better justified. Medtner's most overpowering piano parts occur in his earlier German songs of 1907–10; he set Goethe, Heine and Nietzsche in the original and his treatment of Heine's *Ein Fichtenbaum steht einsam*, Op. 12, No. 2, and Goethe's *Bei dem Glanze der Abendröte*, Op. 18, No. 2, provides two classic examples of what one can only call 'over-composition'. But Medtner, though often accused of being a German at heart, was really happier with Russian poems and it is interesting to observe how at the same period, confronted with Bely's *Epitafiya*, Op. 13, No. 2, he writes not a Russian *Lied* but a *romance*; indeed he even sets Goethe's *Nähe des Geliebten* in a *romance*-like vein (Op. 15, No. 9), though with a close integration of voice and accompaniment rather rare in Russian song. And when he turns in Opp. 24 and 28 to his beloved Fet and Tyutchev and in Opp. 29 and 32 to Pushkin, he is in perfect sympathy with his poets; there is much more restraint, much less overloading of the piano part; these four sets of 1912–14 contain some of his best work. Such Fet songs as *Shopot, robkoe dïkhan'e* ('A whisper, a timid breathing'), Op. 24, No. 7, *Ne mogu ya slïshat' etoy ptichki* ('I cannot listen to this bird'), Op. 28, No. 2, and *Babochka* ('The Butterfly'), Op. 28, No. 3, are the perfect counterparts of the 'Parnassian' poems. And the opening of the Pushkin *Roza*,[47] Op. 29, No. 6, must be quoted to show how beautiful, and how Russian, Medtner can be in extreme simplicity (see Ex. 9).

Rakhmaninov, with all his lyrical *élan*, never achieved anything as exquisite as the best of Medtner's songs though his last set, the six songs by Symbolist poets, Op. 38 (1916), shows him breaking away from his over-rich euphony; the first song, in particular, the Blok *Noch'yu v sadu u menya* ('At night in my garden') is almost Skryabin-

[47] Cf. Glinka's setting, quoted as Ex. 5.

esque in its harmony and its compression – but Skryabinesque like early Skryabin, and Skryabin was already dead.

It is only when one measures them against this beautiful, belated Parnassianism and this belated modernism, that one realizes how shocking the early songs of Stravinsky (b. 1882) and Prokofiev (1891–1953) must have sounded. They are not very important, these Gorodetsky, Verlaine and Balmont songs of Stravinsky's nonage (1907–11). (He also anticipated Rakhmaninov and Medtner in his wordless *Pastoral* of 1908.) Even the still earlier Pushkin 'Favn i Pastushka' ('Faun and Shepherdess') songs with orchestra show talent, and Opp. 6 and 9, with all their obvious debts to Rimsky-Korsakov and Debussy and Mussorgsky, sound far fresher and more individual when set against the background of the contemporary Russian song than when considered simply on their merits. As for the 'Tri stikhotvoreniya iz yaponskoy liriki' ('Three Japanese Lyrics') or the 'Tri pesenki (iz vospominaniy yunosheskikh godov)' ('Three Little Songs, from memories of my childhood'), sophisticated and naïve respectively (1912–13), they could have been written at that date by no one but Stravinsky. The 'Japanese Lyrics' were originally accompanied by an instrumental ensemble (though there is an alternative version with piano), and Stravinsky followed this track further in the 'Pribautki' ('Facetiae') of 1914 and 'Koshach'i kolïbel'nïe pesni' ('Cat's Lullabies') of 1915–16. With these, and the 'Tri istorii dlya detey, ('Three Stories for Children'), with piano, he disappears from the history of Russian song.

The early songs of Prokofiev – of which the most important is *Gadkiy utenok*, Op. 18 – a setting of a cut version of Hans Andersen's 'Ugly Duckling' in prose, made in 1914 – are more straightforward, more diatonic and more euphonious than Stravinský's. Such a typical passage of early Prokofiev as this from *The Ugly Duckling*:

'It would be too heartrending to tell of the hardships he
had to put up with that winter.'

is a long way indeed from the Parnassian *romance* but not really so very far from Mussorgsky.

Soviet Song

After the Revolution, some Russian composers settled abroad, others accepted the new régime. The émigrés continued in their chosen paths and most of them found nothing new on them; the one who continued to develop – Stravinsky – ceased to write songs. But Prokofiev returned to the U.S.S.R., first as a visitor and then permanently, and a glance at his choice of poets before and after his return will be illuminating. Of his early songs, Opp. 9, 18, 23 and 27 (composed 1910–16) and the two sets written in exile, Opp. 35[48] and 36 (composed 1920–1), the majority are settings of Balmont and Anna Akhmatova (one of the 'Perfectionists' who reacted against Symbolism). Those written after his return, Opp. 66, 68, 73, 79, and 121 (1935–50), are (with three exceptions) settings of Soviet poets or popular texts glorifying partisans or Voroshilov or Stakhanov, or on similar themes. Op. 68 are children's songs. The three exceptions are the three Pushkin

48 The five songs of Op. 35 are wordless. The Russian interest in wordless song reached its climax in Glière's two-movement Concerto for coloratura soprano and orchestra, Op. 82 (comp. 1943).

settings, Op. 73, published in 1937 in a Pushkin centennial volume.[49] A similar change occurs in the songs of Prokofiev's older friend Myaskovsky (1881–1950), who never emigrated; Opp. 1, 4, 7, 8 and 16 (1907–14) consist mostly of settings of Hippius, Balmont and Vyacheslav Ivanov; after the Revolution, during 1921–25, came Opp. 20, 21 and 22[50] on Blok, Tyutchev and Delvig; then after a ten-year gap in Myaskovsky's song-writing, the twelve Lermontov songs of Op. 40 (composed 1935–6), two sets, Op. 45 and 52 (1938 and 1940), mostly to words by the Soviet poet Stepan Shchipachev, and various songs without opus-number addressed to Stalin, Romain Rolland, the Soviet Polar explorers, and 'a young warrior'.

The critical change in Soviet music generally, particularly marked in the field of solo song, occurred during the period 1930–34; the firm dividing line was drawn by the pronouncement of the Central Committee of the Communist Party on literature and all the arts in April 1932. Until then, beside the work of such minor conservative talents as Glière and Ippolitov-Ivanov, a good deal of mild modernism – mostly watered-down Skryabin (as in the songs of Alexander Krein) – had flourished under the aegis of A.S.M. (Association for Contemporary Music) (1924–31). The Symbolist poets were still in favour, with lyrics from the Japanese and translations of Sappho. Myaskovsky's Opp. 20–22 belong to this phase. The more pronounced modernist Mossolov even composed in 1926 a cycle of 'Gazetnïe obyavleniya' ('Newspaper Advertisements' – including one *How to get rid of corns*). It is true that there was bitter opposition from R.A.P.M. (Association of Proletarian Musicians) which was against both modernism and the classics, indeed all manifestations of lyricism, and wished composers to abandon the *romance* altogether for the 'mass song' (unison with piano). But both these points of view were swept aside by the pronouncement of 1932. The classics were to be revered, but modernism and all forms of 'subjectivism' or abstract 'formalism' were taboo; 'Socialist realism' was demanded and – despite the very varied definitions officially accepted at different periods – has been demanded ever since. 'Modernism' was not difficult to get rid of; it had never struck very deep roots in Russia; but 'subjectivism' was a different matter, particularly in the field of solo song. Such composers as Myaskovsky found great difficulty in re-orientating themselves and writing simply

[49] *A. S. Pushkin v romansakh i pesnyakh sovetskikh kompozitorov.*
[50] The opus number 22 was originally given to another Hippius set which the composer later suppressed as too modern in idiom.

and 'naturally' enough; some took refuge in the making of folk-song
arrangements, an art in which every generation of Russian composers
from that of Balakirev and Rimsky-Korsakov onward has excelled,
turning not only to Russian songs but to those of the Eastern peoples of
the Soviet Union and to those of Western Europe, English and
Scottish ones always being favourites. Some important composers of
the younger generation – Shostakovich, Khachaturyan, Kabalevsky,
Shebalin, Dzerzhinsky, Khrennikov – have written comparatively
few songs, though most of them paid dutiful tribute to Pushkin (e.g.
Shostakovich's Op. 46 and Khrennikov's Op. 6) just before the centenary
of his death.

On the other hand, the former R.A.P.M. composer Koval (b. 1907)
now found it possible to publish a 'Pervaya tetrad' liriki' (First Book of
Lyrics) in 1934 and actually composed Pushkin ('Pushkiniana', 1932–4)
as well as Nekrassov. It is true that Koval avoided the familiar lyrics
and chose poems that reflect Pushkin's conflict with his environment –
Tak, polden' moy nastal ('So, my noonday hour has struck'), *V Sibir'*
('In Siberia'), and others – and he set them in a rather dry declamatory
style that reminds one of Dargomïzhsky; moreover, the ten songs are
linked by excerpts from Pushkin's diaries and letters which are intended
to be read as a part of the performance.

Much more conventional, but musically much finer, are the
Pushkin songs of Shaporin (b. 1889), a natural conservative. In his
Op. 10 (published in 1937, though some of the songs were written
much earlier) Shaporin was not afraid to turn to such a favourite poem
as *Zaklinanie* ('Evocation'), already composed by Rimsky-Korsakov,
Cui and Medtner, set it to such music as they might have written –
though his melody is actually rather Tchaïkovskian – and (as it happens) surpass all three. So with his cycle of ten Blok songs, 'Dalekaya
yunost' ('Far-off Youth'); they are old-fashioned *romances*, two of them
waltz-*romances*, the music of an epigone but sensitive, beautifully
fashioned music. The same may be said of the Blok and Essenin songs
of Nechaev (b. 1895), who has put the best of himself into his songs.
In other cases, striving for simplicity and 'objectivity' led to unfortunate results. Boris Asafiev, known as historian and critic under the
pseudonym 'Igor Glebov', published a cycle entitled 'Liricheskie
Stranitsi (na temu "Odinochestvo Lermontova")' ('Lyrical Pages, on
the theme of Lermontov's solitude'), in which he took nine of the most
popular of Lermontov's lyrics – *Nochevala tuchka zolotaya*, *Tuchki
nebesnïe* and the rest – and set them to music of incredible feebleness.

The first song, *Solntse* ('Sunshine'), is given the sort of arpeggio accompaniment that nearly died with Glinka; one might imagine that one of the early nineteenth-century dilettanti had come to life again or that the musicologist 'Glebov' was trying his hand at pastiche or parody or leg-pull. But Asafiev was never a very strong creative talent; Myaskovsky, on the other hand, was one of the best of the older composers of the U.S.S.R., a master of his craft, yet his simple and 'objective' treatment of the same poem (Op. 40, No. 5) is, if anything, still more banal:

'How beautiful is the winter sunshine when, breaking through grey clouds, it vainly throws a pale ray on the white snow!'

To try to bridge the gap that separates the modern composer from the modern listener is praiseworthy, but such art as this is not a bridge but a *cul-de-sac*, unworthy of the great tradition of Russian song.

Scandinavia and Finland

PHILIP RADCLIFFE

THROUGHOUT the eighteenth century, the mainstream of European music included a blend of Latin and Teutonic elements which in the works of the greatest composers were so subtly blended as to be hardly separable from each other. But in the nineteenth century composers began to be more conscious both of their own personalities and of their nationalities, both of which were probably intensified by an increasingly vivid response to literature. At the beginning of this century the music of Finland and the Scandinavian countries was simple and unpretentious, showing no influence of the more ambitious developments from that of other European countries; gradually, as the century proceeded, composers acquired more contact with those of other lands, especially Germany. When the music of a country has for a long time been submerged by foreign influences, as was the case with England during the eighteenth and nineteenth centuries, a certain amount of rather self-conscious nationalism may be necessary in order to instil some real individuality into the music. But in the case of Finland and Scandinavia at the beginning of the nineteenth century, it was the contact with other countries that was necessary to enhance the vitality of their music, and to prevent it from being too parochial.

All the Scandinavian countries produced a large mass of popular music; that of Norway was probably the most distinguished, but all three were responsible for simple dance-tunes of great vitality and charm; the following Swedish tune (Ex. 1) is the obvious ancestor of

Ex. 1

many of Grieg's themes. It was a short step from these to the simple songs of the Swedish composers Olof Åhlström (1756–1838) and Adolf Lindblad (1801–1878), which were sung by Jenny Lind. But in neither Sweden nor Denmark has the solo song been more than a pleasant and unpretentious bypath. In Sweden composers such as Franz Berwald (1796–1868), Emil Sjögren (1853–1918), Dag Wiren (b. 1905), and Lars-Erik Larsson (b. 1908) have been more productive of instrumental than of vocal music; others, such as Hilding Rosenberg (b. 1892), have written choral and dramatic works, but the strophic song, or *romance*, has for the most part remained demurely in the background. The same can be said of Denmark, though, for obvious geographical reasons, Danish composers came more quickly into contact with German music than those of the other Scandinavian countries. Niels Gade studied in Leipzig and his style combines a generally Mendelssohnian or Schumannesque manner with touches of a mildly Northern colour.

His songs are of less interest and more conventional than the best of his instrumental works; sometimes, as in *Der Spielmann*, a touch of Scandinavian bleakness enlivens the generally rather colourless idiom. Peter Lange-Müller (1850–1926), was a more prolific and more distinctive song-writer, covering a wider range in his songs and with a far more flexible vocabulary. Some of his most familiar songs, such as *Die Heiligen drei Könige* are simple and homely, but he was also a composer of opera, and in some of his songs, such as *Der Kossak*, *Der Hüne*, and *Der Ostwind*, there is considerable power and originality and sense of atmosphere. Melodically his songs are usually simple and straightforward, but the harmony, though never startling, is often picturesque and unexpected. But in the works of later Danish composers song has not played an important part. Carl Nielsen (1865–1931) was a musician of great independence but his songs, though very popular in their native land, have never had the wide recognition achieved by his strangely original instrumental works. Knud Jeppesen, a pupil of Nielsen, has been polyphonic rather than lyrical in his approach to composition, and Vagn Holmboe, the most distinguished of the later Danish composers, has written more instrumental than vocal music, and solo song has not played much part in his output.

In Norway the development of solo song has been far more significant, both in quantity and quality, and it has had the stimulus of a very rich inheritance of folk-song. The earliest composer of importance was Halfdan Kjerulf (1815–1868), who was a friend of Gade and studied at Leipzig. His style varies: when setting German words it is in an agreeably Schumannesque vein. His setting of Geibel's *Sehnsucht* is an attractive instance, and his *Vöglein, wohin so schnell?*, by the same poet, has considerably more vitality than the rather dull and tentative setting by Franz. But his music is more original and distinctive when he sets words by Björnson. *Synnove's Song*, with its curious, humming refrain, is strongly prophetic of Grieg in his more rhapsodic moods, and although the two composers' settings of the well-known ballad *The Princess* are remarkably similar, Kjerulf's

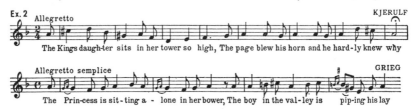

tune has not quite the continuity of Grieg's. He also set some translations from Spanish poems; *Spanische Romanze* makes no attempt at local colour, but has considerable passion. There is a setting of Moore's *Go where glory waits thee* which is more conventional, but finely sustained. Most of his songs are strophic, but some have freer designs, and there are occasional surprises, such as the curious, enigmatic close of *Tauschung*. Kjerulf's style is sometimes commonplace, but his songs on the whole deserve to be more widely known than they are at present.

Those of Grieg, on the other hand, contain much that is extremely familiar, but still more that is inadequately known. From the first he was influenced by some of Kjerulf's Norwegian songs, by the simple folk-like songs of his friend and contemporary Nordraak, and – most of all – by Norwegian folk-song. But his approach to it was highly personal, laying particular stress on certain melodic turns of phrase that attracted him, and which appear more frequently in his own tunes than in the folk-music from which they were derived. Grieg also had a great admiration for Mozart's chromaticism, both harmonic and melodic, especially the opening of the String Quintet in G minor, and traces of this are apt to appear in his work. But, though Grieg's melody is sometimes mannered and is usually rather short-breathed, it has great vitality and charm, which is increased by the pleasantly informal way in which it is presented. Harmonically his music has great individuality, resulting from sudden and vivid modulations to remote keys, and the use of such chords as the dominant ninth and thirteenth in unexpected contexts, often without their normal resolutions; sometimes he dwells sensuously on a pleasant sound for its own sake in a manner prophetic of Delius and Debussy.

His approach to song-writing, as to all kinds of composition, was essentially that of a miniaturist, and he was not concerned with enlarging the formal aspect of the solo song; a surprisingly high proportion of his songs are in simple strophic form. But the emotional content is decidedly varied, especially among the later songs. His settings of German words, unlike those of Kjerulf, do not differ in idiom from the others, and they include some that are thoroughly characteristic, such as *Ein Traum*, but he was more deeply and subtly inspired by Scandinavian poetry. His familiar lyrical manner is seen at its best in the two songs from Op. 33 that he himself afterwards arranged for strings; *Spring* and *The Wounded Heart*. They are both very simple in rhythmic outline, but with much beauty of melody and harmonic detail. Equally successful in its much more concentrated, half-rhapsodical manner is *A Swan*. *The first Meeting* contains one of his favourite melodic finger-prints in the passage describing the horns, and the chromaticism of *With a Waterlily* is particularly characteristic. He was able to use a very simple language to express deep emotion, as in the very beautiful *To Norway*, but in some of the latest songs there is remarkable harmonic variety. *Eros* is a rather unsuccessful attempt at a grandiose Wagnerian manner, but *Rock, oh Wave* has a fine Romantic sweep, and *There cried a Bird*, on the other hand, is impressively bleak and sinister, ending in mid-air on a dissonance. The 'Haugtussa' cycle was a special favourite of the composer; all but two of the songs are strophic, but they have a remarkable intensity and the last song has something of the same resigned pathos of the end of Schubert's 'Die Schöne Müllerin'. The informality of Grieg's songs conceals a very independent and imaginative personality, far more distinguished than that of his Norwegian contemporaries. The songs of Svendsen are pleasant but far more conventional; those of Sinding have more character and include an admirably sardonic setting of Holty's

Totengräberlied, but his setting of *There cried a Bird* falls a long way behind that of Grieg in imaginativeness. It is difficult to predict the future development of song in Norway; at the moment there seems to be no connecting link between the traditionalists at the one end and the atonal style of Fartein Valen at the other.

In Finland, Sibelius is the first composer of importance but his songs are not among his most characteristic works. Sometimes the idiom of the music suggests Grieg, but in general the two composers approached music from widely different angles, Sibelius being not, like Grieg, a natural miniaturist, but a symphonic writer who only occasionally, as in some of the theatre music and the three Sonatinas for piano, was able to express himself with complete individuality on a small scale. In more relaxed works he was always liable to fall into a rather conventional kind of prettiness, and this could happen throughout his life, whether in an early song like *Black Roses* or in the flower-songs of Op. 88. Sometimes, especially in some of the Runeberg songs, Op. 13, the piano writing is turgid, and too suggestive of an orchestral transcription. But among Sibelius's songs there are, inevitably, some that are really fine and characteristic; in such songs as *In the field a Maiden sits* (Ex. 3) from Op. 50, and *The Tree*, from Op. 57, he is able

Ex. 3

Lento assai

und im-mer noch so ei-gen   tönt fern das trau-ri-ge Lied

pp

to compress into a small space something of the sombre, brooding atmosphere that is characteristic of so much of his finest work.

His vocal writing at his best has the austere strength and simplicity that find fuller expression in his great instrumental works. Of the younger Finnish composers Palmgren and Järnefelt have both written songs, though more as a sideline than as an essential part of their output. On the other hand, Yrjö Kilpinen (b. 1892) has concentrated more on song-writing than on any other form of composition, and produced a very large amount. He has set a great variety of words, including much German poetry, and he has always shown great literary sensitiveness and musical versatility. In all these points he shows kinship with Wolf, whom he also resembles at times in his declamation of words. His texture, however, is less elaborate; in quite a number of songs the piano part is definitely an accompaniment, and sometimes, especially in the 'Songs of Death', Op. 62, he is aiming at the stark directness of Mussorgsky. As a song-writer he has many admirable qualities, though behind them there may seem to be a lack of strongly defined personality. Finland so far has shown less interest in the most provocative developments of contemporary music than the Scandinavian countries and perhaps, for this reason, song, the most direct of all musical forms, may flourish there all the more.

Spain

GILBERT CHASE

THE great age of Spanish song was in the sixteenth century. Solo art song with instrumental accompaniment, while somewhat rudimentary as an art form, was cultivated with skill and expressiveness by such musicians as Luis Milán, Luis de Narváez, Alonso de Mudarra, Miguel de Fuenllana, and Esteban Daza, whose books in tablature for *vihuela* were printed during that century. These composers, with their settings of the finest Spanish lyrical poetry of the period, produced, in the words of Paul Henry Lang, 'a musical art of such grace and finish as elevates Spain among the leading musical nations of the Renaissance.'

Comparatively little, on the other hand, is known of Spanish vocal music in the seventeenth century. Most of the collections that have been preserved from this period consist of polyphonic songs, for three or four voices, such as the *Romances y Letras a tres vozes*, dating from the first half of the seventeenth century.[1] Occasionally in these collections one finds songs for a single voice, but they are the exception rather than the rule. Among the more important collections are the *Libro de Tonos Humanos* (a manuscript in the National Library of Madrid, dated 1655), containing over 200 songs by such composers as Mateo Romero, Carlos Patiño, and Francisco Navarro; the *Cancionero de Sablonara* (Staatsbibliothek, Munich), which was transcribed and edited by Jesús Aroca

---

[1] Recently transcribed by Miguel Querol and published by the Spanish Institute of Musicology in Barcelona (1956).

(Madrid, 1916); and the *Tonos Castellanos* in the Library of the Dukes of Medinaceli in Madrid, which includes songs by Juan Blas de Castro, Francisco Gutierrez, and Gabriel Díaz. To these may be added a manuscript of Spanish songs in the library of San Marco in Venice (Codex Girolamo Contarini) containing twenty-five compositions for one voice with basso continuo.

Rafael Mitjana, the pioneer historian of Spanish music, rightly observes that, in contrast to Italian secular music of the seventeenth century, Spanish vocal music of this period is characterized by the relatively little prominence given to the factor of virtuosity. Ornaments are used sparingly, the mordent being the most common. Simplicity and expressiveness, with strong reliance on popular tradition, remain the distinguishing traits of this music. Mitjana cites as examples the *tonadas* of Manuel de Villaflor and Sebastián Durón, and the *solos humanos* (secular songs, as distinct from the religious, which were called *tonos divinos*) of Juan de Navas, especially *Buscaba el Amor* and *Desde el tronco esquivo*. Herewith is a portion of the latter song, as transcribed by Mitjana:

Mitjana draws attention to what he terms 'the eminently national character' of this song, finding it to be an artistic transformation of a very old type of Spanish folk-song called the *petenera*.

One of the most important song composers of the seventeenth century was José Marín (1619–99), of whom there are extant some sixty songs, including *solos humanos*, *tonadas*, and *pasacalles* with guitar accompaniment. His tonada *Así moriré* (Thus I shall die) was published by Felipe Pedrell.[2] Marín was such a character as might have stepped out of a picaresque novel, for he combined a career as composer and church singer with highway robbery and murder. He was condemned to the galleys but managed to escape; the last years of his life were exemplary. His best-known song, *Corazón que en prisión* (Poor imprisoned heart), is an admirably expressive lament; while another song, *Desengañémonos ya* (Let us now be undeceived) is, in the words of Joaquín Nin, 'of an astonishing purity and grace'. Most of Marín's songs remain in manuscript in the National Library of Madrid.

Among the composers whose lives spanned the closing decades of the seventeenth century and the first half of the eighteenth, the most notable were Sebastián Durón (d. 1716), who from 1691 was Master of the Chapel Royal in Madrid; and Antonio Literes (*c.* 1680–*c.* 1755). Following the general practice of the period, both of them wrote music for the theatre as well as for the church. There is an anecdote that the King once asked Durón why things went so much better when he conducted in the theatre than when he conducted in church. To which the musician replied, 'Sire, that is because in the theatre it is the devil who leads the musicians, while in the church I have to do it myself.' The music of Durón is characterized by its rhythmic complexity, revealing the influence of Spanish folk-song. One of his songs in neo-classical vein, *Cloris Hermosa* (Lovely Chloris) was published by Nin in *Classiques Espagnols du Chant*. Also in that collection is an aria by Literes, *Confiado Jilguerito* ('Confiding little finch'), from the zaruela entitled *Acis y Galatea*, produced at the Royal Palace, Madrid, in 1707.

From the seventeenth to the nineteenth centuries, one can scarcely speak of Spanish secular vocal music apart from the theatre. From the earliest times, music figures prominently in the Spanish theatre (as in the delightful eclogues of Juan del Encina), intervening chiefly in the form of incidental songs and dances, and before long there was a great proliferation of minor theatrical forms, such as the *jácara*, the *entremés*, and the *mojiganga*, in which music predominated. The principal musico-dramatic form was the *zarzuela*, which began as an aristocratic courtly entertainment in the seventeenth century and during the

[2] In Volume IV of *Teatro Lírico Español*.

nineteenth century was transformed into a kind of operetta with wide popular appeal.

Thus the solo art-song in Spain did not have a continuous development following its auspicious beginnings in the sixteenth century. When composers were not writing for the church or the theatre (which was very seldom), they generally turned to instrumental music, as in the delightful keyboard sonatas composed by Padre Antonio Soler in the eighteenth century. During the nineteenth century, when the art-song was at the height of its development in certain other countries, vocal music in Spain was almost entirely concentrated either on Italianate opera or on the popular forms of lyric theatre, such as the *zarzuela* and the *tonadilla*. Not until the twentieth century does the solo art-song once more begin to occupy an important place in Spanish musical composition, and it is certainly not without significance that contemporary song-writers, both in their choice of texts and in their musical settings, have frequently returned to the 'Golden Age' of Spanish poetry and song, which flourished so gloriously in the sixteenth century.

With this background in mind, the reader will not be surprised to learn that the majority of Spanish songs that have come down to us from the seventeenth and eighteenth centuries are detached from musico-theatrical forms of one kind or another, chiefly the *zarzuela* and the *tonadilla*. The key word in the foregoing sentence is 'detached', for the theatrical works in which they first appeared are of purely historical interest, with little or no chance of ever being revived on the stage; whereas as the songs themselves, freed from their obsolete theatrical setting, are capable of enjoying an independent and lasting life. Yet it must be confessed that most of these songs would still be buried in archives, or available only in erudite volumes, were it not for the initiative of that remarkable explorer and 'restorer' of early Spanish music, the pianist and composer Joaquín Nin (1879–1949).

In 1926, in Paris, Nin published, with a long historical introduction, his collection of 'Quatorze Airs Anciens d'Auteurs Espagnols' (also known as 'Classiques Espagnols du Chant'), beginning with composers of the late seventeenth century, such as Marín and Durón, and continuing with excepts from some of the more famous composers of tonadillas, such as Literes, Pablo Esteve, and Blas de Laserna. Each song is provided with a complete piano accompaniment that endeavours to recreate the atmosphere in which the tonadillas were originally performed; yet this is accomplished with extraordinary sensibility and artistry, and without a trace of pedantry. It is thanks above all to this

385

collection, which has been a boon to concert singers and their accompanists, that the music with which this chapter is concerned has not remained of purely historical interest, but for more than a quarter of a century has taken its place in the musical activity of our times.

During the eighteenth century, zarzuelas continued to be written, with music by such distinguished composers as José de Nebra (d. 1768) and Antonio Rodriguez de Hita (d. 1787). Before the end of the century, however, the zarzuela was eclipsed in part by the rising tide of Italian opera, and in part by the development of a new and more popular form of the Spanish lyric theatre, known as the *tonadilla*. This term is derived from *tonada*, one of the generic Spanish terms for song, of which it is actually the diminutive form. At first the *tonadilla* was simply a 'little song' interpolated in one of the musical interludes or entertainments, such as the *jácara*, the *entremés*, or *sainete*, that abounded in the Spanish theatre. When these tonadillas began to be sung by two characters in dialogue, they contained the nucleus of a minor theatrical form that was to take shape rapidly from about 1750 onwards, a sort of Spanish counterpart of the German *Singspiel* or the French vaudeville, but with a character completely *sui generis*. The *tonadilla* was always topical and frequently satirical, and dealt generally with popular types, such as the *majos* and *majas* (swashbuckling gallants and their 'lady friends') so often depicted in the tapestries and paintings of Goya. They were usually written for three or four persons and lasted about twenty minutes at the most. They were produced in great quantity and had an ephemeral existence. Some 2,000 works of this type are preserved in manuscript in the National Library of Madrid. The composers who wrote the music for these pieces had to work rapidly in order to meet the incessant demand for new material. They were employed by the theatres and had to supervise and direct the performances as well as write the music. No wonder that their manuscripts contain only the vocal parts completely written out, while the accompaniments, confided to a small orchestra, are indicated in a very summary fashion.

The first noteworthy composer of tonadillas was Luis Misón (d. 1766), who wrote about eighty works in this form. The tonadilla reached its apogee from about 1770 to 1790, during which period the leading composers were Pablo Esteve (d. *c.* 1792) and Blas de Laserna (1751–1816). The latter wrote over 600 works of this type, while Esteve wrote about 400. Nin published two strongly contrasting songs by Esteve; one, of definitely national and popular flavour, is a *Jota*

(Spanish regional dance of vigorous character) from the tonadilla entitled *Los Pasages de Verano* (Madrid, 1779); the other, composed according to the Italian taste, is *Alma, sintamos* ('Suffer, my soul'), a mock-pathetic lament for the feigned death of the immensely popular singer María Antonia Fernández, better known as 'La Caramba' (actually, she had simply run off with a French lover, leaving her company and her leading man in the lurch). These two songs reveal clearly the two poles of attraction between which the tonadilla fluctuated: on the one hand, it was closely linked to national-popular sources, and on the other it could scarcely evade the powerful Italian influence that flooded the Spanish lyric theatre during the eighteenth century and part of the nineteenth. There was also a certain French influence, less important, but not negligible.

Withal, the tonadilla brought the definite emergence and diffusion of what has come to be known as 'the Spanish idiom' in music, and which in turn has exerted its fascination upon so many foreign composers, from Glinka and Bizet to Debussy and Ravel. Certain songs from the tonadilla repertory became extremely popular, detached themselves as independent songs, and circulated widely both in their original form and in arrangements or paraphrases by prominent composers. Such, for example, was the case with the *Tirana del Tripili* by Blas de Laserna, which the Italian composer Mercadente intercalated in his opera *I Due Figaro* (1835), thus making it known all over Europe (the *tirana* is a lively Spanish dance in triple time). Later, it was used by Granados in his suite *Goyescas* for piano and in his opera of the same title (1916). Eliminating the instrumental prelude and coda, the *Tirana del Tripili* consists of the classical *copla* (stanza) and *estribillo* (refrain), the latter remaining invariable while the words of the copla were varied ad infinitum. Here is the melody as transcribed by Subirá from the manuscript in the Municipal Library of Madrid:

Ex. 2

COPLA

La ti - ra - ni - lla en el dí - a es lo que más gus-to da___

Don-de esté este so - ne - ti - llo to-dos se pue-den ca - llar.

ESTRIBILLO

Con el trí-pi - li trí-pi-li trá-pa-la la ti - ra-na se can-tay se bai - la,___

An-da, chi-qui-lla! Da-le con gra-cia, que me ro-bas el al-ma!

As Subirá points out, this melody reveals certain traits that are characteristic of the tonadilla. First, the predominance of an iambic foot (short–long) in the concluding notes, corresponding to a feminine cadence; second, a melodic structure abounding in disjunct intervals based on chordal formation; third, an ornamental tendency that transforms some melodic notes into triplets (this is very common in Spanish songs of all kinds).

Nin had an evident predilection for Laserna, as demonstrated by his inclusion of no less than five songs by this composer in his collection of Old Spanish Airs. Four of these belong to what he calls the 'picaresque' type, with strong popular and topical flavour. In addition to the *Tirana del Tripili*, this group of picaresque songs comprises *Por colación seis abates* ('For their collation, six abbots'), *Las Majas de Paris* ('The "Majas" of Paris'), and *Las Majas Madrileñas* ('The "Majas" of Madrid'), this last being in the form of a *seguidilla*. In contrast to these is another song by Laserna, in the Italianate manner, titled *El jilguerito con pico de oro* ('The Finch with the golden beak'), with its imitative trills, for which Nin has provided a rather elaborate but highly appropriate piano accompaniment.

After 1790 the vogue of the tonadilla began to decline, and after the Napoleonic invasion of Spain in 1810 it soon disappeared. During the twilight of the tonadilla, a name appeared on the scene that was to become famous in the history of Spanish song: that of Manuel García. In 1798 he arrived in Madrid from Cádiz with his wife, the dancer and singer Manuela de Morales, and produced his *tonadilla a duo* called *El Majo y la Maja*, in which he exploited the Andalusian popular songs and dances that were later to figure so prominently in Spanish music. García soon turned to writing operettas, such as *El Poeta Calculista* (The Calculating Poet) and *El Contrabandista* (The Smuggler). The former contains a *polo* – a type of Andalusian popular song – which, like the *Tirana del Tripili*, enjoyed wide and continuous popularity for several generations. Bizet took some of the principal themes for his opera *Carmen* from García's *polo*, which he found in a collection titled *Echos d'Espagne* published at Paris in 1872.

The Nineteenth Century

During the first half of the nineteenth century, the Italian influence was completely dominant in Spanish singing and vocal composition. The Royal Conservatory of Music in Madrid was founded in 1830 under the auspices of the Italian-born Queen María Cristina and with an

Italian, Francesco Piermarini, at its head; all instruction in singing and declamation was given in Italian. Towards the middle of the century a group of young composers began to write *zarzuelas* with Spanish texts and often with marked national character, especially in those of Francisco Asenjo Barbieri (1823–94), who was also a leader in making known the musical treasures of the Spanish Renaissance. It was he who discovered and published the *Cancionero del Palacio*, from the time of Ferdinand and Isabella.[3] Thereafter, the *zarzuela* continued to enjoy enormous favour in Spain and to employ the talents of that country's leading composers, at least until the advent of the modern 'national' movement, initiated by Pedrell, when composers such as Albéniz, Granados, Falla, and Turina, turned to more serious forms of music while continuing to draw on the wealth of Spain's traditional folk-song and dance.

To trace the history of the modern *zarzuela* lies outside the scope of this chapter; while in earlier times the distinction between 'popular' and 'art' music could not always be rigidly drawn, in more recent times the distinction, and the gulf separating the two types of music, become ever more apparent; so that the zarzuela, in spite of some attempts to approach the status of serious opera, remains essentially a popular type of musico-theatrical entertainment. As such, its bearing upon the history of art-song in Spain is entirely peripheral; and it needs to be mentioned chiefly to explain what the majority of Spanish composers were busy with while the symphony, the opera, the various types of chamber music and the art-song, were being developed in other countries. In short, with a few exceptions, such as that of the gifted and short-lived Juan Crisóstomo Arriaga (1806–26), and the ambitious but not entirely successful Felipe Pedrell (who set to music some poems from Victor Hugo's *Les Orientales* and from Théophile Gautier's *Consolations*), almost the whole of the nineteenth century is rather arid as far as the history of art-song is concerned. In view of the paucity of available material, and of Pedrell's great prestige as a precursor of the modern revival of Spanish music, mention may be made here of his various published songs, while admonishing the reader that they are more noteworthy for their historical interest rather than their artistic value. The 'Canciones Arabescas' consist of six songs with Spanish text. The collection titled 'Intimas',[4] comprises twelve songs, some with texts in French, some with texts in Catalan, and others with texts in both languages. The songs of 'Noches de España' (Op. 16 and Op. 46) have Spanish

---

[3] See pp. 71–73.   [4] Published by Manuel Salvat, Barcelona.

texts.The 'Orientales' (Op. 73, Op. 74, and Op. 79) consist of twelve songs to French texts by Victor Hugo.[5] Pedrell also published, under the pseudonym of F. Peláez, a collection of 'Cantos Andaluces' for voice and piano, consisting of arrangements of Andalusian songs in popular style. Of more importance for the history of Spanish music are the four volumes of the 'Cancionero Musical Popular Español' (1918–19), in which Pedrell published a quantity of Spanish vocal music of past centuries.

In the early years of the twentieth century a sort of 'national revival' took place in Spanish music. As already indicated, the precursors of this revival, or renascence, were the scholarly musicians, such as Barbieri and Pedrell, who unearthed the musical treasures of Spain's past while simultaneously drawing upon the wealth of living folk-lore preserved in the popular oral tradition. Among the first composers to follow this direction with success were Isaac Albéniz (1860–1909) and Enrique Granados (1867–1916). The former wrote only a few songs, of relative insignificance (his masterpiece is the suite *Iberia* for piano); but Granados wrote a number of songs, which he called *tonadillas escritas en estilo antiguo* ('tonadillas written in the old style'), that deserve our attention.

Granados wrote twelve tonadillas in all, with texts by his librettist, Fernando Periquet, all evoking the 'majas' and 'majos' of Goya's time, whom the great Spanish painter delighted to depict in his tapestries and canvasses. It should be remembered that for Granados the term tonadilla meant simply a kind of picaresque or romantic song associated with eighteenth-century Madrid; and he thought of it as being accompanied by the guitar, rather than by a small orchestra (as it was in the theatre). Hence his piano accompaniments continually suggest typical guitar figurations. This procedure is especially prominent in the songs titled *El tra la la y el punteado*, *El majo timido*, and *La maja de Goya*. In the last mentioned, the singer is required to recite, *parlando*, a long narrative poem about one of Goya's amorous adventures, while the pianist plays a staccato guitar-like accompaniment; after which the song, properly speaking, begins, *Andantino quasi Allegretto*. A few of the opening measures are quoted here to show how closely Granados adhered to the traditional melodic traits of the tonadilla style (Ex. 3).

Among the tonadillas of Granados is a triptych collectively titled 'La Maja dolorosa' ('The Maja begrieved'), which contains some of his most effective writing in this form. In these three brief but intensively

[5] Published by Ricordi of Milan (n.d.).

Ex. 3 Andantino quasi Allegretto

Voice doubles piano

Yo no ol vi‑da‑ré en mi   vi‑da de Go‑ya la i‑ma‑gen ga‑llar‑da y que‑ri‑da

expressive songs, a *maja* evokes her dead lover, at first with passionate despair, then with romantic ardour, and finally with a kind of exultation as the joys of bygone love are rekindled in her memory. The accompaniment of the first song (*Andantino dramático*) calls for an English horn *ad libitum*. The vocal line, rising and descending in disjunct intervals derived from the chord of the diminished seventh, embraces a range of over two octaves, from A flat above the staff to G natural below. The middle number is the closest to the traditional style of the tonadilla, both in its melody and in its accompaniment.

Although Granados was mostly strongly attracted to the romantic imagery of Goya's Madrid, he was also responsive, as nearly all Spanish (and many foreign) composers have been, to the exotic and sensuous appeal of Andalusia. Among his twelve Spanish Dances for piano, the one that has become a universal favourite is the Fifth, titled *Andaluza*. In 1931 this was published in a transcription for voice and piano, with words by Luis Muñoz Lorente evoking the glamorous image of an idealized Andalusia. The words are well wedded to the music and the whole makes a grateful number for singers in search of unmistakable 'Spanish atmosphere'.

Manuel de Falla (1876–1946) is important in the history of Spanish song above all for his 'Seven Spanish Popular Songs', for voice and piano, completed in 1914. It would be misleading to think of these simply as arrangements of Spanish folk-songs. Taking the traditional melodies of folk-songs from various regions of Spain, Falla has provided them with piano accompaniments which, in the words of J. B. Trend, 'are at the same time brilliantly pianistic and yet thoroughly in keeping with the spirit of the original melodies.' These accompaniments are truly creative, since they disclose indubitable artistry, invention, and intuition, thus providing aesthetic values inherent but not hitherto revealed in the original folk-songs. The seven songs are *Seguidilla murciana*, *El paño moruno*, *Asturiana*, *Jota*, *Nana* ('Lullaby'), *Canción* ('Song') and *Polo*. It seems academic – or rather pedantic – to debate whether or not these are 'pure' art-songs in the strict sense of the term. The fact is

391

they have established a model for contemporary song-writers throughout the Spanish-speaking world, in which popular and artistic elements are so closely and often so inextricably intertwined.

In 1910, whole living in Paris, Falla published 'Trois Mélodies' on poems by Théophile Gautier: *Les Colombes, Chinoiserie, Seguidille*. One remarks in these the same kind of pianistic brilliance, yet always flexible, apt, and unostentatious, that characterizes the accompaniments of the 'Seven Spanish Songs'. Indeed, the third number, *Seguidille*, might be regarded as a fore-runner of the later songs, with the difference that here Falla invents his own 'typical' Spanish melody. How completely typical it is may be seen from the following example:

Ex. 4

In 1927, on the occasion of the tercentenary of the death of Góngora, Falla set to music that poet's magnificent *Sonnet to Cordoba*, for voice and harp, using an austere declamatory style, supported by rich, full-bodied chords, that recalls the vocal and instrumental art of the great Spanish *vihuelistas* of the Golden Age. Of this Sonnet, J. B. Trend has written (with some exaggeration) that 'Falla's setting could only be completely convincing if it were sung by someone who could imagine herself to have, for a moment, the position and attributes of a baroque angel.'

Joaquín Turina (1882–1949) was, like Falla, an Andalusian who spent some years in Paris (1905–14), where he studied composition with Vincent d'Indy at the Schola Cantorum. Nearly all of his music is intimately associated with Andalusia, and particularly with his native city of Seville, which he eloquently evokes in his most important vocal composition, *Canto a Sevilla* (1926) for soprano and orchestra (or piano). This is a setting of four poems by José Muñoz San Román, titled respectively *Semana Santa* ('Holy Week'), *Las fuentecitas del Parque* ('The Little Fountains of the Park'), *El Fantasma* ('The Phantom'), and *La Giralda* (the name of a decorative bell-tower that is a celebrated landmark of Seville). As Irving Kolodin aptly remarks, 'In totality they comprise a kind of rapturous adulation of a city.' In addition, Turina has written several songs for voice and piano, including *Rimas de Béquer*, on poems by the highly Romantic Spanish poet of the nineteenth century, Gustavo Adolfo Bécquer; and *Poema en forma de canciones* ('Poem in the form of songs').

History always becomes more difficult to write as one approaches one's own time. How shall one select from the many composers who have been active in Spain during the last few decades? Some of them, like Conrado del Campo (1879–1953), Jesús Guridi (b. 1886), and Oscar Esplá (b. 1886), enjoy a solid national reputation but are relatively little known abroad. Del Campo, who taught many of the younger composers at the Madrid Conservatory, wrote in a post-Romantic vein with marked German influences. Guridi has devoted himself especially to the music of his native Basque country, while Esplá has written the 'Canciones playeras' ('Seaside Songs') for voice and piano (also orchestrated), based on the songs of Mediterranean fishermen from his native town, Alicante. What this seems to indicate is a strong regional tendency in Spanish music. Indeed, most of what we tend to regard as typically 'Spanish' music is merely that identified with a Spanish region of particularly potent fascination: Andalusia. The prestige of such contemporary composers as Falla and Turina further enhanced the spell of Andalusian music. But other regions of the Peninsula also have their characteristic culture, and in some cases – such as that of Catalonia – their own language and literature also. Two of the most flourishing regional movements in Spanish music today are those centred, respectively, in Valencia and Barcelona.

The leader of the Valencian school is Manuel Palau (b. 1893), who studied in Paris with Koechlin, Bertelin, and Ravel. He has for many years been Director of the Musical Conservatory of Valencia. His early compositions (1920–1926) were deeply coloured by the folk-music of the Valencian region. Thereafter he endeavoured to free himself from strictly folkloristic influences, while maintaining the regional character of much of his music (for example, in his settings of poetic texts in the Valencian dialect). His extensive catalogue includes five cycles of songs for voice and orchestra, some twenty-five songs with orchestral accompaniment, and about twenty songs with piano accompaniment. The majority of them have Valencian texts. However, in his 'Seis Lieder' (Six Lieder') for soprano and piano (also orchestrated, 1950), Palau has taken old Spanish texts, one by Lope de Vega, the others anonymous (including some previously set by Spanish composers of the sixteenth century, such as *De los álamos vengo, Madre*).

In addition to Felipe Pedrell, who was Catalonian and lived in

Barcelona most of his life, the leading figures of the contemporary Catalonian school were Antonio Nicolau (1858–1933) and Enrique Morera (1865–1942), both of whom contributed to enrich the musical life of their native city, Barcelona. Both of them wrote numerous songs with Catalan texts. Today the leading Catalonian composers continue to give an important place to song-writing in their musical production. And they continue to use both Catalan and Spanish texts in their songs, usually giving preference to the former.

Among the older composers, those who have given special attention to song-writing include Juan Altisent (b. 1891), Antonio Massana (b. 1890), and Federico Mompou (b. 1893). The songs of Father Massana (a Jesuit) comprise settings of two poems by the great Catalonian poet Jacinto Verdaguer (texts in Catalan with Spanish translations), 'Dues Cançons' (composed in 1936); Eight Songs with texts by various Catalan poets (composed in 1936); and Five Songs on poems in Spanish by Xavier Criado (composed in 1932). He writes in an attractive lyrical vein, somewhat Neo-Impressionistic, with liberal use of broken chords in his accompaniments.

Federico Mompou strikes a completely individual note in contemporary music. Turina once called him 'the most complete composer' of Spain. Certainly he is the most consistent, never deviating from the aesthetic ambit in which he has chosen to move. His art is intimate, evocative rather than declarative, based on a deliberate simplicity of means, lyrical and poetic, repetitive like a primitive incantation, and full of enchantment (almost in the literal sense). Born in Barcelona, of a Catalonian father and a French mother, Mompou spent many years in Paris, both before and after the First World War, and his point of departure was doubtless the Impressionism of Debussy. Yet he is no mere imitator but a creative artist with a highly personal style. Mompou has written more than twenty songs for voice and piano, with texts in Catalan, French, and Spanish. Some of these, like the six 'Comptines', are based on folk-songs. Others, like the five poems in Catalan on poems by José Janés, collectively entitled 'Cambat del Sonni', are fully developed art-songs (they were composed between 1942 and 1951). Mompou's longest song is the setting of the *Cantar del Alma* ('Canticle of the Soul') by St. John of the Cross. His Spanish settings also include two poems by the late Nobel Prize winner, Juan Ramón Jiménez: *Pastoral* and *Llueve sobre el rio* ('It is raining on the river'), dating from 1945.

Among the younger Catalonian composers, Xavier Montsalvatge

(b. 1912) has distinguished himself as a song-writer with his five
'Canciones Negras' ('Negro Songs'), completed in 1945 for voice and
piano (also orchestrated), on texts by Rafael Alberti, Nestor Luján,
Nicolás Guillén, and Ildefonso Pereda Valdés. It is curious to see this
Catalonian composer turning to Afro-Cuban themes in his settings of
poems by Guillén, such as the *Canto Negro* with its incantatory ejacula-
tions: 'Yambambo, yambambe!' – and its ritualistic jargon: 'Mama-
tomba serembe cuse remba'. He achieves real pathos without sentimentality in the *Canción de cuna para dormir a un negrito* ('Cradle song for a
little Negro boy'), with its delicate evocation of the *habanera* rhythm in
the bass. *Chevere* (text by Guillén) is a succint but dramatic musical
portrait of a 'knife-happy' Negro, while the *Punto de Habanera* is an
eighteenth-century vignette of old Havana, in the tempo of the Cuban
guajiras (folk-song and dance in $\frac{6}{8}$ time). The initial song, *Cuba dentro de
un piano* ('Cuba within a piano'), text by Alberti, is rather difficult to
explain as regards the subject. It is a sort of bitter-sweet evocation of the
fin de siècle, with its *fandangos* and *habaneras*, but which also brought the
end of Spanish domination in the New World, with the loss of Cuba
in the Spanish-American War. So the song ends on a note of anger at
the thought that the Spanish *Sí* has been replaced by the Yankee *Yes!*
Whatever the mixture of nostalgia, local colour, and resentment, the
musical setting skilfully evokes every variety of mood, with its languorous *habanera* rhythm in the left hand, its chromatic sensuousness,
and its violent vehemence at the explosion of the word *Yes!* (spoken),
followed by the calm of resignation as the echoes of the habanera fade
away into silence. Alone with this collection of five songs, Montsalvatge
has definitely established himself as an important figure in the contemporary art-song of Spain.

In the 1930s there were a number of young composers in Madrid
who shared certain ideals in common. They included Ernesto and
Rodolfo Halffter, Gustavo Pittaluga, Rosa García Ascot, Salvador
Bacarisse, Fernando Remacha, and Julián Bautista. To the same
generation belongs the blind Valencian composer Joaquín Rodrigo
(b. 1902), who, however, was in Paris during the 1930s. Several of the
group, including Rodolfo Halffter, Bautista and Pittaluga, migrated to
America after the Spanish Civil War of 1936–39. Halffter settled in
Mexico, while Bautista went-to Argentina.[6]

Ernesto Halffter's best songs were written when he was very young.
They are two songs on poems by Rafael Alberti, titled respectively *La*

[6] See the section on Latin America, p. 304.

Corza blanca ('The white hind') and *La Niña que se va al mar* ('The girl who goes toward the sea'),[7] with French versions by Henri Collet. In these two songs, written in 1927, and particularly in the second, which is much longer and more fully developed, Halffter combines a characteristically Hispanic melodic line with a piano accompaniment of great fluidity, variety, and brilliance. Halffter has also written two songs of lesser importance, with French texts, *Le Lit Laqué Blanc* and *La Chanteuse*, as well as a setting for voice and small orchestra (also available for voice and piano) of the poem *Automne Malade* by Guillaume Apollinaire.

The catalogue of Joaquín Rodrigo's works includes many songs, written for the most part in traditional Spanish style, with strong reminiscences of the 'Golden Age' of Spanish poetry and song. His 'Cuatro Madrigales Amatorios' ('Four amatory madrigals') for voice and piano (also orchestra) are skilful and attractive arrangements of well-known Spanish songs of the sixteenth century. His 'Two Villancicos' for voice and piano, the first a setting of a poem by Lope de Vega, the second anonymous, are very close to the spirit of Spanish folk-song. The first is a courtly pastoral, the second a lively evocation of the Spanish dance, full of verve and fire. Both songs are among the best of their type.

The composer Joaquín Nin-Culmell (b. 1908), son of Joaquín Nin, although he became an American citizen, is associated with the Spanish school through heritage and affinity. He too has turned to the Golden Age in his settings for voice and piano of 'Three Poems by Gil Vicente' (d. *c*. 1536) and of 'Two Poems by Jorge Manrique' (fifteenth century). During a three-year sojourn in Spain (1956–59), Nin-Culmell explored the whole range of Iberian regional folk-song, but concentrated particularly on the region of Catalonia, arranging two series of Catalan folk-songs for voice and piano, in two books of twelve songs each. He has also transcribed for voice and orchestra two of the songs, *Canto Andaluz* and *El Vito*, from his father's collection of 'Chansons Populaires Espagnoles'.[8]

It remains to speak of one of the most successful of contemporary Spanish song writers, Fernando J. Obradors, whose songs appear frequently on concert programmes everywhere, while very little is known of the composer himself. Probably the chief reason for his success is that he epitomizes the popular conception of Spanish song in all of its most typical aspects, from the charming lyrics of the fifteenth century (as in his setting of Juan de Anchieta's *Con amores, la mi madre*)

[7] Both published by Max Eschig, Paris.   [8] Published by Max Eschig, Paris.

to the popular songs of the eighteenth and nineteenth centuries, such as *El Vito*, and the tonadilla entitled *El Majo celoso* ('The jealous Majo'), not forgetting the various folk-songs that he has effectively arranged, such as 'Dos Cantares populares'.

There are, of course, many more Spanish composers of the present time who have written songs for voice and piano, but there is not space to discuss them all. The following names may be listed as a basis for further exploration by singers in quest of unfamiliar material: Alfonso Javier (b. 1905), 'Cinco Canciones Castellanas' (1957); Miguel Asins Arbó (b. 1916), 'Seis Canciones Españolas' on poems by Antonio Machado (National Music Prize, 1950); Salvador Bacarisse (b. 1898), 'Tres Canciones clásicas españoles' (1950); Manuel Blancafort (b. 1897), 'Cuatro Melodías' (1948); Narciso Bonet (b. Barcelona, 1933), 'Vista al Mar', five poems by Joan Maragall (1948); Juan Comellas (b. 1913), 'Seis Tonadas de Ultramar' (1953); José María Franco, 'Canciones de Niños' (1929); Cristobal Halffter (b. Madrid, 1930), 'Two Songs on poems by Gil Vicente' (1952), 'Cuatro Canciones populares leonesas' (1957); Joaquín Homs Oller (b. Barcelona, 1906), 'Poems by J. Carnicer' (1934), 'Cementiri de Sinera' (eight poems by Salvador Espriu, 1952); Carlos Suriñach (b. 1915), 'Tres Cantos de España' (1945); Eduardo Toldrá (b. 1895), 'Seis Canciones sobre poemas del Siglo de Oro' (1942); Esteban Vélez (b. 1906), 'Seis Canciones andaluzas' (Homage to García Lorca), for voice and orchestra (1950); Manuel Walls Gorina (b. 1928), 'Canciones del Alto Duero' (poems by A. Machado, 1950). Among the younger composers, Narciso Bonet and Cristobal Halffter have written songs of considerable merit.

Switzerland

DAVID COX

THE third volume of 'Schweizer Sing- und Spielmusik', edited by
Dr. Willi Schuh, consists of a collection of secular songs by the
great composer of the early sixteenth century, Ludwig Senfl –
songs for four-part mixed voices, which can also be performed by one
tenor voice, with instruments playing the other parts. They may well
have been performed in the latter manner in the sixteenth century, and
other similar examples of 'accompanied solo song' could be quoted.
But the *Schweizer Musikbuch* (also edited by Dr. Willi Schuh) tells us
that it was in the third edition of a collection called 'Geistliche Seelen-
musik', which appeared in the reformed Switzerland in 1700, that Swiss
accompanied solo song, properly so called, had its beginnings. Some of
the items in this collection are marked *Aria, voce sola* – short strophic
pieces of a few bars each, with *basso continuo*. Johann Ludwig Steiner
wrote such songs. Greater freedom and melodic scope are found, however, in the work of Johann Caspar Bachofen, who in the early
eighteenth century was well known for his collections of religious and
patriotic songs. His main work is entitled 'Musikalisches Halleluja' – a
collection of some six hundred songs, a number of which are marked
'*canto solo, con organo*'. They are simple, sincere pieces, dedicated to the
glory of God. And with Johannes Schmidlin's solo songs we find an
accomplished simplicity – as in the 'Schweizer-Lieder' (1769) – but the

figured basses are often harmonized in detail and parts introduced for various instruments. The 'Schweizer-Lieder' was not the first collection of patriotic songs to appear, but it was a sincere expression of something genuinely Swiss, and it had considerable influence.

A highly interesting composer and musical personality appeared in the mid-eighteenth century – F. J. L. Meyer von Schauensee – whose music runs the whole gamut from lighthearted comedy to the expression of the profoundest sorrow. Besides cantatas for solo voice (*Il Trionfo della Gloria* and *Hortus conclusus*), he wrote an extended work under the fanciful title 'Flos vernans in foecundis Helvetiorum Convallibus exortus, harmonico 40 ariarum concentu, a sopri et contr' alto' (1748). This probably means 'The flower that blooms in the fertile valleys of Switzerland, growing from the harmonious confluence of forty airs'. The work is written to the glory of God, and the texts are in Latin. The airs are varied and well written, in the Italian operatic style of the time; some are for soprano and some for contralto, with instrumental accompaniment (two violins, viola, bass and organ).

In the latter part of the eighteenth century the songs of Johann Heinrich Egli had great vogue and several books of them were published. In style they are rather like straightforward Haydn. There is charm and warmth about the twelve 'Kinderlieder' (1789). Perhaps his most interesting work is the collection of forty-nine songs under the title 'Lieder der Weisheit und Tugend zur Bildung des Gesanges und Herzens' (Zürich, 1790) ('Songs of Wisdom and Virtue for the upraising of melody and of the heart'). Many are simple and hymn-like, others a little more complicated – all healthy, clean and uplifting – divided into eight different sections, each dealing with some aspect such as youth, nature, wisdom, and happiness. Some are for mixed voices, but most are for one voice with figured bass. The following may be taken as a typical example.

The songs of Johann Jakob Walder are similar in style to those of Egli, and his '21 Gesänge zum Clavier' (Zürich, 1780) have carefully written accompaniments, and are all secular, with a varied range of subjects – from spring and peasant life to sleep and death.

Nineteenth-century song

The work of the musical educationist and composer Hans Georg Nägeli had considerable influence on Swiss musical life. There are fifteen books of his songs – simple and direct in style – containing some which are still popular in Switzerland. One of them, *Freut euch des Lebens*, had a tremendous vogue in England in the early nineteenth century, under the title *Life let us cherish*. Nägeli was a romantic, seeking in an unpretentious way after new forms. He tried to unify his songs by using a rhythmic motive consistently throughout a song – as in *Die Heiligste der Nächte* – but does not avoid monotony. He was most successful in his patriotic songs, such as *Wir fühlen uns zu jedem Tun entflammet*. The work of Nägeli was to some extent carried on by his friend and follower Xaver Schnyder von Wartensee, who, although he went to live and work in Germany and his music shows strong German influences, remained close in spirit to his native land. His seven 'Geistliche Lieder von Novalis' show accomplishment, contrapuntal interest, and a strong Haydn flavour. He wrote about 150 songs in all.

The Swiss-born composer Louis Niedermeyer is best known for his song *Le Lac* (poem by Lamartine), which made his name famous in Paris before he arrived there in 1823. Saint-Saëns, in the preface to a biography of the composer said: 'Niedermeyer was above all a forerunner; the first to break the mould of the ancient and faded French *romance*, and inspired by the fine poems of Lamartine and Victor Hugo, he created a new and superior type of art, analogous to the German *Lied*. The resounding success of *Le Lac* opened up the way for Gounod and all the others who have followed that path.' This is something of an exaggeration; but his songs have distinction, thanks partly to the excellence of the poems chosen, and mainly for a certain freedom of structure and the matching of the musical style to the mood of the words. Apart from *Le Lac*, three other songs at least deserve to be remembered: *L'Isolement*, *L'Automne*, and *Le Soir*. There is evidence to suggest that Niedermeyer (and not Rossini) wrote the fine aria *Pietà, Signore*, formerly attributed to Stradella.

A good deal of the vocal music, solo and choral, of Karl Attenhofer (who died in 1914) is still popular in Switzerland. His style is uncomplicated and attractive, influenced by Schumann and Brahms. The 'Weihnachtslieder' (Christmas Songs), Op. 42, composed for his own children, are among the many songs for school and family that he wrote. Of his serious art-songs, the 'Fünf Lieder', Op. 26 (1878) – settings of various poets for mezzo-soprano or baritone and piano – are good, characteristic examples. No. 3, *Der Mond scheint durch den grünen Wald* is very effective, with its smooth-flowing semiquaver accompaniment, and the interest equally divided between voice and piano.

Wagner is said to have thought highly of the songs of Wilhelm Baumgartner, who flourished in Zürich as pianist, conductor, composer and teacher in the mid-nineteenth century. His setting of Gottfried Keller's poem *O mein Heimatland* is looked upon by the Swiss as practically a second national anthem.

It seems to be the fate of Joachim Raff to be remembered only by a tiny Cavatina. He wrote many songs which in style look today like a very weakened form of German Lieder; but he was a prominent composer in the Germany of his time. One cycle of songs, however, stands out as being of considerable interest and shows far more depth of feeling than most of his compositions: this is the cycle 'Maria Stuart', Op. 172, in two volumes (Leipzig, 1872). There is something genuinely moving in the sections entitled 'The Lament of Mary Stuart, Queen of France, after the death of her husband', 'Her farewell to France after the birth of her son', and 'Her farewell to the world, before going to the scaffold'.

In the many songs of Friedrich Hegar, a friend of Brahms, we find for the most part pale reflections of German styles, with an occasional exception. The 'Vier Lieder', Op. 7 (Offenbach, 1875) for soprano or baritone and piano, contains a good setting of Goethe's *Im Sommer*, in which the fast murmuring semiquaver accompaniment effectively suggests a summer atmosphere of birds and bees. And of the 'Drei Gesänge', Op. 10 (Leipzig, 1878) for tenor or soprano and piano, the best is a stormy setting of Goethe's *Aussöhnung*, in a dramatic recitative style.

Lavignac's *Encyclopédie de la Musique* describes Hans Huber as 'le plus complet des musiciens suisses'. He was a prolific but rather uncritical composer of extremely uneven output. There is much genuine musical feeling in his 'Mädchenlieder' Op. 61, dedicated to his wife; and in the two books of 'Fiedel-Lieder' (Heinauer, Breslau, 1887) to poems by Theodor Storm, the influence of Schubert and Schumann is very strong; but this is a varied, interesting collection.

Something new appeared in Swiss music in the work of Thomas Fröhlich, who, in a romantic style, recalling Schumann, introduced a soft, dream-like quality into some of his compositions, and there is an original and personal flavour about his work. Some of his solo songs are well known. One of the best is the early *Waldbruders Nachtgesang*, from Op. 3 (composed 1827).

With his five books of 'Geistliche Lieder', the volume of Old German Songs ('Altdeutsche Lieder'), and four volumes of Children's Songs ('Kinderlieder'), the contribution of Walter Courvoisier (who died in 1931) is considerable. His style is a sensitive, personal one, influenced by Hugo Wolf, and also going back to plainsong and early music for its inspiration.

Jaques-Dalcroze and others

Émile Jaques-Dalcroze and Gustave Doret are regarded as the founders of the French-Swiss popular song. Jaques-Dalcroze, a musical educationist and composer, developed a world-famous system which co-ordinated music and bodily movement. Much of what he composed was bound up with this system of eurhythmics, such as the 'Chansons de geste' and the 'Rondes enfantines'. Also, the delightful 'Chansons de l'Alpe' (Jobin, 1905), in simple folk-like style, catch perfectly the spirit of the Swiss scene – *L'Avalanche*, *Le petit clocher de la plaine*, *Les Chèvres*, *L'air tranquille des Plans*, *Le Torrent*; and in *Le Chamois rouge*, patriotic feeling is expressed ('Et nous voulons le chanter . . . Car il est la Suisse libre . . . Celle pour qui nos coeurs vibrent'.) The words, as usual with Jaques-Dalcroze's songs, are by the composer himself. In the 'Chansons rustiques' (Heugel, 1909) he departed from the purely 'popular' style and wrote art-songs, to simple nature poems of his own – often with a certain affectation, as for example in *La Pluie*, which asks: 'The rain – is it not Our Lady weeping with the angels in pity for the scorched land?'

Akin to these are the many simple and charming melodies of Gustave Doret (who was also a noteworthy opera-composer). A most attractive collection is his 'Airs et chansons couleur de temps' (Rouart, Lerolle, 1897 – now Salabert) which contains many fresh, graceful tunes, in particular *Il est un jardin d'amour* and *Dans le bois fleuri*; and, slightly less simple, *Sur le lac où fuit le couchant*, which has an effective arpeggio accompaniment with some unusual twists.

As a pupil of Massenet and Fauré in Paris from 1895 to 1898, Pierre Maurice absorbed the atmosphere of *la mélodie française*, and his settings of French poems reflect many of the characteristics of Fauré, Duparc and Debussy. In his own country, Switzerland, Maurice was one of the most loved and respected of musical personalities. Charles Koechlin, writing about him in 1938 (two years after his death), says: 'Nobody was less pretentious. He had the complete simplicity of one who was extremely sensitive of heart and highly lucid of intelligence. His music says what it set out to say with a profound and natural distinction.' This is very evident in the best of his songs, such as *Vierges mortes* (Henn) or *La Cigale* (Henn; composed 1897–8), in which also the piano can be supplemented by a string quintet, giving extra colour and interest to these, and to *Nocturne* (Siècle musical; composed 1932) and the impressive *L'Attente* (Siècle musical), to words by the composer's daughter. Some attractive settings of translations of Chinese poems – a work composed in 1925 and 1926 and published under the title 'Sept Poésies Chinoises' (O.U.P.; no date) – achieve their effect by conciseness rather than by obvious chinoiserie and become highly personal utterances. They exist also with orchestral accompaniment. Particularly fine is the light, animated, excited song, *Ki-Fong* ('La brise vient d'accourir. Cet arbre a des frissons de jeune fille amoureuse') – also, there is the beautiful and touching lament entitled *Indifférente* ('Sur ma flûte d'ébène, j'ai joué pour toi l'air le plus passionné que je connaissais. Mais tu regardais les pivoines'.)

Rudolf Ganz wrote about a hundred and fifty songs in a clever, eclectic style, not without a sense of humour. And Gustave Ferrari's slight songs suggest Gounod and early Fauré. Volkmar Andreae is more individual in style, as is shown in his 'Vier Gesänge', Op. 12 (Hug, 1907), to words by various poets: there is a real feeling for atmosphere in *Mond am Tage*; and in *Der Schmied* ('The Smith'), a striking rhythmic figure is effectively repeated in the accompaniment. Andreae was also one of the composers who wrote songs in Swiss dialect – for example, his 'Sechs Gedichte in schweizer-deutsch Mundart '(Gebrüder, 1909).

Othmar Schoeck

Othmar Schoeck was one of the strongest personalities in Swiss music, and song was the most important side of his large output. According to the *Schweizer Musikbuch*, we see in his songs the purest and strongest expression of the Swiss character in music. His early style shows the influence of Schubert and Wolf, but gradually as a result of other influences his style developed into a highly varied and personal one, becoming later increasingly economical and penetrating. He has

drawn inspiration from romantic Swiss poets such as Conrad Ferdinand
Meyer, Gottfried Keller, and Karl Leuthold. From the start there has
always been remarkable musical realization of the meaning and spirit
of the many different kinds of poems that he has set. In the Schoeck
Lieder volumes – three published by Hug and five published by Breitkopf – an enormous variety can be found. Volume 3 of the Hug edition
contains fifteen fine songs, from early and late, including the straightforward, atmospheric *Sommerabend* (1907), a setting of Heine; and the
earlier, impressive *Schilflied* from Op. 2, dating from 1905: this is
followed by a number of late songs – settings of Mörike – from Op. 51
(composed between 1931 and 1943) in which a highly personal but
always singable vocal line is supported by a rich, quite elaborate
harmonic texture. Volume 4 of the Breitkopf edition contains four
settings (of 1910) of the Swiss poet Carl Spitteler: of these, *Das beschei-
dene Wünschlein* has an exceptionally fresh and beautiful melodic line,
and *Der Hufschmied* changes its key-signature ten times in the course of
a short song. In the same volume we find Schoeck's very individual
setting of Hebbel's poem *Das Heiligste*:

An important example of his later work is the lengthy song-cycle 'Das
Stille Leuchten' (composed in 1946) – settings of twenty-eight poems
by the Swiss poet Conrad Ferdinand Meyer. The cycle portrays many
moods as suggested by the poet's evocation of the Swiss landscape.

404

Other twentieth-century composers

In the songs of Henri Gagnebin the French influence is very strong. His 'Deux Poèmes des "Heures Claires" d'Émile Verhaeren' (Au Ménestral, 1953) can be warmly recommended. The first, *Le ciel en nuit s'est déplié*, is smooth-flowing and Fauré-like in harmonic subtlety. The second, *Au clos de notre amour*, is in a joyous, $\frac{9}{8}$ dance rhythm. The 'Trois Mélodies' (Henn; no date), to poems by Tristan Derème, are also of unusual interest: *La Girouette* ('The Weathercock') is powerful and declamatory; *Les Éléphants* reminds one of Poulenc with its amusing, mock-contrapuntal style; and *La Barque* calmly floats with an elegance reminiscent of Fauré.

Honegger (see p. 223) was a French-born composer of Swiss parentage. And Ernest Bloch is usually described as an American composer of Swiss birth. Something should, I think, be said here about Bloch's songs. His 'Quatre Poèmes d'Automne' (Schirmer, 1918), are highly individual and musically imaginative settings of poems by Béatrix Rodès, and they are published with French and English words: *La Vagabonde*, *Le Déclin* ('The Waning'), *L'Abri* ('The Shelter'), and *Invocation* – a highly rewarding set for the enterprising singer. The same rich, mature imagination is shown also in 'Historiettes au Crépuscule' (Eschig, 1930(?)) – settings of poems by Camille Mauclair, three for mezzo-soprano or baritone, the other (No. 2) a love song, *Les Fleurs*, for soprano. No. 3, *Ronde*, is an appropriately sinister musical portrayal of a poem about some girls who dance for the Devil.

One of the greatest of Swiss composers, Frank Martin, has not written many solo songs, but special mention must be made of his 'Quatre Sonnets' (Hug, 1921) from *Les Amours de Ronsard*, for mezzo-soprano, flute, viola and cello. The texture is simple and clear – not always the case with Martin – and the peculiar irony of Ronsard is beautifully realized in these settings.

The music of Jean Binet has achieved considerable fame outside his own country. He has a colourful imagination and a lightness of spirit and touch which are the result of strong French influences. His 'Quatre Chansons' (composed 1927), for tenor and eight instruments, to poems by C. F. Ramuz, have been recorded by Hugues Cuenod. In style, Binet is very free, often seemingly meandering, achieving some very interesting effects – and with always a shapely vocal line, singable in spite of some difficult intervals. In his two sets of songs to Existentialist poems by Jean Cuttat – 'Dix Chansons' and 'Six Chansons' (L'Oiseau Lyre, 1949, both) – there is striking conciseness and intensity of expression, reminding one of Poulenc at his best. The spirit of the texts is summed up in the following lines:

> Vois! je suis l'homme sur son rail,
> Lancé sans but avec sa race
> J'entends la mort qui me pourchasse:
> Je vis! et vivre est mon travail.

(Look! I am a man in his rut, sent forth pointlessly with the rest of his race, and hearing death's footsteps ever pursuing me: I live! and living is my job.)

Willi Burkhard, one of Switzerland's most important composers, formed a personal style by eschewing romanticism and going back for inspiration to early contrapuntal styles seen through modern eyes. In his cantata *Herbst*, Op. 36 (Schott, 1933), for soprano, violin, cello, and piano, the inspiration of nature also is strongly felt, and various moods of autumn are effectively conveyed – one of the most effective sections being the second, with its quiet, rushing quavers portraying the south wind. In the 'Neun Lieder', Op. 70 (Bärenreiter, no date), to poems by Christian Morgenstern, suggestive portrayal is also a striking feature: the calmly wandering accompaniment of *Wandernde Stille*, the quiet hovering quaver figures of *Herbst* ('Autumn'), the cold, bare, stark writing of *Erster Schnee* ('First Snow'), the flickering and spurting flames in the accompaniment of *So ziehn zwei Flammen*. It is an exceptionally fine song-cycle.

The large output of Albert Moeschinger includes a small number of solo songs in a somewhat severe and personal style. Besides his two Lenau cycles, his 'Ten Songs on old German poems', Op. 36a (Schott, 1934), deserve to be noted. The poems are all on the subject of love, and the ten short songs reflect many moods in a traditional musical language enriched by modern colouring.

Another composer of large output but few solo songs is Conrad Beck. In the 'Drei Herbstgesänge' ('Three Autumn Songs') (Schott, 1930) – to poems by Rilke – a very free contemporary style, polyphonic and teutonic, is used. The vocal line is always a singable one, provided the singer can hold his own against the complex piano part. The strange absence of any speed indications does not help matters.

Robert Oboussier, a Swiss composer of Belgian origin, combined many elements in his style – traditional, atonal, polytonal, neo-classical, with French and German influences. His songs are highly imaginative, as one can hear in the beautiful recording (by Erna

Berger) of his 'Drei Arien nach Klopstock', for coloratura soprano, oboe, and harpsichord. His most important song-cycle is 'Vie et Mort' (composed 1944-5), for contralto and piano, on twelve poems by the Comtesse de Noailles, published (Bärenreiter) with French and German words.

Grove's Dictionary tells us that Heinrich Sutermeister's music is 'derived from the elements of melody and rhythm and freed from any kind of subjective inflation and complexity . . . sweeping melodic lines, songfulness achieved mainly by diatonic progressions, and generally a manner easily understood by all'. It comes as a shock, therefore, to turn to his 'Vier Lieder' (Schott, 1949) for high voice and piano. The vocal line, in itself, is quite singable; but the style as a whole is so free as to be practically atonal in effect. In the second song, *Sommernacht auf dem Kirchhof*, the atmospheric accompaniment is largely in consecutive sevenths and with no suggestion of key. Only the last song, *Abendlied*, could convincingly be described as diatonic-with-additions, and the effective ending is strongly reminiscent of the conclusion of Stravinsky's *Les Noces*.

In the history of song, Switzerland (with her mixture of styles and of races) has certainly given us much that is of significance and great variety.

United States of America

HANS NATHAN

T HE most significant vocal music in late eighteenth-century America was written by New England composers such as Supply Belcher, William Billings, Jacob French, Oliver Holden, Samuel Holyoke, Jacob Kimball, Andrew Law, Justin Morgan, Daniel Read, Timothy Swan, and others. These were actually artisans and tradesmen (and musicians only on the side), but undeterred by a lack of formal training and fortified by a feeling for the locale, they wrote their psalms, hymns, anthems and occasional rounds (many of them also with secular texts) for the use of singing-schools and other musical gatherings.[1] The popularity of these works, to judge by the number of the so-called tune-books in which they appeared, began in the 'seventies and, increasing in the 'eighties, reached its peak in the next decade. One of their most intriguing aspects is their harmony

Grateful acknowledgement for aid in the preparation of this chapter is made to: American Antiquarian Society, Worcester, Mass.; American Composers Alliance Library, N.Y.; Bethany Beardslee; Professor Allen P. Britton; Professor Arlan R. Coolidge; Elkan-Vogel Co., Philadelphia; Carl Fischer, Inc., N.Y.; Ray Green and the American Music Center, N.Y.; Dr. Donald M. McCorkle, The Moravian Music Foundation; Mercury Music Corporation, N.Y.; Kurtz Myers and The Detroit Public Library (Music and Drama); The New York Public Library (Music Division); Sibley Musical Library (The University of Rochester).

[1] Irving Lowens, *Daniel Read's World: The Letters of an Early American Composer*, in *Notes*, (March, 1952): 'It is true that the singing-school grew out of the church, but during the heyday of the American idiom, it was a secular institution. The use within the church of some of the music selected from the tune-books was quite incidental; the tune-books themselves were compiled to serve secular purposes. In a very real sense, here was the popular music, the music of the people.'

(mostly in four parts) with its open fifths, its consecutive fifths and octaves, its major sevenths and seconds,[2] animated, as Billings wrote,[3] by 'each part . . . striving for mastery and sweetly contending for victory'. In the context of this book, however, we will concentrate on the airs. Appearing in the tenor and usually sung in a 'bold and manly' way[4] by both low and high voices, they were clearly audible over the rest. It was they in particular which were remembered by the people, and Billings's *Chester*, one of the favourites of the Revolutionary Army, is a well-known example.

The style of these tunes has not been fully investigated yet. To make up for it, more than a hundred publications, scattered in American libraries, would have to be examined, for only comparatively little of their contents has been made available in modern reprints.[5] However, with regard to their sources we can rely on a few specific statements. It has been said, for example, that New England composers were influenced by 'the music they heard around them . . . in all likelihood . . . [by] Anglo-Celtic folk-music and its religious offshoot, American hymnody'.[6] This is borne out by the following modal tune,[7] the tenor of *Balloon* by Timothy Swan:

Ex.1

Be - hold__ I__ fall be - fore __ thy__ face, My on - ly re - fuge is thy__

grace; No out - ward form can make me clean, The le - pro - sy lies__ deep with - in.

No bleed - ing bird__ nor bleed - ing beast, Nor hys-sop branch, nor sprink-ling priest; Nor

run - ning brook, nor flood, nor sea, __ Can wash the dis - mal stain__ a - way. No stain a - way.

2 See Goldman's *Introduction* in Richard Franko Goldman and Roger Smith, *Landmarks of Early American Music*, New York, 1943. With regard to the roots of this harmony, see this sentence of the English composer Tans'ur, whose sacred music was well known in America: 'two Fifths or two Eighths (and no more) may be taken together in Three or more Parts (when it cannot be well avoided) rather than spoil the *Air*.' (quoted in Frédéric Louis Ritter, *Music in America*, New York, 1890, p. 79).

3 *The Continental Harmony*, Boston, 1794.

4 Quoted from Jacob Kimball in Oliver Daniel (ed.), *Down East Spirituals*, New York, 1949.

5 Some of it appeared in Goldman and Smith, op. cit. and in editions published by C. C. Birchard, Music Press, and Edward B. Marks Music Corporation. A complete bibliography of the original editions was compiled by Allen P. Britton in his *Theoretical Introductions in American Tune Books to 1800* (thesis), Ann Arbor, Michigan, 1949.

6 Irving Lowens, *John Wyeth's Repository of Sacred Music, Part Second: A Northern Precursor of Southern Folk Hymnody*, in *Journal of the American Musicological Society*, V (1952), p. 114.

7 From *The Village Harmony*, Exeter, 1796. The tune has been furnished by Allen P. Britton.

Many other tunes are, however, in a major or minor tonality and contain no specific folk-song elements, and still others (Jacob Kimball's, for example) are related to the English secular music of the late eighteenth century. Moreover, tunes in duple or common time often share the following features with English psalm tunes:[8] a sustained note at the very beginning, note repetitions, and the division of the melody into brief, almost separate phrases. All this is more pronounced in the American tunes, it seems, and somewhat different. Here notes are frequently repeated on the first three or first two beats, or else on the two last beats of the bar. Also, after the long initial note, the subsequent continuous motion appears precipitate. We might call this a quality of incongruousness. It is also caused, not merely in duple time, by phrases of irregular length amidst regularity,[9] and by melismas and word accents, both apparently unwarranted.

It has justly been said that the New England tunes are in a 'semi-folk idiom'.[10] There is indeed an ingenuousness about them, a disarming awkwardness that has a special appeal to the modern mind. It expresses itself sometimes in terms of a simplicity that borders on the mechanical (the 'jingle', as a nineteenth-century commentator disapprovingly dubbed it[11]), but this is usually counteracted by a strong forward motion that sweeps over all melodic details[12] (Ex. 2). It also results from

Ex. 2

Ye ho-ly throng Of an-gels bright Ye ho-ly throng Of an-gels bright In worlds of light Be-gin the song.

the opposite quality, from a naïve (and wholly charming) attempt to be recherché, as in Ex. 1.

In order to show that the variety of melodic styles is considerably greater than our examples suggest, we quote the following tune, *Columbia*, by Dr. Timothy Dwight, in its original setting (Ex. 3).

One of many patriotic songs in the 1790s, it represents a link between the New England idiom and the Southern folk-hymns[13] of the early nineteenth century, since it is indebted to both. It appeared in a wholly secular publication, a songster entitled *The American Musical Miscellany* of 1798.[14] Like its eighteenth-century models, it was written by a

---

[8] See the music published in Irving Lowens, *The Origins of the American Fuging Tune*, *JAMS*, VI (1953), p. 43.

[9] Referred to by Allen P. Britton, *The Musical Idiom in Early American Tunebooks* (abstract), *JAMS*, III (1950), p. 286.　　　[10] Lowens, *JAMS* (1952).　　　[11] Ritter, op. cit., p. 72.

[12] Republished in full in Lowens, *JAMS* (1953).　　[13] See examples in Lowens, *JAMS* (1952).

[14] 'Printed at Northampton, Massachusetts, by Andrew Wright, For Daniel Wright and Company.'

Ex.3

Co - lum - bia, Co - lum - bia to glo - ry a - rise, The queen of the earth, and the

chief of the skies; Thy ge - nius com - mands thee, with rap - ture be - hold, While

a - ges on a - ges thy splen - dor un - fold. Thy reign is the last, and the

no - blest of time, Most fruit - ful thy soil, most in - vi - ting thy clime: Let

the crimes of the earth ne'er crim - son thy name, Be free - dom and sci - ence, and vir - tue, thy fame.

non-professional, a very literate one this time: Dr. Timothy Dwight, then president of Yale University.[15] That its setting preserves the customary 'hard, naked'[16] sonority is due to the fact that it is actually nothing but a reduction of the usual four-part harmony, in this case like the combination of tenor (if we disregard the octave level) and bass without alto and soprano. A purely vocal performance is possible, since Billings wrote:[17] 'If suitable voices cannot be had, some parts had better be omitted; for . . . two parts well sung, are better than four parts indifferently sung.' But Dr. Dwight's setting may also be understood as a mere abbreviation (as was customary in collections of this time). The bass would then have to be played on a keyboard instru-

[15] See O. G. Sonneck and W. T. Upton, *A Bibliography of Early Secular American Music*, Washington, D.C., 1945, p. 505. The college choir at Yale used to sing New England hymns under Dr. Dwight's direction (mentioned in *The Southern Harmony* of 1835, facsimile edition, Benton, Kentucky, 1939, p. 299, footnote).

[16] Words of a contemporary detractor, see Ritter, op. cit., p. 93.

[17] Quoted in Oliver Daniel (ed.), *Compositions by William Billings*, series I and II, Boston, 1943, 46 and 49.

ment and the harmony filled in, though of course in a stylistically appropriate manner.

Moravians

Very different from the music of New England composers was that of the Moravian Brethren (the followers of John Huss and Count M. L. von Zinzendorf), who had come to America during the eighteenth century and established themselves in Pennsylvania and North Carolina. They quickly developed an extremely active and well-organized musical life, cultivating chamber-music, the chorale, and, in their church service, performing valuable vocal music, usually set for chorus with strings and basso continuo (and, not infrequently, with additional wind instruments). Their repertoire, much of which was used also outside the liturgy proper as at such gatherings as 'Singstunden' and Collegia Musica, was astonishingly large; it consisted of works of major and minor composers of the late eighteenth century, mainly German, as well as of works by Moravians.

What interests us here particularly are the native Moravian compositions for solo voice. While brief pieces with piano accompaniment (for example, by Jacob Van Vleck, which are still unpublished) were called 'ariettas', the term 'geistliche Lieder' can be applied to the entire genre, thus including the larger works, accompanied by instrumental ensembles.[18]

In the few compositions of the latter type that are available (written by J. Antes, J. Dencke, J. Herbst, D. M. Michael, G. G. Müller, J. F. Peter, and S. Peter), a variety of contemporary German influences, sacred and secular, can easily be discovered. Since Protestant and Catholic continental sources were not clearly distinguishable from each other, one might say that both were drawn upon. However, there was also a regard for the Protestant tradition proper, though how strong it was cannot be stated at this point. For instance, in *Meine Seele erhebet den Herrn*[19] (My soul doth magnify the Lord) of 1767, by Jeremiah Dencke, the vocal line is indebted, in several places, to the eighteenth-century Protestant chorale, while one of its rhythmic features (bar 12) traces back to Schütz. On the other hand, the following excerpt from David Moritz Michael's *Ich bin in meinem Geiste*[20] ('I love

[18] Information from Donald M. McCorkle, director of the Moravian Music Foundation, Winston-Salem, North Carolina.
[19] H. T. David.(ed.), *Ten Sacred Songs (Music of The Moravians In America)*, New York, 1947.
[20] Thor Johnson and Donald M. McCorkle (eds.), *Three Sacred Songs for Soprano*, New York, 1958. According to the introductory notes of this edition, Michael lived in America from 1795 to 1815. He was born in Germany in 1751 and died there in 1827.

to dwell in spirit') of about 1800 clearly reveals Haydnesque elements:

Ex.4 Ich bin in mei-nem Gei - ste so gern wo Je - sus ist

Nevertheless, it seems that the piece is more than a copy. To prove this in detail, with such unassuming music, would carry little conviction. More tangible is the question of the originality of the Moravian style as a whole, i.e. as set forth by a large number of compositions. Once this has been answered, we will know whether the Moravian contribution was a mere simplification of European models or a variant in its own right. One specific feature, however, can be pointed out at once: a child-like piety and sincerity – the fruit of a closely-knit, deeply religious community of farmers and artisans. Such ingenuous qualities no longer existed in the far more sophisticated but worldlier sacred music of Central Europe.

Hopkinson, Negro Minstrelsy, and Emmett

Alongside the music of the tune-books, the American public, particularly in the towns, sang all the songs that were current and fashionable in Great Britain, even after the Revolution: those of the public gardens, the regular concerts, the theatres, and operas. These songs circulated in sheets and songsters, which, like the tune-books, grew in number at an ever-increasing rate between the 'sixties and the end of the century. According to the title page of a representative collection of 1797,[21] there existed the following types: 'pathetic and passionate – anacreontic and jovial – comic, ingenious, and witty – sea, hunting, and Masonic songs'. The songster *The American Musical Miscellany*, a mirror of contemporary taste, contains compositions of the English composers Dibdin, Storace, Thomas and Michael Arne, Shield, Samuel Arnold, and James Hook but also 'a large variety of the late Federal American songs, suited to the true spirit of the times'.[22] The latter songs are based on patriotic texts and set by native musicians though in a wholly English style (to say nothing of adaptations to English tunes); they were performed as entr'actes on the stage and most frequently during the politically heated atmosphere of 1798.[23]

21 *The Syren; or Vocal Enchantress*, Wilmington; see Sonneck and Upton, op. cit.
22 From an advertisement of 1799, quoted in Sonneck and Upton, op. cit., p. 20.
23 O. G. Sonneck, *Early Opera in America*, New York, 1915, p. 145.

One of the earliest American composers was Francis Hopkinson, a typical eighteenth-century gentleman: a writer, painter, a prominent political figure and, like Benjamin Franklin, a musician. For example, in the 'eighties he wrote 'An Improved Method of Quilling the Harpsichord' and in the late 'fifties his first songs. In 1788 appeared his 'Seven Songs [actually eight] for the Harpsichord or Forte Piano' to his own texts.[24] They faithfully follow the contemporary English song style, yet, in spite of their semi-professional character, they are fresher than the average continental product. That they are predominantly syllabic would have been welcomed by Benjamin Franklin, though he would have rejected their occasional florid passages, for, rationalist that he was, he expected the vocal line of a song to preserve 'the proprieties and beauties of common speech'[25] and even criticized Handel for violating this principle.

Hopkinson stressed in his preface that his songs were meant 'to please the *young* Performers'. In other words, they were mainly intended for musical entertainment at home. The amateur, indeed, both in the Northern towns and on the Southern plantations, was a key figure in the musical life of the young Republic, not only as a purchaser of music (vocal and instrumental) but as a pupil anxious to learn how to sing, to play, to realize the thorough-bass and even to compose.[26] It was especially the ladies who were expected to be musically proficient, and they must have obeyed the dictates of fashion in preparing their own 'music books', handwritten collections of their favourite songs, hymns, dances and marches.[27] It should be noted at this point that songs were also performed publicly, for concerts, presenting medleys

[24] Facsimile edition, Harry Dichter, *Musical Americana*, Philadelphia, 1954.

[25] Letter of about 1765, reprinted in Gilbert Chase, *America's Music*, New York, 1955, pp. 95 and 96.

[26] Maurer Maurer, *A Musical Family in Colonial Virginia*, in The Musical Quarterly, XXXIV (1948), p. 358, and especially The *'Professor of Musick' in Colonial America*, in The Musical Quarterly, XXXVI (1950), p. 511.

[27] William Dinneen, *Early American Manuscript Music-Books*, in The Musical Quarterly, XXX (1944), p. 50. One of these manuscripts (all of which were written between 1790 and 1800) bears the following notation: 'The charming owner of this musick book, possess'd of every requisite and elegant accomplishment that can fit her to make the happy man who may be her choice dignified, elevated, respectable, will only have to preserve her present disposition to be universally belov'd and esteem'd.' Furthermore, a booklet in verse entitled *Letters Addressed To Young Married Women* (1796; see Sonneck and Upton, op. cit., p. 492) considers music one of the 'most winning accomplishments . . . necessary to preserve the lover in the husband.' Francis Hopkinson, letter of December 21, 1788, with reference to his 'Seven Songs': It is a Book of Songs which I composed, occasionally, for my Daughters . . .' (see O. G. Sonneck, *Francis Hopkinson and James Lyon*, Washington, D.C., 1905). Thomas Jefferson in a letter of 1783 to his daughter Patsy advised her to devote three hours to music every day (see O. G. Sonneck, *The Musical Side of Our First Presidents*, in *Suum Cuique*, New York, 1916).

of instrumental and vocal pieces, had existed since the early part of the century.

It has been said of some minor English composers of the late eighteenth century, who wrote for the stage, that their standard as craftsmen was slight but that they possessed the ability of writing 'catchy . . . and singable tunes'.[28] It was exactly the songs of these composers (mentioned on page 142) that were popular in America. Other composers immigrating mainly from England after the Revolution, had similar talents. Among these were Benjamin Carr, James Hewitt, Victor Pelissier, Alexander Reinagle, and Raynor Taylor; to this group also belonged American-born Peter A. von (or van) Hagen. Their songs, before appearing in print, were first heard on the stage: in plays as incidental music, in pantomimes, and operas. To judge by the few that are available in modern reprints,[29] they are frequently indebted to English sources, but in several of them (by Hewitt, Pelissier, von Hagen) one detects elements related to Mozart operas or the Viennese song of the time. The most talented of the group was Alexander Reinagle. While his piano sonatas, written around 1800, are influenced by C. P. E. Bach and early Haydn, his songs are in the English style.[30] He was completely familiar with the idiom of the Ballad-Opera, and how adroitly he handled it is illustrated by the following spirited passage from 'Some tell us that women are delicate things'[31] in his comic opera *The Volunteers* (performed in Philadelphia in 1795):

Ex. 5

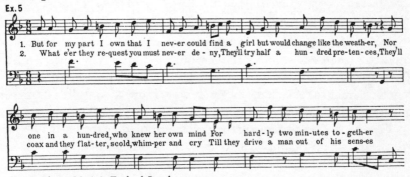

1. But for my part I own that I nev-er could find a girl but would change like the weath-er, Nor
2. What e'er they re-quest you must nev-er de - ny, They'll try half a hun - dred pre-ten-ces, They'll

one in a hun-dred, who knew her own mind For hard - ly two min-utes to - geth-er
coax and they flat-ter, scold, whim-per and cry Till they drive a man out of his sens-es

---

[28] Eric Blom, *Music in England*, London, 1942, p. 113.

[29] In Harold V. Milligan (ed.), *Pioneer American Composers* (2 vols.) Boston, 1921 and 1923; Grenville Vernon, *Yankee Doodle-Doo, A Collection of Songs of the Early American Stage*, New York, 1927; O. G. Sonneck, *Early American Operas*, in *Sammelbände der Internationalen Musikgesellschaft*, Leipzig, 1904–05; John Tasker Howard, *The Music of George Washington's Time*, Washington, D.C., 1931. Facsimiles in William Treat Upton, *Art-Song in America*, Boston–New York, 1930 and Sonneck, *Early Opera in America*, p. 99.

[30] See Sonneck and Upton, op. cit., p. 393 and Chase, op. cit., pp. 115 and 116. Modern edition of Reinagle's *America, Commerce, Freedom*, New York, 1942.

[31] Milligan, op. cit., vol. II.

The American vocal music that was performable in the concert hall showed very little vitality during the greater part of the nineteenth century.[32] Infinitely more distinctive were two humbler types of song: the folk-hymnody of the Southern back-country and the ditties sung by Negro minstrels in circuses and on informal urban and rural stages. With regard to the first, it must suffice (within the frame of this book), to refer to the publications of George Pullen Jackson, through which they have been literally rediscovered.

Negro minstrelsy (the impersonation of the Negro by white comedians) developed from acts such as Charles Dibdin presented in London from the seventeen-eighties on (though not in costume) and from appearances of Negro characters in English plays, as for example the scenes of Mungo, a humorously disreputable servant, in Dibdin's comic opera *The Padlock* (performed in 1768).[33] This kind of entertainment, along with its music, was well known in eighteenth-century and early nineteenth-century America. Stimulated by a primitive Negro population which contrasted strikingly with its Anglo-Saxon environment, it acquired soon after the war with England in 1812 many native features in speech, acting and dancing, although a truly native song style grew more slowly. First, English stage tunes were used; then, in the 'twenties and 'thirties there appeared variants of Scotch, Irish and English folk-song elements. From them, finally, in the early 'forties, emerged a melodic style that had individuality.[34] This was recognized by a European observer,[35] when he spoke of 'a very characteristically national music, if the Americans will allow us to call it so'.

Early Negro minstrel tunes possess some of the blandness of children's songs and some of the fervour of ethnically primitive music. They are jolly (if melody, text and theatrical purpose are considered together) but in a reticent, home-spun way. From this results a dead-pan quality which is wholly in the tradition of American humour.

One of the best songs of the repertoire of the 'forties is *Ole Dad* whose author and composer, as in various other cases, are both unknown. Its preludes and postludes come from the Scotch *Miss McLeod's Reel*; its instrumental interpolations are also in the style of Scotch and Irish reels. For the first part of the song, the initial eight measures of an

---

[32] See John Tasker Howard, *A Program of Early and Mid-Nineteenth Century American Songs*, New York, 1931.

[33] Hans Nathan, *Negro Impersonation in Eighteenth Century England*, in *Notes* (September, 1945).

[34] See S. Foster Damon, *Series Of Old American Songs* (facsimiles), Providence, Rhode Island, 1936.

[35] *Chambers's Encyclopaedia*, J. B. Lippincott, Philadelphia, and W. and R. Chambers, Edinburgh, 1864 (article *Negro Minstrelsy*).

older tune, created in America, have been drawn upon, though without their eighteenth-century features: *A negro song*[36] of *circa* 1801 (linked with a serious English text, well known at that time) by Benjamin Carr. In spite of these borrowings, one of them from local material, the song stands entirely on its own feet:

Its melody consists essentially of a single thematic pattern and yet it has variety: its opening section is of a clearly marked introductory character, and from it grows, appropriately, the more eloquent refrain. The latter, with its restless, inelegant and heavy-footed forward motion, its syncopated, slangy shouts, followed by rapid instrumental passages, and its 'bluesy' timbre (supported by a melodically implicit and harmonically explicit minor tonic) anticipates certain features of jazz.

What the tune has in common with others of its kind is the multiple repetition of short-winded motives, the stress on the fourth as a melodic skeleton (probably suggested by the two highest strings of the banjo, often touched by the minstrel when he played his accompaniment, or else in solos) and the combination of modal (including pentatonic) features with traditional tonality. In various other tunes there is a tone repetition that confirms the beats of their duple metre – in a manner very similar to the airs of eighteenth-century tune-books, though the more direct relation is to folk-hymnody. The repetition of motives (also appearing in Anglo-Celtic fiddle music but less obsessive there within its sinuous context) and, of course, the word-images and the dialect of the text are indebted to the Negro. So are the syncopations which however, in contrast to minstrel banjo music,[37] are rare in the songs, if we may judge by their sheet-music versions.

36 Listed in Harry Dichter and Elliott Shapiro, *Early American Sheet Music*, New York, 1941.
37 Hans Nathan, *Early Banjo Tunes And American Syncopation*, in *The Musical Quarterly*, XLII 1956), p. 455.

417

Alongside the tough, humorous type of Negro minstrel songs, there existed soulful 'ballads', most of them of inferior quality. But towards the middle of the century their standard improved due to the efforts of Stephen Foster (1826–1864). Between the late 'forties and the early 'sixties he supplied the sheet-music market with almost two hundred songs, most of them set to his own texts. About a dozen of them are still remembered – the following five vividly: *Old Folks at home*, *Oh! Susanna*, *Old Black Joe*, *My old Kentucky home*, *Massa's in de cold, cold ground*.

Foster wrote frequently for minstrel shows (performances centring on small ensembles of black-faced musicians), specifically for those of their scenes whose Negro character was faint. Many of his songs (not even counting his Civil War songs and Sunday-school hymns) are therefore in standard English, others in a very mild dialect. He prided himself on having 'done a great deal to build up a taste for the Ethiopian songs among refined people by making the words suitable to their taste, instead of the trashy and really offensive words which belong to some songs of that order'.[38] Although he was apparently opposed to the traditional, non-sentimental minstrel song, he wrote several himself,[39] among them *Oh! Susanna*, the only one, it may be noted, that acquired anything comparable to the anonymity of true folk-music (its use by the gold-miners of 1849 is well known). Otherwise he meant to please a middle class that felt increasingly uneasy about the raw, grotesque style of its popular theatre and wished to have it replaced with something suggestive of more genteel manners. It is significant that his melodies are not only close to Anglo-Celtic folk-song but to the idiom of American hymns as well.[40] This alone ensured a modicum of respectability. Add to this the soft-hearted character of his texts. Replete with words like 'gone', 'far away', 'no more', they offer day-dreams about the old plantation, beautiful young ladies, summer days, and happy youth, a simplified form of romanticism, familiar to readers of family magazines of the time.[41]

Foster's songs, generally more pedestrian than their folk-elements lead us to expect, have been criticized for lacking the genuineness of

[38] Quoted in Chase, op. cit., p. 293.

[39] These are fashioned after earlier minstrel tunes: *Oh! Susanna* after *Gwine Long Down* (1844), *Nelly Bly* after *Clare De Kitchen* (late 1830's), and *Camptown Races* after *Picayune Butler* (1847).

[40] George Pullen Jackson, *Stephen Foster's Debt To American Folk-Song*, in *The Musical Quarterly*, XXII (1936), p. 154.

[41] See Paul Fatout, *Threnodies Of The Ladies' Books*, in *The Musical Quarterly*, XXXI (1945), p. 464.

folk-music.[42] It should be remembered, however, that they are not folk-music. They are (regardless of their use on the stage) 'ballads' for the living-room – musical bric-a-brac perhaps – but within the limitations of this genre surprisingly alive. This is attributable mainly to their inner coherence; the best of them, in spite of their additive structure, have no seams.

Popularity is too weak a word to apply to Foster's songs. Like *The Star-Spangled Banner*, they have become part of the American way of life – so much so that a critical appraisal of them is sometimes considered an act of malice or, at best, of ignorance.

The humorous, primitive type of Negro minstrel songs, after a temporary decline in the early 'fifties, regained its vitality a few years later and flourished until the mid-sixties.[43] Its main representative was Dan Emmett (1815–1904), well known already for two decades. Unlike Foster, he wrote his songs for the part of minstrel shows that had the strongest Negro flavour – the 'Plantation Festival' with which they customarily concluded. This was a grotesquely comical scene, often danced and sung by as many as a dozen performers. According to its choreography, Emmett's songs were called 'walk-arounds'. Their texts, also written by the composer, dealt with Negro life both in the South and the North, usually combining the Negro's statements, spiced with topical allusions, with teasing commentaries about himself. Their tunes are related partly to the minstrel song-and-banjo style of the 'forties and their Anglo-Celtic roots, partly to white hymns (as in *Jonny Roach*, Ex. 7) and even at times to white ballads and marches. Among their few Negro elements is the solo-ensemble alternation in their first part and the repetitiveness of their melodic and textual phrases. Another one is the interval of the minor third (upwards and downwards) which, as in Negro spirituals, often appears in a pentatonic formula (i.e. with a preceding major second), while its larger context is regulated by a major or minor tonality, as well as the dance itself which was suggested by Negro ring dances.

The most famous of Emmett's walk-arounds was *Dixie* (or, more correctly, *Dixie's Land*)[44] of 1859, which, in spite of its New York origin, became the war song of the Confederate armies and is still

[42] For example Rupert Hughes wrote in the preface of his *Songs By Thirty Americans*, Boston, 1904: 'Stephen C. Foster . . . at his best trembled on the razor-edge between the perfect simplicity of folk-song and the maudlin banality of street-song.'

[43] For the subsequent discussion, the author has drawn on his article 'Emmett's Walk-Arounds: Popular Theater in New York', in *Civil War History*, IV (September, 1958).

[44] Hans Nathan, *Dixie*, in *The Musical Quarterly*, XXXV (1949), p. 60.

today in the Southern states considered a kind of national anthem. Though varying a hornpipe pattern (for its opening) and Scotch folk-song elements, it bears an unmistakable individuality as a whole, and it has long been recognized as the most genuinely American product of the nineteenth century.

The details of Emmett's walk-arounds were not unique, but they were welded together into an idiom that had a flavour all its own. One detects it in the heartiness and vigour of the final choruses, and in the compactness and conciseness of the phrases that animate the first part, lending it coherence despite their brevity – as in *Jonny Roach*:

The overall quality of the music is one of rude boisterousness, reminiscent of the frontier (which Emmett knew in his youth) rather than of the drawing-room. It complemented to perfection the efforts of the Bryant's Minstrels in New York, for whom most of the walk-arounds were written, in reviving the flagging art of minstrelsy and the rough-and-tumble style of its early years.

By the middle of the 'sixties the vitality of Negro minstrel music was practically spent: it took a generation until blues and ragtime opened up a new period of indigenous popular music. The old idioms, however, did not disappear at once. They lived on, literally at times, until the 'eighties. Among Emmett's successors was Sam Lucas, among

Foster's James Bland, whose *Carry me back to Old Virginny* (published in 1878) is still sung.

That these two men were Negroes (a phenomenon made possible by the outcome of the Civil War) is of sociological significance, but it meant nothing as far as their music was concerned. For both continued an essentially white tradition, even to the extent of contributing to a genre of entertainment – Negro minstrelsy – that, in its humorous aspects, was a parody of their own race.

The Civil War produced various songs, some of a distinct character, that not only fired the imagination of the combatants but became symbols of their respective causes. Two of the best-known songs of the Southern Confederacy were written by Northerners: the above-mentioned *Dixie*, and *Lorena* (published 1857). Neither had any direct reference to the use to which it was put. *Dixie* could at least be played as a lively military quick-step, while its text referred to the Negro, i.e. as pictured by the ordinary American, as a happy, contented slave. *Lorena*, however, was what someone called a 'home song' – 'a gentle, pure song' for the family[45] – and its heroine, once loved and still remembered, was identical with those described by Foster. Nevertheless, it was precisely in the nostalgia of the song, particularly cloying in its music, that the white Southerners must have recognized their own mournful feelings over an irretrievable past.

Several stirring Northern war songs were written by George F. Root and Henry C. Work. That the former's *The Battle Cry of Freedom* (published 1862) and *Tramp! Tramp! Tramp!* (published 1864) share various features with Sunday-school hymns may be surprising in view of the belligerent character of their words; as a stylistic phenomenon it was nothing unusual. For we must consider that it was William Steffe's Sunday-school hymn that, associated with Julia Ward Howe's text, became *The Battle Hymn of the Republic*, and that the religious genre was occasionally cultivated by writers of secular songs, Foster and Root among them.

Kindred features appear in Work's *Kingdom Coming* (published 1862). However, the tune, as a whole, with its echoes of *Dixie*, its rhythmic verve, and the humorous Negro dialect of its text, was inspired by minstrel music.

Early American Art-Song

The musical scene in America after the middle of the century was

45 William B. Bradbury, *Bradbury's Fresh Laurels For The Sabbath School*, New York, 1867, p. 154.

characterized by two phenomena: the establishment of the professional composer, and, in spite of his cultivation of a variety of musical genres, his preference for art-song.[46] The latter no doubt occurred under the impact of European romanticism with its interest in a form that was brief, lyrical, and verbally articulate. Most of such songs came from the pen of New Englanders like George Chadwick (1854–1931) and Arthur Foote (1853–1937), each of whom wrote about a hundred of them from the 'eighties on over a period of about forty years. Horatio Parker (1863–1919) made his earliest vocal contributions as late as the 'nineties, but the activities of the group actually began thirty years earlier, with songs of minor significance by Dudley Buck (1839–1909).

With regard to the direction of these composers, it is interesting to recall that John Knowles Paine (1839–1906), a representative of the group, still rejected Wagner and Liszt in the 'seventies (though he changed his mind ten years later) and recommended 'for the present and future . . . adherence to the historical forms, as developed by Bach, Handel, Mozart and Beethoven in church music, the oratorio, opera and instrumental music'.[47] He made no reference to song, but from his own few songs, written between 1870 and 1890, we know that he was guided by German models of the very early part of the century.

It was the custom at this time for practically all American composers to study in Germany for a few years. They returned with an infinitely more solid sense of craftsmanship than existed in earlier generations: for example, their piano parts were carefully worked out and written to complement the vocal line and its text, their middle voices and basses showed continuity, and their modulation planning. However, since they were conservative, timidly clinging to worn concepts of early romanticism, their songs remained nondescript.[48] As far as details are concerned, we find, in Chadwick, elements of Mendelssohn, Schubert, Karl Löwe and of the tepid English 'ballad'.[49] In songs of other composers there are faint echoes of Schumann but, of course,

[46] Hughes, op. cit., preface: 'a line drawn through the year 1865 would include on its hither side practically every effort at composition that an American composer has ever made with proper tools and training and serious intent.' Grove's Dictionary of Music and Musicians, edition of 1908 (article Song) stated: 'Song . . . is a form much cultivated by Americans, 'adding that 'It is only within the last fifty years that American song-writers have claimed attention in the musical world.'

[47] M. A. DeWolfe Howe, John Knowles Paine, in The Musical Quarterly, XXV (1939), p. 257.

[48] The same opinion is expressed in Arthur Farwell and W. Dermet Darby, Music in America (The Art of Music, vol. 4), New York, 1915, p. 355.

[49] See Carl Engel, George W. Chadwick, in The Musical Quarterly, X (1924), p. 438, and Grove's Dictionary, edition of 1908 (article Song).

none of Brahms, nor do they appear at any time in later American art songs of consequence.

In the German romantic tradition, Chadwick and Foote, also Parker (though with greater skill in part-writing), composed a few 'Lieder im Volkston', leaning however on the style of Scotch, Irish, and English folk-music.

In view of the formulæ of the group, academic at best, banal at worst, the text in the average song remains a mere caption. Very little thought was given to the inflection of the words and to prosody – a fault that a modern critic like Virgil Thomson still found in too many American songs of his own period.[50] In the following example by Chadwick (*Nocturne*) the text almost sounds like a translation that had been forcibly adapted to the melody:

Ex. 8 Appassionato e poco meno mosso

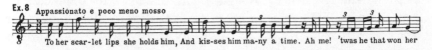

To her scar-let lips she holds him, And kis-ses him ma-ny a time. Ah me! 'twas he that won her

An additional composer may be mentioned here if only for historical reasons: Ethelbert Nevin (1862–1901). In his songs, published from the 'eighties on and enjoying the widest popularity, he is far more adventurous than his New England colleagues. His idiomatic accompaniments draw on the resources of post-Chopin piano music, and in some of his songs, French melodic influence is pronounced. This was something new in America, presaging a change of taste that was about to take place.[51]

Nevin's songs belong to the category of 'salon music', comparable in their shallow elegance to Cécile Chaminade's concoctions. *The Rosary* (published in 1893), widely known in its day and not yet forgotten, is hardly within the confines of art but its sentimentality – exactly parelleling the text (which concludes in this way: 'I kiss each bead, and strive at last to learn to kiss the Cross: sweetheart! to kiss the Cross') – might be admired for the effortless skill of its originator.

Edward MacDowell

Though Edward MacDowell (1861–1908) is very little thought of at present, he was recognized in his time as a man of genuine talent and thorough professional equipment, in fact as the first American composer

[50] See statements of his in William Treat Upton, *A Supplement to Art-Song in America 1930–38*, Philadelphia, 1938, p. 39, and in *The American Song* in his own book *The Art of Judging Music*, New York, 1948.

[51] Arthur Foote, *A Bostonian Remembers*, in *The Musical Quarterly*, XXIII (1937), with reference to 'organ playing', p. 39: 'in the 90's we turned our steps towards Paris instead of Berlin . . .'

of international standing. His artistic horizon was considerably wider than that of the New England group of composers: not only did he know considerably more music than they did[52] but his sense of contemporaneity was keener. He was attracted to Grieg, Tchaïkovsky, Liszt and Wagner and remained faithful to them, untouched by Debussy and Richard Strauss, the avant-gardists of the 'nineties.[53]

Having studied in France as well as in Germany, he combined stimulations from both countries in a distinct, though circumscribed, style of his own. Among a variety of musical genres, he wrote forty-odd songs in spite of the fact that he had many doubts about the validity of song-writing. He was obsessed by the integrity and uniqueness of poetry and tortured by the idea that it could not be translated into adequate musical terms. 'Language and music have nothing in common,' he said; in fact, he thought them 'diametrically opposed'. To him 'the paramount value of the poem is that of its suggestion in the field of instrumental music . . .', probably as a motto or caption. After making 'many experiments for finding the affinity of language and music', he came to the conclusion (even going beyond Wagner who abandoned it in his songs) that the two 'cannot be accurately stated unless one has written both'. This he did in his last three song albums (Op. 56, with the exception of one song; Op. 58 and Op. 60) but only in a handful of his earlier songs.[54]

Of the greatest concern were to him the literary aspects of the vocal line. The latter was to be constructed in a way that 'the attention of the hearer . . . [would] be fixed upon the central point of declamation', and the piano accompaniment, unfortunately 'often . . . a piano fantasie with no resemblance to the melody,' should not detract from it.[55] Indeed, his own accompaniments follow this principle. They faithfully support the voice, with more or less sustained chords in folk-song-like compositions and with more animated and cautiously complimentary rhythms in others. However, MacDowell goes so far as to deprive himself of characteristic motives and thus renounce, perhaps purposely, a major means of psychological suggestiveness. The function of his accompaniment is usually confined to adding a specific, vibrant timbre to the melody. This enhances the individuality

[52] See his lectures on the history of music given at Columbia University and published as *Critical and Historical Essays*, Boston, 1912.

[53] See Lawrence Gilman, *Edward MacDowell*, New York, 1908; edition of 1921, pp. 72 and 74–76.

[54] Gilman, op. cit., pp. 165 and 166.

[55] The above quotations from MacDowell in Gilman, op. cit., pp. 163 – 165.

of the total style but the strong emphasis on prettiness of sound (the harmony is studded with sonorous seventh chords, many secondary dominants among them) tends to make the song decorative and to lend its poetry a flabbily elegant appearance.[56]

What MacDowell was able to achieve with the vocal line by means of imaginative declamation (supported here by exceptionally well-knit harmonic progressions) is shown by an example from *Tyrant Love* in his last song album, Op. 60, published in 1902.

Ex. 9

Light wings hath he As an-y bee Let not him free, For he a-

- lone, Ah me! He a-lone Can rule the king-dom he Hath won, Ah me!

Such a passage is rare in his work, but it suggests his potentialities shortly before his illness and subsequent death.[57]

MacDowell's vocal style, developing from Schumannesque sources, matured slowly. Not until Op. 47 and, more consistently until Op. 56 (published in 1898), did it attain a flavour of its own.

Chromaticism he used sparingly. Instead, in a number of his songs he tended towards a modal folk-song style that, in spite of Scotch and Irish elements (usually varied but more literal in Op. 34 to texts by Robert Burns) was of his own making. Like all romanticists he was attracted to an idiom that guaranteed him a measure of genuineness and historical remoteness.

To the folk-music of his own country he resorted little. However, in preference to the music of the Negro, the 'stern . . . manly and free rudeness'[58] of Indian chant appealed to him, and he let himself be

[56] Daniel Gregory Mason, *Contemporary Composers*, New York, 1918, chapter on *Music in America*: '[MacDowell] frequently cloys by an over-sweet sentimentalism.'
[57] The same thought is expressed in Upton, *Art-Song In America*, p. 124.
[58] Gilman, op. cit., p. 84.

guided by it in the motives and themes of two instrumental works ('Suite No. 2' for orchestra and No. 5 of 'Woodland Sketches' for piano). Basically, he had little sympathy for folkloristic quotation, especially when it was proclaimed to be beneficial to the development of a national style in American music. Moreover, he had serious doubts about the validity of adapting chords to musical folk-lore.[59] However, since his views in this respect were inconsistent,[60] it is uncertain whether he would have rejected, as firmly as we do, piano accompaniments of men like Charles W. Cadman[61] and Arthur Farwell, which, with much literal-mindedness, link Indian chant with the harmonic organization of major and minor tonalities.

The Early Twentieth Century

The history of American song during the first two decades of the twentieth century is marked by a pronounced orientation towards French aesthetics. It is significant that at times even French poetry was set to music as it was significant that Chadwick and MacDowell, in their early works, resorted to German texts.

The songs of John Alden Carpenter (1876–1951), except for a brief excursion into Mahler's folk-song style and the sparse part-writing of his accompaniment,[62] fall entirely under the influence of Debussy's concepts around 1910 and adhere to them for more than ten years. Their delicate sonorities and evocative poetic atmosphere reveal a musician of taste and craftsmanship but only within the limits of a style that was not sufficiently his own. In 1926, when the majority of his vocal works had already been published, he made the attempt to break away from it. In his 'Four Negro Songs' to texts by Langston Hughes he utilized the racy idiom of jazz. He tried to paraphrase it in his own manner (a procedure which Copland was soon to adopt successfully in instrumental music) but actually surrendered to it without achieving the authenticity of a Broadway product.

Charles Martin Loeffler (1861–1935) was born in Alsace and came to America in his early twenties. In contradistinction to Carpenter, who had received his musical education mainly in America (apart from

---

[59] See his *Critical And Historical Essays*, p. 146: 'Folk melodies are, without exception, homophonous [monophonic].'

[60] For example in his *Essays*, chapter XII, he published an 'Arabian Melody' along with an accompaniment in D minor.

[61] Charles Wakefield Cadman, *'Idealization' Of Indian Music*, in *The Musical Quarterly*, I (1915). See the following remark on an Indian chant: 'On account of its buoyancy it seemed to demand the key of B major.'

[62] In *The Cock Shall Crow* (1908), and *Don't Ceäre* (1911).

a few lessons with Edward Elgar), he studied in Germany and France. His songs – mainly set to French texts – were written between the beginning of the century and the mid-'twenties, but most of those that were published appeared between 1903 and 1908. His model was Fauré as well as a style that combined French and Wagnerian elements.[63]

In 1922, Oscar G. Sonneck stated[64] that 'the average American musician . . . [is] ten years behind the times with his taste for modern music, and the average music-lover twenty. . . .' He also found the works of contemporary American composers 'with exceedingly few exceptions . . . rather tame and conventional and old-fashioned, if one discounts naïve excursions into the whole-tone scale of Debussy or rather rare pilgrimages to the now abundantly charted shores of Strawinsky, Scriabin, Schœnberg, and occasional, but somewhat futile and clumsy, compliments to jazz'. These were harsh words, but they must be taken seriously, for Sonneck judged the musical scene not only by published works but also by the large amount of unpublished ones that went through his hands as an editor of G. Schirmer's. However, he might have brightened up his analysis by mentioning Charles T. Griffes (1884–1920). Here was a composer who was well on his way towards developing into a figure of distinction. Indeed his talents had been fully recognized by various professionals (among them Prokofiev, Monteux, Stokowski, Harold Bauer, even Sonneck himself) who, when a premature death ended Griffes's career, publicly declared their 'admiration and respect' for his work and mourned the 'great loss' that the music of America had suffered.[65]

Griffes was the first American-born composer of consequence whose work was closely linked to the international scene of his time. He was familiar with new scores by Debussy, Ravel, Scriabin, Stravinsky, Schoenberg, Busoni, Milhaud, Varèse, and the American Ornstein and thus keenly aware of the new trends – indeed contributing to them – that were transforming the musical vocabulary of the Western world. But he was no mere observer nor an uncritical admirer of the European avant-gardists. Instead, he utilized their stimulus to pursue his own course. Had he lived longer and thus been encouraged

---

[63] See Carl Engel, *Charles Martin Loeffler*, in *The Musical Quarterly*, XI (1925), p. 311. Paul Rosenfeld in his *Musical Portraits*, New York, 1920, p. 265, mentions more specifically the influence of 'the Wagnerizing Frenchmen'.

[64] *The American Composer And The American Publisher*, in *The Musical Quarterly*, IX (1923) p. 122, but delivered as an address one year earlier.

[65] Marion Bauer, *Charles T. Griffes As I Remember Him*, in *The Musical Quarterly*, XXIX (1943), p. 361.

by the musical activities in America that began in the late 'twenties, his gifts would probably have come to full fruition.

As a youngster of seventeen he wrote three songs to French texts. To judge by the facsimile of one manuscript page,[66] they reveal a sense for delicate pianistic sonorities if nothing more. Afterwards came a temporary orientation towards German music under the influence of his study in Berlin (under Humperdinck). Thus his songs written in 1909 and 1910 are not only based on texts of Heine, Eichendorff, Lenau, Geibel and Mosen but are musically in the Brahms – Richard Strauss tradition with a tendency towards the copious piano arrangements of the latter.[67] He soon became critical of Strauss[68] and turned towards French concepts. Between 1911 and 1918 he composed about thirty songs, two-thirds of which have appeared in print. In none of them, not even the late ones of this period, do we find a style that is exclusively of his own making, but there are intriguing aspects everywhere. *The first snowfall* (John B. Tabb) of 1912 is an example. While its melody points in the direction of MacDowell, it is the piano accompaniment that lends value to the song (Ex, 10):

Ex.10 Slowly and softly

The Fir tree felt it with a thrill And mur - mur of con-tent; The

pp

(The accompaniment veiled through a constant use of both pedals)

last dead leaf its ca - ble slipt And from its moor - ings went,

Its harmony (developed from Debussy and Ravel except for its stronger tonality) contains a very original exploitation of dissonances by way of part-writing. It should be stressed in any case that the composer, in

[66] Edward M. Maisel, *Charles T. Griffes*, New York, 1943, p. 31.
[67] Upton, *Art-Song in America*, p. 251.
[68] Maisel, op. cit., p. 110.

spite of his frequent use of impressionist block harmonies, always showed an interest in linearity also. Additional proof of this appears in a passage in *This Book of Hours* (Walter Crane) of 1914 to the words: 'This priceless book is bought with tears untold.' The purity that he attains here, against the *raffinement* of sound, stems from the tranquil motion of quasi-modal voices, regulated by a contrapuntal setting – a procedure reminiscent of Fauré's *Une Sainte en son Auréole*. Two years later, in *Phantoms* (A. Giovannitti), he is again close to Ravel – though he deviates from him in the astonishingly narrow spacing of some of his chords – and in his *Sorrow of Mydath* (John Masefield) of 1917 he follows Debussy and yet at moments goes beyond him by approaching polytonality.

During the first two decades of the century various composers (such as Ravel, Mahler, Stravinsky and Debussy) felt attracted to the Orient. This was partly because of a post-romantic interest in exoticism but even more so because of the encouragement Oriental music and poetry offered them in their efforts to break away from the style of the past. Griffes, too, was affected by this trend. Fascinated by the melodies of the Far East and Oceania, the few with which he became acquainted, by Japanese instruments and Japanese art, he finally believed that 'Modern music tends more and more towards the archaic, especially the archaism of the East.'[69] In his 'Five Poems of Ancient China and Japan' (composed in 1916–17) he therefore used the appropriate pentatonic scales (and one hexatonic one) and, rejecting conventional harmony, he resorted to fourths and fifths (alone or else clearly audible in a three- or four-part setting), recurrent chords and figurations. In his dynamics he avoided Western crescendi and decrescendi. All this remained essentially colouristic; it did not quite attain the structural level of a Whistler, whose fusion of Japanese and Western elements he admired.

Griffes's oriental excursions were only temporary. In his songs of 1918 he returned to a more traditional idiom – to his former luxurious piano settings and sometimes even to the stentorian climaxes of the late nineteenth century. It was rather in music devoid of literary associations – in piano music[70] – that he could realize his artistic intentions at this time.

. . . . .

[69] Maisel, op. cit., p. 205.
[70] See his piano sonata, completed in 1918, and the facsimile of a manuscript page of his 'Five Pieces' for piano of 1919 (in Maisel, op. cit., opposite p. 302).

Compared with Griffes, Carpenter and Loeffler, it was Sidney Homer (1864–1953) who was America's song-writer *par excellence*, producing about one hundred of them (the best between 1899 and 1915[71]) to the almost complete exclusion of instrumental music.

He studied first with Chadwick and then, like his teacher, in Munich with Rheinberger. In spite of the stylistic changes around him, he persistently wrote, throughout a long life, in a style that continued the tradition of a Chadwick and of a Nevin (an 'expurgated' or 'semi-expurgated' one, that is). His songs were widely performed at their time; that they are now largely forgotten is because they tend too often to the facile and the commonplace.

Nevertheless they reveal a grasp of relevant aspects of the genre: above all the fact, as exemplified by the *Lied* or the *mélodie*, that alone paucity and appropriateness of means can translate a brief, poignant poetic statement into its musical equivalent.

The emphasis in Homer's songs is always on the melodic line. Compared with the excessive sinuousness of late romantic music, it is rather a restrained one. It shuns large, charged intervals; and it is predominantly syllabic and symmetrical. The latter aspect is entirely flexible; when phrases are lengthened or shortened, it is usually advantageous to the word accents or to the tempo of the poem. The syllabic style serves the audibility of the words, while pitches and note values underline the declamation, though one elegant in character rather than profoundly interpretative. The melody is therefore more convincing associated with light than with serious verse.

Although the vocal line is restricted, it is wholly cantabile. This is due no little to the accompaniment. Spaced with much deliberation, it supports and at times envelops the upper melody and spells out its inherent rhythm. It owes its own coherence chiefly to the coherence of the lines that delimit its harmony.

It is regrettable that, in spite of details such as these, the end result is thinned out, with very few exceptions, by the conventionality of the composer's harmonic and melodic resources. If this is true, then it is not so much his songs as a whole that can contribute to 'a tradition of American song-writing of higher standards and greater possibilities'[72] (as Samuel Barber would have it), as the neatness and intelligence of their structure.

---

[71] See Samuel Barber (ed.), 'Seventeen Songs By Sidney Homer', New York, 1943. They were selected as representative with the assistance of the composer himself.
[72] Barber, op. cit., preface.

One song of the composer, ·*Pirate Story* (text by Robert Louis Stevenson), published in 1906 and unfortunately not included in Barber's collection ('Seventeen Songs by Sidney Homer'), deserves an extra comment. Very successfully Homer combines here a melody of the Victor Herbert variety but of sharper profile with a rhythm in the accompaniment that may have come from ragtime. The time signature is $\frac{3}{4}$, but it is re-defined by chords, with slight off-beat accentuations, as $\frac{2}{8}$. At a climactic moment this is openly acknowledged (Ex. 11). It is historically interesting that not only this passage,

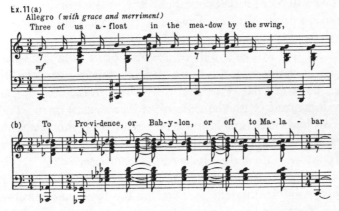

Ex.11(a)
Allegro *(with grace and merriment)*
Three of us a-float in the mea-dow by the swing,

(b) To Pro-vi-dence, or Bab-y-lon, or off to Ma-la-bar

but the entire song, with its literacy and verve, anticipates sophisticated examples of the popular music of the 'twenties and 'thirties.

Charles Ives and others

The numerous songs that Charles E. Ives wrote from 1888 over a period of more than thirty years were not published until 1922[73] (with the exception of a few that appeared later). It took almost a generation until they were listened to with respect and occasional pleasure by the average newspaper critic and the average audience, although their merits had been recognized by various professionals since the 'thirties. It is evident that the time-lag between Ives's creative life and its effect on the outside world was considerable.

Ives (1874–1954) was not a full-time composer. He had chosen the career of a businessman because, as he said in his characteristically disarming way, he disapproved of the man with a family who would let his 'children starve on his dissonances'.[74] How difficult, in the early days of this century, life was for the American musician in America

[73] '114 Songs', Redding, Connecticut, privately published.
[74] Henry Cowell and Sidney Cowell, *Charles Ives And His Music*, New York, 1955, p. 37.

can be gauged by the following statement (a document of epigrammatic candour) that appeared in a serious American publication of
1915:[75] 'Music is not yet generally regarded as a profession for men.
Men go into business; they become brokers, lawyers, or politicians;
they even become newspaper reporters – but not musicians. Music is
still *par excellence* the avocation of long-haired, libidinous foreigners.'

Ives's 'Album of 114 Songs', his first publication, is easy to mis-
understand. First of all, it includes about a dozen songs (written in the
manner of the sentimental ballads and the hit-tunes of the day) to
which the composer himself concedes 'little or no musical value'. They
are merely to prove that 'the fewer . . . [of their kind] are composed,
published, sold or sung the better it is for the progress of music
generally'.[76] Unfortunately, there are also other songs, in fact more
than twice as many, that are of no didactic purpose and yet of equal
banality. They are partly in the same sheet-music idiom, partly in
that of salon-music (with elements from Rubinstein) or in an anaemic
Wagnerian chromaticism. It must be emphasized, however, that the
majority of these songs, trivial by design or by accident, were written
before 1900; they are early efforts of the composer.

Another group of early songs obscure the character of the Album
by almost literally imitating the style of the later nineteenth-century
song type (German and French) along with its respective languages,
or by relying on the Tchaïkovskyan vocabulary.[77]

What remains is a sizeable amount of original songs whose individuality is unmistakable. Nevertheless, here too a word of criticism
is necessary: they often convince not so much in toto (by way of
large-scale musical relations and contrasts) as through an accumulation
of bold details.

The existence of a characteristically American quality in many of
Ives's songs can be demonstrated with the following experiment.
Let them be performed with the subtleties of diction, timbre and
dynamics as demanded by the traditional European vocal repertoire.
The performance will sound stilted; but entirely natural if done by a
singer whose voice and manner are shaped by the informal and
comparatively steady cadences of American speech.

One of the main elements that contribute to the native character
of Ives's songs are quotations from American hymns, which, by the

[75] Farwell and Darby, op. cit., p. 44.

[76] Both quotations from notes that the composer appended to his song album.

[77] Concerning the above analysis, see Aaron Copland, *Our New Music*, New York, 1941,
pp. 155 and 156, who expresses very similar ideas.

way, occur in many of his instrumental pieces as well.[78] Most frequently
the urbanized gospel hymns of the second half of the nineteenth
century (by Lowry, Bradbury and their like, also by the somewhat
earlier Lowell Mason) are made use of but hardly at all folk-hymnody
and its eighteenth-century predecessor. The tune 'Nettleton' by John
Wyeth (in *The Innate*) is among the exceptions,[79] and so are, though
merely by way of suggestion, a few vocal passages based on gapped
scales. Often, however, such passages, especially when they include
pronounced modal progressions of a major second upwards, have a
vaguely archaic and thus a remote and placeless flavour.

It was not so much the artistic merit of these hymns (slight as it is)
that concerned the composer as their value as symbols: there was of
course about them a religious and ethical significance – a relevant
point to a man of Ives's convictions – and it is of interest to know that he
considered those of his songs that contained hymns or parts of them
and appropriate texts as 'suitable for some religious services';[80]
secondly, they were to him signs of American life itself, a 'local color',
as he called it:[81] finally, they incorporated cherished reminiscences of
his youth. The latter can be gathered from two song texts, written by
himself (and these, like many other aspects of his work, have autobiographical overtones) where he utilizes old hymns ('Visions of
homeland . . . strains of childhood')[82] to evoke the atmosphere of the
small Connecticut town in which he grew up.

Other aspects of Ives's songs that are suggestive of the American
scene are quotations from War songs (from the eighteenth century
on), popular songs and ragtime (this, being originally piano music,
usually in the accompaniment), and a cowboy ballad (*Charlie
Rutlage*). At times, colloquial American speech is paralleled in the
vocal line.

All these features (and it must be emphasized that numerous
quotations have no American references whatever) must be understood as the result of the composer's desire to make the details of his
texts as vivid and as realistic as possible. Other composers, during the
nineteenth century, did similar things but, compared with Ives, more
sparingly and with less literal means – frequently confining themselves

[78] Cowell, op. cit., p. 164.

[79] Ives heard it sung in his childhood; see Cowell, op. cit., p. 23.

[80] From the composer's notes at the end of '114 Songs'. See Cowell, op. cit., p. 43.

[81] See also Cowell, op. cit., p. 149, where Ives tries to bring the meaning of this quality into
line with his transcendentalist philosophy.

[82] From *Down East*. Similar references in *The Things Our Fathers Loved*. See Cowell, op. cit.,
pp. 23 and 24.

to a single recurrent motive in the piano accompaniment whose meaning is variable.

In Ives's songs a reference to religion or a moral principle at once elicits the quotation of a hymn or a part of it (or perhaps only of a plagal cadence). The idea of triviality is sometimes underlined by a few measures of a vulgar syncopated dance rhythm. Other examples are equally direct. In the song *Majority*, the concept of the masses is symbolized, visually and aurally, by a multitude of tones in the accompaniment sounded simultaneously – by harsh, powerful tone clusters. At the word 'plunge' in *The Swimmers*, the vocal line makes a precipitate downward motion. In *Grantchester*, at the mention of the word 'faun' (in this satirical context: 'And clever men have seen a faun a-peeping through the green, and felt the Classics were not dead . . .'), a passage from Debussy's *L'après-midi d'un faune* makes its appearance. The frequency of such devices in one song can be shown with an excerpt from *On the Antipodes*:

Here is a contemplation of the various aspects of nature. The feeling of its 'eternity' is conveyed with a long, sweeping melodic line; its 'geometry' by a stiff, artificial rhythm; its 'mystery' by a phrase that is undecided in its direction and vague in its accentuations; its 'nice and sweet' character – the concept of the philistine – by a stale waltz, and so forth.

Such illustrative passages, which are usually concentrated in the voice part, never appear in isolation; they are embedded in a melodic and harmonic context that tends to counteract their literalness.

To what extent a quotation, even an extensive one, can serve as a mere prop can be shown with a few examples. *The Circus Band* and *The Side-Show* are based on music of an appropriate character, but this is varied in such a way (in fact with very slight but effective rhythmic irregularities) that the result is at once a slice of reality and a commentary about it. *General William Booth enters into Heaven* is fashioned after a hymn of the Salvation Army, and yet through melodic changes, interpolations and poignantly suggestive harmony there emerges (in keeping with Vachel Lindsay's text) a mad and powerful panorama of a revivalistic scene in which we participate and which we observe. Here, too, much use is made of stylized declamation. Indeed, the note-values, pitches and tempo of many other of Ives's vocal lines approximate emotionally significant oratory – not merely the explosive statement but the quiet and even humorous one as well.

This brings us to a basic method of Ives's song-writing. He tends to provide each new scene or image with music of its own, i.e. he progresses from one musical idea to another. From this results an additive song structure – a decisive departure from the practice of the nineteenth century. Repetitions exist, however, but they usually occur without delay and chiefly in the accompaniment (as brief ostinati or, more traditionally, as recurrent, rhythmic figurations). Nevertheless, in his *Incantation* (before 1910–21), the ever-experimenting composer exploits the principle of literal repetition not only in the piano part but, to a large extent, in the vocal part also.

It is often said (to stress Ives's originality) that he developed his style from his own resources, but this is only partially true. His melodic vocabulary, for example, consists of three elements, two of them traditional: one (imbued with American hymns) is related to a late eighteenth- or early nineteenth-century Central European idiom; the other to German romanticism (without reference to a specific composer); the third emerged from Ives's desire to preserve the speech quality of his texts by utilizing a large number of repeated and adjacent notes, such intervals as tritones, sevenths, and ninths (usually non-cantabile if unsupported by a triadic harmony), spoken passages, and non-metrical notation. This style appeared for the first time in his songs *The Cage* (adapted in 1906 from an instrumental piece of 1904) and in *Soliloquy* (1907), but kindred ones were in the air at that time and even earlier, and it is most unlikely that the composer was entirely unaware of them. They were of special concern to such post-Wagnerians as Hugo Wolf, Richard Strauss (*Salome*), and the Debussy of *Pelléas et Mélisande*; they inspired Schoenberg's *Waller im Schnee*, a song of 1907, and they made Arthur Farwell, in America, speak of what he called 'sound-speech' as early as 1903.[83]

[83] Quoted by Edward N. Waters, *The Wa-Wan Press*, in *A Birthday Offering to Carl Engel*, New York, 1943.

Ives was too unmethodical a composer to set up two song types with *The Cage* and *Soliloquy* (Ex. 13), which he would follow

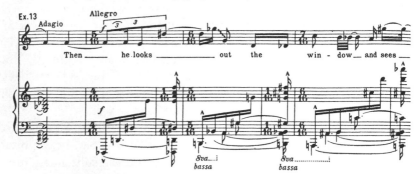

henceforth. While he reserves many major seconds for the former (as parts of a vocal line whose deliberate drabness and incongruous word accents add a touch of surrealist inanity to the story) and many major sevenths for the latter, he makes no attempt to keep the two intervals apart in later songs.

Though Ives resorted to a major or minor tonality when he felt it appropriate to his text, he was fond of atonal chord progressions and non-triadic sonorities brought about by superimposed blocks or radical polyphony. Nor did he hesitate to utilize such chords for the accompaniment of tonal hymns. Since, in his harmony, he anticipated the avant-gardists of the early twentiety century by several years (he knew none of their scores then and, even in later years, negligibly few), one must assume that he developed his harmonic idiom chiefly from personal experiences. There were, first of all, certain Yankee qualities in him that he wished to bring out into the open: showing little regard for triads, 'chords without bites to them',[84] as he called them, he aimed at something considerably more astringent, something that would be in keeping with his own temperament and heritage.[85] Furthermore, he was inspired and encouraged by his father, who was not merely a bandmaster but a musical tinkerer, experimenting with quarter-tones, scale without octaves, unorthodox, percussive chords, and even sounds resulting from several different, only slightly related, compositions played at the same time. Finally, he was inspired by a Thoreauesque communion with nature: in particular by

[84] Quoted in Cowell, op. cit., p. 25.

[85] As early as 1897 he combined vertically C minor and D minor as well as major and minor triads, adjacently placed, in order (to use his own words) 'to represent the sternness and strength and austerity of the Puritan character . . . ' (see Cowell, op. cit., p. 34).

the chance simultaneity of heard and seen phenomena such as rustling trees, church bells, echoes, mist, and their variegated intensities.[86]

The majority of American composers who established their reputation between the late 'twenties and the 'forties, channelled their energies into instrumental, chiefly orchestral, and choral works. Among them were Aaron Copland, Roger Sessions, Roy Harris, Walter Piston, and William Schuman. Their neglect of the art-song resulted partly from their hostility towards a form that was a favourite vehicle of the romantic period, partly from the conviction that a professional career in America was possible only with large-scale statements;[87] and, finally, from the availability, in many American cities, of good orchestras and choral groups.

In the early 'forties there was reason still to complain[88] of an 'over-emphasis on orchestral music' and of the general feeling 'that anything which can be said with less than a chorus of a hundred, or eight horns in unison, is not worth saying'. It was at about that time, however, that the musical scene began to right itself.

The panorama of American art-song during the last twenty-odd years is clouded by a diversity of concepts, influences, and standards.[89] In order to clarify it and at the same time create something like foreground, middle-ground, and background, it seemed essential to be highly selective rather than highly comprehensive. Under the circumstances, a compromise between the two is impossible. Thus only those composers will be discussed who have shown a special interest in the genre. The sequence that has been chosen (apart from a brief, complementary epilogue) may not be ideal, but it does afford a demonstration of certain trends and, roughly, of their chronological order.

First come the song writers who, like their colleagues in the late nineteenth and early twentieth century, are inspired by German or French models, then those who (in spite of European stimulations) tend away from the European scene either by resorting to native sources or by means of the individuality of their style. They are followed by composers who, with their interest in atonality and dodecaphony, have

---

[86] See his songs *Thoreau* and *The Housatonic at Stockbridge* as well as his article *Music and Its Future*, in Henry Cowell (ed.), *American Composers on American Music*, Stanford, California, 1933. With regard to the activities of Ives's father, see Cowell, *Charles Ives And His Music*, pp. 18 – 22.

[87] This was suggested to the author by Roger Sessions.

[88] Samuel Barber, op. cit., preface.

[89] The question of what is American and what is not can hardly be answered without a measure of arbitrariness. Since the line had to be drawn somewhere, significant songs by Erich Itor Kahn, to mention only one of the many European composers who came to the United States as mature artists in the 'thirties and 'forties, have been excluded.

re-established contact with the outside world, by now an international one.

Two composers, whose style is informed by nineteenth-century concepts and who, no doubt for this reason, have a preference for song writing, are Ernst Bacon (b. 1898) and Paul Nordoff (b. 1909).

Bacon's early collection of 'Ten Songs' (published 1928) is set, in the manner of an earlier generation of American composers, to German texts and in a German romantic idiom. This was varied later, but not essentially modified. In the 'forties Bacon wrote his 'Declaration of Independence' in which he quoted Melville's dictum:[90] 'Let us boldly condemn all imitation . . . and foster all originality though at first it be crabbed and ugly as our own pine knots', and then tried his hand at arranging American folk-songs (for example in *Along Unpaved Roads*, published 1944) and settings of American poetry.

Among the latter stand out two songs to texts by Emily Dickinson: *O Friend* and *Velvet People*. It is especially the second that matches its words to perfection – not only their honeyed, girlish sound, but their blend of romantic fancy and epigrammatic observations (Ex. 14). The

means of the composer are chiefly derived from the past century, yet their historical associations make them highly appropriate. They also include the modern device of the rhythmic ostinato which, while adding capricious rhythmic effects to the atmosphere of the music (which is reminiscent of a Mendelssohnian Midsummer Night's Dream), underlines the precision inherent in its language.

The type of song that emerges from Nordoff's earliest publication ('Twelve Songs', 1931–35) adheres to an older convention. It combines elements of the pre-Debussy era with an accompaniment that is less subdued, more eloquent in its figuration and more straightforwardly pianistic than one finds in French music. With this collection the composer staked out a claim, so to speak, which he continued to

[90] *The Southern Literary Messenger*, April, 1940, reprinted with a postscript in the *Bulletin of American Composers Alliance*, vol. VII, No. 2, 1958.

cultivate during the ensuing years up to his 'Four Songs' (1943–48) to texts by E. E. Cummings. In the process, the early style was changed in details. The voice part became more responsive to the exigencies of the poetic declamation and the accompaniment acquired greater subtlety in its relation to the rhythm of the melody and to the poetic images.

Most of Nordoff's lyrical songs tend to rely on the 'atmospheric' function of pianistic sonorities – delicate ones but often too efficiently idiomatic. To judge by the Cummings song *Sam*, written in the manner of a 'slow cake-walk' ('Rain or hail sam done the best he kin till they digged his hole . . .'), it seems that the composer's talents are best applied to the genre that Poulenc has developed so successfully.

Chanler and Thomson

Theodore Chanler (b. 1902) is not one of those composers who gain strength from rebelling against the past. He has openly proclaimed Fauré as his master. Since the 'twenties he has been inspired not merely by his style but even more so by the intelligence that governs it. He admires, to use his own words, 'the subtle simplicity of Fauré's thought, the unexpectedness that is yet always logical, and, most of all, how much he could say with few notes'.[91] Chanler's reference was to Fauré's vocal music and he has applied its principles to his own songs. Accordingly he believes that the vocal part should have 'a recognizable and relatively independent musical shape . . .' but basically result from literary considerations: its 'length, its rhythmic design, even its general contour, are all in one way or another conditioned by the text'. The accompaniment, in spite of a certain amount of 'autonomy', is to act as a 'support' of what he envisions as 'the usually frail structure of the melody'. Here is a 'hierarchy' of elements that, though he wants it to be flexible, seems to him essential to song-writing.[92]

What he admires about Fauré's rhythm is the way it develops out of what he calls 'a regular pulse'. The 'exploitation of a broken pulse of constantly changing measures . . .'[93] (meaning, as it does in earlier Stravinsky, patterns of stresses firmly established and quickly destroyed and the momentary silences that cut open the thread of motion like a gasp) is uncongenial to him. He has avoided this type of rhythm except

[91] *Gabriel Fauré, A Reappraisal*, in *Modern Music*, March–April, 1945.

[92] All quotations are from a statement of the composer in Robert Tangeman, *The Songs Of Theodore Chanler*, in *Modern Music*, May–June, 1945, where there is also a bibliography.

[93] The quotations are from Theodore Chanler, *Rhythm and Habit*, in *Modern Music*, May–June, 1944.

in one song (*Thomas Logge* in 'Eight Epitaphs') where it serves him to convey the oddness and eccentricity of the protagonist of his story.

In some of his songs he lets himself be guided entirely by Fauré's supple motion; in others he makes it more incisive through drier accents and staccati and the clearly defined duration of his tones. Moreover, he is well aware of strictly contemporary concepts. This is already noticeable in his early song *These, My Ophelia*[94] (version of 1925; text by Archibald MacLeish). While in Fauré's melody brief phrases of irregular length assert themselves shyly and never contradict the metre for more than a moment, they are in Chanler's song more irregular and more persistently so. Not only are they supported by the piano but the units into which they crystallize are predominantly asymmetrical (even such a metre as $\frac{9}{8}$ is made to sound like $\frac{4}{4}$ plus $\frac{1}{8}$) and very changeable. However, the cantability of the voice (which, as often in Fauré, is highly restricted in range and intervals) prevents shock effects, and a measure of regularity is introduced by a continuous alternation of the top and bottom part of the accompaniment. It is historically interesting that the static character of the chords, whose flux chiefly depends on cautiously moving middle voices, along with their Fauréan flavour anticipate certain aspects of Stravinsky's *Persephone*.

The Flight (Leonard Feeney; 1944), one of the most mature songs of the composer, shares various features with *These, My Ophelia*. The irregularity of the phrase structure of its vocal line, however, is more abrupt because of a frequent $\frac{5}{16}$ metre that now expands, now contracts, and the unpredictable alternation of three- and two-beat units. The setting as a whole is polyphonic in the sense that, in addition to the voice, its emphasis lies on an almost continuous bass, that, in spite of rests, provides the 'regular pulse' and that most convincingly combines harmonic function with linearity. The melodic style, especially that of the voice is, like Fauré's at times, a blend of French song tradition and Gregorian chant, but for the sake of the biblical subject of the text it leans more heavily on the latter.

Among the small number of Chanler's songs, all of which are distinguished by taste and fine workmanship, stand out *One of us* (in 'The Children', 1945; text by Leonard Feeney) and particularly the 'Eight Epitaphs' of 1937. Both works are very close to Fauré and yet preserve their independence – chiefly because of the grasp of poetic values they reveal.

[94] *Cos Cob Song Volume*, Cos Cob Press (Arrow Music Press), N.Y., 1935.

Indeed the congruity of text and music makes the 'Eight Epitaphs' one of the most valuable contributions to art-song in America. Chanler's tender and terse style fits eminently to Walter de la Mare's lines that evoke the memory of the dead: the young and the old, their virtues and foibles. Neither artist has any use for tearfulness though he knows plenty of pathos and even humour and sarcasm.

Each song of the cycle redefines Fauré's vocabulary in its own way. Though most of them are extremely brief, they are poignant from beginning to end. Their melodic style, derived from one mated to the French language, is nevertheless wholly obedient to English inflection. The subtle nuances of speech of which it is capable – sometimes approaching the recitative – never break the coherence of the vocal line. In the accompaniment aspects are considered that come from chamber-music: the registers, the precise number of voices, lucidity of texture (sometimes a single voice is of telling effect), the doubling of voices, and the distance between them as in *Alice Rodd*:

Virgil Thomson (b. 1896), professed admirer of Gallic mentality, follows the aesthetics of Satie: he aims at an appearance of disarming simplicity, freely resorting to the well known, the well worn and the outright trivial.[95] When qualities such as these occur in Stravinsky, they are usually counteracted by a musically eventful context, but Thomson is less eager to conceal them. Thus in *Preciosilla* (composed in Paris in 1926) he does not hesitate to give full-hearted support to the

[95] See also P. Glanville-Hicks, *Virgil Thomson*, in *The Musical Quarterly*, XXXV (1949), p. 209.

dadaist incongruities of Gertrude Stein's sentences. To quote an example: its concluding words 'Toast - - ed / su-sie is / my - - ice - / cream' are set to an authentic cadence, expanded in conservatory style (*fortissimo* and *maestoso*). In another song, Blake's *The Little Black Boy* (1951), the lachrymose overtones of the poem are inflated by a melody of the genuine silver-threads-among-the-gold variety, modified in the spontaneously jazzy manner of popular 'vocalists'. More subtle is a passage ('Then burst...') in one of the 'Four Songs to Poems of Thomas Campion' (1951): *Follow Your Saint*. In isolation it is a cliché but, in relation to the music that precedes it, it is artless rather than shabby – an effect that fits the text:

The French influence is almost extinct in present-day American song. In earlier years, in addition to Chanler, Thomson and Barber (in his 'Mélodies Passagères' to French texts by Rilke, 1950–51), it even affected a man like Copland. In his *Old Poem* (Arthur Waley, translated from Chinese), composed in 1920 prior to his residence in Paris, he points in the direction of Fauré; and his enthusiasm about that composer reveals itself clearly in an article he wrote a few years later.[96] Finally, in the *Vocalise* of 1928 he combines elements of Debussy with those of his own developing vocabulary (such as the rigid fourth in his melody, the disquieting alternation of two- and three-tone phrases, and the extension of scale-like passages to a ninth). Shortly after that

[96] See Arthur Berger, *Aaron Copland*, New York, 1943, p. 42, and A. Copland, *Gabriel Fauré, A Neglected Master*, in *The Musical Quarterly*, October, X (1924), p. 573.

(in 1930) appeared the 'Five Songs' (to texts from James Joyce's *Chamber Music*) by Israel Citkowitz, which lean towards Milhaud.

Barber, Diamond, Copland, Carter and others

Various aspects of the songs that Samuel Barber (b. 1910) wrote in the late 'twenties and the 'thirties come from a romantic tradition. Reminders of Brahms, for example, appear in the melody and the figuration of the accompaniment and sometimes even in its harmony.[97] Yet the settings are considerably more lucid, and avoiding Brahms's emphasis on metre, they not infrequently counterbalance an unabashed tonality with the modern means of irregular accents and irregular phrase-lengths.

From the early 'forties onwards Barber's melodic style absorbs Stravinskyan concepts. Relinquishing the sweep of traditional canta-bility, it now relies on brief equal note-values and adjacent pitches, and, for its continuity, on the repetition of note-patterns (and the intermittent repetition of single notes) with distinct, shifting accentuations. From this style the composer gains playful effects in *The Queen's Face on the Summer Coin* (1942) and particularly in *Monks and Raisins* of 1943, where the deliberate absurdity of the text ('I have observed pink monks eating blue raisins . . .') is stressed by a melody not dissimilar to a counting rhyme, and through subtle injuries to conventional declama-tion. The same type of melody is exploited with kindred results in *Promiscuity* (No. 7 of the 'Hermit Songs', 1952–3), and in *Knoxville: Summer of 1915*. Applied to more intense vocal parts (as in several of the 'Hermit Songs'), it proves, however, incapable of sustaining the music. Nor is this compensated in other ways. For the accompani-ments, fully professional though they are, are weakened by uneventful chord progressions.

Knoxville, for soprano and orchestra (1947), is considerably longer than an ordinary song; and yet, because of the intimacy of its effects, it has the appearance of a small-scale work.

The composer's agile, elastic melodic idiom served him well in solving the problems of James Agee's poetic prose. The scene is a small American town; it is evening and a child says out aloud what he observes and what he remembers. An initial motive, which, with accentual and melodic changes, reappears in large sections of the score, provides musical and psychological unity. It carries as well

---

[97] Nathan Broder, *Samuel Barber*, New York, 1954, pp. 60–61.

a variety of meanings: it suggests the patter of the child; it indicates, along with the rhythm of its accompaniment, the restfulness of the hour ('when people sit on their porches, rocking gently and talking

Ex.17

gently'); and, like a fragment of a folk tune, evokes the locale. The latter aspect becomes articulate when the talk of the child becomes so intense that a coherent melody is called for. The motive then transforms itself easily into what seems to be a recognizable melody (reminiscent of the music of the Southern Appalachian Mountains) but the prattling character of the story remains:

Ex.18

David Diamond (b. 1915) has cultivated the art-song more consistently than any other American composer of his standing. Between 1940 and the early 'fifties he published about forty songs whose quality is high throughout. Of himself he said:[98] 'The combination of great and tender texts by Melville, St. Teresa of Avila, Joyce, Mansfield, Lovelace, Keats and others, with my particular melodic, polyphonic and harmonic style, makes for the natural continuance of the art-song in our century.' This statement is, no doubt, too sweeping, but it shows at least that the composer is fully conscious of his task and his talent. Indeed, among the variety of forms that he commands, his songs represent his finest achievements.

Elegiac subjects suit his idiom particularly well. *Chatterton* (Keats), *Epitaph* (Melville), *Music when soft voices die* and *Lift not the painted veil* (both by Shelley), *On Death* (John Clare), *My little mother* (Mansfield), *This world is not my home* (anonymous text), speak of a valuable person or a moral quality that has disappeared but is remembered with sad affection.

[98] Quoted in Madeleine Goss, *Modern Music Makers*, New York, 1952, pp. 454–455.

444

Each of his songs is constructed with the same detailed care that is ordinarily given to an instrumental work. Piano parts are usually laid out in separate, independent and continuous lines, while pianistic sonorities are rarely exploited. What counts in performance is the beginning, ending and coherence of phrases, and these must be shown up with the subtlety of stress that would be appropriate to a setting for string quartet.

The bass has even fewer rests than the other lines of the accompaniment. Both fluent and firm, it acts like a counterpart to the voice – reminiscent of Hindemith's *Das Marienleben*.

In spite of this structure, all lines (in the manner of Renaissance music) resemble each other in their tranquil rhythm, their conjunct, cantabile motion, their partial modality, and the slight weight of their metrical accents within a quasi-polyphonic setting. The vocal part is singled out chiefly by rests and occasionally by repeated notes, brief phrases that frequently return to the same note (as equivalents of properties of speech and, indeed, sometimes in the appropriate rhythm), and by more widely arched lines for lyrical moments. It is a characteristic of the style that such lines are not made more sinuous but rather stiffened with a fourth, a fifth, an octave, or a triadic passage whose components remain separate, as in *Chatterton*:

In keeping with the mild, hymn-like character of the melodic style, the harmony confines itself to triadic formations, constantly varying them through the addition of a third or two (now with consonant, now

445

with dissonant effects), and wide and narrow spacings. From this results a balanced sonority that lives less on the variety of chords than on the degree of their fullness or bareness – on warm and cold 'tones', as painters would say.

Diamond's emphasis on musical structure evidently makes relations to the text doubly convincing. Such relations materialize (as the composer stated) by matching a particular kind of poetry with his particular style, but also more specifically: the note-values of the voice, its accents, its direction, the length of rests between its phrases, and even its volume are all highly suggestive of an imaginative reading of the underlying words. In a few instances there exist additional details that illuminate their meaning. Take, for example, this passage in *Billy in the Darbies* of 1944 from *Billy Budd, Foretopman* by Herman Melville, a writer with whom Diamond has a special affinity[99] (Ex. 20):

Ex. 20

I re-mem-ber Taff the Welsh-man ___ when he sank.

And his cheek it was like the bud-ding pink. But me ___ they'll lash me ___

___ in ___ ham-mock, drop me deep fath-oms down fath-oms down, now I'll dream ___ fast a sleep.

Here are three visions that flash through Billy's feverish mind: of Taff, the Welshman, floating dead in the water (a snapshot and as incon-

[99] This song was called to the author's attention by John Edmunds of The New York Public Library.

446

gruous), of himself being thrust into the depth of the ocean (a cry of passionate despair), and of his final sleep amidst the waves (a hallucination, blissful and consoling). A return to reality is a kind of dream too – the stupor of the condemned. The music, vivid in detail and yet detached like a ballad, is evidently so appropriate that it seems to function as a mere poetic ingredient. But it is so well defined in its own terms that it would make sense even if its words were eliminated.

A change of style occurred in the composer's songs of 1950. This led, one year later, to the idiom of *The Midnight Meditation* (Elder Olson), a song-cycle for baritone and piano. In contrast to texts previously drawn upon, its four long, gloomy poems are crowded with disparate images and strained, diffuse metaphors. To match all this, the rhythm has become restless and changeable (this is especially prominent in the accompaniment), the melody tends to an atonal esotericism, and the harmony to highly split sonorities. Crescendi, decrescendi, fortissimo climaxes, and unsteady tempi abound. To project the general 'tenor' of the words would have been inappropriate; the composer instead singles out details in the manner of the later nineteenth century.

In 1949–50 Aaron Copland (b. 1900) wrote his 'Twelve Poems of Emily Dickinson' after more than a decade of predominantly instrumental work. Harmonically they are related to his previous style, and even in the vocal part appear earlier elements such as traces of stylized American mountain tunes (especially in song No. 4), successive fourths moving in one direction, the recurring major third at the opening of song No. 1, which is reminiscent of the opening of *Appalachian Spring*, and in general the principle (originally stemming from Stravinsky) of repeating identical or similar phrases with shifting accentuations. However, the work is marked by a number of features in melody and rhythm (Ex. 21), which, though also resulting from this principle of

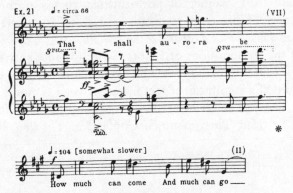

447

repetition, are novel and significant, particularly in their effect on the words.

It is surprising how closely they parallel phenomena in Stravinsky's *The Rake's Progress*, but, though already suggested in *Persephone*, in their present form they were developed independently.

The song-cycle has been hailed by perspective critics as a major work of the composer. Indeed, the expertness of its structure (though not totally effortless) is exemplary: the tight form of each song, the rhythmic interplay of voice and piano, and the high regard for the value of the interval within a motivically animated, essentially harmonic accompaniment. It is debatable, however, whether its text, whose details guided the composer, has received a convincing interpretation. Its declamation is either too regular (also, each line appears too often as a separate musical phrase) or too sober in its inflections, or else it is too abrupt. This and the austerity of the piano part (with such exceptions as song No. 8) tend to contradict the mellifluous and (in spite of its striking metaphors and similes) unemphatic character of the poetry.

Dirge in Woods (Meredith; composed in 1954) reveals a somewhat different style. Dedicated to Copland's former teacher Nadia Boulanger, it is retrospective in perpetuating, in its vocal part, aspects of his Cummings song ('In spite of ev'rything') of 1927.[100]

It seems that Copland is more spontaneous in his 'Old American Songs' (two volumes, completed in 1950 and 1952 respectively) than in more elaborate works for solo voice. In fact, they represent the most genuine arrangement of indigenous folk material that has appeared so far. No wonder, for they have profited from the composer's knowledge and love of the humble and tangy side of American life: of banjo and fiddle tunes, ballads, folk-hymns and ditties, early Negro minstrel melodies, and their manner of performance, to say nothing of the appropriateness of his own vocabulary. Ex. 22 (opposite) presents extracts from *I bought me a cat* and *Zion's Walls*.

Most of the compositions of Elliott Carter (b. 1908) are for instruments, and it is in this medium that he has developed a style of his own and won himself a significant place, in recent years, among American composers. The few songs he wrote in 1943 still follow faithfully the trends of their time. There is much Copland in *The Rose Family* and

---

[100] 'If the Dirge in Woods is like the Cummings song, it was not deliberate on my part' (letter of the composer of early May, 1959). – The Cummings song appeared in the *Cob Cob Song Volume* of 1935.

Dust of Snow[101] (both to texts by Robert Frost), and *Warble for Lilac-Time* (Walt Whitman) and the middle section of *Voyage* (Hart Crane) point to Roy Harris.

Carter's interest in abstract formal aspects reveals itself in a carefully considered rhythm and in his ability to control it throughout the 170-odd measures of the Whitman song. In *Voyage*, however, his attention was chiefly focused on the poem. It fascinated him, and the analysis he made of it[102] was probably his first step. Then, in his effort not merely 'to reflect its . . . lyrical beauty' but details of its 'poetic meaning', he relied heavily on harmony and the nuances in timbre and dynamics that could be expected in performance. The result is inevitably inconclusive but it has its felicitously suggestive moments.

*   *   *   *   *   *

[101] In their published versions, the date of the two songs is given as 1942 in contrast to bibliographies in *Bulletin Of American Composers Alliance*, III (1953), and *The Musical Quarterly*, XLIII (1957).

[102] Published as a preface to the edition of the song.

Although Ben Weber (b. 1916) admires the potentialities of the human voice, he has found most of his structural ideas too expansive for the small-scale form of the song.

Two of his song collections (Op. 6 and Op. 15, composed in 1940 and 1941 respectively) and his song with orchestral accompaniment, Op. 10[103] (Rilke's 'Lied des Idioten'; 1941) are among his early and stylistically tentative works. A few years later he began what finally became Op. 48, but left it unfinished. A long time passed during which he wrote chiefly instrumental music. Then in 1953 followed his 'Four Songs', Op. 40. Though oriented towards atonality (like its predecessors), the work utilizes such traditional elements, particularly in the vocal part, as thirds, chromatic progressions (most frequently downwards and usually one at a time), successive phrases related in length and note values, as well as calm, even, repeated notes. The accompaniment is provided by a solo cello which is half-way between a 'bass' and a concertante part. The work as a whole may not have more impact than a tasteful pastel but it has consistency. For the mild lyricism of its two lines, their idyllic playfulness, complement the texts (a medley of verses by Ezra Pound and of translations from Emperor Hadrian, Euenus, and the Sanskrit) which artfully praise the charms of good living.

In two previous works the *Concert Aria after Solomon* (for soprano and chamber orchestra, Op. 29; 1949) and the *Symphony on Poems of William Blake* (Op. 33; 1950–51), the voice, instead of carrying subtle poetic meanings, rather figures as a vehicle for broad lyrical cantilenas. This structural aspect is reinforced in Op. 33 (a dodecaphonic score and, incidentally, a major contribution to contemporary American symphonic literature), since the voice, appearing here but intermittently, is merely a part within a dense, wholly self-sustaining instrumental context.

In 'Three Songs for Soprano and Strings' (Op. 48; 1957–58),[104] the voice follows the same concepts, except in song No. 1, which originated in 1945. With its full sonority and tranquil rhythm – it relates to the vocal style of *Das Lied von der Erde* – it is set off against the instruments but these claim our attention with equal and often with more than equal intensity. The third song, for example, is a large-scale sonata-form (with a 'developed' recapitulation) in which the voice

[103] The composer, in a letter of April 20, 1959, states that this (unpublished) song, though it may be grouped with Op. 6 and 15, is 'bold and dramatic nevertheless' and 'more advanced in style'.

[104] Published by American Composers Alliance, N.Y.

participates, adding its cantability to the music almost in the manner of a woodwind section in an eighteenth-century symphony.

The sumptuousness of Weber's harmony, caused by 'built-in' seventh and ninth chords (as in *Vigil*), is no throwback to the past,

Ex. 23

for the chords are constantly re-defined, now slightly, now drastically, by notes that result from linear considerations – from a semi-atonal, semi-polyphonic setting. Indeed it is a real 'scale' of degrees of such redefinitions that the composer has established and which he exploits. Thus even wholly traditional chords and chord progressions that breach the delimited area for brief moments sound planned.

The romantic element, facilitated by the non-serial structure of the music, is particularly strong in the second and third song. The soaring, passionate character of many of their instrumental passages points to *Verklärte Nacht*. It is also significant that Weber chose translations of poems by German poets of the early twentieth century: Stefan George, Rilke, and, characteristically, Dehmel. It was verses by Dehmel, we may recall, which Schoenberg used as the literary scaffold of his score as well as in two previous song collections. Weber evidently does not imitate the past; his references to it are indeed so deliberate that he looks upon his work (to use his own words) as an 'hommage à Schoenberg'.

Since Op. 48 Weber's attitude towards song writing has changed. In preparation for future works for solo voice, he is now 'reconsidering

[the] functions of lyrical vocal lines'[105] above and within a contrapuntal setting.

Although Miriam Gideon (b. 1906) is in her aesthetics unrelated to David Diamond and Theodore Chanler, she shares with them a special feeling for poetry. To convey this she has developed a style of considerable individuality. At first glance the vocal part of her songs looks like a recitative. It is marked by brief, repeated notes (both in succession and intermittently), seconds, and narrow range, and it is predominantly syllabic, as in *The Hound of Heaven*:

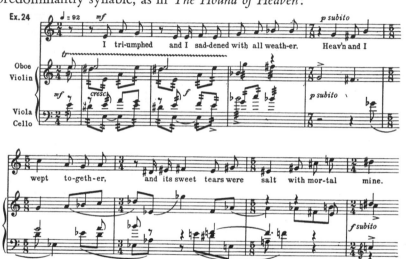

Nevertheless, within these limitations, there exists melodic continuity and even cantability, strengthened by chromaticism and the minor third (used as an interval and as the outline of a phrase). This is particularly true of her 'Three Sonnets from "Fatal Interview"' (Edna St. Vincent Millay 1952); a work oriented towards late romanticism.[106] When the line has a wider span, it sometimes describes a diminished triad or a minor triad (in inversion). Progressions in sevenths and ninths, characteristic of present-day music, are rare. Where they occur, their angularity (and it would be that within the total style) is mitigated, for example, by a minor second going in the opposite direction.

The vocal line materializes through short, restless phrases that rise

---

[105] From a letter of the composer of April 20, 1959.

[106] Other vocal compositions are: *The Hound Of Heaven* (Francis Thompson, 1944) for medium voice, oboe, and string trio; 'Five Sonnets From Shakespeare' (1950) for medium voice, trumpet, and string-quartet; 'Four Epitaphs (Robert Burns; 1952) for low voice and piano; *Mixco* (Miguel Angel Asturias; 1957) for low or medium voice and piano; *To Music* (Robert Herrick; 1957) for low voice and piano. All works of the composer are published by American Composers Alliance, N.Y.

a little and quickly return to their starting point. Thus motion is often hesitant, and when it is just about to expand, it is usually checked. If there is a trend towards fragmentation of the line, it is never carried to extremes since the separate phrases borrow tones, even whole passages, from each other. In this way coherence and even emphasis is attained, reminiscent of the procedure in Wagner's *Im Treibhaus*. What gives life to the line perhaps more than anything else is the system of irregular, sensitive stresses obtained through longer note-values amidst very brief ones and the placement of the notes within a constantly changing metre.

The vocal line disposes freely over all available twelve tones but its centrifugal force is even more restrained than it is in the quasi-atonal opening measures of Bartók's Sixth String Quartet. This is because of much note repetition (considering, above all, the pivotal centres of successive phrases); and with its thirds and triadic implications, at times confirmed harmonically, it provides glimpses of traditional tonality.

Although such abstract elements as the size of the interval and the exact note value count a great deal in the composer's line, the relation to the text is nevertheless intimate. There is always a special regard for prosody but stresses are essentially made according to the poetic significance of the words, and the speed (i.e. the number of notes on a beat) as well as the degree of cohesion among the phrases are regulated just as meaningfully as they would be in recitation. In general, the cautious, shy motion, the half-finished phrase, the mumbling quality of hushed, adjacent tones, the chromaticism – all this fits the poetry, introverted or high-strung as it may be.

Accompaniments, often employing strings, are written in a delicate, lucid chamber-music style. The independence of their lines is not only appropriate in interludes but in combination with the voice as well. For they serve its rhythm not so much by complicating or simplifying it as by increasing or retarding its current. In the process they frequently double its notes in the tradition of French nineteenth-century song writing, but the manner in which they do it is contemporaneous: it involves constant changes of instruments (and thus of timbre) as well as shifts of octave levels.[107]

Wallingford Riegger (b. 1885) is, like many other contemporary American musicians, essentially a composer of instrumental music, but at least one of his three songs *The Dying of the Light* (Op. 59; Dylan Thomas), published in 1956, deserves mention in this context. The way

[107] See George Perle, *The Music of Miriam Gideon*, in *Bulletin Of American Composers Alliance*, VII, 4 (1958).

Riegger, here as elsewhere, applies pan-chromaticism[108] (this, a less historically circumscribed term, is more appropriate than atonality – even in the case of Weber and Gideon), is reminiscent of the Hindemith of the 'twenties,[109] though a few verticalizations of thematic material (bars 54 and 58) and prominent melodic progressions of major sevenths and of ninths suggest the influence of the Schoenberg school. The song, accompanied by piano or orchestra, is primarily a fugue – in the rhythm of traditional counterpoint and even with the traditional entries in fifths at the beginning. The voice (aside from a few chordal passages) is a part of the polyphonic web, though it has a slight edge because of intervals and rhythms that relate to the text. It is true that such relations are more literal than in Stravinsky's setting of the same poem (*In Memoriam Dylan Thomas*). This cannot diminish the fact that Riegger s artistic integrity confirms a standard of song writing that will eventually discourage its facile representatives.

Milton Babbitt (b. 1916) shares the aims of the dodecaphonic *avant-garde*. In his two song-cycles, 'Du', for high voice and piano (August Stramm; 1951) and 'Two Sonnets',[110] for baritone, clarinet, viola, and cello (Gerard Manley Hopkins; 1955) he resorts to only one type of row: the one whose second half is the retrograde of the first, both usually bridged by a tritone. The row (one for each movement) is rarely stated more than once. Instead, segments of it are used and frequently the same ones in succession, though of course in many variants. This method of composition is applied to a kind of pointillism, i.e. the vocal line is split up into small phrases, some consisting of no more than one or two notes, which, separated by rests, have very little coherence among each other:

from *Traum* ('Du', no. 6)

Ex. 25

Flü - - stern plät - - schert

[108] It is suggested that 'panchromaticism' (in slight deviation from the *Harvard Dictionary of Music*, 1944, p. 551, left column) might designate the use of what is sometimes called the chromatic scale (though without a tonic), reserving 'atonality' for its extreme application.

[109] See, for example, Hindemith's Op. 36, No. 3, second movement (miniature score, from K onwards).

[110] The first work is published by Boelke-Bomart, Hillsdale, N.Y.; the second is obtainable in blueprint form from the publisher.

There appear the characteristic large intervals, mainly sevenths, but, discounting intervals between the end of one phrase and the beginning of the next, they are in the minority as compared with more traditional ones. In 'Du', separate phrases considered by themselves are but slightly atonal. Too brief to be of more than ordinary musical interest, they function mainly in support of declamation, underlining the expressionistically disjointed text with accentuations, direction and note values. The accompaniment is even more fragmentized than the voice. Studded with rests, it consists of 'patches' of notes which constantly and unpredictably change their duration and register. Harmony is defined in terms of density, by the number of simultaneous notes and the approximate distance between them (close together, far apart, etc.). While the vocal line parallels specific details of the text, with regard to the accompaniment one is more aware of the correspondence of its fleeting, shadowy, irrational character to general poetic qualities.

In 'Two Sonnets' the composer strives towards a greater degree of melodic coherence than he did before (Ex. 26). The phrases of his voice

Spelt from Sybil's Leaves.

parts are still brief but they are more closely linked with each other, while the accompaniment, unified by one register, no longer operates

455

with what might be called neutral pitches. It thus has a tangible harmony which is occasionally strengthened through the inclusion of traditional consonant intervals. Its rhythm is less spasmodic; it no longer avoids recurrent patterns nor does it refuse to follow the motion of the voice. There is an abundance of dynamic changes. More sudden and more extreme than in the earlier work, they make sense in association with the brusque, demanding fantasy of Hopkins's language.

Coda

A discussion of American art song cannot end here. For what needs to be emphasized is the multitude of efforts. The following then is a list of contemporary composers who have contributed to the genre:[111] George Antheil, Jacob Avshalomov; John J. Becker, Jack Beeson, Arthur Berger, William Bergsma, Leonard Bernstein, Gordon Binkerd, Marc Blitzstein, Paul Bowles, Henry Brant; Henry Cowell, Ruth Crawford, Paul Creston; Richard Donovan; Herbert Elwell; Howard Ferguson, Vivian Fine, Ross Lee Finney, William Flanagan, Lukas Foss; Peggy Glanville-Hicks, Richard F. Goldman, Ray Green; Alexei Haieff, Roy Harris, Everett Helm, Alan Hovhaness; Norman Dello Joio; Harrison Kerr, Gail Kubik; Normand Lockwood; Douglas Moore; Dika Newlin; George Perle, Vincent Persichetti, Daniel Pinkham; Gardner Read, George Rochberg, Ned Rorem; William Schuman, Roger Sessions, Halsey Stevens, Howard Swanson; David Van Vactor, John Verrall; Robert Ward, Adolph Weiss, Hugo Weisgall, Frank Wigglesworth.

If this list were complete, it would include about one hundred names. As it is, condensed and weighted towards the twentieth-century style, it still reveals a confusing variety of orientations as for example postromanticism, neo-classicism, atonality, dodecaphony, and influences of Elizabethan music, American folklore, jazz, the Near and Far East, of contemporary European composers and such native composers as Ives, Copland, Diamond, and Gershwin, to say nothing of the individuality of styles, achieved or attempted.

The songs of Seymour Barab (b. 1921) deserve special mention and perhaps most fittingly at this point. Tuneful and of whimsical humour, they might be taken for encore pieces. But it would be fairer to consider them equivalents of 'light verse' or of the sophisticated illustrations of

---

[111] This list should be supplemented by data in the *Bulletin of American Composers Alliance*, VII, 3 (1958), catalogues of vocal music of the American Music Center, New York, and William Treat Upton, *A Supplement to Art Song in America, 1930–38*, Philadelphia, 1938.

the 'New Yorker' magazine. In such collections as 'Four Songs' (texts by Edmund Waller, Richard Le Gallienne, Thomas Chatterton, and Esther Mathews; about 1952), 'A Child's Garden of Verse'[112] (Robert Louis Stevenson; about 1953) and 'Songs of Perfect Propriety' (Dorothy Parker; about 1957) the composer successfully blends the familiar with the esoteric. On the one hand he draws on 'second-hand' and borrowed material: overworked formulæ of the eighteenth and nineteenth centuries, the nondescript children's songs of the dime stores, musical comedy, and hit-tunes, and, in Le Gallienne's *She's Somewhere in the Sunlight Strong*, brazenly on Satie. On the other hand he makes these elements appear fresh and meaningful by placing them into a musical context which is informed by a knowledge of contemporary devices and animated by a sure feeling for the genre itself. Of this alone the structural interest and the appropriateness of the accompaniments both to the vocal line and the text are clear evidence (Ex. 27):

Go, lovely rose (from 'Four Songs')

During the late nineteenth century there were two main types of popular song: the jolly one in quasi-Irish folk style and the sentimental waltz melody.[113] The latter, appearing in the 'nineties, was considerably heftier than Johann Strauss would have approved of, but it facilitated the success of Victor Herbert (an Irishman who had received a thorough musical education in Germany). Oriented towards the Viennese

[112] Unpublished, like the Dorothy Parker Album, but available on records.
[113] See Sigmund Spaeth, *Read 'em and Weep*, New York, 1939.

457

operetta, he introduced a touch of elegance and cosmopolitan 'finish' into Broadway music and thus gave popular taste, at the turn of the century, a new direction.

What was left of earlier minstrel music went into the so-called 'coon-song' of the 'eighties. From this time on, the Negro influence increased in strength; it appeared in cake-walks, then in ragtime songs and from about 1910 on in the blues. Henceforth jazz was continually drawn upon, and a popular song had to be danceable in order to have a measure of acceptance.[114] All of these sources included not only rhythmic but melodic and harmonic patterns also. To them were eventually added elements of Latin American dances, hillbilly and cowboy songs, Negro spirituals, and anything that had erotic overtones such as Tchaïkovsky, Puccini, Lehár, Debussy, and Ravel. In spite of the heterogeneity of its ingredients, a style emerged that has its own characteristics and that, for better or worse, has been widely imitated abroad.

Set off against a staggering amount of mediocre and tasteless songs are those by Irving Berlin, Cole Porter, Jerome Kern, Richard Rodgers, George Gershwin, Kurt Weill (an outstanding talent, though his change from the style of socio-critical operas in German to the smart Broadway musical was not entirely whole-hearted) and Leonard Bernstein. Some of these men are untutored, purely instinctive composers, others are real professionals who have simplified their concepts of originality and yet have remained literate.

The uniqueness of Gershwin's songs, long recognized by laymen and professionals (Ravel, Stravinsky, and Schoenberg among them), is deceptively covered by the well-worn conventions of New York's sheet-music industry. It could not be otherwise, since it was not the composer's intention to create something totally new but rather to make the most of an established, popular medium. Though this has narrowed his scope, it has not smothered his inventiveness.

What distinguishes Gershwin from the average good song-writer is the precision with which he uses his harmony. Every one of his chords, however fleeting, is chosen with a subtle ear to its intensity, weight, and strength of forward motion within its harmonic context, and, most important of all, to its effect on the tune. Commonplace or trivial by themselves, the tunes become fully valid only through the chords that are added to them: they not merely owe them their special timbre but the organization of their notes into phrases and the degree of fluency

[114] Sigmund Spaeth, *A History of Popular Music in America*, New York, 1948, p. 369.

458

and continuity of their phrases and of composite sections. Take for example the refrain of *I Got Rhythm*:

Ex. 28

I __ got rhy - thm, I __ got mu - sic,__

I __ got my man Who could ask for an-y-thing more?

There is nothing novel about its melody or, for that matter, its accompaniment but the combination of the two, weakened though it is as an excerpt, has the characteristic verve of the composer. Note the easy, elegant sweep from F to C and back to F, and more forcefully up to E flat and the return to B flat as well as the instrumental passage which at once continues the tune and invites its full repetition. And yet for the harmonization sufficed chiefly the basses of the tonic, dominant, and subdominant, secondary dominants (in the form of seventh chords and, in the related middle section of the song, of ninth chords) and chromatic middle voices – devices which occur in other songs also.

Of course the congruency between harmony and tune is not the only noteworthy feature in Gershwin. It is the entire setting with its middle voices, its finely calculated basses, its spacing, its omitted and doubled notes that give life to the song. This explains why the same or similar chord progression has a totally different meaning in each work.

Though Gershwin's best songs, and there must be more than twenty of them, are, like the rest, for quick and casual listening, they are rewarding even when read and studied. How light and sure the hand was that shaped their details: the instrumental interludes and links (*Nobody But You*, refrain; *'S Wonderful*, refrain, bars 2 and 4), the counter-melodies in the tenor register (as in Liszt, for the thumb), the range of dissonances (see the almost consonant sounding, inverted ninth chord at the word 'night' in *Do-Do-Do*, introduction) and of tonality (the refrain of *When Do We Dance* needs no tonic until the very end); above all the modulations – not so much those caused by sequences as the bold, yet so natural, detours (for example from B flat major to its dominant in the ten bars that precede the refrain of *I Got Rhythm*). In all cases the most unassuming, the most obvious of means are employed – or so it seems. This heightens the delight of the critic although it sidetracks his analysis. More and more he feels himself removed from the essence of the music: namely the coherence of the whole and the exhilarating effects it radiates. The predicament, if it may be called that, is the same with Schubert's Ländler, Strauss's and Lanner's waltzes, and Offenbach's cancans and famous barcarolle.

Conclusion

SIR MICHAEL TIPPETT

IF we think of all Dowland's songs and all Schubert's songs, we can
see that the greater part of their production consists of songs in
strophic form, where the verses repeat themselves in a recognizable
pattern. Because of this and because many of these strophic songs have
been so easily acceptable to public taste as to become popular favourites,
the notion arises that all songs are strophic. But Dowland, and even
Schubert, wrote songs which are not strophic. A song like *In darkness
let me dwell* is a kind of melodrama, or scena. It moves in a long line,
without repetition, from beginning to end. The melody in the voice
part is less shaped to a tune in the direction that folk-song is shaped
(folk-song poetry is all strophic), and it seems more dramatized. In
a later form of these scenas, such as those of Purcell two generations
after Dowland, unity of a kind has often been given by a repeated
ground bass upon which the dramatized voice-line rides. An example
like *Music for a while*, besides the repetitions of the ground bass, has at
the end a recapitulation of the beginning, and we feel we are going over
towards the *da capo* aria of Handelian opera. The strophic songs also
move into the sphere of opera, whenever the operatic situation calls
for it.

Clearly the poetry of the strophic song is different from the poetry or prose of the song as scena. For poetry to be recognized as strophic, the strophes must be shaped alike. This is a commonplace which the composer accepts, and by which he is influenced. Unless he is deli-berately wishing to be perverse, he takes the division of the poem into strophes as the division of his song, and within this primary pattern he composes musical verses which will contain the poetic verse of each strophe.

The moment the composer begins to create the musical verses of his song, he destroys our appreciation of the poem as poetry, and substitutes an appreciation of his music as song. This is true of even such simple and exactly corresponding patterns of poetry and music as the endlessly repeatable verses of a folk-song. In fact, it is in my opinion the absolute of the song as a genre. It is not really a matter of the further we go away from the simplicities of folk-song towards the complexities of the songs in a Lieder recital, the more we substitute appreciation of music for appreciation of poetry. As soon as we sing any poetry to a recognizable melody we have at that instant left the art of poetry for the art of music. If it were worth the trouble, we might even demonstrate by experi-ment the moment when chanted recitation of poetry hovers perhaps on the borderline between the two arts; the poetic listener still trying to appreciate the poetry, the musical listener already appreciating the chanting as music. Once the chanting has gone over into song, then our appreciation of the words virtually ceases. If the poem is very fine in its own right, and very well known, then we *imagine* sometimes that we are still appreciating the poetry when it has become a song, but I think this is illusion.

When we hear a good song we are rarely if ever disturbed by the quite possible fact that the poetry is poor. We may discover this later on, as many people have done concerning many Schubert songs. That may make us wonder at the discrepancy. But it is not a discrepancy at all in the sense of the song as a song. It is only a discrepancy to someone who holds to the illusion that we can appreciate a poem as poetry in the act of appreciating the song a composer has made from it. When we consider a poem as poetry, we can of course probe into the mysterious mixture of sound and sense which it is. By this means we may analyze our response to the poem's verbal music and our response to the poem's sense. The fact that we speak of a poem's verbal music, when we are considering its sound to the inner ear, or when recited, is unimportant probably to a poet, but possibly confusing to a musician. The music of a song destroys the verbal music of a poem utterly. I am inclined to think that a composer responds less to a poem's verbal sound, when he chooses that poem as a vehicle for his musical art, than to the poem's situation, lyrical or dramatic. I feel it equally important to distinguish between the response to the verbal music of a poem as a whole, which depends on an extended relationship of vowels and consonants, and the response a composer may make to the sound and rhythm of certain words in the poem. Thus in *Dido's Lament* we appreciate Purcell's response to the words 'remember me' entirely within the song as music; any appreciation of the words of the song as a piece of poetry still being excluded. We connect 'remember me' with the general situation in which Dido finds herself. One supposes that Purcell did so too. We may object that *Dido's Lament* is not a song in the usual sense of the word, because Dido's situation is presented to us beforehand by the operatic action. Yet many well-known Lieder are of this kind. Schubert's *Gretchen am Spinnrade* depends for its full poignancy on our sense of Gretchen's situation at that moment within the Faust tragedy. I am certain Schubert responded to the poem in that knowledge. Yet it is a wonderful song in the concert hall, just as *Dido's Lament* makes a good disc in its own right. Our response to those operatic moments which have crystallized themselves into a situation demanding expression musically in an aria is close to our response to the situation behind a song. Of the same kind is our appreciation of the general situation behind a whole series of songs, like the song-cycle 'Die Winterreise'.

In a general situation covering a whole song-cycle it is not finally necessary that the poet should have arranged already a series of poems within that situation. The composer may do that. This is an experience I know personally. In the gradual composition of my five-poem song-cycle 'The Heart's Assurance' I began with a response to one poem by Sidney Keyes. Considering then the nature of my response to Keyes's poem, I could distinguish between a response arising from my own life – concerning the woman to whom the song-cycle is dedicated and who died as the last war ended; and a response to a more general situation in which my personal experience might be subsumed; Love under the shadow of Death. I had once responded, though never in music, to the bitter poetry of the First World War – to Owen and Sassoon. Now I was responding to the poetry of the Second World War – to a love poetry, it seemed to me, but coloured by the apprehensions of immediate mortality. I was able to discharge my personal emotion into the general poetic expression, and to select from *two* poets, Alun Lewis and Sidney Keyes, the poems that gave me an artistically satisfactory series of poems for songs. To hammer home my chief point about song as an art form, I need only state that when we listen to this song-cycle based on the work of two poets, we are completely unaware of which poet is which.

Now if I am right about the composer responding to the poetic situation rather than to the verbal music of a poem, then we can easily see why the device of relating the instrumental accompaniment to the overall situation of the poem can be so effective in the hands of a composer of taste. Gretchen's situation when she sings at the spinning-wheel is concerned with the anguish of growing realization that Faust has deceived her. It is expressed at once in the poem's first line, 'Meine Ruh' ist hin'.

Schubert's wonderful piano accompaniment does not give immediate expression to Gretchen's anguish as do the words that Gretchen sings, but gives mediate expression through the pictorial image of Gretchen spinning, and by a transliteration of the pictorial image of the girl sitting at the spinning-wheel into an aural image of the sound of the whirring wheel. Then the whirring of the wheel in the song's accompaniment fills out the poem's first line.

Purcell does not give musical expression to Dido's anguish, when Aeneas deceives her, by this kind of means at all. His instrumental accompaniment to Dido's singing is anguished through the use of poignant, plangent harmonies of which he is the great master. (They are to be found – less developed – in Weelkes, and we associate them of course with Monteverdi).

Gluck can achieve a less anguished but infinitely pathetic expression of loss of love, not indeed by deception but by fate, through purely melodic means, as in *Che farò senz' Eurydice?* We can call Schubert's method romantic, and Purcell's and Gluck's classic, but I become less and less sure that the differences are anything more than those of technique.

Not all the poetic situations of songs are of this tragic kind. *Who is Sylvia* or *I attempt from Love's sickness to fly* are lighthearted situations of comedy. There are also situations which do not concern two people in love, but one person alone with nature, or with a state of soul. This situation of the person alone has so often been expressed in poetry that it has given rise to many songs. Yet when I needed to express musically such a personal response to nature felt as mirror for a state of soul, I turned strangely enough to a piece of descriptive prose, not to pastoral poetry. The first reason for this seemed to be merely technical. I wanted to experiment with song as scena, in the form of a short cantata for solo voice. I was being deeply influenced by – for me – newly discovered masterpieces of this genre such as *The Blessed Virgin's Expostulation*. I could not find, in any pastoral poetry that I knew, a strong enough sense of one person singing out from within a clearly-defined situation. In *The Blessed Virgin's Expostulation* the Virgin Mary watches the infant Jesus, and is anguished by her responsibility as a human mother to a child who is God. The situation is summed up poetically in her last words: 'I trust the God but fear the Child'. Within his cantata Purcell uses both dramatic recitative and miniature aria. Each is excellently appropriate. I needed words which would be those of one person singing from a given situation, and from a situation in which the changing moods of the singer could be expressed appropriately through the contrasting techniques of declamation and aria. I could not find the words I wanted in the poetry I knew.

The problem resolved itself through a combination of my own response to nature and my affection for the writings of W. H. Hudson. In the sudden and unexpected manner these things happen, it flashed on me that Hudson, the old man, looking back in his autobiography on himself as a boy of fifteen, when he believed that by going over from boyhood to manhood he might lose his peculiar apprehension of nature, was just the figure singing from within the given situation which I wanted. Hudson's poetic prose proved an easier form of words to handle as a cantata than much poetry could be. But it was not as appropriate as poetry specially written for my purpose could have been. Of course all the verbal music of Hudson's prose is destroyed entirely by the music. If this were not so, a certain arbitrariness in the divisions I have imposed for musical reasons on this piece of prose would become apparent and distracting. The song is saved by the unbroken sense of situation.

I cannot as a composer feel any generic difference between my response to a situation which I want to express by a song, and my response to certain crystallized situations in opera. I am glad to think that one of my colleagues whom I much admire, Benjamin Britten, shows by his songs and his operas that he experiences this unity too. This is not to say that song-writing is the whole of opera. But the techniques of song-writing are some of the techniques of opera. The situations that seem to make good songs are often the situations that crystallize out in the human dramas of opera.

CONCLUSION

Response to situation is the primal gift of the song-writer. Then comes the ability to destroy all the verbal music of the poetry or prose and to substitute the music of music. Felicities of word-painting, such as the 'flying' in *I attempt from Love's sickness to fly* must all be contained within the music of music. The relation of instrumental accompaniment to the poetic situation is I think nearly always at one or more remove.

Index of Names

INDEX OF NAMES

Index of Titles

(Song Cycles are in Roman type)

474